GUIDE TO NORTH AMERICAN

Bed & Breakfasts
and Country Inns

AAA PUBLISHING
1000 AAA Drive, Heathrow, Florida
32746-5063

ST. REMY MEDIA INC.
682 William Street, Montréal, Québec
H3C IN9

AAA

President & CEO: Robert Darbelnet
Executive Vice President, Publishing & Administration: Rick Rinner
Managing Director, Travel Information:
  Bob Hopkins

Director, Product Development: Bill Wood
Director, Sales & Marketing: John Coerper
Director, Purchasing & Corporate Services:
  Becky Barrett
Director, Business Development: Gary Sisco
Director, Tourism Information Development (TID):
  Michael Petrone
Director, Travel Information: Jeff Zimmerman
Director, Publishing Operations: Susan Sears
Director, GIS / Cartography: Jan Coyne
Director, Publishing / GIS Systems & Development:
  Ramin Kalhor

Managing Editor, Product Development:
  Margaret Cavanaugh
AAA Travel Store & e-store Manager:
  Sharon Edwards

TID Regional Managers: Todd Cronson,
  Larry Hamilton, Michel Mousseau,
  Stacey Mower, Patrick Schardin, Bob Sheron
Manager, TID Field Operations: Laurie DiMinico
Project Manager, Travel Information:
  Kim Nicastro
Manager, Travel Information Operations:
  Brenda Daniels
Managing Editor, Points of Interest:
  Suzanne Lemon
Manager, Product Support: Linda Indolfi
Manager, Electronic Media Design:
  Mike McCrary
Project Manager, Systems & Development:
  Robert Miller

Published by AAA Publishing, 1000 AAA Drive,
Heathrow, Florida 32746

*Guide to North American Bed & Breakfasts
and Country Inns* was created and produced for
AAA PUBLISHING by ST. REMY MEDIA INC.

ST. REMY MEDIA INC.

President: Pierre Léveillé
Vice-President, Finance: Natalie Watanabe
Managing Editor: Carolyn Jackson
Managing Art Director: Diane Denoncourt
Production Manager: Michelle Turbide
Director, Business Development:
  Christopher Jackson

Art Director: Michel Giguère
Senior Editor: Elizabeth Lewis
Research Editor: Heather Mills
Editorial Coordinator: Monique Riedel
Writers: Peter Fedun, Robert Labelle
Cartographers: Eric Archambault, Hélène Dion
Illustrators: Gilles Y. Beauchemin,
  Raymond Fong, Rui Laureano Silva,
  Michael W. Yeomans
Photo Researcher: Linda Bryant

Systems Director: Edward Renaud
Pre-Press Production: Martin Francoeur,
  Jean Angrignon Sirois
Technical Support: Danny-Pierre Auger,
  Joey Fraser

*The following people also assisted in the
preparation of this book:*
Andy Brown, Gerard Dee, Lorraine Doré, Gilles
Dumas, Dominique Gagné, Angelika Gollnow,
Pascale Hueber, Kirk Johnson, Liane Keightly,
Anne-Marie Lemay, Rebecca Smollett, Robert
Sonin, Roxanne Tremblay.

St. Remy Media online Website address:
http://www.stremy.com

We believe you're holding the best comprehensive B&B travel guide available for North America. This 2nd edition has been completely updated, with more inns and B&Bs plus additional illustrations to enhance your exploration. You'll quickly discover this truly is a travel guide and not a mere lodging directory.

The colorfully mapped and illustrated regional scenic driving tours, along with dozens of historical and cultural things to see and do along the way, will enhance your experience as no other B&B book can.

This guide was created and designed for the growing segment of *travelers*— as opposed to *tourists*—who seek a personal connection to the places they visit. Virtually any stay at a country inn or bed & breakfast guarantees that connection, which can only be enriched by a driving tour or cultural attraction visit.

No establishment featured in this book paid in any way for the privilege. Nobody received a free night's stay in return for adding a property to the book. To the contrary: **Each lodging included in this book was visited unannounced and evaluated by AAA's full-time, professional staff specifically trained to assess accommodations objectively.**

Our evaluators apply a comprehensive set of inspection criteria—developed just for the B&B/country inn lodging segments—to arrive at the widely respected Diamond Rating for levels of service and amenities. The standards guiding the rating are unique, in that they were developed with input from travelers like you and innkeepers from across the continent who strive to provide a rewarding travel experience.

AAA and publishing partner St. Remy Media Inc. of Montréal, Canada, are confident this adds up to a valuable guide focused on your travel needs. But you judge our success. Have a great journey, and please send your reactions to:

B&B Guide
Product Development – MailStop 66
1000 AAA Drive
Heathrow, Florida 32746-5063

The One That Does It All

For years, people have turned to AAA for their **emergency road service** needs. But AAA is more than towing. Access to AAA's **travel services** can give you the world. Its **financial services** can help you pay for it. And AAA **insurance** can give you the peace of mind to enjoy the ride. Plus, AAA gives you exclusive **Show Your Card & Save®** offers, **bail bond** benefits and **so much more.**

Join AAA and discover the ways AAA can simplify your life. Call or stop by your nearest AAA office today. And make AAA the one for you.

Table *of* Contents

Northeast

Southeast

Southwest

Far West

Northwest

Midwest

Canada

North America

ALASKA
(see inset)

ALASKA

YUKON
TERRITORY

NORTHWEST
TERRITORIES

Northwest

Far West

BRITISH
COLUMBIA

ALBERTA

Midwest

WASHINGTON

MONTANA

OREGON

IDAHO

WYOMING

NEVADA

UTAH

CALIFORNIA

Southwest

ARIZONA

NEW
MEXICO

HAWAII

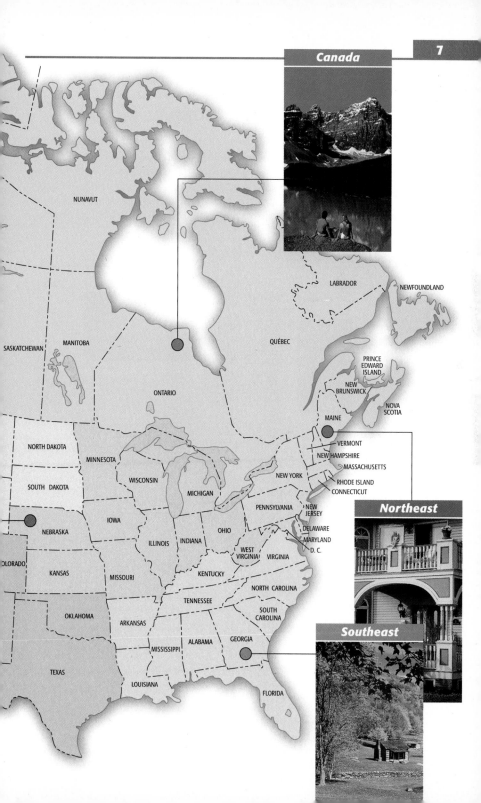

Canada

LABRADOR

NEWFOUNDLAND

NUNAVUT

SASKATCHEWAN

MANITOBA

QUÉBEC

PRINCE
EDWARD
ISLAND

NEW
BRUNSWICK

NOVA
SCOTIA

ONTARIO

MAINE

NORTH DAKOTA

MINNESOTA

VERMONT

NEW HAMPSHIRE

MASSACHUSETTS

WISCONSIN

NEW YORK

RHODE ISLAND

CONNECTICUT

SOUTH DAKOTA

MICHIGAN

Northeast

PENNSYLVANIA

NEW
JERSEY

NEBRASKA

IOWA

OHIO

DELAWARE

MARYLAND

ILLINOIS

INDIANA

WEST
VIRGINIA

VIRGINIA

D. C.

COLORADO

KANSAS

MISSOURI

KENTUCKY

NORTH CAROLINA

TENNESSEE

SOUTH
CAROLINA

OKLAHOMA

ARKANSAS

Southeast

ALABAMA

GEORGIA

TEXAS

MISSISSIPPI

LOUISIANA

FLORIDA

How to Use
This Book

For the purposes of this book, North America is divided into seven regions: Northeast, Southeast, Southwest, Far West, Northwest, Midwest and Canada. Each region starts with a full-color section describing scenic drives through the area. Following this is the listings section for the region, organized alphabetically by state and within the state alphabetically by city. You'll find maps of each state with the listings, as well, indicating which cities have AAA lodgings. We've shown you samples here of how the book works.

Scenic Byways *Regional Map*

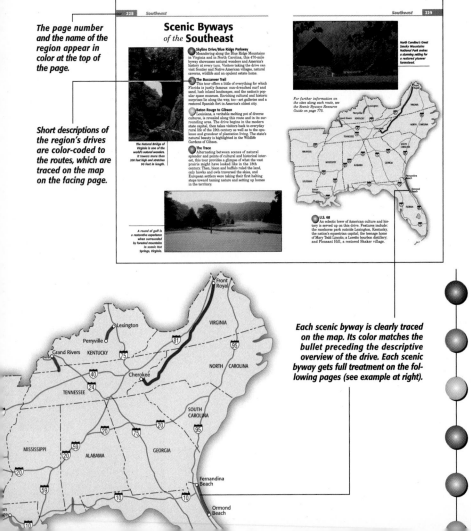

The page number and the name of the region appear in color at the top of the page.

Short descriptions of the region's drives are color-coded to the routes, which are traced on the map on the facing page.

Each scenic byway is clearly traced on the map. Its color matches the bullet preceding the descriptive overview of the drive. Each scenic byway gets full treatment on the following pages (see example at right).

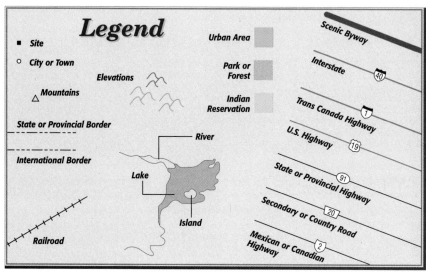

Scenic Byway

Page number, region name and state appear in color at the top of the page.

Byway map has sites and attractions marked by numbered and colored bullets.

Full-color photos of sites in the region have descriptive captions.

Scenic Byway color

Information about sites and attractions along the way. Each site is identified by numbered and colored bullets that refer to the map of the byway. Further information about each site and attraction is found in the Scenic Byways Resource Guide on page 775.

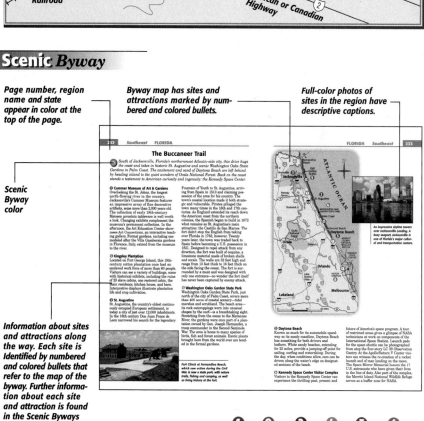

Classification *Indicators*

Bed and Breakfast: *Usually smaller establishments, emphasizing a more personal relationship between operators and guests leading to an at-home feeling. Guest units tend to be individually decorated. Rooms may not include some modern amenities, such as televisions, and may have a shared bathroom. Usually owner-operated, with a common room or parlor, separate from the innkeeper's living quarters, where guests and operators can interact during evening and breakfast hours. Evening and office closures are normal. A continental or full hot breakfast is served and is included in the room rate.*

Country Inn: *Although similar in definition to a bed and breakfast, country inns are usually larger in size, provide more spacious public areas and offer a dining facility that serves at least breakfast and dinner. May be located in a rural setting or downtown area.*

Diamond *Rating*

◆ *Properties meet all listing requirements. They are clean and well maintained.*

◆◆ *Properties maintain the attributes offered at the one diamond level, while showing noticeable enhancement in room decor and quality of furnishings.*

◆◆◆ *Properties show a marked upgrade in physical attributes, services and comfort. Additional amenities, services and facilities may be offered.*

◆◆◆◆ *Properties reflect an exceptional degree of hospitality, service and attention to detail, while offering upscale facilities and a variety of amenities.*

The prestigious Five Diamond Award properties are described beginning on page 12.

Special *Features*

Services
Ⓨ Cocktail Lounge
🐾 Pets Allowed

Accessibility
♿ Fully Accessible
Semi-Accessible
Hearing Impaired

Room Amenities
Coffee Maker in Room
No Cable TV in Room
Non-Smoking Rooms
No Air Conditioning
No Telephones

Sports/Recreation
Pool
Fitness Center

Safety Features
Ⓢ Sprinklers*
Ⓓ Smoke Detectors*
Ⓘ Safe

* Canada only. U.S. properties are all so equipped.

Abbreviations *States & Provinces*

UNITED STATES
AL Alabama
AK Alaska
AZ Arizona
AR Arkansas
CA California
CO Colorado
CT Connecticut
DE Delaware
DC District of Columbia
FL Florida
GA Georgia
HI Hawaii
ID Idaho
IL Illinois
IN Indiana
IA Iowa
KS Kansas
KY Kentucky
LA Louisiana
ME Maine
MD Maryland
MA Massachusetts

MI Michigan
MN Minnesota
MS Mississippi
MO Missouri
MT Montana
NE Nebraska
NV Nevada
NH New Hampshire
NJ New Jersey
NM New Mexico
NY New York
NC North Carolina
ND North Dakota
OH Ohio
OK Oklahoma
OR Oregon
PA Pennsylvania
RI Rhode Island
SC South Carolina
SD South Dakota
TN Tennessee
TX Texas
UT Utah

VT Vermont
VA Virginia
WA Washington
WV West Virginia
WI Wisconsin
WY Wyoming

CANADA
AB Alberta
BC British Columbia
MB Manitoba
NB New Brunswick
NF Newfoundland
NT Northwest Territories
NS Nova Scotia
ON Ontario
PE Prince Edward Island
PQ Québec
SK Saskatchewan
YT Yukon Territory

Rated Listings

Page number, region and state are found at the top of the page.

State maps open each state listing section. Every town or city with properties listed in the book appears on the map in bold blue type.

Listing pages carry the region state and city in color at the top of the page. A left-hand page carries the city of the first property on the page; a right-hand page gives the city of the last property on the page.

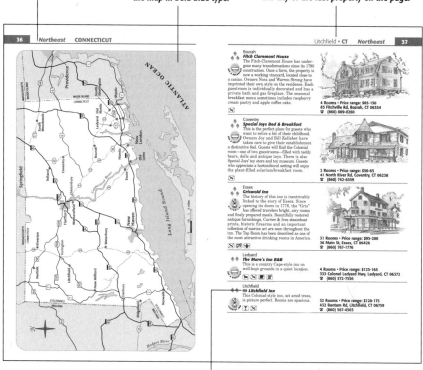

36 | Northeast CONNECTICUT

Litchfield • CT Northeast | 37

Bozrah
Fitch-Claremont House
The Fitch-Claremont House has undergone many transformations since its 1790 construction. Once a farm, the property is now a working vineyard, located close to a casino. Owners Nora and Warren Strong have imprinted their own style on the residence. Each guestroom is individually decorated and has a private bath and gas fireplace. The seasonal breakfast menu sometimes includes raspberry cream pastry and apple coffee cake.

4 Rooms • Price range: $85-150
83 Fitchville Rd, Bozrah, CT 06334
☎ (860) 889-0260

Coventry
Special Joys Bed & Breakfast
This is the perfect place for guests who want to relive a bit of their childhood. Owners Joy and Bill Kelleher have taken care to give their establishment a distinctive feel. Guests will find the Colonial room—one of two guestrooms—filled with teddy bears, dolls and antique toys. There is also Special Joys toy store and toy museum. Guests who appreciate a horticultural setting will enjoy the plant-filled solarium/breakfast room.

2 Rooms • Price range: $50-65
41 North River Rd, Coventry, CT 06238
☎ (860) 742-6359

Essex
Griswold Inn
The history of this inn is inextricably linked to the story of Essex. Since opening its doors in 1776, the "Gris" has offered travelers bright, airy rooms and finely prepared meals. Beautifully restored antique furnishings, Currier & Ives steamboat prints, historic firearms and an important collection of marine art are seen throughout the inn. The Tap Room has been described as one of the most attractive drinking rooms in America.

31 Rooms • Price range: $95-200
36 Main St, Essex, CT 06426
☎ (860) 767-1776

Ledyard
The Mare's Inn B&B
This is a country Cape-style inn on well-kept grounds in a quiet location.

4 Rooms • Price range: $125-165
333 Colonel Ledyard Hwy, Ledyard, CT 06372
☎ (860) 572-7556

Litchfield
Litchfield Inn
This Colonial-style inn, set amid trees, is picture perfect. Rooms are spacious.

32 Rooms • Price range: $120-175
432 Bantam Rd, Litchfield, CT 06759
☎ (860) 567-4503

AAA or CAA indicates Official Appointment properties licensing the right to use our logos in advertising. These properties offer discounts or special amenities to AAA/CAA members.

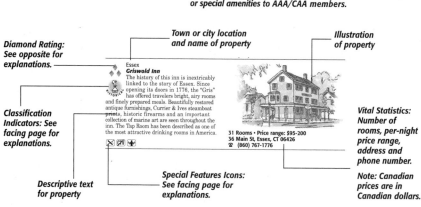

Diamond Rating:
See opposite for explanations.

Town or city location and name of property

Illustration of property

Essex
Griswold Inn
The history of this inn is inextricably linked to the story of Essex. Since opening its doors in 1776, the "Gris" has offered travelers bright, airy rooms and finely prepared meals. Beautifully restored antique furnishings, Currier & Ives steamboat prints, historic firearms and an important collection of marine art are seen throughout the inn. The Tap Room has been described as one of the most attractive drinking rooms in America.

31 Rooms • Price range: $95-200
36 Main St, Essex, CT 06426
☎ (860) 767-1776

Classification Indicators: See facing page for explanations.

Vital Statistics:
Number of rooms, per-night price range, address and phone number.

Note: Canadian prices are in Canadian dollars.

Descriptive text for property

Special Features Icons:
See facing page for explanations.

CROWN OF DIAMONDS BECKONS TRAVELERS TO EXPERIENCE THE EXTRAORDINARY

The diamond's allure is legendary, its appeal multifaceted: enduring quality, consummate luxury, unwavering reliability, sparkling sophistication—and we're not talking gemstones.

Millions of serious travelers appraise the value of diamonds when they are making a lodging selection.

AAA's unique diamond-rating lodging evaluation program is executed annually by dozens of highly trained, full-time inspectors, supported in a regional management system. Their evaluation criteria evolve based on AAA's ongoing communications with the hospitality industry and some 42 million discriminating collaborators: AAA members.

Everyone knows even a single diamond is a good thing to have. Yet thousands of the properties AAA inspects don't merit approval, much less a diamond rating. Those that do

satisfy the requirements of their lodging classification are decorated with from one to five diamonds, AAA's widely respected scale of quality in amenities and service.

Significantly, only a handful of the approximately 26,000 North American lodgings our inspectors approve ever achieve AAA's coveted crown of honor: the Five Diamond Award.

The eight establishments featured in the following pages are the only Five Diamond winners for the lodging classifications presented in this book.

Every AAA diamond-rated lodging assures comfortable accommodations. Indeed, there is a diamond level for every budget and for every occasion.

But a Five Diamond experience transcends all others. The exemplary establishments you are about to meet embody accommodations worthy of a journey.

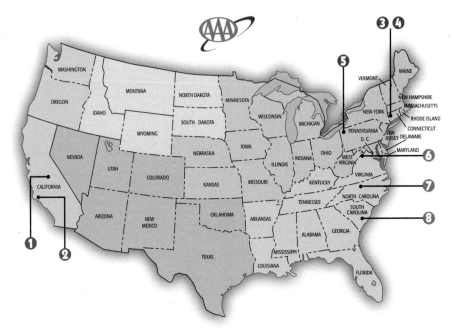

❶ **Chateau du Sureau**
❷ **Simpson House Inn**
❸ **The Mayflower Inn**
❹ **The Inn at National Hall**

❺ **Buhl Mansion**
❻ **The Inn at Little Washington**
❼ **The Fearrington House Inn**
❽ **Woodlands Resort & Inn**

BUHL MANSION

Sharon, Pennsylvania

In 1890, when industrialist Frank H. Buhl began construction of the stone mansion which he and his beloved wife would call home, little did he know that this magnificent architectural gem would endure through the years. That's because he never met the mansion's present owner. For just as Buhl chose Sharon, Pennsylvania, as the site of his "castle," James E. Winner and his wife Donna have made the mansion, now listed on the National Register of Historic Places, the focal point of a personal economic development effort which has brought new luster to the area.

Their contributions include the Vocal Group Hall of Fame Museum and ongoing support of the art world. The result? A part of the mansion houses one of the couple's prestigious art collections. Here visitors can enjoy, as well as buy, the work of some of the region's best-known artists. And what the inn does to nourish the spirit it also does for the body. Buhl Mansion's own state-of-the-art luxury health spa promises to relax, restore and renew.

Body and spirit have also come together in the faithful renovations to the site itself. The results of this $2-million project are impressive. The adjoining greenhouse has been restored to its original magnificent state, and the expansive grounds now possess a manicured, awe-inspiring beauty. Inside the mansion, new stained glass windows grace the halls with multicolored light, while the refurbishing of the Grand Oak stairway has created a glorious showcase for the mansion's intricate woodwork.

As guests ascend to the third floor, they are greeted by a hand-painted mural of formal gardens and cherubs—a fitting welcome to the lavishly appointed guestrooms. Each of the rooms reflects a different aspect of the mansion's original style and incorporates some of the most luxurious of contemporary amenities. The Frank H. Buhl Room, for example, with its "copperlike" ceiling and tones of green and brown, possesses a decidedly masculine ambience befitting its original occupant. The room named after his wife is a work of light and femininity, a study in yellows and blues.

Guestrooms make good use of the mansion's architectural dimensions. The Grand Gables room has 15-foot-high ceilings, while the circular Turret Room showcases a round Jacuzzi for two, a bit of luxury that Mr. Buhl himself certainly would have insisted on if he had lived in the mansion today.

10 Rooms • Price range: $350–$375
422 East State Street, Sharon, PA 16146
☎ **(724) 436-3046**

CHATEAU DU SUREAU

Oakhurst, California

 Tucked away in the tall pines and natural elderberry of the Sierra foothills is a little piece of Provence. Austrian-born owner Erna Kubin-Clanin began with a restaurant on the premises several years ago and its unabashed success prompted the building of this Mediterranean chateau.

From the chateau's signature slate turret to the emblazoned crest on the gates, every detail adds authenticity to this romantic getaway. Tall windows, wrought-iron balconies and terra cotta roofing tiles all testify to a strong European heritage.

Guests are greeted by name at the door and taken on a tour of some of the building's highlights. The richly appointed salon is a show-

case for Kubin-Clanin's collection of European antiques. There is usually a fire going in the fireplace, adding a warm glow to the room's Oriental rugs and hand-painted frescoes. Just off the salon is the turret room, also known as the music tower because it is home to an 1870 Erard grand piano from Paris.

Some creative improvisations have aided the quest for authenticity. The chateau's 40 wooden doors, for instance, were built by a local carpenter who beveled them, then beat them with chains and

even resorted to peppering them with a shotgun to give them an antique look. Similarly "aged" are the limestone floor and stone steps that lead guests to a choice of beautiful rooms.

Each guestroom takes the name of an herb or a flower, determining its color, decor and mood. All rooms are sumptuously furnished with king-size beds, Provençal duvets and Italian linens. Bathrooms include oversize tubs trimmed with hand-painted French tile and separate shower and toilet areas.

Outdoors are a stream-fed pool, pathways through the chateau's gardens, a bocce court and a magical giant chess game.

According to the host, guests may be "outrageously coddled or left in blissful solitude." Within minutes of their arrival, a welcoming tea and basket of delicacies is brought to guests' rooms by the chateau's staff, who are attired in traditional black dresses and white aprons; in the morning, a gourmet French breakfast is served in the Breakfast Room.

But the real treat of the Chateau du Sureau is its Five Diamond restaurant. The Estate of the Elderberries (elderberries is the English translation of *sureau*) serves award-winning French creations and features a distinguished and award-winning wine list.

The culinary delights of France, the romance and charm of another age, all amid the beauty of California: A *séjour* at the chateau is truly a unique experience.

 10 Rooms • Price range: $325-$510
48688 Victoria Lane, Oakhurst, CA 93644
☎ **(559) 683-6860**

THE FEARRINGTON HOUSE INN

Pittsboro, North Carolina

"It's not so much where you go, but how you're treated," comments R.B. Fitch, the proprietor of Fearrington House. His words could well be the motto of this former dairy farm, nestled in the countryside of Chatham County, eight miles south of Chapel Hill. There is no mountain here, no beach. Instead, the charming little village of Fearrington offers pastoral vistas and glorious gardens and seems—at least a little—like paradise.

The focal point of the village is the inn and its adjoining restaurant, the original homestead of the Fearrington family farm.

Established in 1786, the farm passed on from generation to generation until its present owners purchased it and transformed the land into today's country village. Intact, though no longer operational, are the barn and the silo. Cows still graze on the farm, however; the Belted Galloways in the meadow serve in the proud role of village mascots.

The inn's suites stand clustered around a romantic courtyard, while the rooms look out over a 12-acre park. Each is individually decorated with English pine antiques and original art. Distinctive touches include ecclesiastical doors used as headboards, canopied beds and pine flooring imported from a dismantled workhouse along the Thames. The private baths have marble vanities and heated towel racks. Croquet and tennis are available for the energetic. Whirlpools and a wading pool may better suit those looking to de-stress.

One of the best-known features of the inn is its Five Diamond restaurant. Many national magazines have celebrated Executive Chef Cory Mattson's sophisticated Southern cuisine. Mattson says his style is a mixture of Italian, Asian and American cuisine, but his ingredients favor the produce, cured meats and game from the local region.

The village gardens enhance Fearrington's pastoral setting. Walking tours pass through five separate gardens replete with flowers, vines, statuary and birds. Tea is served at the inn's Garden House and the terrace in front of the public Sun Room overlooks Jenny's Garden, with its water sculpture centerpiece. Visitors can purchase more than 200 varieties of plants propagated from those on the grounds at the garden's Potting Shed.

A leisurely stroll around the village reveals a country store, a full-service bar, a fine book store and many other buildings, all sharing the same charming small-town style—as if transported here from a less-hurried era.

31 Rooms • Price range: $195-$385
2000 Fearrington Village Center, Pittsboro, NC 27312
☎ **(919) 542-2121**

THE INN AT LITTLE WASHINGTON

Washington, Virginia

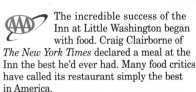 The incredible success of the Inn at Little Washington began with food. Craig Clairborne of *The New York Times* declared a meal at the Inn the best he'd ever had. Many food critics have called its restaurant simply the best in America.

The town of "Little" Washington is beautifully situated between the foothills of Virginia's Blue Ridge Mountains and the Shenandoah Valley just 70-odd miles from the "Big" Washington. It was laid out by a young George Washington in 1749 and actually has first claim to the name.

In 1977 Patrick O'Connell and his partner, Reinhardt Lynch, opened a restaurant in the remains of a local garage and gas station. A few years later, when satisfied guests complained about having to get back in their cars after an evening of wining and dining, O'Connell and Lynch furnished a few rooms above the restaurant. Begun on a tiny budget of $5,000, the inn is today one of the most exclusive establishments in the nation.

Although the inn's exterior seems relatively unimposing, a step through the door reveals turn-of-the-century luxury with a touch of the theatrical. French doors open onto an enchanting garden, transporting the visitor to southern France, while the rich and delightfully eclectic decor of each of the guestrooms was concocted by a London set designer.

But the real drama here is served up in the dining room by O'Connell, a theater student turned chef. In a room draped with William Morris fabrics and lit with lamps shaded by pink silk, guests are treated to course after course of his exquisite inventions. The French-inspired cuisine draws on a variety of other culinary sources and uses the finest local ingredients. Surprising combinations are the result—red pepper soup with Sambucca-laced cream, pastry crescents filled with shiitake mushrooms and Jarlsberg cheese, and seared duck foie gras on polenta with country ham and huckleberries. The *prix fixe* menu offers dozens of choices, including almost 20 spectacular desserts. To observe the act of creation up close, guests can reserve one of the chef's tables right in the gleaming brass and green enamel kitchen.

With the owners' attention to detail and sense of whimsy applied to both the meals and the rooms, the Inn at Little Washington was the first ever to earn AAA's Five Diamond Award for both cuisine and accommodation.

Washington

14 Rooms • Price range: $340-$980
Middle and Main Street, Washington, VA 22747
☎ **(540) 675-3800**

THE INN AT NATIONAL HALL

Westport, Connecticut

 This meticulously restored 1873 Italianate landmark overlooking Westport's Saugatuck River opened in 1993 as a luxury inn.

The results of a five-year, $15-million renovation are impressive. The rose-colored bricks and cast iron of the exterior have been restored to their original splendor, while the interior has been transformed into an oasis of old-world sophistication that is marked by whimsical craftsmanship.

Visitors enter the third-floor lobby by way of a magical elevator, decorated with an array of *trompe l'oeil* leather-bound books. The lobby and the living room are impressively finished with cherry wainscotting, luxurious swag window treatments and large potted plants. The overall theme is Empire opulence and everything is authentic, from the 17th- and 18th-century furniture to the crystal chandelier imported from the Savoy Hotel in London.

Although all the rooms are exquisitely decorated, each has been given its own special touch by way of the artist's brush. Craftsmen under the direction of a master stencil artist from England have created hand-stenciled walls and murals in 18 tasteful themes. All beds have fine linens and European duvets.

Four very special suites feature loft bedrooms, with curving wooden staircases leading to king-size canopy beds. Many of the rooms have 18-foot ceilings.

Other amenities include gas fireplaces, kitchenettes, and limestone and marble-tiled baths equipped with heated towel racks and plush Turkish cotton bathrobes. Many of the long, tall windows offer expansive river views.

Dining at National Hall is always a special event. The entire first floor of the building is devoted to the Miramar Restaurant, which offers gourmet contemporary American-Continental cuisine, an award-winning wine list and fabulous desserts made in the restaurant's pastry kitchen.

Other dining options include the outdoor patio overlooking the river and epicurean private dining in the Versailles Room. Last but not least, the Drawing Room beckons with afternoon tea, canapes and cocktails.

The inn, listed on the National Register of Historic Places, is not the only historic site in Westport. A stroll along the boardwalk of the Saugatuck River reveals a whole district of restored buildings.

Continuing over the bridge, visitors reach a neighborhood known as "Beverly Hills East," offering fashionable boutiques and art galleries as well as Westport's music and summer stock theater scene—considered one of the best in the country.

 19 Rooms • Price range: $225-$485
Two Post Road West, Westport CT 06880
☎ **(203) 221-1351**

THE MAYFLOWER INN

Washington, Connecticut

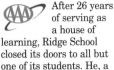 After 26 years of serving as a house of learning, Ridge School closed its doors to all but one of its students. He, a notable local graduate who had gone on to Yale, returned to the historic town and purchased the property, converting it to the Mayflower Inn in 1920. Picturesque Washington, two hours from New York City, soon became a discreet retreat for many of America's most distinguished families—including the Roosevelts—mainly because of the inn's charms.

Over time and through many owners, the inn eventually fell into disrepair. In 1992 two Washington residents, Adriana and Robert Mnuchin, saw the property's potential and used their talents to turn the inn into a hotel of splendid proportions. Art and antiques, gleaned from the owners' many travels through Europe, and a fine eye for landscaping have contributed to creating the elegance and charm of a fine English country house.

The five classic buildings stand on 28 acres of well-tended rhododendrons, stately maples, running streams and rural stone walls. The scene is reminiscent of England's Lake District, with echoes as well of the voices of New England's great poets.

The wide, inviting veranda with its oversize reading chairs greets guests on their way into the lobby, where the richly authentic antique decor indicates the inn's true style. This is a place where comfort and sophistication meet.

Each of the guestrooms has been given its own distinct style, but all have one common signature piece: an 18th-century Chippendale desk. Other common features are fireplaces, spacious marble bathrooms with brass and Limoges fittings, and bed linens by Frette. Guests often visit the inn's piano bar for an aperitif before dining.

And dinner itself has been described by *The New York Times* as "creative, selective and stellar." All of the chef's ingredients come from the local countryside and the nearby Atlantic. Specialties include house-smoked salmon, game sausage and, when in season, organic herbs and produce from the inn's kitchen gardens.

The Mayflower also has a long history as a meeting place. The Teahouse is equipped to handle any occasion, whether a hi-tech business meeting or an intimate reception.

As for sports and leisure, the Mayflower offers its own state-of-the-art fitness club, with steam and sauna facilities, an Omni-surface tennis court, and a superb heated pool. For those looking for a challenge, the Steeprock Reserve, with its acres of hiking trails, is only three minutes away. But one need only bide a while in the wildflower garden or stroll among the maples to savor the New England charm of the Mayflower.

25 Rooms • Price range: $400–$600
118 Woodbury Road, Washington, CT 06793
☎ **(860) 868-9466**

SIMPSON HOUSE INN

Santa Barbara, California

Robert Simpson must have felt he had disembarked on another planet the day he unloaded the first shipment of wood siding from a boat in Santa Barbara harbor. It was 1874. There was no

railway; San Francisco was a 36-hour stagecoach ride away; and electricity was a distant dream. Still, Simpson recognized the allure of the Mediterranean climate and built this wonderful Italianate-Victorian home in what was to become one of the most beautiful cities in the country.

The 20th century was less kind, however, and the home, after surviving an earthquake, nearly met its end under the wrecker's ball. It was rescued in 1976 when the present owners bought the home and began a complete restoration, prompting the city of Santa Barbara to bestow on the inn its Structure of Merit Award.

Since that time, the home's historic barn has been reconstructed, adding four charming rooms to the inn, and several English-style garden cottages have been constructed under the 100-year-old trees.

The accent on all furnishings and decor is Victorian luxury. From the Oriental rugs to the decorative ceiling moldings, everything is authentic. Fringed lampshades, lace curtains and red brocade draperies live in harmony here.

Guestrooms combine English elegance with casual Santa Barbara style. French doors open onto verandas surrounded by magnolias, mature oaks and lush flower gardens. Rooms are graced with goose-down comforters and fresh flowers; some have a fireplace and a whirlpool tub. In-room massages, facials and other beauty treatments are available and guests have access to the nearby Santa Barbara Athletic Club.

Breakfast is a leisurely affair, served on the veranda, in the formal dining room or on a private patio. Afternoon hors d'oeuvres—delicacies such as roasted onions in blue cheese and olive soda bread—are served with a sampling of Santa Barbara's best vintage.

The inn's acre of English gardens with trickling fountains and statues are an inviting place for an evening stroll. Tall green hedges and sandstone walls screen the inn from the tree-lined street.

Not that one should necessarily stay on the grounds. Historic and beautiful Santa Barbara has many sights and guests can begin the so-called Red Tile Walking Tour of downtown right from the door of the inn. Included on the tour are the Alice Keck Park Gardens, the Museum of Art and the Santa Barbara Historical Society.

But guests' greatest pleasure comes in being pampered by Simpson House's professional, service-oriented staff.

14 Rooms • Price range: $215-$435
121 East Arrellaga Street, Santa Barbara, CA 93101
☎ **(805) 963-7067**

WOODLANDS RESORT & INN

Summerville, South Carolina

In 1886 the World Congress of Physicians in Paris declared Summerville, South Carolina, with its pine forests as "one of the healthiest climates in the world." Subsequently, this charming little village 20 miles inland from Charleston quickly became a fashionable winter residence for local travelers as well as elite from abroad.

Woodlands Resort, a classic Revival home built in 1906, was originally one of these residences. Hidden away in 42 private wooded acres, the inn today not only recaptures that genteel era, but also offers visitors all the luxuries of contemporary accommodations.

In the early 1990s Woodlands underwent 18 months of meticulous restoration and reconstruction. New York furniture and interior designer David Eskell-Briggs was brought on board to give each of the 19 rooms personality. Reflected in the rooms' decor is the designer's British background and his travels to India and Jamaica.

It is this same careful attention to detail that also marks the service provided to every guest at the Woodlands. On their arrival, guests are greeted with fresh flowers and an iced split of champagne. Turn-down service includes hand-made chocolates from the Woodlands' talented pastry chef.

The rooms have been appointed in a wonderful combination of comfort and grand style. Some include a sitting room, a fireplace and a whirlpool bath; all are stocked with thoughtful amenities such as monogrammed robes and soothing glycerine soaps.

Special features of the inn include the Five Diamond Dining Room with its innova-

tive "low-country" cuisine, the charming Winter Garden where afternoon tea is served and the elegant lounge. The separate, majestic Pavilion, with its indoor/outdoor fireplaces, its soaring cathedral ceilings and its private dining room, provides a memorable venue for meetings and receptions.

The inn's outdoor facilities are typically English. Guests can choose from tennis, croquet or a walking tour of the grounds' nature trails, ending with a refreshing swim in the climate-controlled pool nestled in the woods.

And the Woodlands hasn't forgotten the original attraction of Summerville: health. The inn's spa provides facials, body treatments of herbal wraps and the rejuvenating touch of an in-house massage therapist.

Although the Woodlands has more than enough to offer any guest, nearby sights beckon. Bicycles are available for touring the charming downtown area of Summerville. Nineteen courses in the area are more than enough to satisfy the most avid golfer. Since it is only 20 miles from the sea, the inn will help plan a day of deep-sea fishing—and the chef will prepare the day's catch.

Summerville

19 Rooms • Price range: $290-$350
125 Parsons Road, Summerville, SC 29483
☎ (843) 875-2600

Northeast

Ocean Grove, NJ, has the largest collection of Victorian architecture in the country.

Scenic Byways
of the Northeast

Yesterday and today come together at Billings Farm and Museum in Woodstock, Vermont, a modern working dairy farm and a museum of state farm life in the 1890s.

Rockland to Bucksport

This tour hugs the Maine coastline, with half a dozen ports of call along the way. From the rugged, unspoiled beauty of Acadia National Park and the historic Fort of Castine to the fishing ports of Rockport and Rockland, the area's rich maritime heritage is in evidence at every turn. But the area is as alive today as it ever was. Fishing boats continue to ply the Atlantic, and lobster is still plentiful and, as always, delicious.

Kancamagus Highway

The trek between Conway and Lost River Gorge offers a reminder of the awesome splendor of Mother Nature. Parallel to the Swift River, the route rises to more than half a mile above sea level at the Kancamagus Pass, displaying some of New Hampshire's most stunning scenery.

Wilmington to Troy

Meandering through the Vermont countryside, this drive is about as far from the hustle and bustle of city life as one can get. Highlights are the resort town of Stowe, a mecca for outdoor-sports enthusiasts, and the Shelburne Museum, with its fascinating collections of folk art.

Sagamore to Orleans

Massachusetts may be the high-tech capital of the east coast, but the history of the Cape Cod area stretches back more than 300 years to when sailors navigated by the stars and sextant. The tour touches on the oldest town in the area, Sandwich, and also visits a fine state park. Additional stops along the way have the unmistakable flavor of the area's seafaring past when whaling dominated the region's economy.

Morning mist envelopes Lake Avalanche in Adirondack Park, a six-million-acre recreation area in upstate New York.

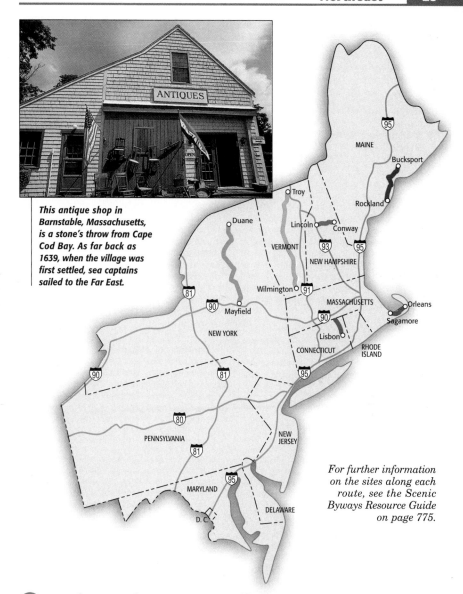

This antique shop in Barnstable, Massachusetts, is a stone's throw from Cape Cod Bay. As far back as 1639, when the village was first settled, sea captains sailed to the Far East.

For further information on the sites along each route, see the Scenic Byways Resource Guide on page 775.

Massachusetts Border to I-395

The strong influence of the sea can be seen in the towns of Connecticut, including Mystic, with its shipbuilding legacy, and New London and Groton, which have witnessed the launching of several generations of seagoing vessels, from 18th-century schooners to nuclear submarines. Inland, the Quinebaug Valley Hatchery raises more than half a million trout annually.

Route 30

This is the tour for dyed-in-the-wool sports fans. From Lake Placid, the site of the 1932 and 1980 winter Olympic Games, through the outdoor enthusiast's paradise of Adirondack Park all the way to the Baseball Hame of Fame in Cooperstown, where the country's athletic heritage plays a starring role.

Rockland to Bucksport

The craggy coast of Maine offers a beguiling collection of coves, inlets and peninsulas. The rich maritime tradition of this area is evident everywhere— from the lobster traps piled up on weathered wharves and the imposing presence of old sea captains' homes to the fishing boats that dot the harbors and the seafood markets that display the catch-of-the-day on roadside signs.

❶ The Farnsworth Art Museum and Wyeth Center

The "Lobster Capital of the World," Rockland is one of Maine's largest fishing ports. The harbor is home to a flotilla of working boats and a fleet of cruise schooners ready to ply the waters of Penobscot Bay. One of the main attractions in town is the Farnsworth Art Museum and Wyeth Center. Along with changing exhibitions of contemporary artwork, the Museum's permanent collection has 19th- and early 20th-century Maine and American art by such notables as Rockwell Kent, Winslow Homer and Andrew Wyeth. The Wyeth Center houses three generations of Wyeth works. Also open to the public is the Farnsworth Homestead, the Greek-Revival home of Lucy Farnsworth, whose estate endowed the Farnsworth Art Museum in memory of her father, William A. Farnsworth.

❷ Rockport

During the 19th century, Rockport produced two million casks of lime a year. The lime was used to make mortar and plaster. Three lime kilns are on display at Rockport Marine Park, along with a statue of André the Seal, known for his migration from Boston to Rockport every summer. The Center for Maine Contemporary Art, which showcases emerging artists, is open year-round, and in the summer the Bay Chamber Concerts take place every Thursday and Friday at the Rockport Opera House.

❸ Camden

When talk turns to identifying the quintessential Maine coastal town, the name Camden is sure to be heard. Known as the town "where the mountains meet the sea," Camden is home to America's largest collection of windjammers, and cruises on board these boats offer a novel way to explore the Maine coastline. Camden was once home to one of America's finest 20th-century poets, Edna St. Vincent Millay, who used to recite her latest creations at the Whitehall Inn. Today the town is a favorite spot for year-round sporting enthusiasts. In the summer, kayaks follow the crenellated coastline near the town, while ice skating, skiing and a toboggan chute prove popular in the winter. One of the best views of the town is from the hills that lie just to the west of the houses that rim Penobscot Bay.

❹ Penobscot Marine Museum

At one time, Searsport was home to close to 300 sea captains, and today many of their homes still line the town's streets. The city boasts one of the best ports on the Maine coast. The Penobscot Marine Museum displays various artifacts from the maritime trade, including shipbuilding and whaling tools and artifacts from the Far East, a reminder that the seafarers traveled far in their endeavors. The museum includes three captains' homes and a half dozen historic buildings. For the antique lover, look no further than the shops that line the nearby stretch of Route 1. In the summer, a flea market is also held on this strip.

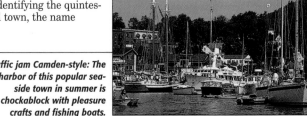

Traffic jam Camden-style: The harbor of this popular seaside town in summer is chockablock with pleasure crafts and fishing boats.

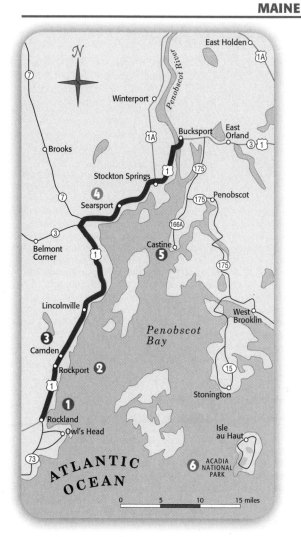

Sailboats get ready to head out for a day on Penobscot Bay, which dominates this portion of the Maine coastline.

❺ Castine

For two centuries, the port town of Castine was fought over by French, British, Dutch, American and Native American forces. The first habitation was a French fort erected in 1613. Today the town is home to the Maine Maritime Academy, which trains merchant marines. Castine also boasts an impressive collection of Federal and Greek-Revival homes as well as white clapboard houses encircling the town common. Tourists can take historic walking tours around town, and enjoy views of yachts and windjammers anchored in the harbor.

❻ Acadia National Park

Acadia National Park draws more than three million visitors a year. And with good reason. The park lays claim to one of the most unspoiled coastlines in the east, with seemingly endless lichen-covered granite hills that spill down into the surf. Part of the park takes up 2,700 acres on Isle au Haut and boasts 20 miles of nature trails. The island is located a half-hour ferry ride from Stonington. The island's deserted cobble beaches offer excellent hiking possibilities and small lean-tos can be reserved in advance for camping.

Kancamagus Highway

"The New Hampshire mountains curl up in a coil," wrote the poet Robert Frost. Nowhere is this more evident than on the Kancamagus Highway (State Route 112). A National Forest Scenic Highway, SR 112 threads its way through the heart of the White Mountains, offering unforgettable scenic vistas of the Granite State.

❶ Lost River Gorge

Lost River Gorge is a tribute to the awesome power of the last Ice Age. This half-mile-long chasm in the Moosilauke River includes waterfalls and caves that visitors can explore by walkways and, in some cases, ladders. Some of the caves require agility to maneuver through, and names such as the Lemon Squeezer are a reminder that these caves are not the best of places for claustrophobics.

❷ Kancamagus Pass

The 34-mile-long Kancamagus Highway—New Hampshire's wildest scenic route—is about as remote a road as you're likely to find in New Hampshire. There are no houses or gas stations along the route—just mile after mile of stunning views. After climbing the rocky hills for 28 miles west of Conway along the course of the Swift River, the road finally reaches an elevation of nearly 3,000 feet at the Kancamagus Pass. Along the way, there are numerous turnouts that reward those who stop with views of sights such as the cascading Sabbaday Falls and the imposing granite-walled Rocky Gorge. From the pass, the highway descends along the east branch of the Pemigewasset River into the town of Lincoln, best known for its water park, the Whale's Tale.

❸ North Conway

The growth of factory outlets has made North Conway a shopping mecca. But there are more reasons to venture here than a deal on designer clothes or kitchen accessories. One of them is the Conway Scenic Railroad depot, which offers a captivating view into railroads of the past. Located in an 1874 station on the Portsmouth Great Falls and Conway Railroad, the twin-towered building includes original furnishings and equipment from the days when telegraphers tapped out messages in Morse code and mailbags were picked up on the fly from a trackside pole. The station also displays old railroad cars, Pullman sleepers and vintage locomotives. From here you can take an 11-mile trip through the Mount Washington Valley in a coach pulled by a steam or diesel engine, or a 5½-hour trip through Crawford Notch.

❹ Crawford Notch State Park

Crawford Notch is named after the family that settled in this area in the late 18th century, and went on to run inns and serve as mountain guides. A few miles north of the notch lies Silver Cascade, a stream that drops 1,000 feet along the flank of Mount Webster. Crawford Notch State Park is a favorite spot for hikers and picnickers.

❺ Franconia Notch State Park

Franconia Notch is perhaps the most celebrated notch in the east, drawing visitors to this cleft in the towering Kinsman and Franconia ranges since the late 18th century. Chief among the attractions is the Old Man of the Mountain—five granite ledges that jut from the cliffs above Profile Lake.

Surrounded by a blanket of green, the pristine waters of Echo Lake beckon vacationers to stop and linger by the shores.

A covered bridge recalls the days of yore when horses and buggies made their way through the New Hampshire countryside.

Together they look uncannily like a human face in profile. Immortalized by Nathaniel Hawthorne in his story *The Great Stone Face*, the visage is so familiar that it has been designated as the state's official trademark. The best spot for viewing this natural wonder is from the eastern shore of the lake. The 6,440-acre Franconia Notch State Park offers many outdoor activities.

❻ Cannon Mountain Aerial Tramway

Driving through the mountains of New Hampshire, one may yearn to soar above the slopes and gaze down at the landscape. Cannon Mountain Aerial Tramway allows visitors to do precisely that. During the summer months, 80-passenger cars whisk people to an observation platform at the summit of the mountain. The 2,022-foot ascent takes less than eight minutes. From the top, visitors drink in the spectacular views. Cannon Mountain has drawn skiers to its slopes since the 1930s. The state-run facility offers trails from novice to expert, with a total vertical drop of 2,146 feet.

Wilmington to Troy

From a starting point near the Massachusetts border to an endpoint tucked against the Canadian border, Vermont State Route 100 meanders through a landscape of covered bridges, farmers' fields and picture-postcard towns. This tour delights the senses every season of the year, treating drivers to a changing panorama of snow-covered fields, budding apple blossoms, cow-grazed meadows and autumn's foliage splendors.

❶ Bennington

Bennington looms large in Vermont's past—and its present. It was here on August 16, 1777, that an American force under General John Stark defeated a British force under General John Burgoyne. The Battle of Bennington is commemorated with a 304-foot-tall obelisk, the tallest battle monument in the world when it was completed in 1891. Today it offers a sweeping view of the nearby countryside from an observation gallery at the top. The oldest part of the city, Old Bennington, is a National Register Historic District, which includes grand 18th- and 19th-century homes clustered around a quintessential village green. Vermont's third-largest city also boasts three covered bridges, as well as renowned Bennington College, founded in 1932.

❷ Stratton Mountain

An outdoor playground year round, Stratton Mountain has some of the best skiing and hiking in Vermont. Since 1982 the site has also hosted the annual U.S. Open Snowboarding Championships, a virtual "Who's Who" of competitive snowboarding. The event is held in mid March.

❸ Manchester

The town of Manchester has been a retreat for the well-heeled since the mid-19th century, when Mary Todd Lincoln brought her young family north to spend part of the summer away from Washington. Her son Robert, the Great Emancipator's only boy to survive to adulthood, eventually made a 24-room Georgian-Revival mansion in the town his vacation home. Known as Hildene, the house and its impressive formal gardens are open to the public. Today

Manchester is popular for its upscale factory outlets and nearby ski resorts, Bromley and Stratton Mountain. To the west stands the imposing Mount Equinox, which boasts Vermont's only mountaintop hotel.

❹ Plymouth

The sleepy hamlet of Plymouth was for one brief moment the center of American political power. Early on the morning of August 3, 1923, after the death of Warren Harding, Calvin Coolidge became America's 30th president at the family home in this village. Coolidge's father, a notary public, administered the oath of office. The town hasn't changed a great deal since then. A visitor still sees the white clapboard houses that were familiar to Coolidge. The President Calvin Coolidge State Historic Site at Plymouth Notch includes a general store that was run by Coolidge's father, the Coolidge residence, the Calvin Coolidge birthplace and the Union Christian Church, an 1840 meeting house still in use.

❺ Shelburne

The 37 buildings making up the Shelburne Museum offer one of the country's most extensive and eclectic displays of American decorative and folk art. There are buildings full of decoys and old woodworking tools, antique toys and rare works of art. One of the most impressive structures is the 220-foot-long sidewheeler *SS Ticonderoga*,

Manchester's Hildene, part of a 412-acre estate, was once the summer home of Robert Todd Lincoln.

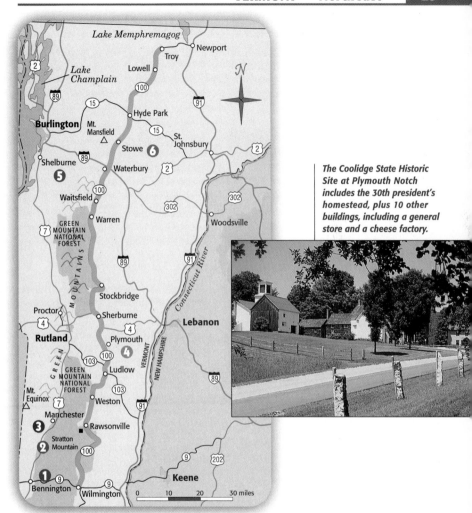

The Coolidge State Historic Site at Plymouth Notch includes the 30th president's homestead, plus 10 other buildings, including a general store and a cheese factory.

which was hauled two miles from Lake Champlain to its landlocked berth at the museum. Nearby Shelburne Farms consists of 1,400 acres landscaped by Frederic Law Olmstead (Central Park's designer), with walking trails, a working farm including a dairy and the shops of working artisans.

⑥ Stowe

Since the 1930s when a rope tow powered by a car engine pulled skiers up the slope for 50 cents a day, the town of Stowe has been synonymous with skiing. The trails on nearby Mount Mansfield, Vermont's highest peak, still provide some of the most challenging runs in the east. Stowe is also the state's most popular summer resort, with an excellent golf course, tennis courts and nearby hiking and biking trails—including the more than five-mile-long Stowe Recreation path, which wends its way to the base of Mount Mansfield through cornfields and meadows dotted with wildflowers. There are also numerous shops and restaurants that cater to the town's year-round visitors.

Sagamore to Orleans

Jutting defiantly into the Atlantic Ocean, the great bent arm of Cape Cod has figured in America's past since the day in 1620 when the Pilgrims sailed by its shores before landing at nearby Plymouth Rock. Today this world of sand dunes and endless beaches offers a salt-scented repose from the stresses of city life.

The Sandwich Glass Museum serves as a reminder of the time when this Cape Cod town made glass that was prized and emulated around the world.

❶ Heritage Plantation

Situated on 76 acres of trees, shrubs and flowers, the Heritage Plantation offers an array of buildings of different architectural styles. Included among the collection is a replica of the round Shaker Barn at Hancock Shaker Village. The barn houses a fine range of vintage automobiles, including Gary Cooper's 1930 Duesenberg. The best time to visit the site is early June, when the rhododendrons are in bloom, covering the grounds with a profusion of colors.

❷ Sandwich

Founded in 1639, Sandwich is Cape Cod's oldest town and boasts a number of impressive homes in its historic district. In fact, many regular visitors to the area consider it the best preserved town on the Cape. Sandwich became prosperous in the 19th century when it was the hub of glassmaking for the region. The Boston & Sandwich Glass Company produced fine-colored glass that was particularly prized. Exhibits of various pieces of tableware and decorative glass are now on display at the Sandwich Glass Museum.

❸ Trayser Museum

The town of Barnstable was settled in 1639 by pioneers who relied on salt hay in the nearby Great Marshes to feed their livestock. Later the town was associated with the whaling trade. Initially settlers trapped whales on the barrier beach called Sandy Neck before taking to the waters off the coast of Cape Cod in locally built ships. History greets the visitor at every turn. The bell in the West Parish of Barnstable church was cast by Paul Revere. And there is the Trayser Museum, housed in the Custom House, which was built in 1856. The museum includes ship models, Native American relics, carpentry tools, nautical equipment and an old wooden jail. Barnstable is also a popular embarkation point for local whale-watching excursions.

❹ Dennis

The clipper ships and schooners that left the Dennis harbor in days gone by often ventured as far as China. Today the town is better known to many visitors for its summer stage: The town lays claim to the oldest professional summer theater in America. Its history is rich with stories of actors and actresses who began their careers here, including Bette Davis and Henry Fonda. Those seeking a bird's-eye view of the Cape should climb the nearby Scargo Hill Tower. From the top, one can see Provincetown at the Cape's sandy fist, more than 20 miles away. Dennis was named after an area minister, Josiah Dennis. His house has been restored and displays furnishings from the 18th century.

Map showing: Cape Cod Bay, N (compass), Sagamore, Sandwich, East Sandwich, West Barnstable, Barnstable, Yarmouth, West Yarmouth, Dennis, Brewster, East Brewster, Orleans, NICKERSON STATE PARK, Harwich Port, Forestdale, Mashpee, Santuit, HERITAGE PLANTATION, ATLANTIC OCEAN. Route numbers 6, 28, 6A, 130, 132. Scale 0, 5, 10, 15 miles.

Lighthouses have been a familiar sight on Cape Cod since before the whaling days of Herman Melville. The one shown at right is found on Nauset Beach at Eastham.

❺ Brewster

Brewster, situated near the elbow of Cape Cod, is home to an impressive collection of stately early 19th-century homes built by the sea captains who once dominated the town's economy. Their legacy is also still evident at the First Parish Brewster Unitarian Church, a white clapboard building containing pews inscribed with the names of some of the town's famous sea captains. Nearby beaches are a popular spot for exploring tide pools. The Cape Cod Museum of Natural History includes interactive exhibits for children. There are also three nature trails that pass through different natural environments of the Cape: beach, woodland and salt marsh.

❻ Nickerson State Park

Nickerson State Park, 2,000 acres of pine trees and oaks punctuated by eight small kettle ponds, is considered by many to be the finest park in Massachusetts. The land was donated to the state in 1934 by Addie Nickerson, widow of railroad magnate Roland Nickerson, who had used the land as his private hunting and fishing preserve. In 1935 the Civilian Conservation Corps planted close to 100,000 trees on the land. Today the park is an oasis for picnickers, canoers and bird-watchers. Cyclists can try out an eight-mile bike path in the park, which connects to the 25-mile-long Cape Cod Rail Trail, a paved path that follows an old railroad bed.

Massachusetts Border to I-395

There is a timeless appeal to Connecticut's rolling green hills and its quaint historic towns anchored around village commons. And the area's connection with the sea runs deep. For centuries, towns, such as Mystic and Groton, have sent mariners to the far ends of the earth.

Mystic Seaport offers an engaging reminder of the past when sailors heading out to sea had to depend on the good graces of the wind to take them to their destination.

❶ Quinebaug Valley Fish Hatchery

Every year the Quinebaug Valley Fish Hatchery raises about 600,000 trout, making it one of the largest hatcheries east of the Mississippi. Visitors can gain a below-the-water view by peering through glass walls in one part of the hatchery. For the avid angler, a public fishing pond is stocked with trout raised at the hatchery.

❷ Roseland Cottage

Sharing three acres with an ice house, an aviary, and a barn containing one of the oldest bowling alleys in the country, Roseland Cottage in Woodstock is a Gothic masterpiece, complete with trompe l'oeil paneled archways, Gothic-Revival furniture and hand-painted tiles. It is also known as the Henry C. Bowen House after its original owner, a silk importer and newspaper publisher who used to spend his summers in Woodstock. Much of the original furniture is in place, such as the large dining table where some of Bowen's illustrious guests dined. Among the visitors during the Fourth of July weekends—a major celebration in this town—were four U.S. presidents: Ulysses S. Grant, Rutherford Hayes, Benjamin Harrison and William McKinley.

❸ Prudence Crandall Museum

The Prudence Crandall Museum, located on the Canterbury green, was the site of an academy for young black women before the Civil War. Students from all over southern New England attended the school until the Connecticut state assembly restricted enrollment to state residents. Later, after a local mob attacked the school with clubs and iron bars, Prudence Crandall reluctantly agreed to close it down in 1834. Fifty years later the state issued an official apol-

ogy and offered her a pension. Today the 13-room Federal-style building has exhibits devoted to local, black and women's history.

❹ Mystic

One of the most important shipbuilding sites in America, the town of Mystic is where some of the fastest clipper ships of the time were constructed. Mystic Seaport, the Museum of America and the Sea, commemorates this legacy, boasting three tall ships, a collection of galleries full of cultural artifacts belonging to seafarers of the past, and the *Charles W. Morgan*, the last of the wooden whaling ships. There is a working shipyard where the freedom schooner *Amistad* was constructed, and a cooperage, shipsmith, printing press, ropewalk and drugstore. Staff at the carve shop demonstrate the techniques used to make the figureheads that graced the bows of America's once-great sailing vessels. Mystic is also home to the Denison Homestead, which dates from 1717 and illustrates home life in New England from the Colonial period to World War II.

❺ Groton

The rich maritime tradition of Groton and New London dates back to the schooners of the 18th century and continues up to the high-tech submarines of today. In 1954 the first nuclear-powered submarine, *Nautilus*,

A trip up to the tower of the Old Lighthouse Museum in Stonington provides a view of three neighboring states.

was launched from Groton. At nearby Avery Point you can board a 55-foot research vessel, the *EnviroLab,* and take a two-and-a-half-hour hands-on educational cruise as part of Project Oceanology. Fort Griswold was the scene of one of the grisliest battles in the War of Independence. A raid by British forces under the command of Benedict Arnold broke through the defending forces at the fort. The patriots surrendered and threw down their weapons, but the attackers took revenge for their heavy losses, killing about 85 militia men, some of whom were boys. A museum on the grounds features a scale model of the fort, and there are superb views from the top of the Groton Monument, a 135-foot-tall obelisk.

⑥ Thomas Lee House Museum

In the rural community of East Lyme, many fine old homesteads are intact. The Thomas Lee House, an excellent example of early Colonial architecture, is believed to be the oldest wooden frame house left in its original condition in the state. Old Lyme was home for many years to Roger Tory Peterson, one of America's best-known naturalists and father of the famous field guides.

Route 30

Winding and hilly Route 30 serves as the jumping-off point for all the sites on this drive. To the east lies the Olympic village of Lake Placid. After a meander through the mountains, there's the sight of Blue Mountain Lake lying at more than half a mile above sea level. To the west are Cooperstown and Howes Cave.

❶ Lake Placid

The village of Lake Placid, situated on the shores of Lake Placid and Mirror Lake, was host to two Olympic games this century, in 1932 and in 1980. Many of the facilities continue to operate. Whiteface Mountain, less than 10 miles north of the village, offers both recreational and competitive downhill skiing. Lake Placid doesn't sit idle when the snow and ice melt: Summer activities are well represented, too. There are miles of bicycle and horseback-riding paths and hiking trails. Public beaches ring the lakes, which are dotted with recreational boats. Golf enthusiasts can choose from among six courses. There are two ways to scale the summit of Whiteface Mountain in summer: by chairlift and via the Whiteface Mountain Veterans' Memorial Highway. For sightseers, there are tours of the facilities at the United States Olympic Training Center and the multipurpose Olympic Center, with its speed-skating oval and hockey and curling rinks.

❷ Blue Mountain Lake

Visitors to the Adirondack Museum can discover the region's history and culture in a pleasant 32-acre setting overlooking Blue Mountain Lake. The museum traces the ways in which people lived, worked and sought recreation in the 19th century in what is now the Adirondack State Park, a six-million-acre wilderness area. The indoor and outdoor exhibits include buildings, furniture, carriages, boats, historic photos and displays of activities such as logging and camping. The drive to and from Blue Mountain Lake itself is breathtaking.

❸ Howes Cave

Howe Caverns in Howes Cave is a treasure trove of subterranean chambers. Elevators take visitors almost 200 feet below ground to the caves, the temperature of which is always a cool 52 degrees Fahrenheit. Brick walkways skirt a prehistoric underground river and pass through caverns with stalagmites and stalactites. The walk leads visitors to the Lake of Venus, where they can enjoy a boat ride. Nearby stands the Iroquois Indian Museum, which celebrates the heritage and culture of the Iroquois people. The museum features contemporary Iroquois art as well as exhibits of archeological and historical artifacts. Hands-on displays are geared to children.

❹ National Baseball Hall of Fame and Museum

From Babe Ruth's practice bat to Mark McGwire's record-breaking home-run ball, the Baseball Hall of Fame in Cooperstown is a shrine to the most revered players of America's national pastime. Three stories high, the hall and adjoining museum are packed with interest, delighting more than 300,000 devotees every year. Thousands of items are on display: tributes to the game's elected members; photos, paintings and

A logging and sawmill village in the 1890s, Tupper Lake in the Adirondacks is now an all-season resort. In summer, in addition to boating, fishing and swimming, the town is an ideal spot for a picnic.

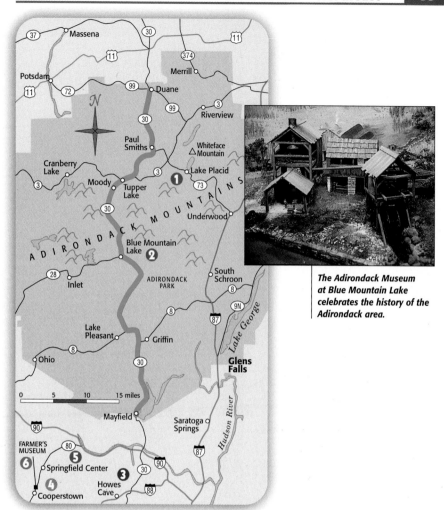

The map shows the Adirondack region with locations including Massena, Potsdam, Merrill, Duane, Riverview, Paul Smiths, Whiteface Mountain, Cranberry Lake, Moody, Tupper Lake, Lake Placid, Blue Mountain Lake, Underwood, Inlet, Adirondack Park, South Schroon, Lake Pleasant, Griffin, Ohio, Lake George, Glens Falls, Hudson River, Mayfield, Saratoga Springs, Farmer's Museum, Springfield Center, Howes Cave, and Cooperstown.

The Adirondack Museum at Blue Mountain Lake celebrates the history of the Adirondack area.

statues of players and special moments; and bats, balls, caps, uniforms and gloves that have played a significant role in baseball's history and lore. The Doubleday Batting Range allows visitors to swing at a fastball. The Ballparks Room displays replicas and actual pieces of baseball stadiums.

❺ Springfield Center
A few miles north of Cooperstown on Lake Otsego, Springfield Center takes visitors from "peanuts and Cracker Jacks" to high culture. Every year the Glimmerglass Opera features four operas performed in repertory at the Alice Busch Opera Theater.

The facility itself is a sight: The side walls are open to the outdoors, revealing the surrounding landscape.

❻ The Farmer's Museum
Just north of Cooperstown on Route 80, the Farmer's Museum recalls life in upstate New York in the 1800s. The museum features household and agricultural tools, as well as artisans who perform traditional skills such as blacksmithing, broom-making, printing and weaving. In the fields are living examples of heritage plant strains and animal breeds, such as Devon cattle and Cayuga ducks.

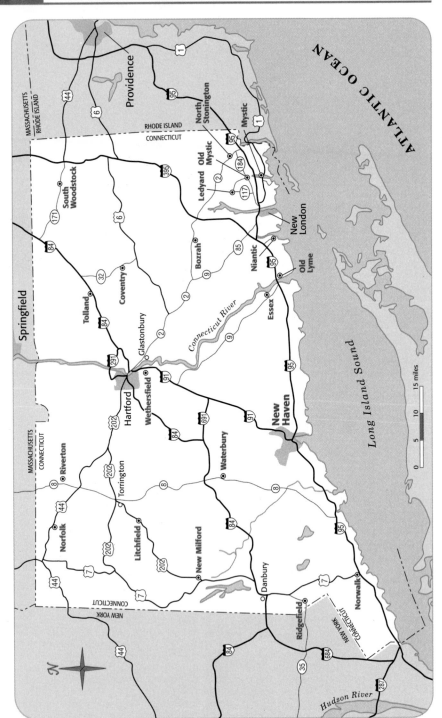

Bozrah
Fitch Claremont House

The Fitch-Claremont House has undergone many transformations since its 1790 construction. Once a farm, the property is now a working vineyard, located close to a casino. Owners Nora and Warren Strong have imprinted their own style on the residence. Each guestroom is individually decorated and has a private bath and gas fireplace. The seasonal breakfast menu sometimes includes raspberry cream pastry and apple coffee cake.

4 Rooms • Price range: $85-150
83 Fitchville Rd, Bozrah, CT 06334
☎ **(860) 889-0260**

Coventry
Special Joys Bed & Breakfast

This is the perfect place for guests who want to relive a bit of their childhood. Owners Joy and Bill Kelleher have taken care to give their establishment a distinctive feel. Guests will find the Colonial room—one of two guestrooms—filled with teddy bears, dolls and antique toys. There is also Special Joys' toy store and toy museum. Guests who appreciate a horticultural setting will enjoy the plant-filled solarium/breakfast room.

2 Rooms • Price range: $50-65
41 North River Rd, Coventry, CT 06238
☎ **(860) 742-6359**

Essex
Griswold Inn

The history of this inn is inextricably linked to the story of Essex. Since opening its doors in 1776, the "Gris" has offered travelers bright, airy rooms and finely prepared meals. Beautifully restored antique furnishings, Currier & Ives steamboat prints, historic firearms and an important collection of marine art are seen throughout the inn. The Tap Room has been described as one of the most attractive drinking rooms in America.

31 Rooms • Price range: $95-200
36 Main St, Essex, CT 06426
☎ **(860) 767-1776**

Ledyard
The Mare's Inn B&B

This is a country Cape-style inn on well-kept grounds in a quiet location.

4 Rooms • Price range: $125-165
333 Colonel Ledyard Hwy, Ledyard, CT 06372
☎ **(860) 572-7556**

Litchfield
Litchfield Inn

This Colonial-style inn, set amid trees, is picture perfect. Rooms are spacious.

32 Rooms • Price range: $120-175
432 Bantam Rd, Litchfield, CT 06759
☎ **(860) 567-4503**

Mystic
Six Broadway Inn

This masterfully restored 1854 Victorian-Italianate home retains much of the charm of the original. Each of the five guestrooms is furnished with exquisite French period pieces. European linens drape queen-size beds. Three of the rooms have views of the majestic Mystic River; one room has its own private porch. Weather permitting, breakfast is served in the gazebo. Downtown Mystic is walking distance.

5 Rooms • Price range: $165-245
6 Broadway Ave, Mystic, CT 06355
☎ **(860) 536-6010**

Mystic
Steamboat Inn
Named after the famous Mystic ships, the Steamboat Inn has as much allure as those old vessels. Six of the rooms, located on the second floor, overlook the Mystic River. The four rooms on the first floor are newer, larger suites. Six rooms have a fireplace and all 10 have whirlpool baths. The inn is within walking distance of attractions such as the Mystic Seaport Museum and the Olde Mistick Shopping Village.

10 Rooms • Price range: $185-275
73 Steamboat Wharf, Mystic, CT 06355
☎ **(860) 536-8300**

Mystic
⏰ Whitehall Mansion

This quintessential New England inn dates back to 1771. It was built by Dr. Dudley Woodbridge, a one-time theologian and minister who later became a successful medical doctor. The restored mansion now houses five guestrooms, featuring antique furnishings, queen-size canopy beds, working fireplaces and modern baths with Jacuzzis. A shuttle is available to transport guests to the nearby casino.

5 Rooms • Price range: $169-219
42 Whitehall Ave, Mystic, CT 06355
☎ **(860) 572-7280**

Mystic
The Adams House
Surrounded by greenery and flower gardens, this place has a homey atmosphere in a Colonial-style setting. Built in 1749, the inn has fireplaces in the dining room and in two bedrooms. All rooms have queen-size beds and private baths.

7 Rooms • Price range: $95-175
382 Cow Hill Rd, Mystic, CT 06355
☎ **(860) 572-9551**

New Haven
The Inn at Oyster Point
Built circa 1903, this charming Victorian house is in Oyster Point National Historic district. Beautifully appointed thematic rooms have upscale furnishings and some antiques. Each unit has access to a shared kitchen.

5 Rooms • Price range: $110-159
104 Howard Ave, New Haven, CT 06519
☎ **(203) 773-3334**

New Milford
⑩ *The Homestead Inn*

This pretty white and green clapboard inn served as the private residence for the Treadwell family from 1853, when it was built, until 1915. After changing hands several times, it was established as an inn in 1928. Each of the rooms—some are located in the adjacent Treadwell house—comes with a private bath, cable television, air-conditioning and a telephone. The hearty breakfast buffet includes English muffins, cheeses and fruit.

15 Rooms • Price range: $86-128
5 Elm St, New Milford, CT 06776
☎ **(860) 354-4080**

New Milford
⑩ *The Heritage Inn of Litchfield County*

This inn combines the friendliness of a small town with access to business services and leisure activities. The property, once visited by Teddy Roosevelt, is a converted tobacco warehouse from the 1800s that now offers guests all the modern amenities.

20 Rooms • Price range: $95-125
34 Bridge St, New Milford, CT 06776
☎ **(860) 354-8883**

Niantic
Inn at Harbor Hill Marina

Located at the top of a hill overlooking marina docks and the Niantic River, this picturesque inn appeals equally to boaters and to landlubbers. All eight comfortable guestrooms offer views of the waterway; some of the rooms even feature a private balcony. The inn's continental breakfast can be eaten on the wraparound porch, where visitors can sit and watch the morning's activities at the nearby marina.

8 Rooms • Price range: $130-195
60 Grand St, Niantic, CT 06357
☎ **(860) 739-0331**

Norfolk
Manor House

Built in 1898 as a residential mansion for a member of the leisure class, the Manor House boasts enormous common areas, Tiffany windows and luxurious guestrooms. The manicured grounds and lush gardens, as well-tended as the house, are visible from all the bedrooms. Special care is taken with the inn's hearty breakfast; condiments include honey taken from the beehives that are kept on the property.

9 Rooms • Price range: $125-250
69 Maple Ave, Norfolk, CT 06058
☎ **(860) 542-5690**

Norfolk
Blackberry River Inn

A charming Colonial inn in the Berkshire foothills. Some rooms have fireplaces.

17 Rooms • Price range: $75-135
536 Greenwoods Rd W, Norfolk, CT 06058
☎ **(860) 542-5100**

North Stonington
Antiques and Accommodations

Two beautifully restored historic homes and a carriage house are set in a well-groomed walled garden. The 1860 house features three guestrooms with private baths. The 1820 garden house has both a two-bedroom and a three-bedroom suite. Both spacious suites have fireplaces. Breakfast is served in the elegant dining room or on the patio. The property is close to North Stonington's antique and artisan's shops.

6 Rooms • Price range: $129-289
32 Main St, North Stonington, CT 06359
☎ **(860) 535-1736**

Norwalk
⊕ *The Silvermine Tavern*

On the banks of the Silvermine River, overlooking a mill pond filled with wild ducks and swans, this 250-year-old Colonial inn features early American decor and folk art, live jazz and award-winning New England cuisine.

11 Rooms • Price range: $90-150
194 Perry Ave, Norwalk, CT 06850
☎ **(203) 847-4558**

Old Lyme
Bee & Thistle Inn

Tucked away on more than five acres of prime terrain, The Bee and Thistle Inn makes a pretty picture along the Lieutenant River. A sunken garden adds to the natural beauty of the landscape. Inside, guests can retreat to cozy nooks to read or write. The carved staircase in the center hall leads to the tastefully decorated guestrooms. The 1756 Dutch-Colonial inn is known for American-style breakfast and dinner cuisine.

12 Rooms • Price range: $79-210
100 Lyme St, Old Lyme, CT 06371
☎ **(860) 434-1667**

Old Lyme
⊕ *Old Lyme Inn*

The Old Lyme has flourished since 1976, its culinary delights drawing high praise from newspapers and magazines. Built in 1850, the property was for a century a 300-acre working farm. Today the 13 large and charming guestrooms are furnished with Empire and Victorian pieces. Facilities include a cocktail lounge and four separate dining rooms, which are available for breakfast, lunch or dinner meetings.

13 Rooms • Price range: $99-175
85 Lyme St, Old Lyme, CT 06371
☎ **(860) 434-2600**

Old Mystic
The Old Mystic Inn

Formerly the village bookstore, this inn is composed of a 1784 home and a modern carriage house. The inn is decorated in a New England country style. A full gourmet breakfast is served. Each of the guestrooms is named after a notable New England author. Some rooms have a working fireplace. Although the village of Old Mystic is off the beaten path, it's an easy drive to area attractions such as Mystic Seaport.

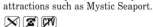

8 Rooms • Price range: $135-165
52 Main St, Old Mystic, CT 06372
☎ **(860) 572-9422**

Ridgefield
West Lane Inn

Surrounded by acres of lawn, flowering shrubs and tall maples, the West Lane Inn is the picture of a gracious New England home. The 1849 inn offers voice mail, color remote cable television and one-day laundry and dry cleaning. All rooms feature four-poster beds and a private bath; some have fireplaces. Continental breakfast is served daily. Restaurants, boutiques and museums are located nearby.

18 Rooms • Price range: $115-195
22 West Ln, Ridgefield, CT 06877
☎ **(203) 438-7323**

Riverton
Old Riverton Inn

This 1796 inn was originally the town stagecoach stop. Units vary in size.

12 Rooms • Price range: $55-210
436 E River Rd (SR 20), Riverton, CT 06065
☎ **(860) 379-8678**

South Woodstock
Inn At Woodstock Hill

Twenty-two suites and guestrooms make up the Inn at Woodstock Hill. Each room in this early 19th-century inn features floral chintz fabrics, four-poster beds and wood-burning fireplaces. The verdant hills and meadows of the surrounding Woodstock countryside are visible from the windows of the inn. Breakfast can be taken in the inn's indoor breakfast nook or in the courtyard overlooking the garden.

22 Rooms • Price range: $95-165
94 Plaine Hill Rd, South Woodstock, CT 06267
☎ **(860) 928-0528**

Tolland
The Tolland Inn

The Tolland Inn, a restored Colonial home of the 1800s, offers seven guest accommodations, including two luxurious suites. The suite on the second floor features a private sitting room and a two-person hot tub. The other suite contains a sitting area with a fireplace and a full bath with an antique ball-and-claw tub. A sumptuous room on the first floor features a queen-size canopy bed and has a private entrance.

7 Rooms • Price range: $65-150
63 Tolland Green, Tolland, CT 06084-0717
☎ **(860) 872-0800**

Waterbury
House on the Hill

The Vandenburghs, the present owners, are only the third family to occupy this home since it was built in 1888. Miraculously, much of the house has not changed, save for a few coats of paint and some modern amenities. All the paneling and intricate woodwork is original. Set in a quiet neighborhood, the house has lavish gardens. The prize hideaways are two rooms tucked into the turrets.

4 Rooms • Price range: $125-165
92 Woodlawn Terr, Waterbury, CT 06710-1929
☎ **(203) 757-9901**

Wethersfield
Chester Bulkley House

The personal touches of innkeepers Frank and Sophie Bottaro make this restored 1830 residence popular with guests. Freshly cut flowers and pillow chocolates are examples of the niceties that help make every stay memorable. Three of the five guestrooms come with a private bath. Wide pine floors and handcarved woodwork add to the ambience of this charming inn, which is situated in the heart of the historical district.

5 Rooms • Price range: $85-95
184 Main St, Wethersfield, CT 06109
☎ **(860) 563-4236**

Notes:

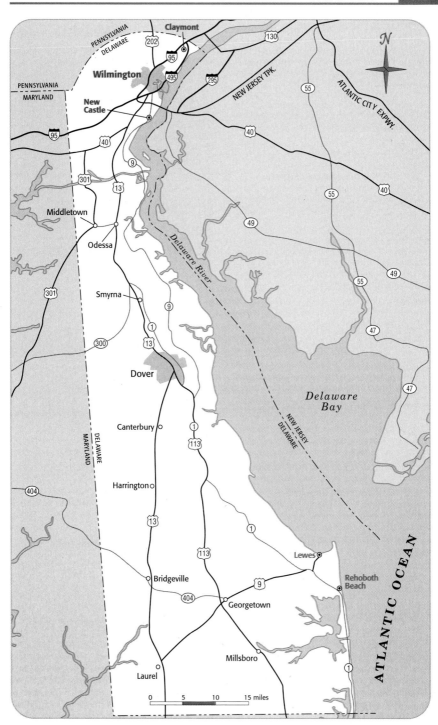

Claymont

Darley Manor Inn Bed & Breakfast
The Darley Manor is a handsomely restored, impressively maintained 19th-century home. The inn was once the residence of one of America's most popular book illustrators, Felix O.C. Darley. All the bedrooms are comfortably furnished and have private baths. Guests can curl up in the parlor with a Charles Dickens novel, illustrated by Darley himself, and be transported back in time.

5 Rooms • Price range: $95-149
3701 Philadelphia Pike, Claymont, DE 19703
☎ **(302) 792-2127**

Lewes

The Inn at Canal Square
This establishment is the only waterfront bed and breakfast in the historic town of Lewes, which serves as a gateway to the Atlantic beaches and the eastern seaboard. Guests can stay in one of the conventional guestrooms located in the main house or on a canal houseboat docked outside. Guestrooms are spacious and all of them have a private bath. Most also have a private balcony and a view of the harbor.

19 Rooms • Price range: $155-185
122 Market St, Lewes, DE 19958
☎ **(302) 644-3377**

New Castle

Armitage Inn
This brick Colonial home, with its walled garden and lovely library, is named after Ann Armitage, the wife of Zachariah Van Leuvenigh who began the inn's tradition of hospitality by providing food and respite for post riders during the Revolutionary War. One wing of the home is believed to have been built in the 1600s. The antique-filled inn sits on the banks of the Delaware River on the edge of Battery Park.

5 Rooms • Price range: $110-185
2 The Strand, New Castle, DE 19720
☎ **(302) 328-6618**

New Castle

William Penn Guest House
William Penn first set foot in the New World at New Castle and this restored 1682 brick guest house that bears his name overlooks the park in the heart of town. The inn offers four guestrooms and boasts the original wide-planked floors.

4 Rooms • Price range: $70-89
206 Delaware St, New Castle, DE 19720
☎ **(302) 328-7736**

Rehoboth Beach

Sea Witch Manor Bed & Breakfast
Victorian elegance, charm and comfort greet guests of this B&B, which is located within walking distance of ocean and beach. The house is furnished with period antiques and bedrooms feature oversize chairs, claw-foot tubs and comforters. The wraparound porch is a great place to relax. Home-baked goods are served every morning in the dining room; afternoon tea is provided in the parlor or on the porch.

5 Rooms • Price range: $140-195
71 Lake Ave, Rehoboth Beach, DE 19971
☎ **(302) 226-9482**

Rehoboth Beach
 Delaware Inn
A traditional 1930s cottage furnished
with antiques and reproductions.

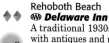

7 Rooms • Price range: $140-210
55 Delaware Ave, Rehoboth Beach, DE 19971
☎ **(302) 227-6031**

Rehoboth Beach
The Mallard Guest House
This property consists of three early
1900s beach resort houses with common outdoor decks. Each house has a
private bath. Guestrooms vary in size

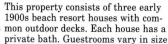

from small to large and all are furnished
with antiques.

17 Rooms • Price range: $95-145
60 Baltimore Ave, Rehoboth Beach, DE 19971
☎ **(302) 226-3448**

Notes:

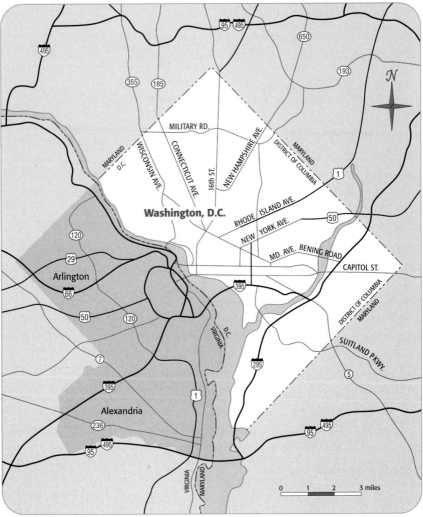

Notes:

Washington

🏵 *The Dupont at the Circle*
Each room in this charmingly restored 1885 Victorian inn is opulently decorated with antiques and reproductions; sumptuous linens and all the modern amenities make for a comfortable stay. The inn's proximity to the Metro provides safe and easy access to museums, galleries, theaters and downtown night life. Guests get a jump-start on the day with a sampling of coffees chosen by the Ecuadorian innkeepers.

8 Rooms • Price range: $155-275
1604 19th St NW, Washington, DC 20009
☎ **(202) 332-5251**

Washington
Swann House
This grand red brick Richardson Romanesque mansion in the heart of the Dupont Circle Historic District has common rooms decorated with fine furnishings. It features elements such as inlaid floors, crystal chandeliers and 12-foot-high ceilings. Thematic guestrooms are sophisticated and luxurious, each with a special architectural detail or decorative flourish. Close to the Metro; a 20-minute walk to the White House.

9 Rooms • Price range: $140-300
1808 New Hampshire Ave NW, Washington, DC 20009
☎ **(202) 265-4414**

Notes:

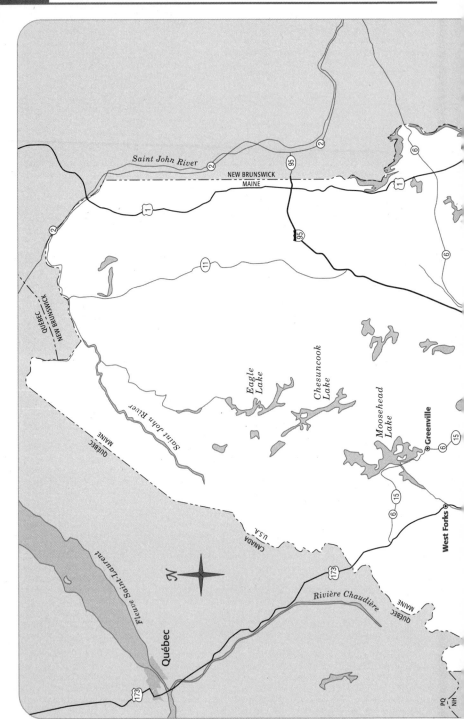

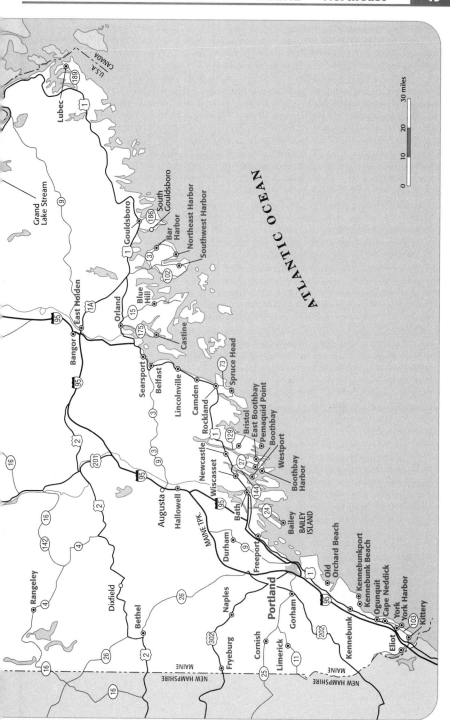

ATLANTIC OCEAN

CANADA
U.S.A.

Lubec

Grand Lake Stream

Gouldsboro
South Gouldsboro
Bar Harbor
Northeast Harbor
Southwest Harbor

East Holden
Bangor
Orland
Blue Hill
Castine
Searsport
Belfast
Lincolnville
Camden
Rockland
Spruce Head

Bristol
East Boothbay
Pemaquid Point
Boothbay
Westport
Boothbay Harbor

Newcastle
Wiscasset
Bath
Bailey
BAILEY ISLAND

Augusta
Hallowell
MAINE TPK.
Durham
Freeport
Portland
Gorham

Rangeley
Dixfield
Bethel
Naples
Fryeburg
Cornish
Limerick

Old Orchard Beach
Kennebunkport
Kennebunk Beach
Kennebunk
Ogunquit
Cape Neddick
York
York Harbor
Kittery
Eliot

NEW HAMPSHIRE
MAINE

0   10   20   30 miles

Bailey Island
Log Cabin & Island Inn

Tucked away on Bailey Island, The Log Cabin offers the atmosphere of a cabin getaway and the convenience of a modern guest house. Most of the appealing rooms have private decks with a view of the Casco Bay harbor. Four rooms come with a kitchen or a kitchenette; one room has a hot tub. The Log Cabin's home-cooked breakfast is traditional Maine fare, including a selection of tasty desserts.

8 Rooms • Price range: $129-219
Rt 24, Bailey Island, ME 04003
☎ **(207) 833-5546**

Bangor
⑩ *The Phenix Inn at West Market Square*

This restored commercial building, circa 1873, has Old-World atmosphere.

32 Rooms • Price range: $90-159
20 Broad St, Bangor, ME 04401
☎ **(207) 947-0411**

Bar Harbor
⑩ *Balance Rock Inn 1903*

This imposing, shingled oceanfront mansion is located on the Historic Shore Path and was constructed in 1903. Guests are treated to breath-taking views overlooking Frenchman's Bay from the covered back porch. Just two blocks from the center of town, the inn is a short walk to shops and other points of interest. The well-appointed guestrooms are decorated with period antiques and some feature fire-places, decks and whirlpools. A lavish buffet breakfast is included, as well as afternoon tea. Other features include a heated oceanfront pool, a cocktail lounge and a fitness room.

16 Rooms • Price range: $225-525
21 Albert Meadow, Bar Harbor, ME 04609
☎ **(207) 288-2610**

Bar Harbor
⑩ *Chiltern Inn*

This cottage-style shingled carriage house is charming and anything but simple. All rooms feature marble bath-rooms, large separate showers and two-person whirlpool tubs. Guests are encour-aged to soak in the spa, relax in the sauna or take a dip in the Chiltern's heated pool, located in a room that also features a fireplace, potted palms and wicker furniture. The loft library has a fireplace and a cozy sofa for curling up in. The foyer antique store carries a selection of fine antiques. Those looking for outdoor activities can take part in lobster or whale-watching excursions or get in a game of golf or tennis.

4 Rooms • Price range: $295-375
3 Cromwell Harbor Rd, Bar Harbor, ME 04609
☎ **(207) 288-0114**

Bar Harbor
Bar Harbor Tides B&B

A newly renovated, 1887 waterfront home, with splendid antique furnishings and decor. High ceilings in the foyer and common areas coupled with large oversized windows allow natural light to warm every room. Guests can enjoy a waterfront view while sitting by the fireplace with a delicious breakfast. All guestrooms have richly colored duvets and pillow accents that complement the antique furnishings.

4 Rooms • Price range: $195-375
119 West St, Bar Harbor, ME 04609
☎ **(207) 288-4968**

Bar Harbor
Black Friar Inn

Old-World comfort in a New-World setting is offered here. The rooms are decorated with period furniture and the woodwork is finely crafted. Breakfast may include Belgian waffles and cinnamon buns; tea cakes and scones are served in the afternoon. Lush pine forests and the Atlantic Ocean are only a short walk away. Animal lovers will be happy to know there is a resident dog on the premises.

7 Rooms • Price range: $85-145
10 Summer St, Bar Harbor, ME 04609
☎ **(207) 288-5091**

Bar Harbor
Briarfield Inn Bed & Breakfast

This cranberry-colored shingle cottage was built by a wealthy publisher in 1887 and has been restored to highlight the original wood floors and period furnishings. The front porch is the place to gather before heading into town to shop or for dinner. Relax by the fireplace or large saltwater aquarium in comfortable period furnishings. Lace curtains, and floral wall coverings accent the decor. Five rooms have fireplaces.

14 Rooms • Price range: $95-165
60 Cottage St, Bar Harbor, ME 04609
☎ **(207) 288-5297**

Bar Harbor
Castlemaine Inn

The former home of an Austro-Hungarian ambassador and his wife, the Castlemaine is a unique and comfortable 1886 home with twisting corridors and sunny alcoves. All rooms have a private bath; some also have a fireplace and a balcony. Four suites are available. A continental breakfast is served buffet-style in the morning room or on the veranda. The inn is a short walk from shops, galleries and restaurants.

17 Rooms • Price range: $109-217
39 Holland Ave, Bar Harbor, ME 04609
☎ **(207) 288-4563**

Bar Harbor
Cleftstone Manor

The Cleftstone Manor is as regal as its name implies. The three-story mansion, located within walking distance of Bar Harbor's waterfront, is one of only a few 19th-century homes on "Millionaire's Row" that survived a severe fire in 1947. Rooms are decorated with period furnishings; some have fireplaces or balconies. The inn offers a well-stocked library and a tasty breakfast that includes blueberry pancakes or quiche.

16 Rooms • Price range: $100-200
92 Eden St, Bar Harbor, ME 04609
☎ **(207) 288-4951**

Bar Harbor
Graycote Inn

The motto of this Victorian inn could well be "a rainy day does not mean a wasted day." That's because owners Pat and Roger Samuel have made a point of stocking the inn with enough indoor activities to make any day enjoyable. Games, a library full of books and even a grand piano are at the disposal of their guests. All of the guestrooms are spacious, large enough for seating at least two people. Some rooms come with a fireplace.

12 Rooms • Price range: $90-169
40 Holland Ave, Bar Harbor, ME 04609
☎ **(207) 288-3044**

Bar Harbor
The Hearthside Bed & Breakfast

Guests can expect a warm welcome and attentive hospitality when they visit this restored circa 1900 home located on a quiet residential street. Guestrooms are decorated in bold, vibrant colors. Three rooms have fireplaces and two have private balconies. A hearty breakfast is served in the dining room or may be taken out to the patio. Acadia National Park is only a five-minute drive away.

9 Rooms • Price range: $95-140
7 High St, Bar Harbor, ME 04609
☎ **(207) 288-4533**

Bar Harbor
Holbrook House

Built in 1876 as Victorian Showplace Inn, Holbrook House is situated right in Bar Harbor's historic corridor. Thus most of the Bar Harbor attractions are just a short walk away and Acadia National Park is only a mile from the inn. All the tastefully decorated rooms were designed with convenience in mind and have a private bath. Two private cottages are also available. A full breakfast is served daily on the enclosed sunporch.

12 Rooms • Price range: $125-170
74 Mt Desert St, Bar Harbor, ME 04609
☎ **(207) 288-4970**

Bar Harbor
 *Ivy Manor Inn*

A European-style lodging on an island off the coast of Maine. Authentic 18th- and 19th-century French and English furnishings grace this circa 1940 Tudor-style cottage. Victorian sofas, armoires and four-poster beds are set in period perfect rooms. The romantic candlelit bistro serves fine French-American cuisine. Guests may also enjoy an after-dinner drink by the fireside in the cordial atmosphere of the English Tavern.

8 Rooms • Price range: $175-350
194 Main St, Bar Harbor, ME 04609
☎ **(207) 288-2138**

Bar Harbor
The Kedge Bed & Breakfast

Built in 1870, this is a good example of Mansard architecture. All common areas and guestrooms have 12-foot-high ceilings and floors featuring black walnut, hard rock maple and heart pine. Located in the historic district, within walking distance of harbor attractions, the inn maintains a serene atmosphere. Guests can relax on a wicker-filled porch or take in the "secret" garden on a private balcony. Full breakfasts are served.

4 Rooms • Price range: $95-170
112 West St, Bar Harbor, ME 04609
☎ **(207) 288-5180**

Bar Harbor
The Ledgelawn Inn

This red-and-vanilla colored 1904 mansion with its own carriage house brings a gracious Old World ambience and charm to the modern world. Some guest units

have four-poster beds, porch, fireplace and whirlpool tub. All are furnished with antiques.

33 Rooms • Price range: $95-275
66 Mt. Desert St, Bar Harbor, ME 04609
☎ **(207) 288-4596**

Bar Harbor
Manor House Inn

Constructed in 1887, the Manor House Inn went through a recent major restoration, after which Congress placed the three-story, 22-room mansion on the National Register of Historic Places. Guests can also stay in either of two nearby Garden Cottages or the original Chauffeur's Cottage. Visitors look forward to a breakfast that may include baked blueberry-stuffed French toast or eggs Florentine.

17 Rooms • Price range: $95-195
106 West St, Bar Harbor, ME 04609
☎ **(207) 288-3759**

Bar Harbor
The Maples Inn

In the early 1900s this elegant inn was the place where the well-to-do visitors to Mount Desert Island would stay. Located on a quiet, residential, tree-lined street, the inn offers a welcome respite from everyday life. For guests who want to explore the area, restaurants and boutiques are within walking distance and the sea is never far away. A hearty breakfast is served daily; refreshments are served in the afternoon.

6 Rooms • Price range: $100-160
16 Roberts Ave, Bar Harbor, ME 04609
☎ **(207) 288-3443**

Bar Harbor
Mira Monte Inn & Suites

The town of Bar Harbor was once named Eden, which befits this idyllic 1864 inn located just five minutes from the 33,000 acres of mountains, seashore and forests of Acadia National Park. The main house offers comfortable guestrooms, many with fireplaces; private two-room suites are located in a separate building. Guests are welcome to breakfast on one of the paved terraces or private balconies.

16 Rooms • Price range: $145-155
69 Mt Dessert St, Bar Harbor, ME 04609
☎ **(207) 288-4263**

Bar Harbor
Primrose Inn

Bar Harbor is one of New England's top resort towns and this striking 1878 Victorian stick-style inn is conveniently located within walking distance of downtown. The tastefully decorated guestrooms are furnished with antiques and period repro-ductions. Some have added conveniences such as gas fireplaces, balconies and whirlpool baths. For longer visits, a one-bedroom suite sleeps four and a two-bedroom can sleep a group of six.

15 Rooms • Price range: $95-175
73 Mt Desert St, Bar Harbor, ME 04609
☎ **(207) 288-4031**

Bar Harbor
The Ridgeway Inn

From the colorful flower gardens in the front yard all the way up to the charming third-floor guestrooms, this lovely Victorian home combines the comforts of home with the hospitality of a country inn. Guests may choose from a variety of room styles and sizes. Most have wicker settees, tables and chairs. One has a two-person Jacuzzi and separate shower. Another has direct access to a side deck. Near all the shops and restaurants.

5 Rooms • Price range: $70-150
11 High St, Bar Harbor, ME 04609
☎ **(207) 288-9682**

Bar Harbor
Wayside Inn Bed & Breakfast

This 1903 Tudor-style home is in a quiet residential neighborhood, one block from Main Street. The large, granite front porch has comfortable wicker furniture and a view of the tree-lined street. The fireplaces in the common areas complement the inn's English and Victorian decor. Oriental rugs, wing chairs, Colonial and period antiques are just a few examples of the furnishings decorating the guestrooms.

7 Rooms • Price range: $125-295
11 Atlantic Ave, Bar Harbor, ME 04609
☎ **(207) 288-5703**

Bar Harbor
Anne's White Columns Inn

Originally a church, this Georgian-style inn has lovely grounds and cozy rooms.

10 Rooms • Price range: $90-135
57 Mt Desert St, Bar Harbor, ME 04609
☎ **(207) 288-5357**

Bar Harbor
◆◆ *The Holland Inn*

This pleasant 1895 former farmhouse is conveniently located close to shops and restaurants. Most guestrooms contain queen-size beds and all are tastefully decorated. Some of the units even have separate sitting rooms.

5 Rooms • Price range: $85-145
35 Holland Ave, Bar Harbor, ME 04609
☎ **(207) 288-4804**

Bar Harbor
◆◆ *Seacroft Inn*

Standing under a canopy of towering oak and pine trees, this 1880 inn boasts beautiful architecture and a luxurious atmosphere. The multi-gabled roof is evocative of Old English grandeur. Guestrooms feature grand beds; several have private decks.

6 Rooms • Price range: $79-109
18 Albert Meadow, Bar Harbor, ME 04609
☎ **(207) 288-4669**

Bath
◆◆ ⑩ *The Galen C. Moses House*

Each of the four rooms available here possesses its own unique qualities. The Victorian Room contains a beautiful bay window and a white marble fireplace. The Moses Room has an antique washstand and plaster frieze walls. The Vintage Room is done in century-old oak and walnut. And the only suite in the inn consists of two sleeping rooms, as well as a private kitchen and bath. All the guestrooms are located upstairs.

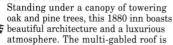

4 Rooms • Price range: $119-159
1009 Washington St, Bath, ME 04530
☎ **(207) 442-8771**

Bath
◆◆ ⑩ *Kennebec Inn*

This grand 1860 Italianate mansion has been decorated throughout in a simple, elegant style with pieces collected by the well-traveled owners. Guestrooms vary in size and decor but all offer modern amenities such as phones, data ports and televisions. Breakfasts, timed for both the early or late riser, are served in the tapestried dining room. The owners and staff are happy to assist guests with plans and activity ideas.

7 Rooms • Price range: $110-175
1024 Washington St, Bath, ME 04530
☎ **(207) 443-5202**

Belfast
◆◆ ⑩ *Belfast Bay Meadows Inn*

For more than 50 years this inn has provided generous hospitality and divine dining. Ornate woodwork and period artworks enhance the traditional Victorian atmosphere. Guests can savor the inn's signature breakfast, which includes lobster, or sample a range of baked goods. Dinner requires a reservation. All rooms have private baths and magnificent views; the grounds extend to Penobscot Bay.

20 Rooms • Price range: $95-185
l92 Northport Ave (US 1), Belfast, ME 04915
☎ **(207) 338-5715**

Belfast

The Jeweled Turret Inn
Each room in this charming and elegant home is designed for the romantically inclined. Windows swathed in lace, carved furniture and ornate trim are reminiscent of Victorian times. All bedrooms have restored private baths and period furnishings. In the afternoon, a silver tea service is set by the fire for high tea. On warm days, guests are served tall glasses of iced tea on the veranda.

7 Rooms • Price range: $89-149
40 Pearl St, Belfast, ME 04915
☎ **(207) 338-2304**

Bethel

L'Auberge Country Inn
Originally constructed in the 1850s as a barn, this quiet country inn has seen many changes over the years. In the 1890s it was disassembled and moved. In the 1920s it was converted to a silent movie theater and the servant's quarters of a hotel. Then in the 1940s it was renovated to its present state as a family home. Antiques, high ceilings and unusual architectural details are featured in the guestrooms.

6 Rooms • Price range: $79-129
22 Mill Hill Rd, Bethel, ME 04217
☎ **(207) 824-2774**

Bethel

The Briar Lea Inn & Restaurant
A cozy parlor offers a warm welcome to visitors when they enter this renovated 1855 farmhouse. All of the guestrooms feature original hardwood floors and private baths and are handsomely furnished with country-style antiques. Outdoor enthusiasts will appreciate the inn's proximity to the Sunday River Ski Resort and Mt. Abrams, an area known for outdoor activities in all seasons.

6 Rooms • Price range: $72-92
150 Mayville Rd (US 2), Bethel, ME 04217
☎ **(207) 824-4717**

Blue Hill
Arcady Down East Bed & Breakfast
An enchanting 19th-century cottage with thoughtfully decorated rooms.

7 Rooms • Price range: $80-160
HC 64, Box 370, Blue Hill, ME 04614
☎ **(207) 374-3700**

Boothbay

Kenniston Hill Inn
Shortly after the Declaration of Independence, David Kenniston bought this Federal home and opened the first tavern in town. Following this tradition of hospitality, the current owners have carefully restored the inn and continue to provide respite from a busy world. Guests can settle into wing chairs by the fireplace or relax on the front porch. Each room is spacious and is equipped with a private bath; five have fireplaces.

10 Rooms • Price range: $95-130
SR 27, Boothbay, ME 04537
☎ **(207) 633-2159**

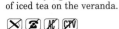

Boothbay Harbor
Admiral's Quarters Inn

This renovated sea-captain's home from the 1830s provides a bird's-eye view of events both on land and at sea. In the summertime, guests have front-row seats on the inn's decks for the Fourth of July festivities. On cooler days, tea is served by the fire in a glassed-in porch. Spend the day cycling or enjoying an old-fashioned clambake on one of many nearby islands. All guestrooms have private decks, bathrooms and entrances.

6 Rooms • Price range: $145-165
71 Commercial St, Boothbay Harbor, ME 04538
☎ **(207) 633-2474**

Boothbay Harbor
Anchor Watch Bed & Breakfast
Family-owned and -run, this converted home sits high on a hill bordering the harbor, a short walk from shops and restaurants. The innkeepers also own

and operate an excursion service, for day-long sailing trips and supper cruises.

5 Rooms • Price range: $135-160
9 Eames Rd, Boothbay Harbor, ME 04538
☎ **(207) 633-7565**

Boothbay Harbor
Atlantic Ark Inn
Set on the eastern side of Boothbay Harbor, many of the guest accommodations at this tranquil inn have a restful water view. Each room is tastefully decorated with antiques, large comfortable beds and white lace curtains. Some have private balconies and all have private baths. The spacious porch is an ideal spot to sit in the sun and watch harbor life drift by. A cottage nestled under the trees is also available.

6 Rooms • Price range: $99-175
62 Atlantic Ave, Boothbay Harbor, ME 04538
☎ **(207) 633-5690**

Boothbay Harbor
Welch House Inn
From its vantage point atop McKown Hill, the Welch House commands a spectacular view of Boothbay Harbor and the surrounding area. Throughout the inn, rooms are richly decorated with antiques, fine furniture and objets d'art collected by the owners on their travels. Both the breakfast room and parlor have been recently redecorated and expanded. Town center and its many pleasures are just a few minutes away.

16 Rooms • Price range: $85-165
56 McKown St, Boothbay Harbor, ME 04538
☎ **(207) 633-3431**

Bristol
The Bristol Inn
This inn on lovely Pemaquid Peninsula offers fine hospitality.

5 Rooms • Price range: $85-90
28 Upper Round Pond Rd, Bristol, ME 04539
☎ **(207) 563-1125**

Camden
⬣ *Inn at Ocean's Edge*

This wonderfully secluded property on Penobscot Bay is well known for its comfortable elegance and for being the perfect place to unwind. Guests are welcome to take a stroll in the surrounding gardens and enjoy the gentle ocean breezes. The accommodations are spacious and very well-appointed, offering such comforts as four-poster king-size beds, double whirlpool tubs and gas fireplaces. The day begins with a delicious breakfast served in the dining room or out on a terrace overlooking the ocean and nearby islands. Other amenities include a fully equipped exercise room.

27 Rooms • Price range: $220-250
PO Box 704, Camden, ME 04843
☎ **(207) 236-0945**

Camden
⬣ *The Inn at Sunrise Point*

Right at the edge of Penobscot Bay, just below the Camden Hills, lies this secluded retreat. Situated on four acres of land with a private seashore, this is an ideal place for all of those looking for a tranquil getaway. Guests can relax in one of the comfortable rooms, all of which have a view of the ocean, or in one of the cottages located on the grounds. All rooms have a wood-burning fireplace, a queen- or king-size bed and a bath with a large tub. All cottages have a double-sized Jacuzzi, a wet bar, and a private deck.

7 Rooms • Price range: $175-375
PO Box 1344, Camden, ME 04843
☎ **(207) 236-7716**

Camden
Abigail's Bed & Breakfast Inn

A friendly, intimate atmosphere permeates this 1847 Federal-style white-clapboard New England inn. Each morning an ample breakfast served around a large table encourages guests to meet and share their stories. Visitors can take a short but invigorating hike that leads to a summit with grand views of the area. The inn boasts two suites in the carriage house and two guestrooms in the main house.

4 Rooms • Price range: $145-185
8 High St, Camden, ME 04843
☎ **(207) 236-2501**

Camden
The Belmont

A 19th-century Edwardian retreat for today's travelers, this inn in a residential area has been carefully restored to reflect the charm of another time. The rooms are immaculate and airy, an elegant mix of old and new. The chef (and co-owner), who has appeared on television as part of a series on "Great Chefs of the East," provides guests with imaginative, intriguing menu choices. There is a pleasant sunporch and garden.

6 Rooms • Price range: $115-185
6 Belmont Ave, Camden, ME 04843
☎ **(207) 236-8053**

Camden
Blue Harbor House, A Village Inn

This classic property is a restored 1810 New England-Cape village inn. Each guestroom is inviting and bright, and furnished with country antiques, hand-fashioned quilts, a canopy bed and a whirlpool bath. Breakfast specialties include blueberry pancakes, chocolate crepes and French toast. Dinner, available only to guests, may be a romantic candlelit affair or an old-fashioned down-east lobsterfest.

10 Rooms • Price range: $95-175
67 Elm St, Camden, ME 04843
☎ **(207) 236-3196**

Camden
Camden Harbor Inn

This inn has welcomed travelers with its old-world ambience and New England hospitality since 1874. Visitors come to enjoy the commanding views of Penobscot Bay as well as the proximity to downhill skiing. Each morning a savory breakfast is served and, in the evening, guests can indulge in dishes made with local produce and the "catch of the day." All of the cozy guestrooms are equipped with private baths.

22 Rooms • Price range: $195-255
83 Bayview St, Camden, ME 04843
☎ **(207) 236-4200**

Camden
The Camden Windward House Circa 1854

Since opening its doors to guests in 1924, this 1854 ship builder's home has offered spacious accommodations in an intimate environment. Bedrooms are furnished with allergy-free feather beds and fine linens. Three comfortable common rooms and spacious grounds provide plenty of opportunity to socialize or relax with a book from the library. Hiking trails around Mt. Battie are just out the back door and the harbor is only a block away.

8 Rooms • Price range: $165-240
6 High St, Camden, ME 04843
☎ **(207) 236-9656**

Camden
Captain Swift Inn

Captain Swift established Maine's first passenger schooner right in this white-clapboard village landmark. The present owners of this inn welcome guests with the traditional salute that Swift gave his passengers. The sun-soaked Federal-style inn, restored with authenticity, is an architect's dream. Each room is decorated with period pieces, creating an ambience that is maintained throughout the inn.

4 Rooms • Price range: $110-130
72 Elm St, Camden, ME 04843
☎ **(207) 236-8113**

Camden
The Elms Bed & Breakfast

For those who marvel at the sight of lighthouses, this inn is a dream come true. The innkeepers have decorated the converted circa 1806 sea-captain's home with lighthouse artworks, books and collectibles and have even organized a lighthouse cruise in hopes of passing on their love of the majestic guardians of the night. Both breakfasts and afternoon teas are lovingly prepared. One guestroom has a fireplace.

6 Rooms • Price range: $90-125
84 Elm St, Camden, ME 04843
☎ **(207) 236-6250**

Camden
Hawthorn Inn

Situated on one-and-a-half private acres of open lawn and mature trees, this restored Victorian Queen Anne-style home has a magnificent view of the harbor. Each room is unique, but all share the same comfortable and warm atmosphere. In the summer, breakfast is served on the deck; winter finds guests seated in front of the fireplace, where Bronson, the resident dog, is most likely napping.

10 Rooms • Price range: $100-205
9 High St, Camden, ME 04843
☎ **(207) 236-8842**

Camden
🅰🅰 Lord Camden Inn

Overlooking the harbor, this inn has many rooms with private balconies.

31 Rooms • Price range: $148-198
24 Main St, Camden, ME 04843
☎ **(207) 236-4325**

Camden
The Victorian By The Sea

Complete with a corner turret and a wide, spindled veranda, this 1881 Queen Anne-style inn is so charming it was chosen by Hallmark to appear on a greeting card. Lush gardens and trees lead down to the ocean from the grand veranda and gazebo. Common rooms include the Piano Room, the Harbor Room and an expanded dining room. Guestrooms and suites are spacious; all have a fireplace and a private bath.

7 Rooms • Price range: $145-215
Rt 1, Seaview Dr, Camden, ME 04843
☎ **(207) 236-3785**

Camden
Whitehall Inn

Steeped in a century-old tradition of refined comfort in a graceful setting, the Whitehall Inn is a Camden landmark. An eclectic mix of antiques from several periods gives each common area and guestroom a unique feeling. The glassed-in dining room and adjacent tavern share a distinct Old World charm. While a guest at the inn, Edna St. Vincent Millay wrote "Renascence," her celebrated ode to the view from atop Mt. Battie.

49 Rooms • Price range: $65-155
52 High St, Camden, ME 04843
☎ **(207) 236-3391**

Cape Neddick
The Cape Neddick House

The Cape Neddick House has been in the Goodwin family for eight generations—ever since it was built in 1885. Daily breakfast may include such old family favorites as cinnamon popovers with raspberry jam, blueberry cheese tortes or strawberry scones. After breakfast, guests can stroll along the river or hike through the Rachel Carson Wildlife Sanctuary. One guest suite has a working fireplace.

5 Rooms • Price range: $90-115
1300 US 1, Cape Neddick, ME 03902
☎ **(207) 363-2500**

Castine
The Castine Inn

Operating since 1898, this inn has rooms with a view of the harbor.

19 Rooms • Price range: $80-210
33 Main St, Castine, ME 04421
☎ **(207) 326-4365**

Castine
Pentagoet Inn

Located in the center of town, this 1894 Victorian inn and adjacent 200-year-old Colonial home offer a variety of rooms, verandas and a cozy pub. The inn was named after Fort Pentagoet, the peninsula's original outpost.

16 Rooms • Price range: $80-150
Main St, Castine, ME 04421
☎ **(207) 326-8616**

Cornish
The Cornish Inn

A 19th-century country inn conveniently located close to the village center.

15 Rooms • Price range: $85-140
Rt 25, Main St, Cornish, ME 04020
☎ **(207) 625-8501**

Durham
The Bagley House Bed & Breakfast

Besides being the oldest house in town, this 1722 country inn has been a place of worship, a temporary school, a store and an important center during the Revolutionary War. Today it is simply a lovely inn with fine country decor, such as handmade quilts and modern conveniences. Breakfast is served in the kitchen around one large table. The resident cat and dog add to the warm hospitality. Convenient to Freeport shopping.

8 Rooms • Price range: $95-160
1290 Royalsborough Rd, Durham, ME 04222
☎ **(207) 865-6566**

East Boothbay
Five Gables Inn

In a quiet country village three miles from Boothbay Harbor stands this beautifully restored, 125-year-old country inn. Situated on a hillside overlooking picturesque Linekin Bay, the inn is an excellent place to enjoy a view of the bay and the islands in the distance. The inn features a large parlor, a spacious wraparound porch and comfortably furnished rooms, all with private baths. Five rooms have working fireplaces.

16 Rooms • Price range: $110-175
Murray Hill Rd, East Boothbay, ME 04544
☎ **(207) 633-4551**

East Boothbay
Linekin Bay Bed & Breakfast

Linekin Bay B&B is a charming 1850 farmhouse-style inn with a wraparound porch and lovely bay views. The entire inn was remodeled and redecorated within the last few years. Several of the spacious guestrooms have electric parlor stoves or fireplaces for those cool Maine evenings. All have hardwood floors with area rugs and comfortable easy chairs or love seats. Guest baths are roomy and newly redecorated.

4 Rooms • Price range: $85-175
531 Ocean Point Rd, East Boothbay, ME 04544
☎ **(207) 633-9900**

East Holden
⚑ *The Lucerne Inn*

With nearly 200 years of service behind it, the Lucerne Inn is expert at pleasing its guests. It is a popular place for business conferences, weddings and weekend getaways. The rooms are all decorated with antique furnishings and have gas fireplaces. Meeting rooms have a view of Phillips Lake and the inn will supply meals and equipment for conferences. A gazebo on the southern lawn provides the perfect wedding setting.

30 Rooms • Price range: $99-199
RR 3, East Holden, ME 04429
☎ **(207) 843-5123**

Eliot
High Meadows Bed & Breakfast

This beautiful Colonial house was built in 1736 by Elliott Frost, a merchant shipbuilder and captain. It is one of the oldest houses in the area and has been transformed into a charming guest house filled with antiques. Original exposed beams, wide floorboards and wood paneling can be found in many of the handsome rooms. Whale-watching and harbor cruises, sandy beaches and outlet shops are all close by.

4 Rooms • Price range: $80-120
2 Brixham Rd, Eliot, ME 03903
☎ **(207) 439-0590**

Freeport
Harraseeket Inn

Tucked away in picturesque Freeport, the Harraseeket Inn offers a charming, rustic setting in the best New England fashion. Built as a private home by a Maine family in 1895, the Harraseeket became an inn in 1984. Since then, it has delighted visitors with its antique furnishings and courtyard gardens. Many rooms have a Jacuzzi or a fireplace; there are six full suites. Common areas include a library, three dining rooms and a ballroom. The day starts with a hearty Maine breakfast (coffee is ready by 6 a.m.) and after a day of exploring the lake region, guests can gather for tea in the mahogany-paneled drawing room.

84 Rooms • Price range: $165-245
162 Main St, Freeport, ME 04032
☎ **(207) 865-9377**

Freeport
181 Main Street Bed & Breakfast

This 1840s Greek-Revival Cape house has been thoroughly and lovingly renovated by the current owners. Comfortable and attractively furnished, the roomy inn has two dining rooms and two parlors along with its seven guestrooms. Handmade quilts, Maine-cherry dining tables and family china and crystal all add a personal touch. There is also a well-maintained garden and a pool.

7 Rooms • Price range: $95-115
181 Main St, Freeport, ME 04032
☎ **(207) 865-1226**

Freeport
Anita's Cottage Street Inn

The inn is located in a quiet residential neighborhood, just a short walk to outlet stores and restaurants. A converted cottage-style home, it has a contemporary feel throughout. The combo dining and sitting room overlooks a backyard bordering on 30 acres of woodlands. In season, breakfast is served on a comfortable patio in this forest setting. Guestrooms are modern, with an emphasis on the Laura Ashley style. One suite has a kitchen.

5 Rooms • Price range: $65-150
13 Cottage St, Freeport, ME 04032
☎ **(207) 865-0932**

Freeport
Brewster House Bed & Breakfast

Located just three blocks north of L.L. Bean, Brewster House now finds itself centrally located in an outlet shopping haven. A beautiful Queen Anne-style home dating back to 1888, the inn was built by a local businessman named Jarvis A. Brewster. It has been restored to its original elegance, with large, comfortably appointed rooms that feature antiques and 19th-century fixtures such as tin ceilings and carved moldings.

7 Rooms • Price range: $100-130
180 Main St, Freeport, ME 04032
☎ **(207) 865-4121**

Freeport
Captain Briggs House B&B

Each room of this 1853 Federal-style sea-captain's home in the heart of town has been restored with special care to preserve the oak, walnut and maple floors. Located on a quiet, tree-lined street and surrounded by gardens, the house has an informal, intimate atmosphere. All rooms have a private bath and guests can choose from king-, queen-, double- or twin-size beds. Breakfast is served in a pleasant, bright breakfast room.

5 Rooms • Price range: $72-130
8 Maple St, Freeport, ME 04032
☎ **(207) 865-1868**

Freeport
Captain Josiah A. Mitchell House Bed & Breakfast Inn

With only 10 days of provisions, Captain Mitchell, the commander of a clipper ship, survived at sea in a longboat for 43 days and drifted 4,000 miles to Hawaii. Mark Twain's retelling of the story put him in the literary limelight. Today the 1779 captain's home is a handsome inn, located in a pretty, residential section of the village just a five-minute walk from outlets and restaurants. Guestrooms are compact and homey.

7 Rooms • Price range: $85-95
188 Main St, Freeport, ME 04032
☎ **(207) 865-3289**

Freeport
Isaac Randall House
This 1823 Federal-style farmhouse has an exceptionally interesting history. It has served as a long-time family home, as a stopping place on the Underground Railroad and as a Prohibition-era dance hall. Today it's an attractive inn with antique-furnished guestrooms and a converted railroad caboose, all with baths. There is also a playground for children on the inn's six wooded acres, as well as a spring-fed pond and a spa.

10 Rooms • Price range: $105-145
5 Independence Dr, Freeport, ME 04032
☎ **(207) 865-9295**

Freeport
The James Place Inn
This charming, Victorian, cottage-style inn is within sight of Freeport's outlet shopping area. It is also near Bradbury Mountain, Wolfsneck State Park and the cross-country ski touring center. The inn features a cafe-style deck and five comfortable guestrooms with private entrances and baths. Some rooms have kitchenettes; some have Jacuzzis. Guests are invited to enjoy a free round of golf at the Freeport Country Club.

5 Rooms • Price range: $95-145
11 Holbrook St, Freeport, ME 04032
☎ **(207) 865-4486**

Freeport
Kendall Tavern Bed & Breakfast
Dating from the 1800s, the building has been renovated to appeal to modern tastes. The guestrooms and two very comfortable common rooms have fireplaces. One of the common rooms has a piano, the other a television, VCR and a collection of movies. The large verandas are perfect for relaxing on a warm afternoon. Only half a mile north of downtown Freeports shops, restaurants and L.L.Bean factory outlet.

7 Rooms • Price range: $85-110
213 Main St, Freeport, ME 04032
☎ **(207) 865-1338**

Freeport
White Cedar Inn

This century-old property was once the home of Arctic explorer Donald B. MacMillan, second-in-command to Robert E. Peary, who in 1909 was the first man to reach the North Pole. Today it is a spacious and comfortable Victorian inn just a short walk from Freeport's outlets. Rooms are air-conditioned with private baths. The Peary-MacMillan Arctic Museum is located at nearby Bowdoin College.

7 Rooms • Price range: $95-130
178 Main St, Freeport, ME 04032
☎ **(207) 865-9099**

Fryeburg
Admiral Peary House

American explorer Robert E. Peary lived here. Today's guests at the inn relax on the screened porch, play billiards and enjoy the outdoor spa and gardens. Guest activities include canoeing and swimming on the Saco River, tennis on the inn's red-clay courts and a hike up Jockey Cap, where the reward is a breathtaking view of the surrounding lakes and mountains. Winter packages are available.

6 Rooms • Price range: $138-148
9 Elm St, Fryeburg, ME 04037
☎ **(207) 935-3365**

Fryeburg
The Oxford House Inn

Breathtaking mountain scenery and a variety of year-round activities such as hiking, skiing, canoeing and golf are all at hand for guests of this distinguished Edwardian home. The inn boasts fine woodwork, spacious rooms and tasteful Victorian furnishings. Each room has a private bath. Full breakfasts are served. The inn's gourmet restaurant is considered one of the finest dining establishments in the Mt. Washington area.

4 Rooms • Price range: $50-125
105 Main St, Fryeburg, ME 04037
☎ **(207) 935-3442**

Georgetown
Coveside Bed & Breakfast

Newly renovated in a circa 1900 seaside cottage style, the inn's open floor plan includes a screened-in porch and comfortable common areas with fireplaces. Each of the individually decorated guestrooms offers a splendid view of Gotts Cove and Sheepscot Bay. Some rooms have a private porch and fireplace but all are without television or phone, providing a welcome reprieve from the distractions of modern life.

6 Rooms • Price range: $115-168
6 Gotts Cove Lane, Georgetown, ME 04548
☎ **(207) 371-2807**

Gorham
Pine Crest Bed & Breakfast

This beautiful Colonial home nestled in the residential area of the village retains much of its 1825 charm. All five sunny guestrooms now have private baths. The inn is located just five miles west of Portland, which means sightseeing and shopping are close enough to be tempting. Portland's Old Port area is also nearby. Beach lovers will be happy to know that there are two beaches in the vicinity: Pine Port and Old Orchard.

5 Rooms • Price range: $109-129
91 South St, Gorham, ME 04038
☎ **(207) 839-5843**

Gouldsboro
The Bluff House

High above Frenchman's Bay, the secluded Bluff House boasts a panoramic view of the mountains and the sparkling water, dotted with lobster boats and sailing ships. The modern rooms are comfortably appointed and have private baths.

8 Rooms • Price range: $59-86
PO Box 249, Gouldsboro, ME 04607
☎ **(207) 963-7805**

Greenville
The Lodge at Moosehead Lake

Majestic, unspoiled Moosehead Lake is the backdrop for this 1917 Cape Cod-Colonial. The inn is awash in rustic charm, with traditional furnishings interspersed with twig tables, magazines in log baskets and old photographs of the area. Guestrooms have beautiful, wooden four-poster beds, each featuring a totemic animal such as a loon, bear or moose. Common areas include the Great Room, with its large stone fireplace, the Moosehead Game Room, equipped with a pool table, and the spacious dining room, which has a whole wall devoted to windows and a view of the lake.

8 Rooms • Price range: $195-475
Upon Lily Bay Rd, Greenville, ME 04441
☎ **(207) 695-4400**

Greenville
Evergreen Lodge Bed & Breakfast

The Evergreen Lodge provides the perfect setting for nature lovers. Constructed of western and northern white cedar, it is situated on 30 acres of private woodland. Just a short distance away lies a wetland, where moose are often seen. In fact, the lodge offers moose safaris on Moosehead Lake on their pontoon boat. All six rooms at the lodge are homey and are named after animals. There is, of course, a Moose Room.

6 Rooms • Price range: $95-135
HCR 76 Box 58, Greenville, ME 04441
☎ **(207) 695-3241**

Greenville
Greenville Inn

Natural beauty surrounds the Greenville Inn. The village of Greenville, on the shores of Moosehead Lake, is visible in the distance, as are the Moose Mountains. The inn also has its own beauty: A leaded-glass window featuring a large spruce tree graces the stairway landing. The four rooms and one master suite have been furnished with a great attention to detail. All rooms have private baths with English tiles; some have soaking tubs.

12 Rooms • Price range: $135-175
PO Box 1194, Greenville, ME 04441
☎ **(207) 695-2206**

Hallowell
Maple Hill Farm B&B Inn

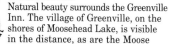

This circa 1890 inn is set on a 62-acre working farm that has a variety of animals, including llamas. Pleasant, rustic guestrooms possess all the mod-

ern amenities. Facilities for meeting are located in a converted barn.

7 Rooms • Price range: $90-110
RR 1, Box 1145, Hallowell, ME 04347
☎ **(207) 622-2708**

Hancock
Le Domaine Inn and Restaurant

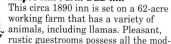

Experience the south of France on the coast of Maine. This charming Provençal-style inn, situated on 85 acres of woodlands, has lovely gardens and walking

trails. Two of the guestrooms are suites with separate sitting areas and gas fireplaces.

5 Rooms • Price: $200
US 1, Hancock, ME 04640
☎ **(207) 422-3395**

Kennebunk
Arundel Meadows Inn

A renovated early-1800s farmhouse with an impressive array of original paintings.

7 Rooms • Price range: $85-145
1024 Portland Rd, Kennebunk, ME 04043
☎ **(207) 985-3770**

Kennebunk
Waldo Emerson Inn

Beautifully restored, this 1750s home has had several well-known owners most notably Mr. Emerson, a shipbuilder and the great-uncle of poet/essayist Ralph Waldo Emerson. Rooms are decorated in an authentic country style with vibrant color combinations. Quilts, made at the quilt shop in the carriage house, adorn the beds.

4 Rooms • Price range: $90-115
108 Summer St, Kennebunk, ME 04043
☎ **(207) 985-4250**

Kennebunk Beach
The Beach House Inn

Nestled at the quiet end of Kennebunk Beach across the street from the ocean, this is the perfect getaway for those seeking a peaceful holiday. Built in 1891, the inn was totally renovated in 1987. An elevator and such safety precautions as a sprinkler system have been effortlessly combined with Old-World Victorian antiques. Two deluxe rooms come with a whirlpool. A room for the handicapped is also available.

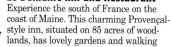

34 Rooms • Price range: $190-350
211 Beach Ave, Kennebunk Beach, ME 04043
☎ **(207) 967-3850**

◆◆ Kennebunkport
◆◆ *Captain Lord Mansion*
Built in 1812 and once a sea-captain's home, this beautifully restored 16-room country inn overlooks Kennebunk River. Listed on the National Register of Historic Places, the inn boasts a sweeping lawn, earning it the nickname "River Green." All rooms are luxurious and have antique four-poster–style beds, many with lace canopies. Fifteen rooms have gas fireplaces; one luxury suite has two fireplaces and a whirlpool tub. Deluxe rooms have small refrigerators. A complimentary three-course full breakfast is served daily. Afternoon tea and sweets are also available every day.

16 Rooms • Price range: $175-299
6 Pleasant St, Kennebunkport, ME 04046-0800
☎ **(207) 967-3141**

◆◆ Kennebunkport
◆◆ *Old Fort Inn*
Visitors will delight in this comfortable and secluded seaside resort. The taste- fully appointed guestrooms are located in a late 19th-century carriage house constructed of red brick and stone. Decorating details such as hand-stenciling on the walls make each room special. All rooms have a wet bar and a private bath. For guests who want to explore beyond the confines of their room, the inn has a large freshwater pool, a private tennis court, horseshoe pits and a shuffleboard. There are two golf courses close by and the ocean is just a short walk away. The gourmet breakfast is served buffet style.

16 Rooms • Price range: $145-350
8 Old Fort Ave, Kennebunkport, ME 04046
☎ **(207) 967-5353**

◆◆ Kennebunkport
◆◆ ⓌⒷ *The White Barn Inn*
In the 1800s this was Boothby boarding- house, a comfortable refuge for weary travelers. Today it is even more accommodating than before. Each of the 18 guestrooms and seven suites has been furnished with coordinated fabrics and New England period antiques. Finishing touches such as fresh flowers, elegant toiletries and thick bathrobes can be found in every guestroom. Visitors can also choose to stay in a pool-house room or a carriage house suite with hotel service. Added attractions include a heated outdoor pool and a fine restaurant for dining. The inn provides bicyles for its guests.

25 Rooms • Price range: $190-550
37 Beach Ave, Kennebunkport, ME 04046
☎ **(207) 967-2321**

Kennebunkport
1802 House Bed & Breakfast Inn

A small informal inn, the 1802 is bounded by the Cape Arundel Golf Club. The Kennebunk River is just a few yards away. All six of the inn's rooms have been recently renovated and have private bathrooms. Most have four-poster queen-size beds; some feature a working fireplace. Each morning, a ship's bell alerts guests that breakfast is ready.

6 Rooms • Price range: $179-379
15 Locke St, Kennebunkport, ME 04046-1646
☎ **(207) 967-5632**

Kennebunkport
Captain Fairfield Inn

James Fairfield and his wife received this handsome Federal mansion in 1813 as a wedding present from the bride's father. Almost 200 years later, the Fairfield Inn is still as well cared for as it was then. Spacious bedrooms, complete with private baths, and, in some cases, fireplaces, are available. Every day, chef and inn owner Dennis Tallagnon offers up a four-course breakfast, including homemade muffins and crepes.

9 Rooms • Price range: $150-195
8 Pleasant St, Kennebunkport, ME 04046
☎ **(207) 967-4454**

Kennebunkport
The Inn at Goose Rocks

Near Goose Rocks Beach, this pleasant inn sits on a knoll above a salt marsh.

32 Rooms • Price range: $125-175
71 Dyke Rd, Kennebunkport, ME 04046
☎ **(207) 967-5425**

Kennebunkport
The Kennebunkport Inn

This inn is actually two buildings: a 34-room, 19th-century mansion and a 1930s river house, which is attached to it. In season, a full breakfast is served. Dinner is also a treat since the inn is known for its freshly caught local seafood and Maine lobster. Guests are invited to relax after dinner in the inn's old-fashioned pub and piano bar. During the day, there's plenty to do, including deep-sea fishing and whale-watching.

34 Rooms • Price range: $99-325
1 Dock Square, Kennebunkport, ME 04046
☎ **(207) 967-2621**

Kennebunkport
Kilburn House

The relaxing Kilburn House offers all the comforts of home. Four guestrooms on the first floor of the 1890s inn come with two double beds and a private bath. A third-floor suite boasts an impressive skylight, two bedrooms and a private living room. Just steps away from the inn lies Kennebunkport's Dock Square, a cosmopolitan shopping area. Guests who crave sandy beaches have only to take a short drive.

5 Rooms • Price range: $95-135
6 Chestnut St, Kennebunkport, ME 04046
☎ **(207) 967-4762**

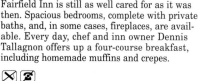

Kennebunkport
Maine Stay Inn & Cottages

Small wonder this tastefully decorated inn is listed on the National Historic Register. It exhibits all the attention to detail expected in a 19th-century home. From the suspended spiral staircase to the sunburst-crystal glass windows, the inn is a delight for the eyes. As well as the rooms of varying sizes, there are several one-bedroom cottages located on the grounds, some of which have a kitchen and a fireplace.

17 Rooms • Price range: $160-250
34 Maine St, Kennebunkport, ME 04046
☎ **(207) 967-2117**

Kennebunkport
Maude's Courtyard Bed & Breakfast
Guests at this pleasant inn have kitchen access. Continental breakfasts.

3 Rooms • Price range: $60-95
74 Western Ave, Kennebunkport, ME 04046
☎ **(207) 967-8433**

Kittery
Inn at Portsmouth Harbor
This three-story Victorian-era brick house is conveniently located to Memorial Bridge across from historic downtown Portsmouth, NH and Kittery's factory outlets. Common rooms feature Victorian watercolors, period furnishings and items collected by the owners on their travels. The Victorian theme is carried over into the guestrooms, but each has a private bath and a direct phone line with voice-mail and data port.

5 Rooms • Price range: $135-175
6 Water St, Kittery, ME 03904
☎ **(207) 439-4040**

Kittery
Enchanted Nights Bed & Breakfast
A few of the guestrooms in this fancifully decorated 1890s Victorian-Gothic home are up in the turret. The inn is close to Kittery outlets and historic downtown

Portsmouth, NH. Cuisine here leans towards the vegetarian.

8 Rooms • Price range: $49-230
29 Wentworth St, Kittery, ME 03904
☎ **(207) 439-1489**

Limerick
Jeremiah Mason Bed & Breakfast
This hospitable 1859 brick home in the center of town has simple spacious rooms.

8 Rooms • Price range: $50-70
40 Main St, Limerick, ME 04048
☎ **(207) 793-4858**

Lincolnville
The Youngtown Inn & Restaurant
This carefully restored 1810-farmhouse is located just five minutes from Camden Harbor in a lovely country setting. A large second-story veranda, furnished with chairs, tables and lounges, overlooks peaceful farmlands. Common areas and guestrooms have pumpkin pine wood floors and country-style decor with wrought-iron accents. The restaurant serves fine French cuisine prepared by a European-trained chef.

6 Rooms • Price range: $99-140
Rt 52 & Youngstown Rd, Lincolnville, ME 04849
☎ **(207) 763-4290**

Lubec
Home Port Inn

Built in 1880, this nicely kept Colonial home sits at the top of a hill on a quiet, tree-lined street. The handsomely decorated common rooms have a genuine homelike ambience. The sitting-room sofas, set before a fireplace, are perfect for curling up on. An air of casual comfort is carried throughout the inn. Each of the cozy guestrooms has a private bath. Campobello Island and Quoddy Head State Park are just a short drive away.

7 Rooms • Price range: $60-85
45 Main St, Lubec, ME 04652
☎ **(207) 733-2077**

Lubec
Peacock House

This jewel of a Victorian home overlooking the Bay of Fundy was built in 1860 by British sea captain William Trott for his bride. The house has hosted some of Maine's most prominent people, including Arctic explorer Donald MacMillan. Splendid public areas and guestrooms are tastefully decorated. The inn provides easy access to fishing, hiking, whale-watching and golfing. Lunch baskets are available for picnics.

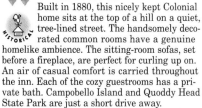

5 Rooms • Price range: $70-90
27 Summer St, Lubec, ME 04652
☎ **(207) 733-2403**

Naples
Inn at Long Lake

This circa 1900 inn overlooking Long Lake in the heart of Maine's lake region harks back to a time when river travel was the norm. These days the inn entices travelers with its floral arrangements, period furniture and hand-stenciled wooden floors. Guests can choose from four deluxe rooms, six standard rooms, four deluxe top-floor rooms and two suites, each with its own special qualities. The Great Room features a fireplace.

16 Rooms • Price range: $72-140
Lake House Rd, Naples, ME 04055
☎ **(207) 693-6226**

Naples
Augustus Bove House

Near the shores of Lake Long, this Victorian era inn was one of the first in the area and is decorated with period antiques. The dining room and parlor, in particular, reflect the Victorian influence. Some guestrooms have fireplaces.

10 Rooms • Price range: $69-175
RR 1 Box 501, Naples, ME 04055
☎ **(207) 693-6365**

Newcastle
The Newcastle Inn

Since 1911 this circa 1840 property on the Damariscotta River has been operated as an inn. Some of the guestrooms have four-poster beds; many have views of the river. There is a comfortable parlor, an all-season porch with wicker furniture and a deck that overlooks the garden and lawn, which sweeps down the hill to the river's edge. The restaurant has been well-reviewed.

14 Rooms • Price range: $125-250
60 River Rd, Newcastle, ME 04553
☎ **(207) 563-5685**

Northeast Harbor
Asticou Inn

Since 1883 the Asticou Inn has been welcoming guests to experience Victorian elegance amid the natural beauty of Mount Desert Island. The main inn and additional cottages offer a variety of room sizes with a choice of ocean or country views. Guests are encouraged to stroll through the beautiful azalea and cutting gardens or venture out for a hike into the adjacent Acadia National Park.

47 Rooms • Price range: $130-355
Rt 3 Peabody DR, Northeast Harbor, ME 04462
☎ **(207) 276-3344**

Ogunquit
Nellie Littlefield House

There is lots to do during a stay at this beautifully restored 1889 Victorian home. Take a walk along the Marginal Way, grab a trolley to Perkins Cove, explore the fascinating seascape or simply relax in one of the inn's air-conditioned rooms. All the rooms have access to a common deck; four have private decks with views of the ocean. Health enthusiasts will be happy to know that there is a fitness center on the grounds.

8 Rooms • Price range: $150-210
9 Shore Rd, Ogunquit, ME 03907
☎ **(207) 646-1692**

Ogunquit
The Pine Hill Inn

This inn is located in a quiet residential section of Ogunquit close to all the activities. The property consists of a Victorian summer house, a rustic cot- tage and a nearby home. Rooms in the main house have canopied European feather beds.

8 Rooms • Price range: $115-150
14 Pine Hill Rd S, Ogunquit, ME 03907
☎ **(207) 361-1004**

Ogunquit
White Rose Inn

An early 20th-century gambrel-style house located near the center of this popular seaside destination. Newly dec- orated guestrooms are available in the main inn as well as the carriage house, which accommodates groups of up to four. Under a canopy of trees, guests may relax on the patio to the soothing sound of the water garden or soak in the hot tub. Convenient to shopping, beaches and The Marginal Trail waterfront path.

8 Rooms • Price range: $95-175
95 Main Street, Ogunquit, ME 03907
☎ **(207) 646-3432**

Ogunquit
Yardarm Village Inn

This vintage inn has a wine and cheese shop. There is a small fee for breakfast.

8 Rooms • Price range: $85-105
142 Shore Rd, Ogunquit, ME 03907
☎ **(207) 646-7006**

Old Orchard Beach
Atlantic Birches Inn

This comfortable Victorian inn, built in 1903 during Old Orchard Beach's heyday, will suit those who want to be close to both shops and the beach. The casually elegant inn is in a quiet residential section; shops and restaurants are only a minute away. The Pier, the amusement area and sandy beaches are a five-minute walk. Both the Victorian Main House and the Cottage house beautiful guestrooms.

10 Rooms • Price range: $85-114
20 Portland Ave, Old Orchard Beach, ME 04064
☎ **(207) 934-5295**

Old Orchard Beach
Old Orchard Beach Inn

Constructed circa 1730, the property began operations as an inn a hundred years later, making it the oldest resort in Maine. Extensive renovations were completed in 2000. Comfortably sized bedrooms conform to their original size and shape. All are decorated with period antiques, patchwork quilts, wall sconces and modern amenities. Guest baths are average-size with contemporary decor and appointments.

18 Rooms • Price range: $65-180/room;
$150-400/suite
6 Portland Ave, Old Orchard Beach, ME 04064
☎ **(207) 934-5834**

Orland
Alamoosook Lodge Bed & Breakfast

Start the day with breakfast in the dining room overlooking Alamoosook Lake. Next, take a walk along the lake or, during the summer months, go swimming, canoeing or fishing. There is lots of wildlife to watch—loons and wood ducks are frequent visitors. During the winter, there is skating, cross-country skiing and ice fishing. At the end of the day, warm up in the lodge's common area by the wood stove.

6 Rooms • Price range: $83-98
PO Box 16, Orland, ME 04472
☎ **(207) 469-6393**

Pemaquid Point
ⓦ *The Bradley Inn at Pemaquid Point*

This is a graceful early 20th-century New England-style home with a gazebo, perennial gardens and tastefully decorated guestrooms, furnished primarily with antiques. Many have fireplaces; some have four poster beds.

16 Rooms • Price range: $135-250
3063 Bristol Rd, Pemaquid Point, ME 04554
☎ **(207) 677-2105**

Portland
ⓦ *Inn On Carleton*

Portland's historic Western Promenade is where you'll find the Inn on Carleton. This 1869 restored Victorian townhouse sits on a quiet residential street close to the center of downtown Portland. From there, it's just a short walk to the Portland Museum of Art and the Performing Arts Center. Also close by is the Old Port area, with its shops and fine restaurants, all connected by cobbled streets.

6 Rooms • Price range: $115-229
46 Carleton St, Portland, ME 04102
☎ **(207) 775-1910**

Portland
West End Inn
An 1871 Victorian inn in the Western
Promenade historic district.

6 Rooms • Price range: $129-199
146 Pine St, Portland, ME 04102
☎ **(207) 772-1377**

Rangeley
North Country Inn Bed & Breakfast
This early 20th-century residence is
surrounded by lakes and mountains.
Tucked away in the middle of Rangeley
Village, the North Country Inn is a
four-season sports resort, offering a variety of
activities such as fishing, hiking, tennis, golf
and, in the wintertime, skiing. The inn has a
private boat dock for guests who are boating
enthusiasts. A homemade country breakfast is
served. Two of the guestrooms have lake views.

4 Rooms • Price range: $85-95
Main St, Rangeley, ME 04970
☎ **(207) 864-2440**

Rangeley
⑩ Rangeley Inn & Motor Lodge
This 1907 four-season resort is on
Haley Pond Lake in western Maine's
Longfellow Mountains. A complete
restoration included adding all the
modern amenities while preserving its historic
country inn charm. Rooms feature antique beds
and furnishings. Some of the private baths have
claw-foot tubs or whirlpools. The dining room
and tavern offer a fine choice of cuisine and
spirits. Many outdoor activities are available.

52 Rooms • Price range: $69-140
51 Main St, Rangeley, ME 04970
☎ **(207) 864-3341**

Rangeley
Country Club Inn
From its lovely location on a hill, the
Country Club Inn overlooks Rangeley
Lake. Accommodations are available in
the main inn or in two motel sections.

All are pleasantly furnished. A public golf course
is located just steps away.

19 Rooms • Price range: $69-96
Country Club Dr, Rangeley, ME 04970
☎ **(207) 864-3831**

Rockland
⑩ Berry Manor Inn
Originally the home of a prominent
Rockland merchant named Charles E.
Berry, this 1898 Victorian mansion is
currently one of the area's premier
B&Bs. Guestrooms, each with private bath, are
decorated in a luxurious 19th-century style.
Early risers can enjoy the morning paper in one
of the lovely parlors, have coffee in the second-
floor library and then eat breakfast a little later
in the remarkable dining room. A guest pantry
is stocked with sweets and other treats for a
late night snack in the gardens or on the front
porch. The residential setting is close to the
harbor and other points of interest.

8 Rooms • Price range: $105-240
81 Talbot Ave, Rockland, ME 04841
☎ **(207) 596-7696**

Rockland
Captain Lindsey House Inn

One of Rockland's first inns, the nine-room 1837 Captain Lindsey House Inn has a long tradition of hospitality. Furnishings from around the world grace each room. All beds have down comforters. Next to the fireplace in the living room is the perfect place to warm up on a cool day and the library is stocked with a large selection of novels. There is a desk and a data port for those who like to mix business with pleasure.

9 Rooms • Price range: $120-175
5 Lindsey St, Rockland, ME 04841
☎ **(207) 596-7950**

Rockland
Lakeshore Inn Bed & Breakfast
Perched in the Dodge Mountains, this attractive and well-maintained home—part of which was built in 1767—offers splendid panoramic views. The smoke-free inn has two guestrooms that open onto a deck; all rooms have an unobstructed view of Lake Chickawaukie. Birds, deer and other wildlife can often be spotted on the grounds. The lake offers freshwater swimming or cruising on a windjammer. Ladies' spa weekends take place off season.

4 Rooms • Price range: $125-155
184 Lakeview Dr, Rockland, ME 04841
☎ **(207) 594-4209**

Searsport
Brass Lantern Inn

This 1850s converted sea captain's home prides itself on providing guests with the utmost tranquillity. Four upper-floor guestrooms have white-noise machines so guests can fall a sleep to the sound of spring rain or ocean waves. Early morning tea or coffee is followed by breakfast. In the colder months, homemade soup, chili and chowder are served later in the day.

5 Rooms • Price range: $80-100
81 W Main St, Searsport, ME 04974
☎ **(207) 548-0150**

South Freeport
Atlantic Seal Bed & Breakfast
An 1850s Cape Cod-style home near the harbor. One guestroom has a fireplace.

4 Rooms • Price range: $95-175
25 Main St, South Freeport, ME 04078
☎ **(207) 865-6112**

Southwest Harbor
The Inn at Southwest
Unlike most inns that were converted into guest houses, this 1884 structure was built as a hotel annex. Each of the rooms is decorated differently and is named after a particular Maine Lighthouse. All come with ceiling fans. Guests are welcomed to relax in the comfortably furnished parlors. A full gourmet breakfast is served daily by candlelight in the dining room or out on the large sunporch.

9 Rooms • Price range: $95-145
371 Main Street, Southwest Harbor, ME 04679
☎ **(207) 244-3835**

Southwest Harbor
The Kingsleigh Inn

The first thing to grab your attention here is the kitchen. It's a warm, welcoming country kitchen, where tea, coffee and cocoa are available all day. The living room also is homey, the walls hung with artworks depicting maritime life adding a nautical touch. The dining-room library has plenty of books, magazines and games for guests to use. All eight guestrooms sport colorful wall coverings and coordinated window treatments.

8 Rooms • Price range: $100-220
373 Main St, Southwest Harbor, ME 04679
☎ **(207) 244-5302**

Southwest Harbor
The Lindenwood Inn

Surrounded by Acadia National Park, Southwest Harbor offers a variety of pleasures for the outdoor enthusiast. Overlooking the harbor, this tastefully decorated inn provides a perfect place to pursue those pleasures. Some guestrooms feature lovely harbor views, decks and gas fireplaces. A third-floor suite has an outdoor hot tub on a private deck. A large shaded porch serves as a breakfast spot in the warmer months.

15 Rooms • Price range: $95-255
118 Clark Point Rd, Southwest Harbor, ME 04679
☎ **(207) 244-5335**

Spruce Head
The Craignair Inn at Clark Island

Formerly a boarding house for quarry-men, this 1928 inn sits on a granite ledge overlooking the sea and Clark Island. The guestrooms vary in size and style; six have private baths. The dining room features local seafood prepared by an award-winning chef. The area's natural beauty and bountiful wildlife make this an ideal spot for those seeking tranquillity and privacy.

21 Rooms • Price range: $48-120
533 Clark Island Rd, Spruce Head, ME 04859
☎ **(207) 594-7644**

West Forks
Inn by the River

Overlooking the Kennebec River, this inn has pleasant common areas with fireplaces and decks. Guestrooms are comfortable and exceptionally clean.

Rooms in the rear of the building are quieter than those at the front.

10 Rooms • Price range: $65-120
US Rt 201, West Forks, ME 04985
☎ **(207) 663-2181**

Wiscasset
The Squire Tarbox Inn

A real country experience awaits guests to this circa 1763 home. Dairy cows are kept on the property providing the milk needed for the cheese served by the inn. The inn prides itself on preparing dinners that suit the mood of the day. After dinner, guests can participate in a game in the barn or take a walk down the pine-needled path that leads to a saltwater marsh. Guestrooms feature braided rugs, patchwork quilts and fireplaces.

11 Rooms • Price range: $107-189
PO Box 1181 Westport Island,
Wiscasset, ME 04578
☎ **(207) 882-7693**

York
Dockside Guest Quarters

This inn, which is located on a small private island, is a classic New England "cottage," complete with wraparound porch and wicker rockers. The porch is an excellent place to take in the view of coastal Maine. The guest house is stocked inside with period furnishings and marine paintings. Most guestrooms have a balcony or a patio. The Dockside Restaurant, overlooking York Harbor and the Marina, specializes in Maine seafood.

25 Rooms • Price range: $85-210
PO Box 205 Harris Island, York, ME 03909
☎ **(207) 363-2868**

York Harbor
Edwards Harborside Inn

This Victorian seaside residence stands in a tranquil, picturesque setting overlooking York Harbor. Ten individually appointed rooms offer cozy comfort and classic New England harbor-front scenery. Local activities include golf, tennis, boating and deepsea fishing. A more leisurely pace can be enjoyed by simply strolling along the beach or visiting historic sights in York. Farther afield are Portsmouth, NH and Kittery's factory outlets.

10 Rooms • Price range: $120-200
Stage Neck Rd, York Harbor, ME 03911
☎ **(207) 363-3037**

York Harbor
Inn At Harmon Park

Fresh-cut flowers, hand-sewn quilts, ceiling fans and wicker furniture add special charm to this gracious inn in a quiet residential area of town. Breakfast is served, weather permitting, on the sunporch. After breakfast, guests can stroll along the river to Harbor Beach or cross "Wriggly Bridge" through a nature preserve into historic York Village to visit shops, galleries and artisan studios.

5 Rooms • Price range: $77-119
415 York St, York Harbor, ME 03911
☎ **(207) 363-2031**

York Harbor
York Harbor Inn

Situated in one of the least crowded and commercialized seaside resort areas, this handsome inn and carriage house offers 35 rooms of varying sizes, each graciously decorated. Additions to the inn's 300-year-old common room reflect a number of different time periods. Of an evening, guests can relax in the inn's comfortable pub, The Wine Cellar. The historic Nubble Light Lighthouse is just down the street.

33 Rooms • Price range: $109-159
York St, York Harbor, ME 03911
☎ **(207) 363-5119**

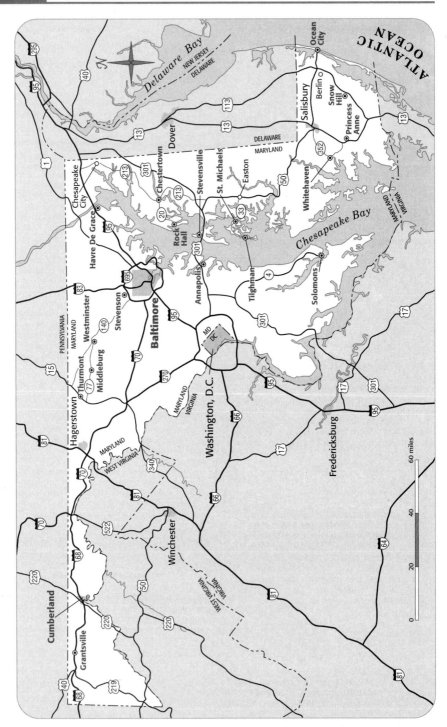

Annapolis
Prince George Inn Bed & Breakfast

The building is more than a century old. It has been extensively renovated to become the first registered B&B in Annapolis. Each of the guestrooms is decorated with antiques and equipped with all the modern amenities. The breakfast room is the place to enjoy a gourmet morning meal, with daily papers and the delicious baked goods of the hostess. In the evening, guests gather around the fireplace in the candlelit parlor.

4 Rooms • Price range: $115-135
232 Prince George St, Annapolis, MD 21401
☎ **(410) 263-6418**

Annapolis
The William Page Inn Bed & Breakfast
The William Page Inn, built in 1908, was the meeting place for the Democratic Club for more than 50 years before being converted to a bed and breakfast. It was further renovated in 1987 and is furnished with antiques and period reproductions. Located in the city's historic district, the inn is a short walk from the waterfront and the Naval Academy. Breakfast is a real treat, with a selection of fresh-baked pastries and breads.

5 Rooms • Price range: $120-210
8 Martin St, Annapolis, MD 21401-1716
☎ **(410) 626-1506**

Annapolis
Maryland Inn
This 18th-century inn has a variety of rooms, some furnished with antiques.

44 Rooms • Price range: $159-249
16 Church Cir, Annapolis, MD 21401
☎ **(410) 263-2641**

Baltimore
Admiral Fell Inn
Originally a seaman's hostel, the inn is now a complex of eight buildings on Fell's Point, Baltimore's lively historic, waterfront district. Period pieces, including several canopy beds, decorate the rooms. A rooftop ballroom has panoramic views.

80 Rooms • Price range: $145-255
888 S Broadway, Baltimore, MD 21231
☎ **(410) 522-7377**

Baltimore
Celie's Waterfront Bed & Breakfast

Located in the historic Fells Point area, the inn was built with luxury and comfort in mind. Some rooms have whirlpool tubs, private balconies or fireplaces. All guestrooms are decorated with antiques, and special attention is paid to details such as fresh cut flowers and terry cloth robes. Guests can enjoy the sweeping views of the harbor from the roof deck or relax on the intimate garden patio.

7 Rooms • Price range: $110-230
1714 Thames St, Baltimore, MD 21231
☎ **(410) 522-2323**

Chestertown
Brampton Bed & Breakfast Inn

Built as a plantation house in 1860, the Brampton retains nearly all its original details and is listed on the National Register of Historic Places. Luxurious rooms have private baths and period furnishings; some have a wood-burning fireplace. The inn has a formal guest parlor and a family room with a VCR and various games. Breakfast and afternoon tea—which include homemade muffins, cakes and cookies—are served daily.

10 Rooms • Price range: $135-255
25227 Chestertown Rd, Chestertown, MD 21620
☎ **(410) 778-1860**

Cumberland
Inn at Walnut Bottom
The multilingual staff of this inn caters to international travelers as well as families with children. The accommodations in two adjacent townhouses are charming and comfortable, with an emphasis on relaxation. The inn offers massages, or "Afspaending," as they are known here. They consist of a unique combination of gentle movements, stretching and mild exercise directed at tension areas.

12 Rooms • Price range: $97-145
120 Greene St, Cumberland, MD 21502
☎ **(301) 777-0003**

Grantsville
Elliott House Victorian Inn
This 1870 Victorian inn is set in the beautiful countryside of the Allegheny mountains and Casselman River. Hiking on the surrounding seven-acre property, or skiing and fishing nearby are possible activities. For relaxation, guests can take refuge on the inn's swings and hammocks and partake in the complimentary tea, coffee and wine. All rooms contain antiques from the original farmhouse and Amish quilt bedspreads.

7 Rooms • Price range: $98-160
146 Casselman Rd, Grantsville, MD 21536
☎ **(301) 895-4250**

Grantsville
Walnut Ridge Bed & Breakfast
This comfortable circa 1864 farmhouse is decorated with antiques and family heirlooms. Guests are welcome to enjoy the front porch swing or walk through the gardens. There are state parks nearby which offer skiing and hiking.

4 Rooms • Price range: $75-85
92 Main St, Grantsville, MD 21536
☎ **(301) 895-4248**

Havre De Grace
Vandiver Inn
A former mayor of Havre de Grace and state treasurer for Maryland, Murray Vandiver, built this Victorian mansion as a wedding present for his bride in 1886. The home is on the National Register of Historic Places and the premises boast a gazebo and pavilion. Many of the guestrooms and suites have a working fireplace or whirlpool tub. Gourmet food is prepared by the hostess, who was once a professional caterer.

17 Rooms • Price range: $64-160
301 S Union Ave, Havre De Grace, MD 21078
☎ **(410) 939-5200**

Middleburg
Bowling Brook Country Inn

This quiet inn was once a farm, built by a Revolutionary War veteran in 1837. Dramatic changes in the 20th century have done little to diminish its original

charm. Tasteful appointments decorate rooms. Guests may use a nearby athletic club.

8 Rooms • Price range: $110-235
6000 Middleburg Rd, Middleburg, MD 21757
☎ (410) 876-2893

Oakland
Carmel Cove Inn

A former monastery for Carmelite friars, the building was sold in 1994 to the present owners who have renovated it to pamper guests. On the shore of the state's largest lake, and surrounded by mountains, the inn has a natural tranquillity. The former chapel is now a common room complete with an antique billiard table and fireplace. Guests are invited to use the tennis court or try their fishing skills from canoes or paddle boats.

10 Rooms • Price range: $100-$160
105 Monastery Way, Oakland, MD 21550
☎ (301) 387-0067

Ocean City
⚓ The Lighthouse Club Hotel, An Inn at Fager's Island

This Chesapeake Bay-style lighthouse on Fager's Island overlooks the Isle of Wight Bay and a nearby wetland teeming with waterfowl. The 23 one-bedroom suites are luxuriously appointed with marble baths, Jacuzzis and gas fireplaces. Services include evening turndown, terry cloth robes and continental breakfast. Dinner and entertainment are just over the footbridge at Fager's Island Restaurant and Bar.

23 Rooms • Price range: $184-295
56th St in-the-Bay, Ocean City, MD 21842
☎ (410) 524-5400

Ocean City
Atlantic House Bed and Breakfast

A lovely, old seaside home a block from the beach and boardwalk. Some of the bright and cheerful bedrooms have private baths and ocean views. An apart-ment is also available by the week. The area offers plenty of activities for the entire family.

11 Rooms • Price range: $95-225
501 N Baltimore Ave, Ocean City, MD 21842
☎ (410) 289-2333

Princess Anne
Waterloo Country Inn

This beautifully restored 1750s dwelling is listed in the National Register of Historic Places. Two luxury suites come complete with a Jacuzzi; some rooms have a fireplace. Situated near a tidal pool, the inn is particularly enjoyable in the summer months, when guests can swim in the outdoor pool, canoe or go biking. Guests are also encouraged to stroll through the gardens or hike in the nearby forest.

6 Rooms • Price range: $100-245
28822 Mt Vernon Rd, Princess Anne, MD 21853
☎ (410) 651-0883

Rock Hall

⊕ *Huntingfield Manor Bed & Breakfast*

A lovely, old seaside home a block from the beach and boardwalk. Some of the bright and cheerful, attractively decorated bedrooms have private baths and ocean views. An apartment unit is also available by the week and has a gas fireplace. The area offers plenty of activities for the entire family. The converted farm house sits on 70 acres that operate as a working farm.

6 Rooms • Price range: $95-145
4928 Eastern Neck Rd, Rock Hall, MD 21661
☎ **(410) 639-7779**

Snow Hill

River House Inn

There's plenty to do during a stay at this 1860s historic home with its two acres of landscaped grounds. Guests can take walking tours or rent canoes or kayaks to explore the scenic river or nearby bays and ocean. There is also a wildlife cruise on The Otter, the inn's pontoon boat. After a day of exploring, guests can relax in one of the comfortable rooms in the main house or in the contemporary cottage units.

10 Rooms • Price range: $99-205
201 E Market St, Snow Hill, MD 21863
☎ **(410) 632-2722**

Solomons

Solomons Victorian Inn

This charming yacht builder's home overlooks Solomons Harbor. The third-floor suite features a whirlpool and has a magnificent view of the waterfront. Some of the other units also have harbor views as well as balconies.

8 Rooms • Price range: $90-175
125 Charles St, Solomons, MD 20688
☎ **(410) 326-4811**

St. Michaels

⊕ *The Parsonage Inn*

This unique brick Victorian home was built in 1883 by Dr. Henry Clay Dodson, a pharmacist and prominent business-man who was appointed Postmaster of St. Michaels by President Lincoln in 1861. Guestrooms are appointed with brass beds and floral linens and they have private baths. Some also have a wood-burning fireplace. Guests are invited to ride the inn's bicycles, sit on the front porch and deck or use the picnic table and grill.

8 Rooms • Price range: $110-185
210 N Talbot St, St. Michaels, MD 21663
☎ **(410) 745-5519**

Stevenson
Gramercy Mansion Bed & Breakfast

Forty-five acres of grounds surround the mansion, which is located just 20 minutes from downtown Baltimore. Guests are close to shops, museums, theaters and other attractions. Nature-oriented activities include strolling along wooded trails or visiting the inn's organic farm. There is also an Olympic-size pool and a tennis court on the grounds. Five main-floor guestrooms have fireplaces and Oriental carpeting.

10 Rooms • Price range: $100-350
1400 Greenspring Valley Rd,
Stevenson, MD 21153
☎ **(410) 486-2405**

Stevensville
Kent Manor Inn

This comfortable inn on the banks of the Chesapeake is a tribute to the charm of days gone by. Guestrooms are decorated with Victorian reproductions. The hosts take pride in their cooking and have won awards for their cuisine. The inn stands on a 226-acre farm where the whole family can enjoy a variety of outdoor activities such as swimming in the Olympic-size pool, using the paddle boats, or following the walking trails.

24 Rooms • Price range: $170-235
500 Kent Manor Dr, Stevensville, MD 21666
☎ **(410) 643-5757**

Thurmont
Cozy Country Inn

This is a unique establishment built in 1929 and still run by the founding family. The rooms and suites of the inn are appointed to commemorate presidents and dignitaries, such as Winston Churchill and John F. Kennedy, who have visited nearby Camp David. As well as having an inviting pub and interesting shops on-site, the inn's Cozy Restaurant prepares wonderful dishes with fresh herbs and vegetables from the gardens.

21 Rooms • Price range: $51-165
103 Frederick Rd, Thurmont, MD 21788
☎ **(301) 271-4301**

Tilghman Island
Chesapeake Wood Duck Inn

Situated on tiny Tilghman Island, the inn and its surroundings offer the ambience of a 19th-century waterman's village. Partake in such sports as sailing or horseback riding or sit by the fireplace with a good book. Eastern-shore charm and hospitality are evident in the tastefully decorated sitting rooms and in the daily gourmet breakfast. The owners like to share stories about the history of the place.

7 Rooms • Price range: $159-219
Gibsontown Rd, Tilghman Island, MD 21671
☎ **(410) 886-2070**

Westminster

Westminster Inn

Originally a schoolhouse, built in 1899, this red-brick building has been transformed into an elegant and luxurious inn. Each room offers a queen-size bed and a private Jacuzzi. The Teacher's Lounge and the Naughty Boy's Pub provide thematic fun and entertainment in the evening. Guests have the use of the East End Athletic Club's heated indoor lap pool and extensive exercise equipment. Breakfast is a continental buffet.

24 Rooms • Price range: $100-195
5 S Center St, Westminster, MD 21157
☎ **(410) 876-2893**

Westminster
Winchester Country Inn
This inn offers a charming and refreshing retreat from everyday life. Built as a home by the founder of Westminster in the 1760s, the establishment was fully restored in 1986. Many local families donated antiques and period furnishings.

5 Rooms • Price range: $85-85
111 Stoner Ave, Westminster, MD 21157
☎ **(410) 848-9343**

Whitehaven
Whitehaven Bed & Breakfast
Guests have a choice of two historic residences, circa 1886 and 1850. Rooms are individually decorated with antique furnishings. Each has a view of the Wicomico River and marsh. Whitehaven offers all the pleasures of a quiet country town.

5 Rooms • Price range: $70-100
23844 River St, Whitehaven, MD 21856
☎ **(410) 873-3294**

Notes:

Notes:

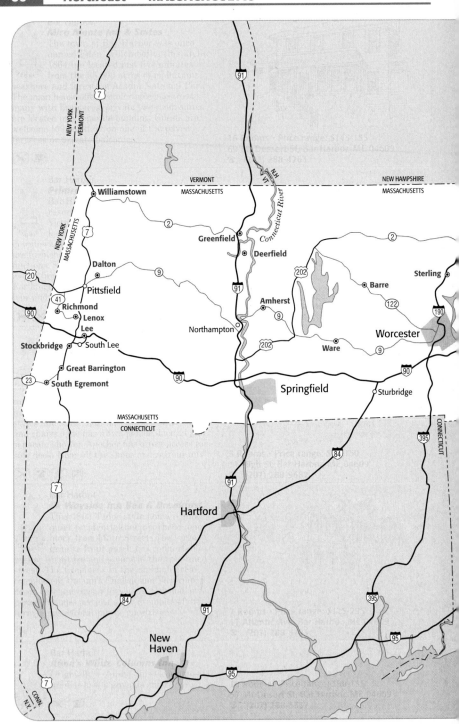

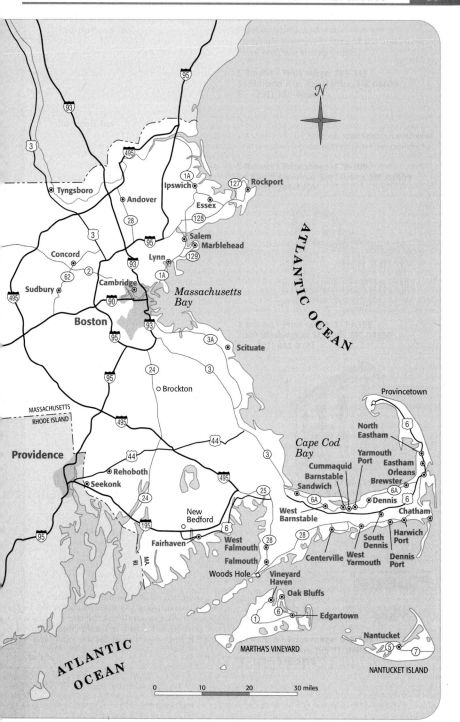

MASSACHUSETTS
RHODE ISLAND

Providence

Tyngsboro
Andover
Ipswich
Rockport
Essex
Salem
Marblehead
Concord
Lynn
Cambridge
Sudbury
Massachusetts Bay
Boston
Scituate
Brockton
Rehoboth
Seekonk
New Bedford
Fairhaven
West Falmouth
Falmouth
Woods Hole
Cape Cod Bay
Provincetown
North Eastham
Yarmouth Port
Eastham
Orleans
Cummaquid
Barnstable
Sandwich
Brewster
Dennis
West Barnstable
Chatham
Centerville
West Yarmouth
South Dennis
Harwich Port
Dennis Port
Vineyard Haven
Oak Bluffs
Edgartown
Nantucket
MARTHA'S VINEYARD
NANTUCKET ISLAND

ATLANTIC OCEAN
ATLANTIC OCEAN

0   10   20   30 miles

Amherst
Allen House Victorian Bed & Breakfast Inn

This vintage 1886 stick-style Queen Anne home has period chandeliers, ornate tile work and original Eastlake fireplace mantels. Each room is homey, featuring lace curtains, trinket boxes, porcelain dolls and, of course, thick quilts. Guests enjoy sinfully delicious meals in the period-wallpapered dining room. The innkeepers pride themselves on providing guests with the utmost in comfort and hospitality.

7 Rooms • Price range: $75-175
599 Main St, Amherst, MA 01002
☎ **(413) 253-5000**

Andover
Andover Inn

This charming 1930s inn is set on the beautifully landscaped grounds of Phillips Academy. There is live music and dancing every Friday evening. A popular Dutch Indonesian buffet (with 20 different dishes) is served Sundays.

29 Rooms • Price range: $105-195
4 Chapel Ave, Andover, MA 01810
☎ **(978) 475-5903**

Barnstable
Ashley Manor Inn

This lovely two-acre estate, with its carefully situated tennis court, is secluded behind high privet hedges and stately trees. The classic fountain garden in the back highlights the charm of the inn, which was built in the mid 1700s. Each room is abeautifully appointed private refuge with fresh flowers, chocolates and fine soaps and lotions. Most rooms have a working fireplace. Breakfast is extravagant.

6 Rooms • Price range: $135-195
3660 Olde Kings Hwy, SR 6A,
Barnstable, MA 02630
☎ **(508) 362-8044**

Barnstable
Beechwood Inn

Named after the two magnificent beech trees that shade the inn, the Beechwood is an authentically restored treasure. Rockers, gliders and wicker furniture overlook acres of quiet lawns, gardens and woods. The inn also boasts original Queen Anne stained-glass windows; one room features a handpainted cottage bedroom suite from the 1860s. All rooms are furnished with lovely antiques; two units have fireplaces.

6 Rooms • Price range: $145-180
2839 Main St (SR 6A), Barnstable, MA 02630
☎ **(508) 362-6618**

Barre
Jenkins Inn

This inn is located on the town green, conveniently close to Brimfield, one of the antique capitals of the world. Theaters and sightseeing opportunities are easily reached. For the outdoor types, there is plenty to do: hiking, fishing, golfing and skiing are all close by. Rooms are cozy and well appointed; all but two units have private baths. The 1834 inn has added modern amenities.

5 Rooms • Price range: $125-165
7 West St, Barre, MA 01005
☎ **(978) 355-6444**

Boston
Newbury Guest House

Built in 1882 as a private home in Boston's fashionable Back Bay neighborhood, this inn was renovated to keep its Old-World charm, while adding modern conveniences. Only a stone's throw from public transportation, the Hynes Convention Center and Copley Place, the inn is convenient for business or vacation travelers. It is also close to some of the region's most famous landmarks as well as the Charles River.

32 Rooms • Price range: $110-180
261 Newbury St, Boston, MA 02116
☎ **(617) 437-7666**

Brewster
The Bramble Inn

The main inn, built in 1861, houses a restaurant on the first floor and lodging on the second. A second building, circa 1849, is just a few doors down. The canopy beds, antique bureaus, art and collectibles enhance the inn's link with the past.

8 Rooms • Price range: $125-175
2019 Main St, Brewster, MA 02631
☎ **(508) 896-7644**

Brewster
Brewster Farmhouse Inn

This farmhouse, built circa 1850, is situated in the heart of the town's historic district, just a short walk from Cape Cod Bay. The guestrooms and common areas are beautifully decorated and speak of graciousness and gentility. The expansive grounds contain a peaceful, landscaped deck and heated pool area, a whirlpool spa, gardens and an orchard. A two-bedroom suite with a shared bath is also available.

8 Rooms • Price range: $100-225
716 Main St, Brewster, MA 02631
☎ **(508) 896-3910**

Brewster
⚐ *Candleberry Inn*

This circa 1800 Federal-style home has original windows, wainscoting and wide-plank wood floors. These details, coupled with beautiful antiques, Oriental carpets and family heirlooms, give the inn a romantic atmosphere. Guestrooms are spacious, attractive and comfortable; three rooms have working fireplaces. The inn, on two landscaped acres, is close to beaches and golf facilities, as well as the summer festivals in Brewster.

9 Rooms • Price range: $95-145
1882 Main St, Brewster, MA 02631
☎ **(508) 896-3300**

Brewster
The Captain Freeman Inn

Elegant architectural details such as a beautiful central staircase are the outstanding features of this restored sea captain's mansion, built in 1860. All rooms are spacious and elegant. Five units have working fireplaces; some have whirlpools and balconies. Plaster moldings and floors of light- and dark-patterned herringbone are found throughout the inn. Meals are served by the pool or by the fire.

14 Rooms • Price range: $155-190
15 Breakwater Rd, Brewster, MA 02631
☎ **(508) 896-7481**

Brewster

Isaiah Clark House

Built as a merchant sea captain's estate, this 1780s home has been restored to mint condition. Antique furnishings, a library and grand piano create a warm and inviting ambience throughout the entire house. When weather permits, breakfast and afternoon tea are served on the raised deck overlooking the gardens. Each of the seven guest quarters has a private bath and some have working fireplaces.

7 Rooms • Price range: $125-150
1187 Main St, Brewster, MA 02631
☎ (508) 896-2223

Brewster
Old Sea Pines Inn

Formerly a girls' finishing school, this inn has remained an exclusive hideaway on the well-kept and secluded grounds of the vast Brewster Estate. The inn is immaculately maintained and has a laid-back, down-east atmosphere for those who just want to relax. It is close to unpopulated beaches, golf courses, fine restaurants and picturesque biking trails. Some of the guestrooms are in outlying buildings.

24 Rooms • Price range: $65-165
2553 Main St, Brewster, MA 02631
☎ (508) 896-6114

Brewster
The Ruddy Turnstone Bed & Breakfast

Situated on three acres of land overlooking a marsh and the bay, this wonderfully restored Cape Cod cottage is a reminder of a seafaring past. Original pine floors, hand-hooked rugs, antique furniture and accessories add to the romantically rustic ambience. The similarly appointed Nantucket Carriage House features barn-board walls and canopy beds. Binoculars are provided for observing the marsh's variety of birds and wildlife.

5 Rooms • Price range: $95-175
463 Main St, Brewster, MA 02631
☎ (508) 385-9871

Brewster
Carriage House Inn

The first thing that greets guests is the parlor's grand piano and those who can play are encouraged to do just that. In addition to the three rooms in the house there are three in the carriage house with fireplaces and private entrances.

6 Rooms • Price range: $170-195
407 Old Harbor Rd, Brewster, MA 02633
☎ (508) 945-4688

Cambridge
A Cambridge House Bed & Breakfast Inn
Meticulously decorated to revive the period in which it was built, this Victorian retreat sits in a modern commercial and residential area. However, looks can be deceiving and in-room amenities such as phones with voice mail and data ports keep guest in touch with the present while they luxuriate in the comforts of the past. Business and pleasure travelers will appreciate the inn's proximity to Harvard and downtown Boston.

15 Rooms • Price range: $189-290
2218 Massachusetts Ave, Cambridge, MA 02140
☎ (617) 491-6300

Centerville
Adam's Terrace Gardens Inn

Originally built in 1830 for Captain John Baker and his family this registered historic home has been a B&B since 1939. In the warmer seasons, breakfast is served bistro-style on a screened deck. Afternoon tea is served daily.

8 Rooms • Price range: $55-110
539 Main St, Centerville, MA 02632
☎ **(508) 775-4707**

Centerville
Long Dell Inn
Attractive Cape-style home with a white picket fence and nicely landscaped grounds. Guests can relax on the backyard hammock or in the comfort of the living room. The carriage house is a fully equipped apartment for up to four people.

6 Rooms • Price range: $79-119
436 S Main St, Centerville, MA 02632
☎ **(508) 775-2750**

Chatham
Captain's House Inn of Chatham
Each of the elegantly furnished guestrooms in this 1839 property has been named after a family member of Captain Hiram Harding, who built the house, or one of the ships that he sailed. Each room has unique attractions, such as four-poster beds with pineapple finials, lacy, white fishnet canopies, plush velvet wing chairs and braided rugs. Guestrooms are also available in the Captain's Cottage, the Carriage House and the comfortable Stables. Breakfast is served daily on fine china; English tea, with scones and cakes, is available in the afternoon.

17 Rooms • Price range: $125-350
369 Old Harbor Rd, Chatham, MA 02633
☎ **(508) 945-0127**

Chatham
Chatham Town House Inn
This 1880s inn consists of four buildings on a two-acre complex in the heart of the village. Each room is decorated with eclectic taste and features amenities such as air-conditioning, a compact refrigerator and cable color television. Some rooms have a balcony or a deck. Two cottages that can accommodate up to four people are available. The inn's Two Turtles Restaurant serves a full breakfast as well as a candlelight gourmet dinner.

25 Rooms • Price range: $195-425
11 Library Ln, Chatham, MA 02633
☎ **(508) 945-2180**

Chatham
The Cranberry Inn of Chatham
The inn's guestrooms feature four-poster queen-size beds and pine flooring. Some rooms in this restored 1830s building have private balconies, beamed ceilings, hand-stenciled wall decorations and wet bars. The common rooms are equally inviting, with Oriental rugs and artworks. Directly behind the inn is an unharvested cranberry bog and nature trail leading to Old Mill Pond. It is just a short walk to the beach.

18 Rooms • Price range: $170-260
359 Main St, Chatham, MA 02633
☎ **(508) 945-9232**

Chatham

Moses Nickerson House Inn

Guests will feel like they've been transported to England when they enter the parlor, which is complete with rose bouquet-covered walls, an Aubusson rug and an antique lyre-based, Duncan Phyfe table. The glass-enclosed dining room, which opens onto the landscaped gardens, is a pleasant breakfast spot. Visitors will be pleased with the guestrooms, with their queen-size beds and hand-made quilts. Some rooms have a fireplace.

7 Rooms • Price range: $149-199
364 Old Harbor Rd, Chatham, MA 02633
☎ **(508) 945-5859**

Chatham
The Old Harbor Inn

With its English-country decor and its setting in a quiet residential neighborhood, this inn provides hospitable and homey surroundings. Guestrooms are comfortably furnished; two of them have been recently renovated and now include a gas fireplace. In the Gathering Room, guests can play parlor games, read the paper or curl up with a good book. The smell of homemade muffins greets visitors in the morning.

8 Rooms • Price range: $139-239
22 Old Harbor Rd, Chatham, MA 02633
☎ **(508) 945-4434**

Chatham

Port Fortune Inn

Situated in the heart of Chatham's historic Old Village, the Port Fortune Inn is within walking distance of restaurants, art galleries and Lighthouse Beach. Guestrooms are supplied with fine linens, plush towels and decorator fabrics. Some rooms have a view of the ocean. There is plenty to do in the summertime: Art and craft fairs, concerts, theater, birding, golf and sailing are all accessible from the inn.

13 Rooms • Price range: $135-200
201 Main St, Chatham, MA 02633
☎ **(508) 945-0792**

Concord
The Colonial Inn

Comprised of three adjoining houses on the village green in Historic Concord Center, this inn has an original section dating back to the early 1700s; it is listed on the National Register of Historic Places. The Main Inn features sophisticated Colonial decor while the Prescott House is appointed with a country theme. For extended visits, the Keyes House Annex offers a pair of fully furnished two-bedroom apartments.

56 Rooms • Price range: $175-225
48 Monument Sq, Concord, MA 01742
☎ **(978) 369-9200**

Concord
The Hawthorne Inn

The inn is an 1870s Colonial-style house east of the town square on the 1775 "Battle Road" on land once owned by Ralph Waldo Emerson and Nathaniel Hawthorne. The rooms and public areas are a gallery for the owners' collection of art and antiques. Room styles vary from traditional New England to Oriental. Oriental or rag rugs accent hardwood floors. Four-poster beds, many with canopy, have handmade quilts.

7 Rooms • Price range: $150-305
462 Lexington Rd, Concord, MA 01742
☎ **(978) 369-5610**

Cummaquid
The Acworth Inn

For those seeking a distinctive and picturesque sanctuary, this inn is perfect. Guests will find light and airy country decor with hand-painted furniture, enchanting rooms, beautiful scenery and attentive hosts. The inn is close to miles of uncluttered beaches; ferries to Nantucket and Martha's Vineyard offer guests a chance to explore further afield. Just-baked muffins are part of the daily breakfast.

5 Rooms • Price range: $100-190
4352 Old Kings Hwy, SR 6A,
Cummaquid, MA 02637
☎ **(508) 362-3330**

Dalton
The Dalton House

Beautifully landscaped grounds surround this welcoming inn, where period antiques and Shaker furnishings share pride of place. An informal breakfast is served daily in the cheerful breakfast room against a backdrop of soft classical music. In the summertime, breakfast is served outdoors under a colorful awning. After breakfast, guests can take a dip in the pool or lounge with a book in a hammock.

11 Rooms • Price range: $115-145
955 Main St, Dalton, MA 01226
☎ **(413) 684-3854**

Deerfield
Deerfield Inn

Situated in the heart of the 300-year-old village of Deerfield, this handsome inn of the same name is a classic New England country establishment. All guestrooms have a private bath. Eleven rooms are located in the inn's South Wing, which is connected to the main house by a covered walkway. Begin the day with an old-fashioned country breakfast and end it with a candlelit dinner. The cuisine is New American all the way.

23 Rooms • Price range: $128-222
81 Old Main St, Deerfield, MA 01342
☎ **(413) 774-5587**

Dennis

Isaiah Hall B&B Inn

Take in the beauty of Cape Cod at this rustic country inn. It was built as a farmhouse back in 1857, but began operating as an inn in 1948. Accommodations are available in the Main House and in the Carriage House, which is decorated with white wicker and knotty pine. Guestrooms feature iron-and-brass beds with warm quilts. Beautiful old homes, sandy beaches and historic Dennis Village are all close by.

10 Rooms • Price range: $111-156
152 Whig St, Dennis, MA 02638
☎ **(508) 385-9928**

Dennis Port
The Rose Petal Bed & Breakfast
Not surprisingly, beautiful rose gardens and white picket fences are a drawing card at this 1872 home. Guestrooms, all located on the inn's second floor, feature queen-size brass or iron beds, hand-stitched quilts and lace curtains. A daily full breakfast features home-baked pastries. The inn is close to the beautiful beaches of Nantucket Sound. Ferries to Nantucket and Martha's Vineyard are easily accessible.

3 Rooms • Price range: $114-125
152 Sea St, Dennis Port, MA 02639
☎ **(508) 398-8470**

Eastham
Whalewalk Inn

This whaling master's home built in the 1830s has been authentically redecorated with quality antique furniture. The inn is made up of the main house and four smaller buildings, including a converted barn and a carriage house. All sit on three acres of gardens and meadowlands 10 minutes from the Cape Cod National Seashore. Thirteen of the guestrooms are equipped with a working fireplaces and all rooms have a private bath.

16 Rooms • Price range: $225-250
220 Bridge Rd, Eastham, MA 02642
☎ **(508) 255-0617**

Edgartown
Captain Dexter House of Edgartown
The informal and relaxed atmosphere of this restored 1840s sea captain's home allows guests the complete enjoyment of all it has to offer. Bedrooms have been thoughtfully decorated with soothing tones, subtle patterns and soft lighting. The parlor is the spot to play a board game, sample the homemade cookies or sip a complimentary aperitif in front of the fireplace. All rooms have private baths. Friendly innkeepers promote island sights.

11 Rooms • Price range: $165-375
35 Pease's Point Way, Edgartown, MA 02539
☎ **(508) 627-7289**

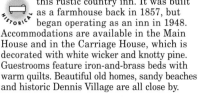

Edgartown
◍ *Colonial Inn of Martha's Vineyard*

Located in the center of Edgartown, the Colonial has operated as an inn since 1911 and is only minutes from the beach, the historic harbor and a variety of restaurants and shops. All rooms have a private bath and air-conditioning. A rooftop veranda provides a relaxing retreat in the afternoons and evenings. Local pleasures include sailing, swimming, tennis and golf. Country auctions and festivals add a touch of small-town charm.

43 Rooms • Price range: $162-262
38 N Water St, Edgartown, MA 02539
☎ **(508) 627-4711**

Edgartown
◍ *Daggett House*

There is a nice selection of rooms and suites to choose from at this harborside property and many of them have either a waterfront or garden view. All rooms have private baths, telephones, televisions and cozy armchairs. The main house dates back to 1660 and is the oldest of the four historic buildings; it houses the restaurant. Guests can enjoy breakfast and lunch on the patio or in the dining room with its original 1660 fireplace.

31 Rooms • Price range: $175-285
59 N Water St, Edgartown, MA 02539
☎ **(508) 627-4600**

Edgartown
Kelley House

This spectacular inn may have modern amenities such as cable television and hair dryers, but the 250-year-old complex still exhibits much of its original charm. Authentic period furniture, colorful quilts and more than 100 pieces of art help to give the five-building inn its distinctive atmosphere. Continental breakfast is served daily and homemade cookies are available for nighttime snacks.

53 Rooms • Price range: $300-775
23 Kelley St, Edgartown, MA 02539
☎ **(508) 627-7900**

Edgartown
The Oak House

Formerly the summer home of a state governor, this 1876 Victorian mansion with its handsome woodwork has been named for the oak paneling that can be found throughout. Several rooms have small balconies that offer a sweeping view of the water. Guests can enjoy their expanded continental breakfast in the dining room or in the large sunroom overlooking the sea. All rooms have private baths, cable TV and telephones.

10 Rooms • Price range: $180-280
Corner of Seaview & Pequot aves,
Oak Bluffs, MA 02557
☎ **(508) 693-4187**

Edgartown
Tuscany Inn

Set back from the street, this B&B is Italianate-Victorian in architecture and decor. All guestrooms are elegantly furnished. Guests may enjoy their frittatas, fresh fruits and homemade breads in the comfort of the beautiful dining room or outside on the patio surrounded by trees and flowers. In the off-season the owner offers weekend-long cooking classes for those interested in the cuisine and culture of Tuscany.

8 Rooms • Price range: $200-395
22 N Water St, Edgartown, MA 02539
☎ **(508) 627-5999**

Edgartown
Ashley Inn

This 1800s sea captain's home with its unique Chinese Chippendale fence and clover leaf window is on historic Main Street. Several rooms have four-poster or canopy beds, whirlpools and fireplaces. Close to downtown shops, restaurants and the beach.

10 Rooms • Price range: $155-310
129 Main St, Edgartown, MA 02539
☎ **(508) 627-9655**

Essex
George Fuller House Inn

Located in the center of historic Essex this 1830 Federal-style house was built by shipwrights and retains much of the original woodworking art. Five of the rooms have working fireplaces. All are furnished with antiques and period reproductions. An interesting salt marsh and the Essex River are visible from the backyard. During an exceptionally high tide, the marsh waters reach the edge of the lawn.

7 Rooms • Price range: $125-225
148 Main St, Essex, MA 01929
☎ **(978) 768-7766**

Fairhaven
Edgewater Bed & Breakfast

Built in 1760 and enlarged in 1880, this rambling Colonial-style Victorian home is perched on the water's edge where the Acushnet River meets New Bedford Harbor. Accommodations in each wing are beautifully decorated and all have harbor views.

5 Rooms • Price range: $75-125
2 Oxford St, Fairhaven, MA 02719
☎ **(508) 997-5512**

Falmouth
The Palmer House Inn

This early 20th-century Queen Anne-style inn combines Victorian charm with the natural beauty of Cape Cod. Stained-glass windows, fine woodwork and antique furnishings adorn the rooms of the main house, while the adjacent Guest House contains four beautiful corner rooms. All guestrooms have a private bath; two have a whirlpool. Breakfast is a special event, with a gourmet menu, lace tablecloths, fine china, soft music and candlelight. Relax on the charming porches, take a short walk to some of Cape Cod's best beaches, visit interesting shops and dine in fine local restaurants.

17 Rooms • Price range: $115-195
81 Palmer Ave, Falmouth, MA 02540
☎ **(508) 548-1230**

Falmouth
The Beach House at Falmouth Heights

Located on a quiet street in a residential neighborhood and just a short walk to the beach, this family-operated B&B has a large sundeck out front and a inviting pool in the backyard. The whimsical and colorful decor is accentuated by fanciful handcrafted furnishings and hand-painted murals by two New England artists. The beauty of nearby Falmouth Heights Beach promises many fond holiday memories.

8 Rooms • Price range: $99-225
10 Worcester Ct, Falmouth, MA 02540
☎ **(508) 457-0310**

Falmouth
⛴ *Captain Tom Lawrence House*

This impressive sea-captain's home has the same circular stairwell, hardwood floors and high ceilings that pleased the captain himself almost 140 years ago. The lovely guestrooms are decorated in soft colors and feature four-poster canopy beds and designer linens. The sitting room has a fireplace and, for the musically inclined, a Steinway piano. Breakfast includes such treats as seafood crepes and quiche.

7 Rooms • Price range: $135-175
75 Locust St, Falmouth, MA 02540
☎ **(508) 540-1445**

Falmouth
⛴ *Grafton Inn*

Here's an early 1900s inn with an ideal beachfront location overlooking Nantucket Sound and Martha's Vineyard. Guests can walk across the street to swim, jog along the beach or take a stroll in the moonlight. Individually decorated bedrooms are bright with pleasing little extras such as fresh flowers, homemade chocolates, white-noise machines and overhead fans. Wine and cheese are served every afternoon.

10 Rooms • Price range: $159-265
261 Grand Ave S, Falmouth, MA 02540
☎ **(508) 540-8688**

Falmouth
The Inn at One Main Street

Built in 1892 by a family of well-known merchants, this gracious shingled and turreted home has been taking in visitors since the 1950s. Located in the Historic District, the inn is within easy walking distance of shops, beaches and the ferry shuttle to Martha's Vineyard. Guests enjoy homemade baked goods and breakfasts that include specialties such as gingerbread pancakes topped with whipped cream and cheese egg puffs.

6 Rooms • Price range: $100-150
One Main St, Falmouth, MA 02540
☎ **(508) 540-7469**

Falmouth
Village Green Inn

This inn was named for its view of the town's historic village green. Built as a Federal-style home in 1804, it was converted to an inn 90 years later and was recently listed on the National Registry of Historic Places. Bicycles are available to guests and bike paths are nearby. A ferry to Martha's Vineyard is accessible, as are whale-watching expeditions. Some guestrooms have a fireplace.

5 Rooms • Price range: $135-170
40 Main St, Falmouth, MA 02540
☎ (508) 548-5621

Falmouth
Wildflower Inn

The Wildflower lives up to its name; the full daily breakfast includes edible wild flowers. The inn itself is more than 100 years old, though it has been restored and updated. The main staircase leads to spacious guestrooms on the second floor, each with a private bath, some with a whirlpool. There is also a cottage with its own private entrance and porch, as well as a full kitchen. Complimentary bicycles are available for use.

6 Rooms • Price range: $125-195
167 Palmer Ave, Falmouth, MA 02540
☎ (508) 548-9524

Falmouth
Woods Hole Passage Bed & Breakfast

A serene setting—two acres of lawn, flowers, herb gardens and shade trees— surrounds this charmingly restored carriage house. There is lots to explore in the area: the Spohr Gardens, Quissett Harbor, Nobska Lighthouse and the Shining Sea Bike Path. On summer afternoons, the inn serves lemonade and cookies; in the winter, hot cider and scones.

5 Rooms • Price range: $120-165
186 Woods Hole Rd, Falmouth, MA 02540
☎ (508) 548-9575

Falmouth
The Moorings Lodge

At this 1905 Gambrel-style house, fresh-fruit compote, homemade granola, fresh baked bread and muffins are served on the glassed-in sunroom facing the beach. Rooms are comfortable and have private baths and refrigerators.

8 Rooms • Price range: $85-150
207 Grand Ave S, Falmouth, MA 02540
☎ (508) 540-2370

Great Barrington
Windflower Inn

Take a step back in time at this restored 1800s Federal-style inn set deep in the heart of the Berkshires. Surrounded by three beautiful acres the inn features spacious living areas with antique furnishings, several working fireplaces, and a lovely dining room. A reading room with books and games also contains a piano for those who can play. Guestrooms have fine antique beds and furniture, some with fireplaces and bay windows.

13 Rooms • Price range: $100-200
684 S Egremont Rd (Rt 23),
Great Barrington, MA 01230
☎ (413) 528-2720

Greenfield
The Brandt House

Set in a quiet neighborhood, this stately early 20th-century Colonial-Revival mansion features mountain views, outdoor patios, wraparound porches and fireplaces. All units are provided with down comforters, robes, fresh flowers and antique or reproduction furnishings. The common living areas are spacious with a modern country-style decor. Outside, a clay tennis court invites players to don their whites.

9 Rooms • Price range: $135-205
29 Highland Ave, Greenfield, MA 01301-3605
☎ **(413) 774-3329**

Harwich Port
Augustus Snow House

One of Cape Cod's fine examples of Queen Anne-style Victorian architecture, this inn is a visual testament to a bygone era. Gabled dormers and a wraparound veranda distinguish the exterior. A mirrored oak fireplace and stained-glass window and window seats are hallmarks inside. A gourmet breakfast is offered daily and traditional Victorian high tea is served in the Garden Room. All units have a working fireplace.

5 Rooms • Price range: $160-190
528 Main St (SR 28), Harwich Port, MA 02646
☎ **(508) 430-0528**

Harwich Port
Dunscroft By-The-Sea B&B Inn

Visitors to this charming, quiet inn set in an exclusive residential area can choose from king- or queen-size canopy, four-poster and sleigh beds and between air-conditioning or fresh ocean breezes. Guests can also opt for a room that has a fireplace, a Jacuzzi or an in-room private bath. The Gathering Room has triple French doors, a baby grand piano, a library and a television.

9 Rooms • Price range: $155-265
24 Pilgrim Rd, Harwich Port, MA 02646
☎ **(508) 432-0810**

Ipswich
Town Hill B&B

Built as Colburn House in 1854, the property became a B&B in 1995. Decor is uncluttered. Most rooms have brass or wrought-iron beds and rocking chairs; some have fireplaces. All but two have a private bath. A short drive to Crane Beach.

11 Rooms • Price range: $90-165
16 N Main St, Ipswich, MA 01938
☎ **(978) 356-8000**

Lee
Applegate, a Bed 'n Breakfast

The Georgian Colonial-style Applegate makes an impression on guests even from the outside. Visitors pass through the iron gate and along the circular driveway through six acres of old apple trees and pines that surround the property. Inside, fine linens, crystal decanters filled with brandy and Godiva chocolates await guests in each room. Several guestrooms have a fireplace; one has a steam shower.

6 Rooms • Price range: $100-330
279 W Park St, Lee, MA 01238
☎ **(413) 243-4451**

Lee
Chambery Inn

Scheduled for demolition due to increasing land needs, the Berkshires' first parochial school, circa 1885, was moved a block in a monumental effort to preserve it. Painstakingly restored, it is now an exceptional European-style small hotel. All rooms are spacious, with private baths, Jacuzzis and king- or queen-size beds. Some rooms have the original school chalkboards. In-room therapeutic massage is available.

9 Rooms • Price range: $110-305
199 Main St, Lee, MA 01238
☎ **(413) 243-2221**

Lenox
Brook Farm Inn

Music and literature play a large role at this 1850s farmhouse. Guests will hear classical pieces, light opera or Broadway tunes as they take a swim in the pool or stretch out in the garden hammock. In the summer, artistic attractions are close by in historic Lennox Village: Hear the Boston Symphony at Tanglewood, see a dance at Jacob's Pillow, view a Shakespearean play outdoors at the Mount or take in a musical comedy at the Berkshire Theater.

12 Rooms • Price range: $120-205
15 Hawthorne St, Lenox, MA 01240
☎ **(413) 637-3013**

Lenox
The Gables Inn

This 100-year-old Berkshire "Cottage" has gone through some noteworthy renovations. Owners Frank and Mary Newton have made improvements such as the circular driveway and new landscaping. And they've re-created some older features such as the eight-sided library. Also of note is the owners' collection of art, which spans five centuries, and the rare documents, books and extensive library of Broadway soundtracks.

17 Rooms • Price range: $90-250
81 Walker St, Lenox, MA 01240
☎ **(413) 637-3416**

Lenox
Seven Hills Country Inn & Restaurant

Visitors will be taken aback by this picturesque inn. The visually stunning property is located on 27 acres of land that includes two hard-surface tennis courts and a 60-foot pool. The Manor House has 15 rooms; another 37 Terrace House guestrooms are available. Throughout the inn, handcarved fireplaces and leaded-glass windows add to the grandeur. The inn's restaurant boasts superb European-influenced cuisine.

52 Rooms • Price range: $120-325
40 Plunkett St, Lenox, MA 01240
☎ **(413) 637-0060**

Lenox
The Village Inn

This 18th-century inn is nestled under a canopy of trees in a quiet Lenox Village residential district. Modern conveniences have been added to the Colonial decor and authentic Hudson Valley paintings grace the walls. Several notable museums are nearby.

32 Rooms • Price range: $85-265
16 Church St, Lenox, MA 01240
☎ **(413) 637-0020**

Lynn
Diamond District Inn

Guests here start off the day with a candlelit meal in the dining room. The sumptuous breakfast menu may include lobster quiche, Belgian waffles, eggs Florentine or breakfast puffs. Vegetarian or low fat meals are also available. Some rooms in this 1911 Georgian-style home, originally the estate of a shoe manufacturer, have a fireplace or a whirlpool. The beach is just a short walk away.

11 Rooms • Price range: $145-200
142 Ocean St, Lynn, MA 01902-2007
☎ **(781) 599-5122**

Marblehead
Spray Cliff on the Ocean

The only oceanfront B&B in Marblehead, this three-story cedar shake house combines waterfront beauty with Old-World hospitality. Most bedrooms have an ocean view; some include queen or king-size beds, down comforters, scented candles and hand-painted furnishings. A continental breakfast is served daily in the Gathering Room. Bicycles and beach towels are available to guests. A public sandy beach is nearby.

7 Rooms • Price range: $150-250
25 Spray Ave, Marblehead, MA 01945
☎ **(781) 631-6789**

Nantucket Island
Seven Sea Street Inn

This recently built guest house, with its widow's walk, features early American furnishings in each of the guestrooms, along with queen-size fishnet-canopy beds for a bit of distinction. A continental breakfast is served daily on fine china and includes fresh fruit salad, cranberry granola, freshly baked bagels and gourmet coffee. Main Street, the Children's Beach and Steamboat Wharf are all just five minutes away.

11 Rooms • Price range: $165-215
7 Sea St, Nantucket Island, MA 02554
☎ **(508) 228-3577**

Nantucket Island
Sherburne Inn

Built in 1835 as the headquarters for the Atlantic Silk Company, the building was converted and became a guest house in 1872. The first and second floor parlors are comfortably set up for reading, watching television or just quietly relaxing in front of their fireplaces. Guestrooms are tastefully decorated, exhibiting a judicious restraint by their lack of clutter. Each room has all the modern conveniences.

8 Rooms • Price range: $165-295
10 Gay St, Nantucket Island, MA 02554
☎ **(508) 228-4425**

Nantucket Island
The Carriage House

Located on a crushed-clamshell lane, in a heavily wooded residential area, this former carriage house may have some space limitations but all rooms

are tastefully decorated and have private baths. The owners provide information on Nantucket.

7 Rooms • Price range: $90-170
5 Ray's Ct, Nantucket Island, MA 02554
☎ **(508) 228-0326**

Nantucket Island
Tuckernuck Inn

Tuckernuck is a comfortable, Country-style inn located just a block from the harbor. It features a restaurant, a library, a widow's walk, a front patio and a backyard with lawn chess. Suites with fully-equipped kitchens are available.

19 Rooms • Price range: $195-195
60 Union St, Nantucket Island, MA 02554
☎ **(508) 228-4886**

North Eastham
Penny House Inn

Originally built in 1690, the Penny House Inn was renovated and converted to an inn in the 1980s. Located about halfway between Hyannis Port and Provincetown, the inn is well situated for those who enjoy bird-watching, whale watching, sailing or deep-sea fishing and those eager to take part in seashore tours. All guestrooms have designer comforters, oversize bath towels and modern private baths.

12 Rooms • Price range: $165-245
4885 Rt 6, North Eastham, MA 02651
☎ **(508) 255-6632**

Oak Bluffs
The Dockside Inn

This is a modern inn with a Victorian flair and lovely views of Oak Bluffs' vibrant harbor. Guests can choose to have their continental breakfasts served in the garden courtyard, the breakfast sunroom or on the front porch overlooking the harbor. All rooms are individually decorated; three are large kitchen suites accommodating up to four guests. Located near ferries, shops, a large park, and moped, bike and car rentals.

22 Rooms • Price range: $150-350
Circuit Ave Ext, Oak Bluffs, MA 02557
☎ **(508) 693-2966**

Orleans
Orleans Inn

Former home of Aaron Snow II and his wife Mary, a descendent of Constance Hopkins who first viewed the Cape from the deck of the Mayflower. The inn has been lovingly restored to include all the modern amenities: TVs, phones and private baths.

11 Rooms • Price range: $125-250
3 Old County Rd, Orleans, MA 02653
☎ **(508) 255-2222**

Provincetown
Crowne Pointe Historic Inn

Perched on a bluff in the heart of Provincetown, this inn has recently undergone a multi-million dollar restoration. Details such as, wallpaper patterns, and paint colors were selected for historical accuracy. Coffered tin and wood moldings were preserved and belt-driven porch fans were repaired. A hot buffet breakfast is served on the large patio deck or in the stately dining room. The list of amenities and services is extensive although not all rooms are identically fitted; it's best to inquire. Ideal for a quiet getaway or as a place to stay when taking in Provincetown's vibrant nightlife.

40 Rooms • Price range: $125-395
82 Bradford St, Provincetown, MA 02657
☎ **(508) 487-6767**

Provincetown
White Wind Inn

Once the home of prosperous ship builder, this gracious 1800s mansion is now welcoming visitors from around the world. A large veranda overlooking Commercial St. is a perfect spot to people watch. Pleasant rooms with private baths.

13 Rooms • Price range: $120-225
174 Commercial St, Provincetown, MA 02657
☎ **(508) 487-1526**

Rehoboth
Five Bridge Inn Bed & Breakfast

This striking and stately inn provides sheer elegance in a country setting. The Georgian retreat is surrounded by 60 acres of land, which can be viewed from the inn's dining room. Following the full daily breakfast, guests are invited to explore nearby wooded trails or visit Duffy, the inn's resident llama. Visitors can also relax in the screened gazebo or by the herb garden; the more active can play tennis or swim.

5 Rooms • Price range: $88-105
154 Pine St, Rehoboth, MA 02769
☎ **(508) 252-3190**

Rehoboth
Perryville Inn Bed & Breakfast

The ghost stories about the inn notwithstanding, the Perryville is a very welcoming and peaceful farmhouse in a rural setting. Handmade quilts adorn the walls, old kerosene lanterns hang from the tall ceilings and the original basswood-carved fireplace mantel still stands. Breakfast may be eaten in the kitchen, in the dining room or on the porch. There is an 18-hole golf course right across the road.

4 Rooms • Price range: $65-105
157 Perryville Rd, Rehoboth, MA 02769
☎ **(508) 252-9239**

Richmond
The Inn at Richmond

Twenty-seven acres of perennial gardens, meadows and woodlands surround this handsome late18th-century farmhouse. The Cottage and Carriage House each include a bedroom, bath, sitting room and fully-equipped kitchen. Luxurious two-room suites with fireplaces are also available. Common areas include the Parlor, the Library, the Garden Room and the Greenhouse. An equestrian center is located on the property.

10 Rooms • Price range: $155-295
802 State Rd (SR 41), Richmond, MA 01254
☎ **(413) 698-2566**

Rockport
Addison Choate Inn

This charming Greek-Revival style house has been in the hospitality business for more than 30 years. Guestrooms all have private baths and king-, queen- or twin-size beds. The buffet breakfast features fresh-ground, private-blend coffee, homemade granola and fresh fruit. During the warmer months, guests can sit on the awning-shaded porch overlooking the garden or take a dip in the in-ground pool.

8 Rooms • Price range: $95-145
49 Broadway, Rockport, MA 01966
☎ **(978) 546-7543**

Rockport
Emerson Inn by the Sea

A short distance from downtown Rockport sits this seaside Federalist-style inn with wide porches overlooking the Atlantic. Constructed in 1846, the inn was moved to its present location in 1912. An informally elegant lobby leads into a formal dining room, which opens onto the front porch. Cozy units with baths are nicely furnished. The fourth floor sundeck and heated saltwater pool are perfect places to spend a relaxing afternoon.

35 Rooms • Price range: $135-295
1 Cathedral Ave, Rockport, MA 01966
☎ **(978) 546-6321**

Rockport
The Inn On Cove Hill

Guests here begin the day with a continental breakfast served on Wedgwood or Royal Doulton English bone china, a breakfast that includes fresh-baked muffins or breads. Guest have their choice of the dining room, one of the umbrella tables in the garden or, when the weather gets chilly, having breakfast in bed. Rooms in this 1791 home are cozy and inviting, with canopy beds and Federal-period antiques.

11 Rooms • Price range: $75-135
37 Mt Pleasant St, Rockport, MA 01966
☎ **(978) 546-2701**

Rockport
Linden Tree Inn

Named after the stately linden that dominates the lawn, this inn prides itself on its landscaped grounds, flowering gardens and the picnic tables and lawn chairs that enable guests to enjoy the natural beauty. There is also much to admire inside the inn: four large guestrooms with a private deck overlooking the garden; a formal living room with eye-catching antiques; and a sunroom filled with flowers.

18 Rooms • Price range: $70-150
26 King St, Rockport, MA 01966
☎ **(978) 546-2494**

Rockport
Old Farm Inn

Situated on the tip of Cape Ann adjacent to Halibut Point State Park, this 1799 homestead has one room in the main house and four modern rooms in the carriage house. Two rooms connect through a butler's kitchen to form a suite.

5 Rooms • Price range: $80-140
291 Granite St, Rockport, MA 01966
☎ **(978) 546-3237**

Rockport
Yankee Clipper Inn

Since 1946 this property, which is comprised of several buildings, has been operated by the same family. The marvelous 1929 Art Deco mansion is the main inn and houses The Veranda Restaurant. An 1840 Greek-Revival home designed by Charles Bulfinch features elegant rooms and suites. At the water's edge is The Quarterdeck with rooms in a slightly more contemporary setting. For stays of a week or more there is a hilltop cottage.

26 Rooms • Price range: $99-299
96 Granite St, Rockport, MA 01966
☎ **(978) 546-3407**

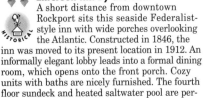

Rockport
Rocky Shores Inn & Cottages

This seaside mansion was built in 1905 by a wealthy Texan on a three-acre hilltop. The inn overlooks the Atlantic Ocean and the twin lighthouses of Thacher Island. Rooms are comfortable and cottages have garden or ocean views.

21 Rooms • Price range: $98-143
65 Eden Rd, Rockport, MA 01966
☎ **(978) 546-2823**

Rockport
⑩ *Seaward Inn*

A lovely collection of buildings that includes a main inn, a lodge, a carriage house and nine cottages around a spring-fed pond situated on five acres of Rockport's lovely coastline. A magical setting that has welcomed guests for more than 50 years.

37 Rooms • Price range: $129-339
44 Marmion Way, Rockport, MA 01966
☎ **(978) 546-3471**

Salem
The Salem Inn

Built by Captain Nathaniel West, the inn is made up of three buildings: the 1834 Federalist brick West House, consisting of three attached townhouses; the smaller 1854 Curwen House; and the Peabody House, an 1874 Colonial structure with two luxury suites and four spacious family suites. Some rooms have fireplaces and Jacuzzis. In warm weather, breakfast is served on the brick patio in the private rose garden.

39 Rooms • Price range: $129-290
7 Summer St, Salem, MA 01970
☎ **(978) 741-0680**

Sandwich
⑩ *Bay Beach*

This secluded beachfront inn overlooking Cape Cod Bay offers travelers a luxurious retreat. Located on a private beach in historic Sandwich, Bay Beach is a fine place to sit back and watch the quiet activity of sailboats and lobster boats. Spacious and bright rooms are comfortably appointed, each with a private bath and a deck. Beautiful grounds are dotted with well-tended gardens. While the inn remains secluded, fishing, golf and biking and walking trails are just minutes away. Also nearby are Sandwich's renowned museums and historic sites, fine restaurants and a marina.

7 Rooms • Price range: $245-345
One Bay Beach Ln, Sandwich, MA 02563
☎ **(508) 888-8813**

Sandwich
The Dan'l Webster Inn

The 300-year-old inn, which is a focal point of the historic downtown district, is a landmark of hospitality, casual elegance and outstanding ambience. The remarkable establishment goes out of its way to pamper guests with impeccably appointed rooms, personalized service and superb cuisine in four dining rooms. The meticulously kept summer gardens are an ideal setting for quiet reflection or friendly conversation.

54 Rooms • Price range: $109-299
winter; $179-399 summer
149 Main St, Sandwich, MA 02563
☎ **(508) 888-3622**

Sandwich
Isaiah Jones Homestead

This elegant 1849 Victorian inn safeguards a piece of Sandwich's history. Guestrooms have been named after distinguished figures of the town's past and are attractively appointed with fine antiques; some have fireplaces and whirlpool baths. The many fine features of this inn include the 11-foot ceiling and crown moldings of the Gathering Room, a curved staircase, beautiful woodwork and lovely porches.

7 Rooms • Price range: $99-175
165 Main St, Sandwich, MA 02563
☎ **(508) 888-9115**

Sandwich
The Captain Ezra Nye House

This vintage captain's house has a cozy early American ambience. Sunny guestrooms are pleasantly appointed with comfortable furnishings and subtle colors. Ranked the oldest town on the Cape, Sandwich boasts many interesting activities.

6 Rooms • Price range: $75-120
152 Main St, Sandwich, MA 02563
☎ **(508) 888-6142**

Scituate
⚇ *The Allen House*

Up on a knoll overlooking Scituate Harbor, this 1905 shingle-style home was renovated in the spring of 2000. Breakfast is often served on the front porch facing the harbor. The bright, cheerful rooms are decorated in a mix of Arts and Crafts and Mission-style furniture. Several rooms overlook the harbor. One has a gas "wood stove," a whirlpool tub under a skylight and glass doors that open to the garden area.

6 Rooms • Price range: $115-215
18 Allen Pl, Scituate, MA 02066-1302
☎ **(781) 545-8221**

Seekonk
Historic Jacob Hill Inn

In the 1920s and 1930s, this 1722 Colonial home was known as the Jacob Hill Hunt Club and hosted some of America's most affluent families for hunts and horse shows. Domed windows and beamed ceilings, paintings of horses and hunting, a pool, stables, and a tennis court are attractions. Combine that with its attention to guest comfort and you've got a winner. There are five suites and a cottage; some have fireplaces and Jacuzzis.

5 Rooms • Price range: $139-359
120 Jacob St, Seekonk, MA 02771
☎ **(508) 336-9165**

South Dennis
Captain Nickerson Inn

This 1879 Queen Anne-style sea captain's home has comfortable and cozy rooms in a warm, homelike environment. Breakfasts are hearty, and bicycles are available for a small fee for those who wish to explore the 20-mile "rail trail" bike path.

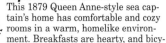

5 Rooms • Price range: $90-127
333 Main St, South Dennis, MA 02660
☎ **(508) 398-5966**

South Egremont
Weathervane Inn

This country inn is nestled in the quaint New England village of South Egremont in the foothills of the Berkshires. The farmhouse was built in 1785 and the inn is made up of a small cluster of buildings on 10 acres of land. Guestrooms are comfortable, with private baths and air-conditioning. Nearby attractions include golf, the Berkshire Theater Festival, the Norman Rockwell Museum and the inn's swimming pool.

10 Rooms • Price range: $85-245
17 Main St, South Egremont, MA 01258
☎ **(413) 528-9580**

Stockbridge
The Inn at Stockbridge

Far back from the road on 12 secluded acres stands this early 20th-century Georgian-style mansion. The inn has been carefully restored and offers elegance and comfort just a mile from downtown Stockbridge. The inn features a pool among the trees and many other charming touches, including a gourmet candlelight breakfast each morning. The area offers music and theater in the summer and skiing in the winter.

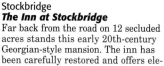

12 Rooms • Price range: $125-270
30 East St, Rt 7, Stockbridge, MA 01262
☎ **(413) 298-3337**

Sudbury
Longfellow's Wayside Inn

Massachusetts Bay Colony laws required anyone operating an inn to provide room for man and beast. That is what this fascinating establishment has been doing since1716, making it America's oldest operating inn. After a fire in the 1950s much of the inn was rebuilt. The one-room red schoolhouse, the carriage house, and the working stone gristmill all add to the pastoral setting. For history buffs, there's a self-guided walking tour.

10 Rooms • Price range: $120-160
72 Wayside Inn Rd, Sudbury, MA 01776
☎ **(978) 443-1776**

Tyngsboro
Stonehedge Inn

This 1988 inn was built with convenience in mind. It even has a helipad and corporate jet access. The most scenic route to the inn is up the long drive, flanked by 30 acres of pastures where retired racehorses graze contentedly. Once at the inn, guests can look forward to 24-hour room service. There are some 30 guest quarters, which feature welcome plates and a turndown service. All rooms come with king-size or double beds; some have balconies, gas-log fireplaces and whirlpool tubs. Guests also have access to tennis and basketball courts, a spa and a pool house.

30 Rooms • Price range: $215-285
160 Pawtucket Blvd, Tyngsboro, MA 01879
☎ **(978) 649-4400**

Vineyard Haven
Martha's Place Bed & Breakfast

Guests at this stately Greek-Revival home are pampered with exceptional service in a luxurious historical setting. Formerly the residence of a descendant of the founder of Martha's Vineyard, the luxurious antique-filled bedrooms are fitted with Egyptian cotton linens and down comforters. A long list of additional amenities ensure that every need is met. Guests will appreciate being situated across from Owen Park Beach in the heart of the historic district. The village shops and restaurants are just a block away as is the ferry dock. Complimentary bicycles are provided for exploring the town.

6 Rooms • Price range: $200-450
114 Main St, Vineyard Haven, Martha's Vineyard, MA 02568
☎ **(508) 693-0253**

Vineyard Haven
Thorncroft Inn
This secluded inn on Martha's Vineyard is exclusively oriented toward couples. The Thorncroft is comprised of three buildings on three-and-a-half acres of landscaped grounds just a block from the ocean. Rooms are furnished with antiques and many of them have wood-burning fireplaces prepared daily by staff, as well as furnished balconies, private entrances and two-person whirlpool tubs. There is also a private cottage with whirlpool available. A full country breakfast and afternoon tea are served daily in the two dining rooms.

14 Rooms • Price range: $225-500
460 Main St, Vineyard Haven, MA 02568
☎ **(508) 693-3333**

Vineyard Haven
Crocker House Inn
On the ultimate weekend getaway destination that is Martha's Vineyard, the Crocker House Inn is a wonderful example of sophisticated simplicity and warm hospitality. The softly monochromatic color scheme of each light-filled bedroom is accented with slightly bolder bedding, carpet and upholstery patterns. In addition to private baths, all rooms have some unique feature, such as an exterior deck, an ocean view or a fireplace.

8 Rooms • Price range: $195-365
12 Crocker Ave, Vineyard Haven, MA 02568
☎ **(508) 693-1151**

Vineyard Haven
Greenwood House B&B
Greenwood House is located in a historic neighborhood four blocks from the ferry dock. Guestrooms of this 1906 inn are attractively appointed, with Arts and Crafts and Stickley furnishings predominating. All rooms have a private bath, air-conditioning and a refrigerator. The grounds feature a garden and Adirondack chairs to relax in, as well as a picnic table and croquet equipment. Full breakfasts are served.

4 Rooms • Price range: $179-269
40 Greenwood Ave, Vineyard Haven, MA 02568-2734
☎ **(508) 693-6150**

Vineyard Haven
The Hanover House
 A short walk up from the ferry dock guests will find a classic shingle-sided seaside home surrounded by trees and hedges. The friendly, personable innkeepers place a great deal of emphasis on housekeeping and the Country-style decor of the guestrooms creates a casual homelike environment. Several rooms have private entrances and open onto sundecks in a large private backyard. Three suites are also available.

15 Rooms • Price range: $138-228
28 Edgartown Rd, Vineyard Haven, MA 02568
☎ **(508) 693-1066**

Vineyard Haven
Tuckerman House
 This remarkably preserved 1836 Greek-Revival home is located in a quiet residential location not far from the ferry landing. Tastefully decorated rooms have little extras, like scented Ralph Lauren pressed linens, cozy robes and large private baths. The back porch overlooking the gardens offers comfortable wicker furniture. Beach towels, chairs and coolers are available for lazy afternoons of soaking in the sun.

5 Rooms • Price range: $185-325
45 William St, Vineyard Haven, MA 02568
☎ **(508) 693-0417**

Vineyard Haven
1720 House
 This 1720 gunstock-style house is a Colonial inn of simple accommodations located in a residential neighborhood minutes away from the town, beach and ferry. A unique feature here is the 350-year-old copper beech tree, the oldest tree on the island.

6 Rooms • Price range: $100-200
152 Main St, Vineyard Haven, MA 02568
☎ **(508) 693-6407**

Vineyard Haven
Captain Dexter House
This sister property of the Captain Dexter House in Edgartown shares the same informal and relaxed ambience. Individually decorated guestrooms are handsomely furnished. A lovely garden has a shady sitting area and the cozy parlor has a fireplace.

8 Rooms • Price range: $125-300
92 Main St, Vineyard Haven, MA 02568
☎ **(508) 693-6564**

Ware
Wildwood Inn Bed & Breakfast
 Pass a peaceful afternoon watching birds and wild rabbits from the wraparound porch or drift down the Ware River in a canoe. A charming Queen Anne-style home with all the familiar comforts of Grandma's house in a pastoral small town.

9 Rooms • Price range: $65-105
121 Church St, Ware, MA 01082
☎ **(413) 967-7798**

West Barnstable
Honeysuckle Hill Bed & Breakfast

Located at the outskirts of the small village of West Barnstable, this 1810 Queen Anne-style seaside cottage offers comfortably elegant accommodations. Rooms are furnished in antiques and white wicker. Lush lawns and gardens surround the inn. Less than two miles away is Sandy Neck, a classic barrier beach that stretches for six miles along Cape Cod Bay. The adjoining conservation area is a scenic spot to hike, canoe, fish and bird-watch.

4 Rooms • Price range: $120-160
591 Old Kings Hwy (Rt 6A),
West Barnstable, MA 02668
☎ **(508) 362-8418**

West Falmouth
Chapoquoit Inn

A 1739 Quaker home with clapboard siding and white picket fence nestled in behind flowering trees and shrubbery. Clean, comfortable rooms with colorful quilts on antique bedsteads. Gorgeous climbing flowers decorate the garden's trellis fence.

8 Rooms • Price range: $140-185
495 Rt 28A, West Falmouth, MA 02574
☎ **(508) 540-7232**

West Yarmouth
Inn at Lewis Bay

This large Dutch-Colonial house in the seaside neighborhood of West Yarmouth was built in 1920 as part of the elegant Hotel Englewood. Today it has been transformed into a charming B&B. Guestrooms are comfortably appointed, all with private baths and two with views of Lewis Bay. Beaches are nearby, as are the ferries to Martha's Vineyard and Nantucket. The area offers golfing, bicycling and whale watching.

6 Rooms • Price range: $98-148
57 Maine Ave, West Yarmouth, MA 02673
☎ **(508) 771-3433**

Williamstown
The Orchards

Although situated on a busy road, this 1985 luxurious hotel was built around a central courtyard to highlight the oversize rooms with their bay windows. All of the spacious rooms are furnished with English antiques and some feature a fireplace. Telephones are located in both the bedrooms and the baths. The dining room is elegant and a huge fieldstone fireplace invites guests into the lounge to relax. The Orchards is conveniently located within walking distance of Williams College. Guests have access to an outdoor swimming pool and an exercise room.

49 Rooms • Price range: $175-275
222 Adams Rd, Williamstown, MA 01267
☎ **(413) 458-9611**

Yarmouth Port
The Inn at Cape Cod

This impressive, Greek-Revival style mansion with its massive Ionic columns has graced the area for more than 200 years. Several patios on the expansive grounds and gardens afford excellent opportunities to relax in peaceful serenity. Rooms are tastefully furnished with European and American antiques. Recipient of Cape Cod Life Reader's Poll 2000 Silver Award. This is a popular spot for weddings and reunions.

9 Rooms • Price range: $125-185
4 Summer St, Yarmouth Port, MA 02675
☎ **(508) 375-0590**

Yarmouth Port
One Centre Street Inn

One Centre Street Inn is a lovingly restored Colonial inn located in a quaint seaside village on Cape Cod's quiet Northside. The circa 1824 inn is listed in the National Register of Historic Places and was once a parsonage for the First Congregational Church of Yarmouth Port. Belgian lace, antique bedsteads and wide-plank pine floors are just a few of the special features. Cranberry toasted-pecan pancakes make breakfast a treat.

6 Rooms • Price range: $105-145
One Centre St, Yarmouth Port, MA 02675
☎ **(508) 362-8910**

Notes:

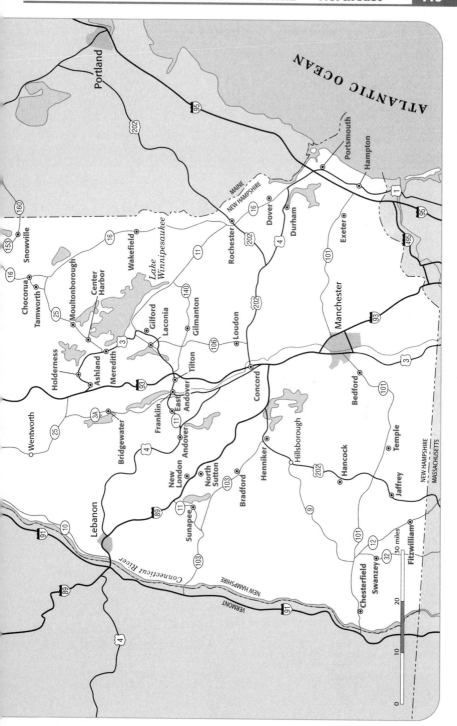

Ashland
Glynn House Victorian Inn

Built in 1895, the inn is a true Victorian home with turrets and gingerbread trim. Just two hours from Boston, the inn is situated in the heart of the White Mountains, an especially breathtaking spot during the fall season. Combining vintage furnishings with modern luxuries, each of the guestrooms has a special decor; some are equipped with a fireplace and a whirlpool bath. A complete gourmet breakfast is included and is served in the elegant dining room.

9 Rooms • Price range: $89-139
59 Highland St, Ashland, NH 03217-0719
☎ **(603) 968-3775**

Bedford
⊕ *Bedford Village Inn*

Built on the site of an 1810 dairy farm, the original buildings making up this historic inn have been beautifully renovated to create an elegant period setting—with all the modern luxuries. Each room features a king-size, four-poster bed, a whirlpool tub and living spaces graced with New England antiques. The award-winning restaurant, with its famed wine cellar, is the perfect spot for dining. The Great Hall accommodates business meetings and receptions, with seating for up to 200 people.

14 Rooms • Price range: $200-410
2 Village Inn Ln, Bedford, NH 03110
☎ **(603) 472-2001**

Bethlehem
⊕ *Adair Country Inn*

This elegant country inn, built in 1927 by attorney Frank Hogan, was named after his daughter, to whom it was given as a wedding gift. Period furnishings and antique reproductions decorate the Tap Room, dining area and guestrooms, many of which have fireplaces. Adair boasts 200 acres of gardens and walking paths designed by the Olmsted brothers of New York Central Park fame. With a backdrop of Mt. Washington and the Presidential Range, the inn has named each of the rooms after its view of a local mountain.

10 Rooms • Price range: $225-360
80 Guider Lane, Bethlehem, NH 03574
☎ **(603) 444-2600**

Bethlehem
The Grande Victorian Cottage

This beautifully restored Victorian mansion has a welcoming circular porch overlooking the spacious grounds and gardens. The guestrooms are cheerful and individually decorated with period antiques. A full American breakfast is served on crystal and china in the dining room, and afternoon refreshments are served on the porch. An 18-hole golf course and a tennis court are within walking distance.

8 Rooms • Price range: $65-120
53 Berkeley St, Bethlehem, NH 03574
☎ **(603) 869-5755**

Bethlehem
The Mulburn Inn at Bethlehem

This English Tudor-style mansion was a summer home of the Woolworths. Built in 1908, it has many original fixtures and stained-glass windows in the parlor. Rooms are large and sunny. Cary Grant and Barbara Hutton honeymooned here.

7 Rooms • Price range: $80-115
2370 Main St, Bethlehem, NH 03574
☎ **(603) 869-3389**

Bethlehem
The Wayside Inn

This homey inn and motel on the banks of the Ammonoosuc River was built in 1825. Rooms are well furnished and grounds are spacious. The inn offers a full-service lounge. The town boasts two golf courses, tennis courts and hiking trails.

26 Rooms • Price range: $59-89
3738 Main St, Rt 302, Bethlehem, NH 03574
☎ **(603) 869-3364**

Bethlehem
⊛ *The Northern Star Inn*

This rustic inn in the heart of the White Mountains is ideal for families.

14 Rooms • Price range: $50-85
157 Maple St, Bethlehem, NH 03574
☎ **(603) 869-4395**

Bradford
Rosewood Country Inn

Country elegance is the hallmark of this inn, with its bordering stone walls, porches and inviting common rooms, set on 12 acres of beautiful property in the Mt. Sunapee Lake Region. The "Candlelight & Crystal" breakfast is always a special occasion, when guests enjoy fresh melon and berries grown locally, homemade muffins or cinnamon apple pancakes. The hosts organize theme weekends around gourmet cooking and baking bread.

11 Rooms • Price range: $95-225
67 Pleasant View Rd, Bradford, NH 03221
☎ **(603) 938-5253**

Bretton Woods
The Bretton Arms Country Inn

This charming 1896 inn, located on the vast grounds of the Mount Washington Hotel, offers the same resort amenities available to hotel clients but with the added bonus of a relaxed, intimate country inn ambience. The mid-size to spacious guestrooms are elegantly decorated and afford some stunning mountain views. Two PGA championship golf courses, 12 tennis courts and alpine ski hills keep guests active year-round.

34 Rooms • Price range: $89-219
US 302, Bretton Woods, NH 03575
☎ **(603) 278-1000**

Bridgewater
The Inn on Newfound Lake

This spacious inn is on the bank of Newfound Lake, where guests can enjoy the private beach and boat dock. The original annex was built in the 1840s. Guestrooms and common areas have been recently refurbished.

28 Rooms • Price range: $75-115
1030 Mayhew Tpke, Bridgewater, NH 03222
☎ **(603) 744-9111**

Center Harbor
Red Hill Inn

The hosts of this inn strive to provide the perfect relaxing getaway for all their guests. The guestrooms are individually decorated and all have natural wood floors. The common areas are large and airy. This is a 100-year-old red-brick mansion, high on a hill on a 60-acre wooded property. Guests can enjoy the view of the White Mountains which rim the sky and hear the call of the loons from Squam Lake.

26 Rooms • Price range: $89-175
Rt 25 B & College Rd, Center Harbor, NH 03226
☎ **(603) 279-7001**

Chesterfield
Chesterfield Inn

Built in 1787, this structure has been completely renovated to create the elegant and welcoming inn it is today. All rooms are spacious and fitted with modern luxuries, and many have terraces or wood-burning fireplaces. The property was once a farm, and today the on-site herb and vegetable gardens furnish produce for the inn's restaurant. The parlor, dining room and terrace are lovely gathering places.

15 Rooms • Price range: $150-275
399 Cross Rd, Chesterfield, NH 03443
☎ **(603) 256-3211**

Chocorua
Mt. Chocorua View House

This inn is perfectly located for a range of activities, as well as being perfectly suited for relaxing inactivity. Each guest room is appointed with antique furniture. The beamed ceilings, wood-burning fireplace and porches create a cozy, comfortable atmosphere any time of year. The surrounding woods offer hiking and walking trails. The hosts are happy to suggest excursions, and provide hot drinks and cookies on your return.

7 Rooms • Price range: $80-115
201 White Mountain Hwy, Chocorua, NH 03817
☎ **(603) 323-8350**

Concord
Centennial Inn

A recent renovation of this 100-year-old home has married the past to the present. Original woodwork, moldings and fireplaces have been restored and each guestroom has been individually decorated to accommodate the business traveler.

32 Rooms • Price range: $129-250
96 Pleasant St, Concord, NH 03301
☎ **(603) 227-9000**

Conway
The Darby Field Inn

Located on scenic Bald Hill, this comfortable mountain retreat offers spectacular views. Each room has a unique decor and most have views of the mountains. A large swimming pool and gardens welcome visitors in summer, while winter activities include nearby cross-country skiing. The inn's dining room serves up a country breakfast and the lounge provides a popular meeting place before dinner.

14 Rooms • Price range: $140-280
185 Chase Hill Rd, Conway, NH 03818
☎ **(603) 447-2181**

Conway
Mountain Valley Manner

A beautifully preserved Victorian home, the Manner is well-situated for the many outdoor activities possible in the White Mountain National Forest. The range of air-conditioned guestrooms includes a three-room family unit. All rooms have private baths and are decorated with classic country decor, featuring comfortable manor-style beds. Included is a full country breakfast, afternoon snacks and bedtime cocoa.

3 Rooms • Price range: $95-135
148 Washington St/Westside Rd,
Conway, NH 03818
☎ **(603) 447-3988**

Dover
⚅ *Silver Street Inn*

Built by a prominent 19th-century industrialist, this large Victorian home boasts the elegant craftsmanship available during the period. Hand-loomed Oriental rugs, ornate plaster ceilings and hand-painted canvas wallpaper make this inn a treasure. Guestrooms blend antique charm with the modern amenities of private bath, telephone and television. A full New England breakfast is included and is served in the dining room.

10 Rooms • Price range: $109-139
103 Silver St, Dover, NH 03820
☎ **(603) 743-3000**

Durham
⚅ *Three Chimneys Inn*

This newly restored 17th-century inn combines Old-World decor with modern luxury. The look is Colonial—exposed beams, wood-burning fireplaces and antique furniture. Rooms are furnished with four-poster beds and rich tapestries, as well as full private baths with Jacuzzis. Two dining rooms, an outside terrace and an authentic tavern with the original 1649 cooking hearth serve traditional cuisine.

23 Rooms • Price range: $159-189
17 Newmarket Rd, Durham, NH 03824
☎ **(603) 868-7800**

Durham
Hickory Pond Inn & Golf Course

Originally a farmhouse, this house was built in the 18th century. The inn maintains its traditional charm, but has modern amenities. The inn also boasts a nine-hole golf course, and nearby attractions include whale-watching and sandy beaches.

18 Rooms • Price range: $59-99
1 Stagecoach Rd, Durham, NH 03824
☎ **(603) 659-2227**

East Andover
⚅ *Highland Lake Inn Bed & Breakfast*

Enchanting in any season, this inn is a wonderful place to relax and breathe the fresh mountain air. The inn is a renovated farmhouse built in 1767 and is surrounded by seven acres. The bedrooms are spacious with private baths, fireplaces and fine bedding. Each morning begins with lavish breakfasts including home-baked breads and muffins, and fresh coffee. The area offers sailing, swimming, golf, skating and skiing.

10 Rooms • Price range: $85-125
32 Maple St, East Andover, NH 03231
☎ **(603) 735-6426**

Exeter
The Inn by the Bandstand

This 1809 Federal townhouse prides itself on spoiling guests with amenities such as terry cloth robes, herbal bath packets and sherry in every room. The guestrooms are enhanced by massive hand-hewn beams and center brick fireplaces. A bridal suite on the second floor includes a fireplace and a Jacuzzi. Mimosas and fresh-baked pastries are served in the breakfast parlor. Phillips Exeter Academy is a short walk away.

9 Rooms • Price range: $120-199
4 Front St, Exeter, NH 03833
☎ **(603) 772-6352**

Exeter
Inn of Exeter

Colorful textiles and wallpaper, aged wood floors and beautiful antiques contribute to the elegant atmosphere of this inn. The home was built in the 1930s and is a wonderful example of Georgian-style architecture. Extensive renovations have fitted each guestroom with modern comforts. There is a rustic lounge where guests can gather, and the award-winning restaurant provides a dining experience of epicurean delights.

46 Rooms • Price range: $95-255
90 Front St, Exeter, NH 03833
☎ **(603) 772-5901**

Fitzwilliam
The Unique Yankee B&B Lodge

Guests receive a warm and friendly welcome at this restored country home. It sits on 18 acres of lake front property and has a commanding view

of Mount Monadnock. Guests enjoy lounging in the lodge's hot tub.

7 Rooms • Price range: $90-140
354 Upper Troy Rd, Fitzwilliam, NH 03447
☎ **(603) 242-6706**

Franconia
Franconia Inn
This historic inn on 107 acres offers spectacular views of the White Mountains and is the perfect setting for downhill and cross-country skiing as well as for hiking and riding. The inn's summer facilities include a swimming pool, tennis courts and a glider port. All of the guestrooms are beautifully appointed and some are equipped with a fireplace and a Jacuzzi. The two dining rooms serve traditional fare with elegance.

32 Rooms • Price range: $96-156
1300 Easton Valley Rd, Franconia, NH 03580
☎ **(603) 823-5542**

Franconia
The Inn At Forest Hills
This 1890s Tudor manor house in the White Mountains is ideally situated for the region's year-round outdoor activities. Each morning a full New England breakfast is served—fireside in the winter, by the French doors in warm weather. The large, beautifully appointed guestrooms each have a private bath. Other facilities include a 45-foot covered veranda, a reading room and a solarium.

8 Rooms • Price range: $130-225
283 Rt 142, Franconia, NH 03580
☎ **(603) 823-9550**

Franconia
Lovett's Inn By Lafayette Brook

Welcoming guests for more than 70 years, this inn has had the pleasure of hosting such celebrities as the Kennedys and Bette Davis. The comfortable atmosphere is popular as a refuge over skiing weekends, or during the foliage season, and guests tend to return year after year. Your hosts can arrange access to the nearby beautiful country club and organize tee times on local golf courses. Dining by the fireplace is another treat.

21 Rooms • Price: $160
1474 Profile Rd, Franconia, NH 03580
☎ **(603) 823-7761**

Franklin
Atwood Inn

In the heart of the Lakes Region, this inn is conveniently located for outdoor activities year-round. A classic brick Colonial-style home built in the 1830s, it was completely restored in 1984. Each guestroom is uniquely decorated; all have private baths and four feature working fireplaces. A full, hearty breakfast is served in the library, on the deck or in the gardens, which are host to a wide variety of birds.

7 Rooms • Price range: $65-90
71 Hill Road; Rt 3A, Franklin, NH 03235
☎ **(603) 934-3666**

Gilford
The Inn at Smith Cove

This Victorian inn, built in 1894 at Smith Cove on Lake Winnipesaukee, has been completely restored with period wall coverings, draperies and natural wood paneling. Each guestroom has its own Victorian personality and a private bath. Also on the property is a private beach, a lighthouse housing a Jacuzzi room and a tea house right on the lake. A full breakfast is served in the dining room.

11 Rooms • Price range: $90-170
19 Roberts Rd, Gilford, NH 03246
☎ **(603) 293-1111**

Gilmanton
⑭ *Temperance Tavern*

Preserved and blessed with many of its original features, the Temperance Tavern has been serving guests since it was built in 1793. Five guestrooms highlight the authentic Federal period atmosphere. There are also several common rooms, including a long wooden tap room and an Indian-shuttered parlor. Those seeking bygone pleasures will find historic Gilmanton charming. Guests looking to explore will enjoy nearby mountains and lakes.

5 Rooms • Price range: $75-125
506 Old Province Rd, Gilmanton, NH 03237
☎ **(603) 267-7349**

Glen
Bernerhof Inn

This small, elegant country inn has well-decorated guestrooms, most with spa tubs and grand brass beds. On-site there is a white-tablecloth restaurant which serves delicious dishes with fresh seasonal ingredients. The pub is another place to spend an evening, either dining or gathering around the fireside. A special feature is the Champagne Breakfast in bed which is awarded to guests on the fourth morning of their stay.

9 Rooms • Price range: $109-175
PO Box 240, Glen, NH 03838
☎ **(603) 383-9132**

Glen
The Covered Bridge House

This cozy B&B boasts its own covered bridge, which has been turned into a charming gift ship, spanning the nearby Saco River. Each guestroom in the house features Colonial-style decor. Four rooms have a private bath; two rooms share a bath, ideal for traveling families or friends. An added feature is an outdoor hot tub. Guest are invited to a hearty breakfast, served daily in the dining room.

6 Rooms • Price range: $59-109
Rt 302, Glen, NH 03838
☎ **(603) 383-9109**

Hampton
The Curtis Field House

Located on 10 country acres just seven miles from the ocean, this restored custom Cape-style home houses three large bedrooms, each graced with antiques and equipped with its own private bath and air-conditioning. A full breakfast is served and a lobster dinner can be ordered in advance. Activities in the area include golfing, tennis, whale-watching and antique shopping.

3 Rooms • Price range: $75-85
735 Exeter Rd (SR 27), Hampton, NH 03842
☎ **(603) 929-0082**

Hampton
Lamie's Inn & Tavern

A traditional stop on the campaign trail of most presidential candidates, this inn and tavern is a landmark. The core of the establishment was built as a

home in the 1740s and additions and modernizations have been made over the years.

32 Rooms • Price range: $88-113
490 Lafayette (US 1) Rd, Hampton, NH 03842
☎ **(603) 926-0330**

Hampton
The Victoria Inn

Built in 1875, this B&B was originally a carriage house. The guestrooms are comfortable, furnished with period antiques and many are lit with chandeliers. European touches from the well-traveled owners enhance the Victorian-style decor. The beaches of the Atlantic Ocean are within walking distance. Other possible activities include harbor cruises, deep-sea fishing, and picking berries and apples from the orchards nearby.

5 Rooms • Price range: $110-140
430 High St, Hampton, NH 03842
☎ **(603) 929-1437**

Hancock
The Hancock Inn

The innkeepers pride themselves on welcoming guests to one of the oldest continuously operating inns in New England. The guestrooms are luxurious and appointed with grand four-poster beds and deep soaking tubs. The living room invites guests to relax and contains a fireplace and an antique checkerboard. There is a lovely pub on-site and delicious food is served from what is the test kitchen for The Old Farmers' Almanac.

15 Rooms • Price range: $120-235
33 Main St, Hancock, NH 03449
☎ **(603) 525-3318**

Harts Location
Notchland Inn

This is a handsome granite mansion built in 1862 and located in the White Mountains close to Crawford Notch. The inn is on a 100-acre property with hiking and walking trails and two ponds for swimming. All rooms have wood-burning fire-places, and suites have outdoor terraces. The sunroom is a perfect place to relax with a book from the eclectic selection in the library or to try your hand at one of the board games.

13 Rooms • Price range: $175-285
Rt 302, Harts Location, NH 03812
☎ **(603) 374-6131**

Henniker
Colby Hill Inn

Weathered barns and a restored carriage house comprise this sprawling farm complex, which appears much as it did 200 years ago. There is a surrounding six-acre property with gardens and a beautiful, secluded swimming pool. Guests may spend time in the parlor, the game room or the gazebo. Full country breakfasts are served, and dinner and drinks are available every evening.

16 Rooms • Price range: $105-195
3 The Oaks, Henniker, NH 03242
☎ **(603) 428-3281**

Henniker
The Meeting House Inn

This 18th-century house was rebuilt in 1840 and is surrounded by woodlands and mountains. An attached barn houses a distinguished restaurant. Henniker is a quaint New England college town and the area boasts excellent cross-country and downhill skiing. The Country Club of New Hampshire provides golf activities in the summer. The gondola at nearby Mount Nunapee State Park offers spectacular views, especially in the fall.

6 Rooms • Price range: $65-115
35 Flanders Rd, Henniker, NH 03242
☎ **(603) 428-3228**

♦♦♦♦ Holderness
 The Manor on Golden Pond
Built on 13 lovely acres in 1907,
this English-style manor was
purchased and then completely
redecorated by its current owners in
1992. Every room is individually decorated
with quality furnishings and fine fabrics.
Many rooms in the main building have fireplaces and private decks, as do rooms in the
Carriage House. Also available are several
cottages on the grounds, two of which are
equipped with kitchens. Other features
include three acres of frontage on pristine
Squam Lake, a large swimming pool and a
tennis court.

25 Rooms • Price range: $195-425
Shepard Hill Rd, Holderness, NH 03245
☎ **(603) 968-3348**

♦♦♦ Intervale
The Forest, A Country Inn
Set on 25 wooded acres in the White
Mountains region, this three-story
inn has been in continuous operation
since the 1890s. Oriental rugs and
period antiques evoke the original Victorian
character. Many of the rooms are equipped
with fireplaces. The well-appointed dining
room serves up homemade breads and muffins.
Facilities include a large veranda and a beautiful
outdoor pool.

11 Rooms • Price range: $115-150
Rt 16A, Intervale, NH 03845
☎ **(603) 356-9772**

♦♦♦ Intervale
The Langley House Inn
This grand country inn was built as a
farmhouse at the turn of the century
and renovated in 1998. Opulence reigns
supreme in the parlor; each guestroom

commemorates an author from the Victorian
era. There is also a pub and a fine restaurant.

6 Rooms • Price range: $95-140
Rt 16A, PO Box 33, Intervale, NH 03845
☎ **(603) 356-9060**

♦♦♦♦ Jackson
 The Inn at Thorn Hill
Located on a knoll overlooking
Jackson village, this 19th-century
inn, designed by Stanford White,
boasts a spectacular view of Mt.
Washington. Furnishings and decorations
are Victorian. The spacious drawing room is
graced with a Steinway baby grand. Besides
the main inn, guests can choose to stay in one
of the several cottages or in the Carriage
House, which is equipped with a deck and a
hot tub. The kitchen staff offer innovative
New England fusion cuisine, with an ever-
changing menu. In summer local produce
stars in many dishes.

19 Rooms • Price range: $175-345
Thorn Hill Rd, Jackson, NH 03846
☎ **(603) 383-4242**

Jackson
Carter Notch Inn

This restored 19th-century inn borders local cross-country ski trails and is minutes away from six downhill ski locations. Summer activities include golf at three major courses, as well as tennis on the inn's courts. The seven pleasant guestrooms are equipped with private baths. Each morning a generous country breakfast is served and winter visitors are invited to an afternoon snack by the living room fireplace.

7 Rooms • Price range: $89-149
PO Box 269, Jackson, NH 03846
☎ **(603) 383-9630**

Jackson
Christmas Farm Inn

This classic inn evokes the merriment of Christmas all year round. Comprised of various buildings, the inn features guestrooms in a variety of styles and deluxe cottages in a spacious setting. Guests are welcome to share a drink in the Mistletoe Pub before sitting down to a delicious candlelit dinner. Outstanding features include the outdoor hot tub, heated swimming pool, sauna and flower gardens.

41 Rooms • Price range: $104-338
Rt 16B, Jackson, NH 03846
☎ **(603) 383-4313**

Jackson
Ellis River House

This romantic inn sits at the base of Mt. Washington near the Red Covered Bridge, dubbed "the kissing bridge." The guestrooms are appointed with period antiques and all have private baths. Many rooms feature a fireplace and a private balcony. A bottle of chilled champagne welcomes honeymooners. Breakfast is offered daily; on Saturday evenings, a gourmet dinner is served.

18 Rooms • Price range: $159-289
Rt 16, Jackson, NH 03846
☎ **(603) 383-9339**

Jackson
The Inn At Jackson

This turn-of-the-20th-century inn blends a relaxed atmosphere with warm hospitality. The handsome wood-paneled living room and spacious guestrooms—all with private baths, several featuring fireplaces—make a homey New England setting. The day starts with a full country breakfast served on the sunporch. Nearby activities include skiing on Jackson's touring trails; local hiking, golf or tennis in the summer.

14 Rooms • Price range: $189-219
Thorn Hill Rd, Jackson, NH 03846
☎ **(603) 383-4321**

Jackson
Nestlenook Farm Resort

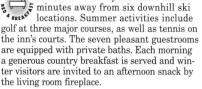

This gingerbread-style inn rests on 65 landscaped acres, near the Emerald Forest. The elegant decor is influenced by the Victorian era. Guestrooms have period antiques and two-person whirlpools; many have four-poster beds and parlor stoves.

7 Rooms • Price range: $175-320
Dinsmore Rd, Jackson, NH 03846
☎ **(603) 383-9443**

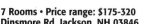

Jackson
◆ ◆ *Dana Place Inn*

Set on 300 acres at the base of Mt. Washington, this Colonial farmhouse has been in the inn-keeping business since 1890. Features include an indoor pool, tennis courts and gourmet cooking. Package specials are available.

35 Rooms • Price range: $99-175
PO Box L, Jackson, NH 03846
☎ **(603) 383-6822**

Jackson
◆ ◆ *Whitneys' Inn*

At the base of Black Mountain, this inn offers comfort and hospitality amid the beauty of nature. The grounds are sprawling and well-tended. Many out-door activities are close at hand. The range of rooms can accommodate any traveler's needs.

30 Rooms • Price range: $142-163
Rt 16B, Jackson, NH 03846
☎ **(603) 383-8916**

Jaffrey
◆ ◆ *The Benjamin Prescott Inn*

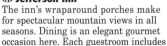

Vintage American furnishings fill this attractive and historic 1853 home. Guestrooms, all equipped with private baths, include a two-room suite with a private sitting room. Cross-country and downhill skiing are available minutes away, while summer activities include hikes on Mt. Monadnock and visits to historic Jaffrey Center, an authentic Colonial village. The inn offers a full breakfast each morning.

10 Rooms • Price range: $85-155
433 Tpke Rd; SR 124 E, Jaffrey, NH 03452
☎ **(603) 532-6637**

Jefferson
◆ ◆ *Jefferson Inn*

The inn's wraparound porches make for spectacular mountain views in all seasons. Dining is an elegant gourmet occasion here. Each guestroom includes books about the establishment's namesake, Thomas Jefferson.

11 Rooms • Price range: $90-160
RFD 1 Box 68A, Jefferson, NH 03583-9306
☎ **(603) 586-7998**

Kearsarge
◆ ◆ *Isaac E. Merrill House Inn*

This gorgeous Colonial home was built in 1773 as a farmhouse. The original owner was Isaac E. Merrill who hosted local artists in exchange for their help on the farm, proving that hospitality was built into the walls. The inn is most popular during the autumn when the views of the fall foliage from the wrap-around porch are particularly striking. Guests are treated to a sumptuous breakfast including the now famous blueberry buttermilk pancakes.

19 Rooms • Price range: $59-169
720 Kearsarge Rd, Kearsarge, NH 03847
☎ **(603) 356-9041**

Laconia
Ferry Point House

Built on the shores of Lake Winnisquam in the early 1800s, this Victorian home was owned by the Pillsbury family. Included on the property is a sandy beach and a gazebo. All rooms have private baths and guests choose from a plentiful breakfast menu. After a day of summer activities—including boating, swimming and riding—the common room, with its fieldstone fireplace, is a great place to relax.

7 Rooms • Price range: $110-135
100 Lower Bay Rd, Laconia, NH 03269
☎ **(603) 524-0087**

Lisbon
Ammonoosuc Inn

Overlooking a river, this inn is a perfect place to unwind. Guests can catch trout from the river. The inn boasts large porches, complete with wicker chairs, as well as a cozy pub and a spacious dining room. Baths feature claw-foot tubs.

9 Rooms • Price range: $45-130
641 Bishop Rd, Lisbon, NH 03585
☎ **(603) 838-6118**

Littleton
Edencroft Inn

The hardwood floors, luxurious bedding, and brass or canopy beds of each guestroom make this turn-of-the-20th-century inn a wonderful place to stay. The library has floor-to-ceiling shelves stocked with books from over the last three centuries. The den is a perfect place to curl up on one of the reclining couches and watch a classic film or play a board game. A five-course breakfast is served daily in the bright breakfast room.

7 Rooms • Price range: $130-180
120 N Littleton Rd, Littleton, NH 03561
☎ **(603) 444-1158**

Littleton
The Beal House Inn

Built in 1833, this property is decorated with an eclectic mix of antiques and contemporary pieces. Bedrooms feature deep claw-foot tubs and cozy down comforters. The inn's jazzy bistro serves fresh fish among other wood-grilled entrées.

7 Rooms • Price range: $95-165
2 W Main St, Littleton, NH 03561
☎ **(603) 444-2661**

Loudon
Lovejoy Farm Bed & Breakfast

This Georgian-Colonial home with its carriage house dates from the 1790s. With original stenciled rooms and antique furniture, the B&B's original rustic appeal has been kept intact. Modern convenience has not been forgotten—all rooms have a private bath. A hearty country breakfast is served in the dining room and complimentary snacks are offered by the fireside in the Family Room.

7 Rooms • Price range: $69-97
268 Lovejoy Rd, Loudon, NH 03301
☎ **(603) 783-4007**

Meredith
Meredith Inn B&B

Built in 1897, this structure was recently renovated to reveal its architectural beauty. Now a warm, striking pink color, the inn is fondly referred to as 'The Painted Lady.' All rooms are bright and airy and are fitted with antique beds covered with pristine white linens. The inn is only a pleasant stroll away from the interesting shops and restaurants of historic Meredith. Two nearby lakes are easily accessible for many activities.

8 Rooms • Price range: $99-159
2 Waukewan St, Meredith, NH 03253
☎ **(603) 279-0000**

Meredith
The Nutmeg Inn

In the heart of the Lakes Region, this 18th-century building still has its original floors, paneling and fireplaces. A historic link in the Underground Railroad, some secret passages still remain. The guestrooms are decorated with period antiques, but not at the expense of convenience and luxury. An exercise room and an outdoor pool are available for guests. Nearby attractions include the Shaker Museum and scenic lake cruises.

8 Rooms • Price range: $90-110
80 Pease Rd, Meredith, NH 03253
☎ **(603) 279-8811**

Moultonborough
Olde Orchard Inn

This historic inn sits on 12 acres of beautiful fruit orchards. Lake Winnipasaukee and an Audubon Society wildlife refuge with hiking trails are both within walking distance. In winter, excellent downhill skiing is available an hour's drive away. All of the inn's guestrooms are decorated with antiques and have private baths; some have a fireplace and a whirlpool. A full country breakfast is served.

9 Rooms • Price range: $75-140
108 Lee Rd, Moultonborough, NH 03254
☎ **(603) 476-5004**

New London
The Inn at Pleasant Lake

Situated in the Sunapee region, this attractive 1790 farmhouse overlooks Pleasant Lake. The inn's sandy beach provides access to swimming and boating, while the boutiques and theaters in nearby New London provide cultural interest. All of the guestrooms have private baths. Other amenities include a full country breakfast served in the dining room and complimentary afternoon tea. A fixed-price dinner menu is also offered.

11 Rooms • Price range: $135-175
125 Pleasant St, New London, NH 03257
☎ **(603) 526-6271**

New London
New London Inn

Located in the centre of town, this Federal-style inn is near Mt. and Lake Sunapee. Built in 1792, it has been renovated in a comfortable elegant style with antiques. The inn has a common room, library, and garden. The inn offers great dining.

25 Rooms • Price range: $75-140
140 Main St, New London, NH 03257
☎ **(603) 526-2791**

North Conway
The Buttonwood Inn

The Buttonwood Inn retains the country atmosphere of its origins in the 1820s. Wide-plank pine floors, antiques, Shaker furniture and period stenciling all serve to reinforce the decor. Just two miles from the village of North Conway, the inn features individually decorated guestrooms; one has a gas fireplace, another has a Jacuzzi and a fireplace. A full breakfast with a choice of entrées is served daily.

10 Rooms • Price range: $130-225
Mt Surprise Rd, North Conway, NH 03860
☎ **(603) 356-2625**

North Conway
Cabernet Inn

This is a renovated 1842 cottage with award-winning gardens and an emphasis on the romantic. Some of the finely decorated guestrooms have fireplaces and all come with the modern comforts. Breakfasts include home-baked muffins, crepes or a made-to-order omelet. Tea is served on Saturday afternoons throughout the year. The inn is convenient to shopping, skiing and hiking trails.

10 Rooms • Price range: $79-199
3552 White Mountain Hwy,
North Conway, NH 03860
☎ **(603) 356-4704**

North Conway
Cranmore Mt. Lodge

Guests are always welcome at this renovated old farmhouse and barn. Babe Ruth spent a lot of time here in the 1940s when the lodge was owned by his daughter, and his favorite room has been maintained as a tribute. Special features of the property include the year-round heated pool, baby ground piano, game room and fireplace. The pond is stocked with trout, and fly-fishing is a popular activity.

18 Rooms • Price range: $79-290
859 Kearsarge Rd, North Conway, NH 03860
☎ **(603) 356-2044**

North Conway
Eastman Inn

This is a restored, three-story 1777 home with a wraparound veranda and sundeck. The parlor and dining room have a comfortable country ambience. Guestrooms have fireplaces and phones. Recently some were also redecorated with a country flavor. Guestrooms with a private entrance are available in an annex. The inn offers easy access to outlet stores and numerous year-round outdoor activities.

14 Rooms • Price range: $110-260
2331 White Mountain Hwy,
North Conway, NH 03860
☎ **(603) 356-6707**

North Conway
The Farm by the River Bed & Breakfast
Situated on land granted by King George III, this farm-turned-inn has been in the same family for seven generations. Guests are invited to enjoy 65 acres of forest, orchards, and river frontage. The farm's stables offer horseback rides, wagon rides and, in winter, sleigh rides. Victorian-style guestrooms feature amenities such as a Jacuzzis. Breakfasts are served fireside in winter, on the patio in summer.

9 Rooms • Price range: $70-189
2555 West Side Rd, North Conway, NH 03860
☎ **(603) 356-2694**

North Conway
Sunny Side Inn Bed & Breakfast
The clean and comfortable guestrooms of this 1850 farmhouse are always inviting. Decorated in pastels and patterns, each room has its own warm character. All cottages are fitted with gas fireplaces and some are geared toward romance with their two-person Jacuzzis. Others are perfect for family holidays with their extra pull-out couch and full kitchen. The flower-trimmed porches are lovely places to relax.

9 Rooms • Price range: $60-119
207 Seavey St, North Conway, NH 03860
☎ **(603) 356-6239**

North Conway
Victorian Harvest Inn
This charming inn is set in the heart of Mt. Washington Valley, offering access to the area's year-round activities. Guestrooms are decorated in Victorian and Colonial styles; two are equipped with a fireplace. A full breakfast is served every morning in the dining room The library provides an extensive selection of books on local hiking and biking trails.

6 Rooms • Price range: $120-220
28 Locust Ln, North Conway, NH 03860
☎ **(603) 356-3548**

North Conway
Wyatt House Country Inn
Attention to detail is key at this lovely inn where guests are welcomed with a glass of sherry, served extravagant breakfasts on English Wedgwood and Irish lace, and treated to afternoon tea. Set in Mt. Washington Valley and on the banks of Saco River, the inn boasts spectacular views and is a great place to stay for a skiing or hiking holiday. A new addition is the romantic two-person Jacuzzi suite.

7 Rooms • Price range: $69-169
3046 White Mountain Hwy,
North Conway, NH 03860
☎ **(603) 356-7977**

North Conway
The 1785 Inn
All rooms are individually decorated. The dining room has two fireplaces is the ideal place for romantic dining.

17 Rooms • Price range: $119-219
3582 N White Mountain Hwy,
North Conway, NH 03860-1785
☎ **(603) 356-9025**

North Sutton
Follansbee Inn on Kezar Lake

Located on peaceful Kezar Lake in sight of the North Sutton town green, this 19th-century country inn is close to local historic sites and skiing and hiking trails. Each guestroom is furnished with antiques, while two common rooms, each with a fireplace, create a warm atmosphere. A full country breakfast is served daily in the family-style lakeside dining room.

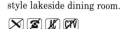

23 Rooms • Price range: $85-130
Kezar Rd, North Sutton, NH 03260
☎ **(603) 927-4221**

North Woodstock
Three Rivers House

Originally built as a hotel, this 1875 inn was one of several carriage stops in its time. Today it stands at the entrance to the Kancamagus Highway, a scenic drive through the White Mountain National Forest. In winter the inn offers week-end ski packages; summer activities include hiking and biking. All rooms have private baths and many are equipped with fireplaces. A hearty breakfast is served daily.

19 Rooms • Price range: $80-185
S Main St, North Woodstock, NH 03262
☎ **(603) 745-2711**

North Woodstock
Woodstock Inn

Ideally situated for year-round activities in the White Mountains, this inn offers lodging with character. The original build-ings have been renovated and all rooms are fitted with modern luxuries. The local railroad station, which has brought holiday-makers to the area since the 1800s, has now been turned into the inn's pub and fine dining room. The on-site brew-ery produces six hand-crafted beers.

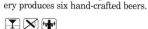

21 Rooms • Price range: $95-155
135 Main St, North Woodstock, NH 03262
☎ **(603) 745-3951**

North Woodstock
Wilderness Inn Bed & Breakfast

Just south of downtown, the inn is conveniently located to year-round activities. Common areas have a com-fortable country feel. Breakfast is served on the all-weather porch. Themed guest-rooms have photos taken by the innkeepers.

8 Rooms • Price range: $80-155
57 Main (Rt 3) St, North Woodstock, NH 03262
☎ **(603) 745-3890**

Portsmouth
Bow Street Inn

The Bow Street Inn has the unique distinction of being housed above the Seacoast Repertory Theatre in a reno-vated 19th-century brewery storage building on Portsmouth's historic waterfront. Rooms are elegantly decorated.

9 Rooms • Price range: $135-180
121 Bow St, Portsmouth, NH 03801
☎ **(603) 431-7760**

Portsmouth
The Inn at Christian Shore

Located in historic Portsmouth, this handsome early 19th-century Federal house combines period charm with modern conveniences. Activities in the area include visiting the town's museums and gardens or taking a day-long trip to the islands from the nearby port. All rooms are air-conditioned; four have private baths. A full New-England breakfast is served daily in the open-beamed dining room.

5 Rooms • Price range: $65-85
335 Maplewood Ave, Portsmouth, NH 03801
☎ **(603) 431-6770**

Portsmouth
Martin Hill Inn

This inn consists of two buildings from the early 1800s. Furnished in period antiques, including canopy and four-poster beds, all guestrooms feature private baths. A garden path links the Guest House and the Main House, where guests are invited to a full country breakfast in the well-appointed dining room. The inn is located in a historic neighborhood minutes from the waterfront and the harbor.

7 Rooms • Price range: $115-130
404 Islington St, Portsmouth, NH 03801
☎ **(603) 436-2287**

Portsmouth
⑩ Sise Inn

This vintage 1881 Queen Anne inn has been restored in style. Each guestroom is decorated with antiques and period reproductions. The living room with its large fireplace and the breakfast room with its fine woodwork are other attractions. Three rooms are also available for all kinds of functions including business meetings and dinner parties. Portsmouth's shops and museums are within walking distance.

34 Rooms • Price range: $165-240
40 Court St, Portsmouth, NH 03801
☎ **(603) 433-1200**

Portsmouth
The Inn at Strawbery Banke

A short stroll from waterfront, this is an attractive early 19th-century inn.

7 Rooms • Price range: $130-150
314 Court St, Portsmouth, NH 03801
☎ **(603) 436-7242**

Rochester
The Governor's Inn

Built in 1920 for former governor Spaulding, this Georgian-Colonial home retains architectural features such as lace woodwork and marble fireplaces. All guestrooms are equipped with private baths. A hot breakfast is served to weekend guests; a continental breakfast is provided weekday mornings. The inn offers the stately Governor's Ballroom for large gatherings, the intimate Huntley Room for small gatherings.

10 Rooms • Price range: $78-148
78 Wakefield St, Rochester, NH 03867
☎ **(603) 332-0107**

Snowville
Snowvillage Inn

A short drive from Mt. Washington, this 18-room inn offers spectacular mountain views and access to winter and summer outdoor activities. All guestrooms are equipped with private baths and furnished with country antiques. The rebuilt Chimney House offers a fireplace in every room. A full country breakfast is served in the dining room, also popular for its fresh-baked pastries and candlelit dinners.

18 Rooms • Price range: $99-249
Stewart Rd, Snowville, NH 03832
☎ **(603) 447-2818**

Sugar Hill
The Hilltop Inn

This attractive early 1900s home is located in a sleepy rural village surrounded by forests and mountains. The mid-sized guestrooms are attractively decorated. There is also a sitting room with a TV and a bright breakfast room.

6 Rooms • Price range: $115-195
1348 Main St, Sugar Hill, NH 03585
☎ **(603) 823-5695**

Sugar Hill
Sunset Hill House

Perched high on a 1,700-foot-high ridge in the White Mountain region, this early 20th-century inn offers nearby skiing in winter and golf, badminton and croquet in summer. Each guestroom has a private bath; some are equipped with a Jacuzzi. The inn also offers fine dining by candlelight and après ski fun in Rose McGee's Tavern. There is also a warming hut for cross-country skiers.

28 Rooms • Price range: $125-395
231 Sunset Hill Rd, Sugar Hill, NH 03585
☎ **(603) 823-5522**

Sunapee
Dexter's Inn

This charming inn has been offering guests comfortable lodgings with beautiful views for 40 years. The inn's tennis club boasts three all-weather courts and a tennis pro is on hand for lessons. Other activities include local golfing, hiking, biking and canoeing. Each guestroom has a private bath and the inn's library lounge and screened-in porch are favorite places to relax. Breakfast and dinner are served daily.

18 Rooms • Price range: $95-165
258 Stagecoach Rd, Sunapee, NH 03782
☎ **(603) 763-5571**

Swanzey
Loafer Inn at the 1792 Whitcomb House B&B

Once the home of a wealthy cotton and wool mogul, this "Old Mansion" was built in 1792. The present owners have been successful in maintaining the splendor of days past, while fitting their inn with all the modern conveniences.

6 Rooms • Price range: $65-85
27 Main St, Swanzey, NH 03446
☎ **(603) 357-6624**

Tamworth
The Tamworth Inn

This "country comfortable" 1830s inn boasts such decorative touches as handmade quilt bedspreads and fresh-cut flowers. The swimming pool and terraced pub are wonderful in the warmer months, the riverside and backyard grounds are gorgeous in autumn, and the nearby skiing is excellent in winter. The on-site barn is home to the "Barnstormers" troupe in July/August, the oldest professional theater group in the U.S.

16 Rooms • Price range: $190-290
15 Cleveland Hill Rd, Tamworth, NH 03886
☎ **(603) 323-7721**

Temple
Birchwood Inn

The Birchwood Inn is a historic inn situated in a quiet rural setting.

7 Rooms • Price range: $64-79
Rt 45, Temple, NH 03084
☎ **(603) 878-3285**

Tilton
Black Swan Inn

This Victorian home built in the 1880s has been tastefully decorated and fur-nished in vintage decor. Each of the seven guestrooms has its own individual style. The Carriage House accommodates two suites, each with a living room and a television. Included is a hearty breakfast served daily in the dining room. Nearby restaurants and year-round outdoor activities make this inn an attractive vacation spot.

9 Rooms • Price range: $70-105
354 W Main St, Tilton, NH 03276
☎ **(603) 286-4524**

Twin Mountain
Fieldstone Country Inn

This 1925 Colonial home rests on five acres of beautiful countryside. Breakfast includes fresh eggs, sausage and bacon from chickens and pigs raised on the property. Golf and ski packages are available, as well as mid-week specials.

7 Rooms • Price range: $75-95
125 Fieldstone Ln, Twin Mountain, NH 03595
☎ **(603) 846-5646**

Wakefield
Wakefield Inn
Built in 1804, this inn has retained many unique features—including a "freestand-ing" spiral staircase and a three-sided fire-place, the focal point of the large sitting room. Each spacious guestroom is equipped with a private bath and attractive furnishings; the owner's homemade quilts are remarkable. Local attractions include historic Wakefield Corner as well as the nearby White Mountains and Maine sea coast.

7 Rooms • Price range: $80-95
2723 Wakefield Rd, Wakefield, NH 03872
☎ **(603) 522-8272**

Wakefield
Lake Ivanhoe Inn
This charming Colonial-style inn is sit-uated at the entrance to Ivanhoe Lake Campground opposite the private beach. The many activities in the area include swimming, canoeing, hiking and biking. A continental breakfast is served to guests daily.

6 Rooms • Price range: $70-80
631 Acton Ridge Rd, Wakefield, NH 03830
☎ **(603) 522-8824**

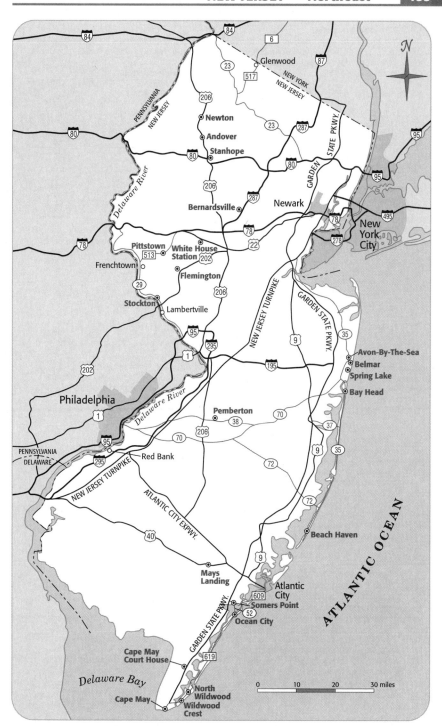

Andover
Crossed Keys B&B

Located in peaceful countryside amid rolling fields and English-style gardens, this large white clapboard home contains a variety of attractive guest units, all decorated with antiques. The glass-enclosed porch is a relaxing place to read.

5 Rooms • Price range: $125-125
289 Peguest Rd (CR 603), Andover, NJ 07821
☎ **(973) 786-6661**

Avon-By-The-Sea
Atlantic View Inn

This inn stands across the street from the beach. Originally built as a grand summer cottage almost a century ago, it is now a comfortable B&B. Mahogany furnishings as well as wicker and hand-painted pieces complement the decor. Breakfast begins with freshly ground coffee, tea or juices, followed by everything from Belgian waffles topped with pears and cream to apple and cheese-stuffed French toast or a vegetable omelet with biscuits.

13 Rooms • Price range: $105-250
20 Woodland Ave, Avon-By-The-Sea, NJ 07717
☎ **(732) 774-8505**

Bay Head
Bay Head Gables

Right at the entry to the fashionable Bay Head area sits this magnificent B&B. With its beautifully manicured lawn, flowering gardens, and 150-foot wraparound porch, this three-story pillared structure is a local landmark. Guests will enjoy the tastefully decorated guestrooms and the atrium-like breakfast room, which gives the feeling of being outdoors. A daily maid service is offered by the inn. The beach is a block away.

11 Rooms • Price range: $140-195
200 Main Ave, Bay Head, NJ 08742
☎ **(732) 892-9844**

Bay Head
Conovers Bay Head Inn

Only one block from the beach, and surrounded by manicured lawns, this inn is perfect for a seaside retreat. Guestrooms are bright and fresh, and the line-dried linens and plush feather beds create a luxurious atmosphere. The spacious outdoor whirlpool is a great place to relax after a day spent in historic Bay Head or at the ocean. Each day begins with a breakfast of baked goods and fresh fruit.

12 Rooms • Price range: $165-300
646 Main Ave, Bay Head, NJ 08742
☎ **(732) 892-4664**

Beach Haven
Amber Street Inn

Innkeepers Michael and Joan Fitzsimmons add their own personal touches to make the Amber Street Inn something special. Joan's English garden adds beauty to the surroundings, Michael's worldwide travels make for some interesting conversations, and they both make breakfast special by preparing it themselves. Fishing trips to the bay, kayaking and golf are some of the many activities close at hand.

6 Rooms • Price range: $145-180
118 Amber St, Beach Haven, NJ 08008
☎ **(609) 492-1611**

Belmar
Down the Shore Bed & Breakfast

This bed and breakfast has a contemporary and homelike atmosphere.

3 Rooms • Price range: $80-100
201 Seventh Ave, Belmar, NJ 07719-2204
☎ **(732) 681-9023**

Belmar
The Inn at the Shore

This spacious and homey inn features a comfortable living room with a working fireplace and a video library, a wrap-around porch and a brick patio. The bedrooms are furnished to reflect the house's 19th-century origins.

12 Rooms • Price range: $75-130
301 Fourth Ave, Belmar, NJ 07719
☎ **(732) 681-3762**

Bernardsville
The Bernards Inn

Long a haven for weary New Yorkers who take the hour's train ride from the city, the Bernards Inn has maintained a high standard of hospitality since 1907. From the entrance welcoming table adorned with a massive floral arrangement to the grand staircase that leads to the deluxe guestrooms and suites, this jewel box of an inn is the epitome of elegance. Meals in the Great Room are a delight, thanks to the chef's fine progressive American cuisine. Expect such delights as lobster bisque. Afterward enjoy the relaxing atmosphere of the Piano Bar.

20 Rooms • Price range: $180-205
27 Mine Brook Rd, Bernardsville, NJ 07924
☎ **(908) 766-0002**

Cape May
The Abbey Bed & Breakfast

This beautiful Gothic villa with an imposing 60-foot tower features authentic Victorian decor. It consists of two adjacent National Register houses, each with seven guestrooms in addition to parlors and verandas. Its location near the beach means water activities and scenic vistas are close at hand. Ornithologists will be delighted since the area lays claim to being one of the best birding hot spots of the East Coast.

14 Rooms • Price range: $100-295
34 Gurney St at Columbia Ave,
Cape May, NJ 08204
☎ **(609) 884-4506**

Cape May
Gingerbread House

One of Cape May's stawart B&Bs, the Gingerbread House used to be a haven for wealthy families. Nowadays the inn welcomes a wide range of travelers drawn to the nearby Atlantic Ocean. Located in Cape May's historic district, the Gingerbread is just a block away from the beach and two blocks from Cape May's Victorian Mall as well as several fine restaurants. A delicious home-baked breakfast is served every morning.

6 Rooms • Price range: $98-250
28 Gurney St, Cape May, NJ 08204
☎ **(609) 884-0211**

Cape May
(AAA) *Hotel Alcott*

An Italianate-bracketed villa, the Hotel Alcott was completely restored in 1998. Cape May's second-oldest property, it was originally known as the Arlington House. The 31-room hotel has made every effort to combine the best of two worlds and is a modern hotel that boasts tastefully chosen antiques. The hotel's restaurant offers a popular dinner buffet or a sumptuous grill menu. The ocean is just steps away.

31 Rooms • Price range: $160-260
107 Grant St, Cape May, NJ 08204
☎ **(609) 884-5868**

Cape May
The Humphrey Hughes House

A spacious and gracious home, The Humphrey Hughes House became an inn in 1980. As such, it retains the atmosphere of a home, while offering guests beautifully appointed rooms with intricate woodwork. The large wraparound veranda with wicker armchairs invites guests to relax outdoors. Or they can enjoy the outdoors from inside the glass-enclosed sunporch. The beach is just a block away. Guests can rinse off sand in the outdoor shower.

10 Rooms • Price range: $140-295
29 Ocean St, Cape May, NJ 08204
☎ **(609) 884-4428**

Cape May
(AAA) *The Inn on Ocean*

A warm and intimate environment awaits visitors to The Inn on Ocean. Each comfortable guestroom contains king- or queen-size premium bedding, fresh flowers, a mini-fridge and a private bath. Here, breakfast makes vacation mornings especially appealing. The day's specialties include treats such as Chardonnay baked apples, pain perdu Louisiana-style, Dutch apple-muffin cake and granola parfait.

5 Rooms • Price range: $129-209
25 Ocean St, Cape May, NJ 08204
☎ **(609) 884-7070**

Cape May
The Mainstay

This elaborately designed inn was constructed by wealthy gamblers in 1872. They spared no expense in making the inn beautiful: 14-foot ceilings, elaborate chandeliers and a sweeping veranda along with the finest walnut furnishings provided more than a touch of class. The inn retains much of that elegance, although modern amenities such as private baths have been added. Breakfast and afternoon tea are served daily.

16 Rooms • Price range: $125-360
635 Columbia Ave, Cape May, NJ 08204
☎ **(609) 884-8690**

Cape May
Manor House

At this inn, breakfast doesn't just mean delicious food; it's also an occasion to figure out what is happening next. After starting the day right, guests can visit a number of fine shops, restaurants and cafes, all close by. Those who want to explore further afield can take a carriage or trolley tour, go biking or hiking or take in a game of golf or tennis. The main attraction in May or June is the Cape May Music Festival.

10 Rooms • Price range: $90-200
612 Hughes St, Cape May, NJ 08204-2318
☎ **(609) 884-4710**

Cape May
The Primrose Inn

Providing the ultimate in relaxation, this inn marries old-style living with modern convenience. Designed in the Italianate-style, the house was built in the local shipyards more than 150 years ago. After a full breakfast, you can borrow a bicycle to explore nearby historic Cape May or take a ride to the beach. Afternoon refreshments will greet you upon your return, to be served on the patio or porch, or in the parlor.

5 Rooms • Price range: $95-250
1102 Lafayette St, Cape May, NJ 08204
☎ **(609) 884-8288**

Cape May
The Queen Victoria

Occupying a prime location in Cape May's Victorian historic district, this inn encompasses two impeccably restored 1880s homes with porches, attractive gardens and a rooftop deck. The guest rooms and suites are furnished with fine Arts and Crafts-style antiques and handmade quilts. Some have whirlpool tubs and/or gas-log fireplaces. A buffet style breakfast is served daily. The old-fashioned parlor features a fireplace and a player piano.

21 Rooms • Price range: $185-285
102 Ocean St, Cape May, NJ 08204
☎ **(609) 884-8702**

Cape May
⏣ *The Southern Mansion*

The Southern Mansion boasts the largest rooms and suites in Cape May. The mansion was built in 1863 when the architectural and social trends of Cape May imitated Southern cities. It went through a two-year renovation, which was completed in 1994. A new southern wing was constructed, providing more guestrooms, a second ballroom, a solarium and two magnificent circular staircases.

24 Rooms • Price range: $140-350
720 Washington St, Cape May, NJ 08204
☎ **(609) 884-7171**

Cape May
Victorian Lace Inn

Guests at the Victorian Lace Inn have the choice of staying in the main house or in the Bantry Cottage, a private hideaway with picket fences located just across the road from the inn. The cottage comes complete with a king-size bed, a double Jacuzzi and a fireplace. Rooms at the main house are no less inviting, featuring private baths, fireplaces and pine floors. Two suites have views of the ocean a block away.

5 Rooms • Price range: $75-250
901 Stockton Ave, Cape May, NJ 08204
☎ **(609) 884-1772**

Cape May
The Virginia Hotel

This circa 1879 country inn is located at the heart of Cape May's historic district. Guests may relax in the intimate lobby, which features a fireplace, grand piano and art and periodical collections. Guestrooms are decorated in Victorian style.

24 Rooms • Price range: $190-250
25 Jackson St, Cape May, NJ 08204
☎ **(609) 884-5700**

Cape May
White Dove Cottage

Attention to detail is what it's all about at this 1866 Second Empire home. American and European antiques are omnipresent. Period wallpaper, soft carpeting and flowers add intimate touches. Particular care is taken in the preparation of breakfast. A grand banquet table is set with lace, fine china and heirloom crystal. Breakfast fare varies with the season, but is always announced by soft music from an antique music box.

6 Rooms • Price range: $110-225
619 Hughes St, Cape May, NJ 08204
☎ **(609) 884-0613**

Cape May
The Brass Bed Inn

The Brass Bed Inn is a restored Gothic-revival Victorian cottage.

9 Rooms • Price range: $75-165
719 Columbia Ave, Cape May, NJ 08204
☎ **(609) 884-2302**

Cape May
Carroll Villa Bed & Breakfast

This 1882 Victorian has cozy rooms and a bustling, popular restaurant.

22 Rooms • Price range: $75-175
19 Jackson St, Cape May, NJ 08204
☎ **(609) 884-9619**

Cape May Court House
The Doctors Inn

Located in the heart of this Cape May County town, this mid-19th century Italianate mansion features parlors and guestrooms elegantly appointed with period antiques. Each guestroom has a gas fireplace and marble bath. Visitors are welcome to take a stroll through the lovely east lawn gardens and rest in the shade of the charming gazebo. A wheelchair lift is available on the premises.

6 Rooms • Price range: $140-175
off season; $160-195 on season
2 N Main St, Cape May Court House, NJ 08210
☎ **(609) 463-9330**

Flemington
Cabbage Rose Inn

The structure and decor of this inn is impressive, from the grand staircase and beautiful sunporch to the stained-glass windows and baby grand piano. Guests are truly pampered here, beginning their days with lavish breakfasts of baked goods and fruits, and later enjoying hot-mulled apple cider, bed-time sherry and treats from the cookie jar. Local activities include canoeing, hot-air ballooning and winery tours and tastings.

5 Rooms • Price range: $75-135
162 Main St, Flemington, NJ 08822
☎ (908) 788-0247

Flemington
Jerica Hill, A Bed & Breakfast Inn

This is Flemington's first B&B and it is located in the historic town center. The building is a Queen Anne-style Victorian and is laden with creature comforts. Guestrooms are fitted with canopy, brass or four-poster beds, bay windows, reading chairs and fresh flowers. The library and porches are places to relax with the daily paper or a book. A complimentary picnic is offered to all guests partaking in the Country Wine Tour.

5 Rooms • Price range: $85-125
96 Broad St, Flemington, NJ 08822
☎ (908) 782-8234

Flemington
Main Street Manor Bed & Breakfast

This impressive late 19th-, early 20th-century family home has been lovingly restored to its original stateliness. Breakfasts are served in an attractive Arts and Crafts-style dining room or, by arrangement, in the second-floor guestrooms. Each of the rooms has a private bath and sitting area. Several have bay window seats and one has an exterior gallery overlooking the nearby woods.

5 Rooms • Price range: $100-150
194 Main St, Flemington, NJ 08822
☎ (908) 782-4928

Mays Landing
Abbott House Bed & Breakfast

This 1860s inn is in the historic Mays Landing area. It offers gorgeous river views from the veranda, and is within walking distance of Lake Lanape.

Guests are treated to breakfasts of fruit-filled pancakes or gourmet omelets.

4 Rooms • Price range: $89-119
6056 Main St, Mays Landing, NJ 08330
☎ (609) 625-4400

Newton
The Wooden Duck Bed & Breakfast

Wildlife abounds on the secluded property that surrounds this white clapboard house. Open fields and woodlands entice guests to take nature walks. A brick patio and outdoor swimming pool also lure guests to wander outdoors. A delicious country breakfast features a variety of homemade breads, eggs, fresh muffins, French toast, pancakes and fruit. Ducks are an omnipresent theme throughout the house.

7 Rooms • Price range: $90-175
140 Goodale Rd, Newton, NJ 07860
☎ (973) 300-0395

North Wildwood
 Candlelight Inn

Perfect for couples seeking a romantic getaway, the Candlelight Inn lives up to its name. Special niceties such as chocolates, fresh flowers and a decanter of sherry may be found in guestrooms. Guests will also find period furniture made of oak, walnut, pine and mahogany throughout the inn. All guestrooms have private baths and brass or antique wooden beds. Some rooms have Oriental rugs, old prints and ceiling fans.

10 Rooms • Price range: $85-230
2310 Central Ave, North Wildwood, NJ 08260
☎ **(609) 522-6200**

Ocean City
 Brown's Nostalgia Bed & Breakfast

This cedar home is just blocks from the beach, the action at the boardwalk, and is close to golf and fishing locations. The wraparound porch is shaded by striped awnings and offers views of the water. Gleaming hardwood floors, colorful stained-glass windows, an exercise room, a games room, comfortable guest units and warm hospitality are found inside. The restaurant offers great food and entertainment.

8 Rooms • Price range: $90-145
1001 Wesley Ave, Ocean City, NJ 08226
☎ **(609) 398-6364**

Ocean City
Castle By The Sea

One block away from the boardwalk and the glistening beaches of Ocean City, you'll find the Castle by the Sea. Adorned with stained-glass windows and a picturesque veranda, the inn also boasts an eye-catching interior: restored hardwood floors, magnificent carved woodwork and stunningly decorated entrance and dining room. A three-course gourmet breakfast and high tea are served daily.

8 Rooms • Price range: $125-229
701 Ocean Ave, Ocean City, NJ 08226
☎ **(609) 398-3555**

Ocean City
  Northwood Inn

Within walking distance of the beach, this 1894 Queen Anne-Victorian house was one of the first houses built on the island. Its bright, airy rooms contain tasteful contemporary furnishings. The inn features a sweeping staircase, hardwood floors, a rooftop whirlpool spa for four, a regulation-size pool table, bicycles, beach and a beach shower and dressing room. A small art gallery is situated on the property.

7 Rooms • Price range: $85-220
401 Wesley Ave, Ocean City, NJ 08226
☎ **(609) 399-6071**

Ocean City
⚅ *Scarborough Inn*

The Scarborough Inn has been an Ocean City landmark since 1895. A European-style inn in the heart of Ocean City's historic district, it is located close to a number of attractions, such as the Music Pier, which features live concerts. The Atlantic Ocean is within walking distance, as is the two-mile-long boardwalk. The inn serves a continental-plus breakfast and is welcoming to families with children.

24 Rooms • Price range: $120-190
720 Ocean Ave, Ocean City, NJ 08226
☎ **(609) 399-1558**

Ocean City
Serendipity Bed & Breakfast

This seaside retreat is minutes away from the boardwalk and sandy beach. The airy guestrooms are cheerful with pastel textiles and wicker furniture.

Guest can explore the island and eat in the seafood restaurant across the street.

6 Rooms • Price range: $87-159
712 9th St, Ocean City, NJ 08226
☎ **(609) 399-1554**

Pemberton
Isaac Hilliard House Bed & Breakfast ... and Beyond

Three guestrooms and one suite are available at the casual Isaac Hilliard House. The guestrooms—Roses, Cranberry and Raspberry—are as individual as their names. For instance, the oversize Raspberry Room features a remote-controlled television and a love seat. In the Isaac Hilliard Suite guests have a large master bedroom and a remote-controlled gas fireplace. Breakfast is served daily.

4 Rooms • Price range: $75-120
31 Hanover St, Pemberton, NJ 08068
☎ **(609) 894-0756**

Pittstown
Seven Springs Farm & Bed 'n Breakfast

Halcyon days are recalled at the 200-year-old, beautifully restored farm house. The rooms are welcoming and feature master cabinetry and attractive

baths. A family-run produce stand sells home-grown vegetables.

4 Rooms • Price range: $85-175
14 Perryville Rd, Pittstown, NJ 08867-4304
☎ **(908) 735-7675**

Somers Point
Mayer's Inn & Marina

This Victorian home has been redesigned for its new incarnation as a country inn. Each romantic guestroom is painted a different atmospheric shade and all are fitted with the amenities of a luxury hotel. The home has patios and sundecks overlooking the marina and the Atlantic City skyline, and the Grandview Dining Room offers a sophisticated menu, emphasizing local seafood and house-grown herbs.

8 Rooms • Price range: $145-275
800 Bay Ave, Somers Point, NJ 08244
☎ **(609) 927-3100**

Spring Lake
The Chateau Inn
 Marble baths, Casablanca ceiling fans, pressed tin ceilings, delicate fabrics and fresh flowers create an ambience of romance at this beautiful inn. Outdoor attractions are just as enticing and include porches, a landscaped courtyard area and brick patios. Guests will receive complimentary beach and tennis passes and a scenic tour of the lake.

38 Rooms • Price range: $79-219
500 Warren Ave, Spring Lake, NJ 07762
☎ **(732) 974-2000**

Spring Lake
Normandy Inn
 Guests will find unique guestrooms and two suites awaiting them at the Normandy Inn. The only inn in Spring Lake to be included on the National Register of Historic Places, the property boasts Colonial-Revival and Neoclassic interiors. Guests will be intrigued by such distinctive items as an antique English tall-case clock, a damask-covered parlor set and several marble sculptures.

18 Rooms • Price range: $93-225
21 Tuttle Ave, Spring Lake, NJ 07762
☎ **(732) 449-7172**

Spring Lake
Seacrest by the Sea
 Visitors will be treated to the inn's specially blended Scandinavian coffee, winner of The New York Times "best coffee in the world" contest. Along with coffee, breakfast consists of buttermilk scones, freshly squeezed orange juice, yogurt and granola. Guestrooms are tastefully furnished, with comfortable feather beds topped by fine Egyptian cotton linens and Belgian lace. Some rooms have a fireplace.

11 Rooms • Price range: $175-275
19 Tuttle Ave, Spring Lake, NJ 07762
☎ **(732) 449-9031**

Stanhope
The Whistling Swan Inn
This Queen Anne-style home, originally built in 1905, has a large porch, charming gardens and a fountain with seating area. Rooms vary in decor and size.

Some have been decorated along certain themes, such as Art Deco or Oriental.

10 Rooms • Price range: $99-150
110 Main St, Stanhope, NJ 07874
☎ **(973) 347-6369**

Stockton
The Woolverton Inn

Centrally located between New York City and Philadelphia, this meticulously renovated 18th-century inn is surrounded by 10 acres of rolling hills. Centuries-old oak and apple trees give the property a majestic feel. The surrounding scenic countryside invites biking, horseback riding, hiking along the Delaware River or a short drive to explore the local wineries. Some rooms feature a fireplace.

9 Rooms • Price range: $115-275
6 Woolverton Rd, Stockton, NJ 08559
☎ **(609) 397-0802**

White House Station
⦿ *Holly Thorn House*

This B&B has been renovated in the style of an English country manor home. It is welcoming, comfortable and filled with a variety of treasures and collectibles. The guestrooms are furnished with antiques and convey a feeling of serenity. Other features include the Billiard Room with wet bar, the outdoor swimming pool and cabana, and the common room with tables piled high with books and shelves of games.

5 Rooms • Price range: $115-145
143 Readington Rd, White House Station, NJ 08889
☎ **(908) 534-1616**

Wildwood Crest
Pope Cottage B&B

Located in a quiet residential neighborhood, just a short walk from the beach and boardwalk, this 1907 Queen Anne-style home blends modern convenience with a mix of antiques and reproductions. Breakfast features fresh fruit, homemade baked goods and freshly brewed coffee. Guests can relax on the wide verandas and enjoy the ocean breezes, or gather around the fire inside to have afternoon tea.

5 Rooms • Price range: $90-150
5711 Pacific Ave, Wildwood Crest, NJ 08260-4355
☎ **(609) 523-9272**

Notes:

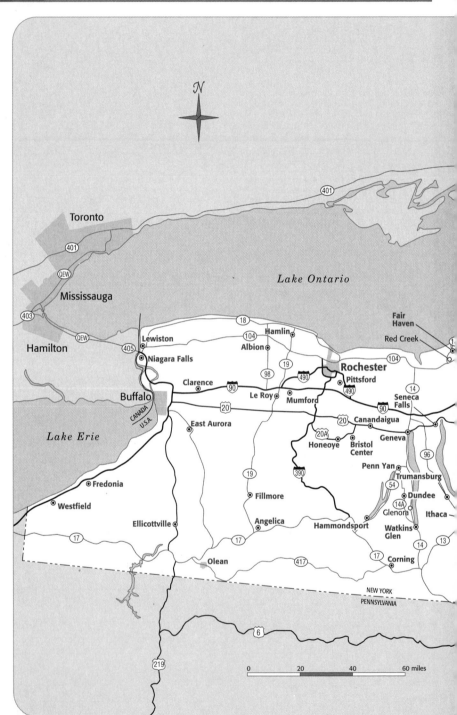

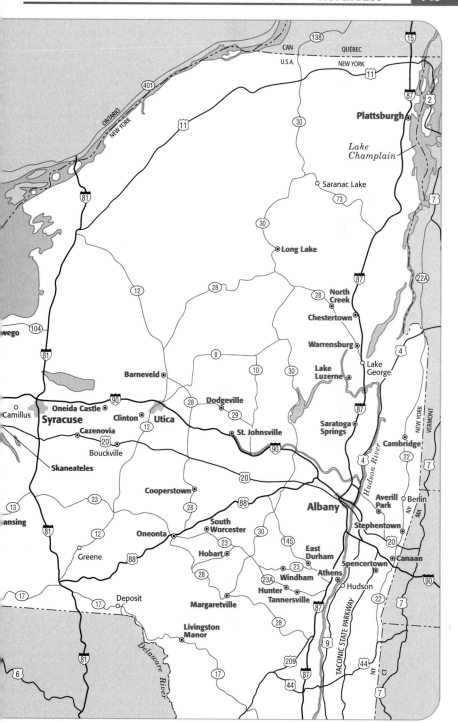

CAN
QUÉBEC
U.S.A.
NEW YORK

138
15
401
11
87
2

ONTARIO
NEW YORK

11
30
Plattsburgh

Lake Champlain

81
Saranac Lake
73
7

30
22A

Long Lake

12
28
28
North Creek
87

Chestertown

104
wego
8
10
30
Warrensburg
4
Lake Luzerne
Lake George

Barneveld
81
28
Dodgeville
29
87
Saratoga Springs

90
Oneida Castle
Camillus
Syracuse
Clinton
Utica
12
St. Johnsville
Cazenovia
20
Bouckville
90
4
Hudson River
Cambridge
22
7

NEW YORK
VERMONT

Skeneateles

13
23
Cooperstown
88
Albany
Averill Park
Berlin

ansing
81
12
28
Stephentown
20
Greene
88
Oneonta
South Worcester
30
145
East Durham
Spencertown
Canaan

17
17
Deposit
Hobart
23
23
Athens
Windham
23A
Hudson
22
7
90

Margaretville
28
Hunter
Tannersville
87

9

6
81
Livingston Manor
28
209
44
TACONIC STATE PARKWAY
44
NY
CT
7

Delaware River
17
87
44

NY MA

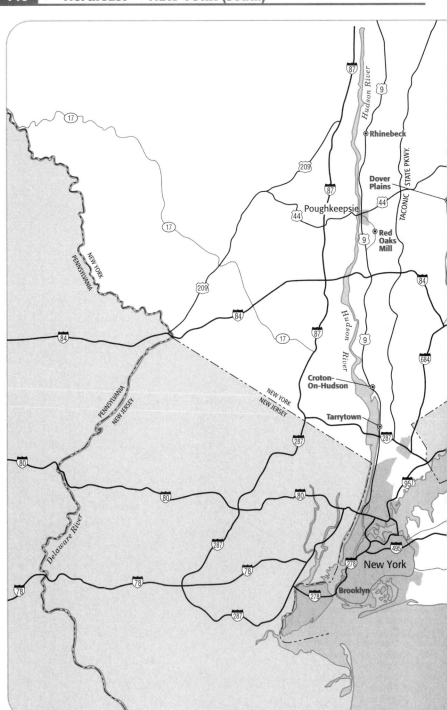

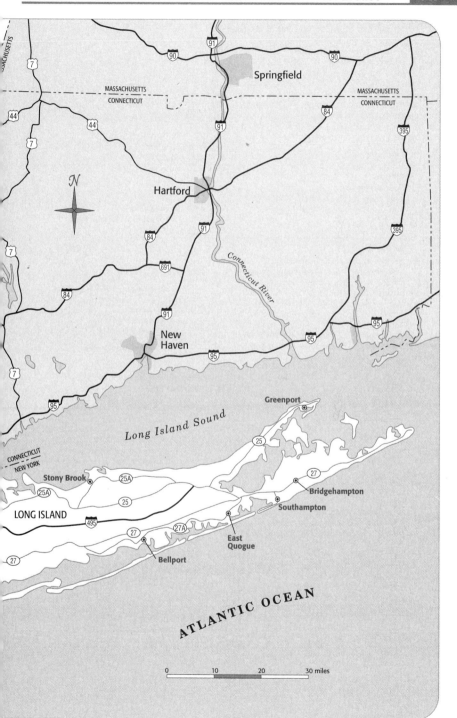

Springfield

MASSACHUSETTS
CONNECTICUT

MASSACHUSETTS
CONNECTICUT

Hartford

Connecticut River

New
Haven

Greenport

Long Island Sound

CONNECTICUT
NEW YORK

Stony Brook

Bridgehampton

Southampton

LONG ISLAND

East
Quogue

Bellport

ATLANTIC OCEAN

0   10   20   30 miles

Albany

⚜ *Albany Mansion Hill Inn & Restaurant*
Located in a quiet, convenient part of one of Albany's historic district neighborhoods, this family-operated inn has eight guestrooms, each with a full private bath. Four meeting spaces—including a professionally landscaped courtyard—are also available to accommodate small gatherings, from cocktail parties to board meetings. Menus can be customized for groups and equipment for meetings is available on request.

8 Rooms • Price range: $125-165
115 Philip St at Park Ave, Albany, NY 12202
☎ **(518) 465-2038**

Albion
Fairhaven Inn
This property has a picturesque locale and comfortable guest units.

4 Rooms • Price: $45-55
14369 Ridge Rd, Albion, NY 14411
☎ **(716) 589-9151**

Angelica

Angelica Inn Bed & Breakfast
This restored Victorian mansion is set on 130 acres. It features spacious rooms, antique furnishings, brass beds and stained-glass windows. Each room has a private bath and a fireplace. Additional lodging can be had at the 1825 Country House, which is decorated in country fashion and features one room with a complete kitchen and a private porch and one two-bedroom suite. The ski hills of Allegany State Park are a short drive away.

5 Rooms • Price range: $60-100
64 W Main St, Angelica, NY 14709
☎ **(716) 466-3063**

Athens
The Stewart House
The stunning views of the Hudson River from this renovated 1883 hotel make it a popular romantic getaway. Amenities include individually decorated guestrooms, an attractive formal dining room, and an old-time bar with bistro menu.

4 Rooms • Price range: $90
2 N Water St, Athens, NY 12015
☎ **(518) 945-1357**

Averill Park
The Gregory House Country Inn & Restaurant
This 1830 Victorian Manor home offers 12 beautifully appointed rooms, each with a private bath. Located in the center of Averill village, nearby attractions include antiques, theater and museums, as well as outdoor activities such as hiking, skiing and horseback riding. Breakfast is served daily in the dining room, and a common room with a working fireplace welcomes guests at the end of the day.

12 Rooms • Price range: $95-125
3016 Rt 43, Averill Park, NY 12018
☎ **(518) 674-3774**

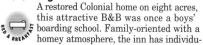

Barneveld
Sugarbush Bed and Breakfast

A restored Colonial home on eight acres, this attractive B&B was once a boys' boarding school. Family-oriented with a homey atmosphere, the inn has individu-ally decorated rooms. Breakfast features home-made waffles; afternoon tea is served.

5 Rooms • Price range: $55-125
8451 Old Poland Rd, Barneveld, NY 13304
☎ **(315) 896-6860**

Bellport
The Great South Bay Inn

This charming property, situated in the heart of Bellport, features six guest rooms, each of which is individually decorated with period antiques. Rooms vary in size. The inn also offers catering for small gatherings.

6 Rooms • Price range: $85-125
160 S Country Rd, Bellport, NY 11713
☎ **(631) 286-8588**

Bridgehampton
The Enclave Inn

Known as the Malibu of the East, the Hamptons boast some of the finest white sand beaches in the world. Located min-utes from the beaches, this handsome inn delivers the feelings of retreat and comfort that have attracted travelers to the region for many years. The newly restored guestrooms, heated swimming pool and manicured grounds all contribute to a relaxing and rewarding stay. A complimentary beach pass comes with each room.

10 Rooms • Price range: $89-279
2668 Montauk Hwy, Bridgehampton, NY 11932
☎ **(631) 537-0197**

Bristol Center
⏣ *Acorn Inn*

Here's a structure that has gone through many incarnations. Today this 200-year-old building today houses elegant guestrooms furnished with charming antiques and queen-size canopy beds. Two rooms have a fireplace; one of them features a whirlpool and a private brick terrace as well. Each room has a modern private bath-room. The atmosphere of the common rooms is warm and inviting, thanks to a Rumford fire-place and a wall lined with interesting books for browsing. The extensively landscaped grounds include a Jacuzzi spa built right into the garden.

4 Rooms • Price range: $115-205
4508 SR 64 S, Bristol Center, NY 14424-9309
☎ **(716) 229-2834**

Brooklyn
Bed & Breakfast on the Park

Ten minutes from bustling lower Manhattan, this is an oasis of art and architecture. Lavishly decorated with antiques, each room has its own attractions, including views of the park, a pri-vate rooftop garden and a working fireplace.

7 Rooms • Price range: $125-300
113 Prospect Park W, Brooklyn, NY 11215
☎ **(718) 499-6115**

Cambridge
Cambridge Inn Bed & Breakfast

The rooms at the Cambridge Inn vary in size and are decorated individually.

8 Rooms • Price range: $48-75
16 W Main St, Cambridge, NY 12816
☎ **(518) 677-5741**

Canaan

The Inn at Silver Maple Farm
This inn combines rustic charm with modern convenience. Great varnished beams and vaulted ceilings distinguish the design of the building and pine floors and antique furnishings grace the guestrooms, each of which is furnished with fine linens and down comforters. The country setting offers great terrain for hiking, biking or just rambling. There is an outdoor heated spa. A hearty breakfast is served daily.

11 Rooms • Price range: $95-275
Rt 295, Canaan, NY 12029
☎ **(518) 781-3600**

Canandaigua

Sutherland House
Surrounded by rolling farmland, this renovated Victorian mansion was built in 1885 by Henry C. Sutherland, a businessman of early Canandaigua days. Guestrooms have full private baths; two of the rooms are equipped with a double Jacuzzi and a fireplace. Located just a mile-and-a-half from Main Street and Canandaigua Lake, Sutherland House is within easy distance of restaurants, festivals and lake activities.

5 Rooms • Price range: $90-175
3179 SR 21 S, Canandaigua, NY 14424
☎ **(716) 396-0375**

Cazenovia

Brae Loch Inn
Family-owned and operated, this authentic Scottish country inn offers fine food amid Scottish heirlooms. Diners are served by kilt-clad attendants in traditional Glengarrie hats. Each of the 14 guestrooms has a private bath and is charmingly furnished with old-world antiques from the British Isles. The Wee Pub offers a wide selection of single malt Scotches, while the Scottish gift shop is central New York's largest.

12 Rooms • Price range: $60-140
5 Albany St, Cazenovia, NY 13035
☎ **(315) 655-3431**

Chestertown

Friends Lake Inn
Turn-of-the-20th-century-style rooms offer a touch of the modern with in-room hot tubs. Most rooms have mountain and lake views. An outdoor sauna and private beach on Friends Lake make it easy to relax before sitting down to the inn's regionally acclaimed New American cuisine. Dinner showcases regional products with the accent on freshness and flavor. The wine list is equally exceptional, with the collection winning the "Grand Award" from Wine Spectator. The inn also boasts its own Ski Touring Center with miles of groomed trails for skiing and hiking.

17 Rooms • Price range: $190-375
963 Friends Lake Rd, Chestertown, NY 12817
☎ **(518) 494-4751**

Clarence

⬙ Asa Ransom House

Asa Ransom was an 18th-century fur trader who built the town of Clarence's first grist mill on the site of the 1853 building which houses today's inn. Some its attractions include a large common room/library with a working fireplace and a spacious veranda. The inn also boasts world-class cuisine served in two dining rooms. All guestrooms are furnished with a private bath and many have working fireplaces and connecting balconies.

9 Rooms • Price range: $89-150
10529 Main St, Clarence, NY 14031
☎ **(716) 759-2315**

Clinton
The Artful Lodger

Located on a historic village green, this 1835 Federal-style residence has been transformed into an elegant five-room inn that showcases the work of regional artists. Queen, king, and twin rooms are available overlooking the village fountain or the tree-lined grounds. In summer, the village green hosts a farmers' market and weekly concerts-in-the-park. All rooms have private baths and ceiling fans.

5 Rooms • Price range: $65-115
7 E Park Row, Clinton, NY 13323
☎ **(315) 853-3672**

Clinton
The Hedges

This inn features original artwork. Guests are greeted by the family dog.

5 Rooms • Price range: $65-125
180 Sanford Ave, Clinton, NY 13323
☎ **(315) 853-3031**

Cooperstown
⬙ Tunnicliff Inn

A Cooperstown landmark since 1802, this Federal-style townhouse has every modern convenience. Each room is furnished with a private bath and accented with period furnishings. There is an elegant dining room and an early 1900s tap room.

17 Rooms • Price range: $125-145
34-36 Pioneer St, Cooperstown, NY 13326
☎ **(607) 547-9611**

Corning
Rosewood Inn

This 145-year-old home was originally a columned Greek-Revival structure and was later revamped in the English Tudor style. The interior, however, is pure Victoriana with period furnishings, Oriental rugs and antiques. Each guestroom is individually decorated, each has a private bath. One ground floor suite includes a kitchenette. Breakfast in the elegant dining room includes homemade breads, muffins and a daily entree.

7 Rooms • Price range: $125-185
134 E 1st St, Corning, NY 14830
☎ **(607) 962-3253**

Croton-On-Hudson
Alexander Hamilton House

A romantic Victorian inn with charming river views, this location is perfect for the many activities of the Hudson River Valley. The accent here is on romance, with a garden gazebo—popular for wedding photos—and the Bridal Chamber with its in-room whirlpool and working fireplace. Full breakfasts include fresh juice, baked goods and hot entrées. Other house specialties include picnic baskets and delicious chocolate-covered strawberries.

8 Rooms • Price range: $75-250
49 Van Wyck St, Croton-On-Hudson, NY 10520
☎ **(914) 271-6737**

Dolgeville
Gatehouse Herbs Bed & Breakfast
This 1893 Victorian on 12 acres over-looks pond and river.

4 Rooms • Price range: $75-85
98 Van Buren St, Dolgeville, NY 13329
☎ **(315) 429-8366**

Dover Plains
Old Drovers Inn

Named for the cattle "drovers" that used to stop here in the mid-1700s, the inn has been offering uninterrupted service for more than 250 years. Historic charm has been retained throughout with such features as working fireplaces in the guestrooms and an arched "barrel-roof" gracing one of the upper rooms. Downstairs, the Tap Room offers hot buttered rum as it did to travelers of yore, while the chef serves fabulous rustic cuisine.

4 Rooms • Price range: $150-395
699 Old Rt 22 (CR 6), Dover Plains, NY 12522
☎ **(845) 832-9311**

Dundee
South Glenora Tree Farm Bed & Breakfast

Located in the heart of the vineyards just above Watkins Glen, this country retreat offers more than 65 acres of wooded hills, meadows and streams to enjoy. Walking and skiing trails weave through the Scotch pine, Fraser and Douglas fir that grow here. After a walk, guests are invited to relax by the fireplace in the Great Room or outdoors on the wraparound porch. They are also welcome to use the picnic pavilion, which contains a gas grill.

5 Rooms • Price range: $99-129
546 S Glenora Rd, Dundee, NY 14837
☎ **(607) 243-7414**

East Aurora
The Roycroft Inn

Ten years after founding the Roycroft Arts and Crafts Community in 1895, writer-philosopher Elbert Hubbard responded to the flood of visitors by opening the Roycroft Inn. Still bearing the names of notable personalities, the rooms are adorned with a collection of original and reproduction furniture and fixtures—as well as all the modern amenities. In addition to the inn itself, the 14-building Roycroft Campus is still going full swing.

22 Rooms • Price range: $130-260
40 S Grove St, East Aurora, NY 14052
☎ **(716) 652-5552**

East Durham
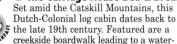 *The Carriage House Bed & Breakfast*

Set amid the Catskill Mountains, this Dutch-Colonial log cabin dates back to the late 19th century. Featured are a creekside boardwalk leading to a water- fall, buggy rides and nature trails. Guests enjoy a full breakfast with menu choices.

5 Rooms • Price range: $68-88
2946 Rt 145, East Durham, NY 12423
☎ **(518) 634-2284**

East Quogue
Carole's Bed & Breakfast

Beautifully restored Victorian home with a large porch; comfortable rooms.

5 Rooms • Price range: $135-160
7 Walnut Ave, East Quogue, NY 11942
☎ **(631) 653-5152**

Ellicottville
Ilex Inn

This turn-of-the-20th-century farmhouse captures all the rural charm of the Allegheny Mountains and adds a few pleasures of its own. A heated in-ground pool and a hot tub spa keep guests pampered, while complimentary pool towels, bathrobes and slippers are provided with each room. Breakfast is served in the formal dining room, as well as on the wide, wraparound veranda in warm weather. Specialties include baked bananas and quiche.

7 Rooms • Price range: $95-185
6416 E Washington St, Ellicottville, NY 14731-1585
☎ **(716) 699-2002**

Ellicottville
Jefferson Inn

The inn is a charming, quiet Victorian home a short walk from downtown. Rooms include one luxury suite and two efficiency units. A large living room with a working fireplace, and a wraparound veranda offer comfortable relaxation areas.

7 Rooms • Price range: $79-159
3 Jefferson St, Ellicottville, NY 14731
☎ **(716) 699-5869**

Fair Haven
Black Creek Farm B & B

As well as the cozy guestrooms in the main house, this renovated inn has a rustic cabin off in the trees for those who'd like an extra-quiet retreat. Overlooking a private two-acre stocked pond, the well-equipped cabin can accommodate a family of up to six. A pedal boat is available for use on the pond. Extensive gardens surround the inn. Hearty breakfasts include homegrown blueberries and apples.

4 Rooms • Price range: $60-85
13615 Mixer Rd, Fair Haven, NY 13064
☎ **(315) 947-5282**

Fillmore
Just A "Plane" Bed & Breakfast

This quiet, rural B&B has an interesting nearby attraction: An adjoining grass airstrip where visitors can take airplane rides. Guestrooms are finished with Amish crafts and quilts. A full breakfast is served in the dining room or sunroom.

4 Rooms • Price range: $50-62
11152 Rt 19A, Fillmore, NY 14735
☎ **(716) 567-8338**

Fredonia
The White Inn

Beautifully restored and decorated with antiques and period reproductions, this circa 1860 hostelry has the comfort and charm of a country manor. The acclaimed dining room offers American and Continental cuisine, while more casual fare can be found in the lounge. The inn's own boat is available for a relaxing sail on Lake Erie, and more lively entertainment can be found at the town's summer bandstand concerts.

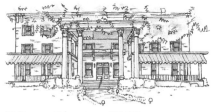

24 Rooms • Price range: $79-179
52 E Main St, Fredonia, NY 14063
☎ **(716) 672-2103**

Geneva
Belhurst Castle

This century-old castle on the shore of Lake Seneca has enjoyed a number of incarnations over the years as a private home, a casino, a speakeasy and as a restaurant. The antique furnishings, art work and Oriental rugs that adorn Belhurst Castle today add to the romantic atmosphere. In the dining room, carved aged-cherry, chestnut and mahogany complement the mosaic-tiled fireplace and beamed cathedral ceiling. With its manicured lawns and a Garden Room that can accommodate up to 300 people, the castle is well suited to such special events as banquets and weddings

13 Rooms • Price range: $105-315
Rt 14 S, Geneva, NY 14456
☎ **(315) 781-0201**

Geneva
⑭ Geneva-On-The-Lake

Located in the midst of the Finger Lake wine district, this elegant villa is a faithful but smaller replica of a villa in Frascati, Italy. The interior is beautifully decorated in the Italian Renaissance style, and guestrooms are furnished with classic American reproductions. The grounds feature formal gardens, classical sculptures, terracotta urns, and a 70-foot swimming pool. Guests are also invited to sample the dining room's gourmet cuisine.

30 Rooms • Price range: $300-467
1001 Lochland Rd, Geneva, NY 14456
☎ **(315) 789-7190**

Greenport
The Bartlett House Inn

Built at the turn of the 20th century, this large Victorian house with Corinthian columns and stained-glass windows was once a convent for the local church.

Nearby Greenport retains the charms of a New England fishing village.

10 Rooms • Price range: $110-140
503 Front St, Greenport, NY 11944
☎ **(631) 477-0371**

Hamlin
Sandy Creek Manor House

Featuring a salmon stream and six wooded acres, this quiet, comfortable European-style B&B is a relaxing place to visit and go for strolls. Open deck

dining, a player piano and an outdoor hot tub are some of the attractions.

4 Rooms • Price range: $60-95
1960 Redman Rd, Hamlin, NY 14464-9635
☎ **(716) 964-7528**

Hammondsport
Blushing Rosé Bed & Breakfast
Tucked away at the southern point of Keuka Lake, the Blushing Rosé Bed & Breakfast offers a cozy, friendly retreat. The area is great for biking, swimming and fishing. Route 54A winds along the lake for 22 scenic miles that are dotted with wineries and marinas. The quaint Hammondsport village square is a pleasant place in the summer months to relax and listen to the music from the bandstand. All rooms have private baths.

4 Rooms • Price range: $85-105
11 William St, Hammondsport, NY 14840
☎ **(607) 569-3402**

Hammondsport
Park Inn
This century-old hotel offers two-room suites furnished with antiques and decorated in an Old-World style. The inn overlooks Hammonsport's charming Village Square and and is minutes away from local attractions such as the Curtiss Museum.

5 Rooms • Price range: $71-81
37-39 Shethar St, Hammondsport, NY 14840
☎ **(607) 569-9387**

Hobart
Breezy Acres Farm Bed & Breakfast
This tastefully renovated farmhouse is situated on 300 acres of woods, pastures and meadows. Cross-country skiers will enjoy the 18 miles of trails that begin near the farm. Downhill skiing, trout fishing, horseback riding and turkey hunting are all nearby. Breezy Acres is a working crop farm and breakfasts are made with homegrown ingredients as well as the farm's maple syrup.

3 Rooms • Price range: $45-90
Rt 10, Hobart, NY 13788
☎ **(607) 538-9338**

Honeoye
Greenwoods Bed & Breakfast Inn
From the vantage point of this inn, guests have fantastic views of Honeoye Lake and the surrounding valleys. Guests can take to the hills for an invigorating walk and relax at the outdoor Jacuzzi spa on their return. All rooms are furnished with European-style linens, hooked rugs, and queen-size beds. In the common room, guests may find the innkeepers' pet keeping warm by the crackling fire.

5 Rooms • Price range: $70-145
8136 Quayle Rd, Honeoye, NY 14471
☎ **(716) 229-2111**

Hunter
Hunter Inn
A dramatic wall of fieldstone with a built-in fireplace warms guests at this friendly and luxurious ski lodge. Located minutes from Hunter Mountain and Ski Windham, this new inn should prove a popular vacation spot for winter sports enthusiasts. Most of the hotel-style guestrooms feature mountain views, whirlpool baths and balconies. The buffet breakfast is designed for outdoor appetites, offering eggs, bacon, pancakes and pastries.

40 Rooms • Price range: $80-195
Rt 23A, Hunter, NY 12442
☎ **(518) 263-3777**

Ithaca
☗ *Rose Inn*

The circular staircase rising from the main hall is the pride of the Rose Inn. Built of solid Honduras mahogany, it ascends two stories to a cupola on the roof. But the spectacular staircase is not the inn's only selling point: There is a formal parlor and various dining rooms where guests can enjoy a full country breakfast and prix-fixe gourmet dinners. All the guestrooms are decorated with period furniture. Four honeymoon suites boast Jacuzzi baths. In warmer months, guests can take advantage of the 20 acres of lawn and gardens that surround the inn.

23 Rooms • Price range: $105-200
813 Auburn Rd, Rt 34 N, Ithaca, NY 14851
☎ **(607) 533-7905**

Ithaca
La Tourelle Country Inn

This inn is set on 70-acres of picturesque rolling hills near Cayuga Lake. Each of the inn's rooms is reminiscent of European country hotels and has a subtle ambience that results from the perfect blend of old-world charm and contemporary comfort. Equally ideal for business or pleasure travelers, the inn can accommodate 200 banquet guests and offers the glamorous Tower Suite to couples.

36 Rooms • Price range: $79-299
1150 Danby Rd, Ithaca, NY 14850
☎ **(607) 273-2734**

Ithaca
Peregrine House Victorian Inn

This delightful brick home was built in 1874 and features a wide front porch. Guestrooms are equipped with private baths and are decorated with lace curtains and Laura Ashley prints. Breakfast is served in the dining room.

8 Rooms • Price range: $59-119
140 College Ave, Ithaca, NY 14850
☎ **(607) 272-0919**

Lake Luzerne
☗ *The Lamplight Inn Bed & Breakfast*

Each of the three buildings here has a personality, ensuring that this inn will please every guest's taste. The main house has been painstakingly restored in luxurious Victorian fashion and has 10 bedrooms. The carriage house, more modern in style, has five suites, each with a Jacuzzi and a fireplace. The spacious sunporch becomes the dining room in summer, where guests may find the innkeepers' pet soaking up the sun.

15 Rooms • Price range: $110-225
231 Lake Ave, Lake Luzerne, NY 12846
☎ **(518) 696-5294**

Lansing
Rogue's Harbor Bed & Breakfast

This historic B&B is located just six miles north of Ithaca. Guestrooms combine modern convenience with the rustic charm of brass- or wood-framed beds. But the real draw here is the dining room with its signature prime rib and seafood fare.

6 Rooms • Price range: $125-150
2079 E Shore DR, Lansing, NY 14882
☎ **(607) 533-3535**

Le Roy
Edson House Bed & Breakfast
Conveniently located near the New York State Thruway, this Victorian offers individually themed rooms, each of which has a private bath. The attractive house also features a wide front porch and comfortable common areas.

4 Rooms • Price range: $69-99
7863 Griswold Circle Rd, Le Roy, NY 14482-0296
☎ **(716) 768-8579**

Livingston Manor
The Magical Land of Oz B&B
Located in a mountain setting, the cozy rooms are filled with "Oz" memorabilia.

7 Rooms • Price range: $75-85
753 Shandelee Rd (CR 149),
Livingston Manor, NY 12758
☎ **(845) 439-3418**

Long Lake
Long View Lodge
Family-owned for four generations, this lodge combines comfortable accommodations with some spectacular mountain views. There is wheelchair access to the restaurant. Continental breakfast is complimentary.

15 Rooms • Price range: $55-90
Rt 28 N & 30, Long Lake, NY 12847
☎ **(518) 624-2862**

Margaretville
Margaretville Mountain Inn Bed & Breakfast
This restored Queen Anne-style home stands on top of Margaretville Mountain and overlooks majestic Catskill Mountain State Park. The building reflects the masterful craftsmanship of a bygone era, and is complemented by tasteful antiques.

7 Rooms • Price range: $65-145
Margaretville Mountain Rd,
Margaretville, NY 12455
☎ **(914) 586-3933**

Mumford
Genesee Country Inn
This inn is a converted stone mill, built circa 1833 and situated on idyllic grounds. The home's storybook exterior is matched by the interior, which is filled with period reproductions. Guests are invited to sit on the dock in the morning and watch the mist rise from the pond. Later in the day, guests can fish for trout or they can go hiking, skiing or to play golf. The course is just a short distance away.

9 Rooms • Price range: $114-150
948 George St, Mumford, NY 14511-0340
☎ **(716) 538-2500**

Niagara Falls
⛽ *The Red Coach Inn*
The Red Coach Inn has been receiving guests since 1923 and welcoming them with warm English country hospitality. Just steps away from Niagara Falls, this Tudor-style inn has nine suites and one double room. Each suite overlooks the thundering rapids and most have a wood-burning fireplace. Guests are presented with champagne and a cheese tray on arrival. A continental breakfast is served daily.

14 Rooms • Price range: $99-179
2 Buffalo Ave, Niagara Falls, NY 14303
☎ **(716) 282-1459**

Niagara Falls
Holley Rankine House

This historic property is part of a quiet residential neighborhood set at a distance from the bustle of downtown. It overlooks the Niagara River and the state park.

The spectacular Niagara Falls are just a 15-minute walk away.

5 Rooms • Price: $60 per person
525 Riverside Dr, Niagara Falls, NY 14303
☎ **(716) 285-4790**

North Creek
The Copperfield Inn

Located at the southern edge of Adirondack Park, this large inn with its distinctive 14-foot-high entranceway windows has much to offer. Guestrooms feature luxurious baths, mini-bars and nightly turn-down service. The inn's facilities include the Trapper's Tavern and the Terrace Ballroom, which can accommodate small or large gatherings. The Gardens dining room is well known in the region for world-class cuisine. Other attractions include a state-of-the-art health club and an all-weather tennis court—and there are year-round activities in the nearby park.

31 Rooms • Price range: $140-250
307 Main St, North Creek, NY 12853
☎ **(518) 251-2500**

North Creek
Goose Pond Inn

As its name suggests, the Goose Pond Inn has a lovely pond at the back of the house and, yes, there are two geese that call it home. Tucked against the foot of Gore Mountain and a stone's throw from the Adirondacks, the inn is ideal for those who want to relax on a raft in the river or hike, bike or ski. The inn's celebrated gourmet breakfast is served each morning with delicacies such as brandied French toast and sautéed apples.

4 Rooms • Price range: $65-115
196 Main St, North Creek, NY 12853
☎ **(518) 251-3434**

Olean
Old Library Inn Bed & Breakfast

This restored 1895 Victorian home, known as the Pink House, is replete with beautiful woodwork and antiques. Each of the rooms is equipped with a private bath and provides the quiet, comfortable atmosphere of another era. The dining room's country breakfast is cooked to order, and the nearby co-owned Old Library Restaurant specializes in seafood, prime rib and antelope. The inn is on the National Register of Historic Places.

8 Rooms • Price range: $65-75
120 S Union St, Olean, NY 14760
☎ **(716) 373-9804**

Oneida Castle
Governor's House Bed & Breakfast

An expansive four-story 1848 brick mansion, this home represents a fine example of Federal-style architecture. Rooms are large and bright, with antique and period furnishings, high ceilings and hardwood floors. Some rooms can accommodate two rollaway beds. Common rooms include two large parlors, a dining room, a library and a fully-stocked complimentary guest kitchen.

5 Rooms • Price range: $83-139
50 Seneca Ave, Oneida Castle, NY 13421
☎ **(315) 363-5643**

Oneonta
Kountry Living, The Sisters B&B

Two sisters own this country-style inn, located near a commercial district.

4 Rooms • Price range: $70-70
576 SR 28, Oneonta, NY 13820
☎ **(607) 432-0186**

Oswego
Oswego Inn Ltd.

This inn's motto "a little country in the city," is taken to heart. A quiet, country atmosphere and cozy, well-appointed rooms make for a soothing retreat in the center of Oswego. The inn displays the work of local artisans throughout.

13 Rooms • Price range: $40-65
180 E 10th St, Oswego, NY 13126
☎ **(315) 342-6200**

Penn Yan
Merritt Hill Manor Bed & Breakfast

Once a stop on the Underground Railroad, this 12-acre country estate overlooks Lake Keuka. The manor has been refurbished. Guestrooms have antiques, canopy beds and private baths. Full country breakfasts are served.

5 Rooms • Price range: $110-125
2756 Coates Rd, Penn Yan, NY 14527
☎ **(315) 536-7682**

Penn Yan
Trimmer House Bed & Breakfast

No expense was spared by the wealthy wine merchant who built Trimmer House in 1891. This fine example of Queen Anne architecture has been restored, with each guestroom combining period furnishings with modern luxury. Some of the house's features include outdoor dining, a library with a working fireplace and a music room. Full breakfasts are served.

5 Rooms • Price range: $75-199
145 E Main St, Penn Yan, NY 14527
☎ **(315) 536-8304**

Pittsford
Oliver Loud's Inn

This 1812 National Register landmark boasts museum-quality antiques and artifacts. The building was moved from its original location on a stagecoach route to its present site by the Erie Canal. All rooms have private baths, and guests are invited to relax in front of the fireplace in the common room or settle into one of the porch rockers overlooking the canal. A continental breakfast basket is delivered in-room every morning.

8 Rooms • Price range: $125-145
1474 Marsh Rd, Pittsford, NY 14534
☎ **(716) 248-5200**

Plattsburgh

Point Au Roche Lodge Bed & Breakfast

Deer, birds and plants flourish on the 851 acres of Point Au Roche State Park, adjacent to this comfortable lodge. Offering views of Lake Champlain, the Adirondacks to the west and the Green Mountains of Vermont to the east, the decks off each room are an extra treat for visitors. The park has a long, protected sandy beach and a picnic area that are open for day use. Trails are open year-round and marked for hiking and skiing.

9 Rooms • Price range: $65-133
463 Point Au Roche Rd, Plattsburgh, NY 12901
☎ **(518) 563-8714**

Red Oaks Mill

⚙ Inn at the Falls

Tucked away on a secluded shore of Wappinger Creek overlooking Mill Pond, this three-and-a-half million dollar contemporary mansion exudes a country-inn personality. Built in an L-shape, the shingle-style inn has a wonderfully spacious interior. Guests can view the creek and falls from the common room's huge windows. Catering to business and leisure travelers alike, the inn offers rooms furnished in a variety of styles, from English Colonial to contemporary. The suite rooms, some with deep-soaking tubs and oversize showers, offer thick, fluffy towels, robes and many other amenities.

36 Rooms • Price range: $155-160
50 Red Oaks Mill Rd (CR 44),
Red Oaks Mill, NY 12603
☎ **(845) 462-5770**

Rhinebeck

Beekman Arms & Delamater Inn and Conference Center

The Beek, as locals call it, dates back to 1766 with the opening of the tavern, which still stands in the center of the inn. The inn's 63 rooms were thoughtfully refurbished and remodeled in 1995, combining period style furnishing with contemporary comforts. The 1844 Delamater House, on the same property, is one of the few examples of American Gothic residences still in existence.

64 Rooms • Price range: $85-160
6387 Mill St, Rhinebeck, NY 12572
☎ **(845) 876-7077**

Rochester

428 Mt. Vernon

This beautifully restored 1917 home is located on two wooded acres adjacent to Rochester's Highland Park, 155 acres of land with trees, wildflowers and birds. The country environment—within city limits—makes the inn a favorite for vacation retreats as well as business meetings. The decor combines Victorian furnishings with the modern amenities private baths and in-room phones. A full generous breakfast is offered each morning.

7 Rooms • Price range: $95-115
428 Mt. Vernon Ave, Rochester, NY 14620
☎ **(716) 271-0792**

Rochester
A Bed & Breakfast at Dartmouth House Inn

Dark paneling, 18-foot ceilings and diamond-paned leaded-glass windows make Dartmouth House an elegant city haven. The stairway landing accommodates an organ that guests are welcome to play—as they are the grand piano in the dining room. Rooms are spacious and professionally decorated. Breakfasts are a gourmet treat. Museums, galleries, shops and restaurants are all within walking distance.

4 Rooms • Price range: $85-125
215 Dartmouth St, Rochester, NY 14607
☎ **(716) 271-7872**

Saratoga Springs
Adelphi Hotel

This spectacular Victorian inn, constructed in 1877, hearkens back to the era when Saratoga was known as "the Queen of the Spas." As with many high Victorian buildings, the Adelphi incorporates many "exotic" features of the British Empire, including the hand-painted stencils in the lobby and the outdoor piazza. But it is the guestrooms that are the the hotel's proudest feature, each of which is elaborately decorated with antiques.

39 Rooms • Price range: $105-400
365 Broadway, Saratoga Springs, NY 12866
☎ **(518) 587-4688**

Saratoga Springs
Longfellows Inn and Restaurant

An imaginative architectural structure made up of two 1915 dairy barns, this inn's design has loft areas in many of the guest suites. A happy marriage of contemporary amenities and rustic charm, the inn offers luxury baths with glass-enclosed showers and Jacuzzis, in-room temperature control and complimentary continental breakfast. The adjoining restaurant prides itself on fine dining, using fresh-picked ingredients.

18 Rooms • Price range: $75-495
500 Union Ave, Saratoga Springs, NY 12866
☎ **(518) 587-0108**

Saratoga Springs
Saratoga Bed & Breakfast

Located on seven acres of pine-filled grounds, this inn consists of two properties. An 1850 restored red brick Federal home was built as a wedding present for a daughter. The small to spacious rooms have tall ceilings, hardwood floors and king-size beds. Across a water garden is the 1860 wood-frame farmhouse, with rooms furnished with queen-size beds and maple and oak antiques.

9 Rooms • Price range: $75-225
434 Church St, Saratoga Springs, NY 12866
☎ **(518) 584-0920**

Saratoga Springs

Union Gables Bed & Breakfast
One of Saratoga's grand Victorians, this Queen Anne home dates back to 1901. The renovations retain the Victorian air, yet provide a feeling of clean, modernity. The large and attractive guestrooms are equipped with private baths and a small refrigerator stocked with Saratoga's sparkling spring water. Other amenities include a tennis court, an outdoor hot tub and a large porch filled with wicker and plants.

10 Rooms • Price range: $110-175
55 Union Ave, Saratoga Springs, NY 12866
☎ **(518) 584-1558**

Saratoga Springs

The Westchester House Bed & Breakfast
This 1885 Queen Anne Victorian was built as a family home and features carefully restored handcrafted moldings, chestnut wainscoting and an elaborately carved parlor fireplace mantle. The colorful exterior is surrounded by gardens. The rooms are comfortably appointed with antique furnishings, ceiling fans and air-conditioning. Racetracks, shops and museums are within easy walking distance.

7 Rooms • Price range: $225-325
102 Lincoln Ave, Saratoga Springs, NY 12866
☎ **(518) 587-7613**

Seneca Falls
The Guion House
In keeping with the landmark history of the area, the comfortably furnished rooms of this Seneca Falls B&B bear the names of early American pioneers of women's rights. The building itself was named for the Civil War hero George M. Guion and is a gorgeous 1876 Second Empire brick house. The Cayuga-Seneca Canal, Van Cleef Lake and the National Women's Hall of Fame are all within walking distance.

6 Rooms • Price range: $75-95
32 Cayuga St, Seneca Falls, NY 13148
☎ **(315) 568-8129**

Skaneateles
Hobbit Hollow Farm Bed & Breakfast
A 100-year-old Colonial-Revival inn set on 300 acres of rolling meadow and forest, this country home offers guests "a world away from the world." Peace, quiet and unspoiled beauty are the main attractions here on this former working farm, now largely returned to nature. Each guestroom is appointed with comfortable furnishings and a private bath. The inn also houses a library, two living rooms, a dining room and a sunporch.

5 Rooms • Price range: $120-270
3061 W Lake Rd, Skaneateles, NY 13152
☎ **(315) 685-2791**

South Worcester
Charlotte Valley Inn Bed & Breakfast
This cozy inn—which is also an antique store—still has its original pine floors and is decorated with American craft quilts. It is set in the pastoral Charlotte Valley. Guestrooms are cozy and have four-poster or canopy beds.

5 Rooms • Price range: $115-125
480 CR 40, South Worcester, NY 12197
☎ **(607) 397-8164**

Southampton
Evergreen on Pine Bed & Breakfast

In the heart of the Hamptons, the Evergreen on Pine offers guests congenial hospitality and accommodations. Built in the late 1800s, this B&B has been kept true to concept by its innkeepers. All rooms are cheerful and comfortable; continental breakfasts are plentiful and healthy. With Long Island's shore a short distance from the inn, a day at the beach is a favorite pastime of guests.

5 Rooms • Price range: $180-275
89 Pine St, Southampton, NY 11968
☎ **(631) 283-0564**

Spencertown
Spencertown Country House Bed & Breakfast

This country house is located at the foothills of the Berkshires in the scenic Hudson Valley—an area with year-round indoor and outdoor activities. Converted from a farm to its current incarnation, the house is steeped in history that dates back to its first owners in the 1800s. In the autumn, when the countryside bursts with color, guests often hike or bike the hills and valleys. In the winter, guests can take to the nearby ski slopes.

9 Rooms • Price range: $70-195
1909 CR 9, Spencertown, NY 12165
☎ **(518) 392-5292**

St. Johnsville
Inn by the Mill

Catering to romance and privacy, this inn is set on extensively landscaped grounds with meandering paths along the Old Mill Stream. All of the rooms in this inn, including the only suite, are located in the century-old miller's home. The kitchen is fully stocked and open to guests to prepare their own breakfasts. The seasonal Hog 'n' Haus Cottage, built in 1888, overlooks a gorge and cascading waterfalls.

5 Rooms • Price range: $100-150
1679 Mill Rd, St. Johnsville, NY 13452
☎ **(518) 568-2388**

Stephentown
Mill House Inn

Built as a sawmill in the early 1940s and converted in 1970 to an inn, this establishment has rough-sawn paneling and beams that give it a warm and rustic atmosphere. Located in the Berkshire Hills, it affords a year-round getaway. In the winter, guests can ski at the many resorts not far away. The fall brings magnificent foliage and excellent hiking. Summer months offer many cultural festivals as well as swimming at the inn.

12 Rooms • Price range: $75-109
Rt 43, Stephentown, NY 12168
☎ **(518) 733-5606**

Stony Brook

⑩ *Three Village Inn*

The original home component of this inn was built in 1751 by farmer Richard Hallock. Majestic murals in two of the rooms are reminiscent of the period in which he lived. Guests can choose to stay in the original wing or in one of the cottages overlooking Stony Brook Harbor. The inn is decorated to reflect each holiday and has planned events for children. Getaway packages are available for guests seeking a romantic weekend.

26 Rooms • Price range: $115-159
150 Main St, Stony Brook, NY 11790
☎ **(631) 751-0555**

Syracuse

The Dickenson House on James

This beautifully restored 1920s Tudor-style home has the atmosphere of a poet's paradise. Each room is named after a British poet and a book of the poet's works lies on the nightstand—just to get you in the mood! The inn has a galley kitchen stocked with the basics, where guests can help themselves to a cup of cocoa and cookies. The third floor of the inn is an elegant loft with skylights. A data port hook-up is available for guests with laptops.

4 Rooms • Price range: $95-120
1504 James St, Syracuse, NY 13203
☎ **(315) 423-4777**

Tannersville

⑩ *The Eggery Inn*

Situated on 12 acres, this inn has a peaceful mountain setting. In the living room, guests will find a Franklin stove—its warmth enjoyed by the owner's dog—an antique piano and spectacular views. Rooms are individually decorated.

15 Rooms • Price range: $99-140
288 Platte Clove Rd, Tannersville, NY 12485
☎ **(518) 589-5363**

Tarrytown
The Castle at Tarrytown

The Castle at Tarrytown overlooks New York's splendid Hudson River Valley from the region's highest hilltop. Constructed at the turn of the 20th century, the majestic castle still shows evidence of its ancient architectural roots, most notably in the Gothic windows and a Romanesque archway. Thirty-one spacious rooms and suites, 24 of which were recently added, are available for guests. Rooms may include such features as handcarved, four-poster king-size beds, exquisite lamps, original European artwork, custom-made chandeliers and marble bathrooms.

31 Rooms • Price range: $275-295
400 Benedict Ave, Tarrytown, NY 10591
☎ **(914) 631-1980**

Trumansburg
Taughannock Farms Inn

Many of the furnishings of this 1873 estate date back to its original owner, John Jones, who shipped them from his residence in Philadelphia, as well as from England and Italy. Today, these pieces, along with the carefully landscaped grounds, make this inn one of the most renowned landmarks of the region. The elegant dining room, graced with linen and silver, offers excellent American fare accompanied by regional wines.

11 Rooms • Price range: $75-375
2030 Gorge Rd, Trumansburg, NY 14886
☎ **(607) 387-7711**

Utica
Rosemont Inn Bed & Breakfast

Located in the heart of Utica's historic district, this 1860 home has been lovingly restored in the Victorian tradition. Each guestroom is furnished with a four-poster queen-size bed, a private bath and period antiques. The working fireplaces make both the parlor and the dining room warm and inviting to winter guests. There are large Victorian porches as well as a well-stocked library. A full breakfast is served daily.

7 Rooms • Price range: $89-145
1423 Genesee St, Utica, NY 13501
☎ **(315) 792-8852**

Warrensburg
Alynn's Butterfly Inn Bed & Breakfast

On 176 acres, only minutes from Lake George, this inn features four individually decorated guestrooms, each with a private bath. The inn also features a wide wraparound porch and a lavish country breakfast, served every morning.

4 Rooms • Price range: $119-149
69 Rt 28 W, Warrensburg, NY 12885
☎ **(518) 623-9390**

Watkins Glen
Longhouse Manor

Situated in the heart of the Finger Lakes near Watkins Glen Gorge, the Longhouse Manor is the perfect getaway. The grounds are secluded within a wooded area that offers enchanting views of Seneca Lake. Guestrooms are finely appointed and spacious, each room has a large private bathroom, a satellite television and a telephone. Guests can swim in the outdoor swimming pool.

4 Rooms • Price range: $110-150
3137 Abrams Rd, Watkins Glen, NY 14891
☎ **(607) 535-2565**

Watkins Glen
The Seneca Lake Watch Bed & Breakfast

This completely restored Queen Anne Victorian with its second- and third-story watch towers provides great views of Lake Seneca. Inside, an elaborate oak staircase leads up to five airy guestrooms, each of which is equipped with a modern private bath. On the main floor, a comfortable guest living room is furnished with a working fireplace, piano and TV with VCR. A gourmet breakfast is served in the adjacent dining room.

5 Rooms • Price range: $85-115
104 Seneca St, Watkins Glen, NY 14891
☎ **(607) 535-4490**

Westfield
The William Seward Inn

Located on a gentle knoll, this historic 19th-century Greek-Revival style mansion provides views of Lake Erie and the surrounding Chautauqua countryside. Palladian windows and majestic columns greet visitors to the main building, while the adjoining Carriage House, newly constructed, reflects the original spirit. Guests enjoy a cozy living room and fireplace and a charming library, but the inn's main pride is the kitchen, which has won awards.

12 Rooms • Price range: $70-185
6645 S Portage Rd, Westfield, NY 14787
☎ **(716) 326-4151**

Windham
Albergo Allegria Historic Bed & Breakfast

This 21-room establishment carries its complete Victorian theme throughout. Two of the original cottages taken from the Osborne House, built in 1892, make up the present-day B&B. A newly built section joins these two cottages. Guestrooms have comfortable down comforters, plush carpeting and full private baths. In addition, the former Osborn horse stables have been converted into five additional suites, each with a 15-foot-high cathedral ceiling and skylight, as well as a double whirlpool. Hearty breakfasts may include stuffed French toast or Belgian waffles.

21 Rooms • Price range: $73-183
43 Rt 296, Windham, NY 12496
☎ **(518) 734-5560**

Youngstown
Cameo Manor Bed & Breakfast

Situated on three secluded acres, this English manor house features a Great Room with fireplaces at either end, a solarium, a library, and an outdoor ter-

race. A full breakfast, which includes a hot entrée, is served family style in the dining room.

4 Rooms • Price range: $70-175
3881 Lower River Rd, Youngstown, NY 14174
☎ **(716) 745-3034**

Notes:

Notes:

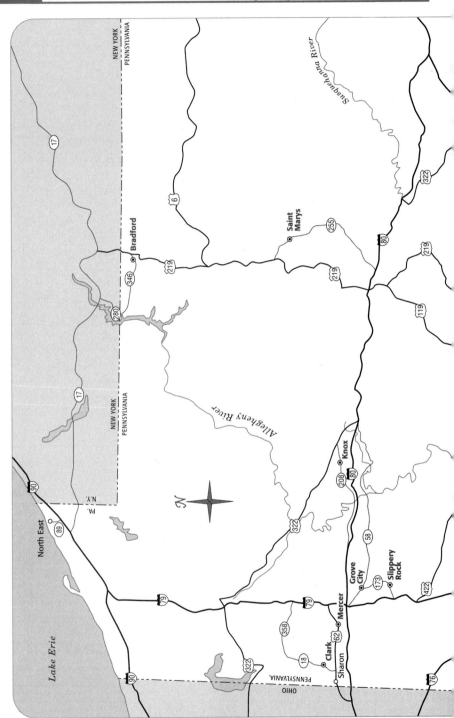

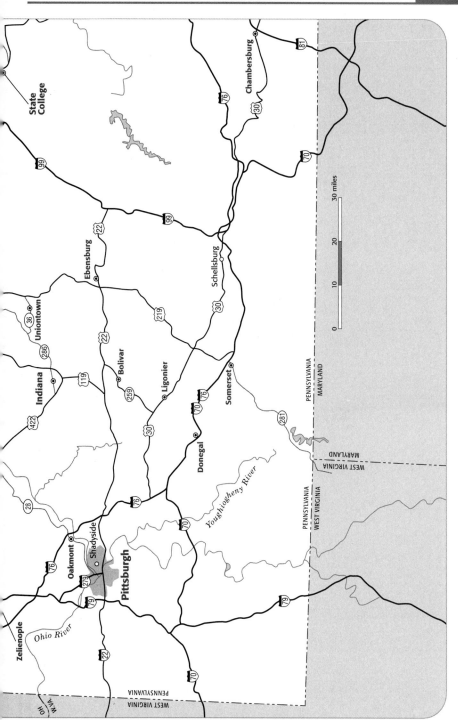

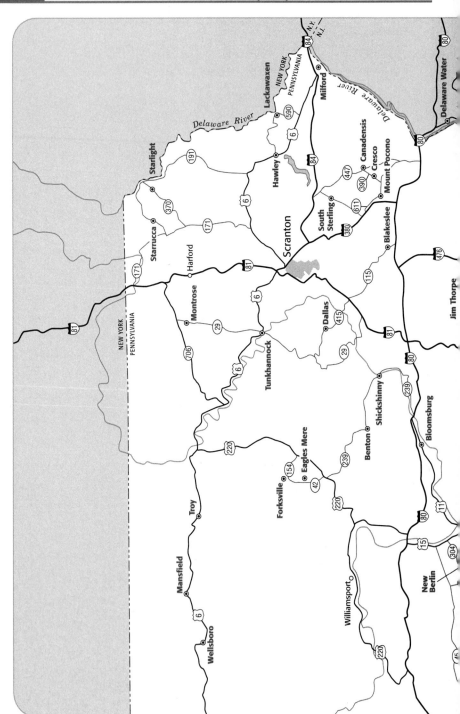

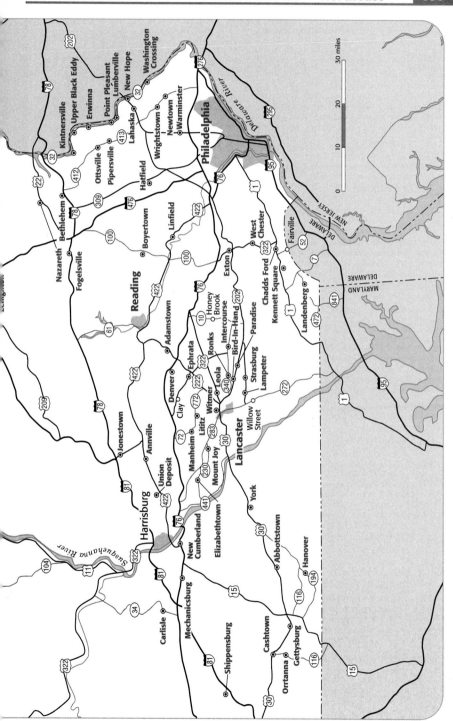

Abbottstown
⊛ *The Inn at the Altland House*

The chestnut woodwork and high ceilings of this recently restored inn hearken back to another era. The contemporary amenities of the guestrooms, however, are state-of-the-art. Guests may also choose to stay at the inn's cozy cottage, which has a full kitchen and fireplace. A complimentary continental breakfast is served daily, and the inn's restaurant, the Berwick Room, offers carefully prepared dinners and a delicious Sunday buffet.

10 Rooms • Price: $89
Center Sq Rt 30, Abbottstown, PA 17301
☎ **(717) 259-9535**

Adamstown
Adamstown Inn

Owners Tom and Wanda Berman have taken great care to create the Victorian look of their inn. Inside, the building features chestnut woodwork and leaded, beveled glass. On the outside, columns and trim are highlighted by shades of red, lavender, green and gold. Guestrooms include antique king- or queen-size beds, two-person Jacuzzis and gas-log fireplaces. The inn sits on a hill and offers a great view of historic Main Street.

4 Rooms • Price range: $68-150
62 W Main St, Adamstown, PA 19501-0938
☎ **(717) 484-0800**

Adamstown
⊛ *The Barnyard Inn*

Located on wooded acres overlooking the countryside, this 150-year-old former German schoolhouse makes a great getaway retreat. The owners' love of animals has led to the assembly of a petting zoo. Rooms are decorated along animal themes.

5 Rooms • Price range: $80-155
2145 Old Lancaster Pike, Adamstown, PA 19501
☎ **(717) 484-1111**

Akron
⊛ *Boxwood Inn*

This circa 1768 farmhouse retains all the charm worthy of its Pennsylvania-Dutch heritage. Traditional handmade Amish quilts and tasteful color schemes grace the guestrooms in the main building, while the Carriage House offers a working fireplace, a Jacuzzi and a private balcony. Other features include a glassed-in porch sitting room and an elegant dining room offering a full, country breakfast with a hot entrée.

5 Rooms • Price range: $115-210
12 Tobacco Rd, Akron, PA 17501
☎ **(717) 859-3466**

Akron
The Bella Vista Bed & Breakfast

Chosen in 1995 to be part of a local collection of historical buildings, Bella Vista is a lavish example of 1912 post-Victorian architecture in a tranquil setting. Guestrooms are individually decorated with original features restored or enhanced.

6 Rooms • Price range: $85-90
1216 Main St, Akron, PA 17501
☎ **(717) 859-4227**

Annville
 Swatara Creek Inn

 Chocolate tycoon Milton Hershey's school for orphan boys is now a picturesque three-story inn overlooking Swatara Creek to the south and the Blue Mountains to the north. Inside it has its own beauty: a formal entry foyer, an intimate sitting room and spacious guestrooms furnished with country decor, including canopy beds. A full breakfast, including homemade baked goods, is served every morning in the dining room.

6 Rooms • Price range: $50-80
10463 Jonestown Rd, Annville, PA
☎ **(717) 865-3259**

Benton
The Red Poppy Bed & Breakfast

 This Victorian home with its screened porches and living room fireplace is cozy and attractive, but its location also makes it a perfect spot for those who need activity when they get away. The area's fishing creek is just across the road and the Mill Race Golf Course and Restaurant is next door. Also close by is Bloomsburg University and Rickett's Glen State Park, which has 21 water-falls. Horseback riding is available.

4 Rooms • Price range: $55-85
RR 2, Box 82, Benton, PA 17814
☎ **(570) 925-5823**

Bethlehem
Wydnor Hall Inn

This 18th-century restored Georgian fieldstone manor house is the perfect setting for those who appreciate classic English-quality design. Guests are pampered with little touches such as down bedding, terry cloth robes, heated towel racks and the inn's custom sparkling water. In the drawing room, guests are invited to browse through a selection of books and magazines. Breakfast includes classic European breads.

5 Rooms • Price range: $100-150
3612 Old Philadelphia Pk,
Bethlehem, PA 18015-5320
☎ **(610) 867-6851**

Bird-In-Hand
Village Inn of Bird-In-Hand

This historic inn in the heart of Lancaster County actually gave its name to the town around it. Built in 1734, the inn is now on the National Register of Historic Places and the innkeepers will happily share the story of its origins. The inn boasts uniquely decorated rooms furnished in antiques. Guests enjoy unspoiled views of the surrounding countryside and are treated to a "continental plus" breakfast.

11 Rooms • Price range: $79-149
2695 Old Philadelphia Pike,
Bird-In-Hand, PA 17505
☎ **(717) 293-8369**

Blakeslee

✪ *Blue Berry Mountain Inn*
On 440 acres amid the Pocono mountains, lakes and ponds stands the Blueberry Mountain Inn. There are modern well-appointed rooms as well as one first-class master suite. The innkeeper serves a full breakfast and, with advance notice, can accommodate those who have special dietary needs. The inn also boasts an indoor heated pool, an outdoor spa and a game room.

6 Rooms • Price range: $90-135
Edmund Dr, Blakeslee, PA 18610
☎ **(570) 646-7144**

Bloomsburg
The Inn at Turkey Hill

Set amid the rolling hills and farmlands of Pennsylvania, this 1839 farmhouse has been in the current owners' family since 1942. Accommodations are located in the main building, the Cottages or the Stables and are furnished with an country motif. Each room is equipped with a private bath and sitting area. The inn also has a handsome lobby with fireplace, a terrace where dinner or drinks are served and a duck pond.

23 Rooms • Price range: $95-103
991 Central Rd, Bloomsburg, PA 17815
☎ **(570) 387-1500**

Bolivar
Champion Lakes Bed & Breakfast at Champion Lakes Golf Course

Champion Lakes has added a perfect complement to its attractive golf course. The rooms of this sports-themed establishment are named after Pittsburgh

Pirate players from the 1960s, and the Patio Bar is a great spot to add up scorecards.

9 Rooms • Price range: $65-85
RD 1, Box 285, Bolivar, PA 15923
☎ **(724) 238-5440**

Boyertown
Twin Turrets Inn
Named for the twin copper turrets that grace its roof, this Victorian home has been beautifully restored in a style faithful to the conception of its original owner, Horace K. Boyer. Modern amenities have been installed to accommodate even the most demanding of business travelers. Breakfast is served in the elegant dining room, lined with stained glass. The inn's gorgeous gardens are a great place to relax.

10 Rooms • Price range: $98.50-130
11 E Philadelphia Ave, Boyertown, PA 19512
☎ **(610) 367-4513**

◆◆ Bradford

Glendorn, A Lodge in the Country
After being a family home for more than five generations, the Glendorn was opened to the public in 1995. The main lodge contains four bedrooms, a dining area and a recreation room for cards, billiards and pool. Several charming cabins offer accommodation outside the main lodge. There are also three tennis courts, a trap and skeet shooting range, a gym and an outdoor swimming pool. Nearby lakes provide the perfect setting for short canoe trips and fishing, while miles of marked trails offer land-lubbers plenty of opportunities to go hiking or picnicking.

10 Rooms • Price range: $375-675
1032 W Corydon, Bradford, PA 16701
☎ **(814) 362-6511**

◆◆ Canadensis
Brookview Manor Bed & Breakfast
Situated on four picturesque acres in a secluded wooded hilltop, this is a great place for hiking, cross-country skiing and trout fishing. After enjoying a night in one of the comfortably decorated rooms, guests are invited to a full country breakfast.

10 Rooms • Price range: $110-150
RR 2 Box 2960, Canadensis, PA 18325
☎ **(570) 595-2451**

◆◆ Carlisle
⚅ *Pheasant Field Bed & Breakfast*
This 200-year-old Federal-style brick farmhouse, built in the 1800s, was a stop on the Underground Railroad. The inn stands in a quiet rural location close to Appalachian Trail. Two of the guestrooms feature private baths, while all benefit from central air-conditioning. A common area includes a sitting area with books, television and VCR and board games. A full breakfast, served daily, includes fruit and homemade bread.

4 Rooms • Price range: $90-175
150 Hickorytown Rd, Carlisle, PA 17013
☎ **(717) 258-0717**

◆◆ Cashtown
Cashtown Inn
The Cashtown, now part of a tranquil village setting, once served as the Confederate headquarters during the Gettysburg Campaign. These days, guests visit to enjoy the inn's elegant dining room, the Tavern Room or one of the comfy guestrooms. An impressive Civil War painting, as well as photos of actor Sam Elliott, who stayed here while filming the movie based on the battle of Gettysburg, hang on the walls.

7 Rooms • Price range: $75-145
1325 Old US 30, Cashtown, PA 17310
☎ **(717) 334-9722**

Chadds Ford
Fairville Inn

Fresh flowers welcome guests to this charming country inn. The inn is made up of three buildings: the Main House, the Spring House and the Carriage House. Eight of the units come with gas fireplaces, several have adjoining decks and all are equipped with private baths. Guests familiar with the paintings of Andrew Wyeth will recognize the haunting beauty of the Brandywine Valley surrounding this inn.

15 Rooms • Price range: $150-205
506 Kennett Pike, Chadds Ford, PA 19317
☎ **(610) 388-5900**

Chambersburg
Shultz Victorian Mansion B&B

This 1880 Victorian home has retained many of the qualities that made it an architectural marvel in the 19th century. Period features and intricate woodwork can be found throughout. Especially notable is the elaborate foyer and the open staircase leading to the third floor. A family collection of antiques adds a personal touch. Four-poster beds and luxurious bedding grace the large rooms. There is a suite-style room with fireplace.

7 Rooms • Price range: $75-85
756 Philadelphia Ave, Chambersburg, PA 17201
☎ **(717) 263-3371**

Clark
Tara, A Country Inn

Based on the classic film, "Gone With The Wind," this 1854 antebellum home is a re-creation of Tara. The inn is a virtual museum of rare and priceless antiques, original works of art and fascinating collectibles. Guests can relax in the European-style spa facilities or take a swim in the outdoor pool. Beautifully landscaped grounds overlook Shenango Lake. Jacket and tie are required at Ashley's, where dinner is a seven-course gourmet meal. Stonewall's Tavern is the area's oldest steak house and has a fine reputation. Many other fine restaurants are situated nearby.

27 Rooms • Price range: $175-275
2844 Lake Rd, Clark, PA 16113
☎ **(724) 962-3535**

Cresco
Crescent Lodge

Nestled in beautiful Paradise Valley in the center of the Pocono Mountains is Crescent Lodge, offering guests a truly luxurious getaway. Accommodations include units in the main house or in one of many cottages on the grounds. Main house rooms are furnished with canopy beds, thick comforters and matching draperies, while the cottages feature fireplaces, sunken Jacuzzis, private patios and decks overlooking the grounds.

30 Rooms • Price range: $95-200
Paradise Valley, Cresco, PA 18326
☎ **(570) 595-7486**

Delaware Water Gap
Water Gap Country Club

Birthplace of the original Eastern Open and host to many other major tournaments, this famed country club welcomes guests to walk in the footsteps of the greatest golfers of all time. The inn features attractive rooms, a restaurant and grill.

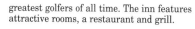

23 Rooms • Price range: $60-70
Mountain Rd, Delaware Water Gap, PA 18327
☎ **(570) 476-0300**

Denver
Cocalico Creek Bed & Breakfast

This is a good jumping-off point from which to explore the history, culture and scenic wonders of Lancaster County. And since Lancaster County is known as the antique capital of America, there are plenty of shops selling unusual items of interest. The 1927 inn is set along Cocalico Creek. Four gorgeous guestrooms are equipped with heated beds, private baths and air-conditioning. Guests are provide with a full gourmet breakfast.

4 Rooms • Price range: $65-110
224 S 4th St, Denver, PA 17517
☎ **(717) 336-0271**

Donegal
⚑ *Lesley's Mountain View Country Inn*

This restored 1850 Georgian farmhouse and converted barn, situated in the heart of Pennsylvania's Laurel Highlands, offers a sweeping view of the nearby Laurel Mountains. The restored chestnut barn is home to Lesley's Restaurant, which serves first-class American cuisine; the seasonal menus depend on the availability of local produce. Afternoon tea is served, as is fine Port, which can be enjoyed in the wine bar.

7 Rooms • Price range: $95-200
10 Mountain View Rd, Donegal, PA 15628
☎ **(724) 593-6349**

Eagles Mere
Crestmont Inn

A delightful inn located on the highest point in Sullivan County, the Crestmont offers gracious hospitality. Ten acres of lawns and nature trails are here to be enjoyed, as well as spectacular rose gardens, a large swimming pool and six Har-Tru tennis courts. Guestrooms with old-fashioned tiger-paw tubs provide period atmosphere. Candlelight sets the tone in the dining room, where meals are prepared by accomplished chefs.

13 Rooms • Price range: $89-198
Crestmont Dr, Eagles Mere, PA 17731
☎ **(570) 525-3519**

Ebensburg
⚑ *The Noon-Collins Inn*

This 1834 historic Federal-style stone country inn once housed a dance studio for Gene Kelly. It later served as the town's community center before being renovated in the 1970s. It is situated at the highest elevation of any inn in the state.

7 Rooms • Price range: $60-65
114 E High St, Ebensburg, PA 15931
☎ **(814) 472-4311**

Elizabethtown
West Ridge Guest House

A luxurious country estate, the West Ridge Guest House is an ideal getaway for those seeking peace and quiet. Tucked away in the rolling hills of Lancaster County, the inn assures guests of a restful stay. Nine guestrooms are offered, each reflecting a different historic style. All rooms feature a private bath. Inn attractions include an exercise room, a hot tub and two fishing ponds. A full breakfast is served daily.

9 Rooms • Price range: $80-140
1285 W Ridge Rd, Elizabethtown, PA 17022
☎ **(717) 367-7783**

Ephrata
Clearview Farm Bed & Breakfast

This 1814 limestone farmhouse provides a touch of class to the 200-acre setting of peaceful farmland. It features an eclectic mix of Victorian and country decor. The original floors are accented with gorgeous area rugs, while the Lincoln Room and the Washington Room display original hand-pegged rafters and exposed stone walls. All rooms feature quality bedding, air-conditioning and private baths. Every morning, fresh flowers and antique crystal greet guests in the dining room, where a lavish gourmet breakfast is served. Outside, a man-made pond is home to a population of ducks and swans.

5 Rooms • Price range: $95-145
355 Clearview Rd, Ephrata, PA 17522
☎ **(717) 733-6333**

Ephrata
Historic Smithton Country Inn

Built in 1763 as a stagecoach inn, the Historic Smithton has been in operation ever since. Period atmosphere reigns here with furnishings that include local antiques, Dutch quilts and four-poster beds. Decoration has been kept true to the original plan with rooms painted white and lit by candlelight—at the request of guests. Breakfast is served in a dining room where wrought iron items and Redware pottery are on display.

8 Rooms • Price range: $75-175
900 W Main St, Ephrata, PA 17522
☎ **(717) 733-6094**

Ephrata
The Inns at Doneckers

This country retreat is made up of several houses. All guestrooms combine Pennsylvania Dutch Country simplicity with contemporary elegance. The decor includes a variety of charming antiques, and many of the rooms and suites are equipped with fireplaces and Jacuzzis. Guests will also find on-site shops featuring art, fashion and furniture, and nearby are a railroad museum and an Americana museum. Breakfast may include homemade treats.

40 Rooms • Price: $69-210
318-324 N State St, Ephrata, PA 17522
☎ **(717) 738-9502**

Erwinna
EverMay on-the-Delaware

Built in the 1700s, this historic inn was enlarged and remodeled in the 19th century, giving it the Victorian flavor it has today. With 25 acres of pasture, woodland and gardens, this country estate sits overlooking the Delaware River. Guest units are found in the manor home, as well as in a carriage house, cottage and reconverted barn, and each is furnished with antiques and collectibles; all have air-conditioning and private baths.

18 Rooms • Price range: $145-350
889 River Rd, Erwinna, PA 18920
☎ **(610) 294-9100**

Erwinna
Golden Pheasant Inn

French country dining is one of the main attractions at this 1857 Bucks County fieldstone inn, which overlooks the Delaware River and Canal. Traditional dining rooms welcome guests; the Tavern Room with its beamed ceiling and fireplace and the candle-lit greenhouse provide the perfect atmosphere for a romantic dinner. Each antique-filled room has a queen-size poster bed and private bath.

6 Rooms • Price range: $75-145
763 River Rd, Erwinna, PA 18920
☎ **(610) 294-9595**

Exton
Duling-Kurtz House & Country Inn

Composed of two 1830s homes, this inn includes a fine restaurant as well as cozy, period lodgings. A red brick walkway connects the two buildings and attractive gardens surround them. Fifteen rooms are available in the old-fashioned stone house, all decorated in a pleasing fashion. Each room has a private bath. Guests are treated to a delicious continental breakfast. The restaurant has an award-wining wine list.

15 Rooms • Price range: $55-120
146 S Whitford Rd, Exton, PA 19341
☎ **(610) 524-1830**

Fogelsville
Glasbern

Located on a former 19th-century farm, this country inn offers a lovely setting for a weekend getaway. Guest units are located in the Farm House, the Carriage House, the Stables, the Gate House, the Garden Cottage and the beautifully converted Pennsylvania German Bank Barn, featuring high-vaulted ceilings, shale walls and hand-hewn wooden beams. Room furnishings seamlessly blend antiques with contemporary comfort.

25 Rooms • Price range: $105-360
2141 Packhouse Rd, Fogelsville, PA 18051
☎ **(610) 285-4723**

Forksville
Morgan Century Farm

Established in 1850, this farm was an important stop on the Underground Railroad. All rooms are clean and comfortable and are equipped with

a private bath. The farm also features a snug, guest house—ideal for a romantic getaway.

5 Rooms • Price range: $68-98
Rt 154, Forksville, PA 18616
☎ **(570) 924-4909**

Gettysburg

🕮 *Baladerry Inn at Gettysburg*

This historic home on four acres of land close to the edge of the battlefield served as a field hospital during the Civil War. It has been fully restored and is now a peaceful getaway. The property features eye-catching flower gardens, a tennis court and a carriage house, which has four guestrooms and is decorated with a large stained-glass window. All rooms are equipped with private baths, and the inn offers a full country breakfast daily.

8 Rooms • Price range: $95-130
40 Hospital Rd, Gettysburg, PA 17325
☎ **(717) 337-1342**

Gettysburg

The Brafferton Inn
This inn is the first house constructed in Gettysburg's historic district and dates back to 1786. Seventy-five years later, the inn found itself in the middle of the Gettysburg conflict; a bullet lodged in the mantel remains there today. There are 10 guest-rooms, including two suites. Each is decorated with 19th-century family antiques, elaborate stencils and portraits. The dining room displays a mural depicting local historical landmarks.

12 Rooms • Price range: $105-120
44 York St, Gettysburg, PA 17325
☎ **(717) 337-3423**

Gettysburg
🕮 *The Brickhouse Inn*

Built for a local banker in 1898, this brick Victorian is within walking distance of the historic battlegrounds as well as Gettysburg's shopping and dining. The building features original slate and tin roofing. Each guestroom is named for a state represented in the battle, and all are accented with quilts, family heirlooms and antiques. Guests are treated to a country breakfast served in the dining room or on the large brick patio.

7 Rooms • Price range: $90-150
452 Baltimore St, Gettysburg, PA 17325
☎ **(717) 338-9337**

Gettysburg
The Gaslight Inn
This 1872 three-story brick home is located within walking distance of the quaint center of Gettysburg with its shops and historic landmarks. The inn's blend of fine furnishings and attention to detail make it a favorite. Some guestrooms include a gas fireplace and private deck, as well as steam showers for two. Guests are also invited to enjoy the old-fashioned front porch, or savor breakfast next to the garden pond on the inn's patio.

9 Rooms • Price range: $100-165
33 E Middle St, Gettysburg, PA 17325
☎ **(717) 337-9100**

Gettysburg

Herr Tavern & Publick House

Twelve rooms are available at the Herr Tavern & Publick House. Five of the rooms are situated in the original historic building; the others are located in a new wing built in 1997. Guestrooms are tastefully appointed in traditional Americana decor. Each unit offers a fireplace, private bath and modern amenities, some feature a Jacuzzi tub. A full breakfast is served in the sunroom, and tea and snacks are available in the afternoon.

12 Rooms • Price range: $65-170
900 Chambersburg Rd, Gettysburg, PA 17325
☎ **(717) 334-4332**

Gettysburg

James Gettys Hotel

Conveniently located in the heart of downtown Gettysburg, this hotel is close to a number of attractions, including some great shops and fine restaurants. Nearby, as well, is the Willis House, where President Lincoln wrote the Gettysburg Address. Eleven suites are available, each featuring a private bath and a kitchenette with a microwave and a refrigerator. A continental breakfast is served daily in the suites.

11 Rooms • Price range: $125-145
27 Chambersburg St, Gettysburg, PA 17325
☎ **(717) 337-1334**

Gettysburg

The Lightner Farmhouse Bed & Breakfast

This 1862 farmhouse combines Federal and Victorian architectural styles. It was used as a field hospital during the Civil War and served as a refuge for the men of the First Corps. Today, this 12-room establishment, with its striking border of tall trees, makes a memorable place to stay. Each room is furnished with a queen-size bed and has a private bath. Guests are invited to relax in the common room by the huge fireplace.

5 Rooms • Price range: $95-100
2350 Baltimore Pike, Gettysburg, PA 17325
☎ **(717) 337-9508**

Gettysburg

Battlefield Bed & Breakfast Inn

This 1809 Civil War-era farmhouse stands on 46 acres bordering the Gettysburg National Military Park. History demonstrations and carriage rides are offered to guests, and a full country breakfast is served by staff in period costumes.

8 Rooms • Price: $74-213
2264 Emmitsburg, Gettysburg, PA 17325
☎ **(717) 334-8804**

Gettysburg

Gettystown Inn Bed & Breakfast

Situated overlooking the spot where Lincoln gave his Gettysburg Address this historic home is furnished as it would have been in 1863—with the addition of present-day comforts. A hearty breakfast is served in the parlor next door.

7 Rooms • Price range: $85-125
89 Steinwehr Ave, Gettysburg, PA 17325
☎ **(717) 334-2100**

Gettysburg
Keystone Inn

This 1913 Victorian welcomes guests onto a wide front porch furnished in wicker—an ideal spot for relaxing. A chestnut staircase leads to the second and third floors and the individually decorated rooms, each of which has a private bath.

5 Rooms • Price range: $79-99, Suite $119
231 Hanover St, Gettysburg, PA 17325
☎ **(717) 337-3888**

Grove City
Lynnrose Bed and Breakfast

Surrounded by rolling hills, this distinctive Victorian home offers guests four spacious rooms, each furnished with antiques. French doors lead from the dining room onto a large garden where guests can enjoy after-breakfast coffee.

4 Rooms • Price range: $65-85
114 W Main St, Grove City, PA 16127
☎ **(724) 458-6425**

Grove City
Snow Goose Inn

This former doctor's house offers comfortable rooms with private baths.

4 Rooms • Price range: $65
112 E Main St, Grove City, PA 16127
☎ **(724) 458-4644**

Hanover
The Beechmont Inn

This Federal-style home, dating back to the early 19th century, is decorated in period elegance, offering guests a comfortable refuge from the modern-day world. Accommodations include four large rooms and three suites equipped with such amenities as a fireplace, private balcony or whirlpool. Breakfast is served in the dining room or to guests in bed and can include such delicacies as herb cheese tart with ambrosia cup.

7 Rooms • Price range: $80-135
315 Broadway, Hanover, PA 17331
☎ **(717) 632-3013**

Hatfield
John Kindig House Bed & Breakfast

Built in 1864, this former farmhouse, welcomes guests to a tasteful blend of antique furnishings and contemporary amenities. The four guestrooms feature four-poster beds, handmade quilts and original artwork. All are equipped with private baths. Guests are also invited to enjoy the wraparound porch, in-ground swimming pool, and to explore the garden with its pond and gazebo.

4 Rooms • Price range: $95-105
244 W. Orvilla Rd, Hatfield, PA 19440
☎ **(215) 361-3200**

Hawley
The Settlers Inn at Bingham Park

Stone patios and flower and herb gardens mark the way to this restored Tudor manor. Rooms are furnished in authentic English Arts and Crafts-style. The dining room is known for its creative regional cuisine. Lake Wallenpaupack, with surrounding woodlands and 52 miles of shoreline, is situated nearby, as are the Dorflinger-Suydam Glass Museum, The Ritz Company Playhouse and the Zane Grey Museum.

20 Rooms • Price range: $85-195
4 Main Ave, Hawley, PA 18428
☎ **(570) 226-2993**

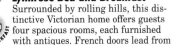

Hawley

The Falls Port Inn & Restaurant

This early 20th-century inn was constructed by Baron von Eckelberg and has been restored to the elegance of the Baron's era. Quaint guestrooms are furnished in period antiques. Affordable quality cuisine can be found at the inn and in the area.

9 Rooms • Price range: $75-100
330 Main Ave, Hawley, PA 18428
☎ **(570) 226-2600**

Indiana
Charbert Farm Bed and Breakfast

This renovated 1850's farmhouse is set on 108 acres of countryside. The four bedrooms each offer a lovely view of the garden. Guests are invited to a bountiful breakfast in the Victorian-style dining room, or to join in a sing-along in the Music Room.

4 Rooms • Price range: $55-95
2439 Laurel Rd, Indiana, PA 15774
☎ **(724) 726-8264**

Intercourse
Intercourse Village Bed & Breakfast Suites

Located in the heart of picturesque Amish country, this romantic village B&B offers an intimate setting for couples. The elegant 1909 main house has been restored to its original Victorian elegance, while the three new outbuildings have been given a more rustic country atmosphere. Rooms in all four buildings are equipped with private baths and working fireplaces, while the intimate two-room suite that is located in the Summer House boasts a heart-shaped Jacuzzi. Each morning, guests are invited to a three-course candlelight breakfast served in the formal dining room.

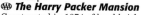

12 Rooms • Price range: $99-189
Rt 340-Main St-PO Box 340,
Intercourse, PA 17534
☎ **(717) 768-2626**

Jim Thorpe

The Harry Packer Mansion

Constructed in 1874 of local brick and New England sandstone, this Second-Empire Italianate mansion is the former home of an industrial magnate. The building has been restored, complete with the original detailed Minton tiles, bronze chandeliers and Tiffany windows. Guestrooms in the mansion and the adjacent carriage house are as elegant as when the mansion was built—with the added luxury of contemporary amenities. Weekends year-round are devoted to murder mysteries, in which guests are assigned roles in plots revolving around the Packer fortune and its hopeful heirs.

12 Rooms • Price range: $125-225
Packer Hill, Jim Thorpe, PA 18229
☎ **(570) 325-8566**

Jim Thorpe
Arbor Glen, A Country Retreat

Standing on 65 wooded acres, this luxury B&B makes the most of its serene rural setting. The region's fresh air can be enjoyed on the inn's elegant porch or by strolling near the stone-strewn stream. Also on the property is a pond stocked with trout. The proprietors pride themselves their guestrooms, which are large, carpeted suites, featuring queen-size canopy or four-poster beds, fireplaces and granite bathrooms with Jacuzzis.

4 Rooms • Price range: $195-225
3585 Fairy Land Rd, Jim Thorpe, PA 18229
☎ **(570) 325-8566**

Jim Thorpe
🆎 *The Inn at Jim Thorpe*

This New Orleans–style grand hotel with its beautiful wrought iron balconies sits in the center of Jim Thorpe's historic district. The inn has hosted some remarkable people of the 19th century, including Ulysses S. Grant and Thomas Edison. Rooms are elegantly appointed, with private baths equipped with pedestal sinks and marble floors. The independently operated Emerald Restaurant offers fine Irish-American cuisine.

36 Rooms • Price range: $99-129
24 Broadway, Jim Thorpe, PA 18229
☎ **(570) 325-2599**

Jonestown
Strawberry Patch Lodge Bed & Breakfast

This spacious log home is situated on top of a hill, surrounded by 10 acres of forest and farmland. Guests enjoy relaxing in the large comfortable parlor or loft area with its breathtaking 30-foot cathedral ceiling, or they can admire the view on the large wraparound veranda. Each room is decorated in antiques with Victorian charm. A full breakfast is served in the dining room, and the B&B's tea room provides afternoon tea daily.

7 Rooms • Price range: $95-149
115 Moores Rd, Jonestown, PA 17046
☎ **(717) 865-7219**

Kennett Square
🆎 *Scarlett House*

A stone manor built in Foursquare architectural style, Scarlett House is located in historic Kennett Square. Rooms are spacious and homey, filled with Victorian-era furnishings. Two parlors with fireplaces and a private sitting room are available for guests to enjoy. Inviting country roads surround Kennett Square and the area has museums, the Franklin Mint and outdoor activities such as canoeing on the Brandywine River.

4 Rooms • Price range: $90-139
503 W State St, Kennett Square, PA 19348
☎ **(610) 444-9592**

Kintnersville
The Bucksville House

Two hundred years of history stand behind the Bucksville House. This 1795 restored stagecoach inn is decorated with antique and country-style furnishings. All rooms have private baths, and some are equipped with fireplaces. The daily breakfast is served either in the gazebo or in front of the fireplace. Guests can read in the cozy common room or take a stroll on the brick patio with its grape arbor and water garden.

5 Rooms • Price range: $100-130
4501 Durham Rd, Rt 412,
Kintnersville, PA 18930-1610
☎ **(610) 847-8948**

Kintnersville
Lightfarm

Built in 1815, this inn is also an archeological site. Guests can take part in open-hearth cooking lectures, and they can participate in farm chores if they wish. The farm has lovely common areas with period furnishings, and some guestrooms have canopied beds and gas fireplaces. Seasonal produce fresh from the inn's farm is served and proprietors are willing to try to satisfy any special nutritional needs.

4 Rooms • Price range: $79-150
2042 Berger Rd, Kintnersville, PA 18930
☎ **(610) 847-3276**

Knox
Wolf's Den Bed & Breakfast

This circa 1831 farmhouse is set in a secluded garden of tall white pine overlooking a beautiful lake and golf course. Two of the four charming guestrooms offer private baths, and guests are invited to a full breakfast served daily.

4 Rooms • Price range: $65-85
RD 3, Knox, PA 16232
☎ **(814) 797-1105**

Lackawaxen
Roebling Inn on the Delaware

Once the home of the superintendent for the Delaware and Hudson Canal, this 1870 Greek Revival home is furnished in antiques and overlooks the Delaware River. Each room is equipped with a private bath, and a full breakfast is served daily.

6 Rooms • Price range: $70-140
155 Scenic Dr, Lackawaxen, PA 18435
☎ **(570) 685-7900**

Lahaska
⊕ Golden Plough Inn

The Golden Plough Inn is located in an area known as Peddler's Village, 42 acres of winding brick walkways, colorful gardens and specialty shops. The inn's 66 guest units are located throughout the village. Each of the rooms and suites are appointed with elegant fabrics and wall coverings, and many are equipped with gas fireplaces and large whirlpool baths. The village also features eight fine restaurants.

66 Rooms • Price range: $115-340
SR 202 & Street Rd, Lahaska, PA 18931
☎ **(215) 794-4004**

Lampeter
Australian Walkabout Inn B&B

This authentic Australian-style B&B is situated on an acre of landscaped property in the heart of the Amish countryside. English gardens, a water-lily pool and a wraparound porch work together to give this restored Mennonite home a special charm. Jacuzzis and fireplaces can be found in some of the rooms. Luxury Anniversary and Honeymoon Suites are available and guest are invited to a full, candlelight breakfast.

5 Rooms • Price range: $99-229
837 Village Rd, Lampeter, PA 17537
☎ **(717) 464-0707**

Lampeter
The Manor Bed & Breakfast

The Manor is a cozy, period farmhouse set in Pennsylvania Dutch country and is close to many shops and restaurants. This B&B offers wonderful country views, a beautiful outdoor pool and a variety of lawn games.

6 Rooms • Price range: $89-99
830 Village Rd, Lampeter, PA 17537
☎ **(717) 464-9564**

Lancaster
Gardens of Eden Bed & Breakfast

This graciously appointed Victorian house sits on a three-and-a-half-acre site overlooking the Conestoga River. The terraced gardens are filled with perennials and a remarkable variety of wildflowers. Trails for hiking and spotting wildlife meander through the surrounding grounds. Summer activities include canoeing, rowboating and fishing on the river, as well as garden tours and biking along routes that pass by the house.

4 Rooms • Price range: $90-150
1894 Eden Rd, Lancaster, PA 17601
☎ **(717) 393-5179**

Lancaster
The King's Cottage

With its red-tile roof and stucco walls, this Spanish mission-style mansion holds its own in the middle of Amish country. The elegant interior includes stained-glass windows, a sweeping staircase, airy porches and crystal chandeliers. The inn is a delightful mix of 18th-century reproductions and antiques, hardwood floors and Oriental rugs. The Carriage House at the back of the main inn, features a fireplace and Jacuzzi for two.

8 Rooms • Price range: $105-220
1049 E King St, Lancaster, PA 17602
☎ **(717) 397-1017**

Lancaster
O'Flaherty's Dingeldein House Bed & Breakfast

A Dutch-Colonial-style home located in Lancaster County, O'Flaherty's Dingeldein House is an inviting stopover. Constructed in 1910, portions have since been added, making it spacious and comfortable. Rooms are traditionally appointed, most of them with private baths and all with air-conditioning. Guests are invited to enjoy the wide porch, the pretty gardens and the various common areas with fireplaces.

6 Rooms • Price range: $95-115
1105 E King St, Lancaster, PA 17602
☎ **(717) 293-1723**

Landenberg
Cornerstone Inn Bed & Breakfast

The original Cornerstone house was built in the early 1700s, while the larger version of the building that stands today was completed in 1820. The facade is constructed from "plum pudding" fieldstone, a vari-colored stone from a nearby quarry. The guestrooms are elegantly furnished with 18th- and 19th-century antiques. The inn also includes cottages converted from outbuildings, some of which are equipped with fireplaces.

16 Rooms • Price range: $100-250
300 Buttonwood Rd, Landenberg, PA 19350
☎ **(610) 274-2143**

Lebanon
⑭ *Inn 422*

Originally built in the early 1800s, this charming country inn was reconstructed in the 1880s with its current Victorian appearance. The grounds are beautifully landscaped with a terraced garden, flagstone patio, fountains and gazebos. The large guestrooms are elegantly furnished with a mix of antiques and period reproductions, while the inn's three dining rooms offer fine dining based on the best of local seasonal produce.

5 Rooms • Price range: $95-175
1800 W Cumberland St, Lebanon, PA 17042
☎ **(717) 274-3651**

Lehighton
Sweet Reflections B&B

Originally part of a Mahoning Valley farm, this brick home features high ceilings, and original wood floors. The proprietors promise guests a visit as comforting as "Thanksgiving at Grandma's house," and offer a hot country-style breakfast.

4 Rooms • Price: $85
574 Oak Grove Dr, Lehighton, PA 18235
☎ **(570) 386-5406**

Leola
Leola Village Inn & Suites

Surrounded by lush farmlands, Leola Village offers guests traditional comforts with some luxurious modern amenities. Each room is tastefully decorated with comforters, genuine Amish quilts and period furnishings. In addition to the guest accommodations, Leola Village offers delightful shops, fine restaurants and services. A continental breakfast is served in the converted tobacco barn which features a working fireplace.

30 Rooms • Price range: $129.95-179.95
38 Deborah Dr, Leola, PA 17540
☎ **(717) 656-7002**

Ligonier
⑭ *Lady of the Lake Bed & Breakfast*

A delightful 60-acre retreat in the heart of the Ligonier Valley, Lady of the Lake lies right next door to Idlewild Park and Storybook Forest. In summer, an in-ground pool and a tennis court are available for guests to enjoy.

5 Rooms • Price range: $85-135
157 Rt 30 E, Ligonier, PA 15658
☎ **(724) 238-6955**

Ligonier
Campbell House B&B

This 100-year-old cottage is a peaceful retreat or a stopover while visiting the nearby Laurel Highlands. Each room is comfortably decorated and equipped with a private bath. Complimentary snacks and beverages are available for guests in the pantry.

4 Rooms • Price range: $80-155
305 E Main St, Ligonier, PA 15658
☎ **(724) 238-9812**

Linfield
Shearer Elegance Bed & Breakfast

Built in 1897, this salmon-stoned, Victorian is situated amid three acres of gardens. Master craftsmen originally constructed this 10,000-square-foot building, which was lovingly restored in the 1980s. The mansion's guestrooms all have private baths, and each is decorated in vintage style. The newly designed suite features a sitting room, two balconies, and a Jacuzzi.

7 Rooms • Price range: $90-140
1154 Main St, Linfield, PA 19468
☎ **(610) 495-7429**

Lititz
Alden House Bed & Breakfast

Located in the center of one of Lancaster County's most delightful little towns, this 1850 Victorian Colonial-style home has been restored to its original charm. The inn consists of two guestrooms and three spacious suites, all of which are beautifully decorated in period style, while featuring contemporary amenities. Guests are encouraged to explore historic Lititz with its many fascinating antique shops.

5 Rooms • Price range: $85-90
62 E Main St, Lititz, PA 17543
☎ **(717) 627-3363**

Lititz
Swiss Woods Bed & Breakfast

The open beams, natural woodwork and handcrafted furniture of this pleasant inn contribute to a warm yet airy atmosphere reminiscent of Switzerland. Rooms have private baths and open onto a patio or a balcony bright with petunias and begonias. Local outdoor activities include canoeing and fishing, or simply strolling by the nearby lake. The busy kitchen offers meals influenced by Swiss, German and Austrian cuisine.

7 Rooms • Price range: $99-175
500 Blantz Rd, Lititz, PA 17543
☎ **(717) 627-3358**

Lumberville
1740 House

This pre-Revolutionary War structure is filled with rustic charm. Guests are invited to relax in the sitting room around a large stone fireplace or enjoy the view of the Delaware River on the terrace or balcony adjoining each guestroom. The atmosphere and charm of the inn prompted Harpers Bazaar magazine to pick it as one of the 10 outstanding inns in the country! Nearby are historic sites, museums, and shops.

24 Rooms • Price range: $70-140
3690 River Rd, Lumberville, PA 18933
☎ **(215) 297-5661**

Manheim
Rose Manor Bed & Breakfast

It is herbs that figure large in this comfortable old-fashioned inn. In the names
of the rooms, in the food and outdoors in
the garden, herbs are abundant. All
rooms are tastefully furnished with beautiful fabrics and antiques. Rose Manor also features an
indoor swimming pool, a backyard patio and a
warming fireplace in the parlor. Guests are invited to afternoon teas served with baked goods.

5 Rooms • Price range: $60-120
124 S Linden St, Manheim, PA 17545
☎ **(717) 664-4932**

Mansfield
Crossroads Bed & Breakfast

This Georgian home offers guests a
spacious living room and sunporch on
which breakfast is served amid fresh
flowers and candlelight. Each guest

room is equipped with a large personal closet,
European duvet coverlets and quilts.

4 Rooms • Price range: $59-109
131 S Main St, Mansfield, PA 16933
☎ **(570) 662-7008**

Mechanicsburg
⊕ Ashcombe Mansion Bed & Breakfast

A beautifully restored Victorian Queen
Anne-style mansion, Ashcombe boasts
an expansive central hallway and large,
elegant formal rooms. Details, including
intricately patterned parquet floors and carved
ornamental woodwork, fill out each richly
appointed guestroom. The property is made up
of 23 acres of countryside, ideal for long, pleasant
walks. Wild ducks, geese and herons can be
found on the bordering pond.

6 Rooms • Price range: $120-180
1100 Grantham Rd, Mechanicsburg, PA 17055
☎ **(717) 766-6820**

Mercer
Mehard Manor Bed & Breakfast

Constructed in 1913, Mehard Manor
has been well preserved, providing
visitors a glimpse into the elegance of
an earlier period. This spacious inn is
richly embellished with wainscoting, molded
plaster ceilings, crown moldings and Doric
columns. Guestrooms are all located at the
corners of the building, creating a greater
sense of privacy, and each is furnished with
antiques and reproductions.

4 Rooms • Price range: $75-85
146 N Pitt St, Mercer, PA 16137
☎ **(724) 662-2489**

Milford
⊕ Cliff Park Inn & Golf Course

The Cliff Park Inn has been in the
Buchanan family for five generations
and the original character of this former
farmhouse has been maintained. The
inn has cozy parlors with working fireplaces.
Each of the 18 guestrooms has a private bath
and climate control; two are equipped with gas
fireplaces. In season, the inn serves three full
meals; breakfast may include the inn's trademark
cinnamon French toast.

18 Rooms • Price range: $90-175
155 Cliff Park Rd, Milford, PA 18337
☎ **(570) 296-6491**

Milford
🏩 *Black Walnut B&B Country Inn*

This century-old farmhouse is situated in the beautiful rolling hills of the Pocono Region, amid 160 acres of black walnut trees. The rooms feature double and queen-size beds, a private or semiprivate bathroom and antique furnishings.

12 Rooms • Price range: $85-130
179 Fire Tower Rd, Milford, PA 18337
☎ **(570) 296-6322**

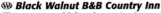

Montrose
🏩 *Ridge House*

This circa 1866 Eastlake Octagonal Victorian home, furnished in antiques, prides itself on making guests feel at home. House goodies include after- breakfast coffee served on the front porch, and teddy bears for visiting children.

4 Rooms • Price range: $35-55
6 Ridge St, Montrose, PA 18801
☎ **(570) 278-4933**

Mount Joy
Hillside Farm B&B

Aptly named for its perch atop a hill, this B&B offers guests magnificent rural views. The two-acre grounds are convenient to local attractions such as antique shops and traditional Amish farms, yet are secluded enough for a getaway retreat.

6 Rooms • Price range: $65-175
607 Eby Chiques Rd, Mount Joy, PA 17552
☎ **(717) 653-6697**

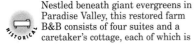

Mount Pocono
Farmhouse Bed & Breakfast

Nestled beneath giant evergreens in Paradise Valley, this restored farm B&B consists of four suites and a caretaker's cottage, each of which is equipped with a private bath. Suites also open onto a screened porch.

5 Rooms • Price range: $60-115
Grange Rd, Mount Pocono, PA 18344
☎ **(570) 839-0796**

Nazareth
Classic Victorian Bed & Breakfast

Each of the three intimate and inviting guestrooms here features period furnishings, lace curtains and Oriental carpets. This 1900 B&B provides a hearty breakfast in the dining room or, weather permitting, on the front veranda or the second-floor balcony. Meals are enhanced by fine china, linens and flatware. On request, breakfast is available in a basket that is left outside the door of your guestroom.

3 Rooms • Price range: $90-115
35 N New St, Nazareth, PA 18064
☎ **(610) 759-8276**

New Berlin
🏩 *The Inn at New Berlin*

Innkeepers Nancy and John Showers have transformed this turn-of-the-20th-century structure into a modern inn while keeping the charm of the original Victorian home intact. Spacious rooms with high ceilings, exquisitely carved woodwork and comfortable nooks can be found throughout. The inn provides additional accommodation in two nearby buildings. Business travelers will appreciate the data ports and the inn's fax service.

9 Rooms • Price range: $99-179
321 Market St, New Berlin, PA 17855-0390
☎ **(570) 966-0321**

New Castle
The Jacqueline House Bed & Breakfast

Although it was built in 1992, this charming B&B actually reflects an era from days past. Period architecture from estates throughout the Northeast was used as inspiration. Decorated in appealing Victorian and Amish country decor, each guest unit is also equipped with contemporary amenities. Guests are invited to a full breakfast and are welcomed to use the in-ground pool and spacious wraparound porch.

6 Rooms • Price: $90
Mercer-New Castle Rd, New Castle, PA 16105
☎ **(724) 946-8382**

New Cumberland
Farm Fortune Bed & Breakfast

This Colonial-style B&B is a preserved 1700s limestone farmhouse nestled on wooded, landscaped grounds, overlooking Yellow Breeches Creek. With large open fireplaces and wooden floors, the kitchen and sitting rooms maintain the feel of the 1700s. The guestrooms, each of which is decorated differently, are equipped with modern amenities, yet still have an old-fashioned charm. A full breakfast is served in the dining room.

5 Rooms • Price range: $75-95
204 Limekiln Rd, New Cumberland, PA 17070
☎ **(717) 774-2683**

New Hope
⊕ *The Mansion Inn*

Bucks County's "Grand Old Lady" has been restored to its original standing; the 1865 manor home continues to represent a fine example of Baroque-style architecture of the Second French Empire. Located right in the heart of New Hope's Historic District, the inn is within a short walking distance of a number of attractions, including shops, galleries and the Bucks County Playhouse. The inn boasts spacious suites, each featuring a private bath. Some room come with a whirlpool and a fireplace. The garden gazebo is a favorite lounging spot during the warmer months.

9 Rooms • Price range: $195-285
9 S Main St, New Hope, PA 18938
☎ **(215) 862-1231**

New Hope
Aaron Burr House Inn & Conference Center

Part of the New Hope Historic District, the Aaron Burr House Inn is also eligible for the National Register of Historic Places. Built in 1873 and renovated in 1990, the inn features original Victorian-era high baseboards, carved moldings, paneled doors, high ceilings and tall arched windows. This visually stunning inn also boasts 2,000 square feet of Pennsylvania black-walnut floors throughout the central halls and staircases.

7 Rooms • Price range: $90-255
80 W Bridge St (SR 179), New Hope, PA 18938
☎ **(215) 862-2520**

New Hope
The Fox & Hound Bed & Breakfast of New Hope

On the banks of the Delaware River, this 1850s stone manor house offers a diverse array of activities. Guests are invited to explore the perennial gardens, relax on the outdoor patio or enjoy biking or hiking along the Delaware Canal. Shops and historic sights are located nearby in New Hope village. Eight guestrooms are available, some with a fireplace and a Jacuzzi. A continental breakfast is served in the dining room.

8 Rooms • Price range: $80-180
246 W Bridge St, New Hope, PA 18938
☎ **(215) 862-5082**

New Hope
Pineapple Hill Bed & Breakfast

This 1790 restored manor house rests on six acres of land and is situated between New Hope village and Washington Crossing Park. Outdoors, guests can enjoy the hand-tiled pool which is surrounded by the walls of a stone barn, or the beautifully maintained rose garden. Local antiques decorate each of the five guestrooms and three suites. All suites have a separate living room, and one also features a fireplace.

9 Rooms • Price range: $75-235
1324 River Rd, New Hope, PA 18938
☎ **(215) 862-1790**

New Hope
The Wedgwood Inn of New Hope

This inn's grounds were the site of a Revolutionary War encampment in December, 1776, just prior to George Washington's famous crossing of the Delaware River. Today the inn and its two acres of manicured grounds are more peaceful. The large attractive building features a veranda, a porte cochere and a gazebo. Guests will also appreciate the original art and Wedgwood pottery found throughout the inn.

18 Rooms • Price range: $85-260
111 W Bridge St (SR 179), New Hope, PA 18938
☎ **(215) 862-2570**

Newtown
The Brick Hotel

This circa 1764 inn was initially constructed in 1764 and enlarged in 1821 by Joseph Archambault, an officer and confidant of Napoleon Bonaparte. The property features a glass-enclosed veranda dining room, a brick patio and an exquisite perennial garden. Guest units are carefully restored in Victorian decor with four-poster and canopy beds. The hotel is located near the small retail outlets of this vibrant small-town area.

15 Rooms • Price range: $90-150
1 E Washington Ave, Newtown, PA 18940
☎ **(215) 860-8313**

Newtown
Ye Olde Temperance House

Often the site of temperance gatherings, this pre-Revolutionary War inn was constructed in 1772. Guest units are decorated to reflect the ambience of the late 18th and early 19th centuries. Guests are invited to visit the inn's four distinctly decorated dining rooms, one of which features murals painted in the fashion of Edward Hicks, Newton's renowned Colonial folk artist. The inn is also famed for its Dixieland jazz brunches.

13 Rooms • Price range: $100-150
5 S State St, Newtown, PA 18940
☎ **(215) 860-0474**

Oakmont
The Inn at Oakmont

This B&B was built in 1994 to reflect the service and charm of an earlier, more gracious era. All eight guest rooms have private baths, televisions and telephones, while two of the rooms have fireplaces and whirlpool baths. One of the rooms also has its own porch which overlooks a beautiful flower garden in summer. Guests are greeted in the dining room each morning by the aroma of a deliciously prepared gourmet breakfast.

8 Rooms • Price range: $100-150
300 Rt 909, Oakmont, PA 15139
☎ **(412) 828-0410**

Orrtanna
Hickory Bridge Farm Bed & Breakfast

Dating all the way back to the 1700s, Hickory Bridge Farm remains a working farm operaation to this day. The rooms are decorated in farmhouse style with comfortable furnishings. Rustic cabins are available and are equipped with working fireplaces. A full breakfast is served daily in the farmhouse, and on weekends guests are invited to a real down-home country dinner served in the 150-year-old chestnut barn.

7 Rooms • Price range: $85-145
96 Hickory Bridge Rd, Orrtanna, PA 17353
☎ **(717) 642-5261**

Ottsville
Frankenfield Farm Bed & Breakfast

This 1879 stone and stuccoed brick dwelling is situated on 12 scenic acres of Bucks County countryside. Appointed with cozy upholstered furnishings, the common room offers a perfect place for conversation or just relaxing with a book. Guestrooms are decorated with period reproductions. A large guest unit is also available, and is located in a separate house. Outdoor activities include hiking, biking and horseback riding.

4 Rooms • Price range: $110-150
93 Frankenfield Rd, Ottsville, PA 18942
☎ **(610) 847-2771**

Paradise
The Beiler's Bed & Breakfast & Efficiencies

Lovely 19th-century Colonial-style brick home set off by immaculate landscaping.

8 Rooms • Price range: $65-95
3153 Lincoln Hwy E, Paradise, PA 17562
☎ **(717) 687-8612**

Philadelphia

🏾 *1011 Clinton*
Set on a quiet, tree-lined residential street, this 1836 Federal-style townhouse is set in a historic urban setting. Each guestroom is a large apartment elegantly decorated with a mix of contemporary upholstered furniture and historic reproductions. Each unit also includes a kitchen area and gas fireplace. A relaxing, flower-lined, private courtyard is available during the months when the weather is warm.

7 Rooms • Price range: $145-200
1011 Clinton St, Philadelphia, PA 19107
☎ **(215) 923-8144**

Philadelphia
Alexander Inn

Situated downtown, just a few blocks from the theater district and a variety of restaurants, this attractive 1890 seven-story brick structure blends the charm of a period B&B with modern-day comfort. The guestrooms feature Art Deco furnishings reminiscent of the cruise ships of the 1930s, and all are equipped with private baths and fluffy towels. A breakfast buffet offers guests fresh baked goods, cereals, fruits and juices.

48 Rooms • Price range: $99-149
Spruce at 12th St, Philadelphia, PA 19107
☎ **(215) 923-3535**

Philadelphia
Shippen Way Inn

This historic inn is part of a section of early Philadelphia row housing dating back to 1750. Each room is appointed in Colonial, Country or Southwestern style and ranges from tiny to master-size. The most popular room overlooks a backyard garden.

9 Rooms • Price range: $80-120
418 Bainbridge St, Philadelphia, PA 19147
☎ **(215) 627-7266**

Philadelphia
🏾 *The Thomas Bond House*

Dr. Thomas Bond helped found the first public hospital in the U.S. His house, located in the city's Independence National Historic Park, is a restored 1769 Georgian townhouse offering Federal-style accommodations.

12 Rooms • Price range: $95-175
129 S 2nd St, Philadelphia, PA 19106
☎ **(215) 923-8523**

Pipersville
The Victorian Peacock Bed & Breakfast

Located in scenic Bucks County and situated on five park-like acres, this inn offers an interesting mix of the contemporary with the charm of another era. The mansion is actually a modern recreation of a classic Victorian home. Its wraparound veranda and public areas are decorated in comfortable modern fashion, while the guestrooms are furnished with antiques, oversize beds, fine linens and plush comforters.

5 Rooms • Price range: $90-160
309 E Dark Hollow Rd, Pipersville, PA 18947
☎ **(215) 766-1356**

Pittsburgh
Appletree Bed & Breakfast

A beautifully restored Victorian home, this property is conveniently located close to a number of attractions.
Standing in the heart of Pittsburgh's historic Shadyside neighborhood, the B&B is less than two blocks away from Walnut Street, with its art galleries, craft shops and some of the best restaurants in the city. The 1884 inn boasts attractive guestrooms, fireplaces and original wood flooring.

8 Rooms • Price range: $130-180
703 S Negley Ave, Pittsburgh, PA 15232
☎ **(412) 661-0631**

Pittsburgh
⑭ *The Priory, A City Inn*

Built in 1884, this large B&B used to host Benedictine priests who came to Pittsburgh. Rooms are individually decorated with Victorian-style furnish-

ings and vary in size. Guests are invited to a continental breakfast, served each morning.

24 Rooms • Price range: $114-160
614 Pressley St, Pittsburgh, PA 15212
☎ **(412) 231-3338**

Point Pleasant
Tattersall Inn

Part of a quiet Delaware River village, this historic 18th-century manor home is conveniently placed for visiting restaurants and shops. Antique-filled rooms

and the formal dining room, with its marbled fireplace, welcome guests.

6 Rooms • Price range: $90-140
16 Cafferty Rd, Point Pleasant, PA 18950
☎ **(215) 297-8233**

Reading
Hunter House Bed & Breakfast

This 1847 Greek-Revival townhouse is furnished with a tasteful mix of antiques and contemporary furnishings. The B&B is part of the Callowhill

Historic District, which offers visitors an interesting range of architectural styles.

4 Rooms • Price range: $95-115
118 S Fifth St, Reading, PA 19602
☎ **(610) 374-6608**

Ronks
Candlelight Inn Bed & Breakfast

This B&B is located in the heart of Pennsylvania Dutch country and is surrounded by Amish farmland. The proprietors offer an elegant, relaxing ambience, featuring Victorian antiques, fresh flowers and a candlelight breakfast. Each guestroom includes a private bath, fluffy towels and bathrobes. In spite of its rural location, the Candlelight is just minutes away from shops, restaurants and theaters.

7 Rooms • Price range: $79-149
2574 Lincoln Hwy E, Ronks, PA 17572
☎ **(717) 299-6005**

Shickshinny
The Blue Heron Bed & Breakfast

This charming B&B is set on expansive grounds in a tranquil rural area.

6 Rooms • Price range: $60-90
RR 2, Box 2212, Shickshinny, PA 18655
☎ **(570) 864-3740**

Shippensburg
McLean House

This 18th-century home sits in Shippensburg's historic district and is a short walk from shopping, dining and the local university. Built as a two-family residence, the manor features two parlors, a large dining room, screened porches, a pool and an expansive lawn. All rooms are spacious and decorated with antiques and family heirlooms. Branch Creek, which borders the property, is home to trout and mallard ducks.

4 Rooms • Price range: $35-50
80 W King St, Shippensburg, PA 17257
☎ **(717) 530-1390**

Slippery Rock
Applebutter Inn

Set amid the rolling hills of Western Pennsylvania, the Applebutter Inn was built in 1844 on land granted to encourage westward settlement. The original six-room farmhouse was built of bricks formed and fired on the premises. Inside, guests will find restored woodwork, exposed brick fireplaces and original chestnut and poplar flooring. Each guestroom is individually decorated with antiques and treasures from the 1800s.

11 Rooms • Price range: $59-125
666 Centreville Pike, Slippery Rock, PA 16057
☎ **(724) 794-1844**

Somerset
The Inn at Georgian Place

Perched atop a hill in the heart of the Laurel Highlands, this mansion boasts exceptional views of the mountains and Lake Somerset. Built in 1915 by a local cattle and coal baron, the interior still features original oak paneling and an expansive marble foyer. Guestrooms reflect comfort and privacy and offer a variety of amenities. A gourmet breakfast is served every morning in the elegant dining area, where tea-time is also observed.

11 Rooms • Price range: $95-185
800 Georgian Place Dr, Somerset, PA 15501
☎ **(814) 443-1043**

Somerset
Quill Haven Country Inn

Set in the mountains of Pennsylvania, this pleasant 1918 home was built in the Arts and Crafts style and combines original decor with modern convenience. Antiques and fine woodwork are seamlessly blended with the new, such as the renovated private baths which complete every room. Nearby attractions include skiing and white-water rafting, as well as Frank Lloyd Wright's architectural masterpiece, Falling Water.

4 Rooms • Price range: $75-95
1519 N Center Ave, Somerset, PA 15501
☎ **(814) 443-4514**

South Sterling
The French Manor

A tree-lined lane bordered with ivy-covered stone walls lead to this mountain-top retreat. Fashioned after a stone chateau in the south of France, the inn features imported Spanish slate, which crowns the structure, and a Romanesque arch at its entrance. Breakfast and tea are served on the veranda with its view of the mountains, and guests are invited to sample the inn's fine French cuisine in the dining room.

15 Rooms • Price range: $135-275 per couple, per night
Rt 191 Huckleberry Rd, South Sterling, PA 18460
☎ (570) 676-3244

St. Marys
⑩ *Towne House Inn*

This converted 1899 Tudor-Revival landmark was once the home of affluent musicians. Its magnificent stairway is trimmed with quarter-sawn oak, and mahogany was used in the construction of the interior cabinets. The property also includes a restored example of a Queen Anne-style residence known as the Willows. Nearby, the Allegheny National Forest offers visitors a wide variety of outdoor activities.

59 Rooms • Price range: $49-125
138 Center St, St. Marys, PA 15857
☎ (814) 781-1556

St. Marys
⑩ *Old Charm Bed & Breakfast*

Set in a residential area, and made up of a main house and carriage house.

6 Rooms • Price range: $52
444 Brussells St, St. Marys, PA 15857
☎ (814) 834-9429

Starlight
The Inn at Starlight Lake

Surrounded by acres of forest and farmland meadows, this 1909 country resort features 26 rooms, including 10 cottage rooms, each decorated with early 20th-century furnishings. Full breakfasts and dinners are served in the dining room.

26 Rooms • Price range: $85-165
SR 4020, Starlight, PA 18461
☎ (570) 798-2519

Starrucca
The Nethercott Inn B&B

This Victorian home is furnished with antiques and country decor.

7 Rooms • Price range: $90-115
1 Main St, Starrucca, PA 18462
☎ (570) 727-2211

State College

⑭ *Carnegie House*

Overlooking a championship golf course on 170 acres of land that once belonged to Andrew Carnegie, the Carnegie House is fashioned after the country inns of Scotland. Complete with dormers and cupolas, this 22-guestroom B&B also has a library with cushioned window seats and a teak-decked veranda. All bedrooms are equipped with king-size or double beds, a sitting room, a spacious bathroom and such comfortable little touches as woolen throws and colorful pillows. Carnegie House also boasts the Thistle Bar, said to be the town's tiniest bar serving the biggest drinks!

22 Rooms • Price range: $150-195
100 Cricklewood Dr, State College, PA 16803
☎ **(814) 234-2424**

Strasburg
⑭ *Historic Strasburg Inn*

Located in the heart of Pennsylvania Dutch country, the Historic Strasburg Inn is completely surrounded by the tilled fields of Amish farmland. Guestrooms are accented with dried floral arrangements, handsome moldings, and inviting rocking chairs. The inn offers a variety of activities to keep visitors busy—swimming in the heated pool, horse and carriage rides, volleyball and even hot-air balloon rides.

101 Rooms • Price range: $139-159
One Historic Dr, Strasburg, PA 17579
☎ **(717) 687-7691**

Strasburg
⑭ *Strasburg Village Inn*

The Strasburg Village Inn, originally a tavern dating back to 1788, is an attractive, urban B&B graced with antiques and period artwork. A theater, shops and a variety of restaurants are all within walking distance.

10 Rooms • Price range: $94-159
1 W Main St, Centre Sq, Strasburg, PA 17579
☎ **(717) 687-0900**

Troy
Golden Oak Inn Bed & Breakfast

A strong Civil-War theme runs throughout this Queen Ann–style B&B, tucked away in the northern mountains of Pennsylvania. The proprietor's interest in Civil War history is reflected in the names of the guestrooms, such as The South and North Rooms, which are graced with portraits of Union and Confederate generals. The proprietor's interests also include gourmet cuisine, and he is a graduate of the Culinary Institute of America.

5 Rooms • Price range: $60-110
196 Canton St, Troy, PA 16947
☎ **(570) 297-4315**

Tunkhannock
Shadowbrook Inn & Resort
This inn features a challenging 18-hole course, as well as a mini-putt course. Other activities include swimming and racquetball. Rooms are large and ultra-modern, and the Dairy Bar Restaurant offers the inn's own homemade ice cream.

73 Rooms • Price range: $59-129
615 SR 6 E, Tunkhannock, PA 18657
☎ **(570) 836-2151**

Tunkhannock
Sharpe's House Bed & Breakfast
This turn-of-the-20th-century house is
set in the Endless Mountains area.

2 Rooms • Price range: $55-65
259 Bartron Rd, Tunkhannock, PA 18657
☎ **(570) 836-4900**

Union Deposit
Union Canal House Country Inn
All the guestrooms in this comfortably
furnished inn are equipped with baths.

7 Rooms • Price range: $75-195
107 S Hanover St, Union Deposit, PA 17033
☎ **(717) 566-0054**

Uniontown
Ⓐ Inne at Watson's Choice
This 1820 country farmhouse is an
example of traditional German rural
architecture. Guests are greeted by
attractive landscaping, a wraparound
porch and public areas decorated with country
charm. The inn is located near attractions such
as antique and crafts shops and fine restaurants.
Local outdoor activities include hiking, white-
water rafting and horseback riding. A hearty
country breakfast is served daily.

7 Rooms • Price range: $79-125
234 Balsinger Rd, Uniontown, PA 15401
☎ **(724) 437-4999**

Upper Black Eddy
The Bridgeton House on the Delaware
This lovely 1836 brick-and-stucco inn
stands by the scenic Delaware River,
protected under the Federal Wild and
Scenic designation. The inn was completely renovated in 1981 to reveal original wood
flooring and fireplaces. These fireplaces grace
the distinctive guestrooms, which are furnished
with canopy beds, country antiques and balconies
offering river views. The inn also features a
pleasant backyard patio and fountain.

11 Rooms • Price range: $99-279
1525 River Rd, Upper Black Eddy, PA 18972
☎ **(610) 982-5856**

Warminster
Ravenhead Inn
Set in a rural location on two landscaped
acres, this restored manor house was
originally constructed in 1849. The
high-ceilinged, individually themed
guestrooms are decorated with antiques and
collectibles, as are all of the common areas. A
hearty breakfast is served in the dining room or
al fresco on the private patio. The attractions of
Buck's County include a variety of antique dealers,
galleries and restaurants.

4 Rooms • Price range: $175-190
1170 Bristol Rd, Warminster, PA 18974
☎ **(215) 328-9567**

Washington Crossing
Inn to the Woods Bed & Breakfast

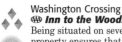

Being situated on seven acres of wooded property ensures that Inn to the Woods B&B will always live up to its name. Guests can relax in the sitting room by the stone fireplace, by the indoor garden and fish pond, or they can stroll the walking trails. Each guest unit has its own character and is equipped with modern amenities such as telephones, TVs and VCRs. The inn is closed on Monday and Tuesday.

4 Rooms • Price range: $85-300
150 Glenwood Dr, Washington Crossing, PA 18977
☎ **(215) 493-1974**

Wellsboro
Blue Moon Inn

Located in the Gas-Lit district, this grand William Morris Victorian was built in 1903 as a wedding present. Completely renovated and redecorated in 1998, the inn features faux-marble walls and raised paneling. Guests are invited to relax on the wide front porch with its wicker furniture or by the fireside in the Lodge Room. A delicious, full breakfast is served daily in the formal dining room.

4 Rooms • Price range: $79-149
129 Main St, Wellsboro, PA 16901
☎ **(570) 724-0942**

West Chester
Whitewing Farm Bed & Breakfast

This 1700's Pennsylvania farmhouse is surrounded by natural beauty. Greenhouses, flower gardens, a barn and stables along with a guest cottage by a pond are some of the attractions found on the 43-acre property. Breakfast specials may include sautéed apples on English muffins or pancakes with raspberry sauce. Other treats such as homemade breads or lemon sugar cookies are always available in the kitchen.

10 Rooms • Price range: $125-259
370 Valley Rd, RD 6, West Chester, PA 19382
☎ **(610) 388-2664**

Witmer
Folk Craft Center Bed & Breakfast

The Folk Craft Center B&B offers the elegance and simplicity of a 150-year-old farmhouse with the conveniences of contemporary amenities. Built entirely of old materials salvaged throughout Lancaster County, this half-timbered and brick building includes a museum with two floors of antiques and artifacts interpreting early Pennsylvania life. Guests can enjoy a full country breakfast served in the dining room or summer kitchen.

4 Rooms • Price range: $100-175
441 Mt Sidney Rd, Witmer, PA 17585
☎ **(717) 397-3676**

Wrightstown
Hollileif Bed & Breakfast

Surrounding this inn are antique shops, restaurants and historical attractions.

5 Rooms • Price range: $75-160
677 Durham Rd (SR 413),
Wrightstown, PA 18940
☎ **(215) 598-3100**

Zelienople
The Inn On Grandview

Built in the late 19th century and originally known as the Zimmerman Hotel, this inn's original style has been maintained with such charming period amenities as pedestal sinks, claw-foot tubs and exposed beams. Some rooms also feature gas-log fireplaces and private balconies. Rocking chairs on the front porch invite guests to relax, while the back porch is a popular spot for breakfast in warm weather.

4 Rooms • Price range: $85-115
310 E Grandview Ave, Zelienople, PA 16063
☎ **(724) 452-0469**

Notes:

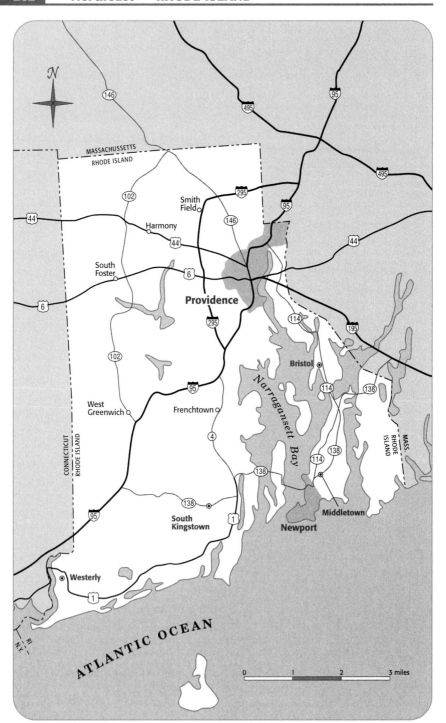

Bristol
Bradford-Dimond-Norris House Bed & Breakfast

 In 1778 the original house was burnt down during a British raid. It was then rebuilt in 1792. Subsequent owners and additions have made the house what it is today—a majestic, multi-tiered Federal-style building , which has been dubbed the "wedding cake house." Each of the guestrooms has a modern bathroom and individually controlled air-conditioning. They can also be opened up to accommodate a third guest.

4 Rooms • Price range: $95-120
474 Hope St, Bristol, RI 02809
☎ (401) 253-6338

Bristol
Rockwell House Inn

 This 1809 home is a veritable catalogue of architectural styles, exhibiting Federal, Georgian, Greek Revival, Italianate and Victorian features! The interior boasts impressively high ceilings, three fireplaces and spectacular stenciling work. The breakfast room serves up entrées such as Dutch puffed pancakes and French toast, while other niceties include afternoon tea, evening sherry and a nightly turn-down service.

4 Rooms • Price range: $110-145
610 Hope St, Bristol, RI 02809-1945
☎ (401) 253-0040

Bristol
William's Grant Inn

 This beautiful, five-bay Federal-style home is located on a quiet, tree-lined street in a residential neighborhood. The guestrooms are charming and well-appointed, but the real star here is breakfast, featuring entrées such as a fresh spinach and mushroom omelet. Guests are invited to work off breakfast by taking a walk to the nearby waterfront, with its 30-mile bike trail, or to visit downtown Bristol's antique shops.

5 Rooms • Price range: $95-110
154 High St, Bristol, RI 02809
☎ (401) 253-4222

Middletown
Polly's Place
Cape-style home situated in a quiet, residential area. Nicely landscaped.

4 Rooms • Price range: $60-150
349 Valley Rd, Middletown, RI 02842
☎ (401) 847-2160

Newport

⊕ *Vanderbilt Hall*
This mansion-style hotel is situated in the historic Hill District just off the harbor walkway. A curved split staircase hints at a more upper-crust and genteel past, when the front mezzanine opened onto a ballroom and a theater. Alfred Vanderbilt donated the 1909 building to the town and for years it functioned as a YMCA. A muraled subterranean pool serves as a reminder of this period of its past. Restoration has made the most of the grand house; the owners have furnished each guestroom differently but always with elegance. A roof deck offers views of sunsets and of the city.

50 Rooms • Price range: $195-795
41 Mary St, Newport, RI 02840
☎ **(401) 846-6200**

Newport

⊕ *Beechtree Inn*
This Victorian inn, built in 1887, has recently been renovated and enlarged, offering spacious rooms, each with private baths. Many of the rooms also include working fireplaces, Jacuzzis and even sun decks. Breakfast is termed "the biggest in Newport," but in-house treats don't stop there. Guests are offered a bowl of local clam chowder on Friday evenings and, in the afternoons, are invited to have tea or a glass of sherry.

8 Rooms • Price range: $165-295
34 Rhode Island Ave, Newport, RI 02840
☎ **(401) 847-9794**

Newport

The Clarkeston
Dated at circa 1705, The Clarkeston is listed on the National Register of Historic Places as one of the oldest inns in Newport. Intact are the original wide board wooden floors, and a decor of period furnishings. The guestrooms themselves are a lesson in Newport history as each has been decorated around one of the town's most famous or infamous characters. Rooms also include such amenities as fireplaces and Jacuzzis.

9 Rooms • Price range: $105-245
28 Clarke St, Newport, RI 02840
☎ **(401) 848-5300**

Newport

Cleveland House Inn
This inn's motto "offering today's amenities with yesterday's style" is borne out by rooms that are furnished with canopy, sleigh or four poster beds but which are also equipped with a variety of modern amenities such as Jacuzzis.

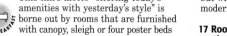

17 Rooms • Price range: $85-265
27 Clarke St, Newport, RI 02840
☎ **(401) 849-7397**

Newport
La Farge Perry House

The La Farge Perry House is an elegantly restored oasis of calm located in Newport's posh residential area known as the Hill. The downtown area and waterfront are within easy walking distance, but the Hill is far enough away to provide a restful atmosphere and retreat from the bustle of tourist throngs. The inn offers gourmet breakfasts, Jacuzzis and working fireplaces, but is especially renowned for its tranquil gardens.

5 Rooms • Price range: $195-350
24 Kay St, Newport, RI 02840
☎ **(401) 847-2223**

Newport
The Francis Malbone House Inn

This meticulously restored mansion is both comfortable and charming. Built in 1760, its Colonial heritage is reflected in the magnificent height of the ceilings and the size of its rooms. The common sitting rooms have wood-burning stoves. All guestrooms are exquisitely decorated, the most luxurious of them is the Counting House; 33 feet long, it includes a double whirlpool tub, a king-size bed and a spacious sitting area.

20 Rooms • Price range: $275-395
392 Thames St, Newport, RI 02840
☎ **(401) 846-0392**

Newport
🏵 *Hydrangea House Inn*

This charming inn was built in 1876 and is decorated in antiques and works of art. The name is taken from the local story that gardeners who worked on the Newport mansion grounds used to take home cuttings of the exotic plants they cared for— among them the hydrangea, which, as a result, now blooms all over Newport. The inn boasts its own hydrangea garden, onto which one of the rooms has its own private access.

7 Rooms • Price range: $145-300
16 Bellevue Ave, Newport, RI 02840
☎ **(401) 846-4435**

Newport
The Melville House

Built in 1750, this home is situated on a quiet street lit by gas lamps and lined by many historic properties. Although Newport is often known for the splendid summer homes of America's "royalty," this inn remains dedicated to the simpler style of the Colonial era. Some rooms have private baths; one suite has a fireplace. The inn offers tea and sherry in the afternoon. Nearby attractions include the Brick Market and harbor front.

7 Rooms • Price range: $145-175
39 Clarke St, Newport, RI 02840
☎ **(401) 847-0640**

Newport
The Old Beach Inn

Not far from this gracious inn are some of Newport's most popular sites: the historic waterfront, the famed mansions and the scenic Cliff Walk. Built in 1879, this Victorian home was renovated and refurbished with many period pieces. Room decor varies from whimsical hand-painted furniture to pencil-post canopy beds. The courtyard is beautifully landscaped making it the perfect place to relax over breakfast in warm weather.

9 Rooms • Price range: $135-275
19 Old Beach Rd, Newport, RI 02840
☎ **(401) 849-3479**

Newport
Sarah Kendall House B&B

This stately three-story Victorian home, built in 1871, is listed on the National Register of Historic Places and faces Newport Harbor. Open year-round, the green and beige inn is a popular honeymoon retreat and is just a five-minute walk from both downtown Newport and the historic district. Guestrooms here are air-conditioned, have color televisions and feature private baths. Guests are provided with off-street parking.

5 Rooms • Price range: $145-225
47 Washington St, Newport, RI 02840
☎ **(401) 846-7976**

Newport
⚫⚫ Stella Maris Inn

Built in 1853 from brownstone imported from Connecticut, this inn was first a year-around home, then a summer home and finally a convent before opening its doors as an inn in 1990. Located a few blocks from Newport's theater, shopping and restaurants, the inn's guestrooms are all tastefully furnished. Some have ocean views and working fireplaces. Stella Maris is ideal for weddings, conferences or romantic weekend getaways.

9 Rooms • Price range: $140-225
91 Washington St, Newport, RI 02840
☎ **(401) 849-2862**

Newport
Brinley Victorian Inn

Set on a quiet street, the inn is filled with Victorian wallpaper and early 20th-century antiques. The suites have fireplaces. Guests can read on the porch swing, sunbathe in the courtyard or visit the shops of Newport.

16 Rooms • Price range: $129-229
23 Brinley St, Newport, RI 02840
☎ **(401) 849-7645**

Newport
⚫⚫ The Burbank Rose

This historic 1850 inn is conveniently located close to the waterfront area.

5 Rooms • Price range: $99-199
111 Memorial Blvd W, Newport, RI 02840
☎ **(401) 849-9457**

Newport
James B. Finch House Inn
Built in 1866 in the Renaissance style, this inn is a Champlin Mason creation.

6 Rooms • Price range: $125-250
102 Touro St, Newport, RI 02840
☎ **(401) 848-9700**

Newport
Pilgrim House Inn
This inn commands a spectacular harbor view, especially from the rooftop patio, where guests can enjoy peace and solitude. All the rooms are decorated

with period furniture and are equipped with private baths. Parking is available for a fee.

11 Rooms • Price range: $100-205
123 Spring St, Newport, RI 02840
☎ **(401) 846-0040**

Newport
Spring Street Inn
This 1858 Empire Victorian offers cozy, comfortable units, including one large suite on the top floor with a private deck overlooking the harbor. Antique

historical prints hang from the walls in the public areas.

7 Rooms • Price range: $150-279
353 Spring St, Newport, RI 02840
☎ **(401) 847-4767**

Providence
State House Inn
This beautifully restored 100-year-old Colonial-Revival inn stands in a quiet residential neighborhood conveniently located near the State Capitol. Guestrooms are decorated in both Colonial and Shaker style. All have private baths, and some of them are equipped with canopy beds and working fireplaces. The inn has several inviting common areas including a small library and a cheerful breakfast room.

10 Rooms • Price range: $89-169
43 Jewett St, Providence, RI 02908
☎ **(401) 351-6111**

Providence
What Cheer B&B
This attractive B&B is a restored Victorian house, located in an historic section of the city that celebrates Providence's past. Each guest unit

is a two-room suite consisting of a separate sitting area and a bedroom.

5 Rooms • Price range: $129-229
73 Holden St, Providence, RI 02908
☎ **(401) 351-6111**

South Kingstown
The Kings' Rose Bed & Breakfast Inn
Guests at this 1930s Colonial-style Williamsburg house are minutes from state and town beaches, fishing, golf, antique shopping, summer theater and a variety of restaurants. Set on two-and-a-half acres of lawn and lovely English gardens, the inn is a great spot to relax. Breakfast includes fresh fruit, home-baked muffins and a range of choices from the grill; if guests make prior arrangements, they may ask friends to breakfast.

5 Rooms • Price range: $90-130
1747 Mooresfield Rd,
South Kingstown, RI 02879
☎ **(401) 783-5222**

Wakefield
Brookside Manor

This historic Colonial home dating to the late 17th century has been carefully restored. Named for the small stream that runs through the property, the inn includes eight acres of landscaped gardens and brick and stone terraces. The uniquely decorated guest accommodations have been given names such as the Ottoman Suite and the French Toile Salon in keeping with their international decor.

5 Rooms • Price range: $195-250
380B Post Rd, Wakefield, RI 02879
☎ **(401) 788-3527**

Westerly
The Villa Bed & Breakfast

This inn has the feel of a luxurious Mediterranean villa retreat. Each of the seven rooms is decorated with original art and colorful linens. The European-style courtyard has an in-ground swimming pool with a floating fountain, a hot tub and inviting lounge chairs. The inn also includes two luxurious suites, one with a Jacuzzi under a skylight. If guests ever wish to leave, the ocean and miles of white-sand beaches are only minutes away.

6 Rooms • Price range: $165-245
190 Shore Rd, Westerly, RI 02891
☎ **(401) 596-1054**

Westerly
Shelter Harbor Inn

This inn, which is located a short distance from historic Watch Hill, was converted from a 1911 farmhouse and its outbuildings. Three of the units in the main house have balconies, several have fireplaces and second-floor or rooftop sun decks.

24 Rooms • Price range: $88-162
10 Wagner Rd, Westerly, RI 02891
☎ **(401) 322-8883**

Notes:

Notes:

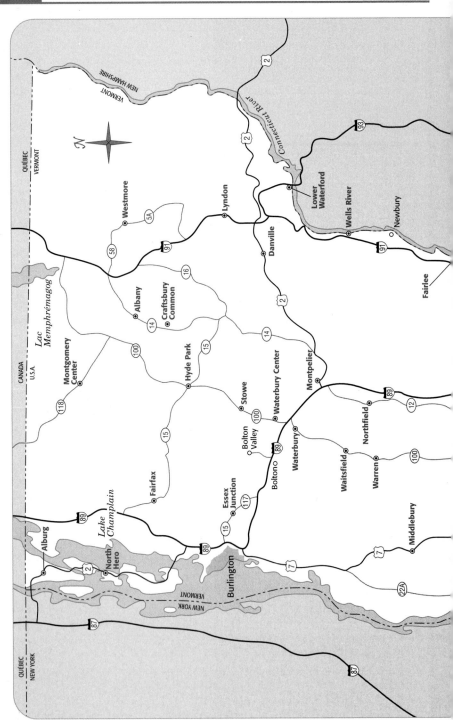

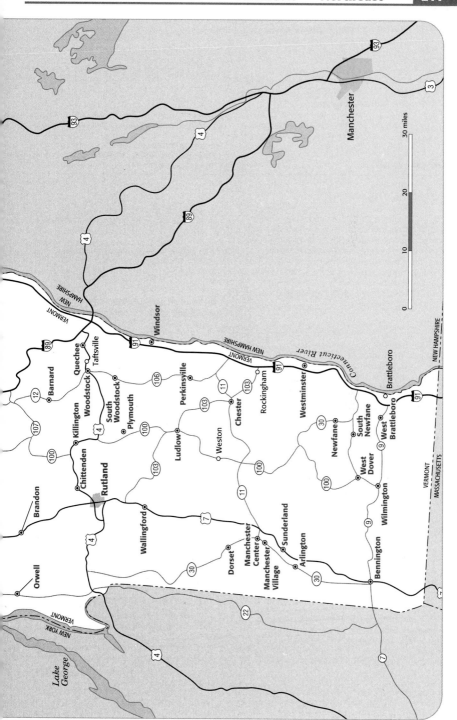

Albany

The Village House Inn of Albany
Perfect for families, this restored Victorian-style home has cozy rooms.

8 Rooms • Price range: $75-85
Rt 14, Albany, VT 05820
☎ (802) 755-6722

Alburg

The Ransom Bay Inn
This large stone house began its life as an inn and tavern 200 years ago, and the tradition of hospitality continues today. The guestrooms are spacious and tastefully decorated. The common rooms are warmed by fireplaces and a wood-burning stove.

4 Rooms • Price range: $60-75
4 Center Bay Rd, Alburg, VT 05440
☎ (802) 796-3399

Arlington

The Arlington Inn
This 1848 Greek-Revival mansion houses a country inn and a large dining room. Additional annexes located next door are known as the Carriage House, the Old Parsonage, and the Deming House. The inn is rich with local history, antiques and spacious common areas. Each morning, a full country breakfast is served in the solarium, while the dining room enjoys an international reputation for fine cuisine.

22 Rooms • Price range: $100-265
3904 Historic SR 7A, Arlington, VT 05250
☎ (802) 375-6532

Barnard

The Maple Leaf Inn
Tucked into a village of white-steepled churches and mountain views, this inn is a delightful getaway. The newly built Victorian-style farmhouse is set on 16 acres of land covered with maple and birch trees and displays features such as gables, gingerbread trim and a wraparound porch with a gazebo. Spacious guestrooms include sitting rooms, fireplaces and luxurious bathrooms with whirlpool tubs. Badminton and croquet can be played on the grounds. The area offers skiing and golf, craft shops and covered bridges. Home-baking makes breakfast a treat; dinners can be arranged on request.

7 Rooms • Price range: $120-230
Rt 12, Barnard, VT 05031
☎ (802) 234-5342

Bennington

Alexandra Bed & Breakfast Inn
This 1859 farmhouse offers an elegant, understated respite for business travelers and vacationers alike. Orchards and farmland provide a countryscape just five minutes from the business district, shops and historic Old Bennington. Bright rooms are comfortably appointed with four-poster beds and modern baths. The area is rich in pre-Revolutionary War history and summer brings theater, golf and antique auto shows.

12 Rooms • Price range: $75-150
916 Orchard Rd (SR 7A), Bennington, VT 05201
☎ (802) 442-5619

Bolton Valley
The Black Bear Inn
With a panoramic view of the Green Mountains and 6,000 acres of surrounding forest to explore, this mountaintop inn is truly a country retreat. Almost 50 downhill ski trails and 60 miles of cross-country ski trails are directly accessible from the inn. Rooms are comfortably adorned with patchwork quilts, Vermont stoves or fireplaces and private baths. Guests may enjoy the heated pool and the outdoor hot tubs—as well as the fine dining.

24 Rooms • Price range: $70-160
4010 Bolton Access Rd, Bolton Valley, VT 05477
☎ **(802) 434-2126**

Brandon
The Lilac Inn
With its five-arched facade and grand proportions, this Greek-Revival mansion is an elegant place for a romantic weekend or a wedding. The inn boasts a ballroom, library, tavern, dining room and backyard gazebo along with comfortable, well-appointed rooms. A spacious Bridal Suite is also available. Cultural events are held at the inn, including a music series showcasing chamber ensembles and full orchestras.

9 Rooms • Price range: $90-275
53 Park St, Brandon, VT 05733
☎ **(802) 247-5463**

Chester
The Inn at Cranberry Farm
This newly built post-and-beam house is located on 60 acres of pastoral landscape overlooking the Williams River. All guestrooms have private baths, and large wood-frame windows, and the inn's Great Room is furnished with thick, luxurious sofas grouped around a fireplace. The inn also offers art classes at its own craft center, and each morning a Vermont-style breakfast readies guests for nearby outdoor activities.

11 Rooms • Price range: $120-190
61 Williams River Rd, Chester, VT 05143
☎ **(802) 463-1339**

Chester
The Stone Hearth Inn
The attached barn of this comfortable brick farmhouse has been converted into a large common room with a fieldstone fireplace as well as tables for table tennis and pool. The inn boasts an interesting German nutcracker collection.

10 Rooms • Price range: $119-149
698 Rt 11 W, Chester, VT 05143
☎ **(802) 875-2525**

Chittenden
Mountain Top Inn
Situated on nearly 1,000 acres, this great Vermont resort offers an expansive trail system for hiking and cross-county skiing. Additional activities may include horseback riding, bicycling, trapshooting and horse-drawn sleigh rides in the winter months. Guestrooms have a cozy, rustic flair and are located in either the main inn or the surrounding cottages or chalets. The inn also offers superb dining.

45 Rooms • Price range: $156-268
195 Mountain Top Rd, Chittenden, VT 05737
☎ **(802) 483-2311**

Craftsbury Common
The Inn on the Common

Three meticulously restored classic Colonial buildings make up this handsome inn. Set in the tranquil village of Craftsbury, the inn is an ideal retreat for lovers of the outdoors. In addition to the attractions of rural Vermont, the 10-acre property features a tennis court and a landscaped pool. Rooms are tastefully furnished with antiques and all have private baths. The inn also offers excellent meals and an extensive wine list.

16 Rooms • Price range: $255-310
1162 N Craftsbury Rd, Craftsbury Common, VT 05827
☎ **(802) 586-9619**

Danville
Danville Inn

The Danville Inn is a Victorian-style home with modest rooms.

4 Rooms • Price range: $60-70
86 US 2 W, Danville, VT 05828
☎ **(802) 684-3484**

Dorset
Inn at West View Farm

Located in the charming village of Dorset, this inn has welcomed guests since the turn of the 20th century. A restored farmhouse, the inn offers full-service amenities in a pastoral setting. Each of the guestrooms has a comfortable sitting area, while beds are covered in luxurious comforters. The inn's full country breakfast fortifies guests for the day's activities, and at day's end complimentary wine and cheese are served.

10 Rooms • Price range: $140-225
2928 Rt 30, Dorset, VT 05251-9633
☎ **(802) 867-5715**

Essex Junction
The Inn At Essex

The stately Colonial-style buildings that make up this inn provide visitors with a panoramic view of the Adirondacks and the Green Mountains. Guests also have easy access to the shores of historic Lake Champlain, which is just a few minutes away. All the inn's guestrooms are distinctively decorated. Some have whirlpool tubs, others have fireplaces. For dining, guests can choose from the inn's Butler Restaurant or the Tavern Restaurant and Lounge, both of which offer the best in American fare and traditional cuisine. Nearby activities include skiing and golfing.

121 Rooms • Price range: $175-209
70 Essex Way, Essex Junction, VT 05452
☎ **(802) 878-1100**

Fairfax
The Inn at Buck Hollow Farm

This restored 1790s carriage house is set on 400 acres of rolling meadows and woodlands. The inn is truly a four-season attraction, but never so much as in the fall when autumn paints the surroundings. All four guestrooms are furnished with queen-size canopy beds, while the inn's terraced grounds feature a whirlpool tub and a swimming pool. A full breakfast is served in the sunroom.

4 Rooms • Price range: $53-83
2150 Buck Hollow Rd, Fairfax, VT 05454
☎ **(802) 849-2400**

Fairlee
Silver Maple Lodge & Cottages

This inn is made up of several knotty-pine cottages as well as a restored farmhouse. Most rooms have private baths and several cottages have kitch-

enettes and fireplaces. Hot-air ballooning is one of the many activities in the area.

15 Rooms • Price range: $55-89
520 US 5 S, Fairlee, VT 05045
☎ **(802) 333-4326**

Hyde Park
The Fitch Hill Inn

Situated on a high wooded hill overlooking the Green Mountains, this 18th-century Colonial house offers a relaxing retreat. The inn boasts maple floors, 12-foot-high ceilings, flower gardens and two comfortable porches. It also houses a Civil-War library and photograph collection. Rooms are pleasantly appointed, each with a private bath. Breakfasts are gourmet and five-course dinners are available by reservation.

6 Rooms • Price range: $139-159
258 Fitch Hill Rd, Hyde Park, VT 05655
☎ **(802) 888-3834**

Killington
Birch Ridge Inn

This inn is located high on a ridge dotted with silver and white birch trees, and is distinguished by its twin A-frame buildings. All of the guestrooms are equipped with private baths, while some feature working fireplaces and whirlpool tubs. One of the inn's main attractions is the Great Room with its fireplace constructed from slate cut at a local quarry. Guests are also invited to sample the inn's fusion-style cuisine.

10 Rooms • Price range: $145-200
37 Butler Rd, Killington, VT 05751
☎ **(802) 422-4293**

Killington
The Peak Chalet

This charming European-style B&B is located in the heart of Killington Ski Resort. Downhill and cross-country skiing, golf and theater are just minutes away. The guest living room of this modern inn features a stone fireplace and offers panoramic views of Killington and the Green Mountains. All rooms have a private bath. A fully equipped, one-bedroom condo is also available.

5 Rooms • Price range: $88-159
184 S View Path, Killington, VT 05751
☎ **(802) 422-4278**

Killington
Snowed Inn

In spite of the name, this inn is a welcomed retreat in any season. Tucked away in a quiet, woodland setting in the heart of the beautiful Killington mountains, it offers the beauty and activities of outdoor Vermont year-round. Guests gather in the lounge with its fireplace, or had for the games room or the exercise room, which has a weight machine, exercise bicycle and treadmill.

20 Rooms • Price range: $70-240
104 Miller Brook Rd, Killington, VT 05751
☎ **(802) 422-3407**

Killington
⚙ *The Vermont Inn*

This 1840 inn is situated on six acres in the Green Mountains. Several indoor common areas sport country-style decor, complete with original wood beams and fireplaces. The lodge is particularly handsome, with a wood stove and a view of the mountains. A sauna, a hot tub, a tennis court and a swimming pool are also available. A full country breakfast is served, featuring the inn's French toast and maple syrup.

18 Rooms • Price range: $80-215
69 US 4, Killington, VT 05751
☎ **(802) 775-0708**

Lower Waterford
⚙ *Rabbit Hill Inn*

Set on 15 acres in a tiny village overlooking the Connecticut River Valley, this New England inn was first opened in 1795 to traders and loggers. An annex was added in 1850 and today the two buildings house 21 delightfully furnished guestrooms. Skylights, vaulted ceilings, sun decks, fireplaces and whirlpools give these rooms added comfort. Large, attractively furnished common rooms and a pub have been set up for guests to enjoy. The inn also boasts a greenhouse and a garden. Breakfast features generous gourmet fare; tea and scones are served in the afternoon.

21 Rooms • Price range: $325-375
Lower Waterford Rd, Lower Waterford, VT 05848
☎ **(802) 748-5168**

Ludlow
⚙ *The Andrie Rose Inn*

This 1829 inn sits at the base of Okemo Mountain and is just one block from Ludlow Village. The elegant country house has nine guestrooms furnished with designer linens, down comforters and fluffy terry cloth towels. All rooms are equipped with private baths, while some feature skylights and whirlpool tubs. Additional suites are located in an adjacent guest house and in the recently renovated 1840 Greek-Revival property, Solitude. The full Vermont breakfast may include golden buttermilk waffles with Ben & Jerry's homemade Vermont ice cream.

20 Rooms • Price range: $140-320
13 Pleasant St, Ludlow, VT 05149
☎ **(802) 228-4846**

Lyndon
 Branch Brook Bed & Breakfast

Dating from the 1830s, this restored Federal-period home is set amid country surroundings near the Burke Mountain ski area. Rooms are comfortable and meals are cooked on an English-style wood cooker that guests are also invited to use. Honey and maple syrup are home-produced at Branch Brook. Landscaped grounds overlook a brook, while lakes, rivers, country roads and mountains are all easily accessible.

5 Rooms • Price range: $60-85
36 Branch Brook Ln, Lyndon, VT 05849
☎ **(802) 626-8316**

Manchester Center
 The Inn at Ormsby Hill

This inn, dating back to 1764, is a handsome Federal-style mansion and one of Ormsby's oldest structures. Today, it is one of the most highly acclaimed inns in the Northeast. Aside from luxurious rooms, gorgeous surroundings and sumptuous dining, the inn's secret to success is a strong attention to detail. Candlelight for the Jacuzzi, plenty of large, thick towels and wineglasses with corkscrews are some of the things that make this inn special. A multi-course breakfast is served in the conservatory, a land-locked "ship" with stern windows overlooking the garden and the mountains.

10 Rooms • Price range: $190-410
1842 Main St (Rt 7A), Manchester Center, VT 05255
☎ **(802) 362-1163**

Manchester Village
The Village Country Inn

This enchanting country inn can be found in the heart of the village of Manchester. A number of activities are easily accessible from the inn, including skiing and sleigh rides in the winter time. The inn offers a wide range of guestrooms, everything from luxury suites to large and mid-size rooms. Start the day with a full country breakfast, and end it with a four-course candlelight dinner in the romantic Rose Room.

32 Rooms • Price range: $119-295
3835 Main St, Manchester Village, VT 05254
☎ **(802) 362-1792**

Middlebury
 Swift House Inn

This inn is made up of three buildings: the Main House, the Victorian Gatehouse and the Carriage House. In total, 21 guestrooms of varying sizes are available, all of them featuring oversize four-poster beds. Some rooms also have a fireplace, a whirlpool tub and a private terrace. This 1812 Federal-style home, once the home of a former Vermont governor, also has several sitting rooms, a library, a sauna, a steam room and outdoor lawn games. Guests can fish in nearby Otter Creek or go hiking in the summer; in the winter, there is skiing.

21 Rooms • Price range: $110-245
25 Stewart Ln, Middlebury, VT 05753
☎ **(802) 388-9925**

Middlebury
 The Middlebury Inn

 For more than 170 years, this inn has offered lodging and fine dining to travelers. Three properties are ready to accommodate visitors. The Main House has rooms of different sizes, all with private baths. Guestrooms at The Contemporary Motel offer modern amenities such as hair dryers and direct-dial phones. The Porter House Mansion features a rare marble fireplace and a fine leaded-fan doorway.

75 Rooms • Price range: $76-225
14 Court Square, Middlebury, VT 05753
☎ **(802) 388-4961**

Montgomery Center
The Inn On Trout River

A trout stream runs behind this attractively restored Victorian home.

10 Rooms • Price range: $72-132
241 Main St, Montgomery Center, VT 05471
☎ **(802) 326-4391**

Montpelier
 The Inn at Montpelier

 Two stately historic buildings make up the Inn at Montpelier, both of which were built in the early 1800s. Classic Federal in design, these buildings feature Greek- and Colonial-Revival woodwork, 10 fireplaces, gracious front staircases and glass-fronted china cupboards. Each guestroom has a private bath, a television and fine antiques and reproductions. A continental breakfast is served daily.

19 Rooms • Price range: $114-177
147 Main St, Montpelier, VT 05602
☎ **(802) 223-2727**

Montpelier
Betsy's B&B

Two pleasant adjacent Victorian homes with attractive rooms in a quiet area.

12 Rooms • Price range: $70-100
74 E State St, Montpelier, VT 05602
☎ **(802) 229-0466**

Newfane
Four Columns Inn

Built in 1832, the Four Columns Inn is designed in the Greek-Revival style, giving it the look of a Southern mansion. Set on 150 wooded acres, this striking building faces one of New England's most photographed town greens. Guestrooms are beautifully furnished and offer both fireplaces and Jacuzzis as options. Chef Greg Parks, honored by the James Beard Foundation, has earned the inn's restaurant a Four-Diamond designation.

15 Rooms • Price range: $140-280
21 West St, Newfane, VT 05345
☎ **(802) 365-7713**

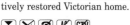

North Hero
North Hero House

This marvelous property consists of four historic buildings. The main house offers nine comfortable guestrooms, as well as a library, dining rooms and a pub. The other three buildings, which sit right on the shores of the lake, house the remainder of the 26 rooms. Guests are invited to swim in the lake, stretch out on the sandy beach, go boating or take part in a match of tennis or in a round of golf.

26 Rooms • Price range: $89-249
Rt 2, North Hero, VT 05474
☎ **(802) 372-4732**

Northfield
Northfield Inn

The Northfield Inn offers a variety of activities, including lawn games, hiking, tennis, golf, ice skating and skiing. Tucked away in Northfield's Green Mountains, the inn offers just as much in the way of comforts: period furnishings and interesting collections. Guestrooms have private baths and European feather bedding. There is also a fitness room and a library. A multi-course breakfast is served daily.

12 Rooms • Price range: $85-159
228 Highland Ave, Northfield, VT 05663
☎ **(802) 485-8558**

Orwell
Historic Brookside Farms

This 1789 farmhouse reflects a Neoclassic Greek-Revival style. Shimmering white Ionic columns at the front of the mansion foreshadow the grand interior decor. A working farm, the Brookside produces maple syrup and its 300 acres are home to many animals. An impressive 10,000-volume library is available inside, as well as nine antique-filled guestrooms. A country breakfast, afternoon tea and a five-course gourmet dinner are served daily.

6 Rooms • Price range: $75-175
183 Rt 22A, Orwell, VT 05760
☎ **(802) 948-2727**

Perkinsville
The Inn at Weathersfield

The country-style ambience of the Inn at Weathersfield is highlighted by such features as authentic wide-planked floors, exposed wooden beams, handmade quilts and an array of antique furnishings. Other attractions include the open hearth and beehive oven in the 202-year-old keeping room, the antique parlor with its resident ghosts, the Steinway grand piano in the dining room, and the games room with its Finnish sauna.

7 Rooms • Price range: $95-185
Rt 106, Perkinsville, VT 05151-0165
☎ **(802) 263-9217**

Plymouth

Salt Ash Inn

Conveniently located near some of Vermont's most popular ski hills, this 19th-century stagecoach stop makes an ideal home base for downhill skiers and other winter enthusiasts. Summer outdoor activities are also plentiful. The innkeepers maintain a very friendly country-style environment with a strong emphasis on fun. All but one guestroom has a private bath. An outdoor Jacuzzi holds up to eight. Pets are welcome.

18 Rooms • Price range: $98-130
4758 Rt 100A, Plymouth, VT 05056
☎ **(802) 672-3748**

Quechee
The Quechee Inn at Marshland Farm

Located off the beaten path near the banks of the Ottauquechee River where you can fish, hike and relax. The inviting taproom located off the lobby has exposed beams, comfortable sofas and grand piano. Each room is individually decorated.

24 Rooms • Price range: $100-210
1119 Quechee Main St, Quechee, VT 05059
☎ **(802) 295-3133**

Rutland
The Inn at Rutland

This Victorian mansion has been firmly planted on Main Street since 1889. Wonderfully preserved details include a grand oak staircase, leaded glass windows and molded plaster ceilings. Spacious guestrooms are set with antique bedsteads and furnishings. Morning meals are presented on fine china in the dining room, which features leather wainscoting. Year-round outdoor and cultural activities are easily accessible.

12 Rooms • Price range: $125-205
70 N Main St (US 7), Rutland, VT 05701
☎ **(802) 773-0575**

South Newfane
The Inn at South Newfane

Surrounded by 100 acres of woodlands, this turn-of-the-20th-century inn encourages guests to slow down and relax. From the rocking chairs on the grand front porch to the comfortably appointed bedrooms, everything is designed for comfort. Breakfast is prepared by a European-trained chef who just happens to be one of the innkeepers. A spring-fed pond for swimming is a summer treat.

6 Rooms • Price range: $85-130
369 Dover Rd, South Newfane, VT 05351
☎ **(802) 348-7191**

South Woodstock
Kedron Valley Inn

One of Vermont's oldest inns, the Kedron Valley has played many roles in its life, one of which was as a refuge for fugitive slaves during the 1860s. These days, the inn acts as a comfort spot; guestrooms feature canopy beds and fireplaces or wood stoves; some have private decks. The inn's cuisine ranks among the best in Vermont. In the summertime, guests can take advantage of the large, spring-fed swimming lake.

28 Rooms • Price range: $186-309
Rt 106, South Woodstock, VT 05071
☎ **(802) 457-1473**

Stowe
⊕ *1066 Ye Olde England Inne*

Ye Olde English Inne prides itself on catering to diverse needs. Guest accommodations range from cozy cottage-style to super-luxury suites, all of which have spacious bathrooms with whirlpool tubs. Some have private porches and spectacular mountain views. Various activities are close at hand, including biking, swimming, tennis and golf. As well, some of New England's finest downhill and cross-country skiing is easily accessible.

30 Rooms • Price range: $179-299
433 Mountain Rd, Stowe, VT 05672
☎ **(802) 253-7558**

Stowe
Brass Lantern Inn

The 200-year-old village of Stowe is the home of the Brass Lantern. This 1800 farmhouse boasts nine guestrooms furnished with handmade quilts and antiques. All rooms have private baths; some have fireplaces. A full country breakfast is served daily. Guests are invited to sit in front of the fireplace in the living room or, in good weather, out on the patio for wine, tea or coffee and dessert.

9 Rooms • Price range: $110-225
717 Maple St, Stowe, VT 05672
☎ **(802) 253-2229**

Stowe
Butternut Inn at Stowe

This inn boasts 18 guestrooms, each decorated with antique furniture. A variety of homemade goodies is available, including pumpkin pie, cinnamon raisin bread and cobblers. A mountain stream runs through the spacious grounds.

18 Rooms • Price range: $89-170
2309 Mountain Rd, Stowe, VT 05672
☎ **(802) 253-4277**

Stowe
⊕ *Edson Hill Manor*

Set amid 225 acres of forest and rolling hills, this restored manor offers a taste of country life. Relax around a large fireplace in the wood-paneled parlor. Dine in a setting with a breathtaking view of the mountains before retiring to a cozy country-style bedroom. Stables and a fishing pond are a short walk down a tree-lined lane. There's a swimming pool in summer, sleigh rides in winter.

25 Rooms • Price range: $90-250
1500 Edson Hill Rd, Stowe, VT 05672
☎ **(802) 253-7371**

Stowe
⊕ *Green Mountain Inn*

Built in1833, this historic inn has been meticulously restored to its original condition. Many of the decorative details, like wallpapers, drapes and furniture, are carefully reproductions. Tastefully decorated rooms and suites reflect the grace and charm of the era with the added convenience of modern amenities. The outdoor pool is heated year-round and a fully equipped health club offers massage services.

78 Rooms • Price range: $99-389
18 S Main St, Stowe, VT 05672
☎ **(802) 253-7301**

Stowe
Honeywood Inn
Charming Swiss chalet-style home with nice rooms and accommodating hosts.

10 Rooms • Price range: $99-169
4583 Mountain Rd, Stowe, VT 05672
☎ **(802) 253-4846**

Stowe
⊕ Andersen Lodge, An Austrian Inn
Austrian mountain lodge with large comfortable public areas and nicely decorated rooms of various sizes. A game room, sauna, Jacuzzi, heated pool

and tennis court are all on-site. The Austrian hosts have created a warm European ambience.

18 Rooms • Price range: $78-178
3430 Mountain Rd, Stowe, VT 05672
☎ **(802) 253-7336**

Stowe
⊕ Scandinavia Inn & Chalets
Each of the rustic chalet units has a barbecue and a picnic table.

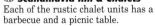

21 Rooms • Price range: $69-119
3576 Mountain Rd, Stowe, VT 05672
☎ **(802) 253-8555**

Stowe
Stowehof Inn
This is a rustic property on 30 acres of forested and landscaped grounds. Large cozy public areas with fireplace. Many units have either a balcony or patio and

magnificent mountain views. Some smaller units are quite modest.

50 Rooms • Price range: $150-275
434 Edson Hill Rd, Stowe, VT 05672
☎ **(802) 253-9722**

Sunderland
Hill Farm Inn
A complimentary jar of homemade jam welcomes guests to this pleasant inn.

15 Rooms • Price range: $95-185
458 Hill Farm Rd, Sunderland, VT 05250
☎ **(802) 375-2269**

Waitsfield
The Inn at Round Barn Farm
Mountains, meadows and ponds surround this establishment. The inn boasts a 60-foot indoor lap pool that extends into a greenhouse filled with bougainvillaea and hibiscus—and the rest of the inn is just as impressive. Rooms with Jacuzzis, fireplaces, steam showers and canopied beds offer every comfort. Guests can enjoy seasonal activities right on the inn's property.

12 Rooms • Price range: $155-290
1661 E Warren Rd, Waitsfield, VT 05673
☎ **(802) 496-2276**

Waitsfield
⊕ Tucker Hill Inn
A charming, newly renovated Colonial inn with attractively decorated guest rooms, two clay tennis courts and an outdoor pool. A few rooms have private balconies and one has a whirlpool and wood-burning fireplace. The landscaped lawns are surrounded by 14 acres of woods. The restaurant was also renovated to bring in the light and expose the view. Named Inn of the Month in Ski Magazine's February, 2000 edition.

16 Rooms • Price range: $79-199
65 Marble Hill Rd, Waitsfield, VT 05673
☎ **(802) 496-3983**

Waitsfield
1824 House Inn
This restored farmhouse with pleasant rooms is located on 22 wooded acres.

8 Rooms • Price range: $115-145
2150 Main St, Waitsfield, VT 05673
☎ **(802) 496-7555**

Wallingford
I. B. Munson House Bed & Breakfast Inn

Set in an historic New England village, this restored 1856 Italianate-Victorian home features large porches, working fireplaces and elegant rooms. Three covered porches are perfect spots to enjoy the gardens or a view of the mountains. The guestrooms feature fine antique furniture and comfortable beds. Three rooms have a fireplace and two have antique claw-foot tubs. A perfect romantic haven.

7 Rooms • Price range: $110-180
37 S Main St, Wallingford, VT 05773
☎ **(802) 446-2860**

Warren
⊕ *The Sugartree, A Country Inn*

Set in the Mad River Valley, The Sugartree is bordered by the Green Mountains on one side and farmlands on the other. Just half a mile from the Sugarbush ski area and minutes from Mad River Glen, the inn affords guests a wide variety of year-round recreational opportunities. All nine rooms are individually decorated with the innkeepers' crafts, handmade quilts and antiques; some have canopy beds.

9 Rooms • Price range: $115-175
2440 Sugarbush Access Rd, Warren, VT 05674
☎ **(802) 583-3211**

Waterbury
Thatcher Brook Inn
This is a gracious, renovated 1899 Victorian home with newer wings. Guestrooms are a very good size and are newly decorated with hardwood trim enhancements. Some rooms have their own working fireplace.

22 Rooms • Price range: $80-195
1017 Waterbury-Stowe Rd, Waterbury, VT 05676
☎ **(802) 244-5911**

Waterbury
Inn at Blush Hill
This restored 1790's stagecoach inn is in the heart of Vermont's recreational crossroads. All the rooms are cozy and the sunny breakfast room overlooks meadows and mountains. Package specials are available with lift tickets and dinner included.

5 Rooms • Price range: $110-150
784 Blush Hill Rd, Waterbury, VT 05676
☎ **(802) 244-7529**

Waterbury
⊕ *The Old Stagecoach Inn*
All rooms in this inn, originally a stagecoach stop, are furnished with antiques.

11 Rooms • Price range: $55-200
18 N Main St, Waterbury, VT 05676
☎ **(802) 244-5056**

Waterbury Center
🏵 *The Black Locust Inn*

Len, Nancy and Valerie, and Lady, their golden retriever, are the gracious hosts at this charmingly restored 1830s farmhouse. All guestrooms are cheerfully furnished and decorated with hand-crafted art. Country breakfasts are carefully prepared and diet-restricted selections are available. Len serves a choice of international wines during social hour. Wine-tastings and other catered events can be organized.

6 Rooms • Price range: $115-212
5088 Waterbury-Stowe Rd,
Waterbury Center, VT 05677
☎ **(802) 244-7490**

Wells River
The Whipple-Tree B&B

A long, meandering mountain road climbs up to this charming B&B with the breathtaking view of the White Mountains. The guestrooms are large and beautifully decorated, some with gas fireplaces. Much of the furniture was made by Vermont craftsmen and the finely worked wood shows a great attention to detail, as does the entire property. Activities for all seasons are close at hand for those who tire of relaxing.

6 Rooms • Price range: $140-190
487 Stevens Pl, Wells River, VT 05081
☎ **(802) 429-2076**

West Brattleboro
Meadowlark Inn Bed & Breakfast

High on a hill overlooking the rolling countryside stands this picture-perfect 1870 farmhouse in a storybook setting. Full breakfasts are served beside the dining room fireplace or in the library. It is best to inquire which of the inviting rooms have the desired amenities: a Jacuzzi, a fireplace, a refrigerator, a spectacular view. Relax on the screened-in porch while deer roam across the property to a chorus of frogs in the nearby pond.

7 Rooms • Price range: $95-150
13 Gibson Rd, West Brattleboro, VT 05303
☎ **(802) 257-4582**

West Dover
🏵 *Snow Goose Inn*

Nestled among maple, pine and birch trees, this grand country inn enjoys a commanding view of Deerfield Valley. Lovely guestrooms are individually decorated with antiques and feather beds with fine linens. Several have whirlpools, fireplaces and private decks. A full country breakfast is served each morning to B&B guests only. Guests are invited to enjoy drinks and hor d'oeuvres during the afternoon cocktail hour

13 Rooms • Price range: $105-300
259 Rt 100, West Dover, VT 05356
☎ **(802) 464-3984**

Westmore
🏵 *Willough Vale Inn on Lake Willoughby*

This is a modern country inn with attractive guestrooms.

12 Rooms • Price range: $119-235
793 Rt 5A, Westmore, VT 05860
☎ **(802) 525-4123**

Wilmington
Nutmeg Inn

The grounds of the Nutmeg Inn offer guests the opportunity to hike into the wilderness on one of the many trails found next to the inn. In the winter, guests will return to the inn to wonderful aromas: wood burning in the fireplace, tea on the stove and the innkeepers' delicious bread baking in the oven. Guestrooms are individually decorated and have private baths; most have a fireplace. The four suites also have two-person Jacuzzis.

14 Rooms • Price range: $109-329
153 SR 9 W, Wilmington, VT 05363
☎ **(802) 464-7400**

Windsor
Juniper Hill Inn

The Juniper Hill Inn is a circa 1900 Colonial-Revival mansion set amid formal gardens and expansive manicured lawns. On entering the inn, guests will discover high ceilings, elaborate honey-colored oak paneling and fireplaces from a time when no expense was spared to create elegance in a country setting. All of the bedrooms are individually decorated and many have fireplaces.

16 Rooms • Price range: $95-175
153 Pembroke Rd, Windsor, VT 05089
☎ **(802) 674-5273**

Woodstock
Canterbury House A Bed & Breakfast

Refurbished to add modern comforts, this 1880 Victorian home has still managed to preserve a feeling of historic authenticity. Furnished with antiques that reflect fine craftsmanship, the inn is hospitable and charming. Hearty breakfasts are served at a common table. Within a block or so of the inn, guests will find excellent shops, antique stores and museums. A Robert Trent Jones-designed golf course is located nearby.

8 Rooms • Price range: $100-175
43 Pleasant St (US 4), Woodstock, VT 05091
☎ **(802) 457-3077**

Woodstock
Carriage House of Woodstock

A wonderfully restored 1830 Victorian home with a large porch and an attached carriage house in what it one of New England's top travel destinations. Immaculate guestrooms feature a tasteful mix of beautiful Victorian and modern furnishings. All rooms have private baths, one has a fireplace. Breakfasts are a delightful blend of tradition and creativity. The lovely parlor is a pleasant place to converse, read or listen to music.

9 Rooms • Price range: $95-185
455 Woodstock Rd, Rt 4 W,
Woodstock, VT 05091
☎ **(802) 457-4322**

Woodstock
Deer Brook Inn

This 1820 Colonial farmhouse was once the main house of a large dairy farm. Renovated to combine the warmth and character of yesterday with today's conveniences, the inn exudes country comfort. Each guestroom is spacious and very well maintained. Rooms have king- or queen-size beds, homemade quilts and cheerful furnishings. Four of the rooms are located on the second floor; the two-room suite is situated on the first floor.

5 Rooms • Price range: $90-120
535 US Rt 4, Woodstock, VT 05091
☎ **(802) 672-3713**

Woodstock
⟨⟨⟩⟩ *The Jackson House Inn*

A lovely getaway, with four acres of beautiful gardens, offering gourmet dining, charming, intimate guestrooms and exceptional hospitality. Common rooms are elegant. Some guestrooms are cozy and others spacious, but all are beautifully decorated. The innkeepers are happy to cater to special needs or requests. A short drive away are the unique galleries and shops on Woodstock's bustling main street.

15 Rooms • Price range: $195-380
114-03 Senior Ln, Woodstock, VT 05091
☎ **(802) 457-2065**

Woodstock
⟨⟨⟩⟩ *The Winslow House*

Expect to be well cared for by charming hosts with a wry sense of humor at this nicely restored 1872 Colonial-style farmhouse. Each room features pieces from the innkeeper's extensive collection of period antiques. Four of the guestrooms have separate sitting areas and all have private baths. A hearty candlelight breakfast is served in the dining room and guests are welcome to relax in the sitting room. Casual and unpretentious.

4 Rooms • Price range: $85-150
492 Woodstock Rd (Rt 14),
Woodstock, VT 05091
☎ **(802) 457-1820**

Woodstock
The Woodstocker Bed & Breakfast

A charming Cape-style home, circa 1830, on a tree-lined street.

9 Rooms • Price range: $135-155
61 River St, Woodstock, VT 05091
☎ **(802) 457-3896**

Southeast

Autumn colors blaze behind a cabin in Virginia's historic Shenandoah Valley.

Scenic Byways
of the Southeast

The Natural Bridge of Virginia is one of the world's natural wonders. It towers more than 200 feet high and stretches 90 feet in length.

Skyline Drive/Blue Ridge Parkway
Meandering along the Blue Ridge Mountains in Virginia and in North Carolina, this 470-mile byway showcases natural wonders and America's history at every turn. Visitors taking the drive can visit frontier and Native American villages, natural caverns, wildlife and an opulent estate home.

The Buccaneer Trail
This tour offers a little of everything for which Florida is justly famous: sun-drenched surf and sand, lush inland landscapes, and the nation's popular space museum. Enriching cultural and historic surprises lie along the way, too—art galleries and a restored Spanish fort in America's oldest city.

Baton Rouge to Gibson
Louisiana, a veritable melting pot of diverse cultures, is revealed along this route and in its surrounding area. The drive begins in the modern state capital, then takes visitors back to everyday rural life of the 19th century as well as to the opulence and grandeur of plantation living. The state's natural beauty is highlighted in the Wildlife Gardens of Gibson.

The Trace
Alternating between scenes of natural splendor and points of cultural and historical interest, this tour provides a glimpse of what the vast prairie might have looked like in the 18th century. Then, bison and buffalo ruled the land, only hawks and owls traversed the skies, and European settlers were taking their first halting steps toward taming nature and setting up homes in the territory.

A round of golf is a restorative experience when surrounded by forested mountains in scenic Hot Springs, Virginia.

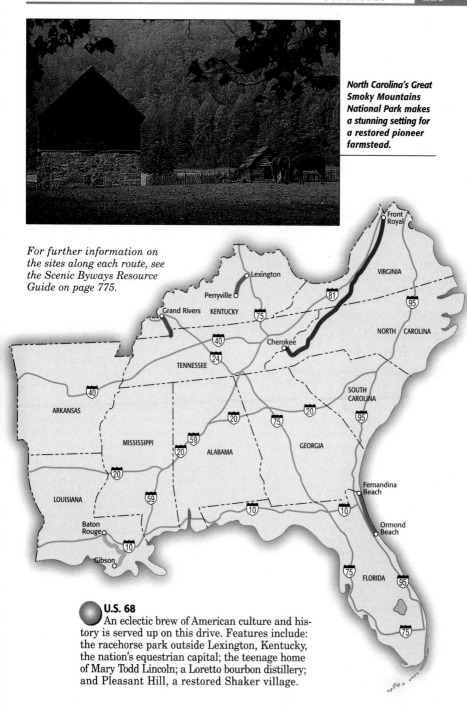

North Carolina's Great Smoky Mountains National Park makes a stunning setting for a restored pioneer farmstead.

For further information on the sites along each route, see the Scenic Byways Resource Guide on page 775.

Front Royal

VIRGINIA

Lexington

Perryville

Grand Rivers   KENTUCKY

Cherokee

NORTH CAROLINA

TENNESSEE

SOUTH CAROLINA

ARKANSAS

MISSISSIPPI

ALABAMA

GEORGIA

Fernandina Beach

LOUISIANA

Ormond Beach

Baton Rouge

Gibson

FLORIDA

U.S. 68
An eclectic brew of American culture and history is served up on this drive. Features include: the racehorse park outside Lexington, Kentucky, the nation's equestrian capital; the teenage home of Mary Todd Lincoln; a Loretto bourbon distillery; and Pleasant Hill, a restored Shaker village.

Skyline Drive/Blue Ridge Parkway

From Front Royal, a frontier village in the northwest corner of Virginia, to the natural splendor of Luray Caverns, this tour skirts the crest of the Blue Ridge Mountains, connecting Shenandoah National Park and Great Smoky Mountains National Park in North Carolina. Outside the park, a French Renaissance château contrasts with a traditional Native American village.

❶ Warren Rifles Confederate Museum
The Warren Rifles Confederate Museum in Front Royal, Virginia, contains exhibits of Confederate uniforms, guns, documents and photographs. Letters written by Confederate soldiers, as well as personal items owned by Gens. Robert E. Lee, Stonewall Jackson, Jubal Early and Turner Ashby make fascinating displays.

❷ Luray Caverns
Just west of Skyline Drive lie the Luray Caverns, eastern America's largest and most popular show caves. Well-lighted, paved walkways lead visitors through cathedral-sized rooms with ceilings 10 stories high, where enormous chambers are filled with towering stone columns, shimmering draperies and crystal-clear pools.

❸ Shenandoah National Park
Extending 105 miles along the crest of the Blue Ridge Mountains, Shenandoah National Park is one of the most picturesque and historic areas of the east. Mountainous ridges divide the timbered hills and fields of the piedmont on the east from the Shenandoah Valley on the west. Cascading streams and deep wooded hollows provide unforgettable vistas between the ridges. Along the way are several high points: Hawksbill Peak and Stony Man, both standing more than 4,000 feet high. Embracing close to 200,000 acres, the park is home to diverse flora and fauna. Almost 100 tree species, mainly hardwoods—some

of them 300 years old—grow here, producing a blaze of autumn color. More than 1,000 species of flowering plants, including wildflowers, azaleas and mountain laurel, bloom throughout the spring. A wildlife sanctuary, the park harbors some 50 species of mammals, from groundhogs and squirrels to deer and bears. Bird and reptile species number in the hundreds. Skyline Drive, a two-lane road that meanders through the park, has no billboards, stoplights or truck traffic to spoil the view.

❹ Blue Ridge Parkway
Linking Shenandoah National Park and Great Smoky Mountains National Park in North Carolina and Tennessee, the Blue Ridge Parkway offers sweeping panoramas of the southern highlands. The Virginia leg of the road reveals a variety of highlights including Humpback Rocks, Otter Creek and Smart View. In North Carolina, you'll drive past Cumberland Knob, Doughton Park and Linville Falls. Hiking trails, picnic areas and drinking water are available along the parkway. Although the road is open year-round, ice or snowy weather may close it temporarily. At Humpback Rocks Visitor Center, near Afton, Virginia, a restored pioneer mountain farm is a worthwhile stop. Blue Ridge Mountain frescoes (biblical paintings) decorate two churches along the route in North Carolina. One is in Glendale Springs, the other in West Jefferson. Just west of Blowing Rock, at milepost 294 along the route, stands the Parkway Craft Center, where mountain crafts are demonstrated and sold in a refurbished manor house.

Mabry Mill, located just off the Blue Ridge Parkway in Virginia, displays slices of pioneer history with a blacksmith shop, gristmill and sawmill.

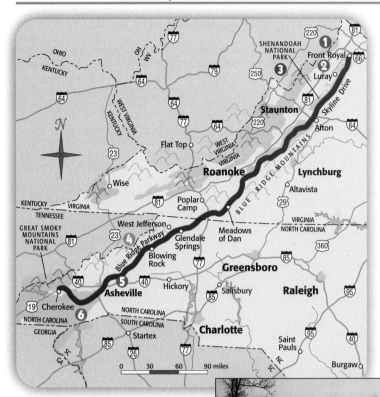

This manor house in Moses H. Cone Park near Blowing Rock, North Carolina, is now the Parkway Craft Center, showcasing mountain crafts.

⑤ Biltmore Estate

In the popular mountain resort of Asheville, North Carolina, the Biltmore Estate harks back to the grandeur of the 19th century. Built at the close of the century by George Washington Vanderbilt, the château and grounds feature a 40-acre garden, a greenhouse and a winery in the restored dairy. The 250-room mansion was ahead of its time: The servants of Vanderbilt family worked with such conveniences as electrical dumbwaiters, clothes washers and driers—amenities that were not available to the public until years later.

⑥ Oconaluftee Indian Village

The end of this drive is a beginning—of sorts. Oconaluftee Indian Village, just outside Cherokee, North Carolina, provides an authentic re-creation of 18-century Native American heritage and culture. Visitors on guided tours of the site glimpse members of the Cherokee tribe practicing traditional skills in period dress. Women pound corn into meal with wooden utensils. Men show how to blow darts through hollow reeds, their method of hunting small game. Artisans are busy weaving baskets, making pottery and carving wooden tools.

The Buccaneer Trail

South of Jacksonville, Florida's northernmost Atlantic-side city, this drive hugs the coast and takes in historic St. Augustine and scenic Washington Oaks State Gardens in Palm Coast. The excitement and sand of Daytona Beach are left behind by heading inland to the quiet wonders of Ocala National Forest. Back on the coast stands a testament to American curiosity and ingenuity: the Kennedy Space Center.

❶ Cummer Museum of Art & Gardens
Overlooking the St. Johns, the longest north-flowing river in the country, Jacksonville's Cummer Museum features an impressive array of fine decorative artifacts, some more than 2,000 years old. The collection of early 18th-century Meissen porcelain tableware is well worth a look. Changing exhibits complement the museum's permanent collection. In the afternoon, the Art Education Center showcases Art Connections, an interactive teaching gallery. Formal gardens, including one modeled after the Villa Gamberaia gardens in Florence, Italy, extend from the museum to the river.

❷ Kingsley Plantation
Located on Fort George Island, this 19th-century cotton plantation once had an enslaved work force of more than 60 people. Visitors can see a variety of buildings, some with historical exhibits, including the ruins of 23 slave cabins, one restored cabin, the main residence, kitchen house, and barn. Interpretive displays illustrate plantation life and crop cultivation.

❸ St. Augustine
St. Augustine, the country's oldest continuously occupied European settlement, is today a city of just over 12,000 inhabitants. In the 16th century Don Juan Ponce de Leon narrowed his search for the legendary Fountain of Youth to St. Augustine, arriving from Spain in 1513 and claiming possession of the area for his country. The town's coastal location made it both strategic and vulnerable. Pirates pillaged the town many times in the 16th and 17th centuries. As England extended its reach down the American coast from the northern colonies, the Spanish began to build in 1672 what remains as St. Augustine's main attraction: the Castillo de San Marcos. The fort didn't stop the English from taking over Florida in 1763, however. Twenty years later, the town was traded back to Spain before becoming a U.S. possession in 1821. Designed to repel attack from any direction, the fort was built of coquina, a limestone material made of broken shells and corals. The walls are 32 feet high and range from 13 feet thick to 16 feet thick on the side facing the ocean. The fort is surrounded by a moat and was designed with only one entrance—no wonder the fort itself has never been captured by enemy attack.

❹ Washington Oaks Garden State Park
Washington Oaks Garden State Park, just north of the city of Palm Coast, covers more than 400 acres of coastal scenery—tidal marshes and scrubland. The beach area—its rock outcroppings worn into unusual shapes by the surf—is a breathtaking sight. Stretching from the ocean to the Matanzas River, the gardens were once part of a plantation owned by Gen. Joseph Hernandez, a troop commander in the Second Seminole War. The area is home to many species of birds, fish and forest animals. Exotic plants brought here from the world over are tended in the formal gardens.

Fort Clinch at Fernandina Beach, which saw action during the Civil War, is now a state park, with nature trails, fishing and camping, as well as living history at the fort.

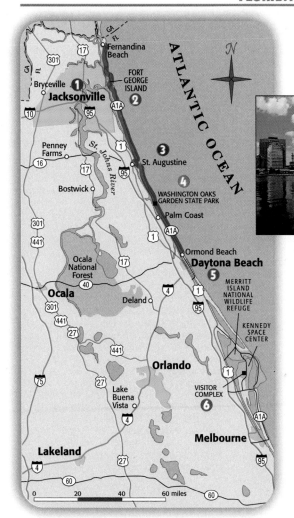

An impressive skyline towers over Jacksonville Landing. A busy seaport, Jacksonville is one of Florida's major cultural and transportation centers.

❺ Daytona Beach

Known as much for its automobile speedway as its sandy coastline, Daytona Beach has something for both drivers and bathers. White sandy beaches, extending for 23 miles, provide a jumping-off point for sailing, surfing and waterskiing. During the day, when conditions allow, cars can be driven along the water's edge on designated sections of the beach.

❻ Kennedy Space Center Visitor Complex

Visitors to the Kennedy Space Center can experience the thrilling past, present and future of America's space program. A tour of restricted areas gives a glimpse of NASA technicians at work on components of the International Space Station. Launch pads for the space shuttle can be photographed from atop the four-story LC 39 Observation Gantry. At the Apollo/Saturn V Center visitors can witness the re-creation of a rocket launch and of man landing on the moon. The Space Mirror Memorial honors the 17 U.S. astronauts who have given their lives in the line of duty. Also part of the complex, the Merritt Island National Wildlife Refuge serves as a buffer zone for NASA.

Baton Rouge to Gibson

The bustle of Louisiana's state capital in Baton Rouge contrasts vividly with the re-creation of pre-industrial life at Louisiana State University's Rural Life Museum. A short drive through bayou country takes visitors to three well-kept plantation homes before reaching a natural swamp and wildlife garden in Gibson.

❶ Baton Rouge
There's no better example of modern know-how juxtaposed with tradition than in Baton Rouge, Louisiana's second-largest city and state capital. The Old State Capitol, completed in 1850, is a Gothic-Revival castle standing guard over the Mississippi; the building now houses exhibits about Louisiana politics and history. In contrast, the current capitol building is a 34-story Art Deco edifice, built in 1932 using marble from every marble-producing country in the world—26 varieties. In 1935 that marble was chinked by the assassin's bullet that killed Sen. Huey P. Long, earlier Governor of Louisiana. Long is buried in the sunken garden on the grounds outside the building. Today's sightseers can visit the information center on the first floor and the observation platform on the 27th floor. A few miles down Highway 10, the LSU Rural Life Museum re-creates Louisiana plantation life and culture in the 1800s. The Plantation area embraces a complex of buildings including a gristmill, blacksmith shop, school house, sick house and slave cabins. Inside period furniture and equipment provide a feeling of authenticity. The Barn area includes everyday items, such as farming tools and household implements, dating from prehistoric times to the beginning of the 1900s. The Folk Architecture area demonstrates a variety of the building styles inhabited by early settlers in the region.

❷ Plaquemine
A few miles south of Baton Rouge on Route 1 lies the town of Plaquemine, named after a nearby bayou. A navigable waterway until a levee built after the Civil War cut its link to the Mississippi, the bayou was made navigable again in 1909 with the construction of the Plaquemine Lock. The lock and lock house were closed in 1961 and are now a museum. The top of the levee offers a commanding view of the river.

❸ Nottoway Plantation
A little farther south, in White Castle, Nottoway Plantation is an impressive remnant of the South before the Civil War. Built in 1859, the house was the largest residence in Louisiana at the time. The heart of a self-sufficient plantation, the home boasts three stories, 64 rooms, 22 massive columns in the Greek-Revival and Italianate styles, a commanding view of the river, and a ballroom with marble mantels, crystal chandeliers and windows more than 10 feet high—all restored and furnished in keeping with the period. The palatial house was avant-garde for its time, offering indoor bathrooms, gas lamps and an intercom system with silver call bells.

❹ Tezcuco Plantation
On the opposite bank of the Mississippi stands the Tezcuco Plantation in Darrow. About 10 years older than Nottoway, this raised brick cottage in the Greek-Revival style houses collections of art, crystal, pottery and silver. Today the Tezcuco operates as a bed and breakfast, offering rooms that are furnished in the period. Visitors can begin to get a feel for what it was like to live on a Southern plantation.

Once a shortcut to the Mississippi, the Plaquemine lock system is commemorated by the old lock house, which now serves as a museum.

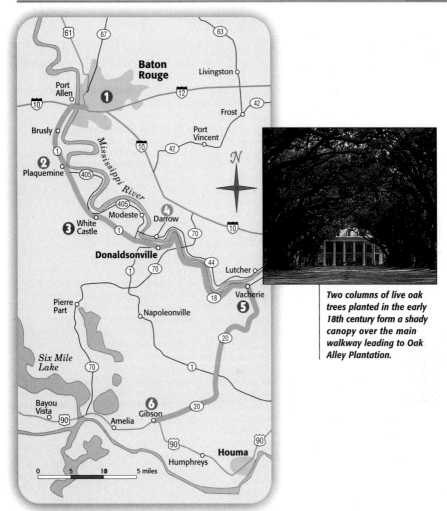

Two columns of live oak trees planted in the early 18th century form a shady canopy over the main walkway leading to Oak Alley Plantation.

❺ Oak Alley Plantation

One mile west of Vacherie on Route 18, Oak Alley Plantation lives up to its name. The main walkway leading to the palatial house is covered by a quarter-mile-long canopy formed by 28 mature live oak trees, planted more than a century before construction was completed in 1839. Restored to its pre–Civil War splendor after suffering decades of neglect, the Greek-Revival mansion features several rooms that recall what plantation life was like more than 150 years ago. Furnishings, decor and accessories have been reproduced with authenticity. Mahogany chairs and a blue-velvet sofa set around a handwoven wool rug grace the living room. In the dining room, a shoofly fan, used to cool off guests and chase away flies, hangs over the table.

❻ Wildlife Gardens

South of the junction of routes 90 and 20, Wildlife Gardens in Gibson delights visitors all year round. On a walking tour of the site, which takes about 90 minutes, visitors explore the many riches of the gardens. At the center is a natural swamp, complete with native fauna and flora.

The Trace

This tour meanders through the wooded peninsula that is Land Between the Lakes National Recreation Area and is punctuated by living-history museums and other 19th-century heritage sites. The drive recalls simpler, more tranquil times, when birds and mammals ruled the land and early Americans were beginning to set up their homes and farms in the rural landscape.

❶ Adsmore Living History Museum

Just off the Western Kentucky Parkway, the Adsmore Living History Museum in Princeton provides glimpses of life in the last half of the 1800s. Built near the middle of the 19th century as a mansion for the Smith-Garrett families, the refurbished site includes the residence, a log house and a gun shop. Each building is decorated and furnished in accordance with a specific period in the lives of the families.

❷ The Trace

Between I-24 in western Kentucky and Route 79 in northern Tennessee, a picturesque two-lane, 40-mile-long road called The Trace runs through the Land Between the Lakes National Recreation Area. Featuring wildlife, history and hundreds of miles of outdoor enjoyment, the area is one of the largest inland bird sanctuaries in the eastern United States. More than 230 species have been sighted in the 170,000-acre park. Eagle-watching is a popular activity along the banks of the two lakes, Barkley and Kentucky, that flank the drive. But birding isn't the only attraction here. Visitors are just as likely to spy buffaloes. On the Tennessee side of the area, herds of the big beasts roam a 200-acre range. A highlight of the area is the Elk and Bison Prairie, a 750-acre habitat for some of the species that ruled the area in the 1700s. Driving along the 3.5-mile prairie loop, visitors may observe birds such as osprey and owls as well as bison, coyotes, deer and elk.

Managed by the Tennessee Valley Authority, the area attracts anglers, hunters, campers and boating enthusiasts. It also features hundreds of miles of trails for hiking, horseback riding and mountain biking. Several of the trails lead to scenic views and points of historical interest.

❸ Golden Pond Visitor Center

The Golden Pond Visitor Center is located smack in the middle of the recreation area, just on the Kentucky side of Route 68. Its interpretive displays, audiovisual orientation programs and planetarium/theater are well worth a stop. Visitors to the area during December can view the planetarium's annual Christmas show, "'Tis the Season."

❹ The Homeplace-1850

The Homeplace, a living-history farm, sits on the eastern side of The Trace in Tennessee. Guides on the site dress in period clothing and perform everyday chores to help visitors get a sense of rural life in the area in the mid-19th century.

❺ Fort Donelson

The capture of Fort Donelson by Union General Ulysses S. Grant and a fighting force of 17,000 troops in February 1862 was a turning point in the Civil War. The attack marked the first major victory for the North during the conflict. The fort defended the Cumberland River in Tennessee and taking it opened up the South for Union forces. Southern Kentucky and parts of

In the Land Between the Lakes Recreation Area, The Homeplace-1850 re-creates antebellum farm life. The site features 14 original log structures.

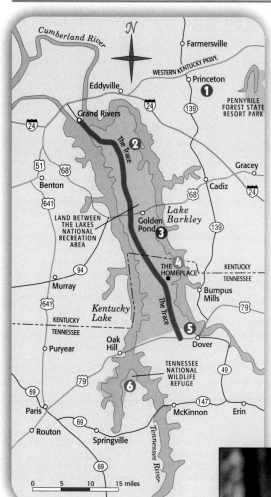

Both the Tennessee National Wildlife Refuge and the bird sanctuary within the Land Between the Lakes offer birders the chance to spot hundreds of species.

Tennessee fell in short order. Visitors can tour the site, reliving the engagement at the fort's National Battlefield in Dover, Tennessee. The battlefield park contains the original fort, Confederate earthen rifle pits and river batteries and a national cemetery, set up in 1867 for the remains of Union troops and other American veterans.

❻ Tennessee National Wildlife Refuge

The Tennessee National Wildlife Refuge, just south of the recreation area, is home to migratory ducks and geese. More than 226 bird species, including eagles and herons, find refuge in its 50,000-plus acres.

U.S. 68

This tour offers changes of speed—and scenery. From the Kentucky Horse Park in Lexington, where horseracing is celebrated, visitors step into the girlhood home of Mary Todd Lincoln. Farther on down the road, tradition, simplicity and a sense of history prevail at a restored Shaker village and at Old Fort Harrod.

❶ Kentucky Horse Park

Some of the world's most celebrated horse farms ring the outskirts of Lexington, the heart of bluegrass country. Along with the breeding, rearing and training of thoroughbred, standardbred, saddlebred and show horses, Lexington has seen horseracing for more than 200 years. By the end of the 18th century, the city's jockey club, the first to be organized in Kentucky, was formed. Just a scant thoroughbred race from downtown Lexington lies Kentucky Horse Park, an attraction that occupies more than 1,000 acres. The park celebrates man's relationship to the horse. Visitors to the park can explore the facility on foot and take a short tour on a trolley pulled by—big surprise— horses. A highlight is the memorial where the incomparable Man o' War is interred. Every day between March 15 and October 31, the Parade of Breeds takes place on the grounds. The International Museum of the Horse traces the 58-million-year history of the horse through paintings, photographs and special equestrian exhibits.

❷ Mary Todd Lincoln House

Mary Todd lived with her family in this residence on Main Street in downtown Lexington from the age of 14 until she was 21 years old. Three years after leaving this house she married Abraham Lincoln, the man who in 1860 became the 16th president of the United States. The late Georgian brick home, constructed between 1803 and 1806, has been restored and furnished in the period. Mary Todd Lincoln possessed an impressive Meissen collection and a portion of it is on display in the house. Visitors can also view items belonging to the Lincoln-Todd families.

❸ Shaker Village of Pleasant Hill

In 1806, a small assemblage named the United Society of Believers in Christ's Second Appearing founded the colony of Pleasant Hill, just off what is now Route 68. These Shakers, so-called because of their dancing and twirling during religious ceremonies, believed in living a simple life. Nonetheless, they made substantial contributions to society, inventing such devices (usually unpatented) as the circular saw, a threshing machine and the common clothespin. The restored village of Pleasant Hill, overlooking the Shawnee Run Creek, recalls the Shakers' spirit. The 33 buildings on the site have been faithfully maintained. Rooms are decorated with authentic Shaker furniture and guides in traditional costume perform original Shaker music.

❹ Old Fort Harrod

At the junction of Routes 68 and 127, visitors can learn the craft of broom-making and other traditional skills through living-history presentations at Old Fort Harrod in Harrodsburg. Fort Harrod is the site of the first permanent settlement in Kentucky. Now operated as a state park, the reconstructed fort features two-story blockhouses in three of its corners. A freshwater spring flows through the fourth corner.

Founded in 1806, Shaker Village of Pleasant Hill is the largest restored Shaker village in the United States.

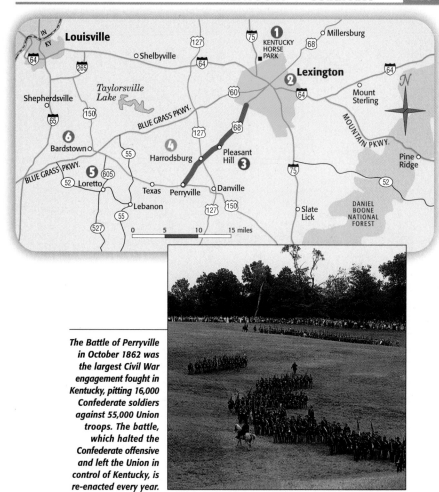

The Battle of Perryville in October 1862 was the largest Civil War engagement fought in Kentucky, pitting 16,000 Confederate soldiers against 55,000 Union troops. The battle, which halted the Confederate offensive and left the Union in control of Kentucky, is re-enacted every year.

❺ Maker's Mark Distillery

A couple of miles off Route 52, Maker's Mark Distillery continues to make what it is famous for: bourbon. Visitors can take a guided tour of the facility. Points of interest include the still house, where the bourbon is handmade; the bottling house, site of the wax-dipping operation; and the warehouse.

❻ My Old Kentucky Home State Park

Kentucky's second-oldest city, Bardstown, was settled in the late 18th century. Once a political and social hub, the city now boasts distilling as one of its main industries. My Old Kentucky Home State Park, just out-side town on Route 150, is so-called because Stephen Foster is thought to have composed "My Old Kentucky Home, Good-night!" here in 1852. But the main attrac-tion is the mansion where he stayed. It was built in 1818 by Foster's cousin Judge John Rowan, who served on the Kentucky Court of Appeals, in the House of Representatives and in the U.S. Senate. The Rowan house, called Federal Hill, is furnished with old paintings and heirlooms. The grounds con-tain the family cemetery, a garden and a replica of the Judge's law office. Guides dressed in pre–Civil War clothing take visitors on tours of the site.

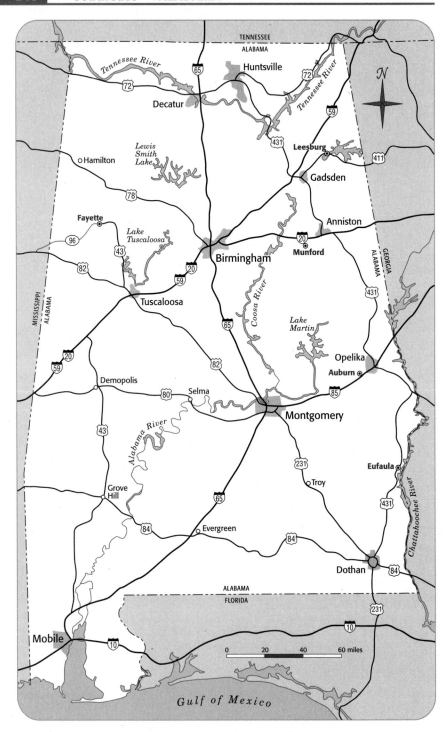

Auburn

 *The Crenshaw Guest House*
Nestled amid an acre of giant oaks and pecan trees, this Victorian home was built by an Auburn University professor in 1890. Original architectural details such as bay windows and gingerbread trim are tastefully combined with modern comfort and convenience. Each guestroom has a private bath, study desk and computer data port. In the separate Carriage House each unit overlooks the garden and includes a kitchenette.

6 Rooms • Price range: $48-100
371 N College St, Auburn, AL 36830
☎ **(334) 821-1131**

Eufaula
Kendall Manor Inn
This 1872 mansion, with its distinctive tower rising above the treetops, overlooks historic Eufaula. In the tradition of Southern hospitality, guests are greeted with a seasonal beverage and then invited to "sign in" on the plaster walls of the staircase leading up to the tower room. Guestrooms are decorated with period antiques and are equipped with private baths. Breakfast may be served outdoors by the garden.

6 Rooms • Price range: $129-149
534 W Broad St, Eufaula, AL 36027
☎ **(334) 687-8847**

Fayette
Rose House Inn
This circa 1900 Victorian house has been sensitively restored and beautifully decorated. In addition to the six rooms in the main house, Rose Cottage offers four additional rooms, each with a private bath. Each room is also equipped with cable television and two phone lines to accommodate voice mail. Local attractions include historic Fayette's museums. A continental breakfast is offered every morning.

10 Rooms • Price range: $55-75
325 2nd Ave NW, Fayette, AL 35555
☎ **(205) 932-7673**

Leesburg
The Secret Bed & Breakfast Lodge
Sitting high on a mountain top, this romantic lodge boasts views of sparkling Weiss Lake and the valley below. Guests can relax in the lodge, which has a fireplace and a vaulted 20-foot-high ceiling, or swim in the spectacular rooftop pool.

6 Rooms • Price range: $95-145
2356 Hwy 68 W, Leesburg, AL 35983-4000
☎ **(256) 523-3825**

Munford
The Cedars Plantation Historic B&B
A veritable piece of history, this home was built pre-Civil War and has endured many generations and reincarnations. The house has been recently renovated to welcome guests into the high-ceilinged parlors and the well-stocked library. The surrounding 30-acre property is also enticing with a pool, tennis court and walking trails. Nearby lies the Talladega National Forest, Cheaha State Park, museums and antique shops.

4 Rooms • Price range: $70-120
590 Cheaha Rd, Munford, AL 36268
☎ **(256) 761-9090**

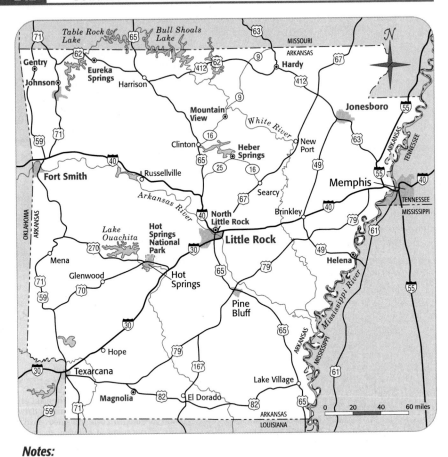

Notes:

◆ ◆ Eureka Springs
◆ ◆ **🏠 *Angel at Rose Hall***

Nestled in the trees of the Ozark Mountains, this home is a treasure of hospitality and opulence. Guests arrive to fresh flowers and chocolates, and are offered a bottle of champagne each evening of their stay. The home has a sophisticated decor using warm hues and luxurious textiles, and is distinguished by stained-glass windows, fireplaces and antiques. The result is a perfect setting for a special getaway. Each guestroom boasts designer linens, a private bath and a double Jacuzzi. The backyard gazebo overlooks a small pond and is a good place to listen to birds and the nearby waterfall.

5 Rooms • Price range: $125-185
56 Hillside, Eureka Springs, AR 72632
☎ (501) 253-5405

◆ Eureka Springs
◆ ◆ **🏠 *Arsenic & Old Lace B&B***
◆

This graceful Victorian home in historic Eureka Springs has been beautifully restored and decorated in period style with antiques and imported wallpapers. It is situated on a deeply wooded hillside and its grounds are accented with flowering shrubs and pathways. Each guestroom in this B&B is equipped with a private bath and Jacuzzi. A gourmet breakfast is served daily in the elegant dining room.

5 Rooms • Price range: $130-185
60 Hillside Ave, Eureka Springs, AR 72632
☎ (501) 253-5454

◆ Eureka Springs
◆ ◆ ***A Cliff Cottage & The Place Next Door, A Bed & Breakfast Inn***

Built in 1892, this historic cottage was the home of the first mayor of Eureka. Nestled against a bluff, the two buildings of the inn are surrounded by award-winning gardens. The decor of the guestrooms is an eclectic mix of Victoriana and art brought back from trips by the well-traveled owner. The recently built Place Next Door complements the Cottage's style and houses two guestrooms, each with a private veranda.

4 Rooms • Price range: $135-195
42 Armstrong St, Eureka Springs, AR 72632
☎ (501) 253-7409

◆ Eureka Springs
◆ ◆ **Crescent Cottage Inn**

For a breathtaking view of the Ozark Mountains the back porches of the Crescent Cottage Inn are the place to be. Originally built for the state's first post-Civil War governor, this Victorian "Painted Lady" combines Old World charm with all the modern comforts. Some rooms have private verandas with swings for lazy afternoons soaking in the mountain view. Listed on the National Register of Historic Places.

4 Rooms • Price range: $99-149
211 Spring St, Eureka Springs, AR 72632
☎ (501) 253-6022

Eureka Springs
 *Heartstone Inn & Cottages*

This rambling wood structure in the historic section of Eureka Springs is a Victorian-style gem. Guests can take advantage of the soft breezes of warm Southern evenings on the inviting veranda, deck or in the gazebo. Each room is equipped with a private bath, and two have a Jacuzzi. There is also an in-house massage therapy studio. Heartstone's gourmet breakfast has been called the best in the Ozarks.

12 Rooms • Price range: $89-139
35 Kings Hwy, Eureka Springs, AR 72632
☎ **(501) 253-8916**

Fort Smith
Beland Manor Inn

This Colonial-style inn has individually decorated guestrooms with a personal touch of Southern hospitality. In-room luxuries range from Jacuzzis and fireplaces to massages and game and video libraries. Guests are welcome to relax on the patio, in the garden, or visit the grounds of the St. Scholastica Monastery across the street. The wild, wild west is close at hand at the various monuments of Fort Smith's National Historic Site.

8 Rooms • Price range: $79-165
1320 S Albert Pike, Fort Smith, AR 72903
☎ **(501) 782-3300**

Fort Smith
Michael's Mansion

This Neo-Classic home boasts oak woodwork and elegant stained glass.

5 Rooms • Price range: $57-147
2900 Rogers Ave, Fort Smith, AR 72901
☎ **(501) 494-3700**

Gentry
Apple Crest Inn Bed & Breakfast

This grand Victorian mansion and carriage house is tucked into a corner of the Ozark wilderness known locally as Sleepy Hollow. The thematically decorated rooms are inspired by places as far away as Australia; the Down Under suite sleeps up to four. Jacuzzis are available in three rooms and the rest have antique claw-foot tubs with showers. Antique shops, a golf course and two state parks with great fishing are located nearby.

6 Rooms • Price range: $85-170
12758 S Hwy 59, Gentry, AR 72734
☎ **(501) 736-8201**

Hardy
Olde Stonehouse Bed & Breakfast Inn

These cozy accommodations are decorated with beautiful antiques.

8 Rooms • Price range: $65-125
511 Main St, Hardy, AR 72542
☎ **(870) 856-2983**

Heber Springs
The Anderson House Inn

In its original incarnation in the 1880s, The Anderson House was Heber Springs' theater. Today the inn is decorated with antiques, and the guestrooms are supplied with handmade quilts from local artisans. Each room has a private bath and is air-conditioned. Local attractions include antique and craft shops, and the nearby Ozark foothills offer many outdoor activities. A full breakfast buffet is served in the large common room.

15 Rooms • Price range: $62-84
201 E Main, Heber Springs, AR 72543
☎ **(501) 362-5266**

Helena
Edwardian Inn

This Colonial-Revival mansion was built at the beginning of the 20th century. The woodwork of the home is remarkable, and much of the paneling, mantel-work and hardware is original. Rooms are elegantly furnished and spacious with private baths. Breakfast is always a treat with lots of fresh food and coffee. Helena was significant in the Civil War; battles for the Mississippi River were fought near here, and many landmarks remain.

12 Rooms • Price range: $60-125
317 Biscoe, Helena, AR 72342
☎ **(870) 338-9155**

Hot Springs National Park
Stitt House Bed & Breakfast

This jewel in the heart of Hot Springs National Park is the town's oldest standing dwelling. The pre-Victorian mansion is the epitome of Southern grace with hardwood floors and tasteful decor. The sprawling lawns feature lush greenery, a lovely fountain, a heated swimming pool and a new Jacuzzi. Superior hospitality is offered, from the morning's gourmet breakfast to the evening's turndown service.

4 Rooms • Price range: $105-130
824 Park Ave, Hot Springs National Park,
AR 71901
☎ **(501) 623-2704**

Johnson
Inn at the Mill, A Clarion Carriage House

Historic Johnson Mill, with its striking waterwheel, was partially destroyed during the Civil War, then reconstructed in 1867. Its present incarnation combines a timeless wooden exterior with an interior of sweeping, modern lines. The mill and its buildings feature 48 guestrooms, including six suites, each inspired by a famous artist. A continental breakfast is served, and the inn also boasts Arkansas' highest-rated restaurant.

48 Rooms • Price range: $99-165
3906 Greathouse Springs Rd, Johnson, AR 72741
☎ **(501) 443-1800**

Jonesboro
West Washington Guest House

The personable hosts here have created a lovely home away from home.

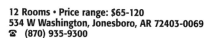

12 Rooms • Price range: $65-120
534 W Washington, Jonesboro, AR 72403-0069
☎ **(870) 935-9300**

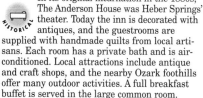

Little Rock

🏅 *The Empress of Little Rock Bed & Breakfast*

The Hornibrook Mansion was completed in 1888 and is a fine example of Gothic Queen Anne-style architecture. Its features include the distinctive three-and-a-half-story corner tower, a stained-glass skylight and octagonal rooms. Restored in 1994, the halls and guestrooms have been decorated with careful attention to detail. Breakfast is served on the veranda or in the dining room with silver service—a delightful combination of English crumpets and Southern hospitality. More than luxury lodgings, the Empress is a step back in time to a more graceful era.

5 Rooms • Price range: $125-195
2120 S Louisiana, Little Rock, AR 72206
☎ **(501) 374-7966**

Magnolia

Magnolia Place Bed & Breakfast

This 1910 inn is furnished with antiques and is located downtown.

5 Rooms • Price range: $99-129
510 E Main St, Magnolia, AR 71753
☎ **(870) 234-6122**

Mountain View

The Inn at Mountain View

After a deep sleep on beds with fine linens and handmade quilts, guests will awake to a seven-course breakfast with bottomless cups of coffee. Built as an inn in 1886, this hostelry has welcomed many guests and kept them returning to enjoy its warm hospitality. Guests can enjoy the breeze, relax on a rocker on the large front porch, fish for trout in the nearby White River, or visit the Ozark National Forest.

11 Rooms • Price range: $63-98
307 W Washington St, Mountain View, AR 72560
☎ **(870) 269-4200**

North Little Rock

The Baker House Bed & Breakfast

A majestic example of Southern comfort, Baker House offers an enchanting stay. Visitors entering this inn are greeted by an ornate, circular pine staircase that leads to comfortably furnished guestrooms. Carved oak is featured throughout, on furniture, mantles and doorways. The second-floor walk-way offers a magnificent view of the water and the city's skyline. Guests can help themselves to treats from the butler's pantry.

5 Rooms • Price range: $88-139
109 W 5th St, North Little Rock, AR 72114
☎ **(501) 372-1268**

Notes:

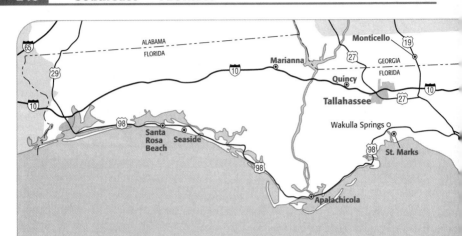

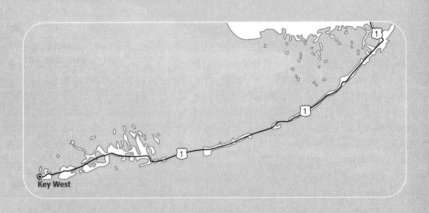

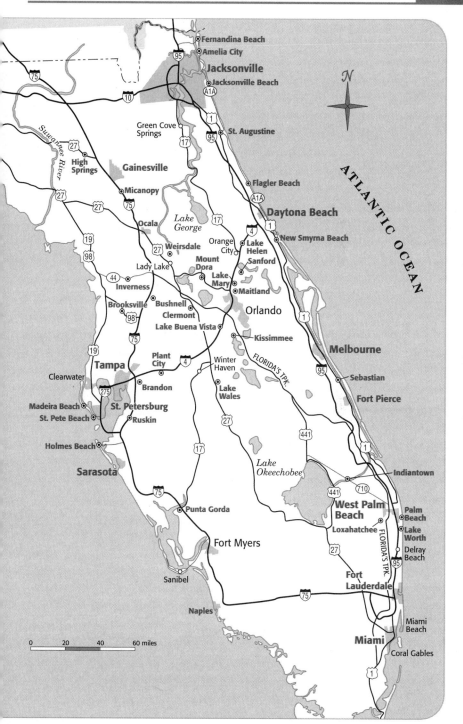

Amelia City

⊕ *Elizabeth Pointe Lodge*
The main house has 20 sunny rooms with oversize Roman tubs. Services include a morning newspaper delivery. There are two other buildings on the grounds: Harris Lodge, which has four guestrooms with large sitting rooms and the Miller Cottage, with two baths and two bedrooms. Guests can find long stretches of oft-deserted beaches just steps from the inn.

25 Rooms • Price range: $155-280
98 S Fletcher Ave, Amelia City, FL 32034
☎ **(904) 277-4851**

Apalachicola
⊕ *The Gibson Inn*
The Gibson Inn is a restored late 19th-century inn listed on the National Register of Historic Places. Each room is tastefully decorated with Victorian-era antiques from around the world. Fall is a splendid time to visit, when the Gulf waters are still warm and the evenings on the veranda are cool. The inn offers Murder Mystery Weekends as well as special traditional holiday dinners.

30 Rooms • Price range: $85-100
Market St & Ave C, Apalachicola, FL 32329
☎ **(850) 653-2191**

Brandon
Behind the Fence Bed & Breakfast
A visit to the Behind the Fence B&B is a retreat to the simplicity and tranquillity of life as it was in the 1800s. The inn is authentically decorated with Country-style antiques, hand-dipped candles and dried herbs. The B&B's central location—near universities and tourist attractions, as well as fishing, horseback riding, golf and scenic river canoeing—makes it a great jumping-off point for a variety of enjoyable day trips.

5 Rooms • Price range: $69-89
1400 Viola Dr, Brandon, FL 33511
☎ **(813) 685-8201**

Brooksville
⊕ *Verona House B&B*
This is a nice family-owned and operated establishment that was built in 1925. It is one of the few original Sears and Roebuck Catalog Houses still in existence and is on the National Register of

Historic Places. Guestrooms are comfortably furnished; full breakfasts are served.

4 Rooms • Price range: $77-100
201 S Main St, Brooksville,
FL 34601
☎ **(352) 796-4001**

Bushnell
Cypress House Bed & Breakfast
Surrounded by magnificent moss-draped oaks, the Cypress House suits its rustic, peaceful setting. The inn is a modern log home with cozy Country-style decor and a wide wraparound veranda with rockers. It sits on 10 acres of farmland, which provide guests with plenty of outdoor recreational possibilities, including badminton, croquet and horseshoes. There are also trails for mountain biking. Most of the five rooms have a private bath.

5 Rooms • Price range: $60-80
CR 476 B, 5175 SW 90th Blvd, Bushnell,
FL 33513
☎ **(352) 568-0909**

Clermont

Mulberry Inn B&B
This 1890 inn is situated near parks and lakes as well as the historic downtown area of Clermont. The main house and carriage house are surrounded by a white picket fence, giving the establishment a cozy feel. Rooms are comfortably furnished.

5 Rooms • Price range: $70-105
915 W Montrose St, Clermont, FL 34711
☎ **(352) 242-0670**

Daytona Beach

The Coquina Inn Bed & Breakfast
Built in 1912 to serve as the parsonage for the First Methodist Church, the Coquina Inn is listed on the National Register of Historic Places. The inn has beautifully appointed rooms and parlors. Guests are welcome to play the baby grand piano while sipping complimentary sherry, or they can relax in the sunroom with a cup of tea. The inn is close to all of Daytona's greatest attractions, including beaches, fine dining and golfing.

4 Rooms • Price range: $80-110
544 S Palmetto Ave, Daytona Beach, FL 32114
☎ **(904) 254-4969**

Daytona Beach
Live Oak Inn
Each of the inn's guestrooms overlooks the gardens of the property or the nearby Halifax Harbor Marina. The rooms are all decorated differently, representing people or events that have helped shape Florida's history. All rooms have baths; some have Jacuzzis, others have Victorian soaking tubs. The inn's restaurant dining room is open for both lunch and dinner and can also accommodate private parties.

12 Rooms • Price range: $80-90
444-448 S Beach St, Daytona Beach, FL 32114
☎ **(904) 252-4667**

Daytona Beach
The Villa Bed & Breakfast
This beautifully decorated 1920 Florida Spanish-style mansion boasts a gated entrance to two acres of landscaped grounds. Flowering gardens surround the tiled patio which has a pool and a spa. Rooms feature Russian icons, Chinese jade and stunning period antiques. Within easy walking distance of the beach. Listed on the National Register of Historic Places.

4 Rooms • Price range: $125-250
801 N Peninsula Dr, Daytona Beach, FL 32118
☎ **(904) 248-2020**

Fernandina Beach
Addison House
The Addison House is a historic 1876 Victorian home that forms the main part of an inviting inn, which includes two other buildings. Many of the 13 rooms have a king-size bed and are equipped with a whirlpool, and most open onto a porch overlooking the landscaped courtyard. A full breakfast is served on the covered porch—weather permitting—and the innkeepers can make special arrangements for picnic lunches.

13 Rooms • Price range: $99-225
614 Ash St, Fernandina Beach, FL 32034
☎ **(904) 277-1604**

Fernandina Beach

Bailey House

One of the most photographed Victorian homes of the South, the Bailey House has enormous charm. It is listed on the National Register of Historic Places. Construction began in 1895 under the direction of owner E.W. Bailey, and the house remained in the family for 70 years. The influence of those early years is readily apparent in the intricately carved marble-and-wood fireplaces and the stained-glass windows.

10 Rooms • Price range: $125-185
28 S 7th St, Fernandina Beach, FL 32034
☎ **(904) 261-5390**

Fernandina Beach
The Fairbanks House

The Fairbanks' quaint courtyard lulls guests into a state of relaxation with the scent of roses and the soothing sound of water lapping at the pool's edge. The house is situated on an acre of land and is a combination of an 1885 Italianate villa and cottages, including one that dates from 1880 and was previously a schoolhouse. Each of the charming guestrooms has a private bathroom featuring a Jacuzzi or claw-foot tub.

12 Rooms • Price range: $150-250
227 S 7th St, Fernandina Beach, FL 32034
☎ **(904) 277-0500**

Fernandina Beach
Florida House Inn

One of the state's most venerable hotels, the Florida House Inn is a B&B that also serves meals to the public. The original inn once entertained such notable guests as the Rockefellers and the Carnegies. It remains steeped in historic charm while still providing its clientele with all the modern conveniences one would expect to find in a fine inn. All the rooms are decorated with antiques.

15 Rooms • Price range: $79-179
22 S 3rd St, Fernandina Beach, FL 32035
☎ **(904) 261-3300**

Fernandina Beach
Hoyt House B&B

The Queen Anne-style Hoyt House was built in 1905 and is an outstanding example of late-Victorian architecture. The guest chambers have antique furnishings, a private bath and all the amenities necessary for comfort. The B&B is located in the downtown historic district of Amelia Island, where guests will find antique emporiums, museums and excellent restaurants.

10 Rooms • Price range: $119-164
804 Atlantic Ave, Fernandina Beach, FL 32034
☎ **(904) 277-4300**

Flagler Beach
Shire House Bed & Breakfast

This inn wraps guests in both Southern charm and Old World elegance. All rooms have whirlpools and wet bars. The ocean is just across the street, and guests are welcome to use the inn's heated pool.

5 Rooms • Price range: $95-160
3398 N Oceanshore Blvd, Flagler Beach, FL 32136
☎ **(904) 445-8877**

Flagler Beach
The White Orchid Oceanfront Inn

Directly on the beach, this breezy inn is an ideal location to indulge in the pleasures of life. Rooms are decorated in a sleek Art Deco style and offer amazing oceanfront views. You will be treated to expanded continental breakfasts, afternoon wine and appetizers, and offered beach chairs, umbrellas and bicycles to enhance your enjoyment of the beach. Also on-site is a gourmet restaurant, a heated pool/spa and Jacuzzis.

8 Rooms • Price range: $119-179
1104 S Oceanshore Blvd, Flagler Beach, FL 32136
☎ **(904) 439-4944**

Fort Lauderdale
⑭ Caribbean Quarters, A Bed & Breakfast
The close proximity to the beach and the Caribbean architecture of this inn give it a tropical ambience. Plantation-style wooden verandas overlook the lush vegetation in the courtyard. Rooms are decorated in vibrant, floral patterns.

12 Rooms • Price range: $95-225
3012 Granada St, Fort Lauderdale, FL 33304
☎ **(954) 523-3226**

Fort Lauderdale
⑭ Eighteenth Street Inn

This ranch-style inn is in the bustling centre of "America's Venice," Fort Lauderdale. Each guestroom features sculpture, paintings or photographs by artists from different regions in America. The grand outdoor pool has waterfalls and fountains and is surrounded by a variety of exotic palm trees and other tropical vegetation. Guests are welcome to pick fruit from the grapefruit and orange trees that grow on the property.

6 Rooms • Price: $95-205
712 SE 18th St, Fort Lauderdale, FL 33316
☎ **(954) 467-7841**

Fort Pierce
⑭ The Mellon Patch Inn

Early risers at this modern inn can pick up their coffee and stroll across the road to the beach, where they can witness unforgettable sunrises. Popular nearby activities include playing tennis, golfing, and picnicking on a secluded stretch of beach. The boutiques and galleries of Vero Beach also offer visitors a pleasant way to spend an afternoon. Individually decorated rooms are bright and airy. The grounds run down to a lagoon.

4 Rooms • Price range: $140-165
3601 N A1A, Fort Pierce, FL 34949
☎ **(561) 461-5231**

Fort Pierce
Villa Nina Island Inn Beach Bed & Breakfast

Standing between the Atlantic Ocean and the Indian River, this inn is across the street from a private beach, and sits on acres of river-view property. All guestrooms have private entrances, feature tropical decor and are fitted with modern amenities. The heated pool and fountains enhance the inn's relaxing atmosphere. Local activities include canoeing and snorkeling.

4 Rooms • Price range: $105-205
3851 N A1A, Fort Pierce, FL 34949
☎ **(561) 467-8673**

Gainesville
 Sweetwater Branch Inn Bed & Breakfast

This restored 1885 Victorian home is conveniently located adjacent to the University of Florida and the city's historic district. The gracefully proportioned rooms feature hardwood floors and antique furnishings. Three of the rooms have a working fireplace. Guests can stroll through the lush gardens listening to the soft murmur of the flowing fountains. Breakfast includes the inn's famous crepes and can be served in bed.

13 Rooms • Price range: $85-150
625 E University Ave, Gainesville, FL 32601
☎ **(352) 373-6760**

High Springs
Grady House Inn

The Grady House is a 1917 home listed on the National Register of Historic Places. The innkeepers have decorated the place with their extensive collection of artworks and have restored the home to its original charm. The inn hosts many different planned events, such as a two-day basket-weaving workshop, a Valentine's Day Weekend and moonlight canoe trips to nearby Lily Springs.

5 Rooms • Price range: $89-119
420 NW 1st Ave, High Springs, FL 32655
☎ **(904) 454-2206**

Holmes Beach
 Harrington House Beachfront Bed & Breakfast

This wonderfully decorated coquina brick beachfront home is an ideal location to enjoy the pristine white sands of the Gulf of Mexico. Most guestrooms feature French doors that open onto balconies overlooking the heated pool, the beach or the gulf itself. Breakfast is served in the sunny, citrus-colored dining room. Guests can swim, kayak or roam the beach all day, and then enjoy the evening's spectacular sunsets.

16 Rooms • Price range: $179-249
5626 Gulf Dr, Holmes Beach, FL 34217
☎ **(941) 778-5444**

Indiantown
Seminole Inn

When S. Davies Warfield built this inn in 1926, he envisioned it as the focal point of the community. Today it is still centrally located, and with its original hardwood floors, fixtures and chandeliers, it captures the ambience of the Old South. The restaurant in the inn is architecturally stunning and features Sunday buffets as well as a "Charles Dickens' Christmas," complete with a special tree-lighting event.

23 Rooms • Price range: $75-95
15885 SW Warfield, Indiantown, FL 34956
☎ **(561) 597-3777**

Inverness
The Crown Hotel

Once a fishing lodge, this structure has been restored in the style of an English manor. Rooms are cozy and well decorated. Guests can enjoy tea or wine by the fireside or take in the view of the lake from the porch. Many outdoor activities are nearby.

34 Rooms • Price range: $40-80
109 N Seminole Ave, Inverness, FL 34450
☎ **(352) 344-5555**

Jacksonville
⚜ *Plantation Manor Inn*

Built in 1905, this gracious plantation home has been restored to its earlier splendor. Rejuvenated pine floors and cypress wainscoting add to the elegant and spacious feel of this Greek-Revival style home. The nine rooms are tastefully appointed with antique furnishings, Oriental rugs, and Ralph Lauren and Laura Ashley prints. Some guestrooms have a fireplace; all have a private bath. A wraparound porch is supported by Greek-Revival Doric columns, while a lap pool and hot tub are bordered by orange trees set amid a charming English garden.

9 Rooms • Price range: $135-175
1630 Copeland St, Jacksonville, FL 32204
☎ **(904) 384-4630**

Jacksonville
House On Cherry Street

This 1909 inn has a large lawn and overlooks the St. Johns River. The home is comfortably decorated with American antiques from the Queen Anne period. The warm atmosphere is enhanced by many Oriental rugs. Bedrooms have grand four-poster beds, fresh flowers and a private bath. After a full breakfast, guests can enjoy coffee on the outdoor terrace. The owners keep a refrigerator stocked for guest use.

4 Rooms • Price range: $90-115
1844 Cherry St, Jacksonville, FL 32205
☎ **(904) 384-1999**

Jacksonville
River Park Inn, the 1887 House

At this inn, the tone is set by the porch swing and double rocker on the veranda where guests can enjoy cooling breezes off the river. Inside guestrooms are cozy with large quilted beds. Across the street there is a pool fed by a mineral spring.

5 Rooms • Price range: $65-100
103 S Magnolia Ave, Jacksonville, FL 32043
☎ **(904) 284-2994**

Jacksonville Beach
Pelican Path B&B by the Sea

A friendly welcome from hospitable owners awaits guests of this inn by the sea, which is reminiscent of the houses built on San Francisco hillsides. Bay windows provide all guestrooms with a view of the ocean, two have private balconies and spa tubs. Enjoy a hearty breakfast with fresh fruit and the house specialty, pan dowdy. Golf and tennis facilities are nearby as is the Jacksonville Zoo. Bicycles are available for guest use.

4 Rooms • Price range: $80-165
11 N 19th Ave, Jacksonville Beach, FL 32250
☎ **(904) 249-1177**

Key West
Heron House
Elegant and unpretentious, Heron House takes its cue from the Florida Keys' natural environment. Four renovated conch houses, dating as far back as 1856, surround tropical gardens filled with homegrown orchids and a variety of local plants. The Heron House's luxurious rooms are decorated in contemporary tropical decor and have large private decks and balconies. Some rooms are equipped with a whirlpool. All of them have a private bath. Patios, multilevel decks and an in-ground pool provide plenty of opportunity to relax.

23 Rooms • Price range: $189-209
512 Simonton St, Key West, FL 33040
☎ **(305) 294-9227**

Key West
Andrews Inn
The hosts of this atmospheric inn have named each of their guestrooms after a setting from a Hemingway novel. The rooms are airy with large windows and vaulted ceilings, and many are painted deep pastel colors. The grounds have delicate stone fountains and a secluded courtyard filled with aromatic palm, hibiscus and jasmine trees. Guests can stroll or cycle to many nearby attractions, including boutiques and restaurants.

6 Rooms • Price range: $115-359
0 Whalton Lane, Key West, FL 33040
☎ **(305) 294-7730**

Key West
Blue Skies Inn
Just one block from the beach, this inn offers homey comforts and resort-style luxury all at once. The size of rooms vary; some have a living area and kitchenette. All have clean, large bathrooms and are beautifully decorated with hardwood floors, private patios, fireplaces, Parisian linens or king-size beds. Guests can enjoy the front porch or grand sundeck. Nearby activities include sky diving and flats fishing.

5 Rooms • Price range: $155-195
630 South St, Key West, FL 33040
☎ **(305) 295-9464**

Key West
Center Court Historic Inn & Cottages
This spacious property has won awards for the craftsmanship of its recent renovation. The tranquil and exotic grounds boast lush gardens and a fish-stocked pond. Other features include a heated pool, spa, sundeck and exercise pavilion.

6 Rooms • Price range: $88-388
915 Center St, Key West, FL 33040
☎ **(305) 296-9292**

Key West
⚙ *Chelsea House*

The many windows, tall doors and light linens in this comfortably decorated inn create a pleasant tropical ambience. The establishment is large with a variety of spacious rooms and suites and an expanse of outdoor grounds. A winding brick path leads guests through the tropical gardens and around the sundecks to a refreshing and sparkling pool. Enjoy breakfast on the patio.

21 Rooms • Price range: $85-245
707 Truman Ave, Key West, FL 33040
☎ **(305) 296-2211**

Key West
The Conch House Heritage Inn

Located in the heart of "Old Town" Key West, The Conch House is one of the island's earliest historic family estates. High ceilings, wood shutters, wraparound spindled porches and picket fences give the inn an old-fashioned charm. Guests can choose to stay in the spacious and elegant rooms in the main house, the Caribbean-style wicker rooms in the poolside cottage or a cozy tropical cabana. All rooms have a private bath.

8 Rooms • Price range: $148-228
625 Truman Ave, Key West, FL 33040
☎ **(305) 293-0020**

Key West
Curry Mansion Inn

Nestled on the grounds of the former Curry estate, this elegant inn offers a luxurious retreat. Curry Mansion is home to many extraordinary antiques and unusual items, including Ernest Hemingway's big game gun and Henry James' grand piano. Well-appointed rooms feature wicker, antiques and handmade quilts, as well as air-conditioning, a ceiling fan, and a private bath. A pool and hot tub are available to guests.

28 Rooms • Price range: $180-325
511 Caroline St, Key West, FL 33040-6552
☎ **(305) 294-5349**

Key West
⚙ *Cypress House Bed & Breakfast*

This preserved 110-year-old Bahamian-style mansion is set amid lush gardens. Many rooms open onto verandas, decks or surrounding gardens. In-room amenities include terry cloth robes, refrigerators and ceiling fans. Cocktails are served by the pool.

15 Rooms • Price range: $140-350
601 Caroline St, Key West, FL 33040
☎ **(305) 294-6969**

Key West
Duval House

Built in the 1890s, this inn was originally a cigar factory. Seven cottages surround a garden and are decorated with pastels and Caribbean-style wicker furniture. Guests enjoy poolside breakfasts and the inn's location on famous Duval Street.

28 Rooms • Price range: $180-335
815 Duval St, Key West, FL 33040
☎ **(305) 294-1666**

Key West

Frances Street Bottle Inn

Like the town, this lovely Conch-style building has an interesting history. In 1926, in one of its incarnations, it was a grocery store. Since then it has also been a church, a boarding house and even a set for a television series. Today it offers a tastefully decorated tropical environment that includes a palm-shaded patio with a spa. Rooms are nicely decorated in soft Caribbean pastels. Daytime activities and an exciting nightlife are a short walk away.

8 Rooms • Price range: $135-165
535 Frances St, Key West, FL 33040
☎ **(305) 294-8530**

Key West

Island City House Hotel

This hotel is made up of three unique buildings: the Island City House is a three-story Victorian mansion with handsome rooms, hardwood floors and antiques; the Arch House is a carriage house with casual island decor; and the Cigar House, a replica of a cigar factory, stands in the rear garden and overlooks the pool and Jacuzzi deck. It houses six spacious parlor suites and is nicely appointed with rattan furnishings.

24 Rooms • Price range: $175-240
411 William St, Key West, FL 33040
☎ **(305) 294-5702**

Key West

Key Lime Inn

This mid-19th century family estate, with its white picket fences, verandas and tin roofs, is a fine example of British Caribbean elegance. Guests may choose to stay in the Main House, the one-room Garden Cottages or the Pool Cabana. Many of the accommodations have verandas or patios. Lounge chairs and towels are provided for those afternoons spent lingering by the pool. Listed on the National Register of Historic Places.

37 Rooms • Price range: $149-235 winter;
$98-146 summer
725 Truman Ave, Key West, FL 33040
☎ **(305) 294-5229**

Key West

Lightbourn Inn

This attractive 1903 Queen Anne-style mansion is located on a tree-lined residential avenue just a few blocks from downtown and the waterfront. Its extensive public areas are furnished with antiques and artifacts from the owners' many years of travel. The inn is charmingly appointed with refinished wood floors, 11-foot ceilings and antiques. It also houses the largest private collection of teddy bears and signed memorabilia in Key West.

10 Rooms • Price range: $128-258
907 Truman Ave, Key West, FL 33040
☎ **(305) 296-5152**

Key West
La Mer Hotel & Dewey House

Dewey House, originally the home of philosopher and educator John Dewey, and its neighbor, the intimate La Mer Hotel, are located on South Beach overlooking the Atlantic. Spacious and attractively furnished guestrooms feature marble baths and sunlit balconies overlooking tropical gardens and the ocean. Many rooms have a Jacuzzi, and guests have beach and pool privileges.

19 Rooms • Price range: $220-330
504-506 South St, Key West, FL 33040
☎ **(305) 296-5611**

Key West
⑩ La Pensione

Erected in 1891 as the private residence of the vice-president of the Cortez Cigar Company, this handsome classic Revival mansion hearkens back to earlier days when the island was at the heart of a vast cigar-making empire. Seven intimate rooms are decorated in a casual Key West style, each with a private modern bath and air-conditioning. The inn features a peaceful, secluded pool and lounge deck as well as spacious verandas.

9 Rooms • Price range: $168-178
809 Truman Ave, Key West, FL 33040
☎ **(305) 292-9923**

Key West
⑩ Watson House

The mid-19th century Watson House has been restored to its original style. Guestrooms in the main house and the poolside cabana feature hardwood floors and are comfortably outfitted, with wooden paddle fans, wicker and rattan furnishings. The exterior has private decks overlooking the pool and tropical gardens. The garden boasts a waterfall that leads from the heated spa into the swimming pool.

3 Rooms • Price range: $105-500
525 Simonton St, Key West, FL 33040
☎ **(305) 294-6712**

Key West
The Weatherstation Inn

This inn is distinguished by Bahama shutters, lush vegetation, natural wood floors, harbor views and rooms painted in gorgeous pastel tones. The inn stands in a private gated community, centrally located in the heart of the Old Town.

8 Rooms • Price range: $195-315
57 Front St, Key West, FL 33040
☎ **(305) 294-7277**

Key West
Blue Parrot Inn

This lovely whitewashed home, built in 1884, features grand upper- and lower-level balconies. Room decoration varies; some are particularly cozy with wood-paneled walls. The gem of this inn is the large pool surrounded by colorful tropical flowers.

10 Rooms • Price range: $79-209
916 Elizabeth St, Key West, FL 33040
☎ **(305) 296-0033**

Key West

♦ ♦ ⊕ *La Casa de Luces*

This pretty home has many windows to let the warm Florida sun shine in. The mini-suites and rooms are clean and comfortable and feature 14-foot-high

ceilings. The rear garden boasts a Jacuzzi; the veranda has antique Cuban rockers.

8 Rooms • Price range: $149-279
422 Amelia St, Key West, FL 33040
☎ **(305) 296-3993**

Key West
♦ ♦ ⊕ *The Palms Hotel*

There are many types of accommodations in the 1889 main house and set around the tropical courtyard area. Guestrooms are furnished with comfort-

able white wicker. A bar runs around the deck area and the pool.

21 Rooms • Price range: $160-185
820 White St, Key West, FL 33040
☎ **(305) 294-3146**

Key West
♦ ♦ ⊕ *Westwinds*

A gingerbread, clapboard home located in the historic 'Old Town' of Key West, this tropical getaway is both clean and comfortable. Enjoy a continental break-

fast by the pool or in the garden. Hibiscus, banana and banyan trees grow in the garden.

22 Rooms • Price range: $90-250
914 Eaton St, Key West, FL 33040
☎ **(305) 296-4440**

Kissimmee
♦ ♦ ♦ ⊕ *Wonderland Inn*

This property on the National Register of Historic Places has had its original architectural beauty completely restored. Each guestroom features a white wicker rocker, hand-painted murals, private tiled baths with pedestal sinks and terry cloth robes, and a juicer for oranges grown on the property. The gardens feature more than 30 types of flowers and many butterflies and birds. Guests are invited to a nightly wine-and-cheese party.

11 Rooms • Price range: $79-139
3601 S Orange Blossom Tr, Kissimmee, FL 34741
☎ **(407) 847-2477**

Lake Buena Vista
♦ ♦ *Perri House Bed & Breakfast Inn*

Perri House is a quiet country estate on 20 acres of land adjacent to the Walt Disney World Resort. Surrounded by wooded areas and orange groves, the estate has been transformed into a bird sanctuary and wildlife preserve. A front porch overlooks the central gardens' bird fountain and feeders. The inn also features a sundeck, pool and hot tub, and has its own Bird House Museum. Disney World is a five-minute drive away.

8 Rooms • Price range: $90-140
10417 Centurion Ct, Lake Buena Vista, FL 32836
☎ **(407) 876-4830**

Lake Helen

🏛 *Clauser's Bed & Breakfast*

This 1890s Victorian inn is a quiet country retreat. A two-story carriage house has six modern rooms—some with a Jacuzzi, most with a private screened porch and all with private baths. The inn also features a small English pub, as well as a hot tub built into the gazebo in the courtyard. A walking path leads to the lake. Guests may borrow one of the inn's bicycles to explore the area's country lanes.

8 Rooms • Price range: $85-140
201 E Kicklighter Rd, Lake Helen, FL 32744
☎ **(904) 228-0310**

Lake Mary
Cherry Laurel Inn

This inn boasts attractively appointed bedrooms and common areas.

5 Rooms • Price range: $130-170
2461 Cherry Laurel Dr, Lake Mary, FL 32795
☎ **(407) 323-5515**

Lake Wales
🏛 *Chalet Suzanne Country Inn & Restaurant*

This inn stands on 70 acres of land, with a private lake and airstrip. A combination of architectural styles has endowed this inn with a fairy-tale quality; inside the antiques and stained glass only add to its charm. Rooms are attractively appointed and each has its own private entrance. The inn is well known for its fine cuisine, as well as the commercial soups and sauces that have been made in its cannery for the last 40 years.

30 Rooms • Price range: $139-189
3800 Chalet Suzanne Dr, Lake Wales, FL 33853
☎ **(863) 676-6011**

Lake Wales
The G.V. Tillman House Bed & Breakfast

Here, guests will enjoy a deep sleep on feather beds and plump pillows, awakening to fresh coffee and a delicious breakfast. Porches overlooking Crystal Lake are a perfect place to relax. For adventurous guests, the innkeeper organizes bass fishing.

5 Rooms • Price: $95
301 E Sessoms Ave, Lake Wales, FL 33853
☎ **(863) 676-5499**

Lake Worth
Sabal Palm House B&B Inn

Gleaming oak floors and high, molded ceilings create the first impression when visitors come to this inn, where each bedroom is named after and features the work of a master artist such as Renoir or Chagall. All rooms have covered balconies, luxury linens, designer towels and fresh-cut flowers. Each day brings a gourmet breakfast, tea and sweets at mid-day, and wine and cheese in the afternoon. Services offered include nightly turn-down and reservation-making at local restaurants, theaters and comedy clubs. The courtyard is filled with tropical plants and the ocean is just a stroll away.

7 Rooms • Price range: $75-180
109 N Golfview Rd, Lake Worth, FL 33460
☎ **(561) 582-1090**

Loxahatchee
Southern Palm Bed & Breakfast

This well-designed modern B&B under the trees on 20 acres of the northern Everglades is ideal for relaxing getaways. Antiques accentuate the spacious rooms. Private balconies overlook a tropical pond and nearby forests.

5 Rooms • Price: $125
15130 Southern Palm Way, Loxahatchee, FL 33470
☎ **(561) 790-1413**

Madeira Beach
The Lighthouse Bed & Breakfast Motel

Just a short walk from the water stands this faux lighthouse B&B. Individual units with private entrance are arranged in a circle around a courtyard and gazebo. Full breakfasts are served. Each guestroom has air-conditioning.

6 Rooms • Price range: $80-95
13355 2nd St E, Madeira Beach, FL 33708
☎ **(727) 391-0015**

Maitland
Thurston House

Located on five acres of wooded land overlooking Lake Eulalia, this B&B is a tranquil retreat, just five miles north of Orlando. The Victorian style of this former private home has been authentically restored, with impressive cypress moldings and paneling. Each guestroom is equipped with a private bath and is furnished with a queen-size bed and charming country decor. A generous continental breakfast is served daily.

4 Rooms • Price range: $130-160
851 Lake Ave, Maitland, FL 32751
☎ **(407) 539-1911**

Marianna
Hinson House Bed & Breakfast

This bungalow-style inn sits on the exact location of the Civil War's Battle of Marianna. Guests can read about this fascinating event in the library and visit nearby historical sites. The home is spaciously designed and features tall French doors and many large windows to let in the ocean breezes. All guestrooms and suites are tastefully decorated in vibrant colors and have full private baths.

5 Rooms • Price range: $65-95
4338 Lafayette St, Marianna, FL 32446
☎ **(850) 526-1500**

Melbourne
Crane Creek Inn Waterfront Bed & Breakfast

Built in 1925 this bright and cheery inn is blessed with a commanding view of picturesque Crane Creek. All of the individually decorated rooms have waterfront views. The riverside pool and spa are surrounded by lush tropical foliage and palms. Melbourne's central location puts it within driving distance of NASA, Cape Canaveral, Disney World and Cocoa Beach.

5 Rooms • Price range: $75-110
907 E Melbourne Ave, Melbourne, FL 32901
☎ **(321) 768-6416**

Miami
Miami River Inn

Soaring palms surround this historic inn, which is Miami's only B&B. Rooms feature hardwood floors, brass, wood or wicker furniture, and boast river or city views or a porch onto the garden. There is a pool, a Jacuzzi and a garden on the premises.

40 Rooms • Price range: $99-199
118 SW South River Dr, Miami, FL 33130
☎ **(305) 325-0045**

Micanopy
Herlong Mansion

This circa 1840 mansion, renovated in the Greek-Revival style, offers high ceilings, stained-glass windows, beautiful woodwork and elegant decoration. Some guestrooms feature canopy beds and fireplaces. Tall oak and pecan trees stand nearby.

11 Rooms • Price range: $70-179
402 NE Cholokka Blvd, Micanopy, FL 32667
☎ **(352) 466-3322**

Monticello
Palmer Place B&B

Listed on the National Register of Historic Places, this antebellum home maintains the gracious style of a time long since past. Modern conveniences, however, have not been forgotten. Each of the spacious rooms is equipped with a full private bath and phone. Each morning, guests are invited to a full breakfast on the sunporch, while the inn's Grand Hall welcomes small or large parties for dinners and receptions.

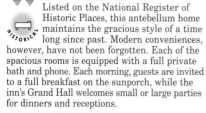

5 Rooms • Price range: $70-95
625 W Palmer Mill Rd, Monticello, FL 32345
☎ **(850) 997-5519**

Mount Dora
Darst Victorian Manor

Set overlooking Lake Dora, this authentic replica of an 1800s manor recreates Victorian luxury with all the conveniences you would expect from a first-class inn. Each of the six rooms has been individually decorated with antiques and period reproductions. Fresh flowers and a velour bathrobe await each new guest. A terrace on the second floor provides perfect views of the lake, while the large, beautifully decorated parlor makes a great place to recount the day's events. Guests are invited to a gourmet breakfast, and afternoon tea is served on china and silver in the dining room.

5 Rooms • Price range: $125-220
495 Old Hwy 441, Mount Dora, FL 32757
☎ **(352) 383-4050**

Mount Dora
⚛ *The Emerald Hill Inn*

This expansive limestone home with its coquina rock fireplace and cathedral ceilings is an airy, inviting lodge. Overlooking Victoria Lake and surrounded by two acres of orange groves, the setting is perfect for a tranquil getaway. Each room is equipped with a private bath and has been individually decorated. Nearby attractions include Disney World—an hour's drive away—and Ocala National Forest.

4 Rooms • Price range: $99-149
27751 Lake Jem Rd, Mount Dora, FL 32757
☎ **(352) 383-2777**

Naples
Inn by the Sea

Naples has grown from a small 19th-century fishing village into a gem of the Gulf Coast. This 1937 home was the town's first guesthouse. Cozy quarters are comfortably furnished and have polished pine floors and plenty of sunlight. The inn is only two blocks from miles of white sand beaches or the upscale Third St. shops. The innkeepers, who live next door, speak English, Italian, Dutch, French and Russian.

5 Rooms • Price range: $94-189
287 Eleventh Ave S, Naples, FL 34102-7022
☎ **(941) 649-4124**

New Smyrna Beach
Little River Inn B&B

A nature lover's dream, this inn sits on two acres of oak-canopied land and is visited by blue herons and manatees from the nearby Indian River Lagoon nature preserve. Guests will enjoy elegant bedrooms and sweeping views from wide verandas.

6 Rooms • Price range: $80-160
532 N Riverside Dr, New Smyrna Beach, FL 32168
☎ **(904) 424-0100**

New Smyrna Beach
⍟ _Night Swan Intracoastal Bed & Breakfast_

Overlooking the Intracoastal Waterway of New Smyrna Beach, this inn is made up of two circa 1900 homes. The interiors have been furnished with period antiques, and the sweeping front porches provide a terrific setting for watching the water and just plain relaxing. Each of the spacious rooms is equipped with a private bath, and some have a whirlpool tub. A full breakfast is served in the dining room.

15 Rooms • Price range: $85-160
512 S Riverside Dr,
New Smyrna Beach, FL 32168
☎ **(904) 423-4940**

New Smyrna Beach
⍟ _Riverview Hotel_

For luxury lodging, gourmet dining on the waterway and clean ocean beaches only a stroll away, look no further. This inn features natural wood throughout, big comfortable beds and ornate ceiling fans in all guestrooms. Each day begins with an extended continental breakfast and ends with a nightly turn-down service. Guests can swim in the large clear pool, surrounded by tropical flowers and palm trees.

19 Rooms • Price range: $80-200
103 Flagler Ave, New Smyrna Beach, FL 32169
☎ **(904) 428-5858**

Ocala
Seven Sisters Inn

Guests are treated to luxury here in the form of canopy beds with fine linens, full breakfasts with the daily paper and rooms with fireplaces, Jacuzzis and soaking tubs. Evening brings candlelight dinners and murder mystery events.

8 Rooms • Price range: $95-185
820 SE Fort King St, Ocala, FL 34471
☎ **(352) 867-1170**

Palm Beach
⊕ *Palm Beach Historic Inn*

Built in 1921, this inn has maintained its high standard of hospitality over the years. All rooms are tastefully and individually decorated. Since the inn is just steps from the white beaches of the Atlantic, guests can enjoy the sun and sand, or go golfing, play tennis and go horseback riding. Guests will also love what Palm Beach has to offer, from boutique shopping to evenings at the opera, the ballet, the theater or comedy clubs.

13 Rooms • Price range: $150-325
365 S County Rd, Palm Beach, FL 33480
☎ **(561) 832-4009**

Plant City
Rysdon House Bed & Breakfast

No expense was spared in the creation of this beautiful Victorian house, built in 1910 by a wealthy lumber magnate. Guests can relax on the wicker rockers and porch swings on the wraparound porch or enjoy the enclosed Jacuzzi and large pool.

4 Rooms • Price range: $85-105
702 W Reynolds St, Plant City, FL 33566
☎ **(813) 752-8717**

Punta Gorda
Gilchrist Bed & Breakfast Inn

This cozy circa 1914 home rests in a water wonderland, the Punta Gorda County, which boasts 120 miles of shoreline. Guests will be in the middle of the interesting historic district and only half a block from Peace River waterfront.

3 Rooms • Price: $95
115 Gilchrist St, Punta Gorda, FL 33950
☎ **(941) 575-4129**

Quincy
McFarlin House Bed & Breakfast Inn

This impressive Queen Anne-style Victorian home is located in the Historical District of Gadsden county. Distinctive features of the inn include a 42-pillar porch encompassing three sides of the house and a third-floor turret. Well-tended gardens add to the romantic atmosphere. Guestrooms are furnished with antiques and many are equipped with a Jacuzzi. A full breakfast is served daily.

9 Rooms • Price range: $85-175
305 E King St, Quincy, FL 32351
☎ **(850) 875-2526**

Quincy
Allison House Inn

Built by a former Florida governor in 1843, this Greek-Revival home is located in the historic district. Rooms and suites are large and sunny. The gracious hosts are known for their homemade goodies, especially the granola and biscotti.

5 Rooms • Price range: $70-95
215 N Madison St, Quincy, FL 32351
☎ **(850) 875-2511**

Ruskin
Southern Comfort Bed & Breakfast

Guests will find everything they need at this 6,800-square-foot house, shaded by trees and set in a peaceful country locale. The grand pool and private deck are wonderful places to relax and enjoy the sun. There are golf and tennis facilities on-site.

4 Rooms • Price range: $85-95
2409 Ravine Dr W, Ruskin, FL 33570
☎ **(813) 645-6361**

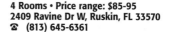

Sanford

∰ The Higgins House Bed & Breakfast

This Queen Anne-style house was built as a private residence in 1894. The B&B features a large Victorian parlor and an upstairs veranda. There are three guestrooms and one cottage available. All guestrooms have a private bath. Cochran's Cottage has two bedrooms, two baths, a living room, a complete kitchen and a porch. A continental breakfast is served daily.

4 Rooms • Price range: $80-120
420 S Oak Ave, Sanford, FL 32771
☎ **(407) 324-9238**

Santa Rosa Beach

A Highlands House Bed & Breakfast

This charming Gulf Coast B&B will delight any visitor who longs to be close to the water. A re-creation of an antebellum-style home, the B&B boasts four-poster beds and wingback chairs in each of the guestrooms. Comfortable wicker chairs on the extra-wide porch invite guests to sit and listen to the sound of the surf—a comforting reminder of the nearby beach—and view the sunset. Breakfast is served in the dining room.

8 Rooms • Price range: $90-200
4193 W Scenic SR 30A,
Santa Rosa Beach, FL 32459
☎ **(850) 267-0110**

Sarasota

The Cypress, A Bed & Breakfast Inn

The Cypress B&B has a wonderful tropical feel to it. Surrounded by palms, mango trees and moss-covered oaks, the inn is located on historic grounds overlooking Sarasota Bay. Inside guests will find a tasteful mix of American and European antiques. Each of the guestrooms has its own distinct charms, like the Martha Rose master suite, which has a balcony view of the Gulf of Mexico.

4 Rooms • Price range: $150-210
621 Gulfstream Ave S, Sarasota, FL 34236
☎ **(941) 955-4683**

Seaside

Josephine's French Country Inn

Situated on 80 acres of prime Gulf Coast land, this inn overlooks one of the best beaches in the region. All guestrooms come with a private bath, bar sink, microwave oven, coffee maker and a fireplace. One room has been modified for the physically disabled. A gourmet breakfast is served, and the award-winning dining room offers inn specialties such as crab cakes and Caribbean seafood chowder.

9 Rooms • Price range: $165-240
38 Seaside Ave, Seaside, FL 32459
☎ **(850) 231-1940**

Sebastian

The Davis House Inn

The views of the Indian River from the balconies of these efficiency suites are breathtaking. After a lavish breakfast over the morning paper, guests can soak up the sun on the deck. The evening brings festivities in the inn's self-serve bar and grill.

12 Rooms • Price: $80
607 Davis St, Sebastian, FL 32958
☎ **(561) 589-4114**

St. Augustine
🏛 *Alexander Homestead Bed & Breakfast*

The 1888 Alexander Homestead is located only steps away from the St. Augustine Historic District. The guestrooms offer a mix of family heirlooms and eclectic treasures. The parlor is warmed on cool evenings by a crackling fire. The formal dining room boasts a handsome sideboard displaying crystal, china and silver. The inn serves tasty breakfasts, which include French apple casserole and homemade granola.

4 Rooms • Price range: $125-175
14 Sevilla St, St. Augustine, FL 32084
☎ **(904) 826-4147**

St. Augustine
Bayfront Westcott House

The Westcott House is well situated on the Intracoastal Waterway, a half block from St. Augustine's Yacht Pier and a short distance from the city's many beaches. Originally built in the late 1800s, the guest house has been completely renovated and now it features guestrooms furnished with American and European antiques. Each room has a queen- or king-size bed and a private bath.

9 Rooms • Price range: $135-195
146 Avenida Menendez,
St. Augustine, FL 32084-5049
☎ **(904) 824-4301**

St. Augustine
🏛 *Casa de la Paz Bayfront Bed & Breakfast*

The innkeepers of this 1915 Mediterranean-style B&B overlooking the bay pride themselves on their cooking. Breakfast is a treat and homemade baked goods are served throughout the day. The inn owns 47 antique music boxes.

6 Rooms • Price range: $120-250
22 Avenida Menendez, St. Augustine, FL 32084
☎ **(904) 829-2915**

St. Augustine
Casa De Solana Bed & Breakfast Inn

This Spanish Colonial-style house, built in 1763, features four suites, some with a fireplace, some with a balcony overlooking the garden and some with a view of Matanzas Bay. All have a private bath. Chocolates and a crystal decanter of sherry add a special touch to each room. Breakfast is served every morning in the formal dining room. The historic sights of St. Augustine are just steps away.

4 Rooms • Price range: $95-229
21 Aviles St, St. Augustine, FL 32084
☎ **(904) 824-3555**

St. Augustine
🏛 *Casa de Suenos Bed & Breakfast*

Nicknamed "The House of Dreams," this circa 1900 Mediterranean-style home features arches, pine floors and rooms tastefully decorated with fine furnishings. Some rooms have a fireplace; all have a private bath. Guests can enjoy live entertainment at gatherings held every weekend evening. Located in the heart of this historic town, the Casa de Suenos B&B is close to shops, restaurants and landmarks.

6 Rooms • Price range: $120-190
20 Cordova St, St. Augustine, FL 32084
☎ **(904) 824-0887**

St. Augustine
Casablanca Inn on the Bay

This 1914 Mediterranean-Revival historic home is listed on the National Register of Historic Places. It sits overlooking Mantanzas Bay. Rooms and suites are decorated with fine antiques. Some have special amenities like a Jacuzzi, private entrance and a bay-front view. The porch features rocking chairs and ceiling fans that stir the warm tropical breezes. A hearty full breakfast is served on the grand front porch.

20 Rooms • Price: $89-199
24 Avenida Menendez, St. Augustine, FL 32084
☎ **(904) 829-0928**

St. Augustine
Cedar House Inn Victorian B&B

The innkeepers of this restored 1893 Victorian home put the emphasis on hospitality and comfort. Refreshments are served on the veranda. The library boasts an interesting collection of books, and a player piano stands in the parlor. Guestrooms are comfortably furnished and have a queen-size bed, as well as a private balcony. Each room has its own private bathroom with either a Jacuzzi or a claw-foot tub.

6 Rooms • Price range: $99-129
79 Cedar St, St. Augustine, FL 32084-4311
☎ **(904) 829-0079**

St. Augustine
🏧 *Centennial House Bed & Breakfast*

Set in the heart of the oldest European settlement in North America, this historic home has been meticulously restored to enhance its Old World charm and provide all the modern conveniences. The beautifully appointed rooms exhibit refined comfort. The Carriage House room features cathedral ceilings, a sitting area and a private balcony. All have private baths and most have whirlpools. Steps away from 500 years of Spanish Colonial history.

7 Rooms • Price range: $105-215
26 Cordova St, St. Augustine, FL 32084
☎ **(904) 810-2218**

St. Augustine
Old City House Inn

This 1873 classic Colonial-Revival house was originally built as a stable. After going through several changes, including being a hat shop and an antique store, it emerged as a B&B in 1990. Each guestroom provides modern conveniences such as cable television and air-conditioning, as well as a private bath. A central courtyard and a veranda are accessible to all guests. A full breakfast is served every morning.

7 Rooms • Price range: $79-179
115 Cordova St, St. Augustine, FL 32084
☎ **(904) 826-0113**

St. Augustine
St. Francis Inn

In the heart of the historic district of the 'Oldest City,' this inn dates back to the late 1700s. Rooms and suites vary in size and in style; several have fireplaces, kitchenettes or whirlpool tubs. Guests are treated to lavish breakfasts, and coffee and iced tea all day. Wine or beer are served at the evening socials. The pool is great for a swim and some sun, and the courtyard garden is a tranquil place to stargaze.

11 Rooms • Price range: $95-199
279 St George St, St. Augustine, FL 32084
☎ (904) 824-6068

St. Augustine
Castle Garden Bed & Breakfast

This inn was built around 1860 to serve as a carriage house for the mansion across the street, which now houses Ripley's Believe It or Not Museum. The building's exterior, foundation and chimney are original and have remained untouched.

6 Rooms • Price range: $65-165
15 Shenandoah St, St. Augustine, FL 32084
☎ (904) 829-3839

St. Marks
Sweet Magnolia Inn

Nature lovers will appreciate the location of this inn within walking distance of several salt marshes as well as the confluence of the St. Marks and the Wakulla rivers. Visitors will catch a glimpse of the different wildlife attracted to this area. The inn includes seven guestrooms, five of which have a Jacuzzi. Breakfast is served and dinner is available upon request. Nearby attractions include the St. Marks Wildlife Refuge.

7 Rooms • Price range: $85-115
803 Port Leon Dr, St. Marks, FL 32355
☎ (850) 925-7670

St. Pete Beach
Pasa Tiempo Bed & Breakfast

Passing through the gates of Pasa Tiempo's walled courtyard, guests enter a flowering tropical paradise. The Spanish-Colonial architecture influences the decorative touches of the common rooms and the bold but sophisticated use of color in the guest suites. Watch the sunrise while breakfast is served on the bay-side deck or sip a glass of wine and enjoy the deep hues of a spectacular sunset.

8 Rooms • Price range: $115-200
7141 Bay St, St. Pete Beach, FL 33706
☎ (727) 367-9907

St. Petersburg
Sunset Bay Inn

This inn, built in 1911, has been beautifully restored and is now designated a historic landmark. Made up of a main house and the carriage house, the inn combines various styles of architecture, from Colonial-Revival to Georgian. Scrumptious breakfasts in the enchanting dining room are a memorable affair. Each of the tastefully decorated bedrooms includes such amenities as a private bath with a whirlpool tub and shower, comfortable queen- or king-size bed and a telephone with a modem hookup. Recipient of the Architectural Society of America 1999 Preservation & Restoration Award.

6 Rooms • Price range: $170-250
635 Bay St NE, St. Petersburg, FL 33701
☎ **(727) 896-6701**

St. Petersburg
Bayboro House Bed & Breakfast On Old Tampa Bay

A relaxing getaway in Old Tampa Bay, this inn offers down-home hospitality, as well as beautifully furnished facilities. Each guestroom features a private bath, air-conditioning, television, beach chairs and a morning newspaper at the door. A romantic three-room guest suite offers special amenities such as a private deck overlooking Tampa Bay and a fully equipped kitchen, along with a dozen roses and a bottle of wine.

6 Rooms • Price range: $155-195
1719 Beach Dr SE, St. Petersburg, FL 33701
☎ **(727) 823-4955**

St. Petersburg
Bayboro Inn & Hunt Room Bed & Breakfast

The Bayboro Inn & Hunt Room has been welcoming guests since 1914. Renovated in 1994, this inn features six guestrooms, each decorated in a particular theme, using motifs from the Renaissance, Egypt and Key West. Each guestroom has a private bath. Wood-burning fireplaces grace the dining and living room areas. There is also an outdoor patio for warm evenings. Breakfast is served upon request.

6 Rooms • Price range: $75-110
357 3rd St S, St. Petersburg, FL 33701
☎ **(727) 823-0498**

St. Petersburg
The Claiborne House at Bay Gables

Designated a local landmark, this charming inn features a garden with a gazebo area and a fine dining restaurant. Guests are only half a block from the waterfront, and within walking distance of museums and other local attractions.

9 Rooms • Price range: $95-115
340 Rowland Ct NE, St. Petersburg, FL 33701
☎ **(813) 822-8855**

St. Petersburg
Mansion House B&B and The Courtyard on Fifth

The Mansion House B&B is made up of two historic homes, built between 1904 and 1912. Situated right in the heart of St. Petersburg's arts and entertainment district, the inn is a short walk away from art galleries and antique emporiums. The floors are made of Georgia pine, and the furnishings are a mix of antique and traditional, with a variety of eclectic items. There is a swimming pool for guests to enjoy.

12 Rooms • Price range: $115-165
105 5th Ave NE, St. Petersburg, FL 33701
☎ **(800) 274-7520**

Tallahassee
Calhoun Street Inn Bed & Breakfast

Spanish moss and rows of oak trees shade the area around this historic 1907 Colonial-Revival home. Rooms are spacious and have gleaming pine floors; many have fireplaces or claw-foot tubs. Other pleasing details are the handmade quilts and fresh-cut flowers that decorate the rooms. Guests are greeted by the smell of baked goods and then are truly pampered by being served their breakfast in bed.

4 Rooms • Price range: $65-95
525 N Calhoun St, Tallahassee, FL 32301
☎ **(850) 425-5095**

Tampa
Gram's Place Bed, Breakfast & Music

This B&B is designed with music lovers in mind. There are two Key West-style courtyards to relax in and instruments and a recording studio are available for guests' use. Rooms are decorated in musical themes, including blues, rock, jazz and folk.

6 Rooms • Price range: $15-95
3109 N Ola Ave, Tampa, FL 33603
☎ **(813) 221-0596**

Venice
Banyan House Historic Bed & Breakfast

This 1926 inn is surrounded by parklike grounds and beautiful gardens.

5 Rooms • Price range: $99-129
519 Harbor Dr S, Venice, FL 34285
☎ **(941) 484-1385**

Weirsdale
Shamrock Thistle & Crown

Built in 1887, this three-story Victorian house is located in the rolling countryside of Marion County. The inn boasts six distinctive rooms, ranging from cozy to elegant. Suites with a whirlpool are available, and some are equipped with a fireplace. Common areas include a game room and a library with fireplace. A cottage with a Jacuzzi, fireplace and private deck is also available. Golfing and beaches are close by.

7 Rooms • Price range: $79-185
12971 SE CR 42, Weirsdale, FL 32195
☎ **(352) 821-1887**

West Palm Beach
Hibiscus House Bed & Breakfast

Mayor David Dunkle built the Hibiscus House during the Florida land boom of the 1920s. This B&B has much to offer its guests, both inside and out. Lush landscaping and tropical gardens provide many private areas in which to relax, and guests can sip complimentary cocktails by the secluded heated pool. A full two-course breakfast is served daily on china, silver and Waterford crystal in the formal dining room or poolside.

4 Rooms • Price range: $95-180
501 30th St, West Palm Beach, FL 33407
☎ **(561) 863-5633**

West Palm Beach
Royal Palm House B&B

This inn promotes peace and quiet in a tranquil, tropical setting. Each guest room is named after a different type of palm tree. The pool is surrounded by exotic plants and a butterfly garden, and the tropical garden itself is full of citrus trees that can be picked for their ripe fruit. A hot full breakfast is served in the cheerful Morning Room and evening cocktails are served in the tastefully decorated Florida Room.

5 Rooms • Price range: $75-125
3215 Spruce Ave, West Palm Beach, FL 33407
☎ **(561) 863-9836**

West Palm Beach
Tropical Gardens Bed & Breakfast

With its sunshine-yellow exterior, green-striped awnings and white picket fence, this 1937 cottage-style building retains much of its "Old Florida" charm. Rooms have modern amenities such as air-conditioning, ceiling fans and cable television. An expanded continental breakfast is served daily, featuring favorites such as fresh-squeezed Florida orange juice, tropical fruit salad and fresh-baked scones.

4 Rooms • Price range: $75-125
419 32nd St, West Palm Beach, FL 33407-4809
☎ **(561) 848-4064**

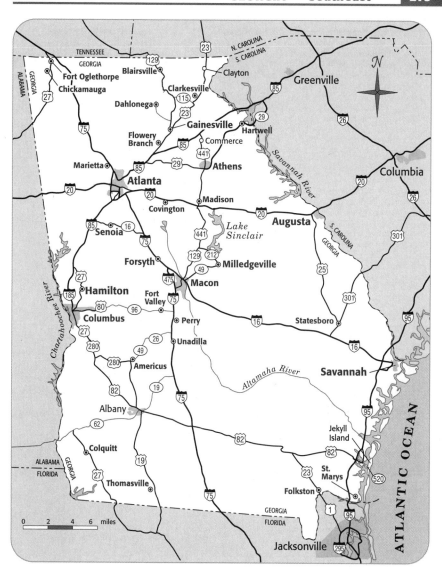

TENNESSEE
GEORGIA
ALABAMA
GEORGIA

Fort Oglethorpe
Chickamauga

Blairsville
Clayton
Clarkesville
Greenville

Dahlonega

Gainesville
Hartwell

Flowery
Branch
Commerce

Marietta

Atlanta
Athens
Columbia

Covington
Madison
Augusta

Senoia
Lake
Sinclair

Forsyth
Milledgeville

Hamilton
Macon

Fort
Valley
Columbus
Perry
Statesboro

Unadilla
Savannah

Americus

Albany
Jekyll
Island

Colquitt
St.
Marys

Thomasville
Folkston

ALABAMA
FLORIDA
GEORGIA

GEORGIA
FLORIDA

0   2   4   6 miles

Jacksonville

ATLANTIC OCEAN

Chattahoochee River
Savannah River
Altamaha River
S. CAROLINA
N. CAROLINA
S. CAROLINA

Americus
1906 Pathway Inn Bed & Breakfast

There's plenty to do at the 1906 Pathway Inn B&B. Guests can visit the Civil War town of Andersonville, hike across Providence Canyon or visit Westville, a village that authentically re-creates life from the mid-19th century. After a day's exploring, guests can relax in rooms that feature a king- or queen-size bed, ceiling fan and a private bathroom. A candlelight breakfast is served daily in the dining room.

5 Rooms • Price range: $65-125
501 S Lee St, Americus, GA 31709
☎ **(912) 928-2078**

Athens
The Nicholson House

The Nicholson House provides a tranquil getaway in the heart of Athens. Built in 1820, the house has been carefully restored, and now includes such modern amenities as central heating and air-conditioning in each bedroom. As well, each room has a private bath and a telephone. Guests can stroll through six wooded acres of rolling hills and enjoy the magnolias and wild azaleas.

7 Rooms • Price range: $100-120
6295 Jefferson Rd, Athens, GA 30607
☎ **(706) 353-2200**

Atlanta
⚑ *Ansley Inn*

A renovated 1907 Tudor-style home in an upscale residential neighborhood.

22 Rooms • Price range: $109-199
253 15th St, Atlanta, GA 30309
☎ **(404) 872-9000**

Atlanta
The Gaslight Inn B&B

This inn offers something for everyone. Guestrooms range from affordable, elegant rooms to luxurious suites. Some rooms feature 18th-century hand-painted furniture, while others include a whirlpool, a separate steam bath, and a private deck overlooking the gardens. There are several nearby places to visit, such as the Fernbank Natural History Museum, the Carter Presidential Library, and the Callanwolde Fine Arts Center.

6 Rooms • Price range: $95-195
1001 St Charles Ave NE, Atlanta, GA 30306
☎ **(404) 875-1001**

Atlanta
Shellmont Inn

The Victorian architecture of this 1890 building has been carefully restored, and details such as Tiffany windows, magnificent woodwork and authentic furnishings are sure to beguile its guests. Guestrooms feature a modern bath, complete with special soaps, shampoo and bath foam. Guests will also find flowers and a welcome basket with candies and fruit on the dresser.

5 Rooms • Price range: $115-160
821 Piedmont Ave NE, Atlanta, GA 30308
☎ **(404) 872-9290**

Augusta
The Azalea Inn
This Victorian home on a tree-lined street has charming rooms.

20 Rooms • Price range: $99-179
314-316 Greene St, Augusta, GA 30901
☎ **(706) 724-3454**

Blairsville
⏣ *Misty Mountain Inn & Cottages*
Each room at this inn has a fireplace, while the cottages feature loft bedrooms.

10 Rooms • Price range: $50-90
4376 Misty Mountain Ln, Blairsville, GA 30512-5604
☎ **(706) 745-4786**

Chickamauga
The Gordon-Lee Mansion Bed & Breakfast
One of the South's older and more gracious homes, the Gordon-Lee Mansion was built in 1847 and served as the local headquarters for the Union Army during the Civil War. Decorated with Oriental rugs, crystal and brass chandeliers, and ornate millwork, this B&B is set on seven acres of manicured land with many trees. The property also includes a formal English garden.

5 Rooms • Price range: $65-125
217 Cove Rd, Chickamauga, GA 30707
☎ **(706) 375-4728**

Clarkesville
Burns-Sutton Inn
This spacious three-story B&B was built in 1901 by two master carpenters, and showcases Victorian architecture. The inn has several eye-catching features, such as stained-glass windows, hand-carved fireplace mantles and delicate cutwork in the balustrades. There are seven guestrooms, including three suites and one luxury room with a double whirlpool tub. Several rooms have a fireplace.

7 Rooms • Price range: $65-125
855 Washington St, Clarkesville, GA 30523
☎ **(706) 754-5565**

Colquitt
⏣ *Tarrer Inn*
Originally built as a boarding house in 1861, the Tarrer House began offering lodgings in 1905. Recently renovated, the inn features 12 guestrooms, each decorated with period antiques, embroidered linen and a hand-painted fireplace. The inn's Southern menu includes many tempting dishes including succulent stuffed roast pork loin topped with Tarrer Inn Mayhaw gravy and grilled marinated quail breasts.

12 Rooms • Price range: $89-105
155 S Cuthbert St, Colquitt, GA 31737
☎ **(912) 758-2888**

Columbus

Rothschild-Pound House Inn

Rescued from the wrecking ball and moved to the safety of the historic district, this marvelous example of Second Empire-Victorian architecture has been reborn as an elegant B&B. Hardwood floors, 14-foot-high ceilings and leaded-glass windows are superbly integrated with modern amenities. Every evening guests may enjoy a cocktail in the parlor before stepping out for dinner at one of the fine local restaurants.

10 Rooms • Price range: $97-255
201 7th St, Columbus, GA 31901
☎ **(706) 322-4075**

Covington
2119, The Inn
Located in rural Georgia, this inn is a restored 1905 home.

5 Rooms • Price range: $65-95
2119 N Emory St, Covington, GA 30014
☎ **(770) 787-0037**

Dahlonega
⑩ Lily Creek Lodge

This is a European-style hunting lodge in the forested foothills of the Blue Ridge Mountains. Antique-decorated guestrooms have fine linens, down comforters, private entrances and baths. Naturelovers will enjoy staying here all year round. Such outdoor features as a tree-house deck and a pool with a waterfall make the most of the lodge's natural setting. Bring binoculars for observing wildlife in the surrounding forest.

12 Rooms • Price range: $99-159
2608 Auraria Rd, Dahlonega, GA 30533
☎ **(706) 864-6848**

Dahlonega
The Smith House

In 1884 a man named Captain Hall was refused the right to mine the rich vein of gold on his property because it was too close to the town square. Frustrated with his situation, he built a house on top of it. In 1922 the house was sold and turned into an inn that has been entertaining guests with Southern hospitality and home-style cooking ever since. Guestrooms and two villa suites have all the modern comforts.

18 Rooms • Price range: $55-149
84 S Chestatee St, Dahlonega, GA 30533
☎ **(706) 867-7000**

Flowery Branch
Whitworth Inn

The Whitworth Inn offers a quiet country atmosphere and a peaceful getaway. Each of the guestrooms features a private bath. A full breakfast is served every morning in the dining room, which overlooks the gardens and a backyard gazebo. Lake Lanier, located only a few minutes away, offers a variety of activities such as sailing and golfing. Chateau Elan winery/golf course is also nearby.

9 Rooms • Price range: $59-85
6593 McEver Rd, Flowery Branch, GA 30542
☎ **(770) 967-2386**

Folkston
The Inn at Folkston

Guests visiting this property will start to relax the minute they pass the fountain flowing in the inn's Garden of Meditation. Located in a small town in the southeast corner of Georgia, this 1922 inn is situated on two acres of land, just a short distance from the town of Folkston and the Okefenokee National Wildlife Refuge. Each of the four guestrooms features a feather bed, fresh flowers and a private bath. Breakfast is served daily.

4 Rooms • Price range: $85-135
509 W Main St, Folkston, GA 31537
☎ **(912) 496-6256**

Forsyth
Forsyth Square Bed & Breakfast Inn

Restored 1925 boarding house with nice decor and modern amenities.

12 Rooms • Price range: $59-69
22 W Main St, Forsyth, GA 31029
☎ **(912) 994-2165**

Fort Oglethorpe
The Captains Quarters B&B Inn

This beautifully renovated Renaissance-Revival duplex was originally built for two cavalry captains and their families. Today, the inn offers travelers two large suites and five guestrooms. Each room has a private bath; four of them have a fireplace and a king-size bed. Common rooms are decorated with antiques and collectibles. A three-course breakfast is prepared daily, and is served on china and silver.

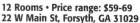

9 Rooms • Price range: $99-139
13 Barnhardt Cir, Fort Oglethorpe, GA 30742
☎ **(706) 858-0624**

Fort Valley
The Evans-Cantrell House

The lovely guestrooms at the Evans-Cantrell House, a 1916 Italian Renaissance-Revival home, are furnished with period reproductions. All rooms, including a two-room suite with a sitting room and a day bed, are on the second floor and each features a private bath. Guests can explore the little town of Fort Valley and the Everett Square Historic District. A hearty Southern breakfast is served daily.

4 Rooms • Price range: $75-105
300 College St, Fort Valley, GA 31030
☎ **(912) 825-0611**

Gainesville
Dunlap House Bed & Breakfast Inn

The Old South is in full splendor in this elegant 1910 inn. Completely renovated in 1985, the inn's guestrooms have designer linens and oversized cotton bath towels. All rooms are equipped with cable television, a telephone and a king- or queen-size bed. Some rooms also have a working fireplace. A complimentary breakfast is served either in your room or on the wicker-furnished veranda.

10 Rooms • Price range: $75-155
635 Green St NW, Gainesville, GA 30501
☎ **(770) 536-0200**

Hamilton
Magnolia Hall Bed & Breakfast

Directly behind the courthouse in this picturesque town is Magnolia Hall. An 1890s Victorian cottage-style home, this B&B features white gingerbread trim and a wraparound porch. Among the 100-year-old hollies outside is a splendid magnolia tree that is stunning when in blossom. Inside features include antique decor, high ceilings and a piano in the sitting-room. The B&B is only five minutes away from Callaway Gardens.

5 Rooms • Price range: $95-115
127 Barnes Mill Rd, Hamilton, GA 31811
☎ **(706) 628-4566**

Hartwell
The Skelton House

The Skelton House was built in 1896 by Jim Skelton and his wife. The couple raised 10 children here and today this B&B is run by their descendants. Some of the comfortable guestrooms are named after the original family's children and decorated with their memorabilia. Breakfasts, prepared with fresh herbs from the kitchen garden, include homemade jams and jellies. The spacious grounds are often used for weddings and parties.

7 Rooms • Price range: $85-125
97 Benson St, Hartwell, GA 30643
☎ **(706) 376-7969**

Macon
⏚ *1842 Inn*

This Greek-Revival dazzler, named for the year when it was built, is steeped in antebellum architectural detail. After dark the inn only gains in charm, as its verandas sparkle with hundreds of lights. Former Macon mayor and cotton merchant John Gresham built the mansion and his ghost is rumored to haunt the master suite that bears his name. The Taft Library is named after the former president— and one-time guest. Although there is no restaurant on the premises, an off-site private club provides guests with dining and recreation.

21 Rooms • Price range: $165-245
353 College St, Macon, GA 31201
☎ **(912) 741-1842**

Marietta
The Stanley House Bed & Breakfast

This four-story Queen Anne home was built in 1895 for Felie Wilson, Woodrow Wilson's aunt. Renovated in 1985, the antique-furnished guestrooms now feature private modern baths. A sunny front garden is a pleasant place to sit and watch the world go by. The town square park holds regular art shows under the shade of its grand old trees. There are also shops and interesting antique stores set around the square.

5 Rooms • Price: $100
236 Church St, Marietta, GA 30060
☎ **(770) 426-1881**

Marietta
The Whitlock Inn Bed & Breakfast

This restored 1900 residence is located in a National Register Historic District. The inn includes five guestrooms, each with private bath, and either queen-size or twin beds. Each room also features a ceiling fan, cable TV, telephone, writing desk and central heating and air-conditioning. A 100-seat ballroom is available to rent for receptions or business functions. A continental breakfast is served daily.

5 Rooms • Price: $145
57 Whitlock Ave, Marietta, GA 30064
☎ **(770) 428-1495**

Milledgeville
Antebellum Inn

This grand Greek-Revival mansion, circa 1890, is located on Georgia's historic Antebellum Trail in Milledgeville. Elegant guestrooms include amenities such as televisions with VCRs, private telephones with answering service, modem hookups and writing desks. Two spacious parlors and a large outdoor porch are perfect for resting after a day of sightseeing. A dip in the outdoor pool is a refreshing way to start the day.

5 Rooms • Price range: $65-99
200 N Columbia St, Milledgeville, GA 31061
☎ **(912) 454-5400**

Perry
Henderson Village

With nine historic houses on 18 acres, the Henderson is a genuine village resort. The homes have been beautifully restored and renovated with nothing but luxury in mind. Each has a columned porch overlooking lovely gardens or landscaped yard. Breakfast may be taken at the Langston House restaurant or delivered to the room. The outdoor pool is open year-round as is the aviary. This inn is a remarkable resort in every way.

24 Rooms • Price range: $175-350
125 S Langston Circle, Perry, GA 31069
☎ **(912) 988-8696**

Savannah
Ballastone Inn

Situated in historic Savannah, this restored 1838 antebellum mansion boasts guestrooms decorated with antiques and period reproductions. Most rooms also have a fireplace, a king-size bed and a sitting area; some feature a balcony and whirlpool tub. Terry-cloth robes and slippers can be found in every room. The inn also has a parlor, a lounge with an antique bar and a courtyard. Tennis equipment and bicycles are provided. Breakfast, lunch and afternoon tea are served in the Tea Room. Here is Southern hospitality at its most gracious.

17 Rooms • Price range: $255-415
14 E Oglethorpe Ave, Savannah, GA 31401
☎ **(912) 236-1484**

♦♦ Savannah
♦♦ **The Gastonian**

There is no more indulgent introduction to the delights of Savannah, than a stay in one of these two opulent 1868 Italianate Regency-style mansions, which are connected by a curving back porch. Each guestroom is beautifully appointed with English antiques and all feature luxurious canopy beds, fireplaces, deluxe baths (some with whirlpools) and tastefully coordinated linens, drapes and carpets. Some rooms have their own private entrance to a courtyard garden. The Gastonian continues to be a favorite hideaway for movie stars.

17 Rooms • Price range: $225-320
220 E Gaston St, Savannah, GA 31401
☎ **(912) 232-2869**

♦♦ Savannah
♦♦ **Hamilton-Turner Inn**

Built in 1873 and fully restored in 1998, this fine example of Second Empire architecture is adorned with Eastlake, Empire and Renaissance-Revival antiques. Several rooms have claw-foot bathtubs or whirlpools, fireplaces and balconies with views of Lafayette Square. A full Southern breakfast is served in the tearoom. The parlor is a cozy spot for soft music and conversation in front of the fire. A two-bedroom carriage house is also available. Trivia buffs will be interested to know that the previous owner was the character Mandy from John Berendt's book "Midnight in the Garden of Good and Evil."

14 Rooms • Price range: $169-358
330 Abercorn St, Savannah, GA 31401
☎ **(912) 233-1833**

♦♦ Savannah
♦♦ **The Kehoe House**

Located in Columbia Square in Historic Savannah, this 1892 inn has been restored to its original stately elegance. One of Consul Courts, luxury European-style inns, The Kehoe House features 15 suites furnished with period antiques. Some of the guestrooms have their own private veranda. A complimentary breakfast is offered every morning, tea is served in the afternoon and cocktails along with hors d'oeuvres are served in the parlor every evening. The inn's conference room is available for business meetings or executive seminars.

15 Rooms • Price range: $205-275
123 Habersham St, Savannah, GA 31401
☎ **(912) 232-1020**

Savannah
🏛 *East Bay Inn*

This 1853 restored cotton warehouse features Georgian-style rooms and 18-foot-high ceilings. All guestrooms have 18th-century period furnishings, a queen-size four-poster rice bed, Oriental carpets, hardwood floors and a private bath. Coffeemakers are in each room and complimentary coffee and tea are provided. The East Bay Inn also provides other special touches, including evening wine and sherry.

28 Rooms • Price range: $149-199
225 E Bay St, Savannah, GA 31401
☎ **(912) 238-1225**

Savannah
Eliza Thompson House Inn

The inn dates to 1847, when a rich socialite, Eliza Thompson, built her fabulous home in the center of the trading district. Located in the heart of Savannah's historic district, the inn that still bears Miss Thompson's name is close to a variety of captivating sights, including antique shops, museum houses and Civil War memorials. The inn includes 25 guestrooms. A deluxe full breakfast is offered daily.

25 Rooms • Price range: $119-260
5 W Jones, Savannah, GA 31401
☎ **(912) 236-3620**

Savannah
🏛 *Foley House Inn*

This restored Victorian townhouse boasts large, comfortable guestrooms (and some smaller units in the carriage house), combining traditional decor and modern amenities. All have private baths, and some come with an oversized Jacuzzi. Guests can use the inn's well-stocked film library. Many of Savannah's historic sites, such as the fabled waterfront district and the beautiful park on Chippewa Square, are steps from the door.

18 Rooms • Price range: $205-350
14 W Hull St on Chippewa Sq,
Savannah, GA 31401
☎ **(912) 232-6622**

Savannah
The Forsyth Park Inn

This Victorian mansion, overlooking Forsyth Park, has been carefully restored to its original 19th-century splendor. The inn features high ceilings, tall windows, huge carved oak doors and period furnishings. Each guestroom has a four-poster king- or queen-size bed, a fireplace, and an antique marble bath or a whirlpool tub. A private carriage cottage is also available. Continental breakfast is served in the parlor.

10 Rooms • Price range: $135-240
102 W Hall St, Savannah, GA 31401
☎ **(912) 233-6800**

Savannah
Gaston Gallery Bed & Breakfast

This 1876 Italianate townhouse is located in Savannah's historic district.

15 Rooms • Price range: $90-200
211 E Gaston St, Savannah, GA 31401
☎ **(912) 238-3294**

Savannah
Magnolia Place Inn

Forsyth Park, created in 1851, is a 20-acre green space in the middle of downtown Savannah's historic district. The homes around the park's perimeter are some of the city's most beautiful and the 1878 Magnolia Place Inn is no exception. Elegant English antiques, porcelains and richly hued fabrics grace every room. The spacious guest quarters have four-poster beds, many have Jacuzzi baths and gas fireplaces.

13 Rooms • Price range: $145-325
503 Whitaker St, Savannah, GA 31401
☎ **(912) 236-7674**

Savannah
⚅ *Olde Harbour Inn*

It is hard to imagine that this lovely inn was originally an 1892 riverfront warehouse. The decor is a successful blend of antique furnishings and modern interior design. The one- and two-bedroom suites with full kitchens and private baths are beyond spacious. For example, the suites on the fourth-floor have 23-foot-high ceilings. Breakfast is served in the Marine Room overlooking the river. Evening cocktails are served in the parlor.

24 Rooms • Price range: $129-229
508 E Factors Walk, Savannah, GA 31401
☎ **(912) 234-4100**

Savannah
⚅ *Planters Inn*

Located in historic Reynolds Square, the Planters Inn is surrounded by live oak trees and flowering azaleas. Step out the front door and you will probably see horse-drawn carriages passing by. From here, it's a short stroll to Savannah's bustling riverfront, where renovated cotton warehouses have been converted into quaint shops. Guestrooms and suites at the inn are decorated in fine fabrics. A complimentary breakfast is served daily.

56 Rooms • Price range: $125-185
29 Abercorn St, Savannah, GA 31401
☎ **(912) 232-5678**

Savannah
The President's Quarters Inn & Guesthouse

True to its name, the President's Quarters offers seven suites named after presidents who have visited Savannah. There are also nine guestrooms. This inn features antiques and period furnishings, and each room has a fireplace, a balcony, and a four-poster bed, a canopy bed or an old-fashioned high bed. Guests enjoy complimentary afternoon tea with cakes, a nightly turndown service with cordials and sweets.

19 Rooms • Price range: $137-250
225 E President St, Savannah, GA 31401
☎ **(912) 233-1600**

Savannah
River Street Inn

Situated on a bluff overlooking River Street and the Savannah River, the rooms in this mid-19th-century inn offer contemporary comforts in a cozy historic setting. French-style balconies provide views of the river to the north or the city to the south. Two in-house restaurants have cocktail bars that feature local entertainment. The location is ideal for exploring historic Factor's Walk and River Street's shops.

86 Rooms • Price range: $179-239
124 E Bay St, Savannah, GA 31401
☎ **(912) 234-6400**

Savannah
Joan's on Jones B&B

The spacious suites in this Victorian townhouse have private entrances.

2 Rooms • Price range: $145-170
17 W Jones St, Savannah, GA 31401
☎ **(912) 234-3863**

Senoia
The Veranda

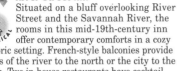

At the turn of the 20th century it was the Hollberg Inn. Today, this Greek-Revival inn, restored to its original glory, has been named after its columned wraparound veranda. The unpretentious Southern Country-style decor reflects the hosts' taste. A large collection of antiques and curios includes a Wurlitzer player piano and more than 1,000 kaleidoscopes. Breakfasts are lavish.

9 Rooms • Price range: $85-155
252 Seavy St, Senoia, GA 30276-0177
☎ **(770) 599-3905**

St. Marys
Spencer House Inn Bed & Breakfast

Listed on the National Register of Historic Places, this 1872 building is a fine example of Greek-Revival architecture. The day starts here with a delicious breakfast buffet. Each of the guestrooms has a ceiling fan, central air-conditioning and heating, cable television, and a private bath. The Spencer House makes elegant use of selected fabrics, rugs and furnishings. The three-story inn also has an elevator and an outside ramp for added convenience.

14 Rooms • Price range: $80-145
101 E Bryant St, St. Marys, GA 31558
☎ **(912) 882-1872**

Statesboro
Statesboro Inn & Restaurant

A Victorian house built in the early 1900s, this inn has been meticulously restored to conform with the stringent National Historic Register guidelines. Today the inn has polished hardwood floors, elegant antiques and old-fashioned lighting. Some guestrooms feature working fireplaces, whirlpool baths or porches. The dining room offers breakfast, lunch and dinner.

18 Rooms • Price range: $95-150
106 S Main St, Statesboro, GA 30458
☎ **(912) 489-8628**

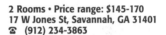

Thomasville
1884 Paxton House Inn

This Gothic Victorian home has a meticulously kept front yard and a charming back garden with secluded guest cottages tucked away under the trees. The main house is elegantly decorated with antiques and collectibles. Guests enjoy complimentary robes, down pillows and an evening turn-down service. Early risers can drink their coffee on the spacious veranda while watching the sunrise.

10 Rooms • Price range: $85-250
445 Remington Ave, Thomasville, GA 31792
☎ **(912) 226-5197**

Thomasville
Serendipity Cottage Bed & Breakfast

This is a grand 1906 "Four Square" with features such as leaded-glass windows, oak columns and pocket doors. The oak wainscoting in the dining room is topped with a grooved plate rail to display the original owner's collection of trophies. Rooms are appointed with queen-size beds and private baths. Evening turn-down service includes a little gift of chocolate and morning coffee will be brought to the room on request.

4 Rooms • Price range: $80-120
339 E Jefferson St, Thomasville, GA 31792
☎ **(912) 226-8111**

Unadilla
Sugar Hill Bed & Breakfast

This 1850 farmhouse is a delight any season of the year. Guests visiting in the winter will appreciate the inn's three strategically placed fireplaces. In the summertime, there is a pool for cooling off. But whatever the season, visitors can look forward to charming guestrooms, each with a private bath, ceiling fan, and central air-conditioning and heating. Two common rooms contain books, games and a television.

4 Rooms • Price range: $50-75
2540 Sugar Hill Rd, Unadilla, GA 31091
☎ **(912) 627-3557**

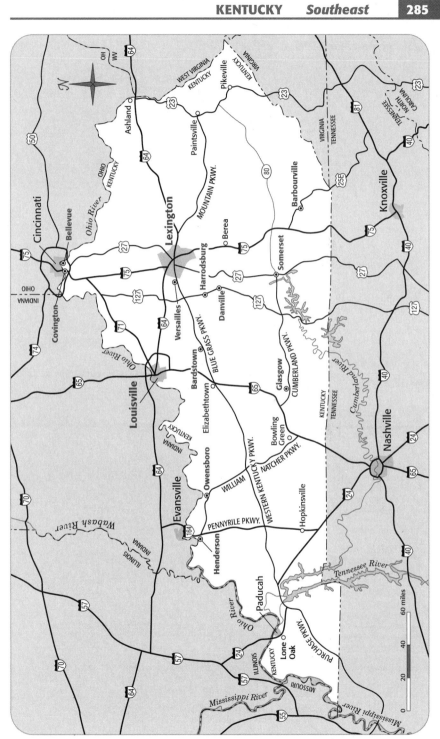

Barbourville
Appletree Inn
Guests can choose to take advantage of the no-phone option for a quiet stay.

4 Rooms • Price range: $82-112
231 Knox St, Barbourville, KY 40906
☎ **(606) 546-5328**

Bardstown
Arbor Rose

The original section of this historical home dates back to 1820. Named after a song by Bardstown's most famous son, Stephen Foster, this B&B is near all the local attractions. The house has five fireplaces and each guestroom is comfortably furnished and equipped with a private bath. Breakfast is served on the garden patio.

5 Rooms • Price range: $99-129
209 E Stephen Foster Ave, Bardstown, KY 40004
☎ **(502) 349-0014**

Bardstown
Beautiful Dreamer Bed & Breakfast

This replica of a Federal beauty charms guests with its delightful ambience. Furnished with antiques, the 3,800-square-foot expanse features a graceful central staircase and wood-burning fireplace in the dining room. All four bedrooms are equipped with a private bath, and one boasts a double Jacuzzi. Guests are invited to gather around the piano in the evenings for sing-alongs.

4 Rooms • Price range: $99-119
440 E Stephen Foster Ave, Bardstown, KY 40004
☎ **(502) 348-4004**

Bellevue
Cincinnati's Weller Haus Bed & Breakfast

Two side-by-side Gothic-Victorian homes make up this charming B&B. Only 1.7 miles from downtown Cincinnati across the Ohio River, Bellevue retains all the charm and hospitality of small-town Kentucky. The gardens are a great place for guests to relax and listen for the sounds of the local church bells. Each guestroom is decorated for comfort and equipped with a private bath.

5 Rooms • Price range: $89-158
319 Poplar St, Bellevue, KY 41073
☎ **(859) 431-6829**

Covington
⚫ Amos Shinkle Townhouse Bed & Breakfast

Covington entrepreneur Amos Sprinkle built his Riverside District home in 1854. Today, it is the only B&B in the area listed on the National Trust for Historic Preservation. A simple exterior gives way to a detailed interior. A grand entrance hall stairway, 16-foot-high ceilings with crown moldings, richly decorated guestrooms and gracious hosts make this one of the area's favorite romantic getaways.

7 Rooms • Price range: $84-160
215 Garrard St, Covington, KY 41011-1715
☎ **(859) 431-2118**

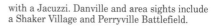

Danville
Twin Hollies Retreat

An 1833 antebellum mansion built for a Virginian judge. Spacious antique-filled guestrooms are surrounded by four acres of woods and a formal garden with a Jacuzzi. Danville and area sights include a Shaker Village and Perryville Battlefield.

3 Rooms • Price range: $80-80
406 Maple Ave, Danville, KY 40422
☎ **(859) 236-8954**

Glasgow
Four Seasons Country Inn

Nestled in the rolling hills of southern Kentucky, this large Victorian-style home combines quaint beauty with modern luxury. Conveniences include a private bath, four-poster bed and HBO in every room. Local outdoor attractions include Mammoth Cave National Park and Barren River State Park with its miles of hiking trails. Guests are invited to a generous complimentary breakfast served daily.

21 Rooms • Price range: $78-140
4107 Scottsville Rd, Glasgow, KY 42141
☎ **(270) 678-1000**

Harrodsburg
Beaumont Inn

The Beaumont Inn was originally a college for young ladies, which is evident by the names and dates still found inscribed in the mortar. Its spacious guestrooms, each equipped with a private bath, are furnished with antiques, setting a gracious tone of southern hospitality typical of the Bluegrass region. Other facilities include parlors and meeting rooms, a large outdoor pool, and a charming dining room.

33 Rooms • Price range: $65-125
638 Beaumont Inn Dr, Harrodsburg, KY 40330
☎ **(859) 734-3381**

Harrodsburg
Shaker Village of Pleasant Hill

Nestled in a 19th-century farm village, the rooms feature Shaker reproductions.

81 Rooms • Price range: $60-90
3501 Lexington Rd, Harrodsburg, KY 40330
☎ **(859) 734-5411**

Henderson
L & N Bed & Breakfast

The L & N stands beside train tracks of the railway that gave it its name. The interior design and furnishings of this Victorian home have been carefully chosen in keeping with an antique railway theme. Stained-glass windows, decorative fireplaces and an intricately carved oak staircase make this B&B a special place. Each of the spacious, individually decorated guestrooms is equipped with a private bath and cable television.

4 Rooms • Price: $75
327 N Main St, Henderson, KY 42420
☎ **(270) 831-1100**

♦♦ Lexington
♦♦ **Brand House at Rose Hill**
♦♦ This dignified, Federal-style 1812
home was constructed by Scottish
entrepreneur John Wesley Hunt, a
testament to the man's prosperity
in the New World. Brand House is now
listed in the National Register of Historic
Places and its floor plan is registered with
the Library of Congress. Faithful renovations
to the house have not shortchanged modern
luxury. Each guestroom is equipped with a
private bath, including a whirlpool tub; some
rooms feature a fireplaces. Breakfast includes
such delicacies as country ham soufflé and
blueberry mousse.

5 Rooms • Price range: $109-239
461 N Limestone St, Lexington, KY 40508
☎ **(859) 226-9464**

♦ Louisville
♦♦ **Aleksander House Bed & Breakfast**
♦ Located in historic Old Louisville, this
three-story Italianate-Victorian home
was built in 1882. Completely renovated,
the house features 14-foot-high ceilings,
original fireplaces, and oak and walnut floors.
The spacious rooms offer a private or shared
bath. Guests are invited to a full gourmet
breakfast daily. Aleksander House is conveniently
located near the airport as well as Louisville's
many attractions.

4 Rooms • Price range: $95-149
1213 S First St, Louisville, KY 40203
☎ **(502) 637-4985**

♦ Louisville
♦♦ **Central Park Bed & Breakfast**
♦ Historic Louisville is a neighborhood of
19th-century homes and buildings num-
bering in the thousands, making it the
nation's largest Victorian district. This
inn across from Central Park has 11 fireplaces
with hand-carved oak mantels, 12-foot-high
doors and stained-glass windows. The period
furnishings are complemented by data ports,
TV/VCRs and private baths. Museums, shopping and fine restaurants are all nearby.

8 Rooms • Price range: $89-169
1353 S Fourth St, Louisville, KY 40208
☎ **(502) 638-1505**

♦ Louisville
♦♦ **The Columbine Bed & Breakfast**
♦ This stately 1896 Greek-Revival mansion
with a massive columned portico is set
in a gentrified neighborhood. The richly
colored rooms accent the antique furnishings and the handsome mahogany, oak and
cherry woodwork. A grand central staircase
with a marvelous balustrade leads to the tastefully
furnished guestrooms. Guests can choose what
they wish for breakfast and authentic northern
Italian cuisine is available for dinner.

5 Rooms • Price range: $70-140
1707 S 3rd St, Louisville, KY 40208
☎ **(502) 635-5000**

Owensboro
WeatherBerry Bed & Breakfast

This stately Kentucky farmhouse, built in 1840, is on the National Register of Historic Places. The rooms are filled with beautiful antiques and each has a private bath. A day-lily garden is the highlight of the seven acres surrounding the house. A city park is across the street, perfect for an early-morning stroll. A little farther afield lies the airport, a golf course, the Ben Hawes State Park and the Conference Center.

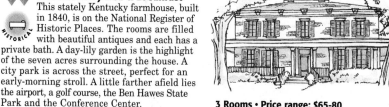

3 Rooms • Price range: $65-80
2731 W 2nd St, Owensboro, KY 42301
☎ **(270) 684-8760**

Somerset
The Osbornes of Cabin Hollow B & B

Set on a wooded hilltop, this log cabin has porches that offer a fine view of the woods during the day and the lights of the city at night. Homemade biscuits, jams and jellies are served with a hearty breakfast. This is a quiet retreat in a lovely spot.

3 Rooms • Price range: $55-70
111 Fietz Orchard Rd, Somerset, KY 42501
☎ **(606) 382-5495**

Versailles
1823 Historic Rose Hill Inn
A large home built in 1823, Rose Hill Inn sits on three acres of land minutes from downtown Versailles. A one-time Civil War hospital, the rambling white structure with its broad front pillars and the adjacent brick cottage now boast period furnishings and modern amenities. Each room has been named after a previous resident and is equipped with a private bath. Breakfast is served in the main dining room.

6 Rooms • Price range: $69-139
233 Rose Hill, Versailles, KY 40383
☎ **(859) 873-5957**

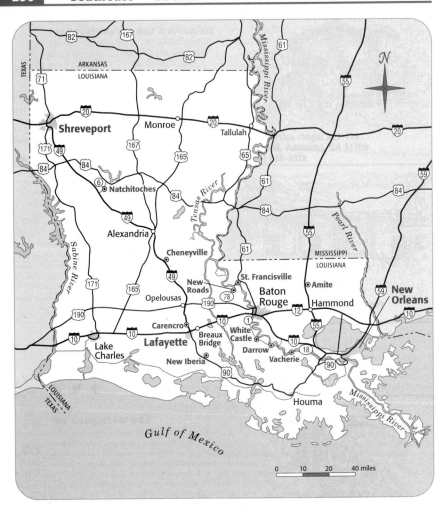

Amite
Elliott House

Set among oaks, camellias and dogwoods, this historical home is one of Amite's oldest buildings. Guests can relax in rockers on the wide colonial gallery, read a book selected from the extensive library or retreat to a comfortable chair in front of the wood-burning fireplace in their room or the parlor. The inn offers down-home cooking and a four-course candlelight dinner for special occasions.

3 Rooms • Price range: $70-90
801 N Duncan Ave, Amite, LA 70422
☎ (504) 748-8553

Carencro
La Maison de Campagne, Lafayette

This former sugarcane and cotton plantation is right in the heart of Cajun country, 15 minutes outside Lafayette. Each of the three guestrooms has been decorated with antiques. A former sharecropper cottage located near the outdoor pool is available for guests who plan to stay more than two days. Guests have the option of several nearby activities, which include biking on the Wilderness Trail along the Vermillion River.

4 Rooms • Price range: $120-135
825 Kidder Rd, Carencro, LA 70520
☎ (337) 896-6529

Cheneyville
Loyd Hall Plantation

Situated on the banks of the Bayou Boeuf, this 1800s plantation has been fully restored to its original glory. The 640-acre plantation has been in continual use for more than a century. These days it provides guests with an opportunity to see cattle and crop farming, including fields of corn and cotton. The inn itself features ornate plaster ceilings, suspended staircases and rare antiques.

6 Rooms • Price range: $100-170
292 Loyd Bridge Rd, Cheneyville, LA 71325
☎ (318) 776-5641

Darrow
⊛ *Tezcuco Plantation B&B*

This large plantation has rooms in the main house and in smaller cabins.

20 Rooms • Price range: $65-165
3138 Hwy 44, Darrow, LA 70725
☎ (225) 562-3929

Lafayette
Alida's Bed & Breakfast

This B&B is a restored late 19th-century cottage located near Highway 90.

4 Rooms • Price range: $85-150
2631 SE Evangeline Thrwy, Lafayette,
LA 70508-2168
☎ (337) 264-1191

Natchitoches
⊛ *Fleur de Lis Bed & Breakfast*

Circa 1903 Queen Anne Victorian-style home with wraparound porch.

5 Rooms • Price range: $65-85
336 2nd St, Natchitoches, LA 71457
☎ (318) 352-6621

New Iberia
Le Rosier Country Inn Bed & Breakfast

This charming circa 1870 home with its recently built carriage house is set deep in South Louisiana's Cajun country. The accent is on Acadian-style food with the operation of the inn's two dining rooms under the helm of owner Hallman Woods and his acclaimed chef son, Hallman III. The two buildings are linked by a beautiful rose garden, hence the inn's name. The guestrooms overlook an inviting veranda bordering the garden.

6 Rooms • Price range: $95-115
314 E Main St, New Iberia, LA 70560
☎ **(337) 367-5306**

New Orleans
Bed & Breakfast As You Like It

Located just three miles from the French Quarter, this Mediterranean-style home provides easy access to a number of attractions, including the Convention Center, the Superdome and the Casino. Among other nearby attractions are the Audubon Park and Zoo and the Mississippi River Cruise. This B&B features two large rooms, each with a private bath, phone and television. One has a sitting room. A continental breakfast is served daily.

2 Rooms • Price range: $80-150
3500 Upperline St, New Orleans, LA 70125
☎ **(504) 821-7716**

New Orleans
⚅ The Chateau Hotel

Tjis 1820s residence offers many rooms overlooking the courtyard and the pool.

45 Rooms • Price range: $79-149
1001 Chartres St, New Orleans, LA 70116
☎ **(504) 524-9636**

New Orleans
Grenoble House

This three-story brick Creole townhouse in the French Quarter was built in 1834 and features tastefully renovated suites with exposed brick walls, fireplaces and fully equipped kitchens. The courtyard has a pool and a barbecue/bar area that guests are welcome to use. It is ideally located three blocks from the lively French Quarter, which means it's far enough away to be quiet but conveniently close to the fun.

17 Rooms • Price range: $179-279
329 Dauphine St, New Orleans, LA 70112
☎ **(504) 522-1331**

New Orleans
⚅ The Historic French Market Inn

Built in the 1800s near the banks of the Mississippi for Baron Joseph Xavier de Pontalba this remarkable inn is hidden away in the heart of the French Quarter. Comfortable guestrooms featuring exposed brick walls and antique furniture are modernized with all the amenities. Enjoy breakfast on a romantic, secluded courtyard or bask in the sun by the pool. The sounds and the sights of Bourbon Street are two blocks away.

93 Rooms • Price range: $89-299
501 Rue Decatur, New Orleans, LA 70130
☎ **(504) 561-5621**

New Orleans

LaFitte Guest House
This restored French manor house, originally built in 1849, is situated right on the ever-entertaining Bourbon Street. All guestrooms are carpeted, and have either a king- or queen-size bed. Guests can take advantage of tranquil sound machines and silk sleep masks. The staff will help you with everything from making restaurant reservations to arranging tours. A continental breakfast is served daily.

14 Rooms • Price range: $149-219
1003 Bourbon St, New Orleans, LA 70116
☎ **(504) 581-2678**

New Orleans

Lamothe House Hotel
The former home of a Louisiana sugar baron, this 1839 hotel is one of New Orleans' most beautiful. A perfect example of the aristocratic charm of French Louisiana, the hotel boasts hand-turned mahogany banisters, interior millwork and exquisite plasterwork. Hand-hewn cypress floors, rolled-glass window panes and ceiling timbers add to the beauty. Antique furnishings are found throughout. There is an attractive courtyard open to guests.

20 Rooms • Price range: $79-200
621 Esplanade Ave, New Orleans, LA 70116
☎ **(504) 947-1161**

New Orleans

Maison Esplanade Guest House
This restored guest house features accommodations ranging from small rooms to spacious suites. A total of 10 rooms are available here, each with a four-poster bed. There are also two suites, as well as rooms that accommodate pets.

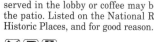

10 Rooms • Price range: $89-159
1244 Esplanade Ave, New Orleans, LA 70116
☎ **(504) 523-8080**

New Orleans

The Queen Anne Hotel
This 1890 Queen Anne-Victorian mansion has been painstakingly restored to its original grandeur by the owners of the Prytania Park Hotel. The B&B features floor-to-ceiling windows, cornices, tapestries, Oriental carpets, hardwood floors and exquisitely decorated rooms. A continental breakfast is served in the lobby or coffee may be had on the patio. Listed on the National Register of Historic Places, and for good reason.

12 Rooms • Price range: $149-269
1625 Prytania St, New Orleans, LA 70130
☎ **(504) 524-0427**

New Orleans
Avenue Bed & Breakfast
Built in 1892 for a sugar plantation owner, this B&B is ideally located near the sights, sounds and flavors of the famous French Quarter. The guest-rooms are spacious, some have small sitting areas. A continental breakfast is served.

6 Rooms • Price range: $89-199
4125 St Charles Ave, New Orleans, LA 70115
☎ **(504) 269-2640**

New Orleans
Chateau du Louisiane

A few steps from this 1885 mansion guests can catch a ride on the historic St. Charles Streetcar or, during Mardi Gras, watch one of the many passing parades. Guestrooms have private baths and phones with voice-mail.

5 Rooms • Price range: $89-159
1216 Louisiana Ave, New Orleans, LA 70115
☎ **(504) 269-2600**

New Orleans
Fairchild House Bed & Breakfast

This is a nicely decorated 1841 Greek-Revival home in the lower Garden District. Guestrooms are spacious and fully equipped with modern conve- niences. The dense foliage in the back garden creates a cool, shady spot on hot days.

14 Rooms • Price range: $75-145
1518 Prytania St, New Orleans, LA 70130
☎ **(504) 524-0154**

New Orleans
Garden District Bed & Breakfast

This historic property features kitchens in four of the comfortable guestrooms.

5 Rooms • Price range: $80-90
2418 Magazine St, New Orleans, LA 70130
☎ **(504) 895-4302**

New Orleans
Jude Guest House

This refurbished house is located at the entrance to a campground.

5 Rooms • Price range: $75-120
7400 Chef Menteur Hwy,
New Orleans, LA 70126
☎ **(504) 241-0632**

New Orleans
The Olivier Estate, a Bed & Breakfast

Two homes and a cottage make up this former family estate: a Spanish-style mansion from 1855; an 1871 Greek-Revival mansion; and a cottage built in 1878. All have been restored to include modern baths, big screen TVs and sound systems.

6 Rooms • Price range: $80-125
1425 N Prieur St, New Orleans, LA 70116-1744
☎ **(504) 949-9600**

New Orleans
Rathbone Inn

Constructed in 1850, the Rathbone Inn is a Greek-Revival style mansion. The sunny guestrooms have high ceilings, kitchenettes and private baths. The inn is located two blocks from the French Quarter and four from Bourbon Street.

9 Rooms • Price range: $59-259
1227 Esplanade Ave, New Orleans, LA 70116
☎ **(504) 947-2100**

New Orleans
Rue Royal Inn

This historic building dating back to the 1800s has a stone and brick court-yard, a nice selection of rooms and the convenience of being located in the French Quarter. Some rooms have a sitting area, a balcony, a wet bar and a Jacuzzi.

17 Rooms • Price range: $85-165
1006 Royal St, New Orleans, LA 70116
☎ **(504) 524-3900**

New Orleans
Whitney Inn

This inn is a 19th-century town house situated in the Lower Garden District. The neighborhood is very active during Mardi Gras as St. Charles Ave. is one of the major parade routes. The inn is located close to the French Quarter.

21 Rooms • Price range: $80-130
1509 St Charles Ave, New Orleans, LA 70130
☎ **(504) 521-8000**

New Roads
Sunrise on the River

Situated on the banks of the picturesque False River in a small South Louisiana town, this B&B offers peace, quiet and the sight of the sun rising above the river. The gazebo at the end of the private pier offers an idyllic setting for a lazy afternoon spent dozing in a hammock. The patio is the perfect spot to sit with a cup of morning coffee and watch for birds. Restaurants and antique shops are located nearby.

3 Rooms • Price range: $125-240
1825 False River Dr, New Roads, LA 70760
☎ **(225) 638-3642**

Shreveport
Slattery House

This 1903 Victorian home is located in the Highland Historic District and is listed in the National Register of Historic Places. Situated on more than an acre of land, this three-story house has spacious rooms furnished with antiques from the 1800s. Each guestroom has a private bath, television and telephone. Guests can also take advantage of the private pool. A full country breakfast is served daily.

6 Rooms • Price range: $99-195
2401 Fairfield Ave, Shreveport, LA 71104
☎ **(318) 222-6577**

St. Francisville
Green Springs Inn & Cottages

This inn is a reproduction of an early 1800s West Feliciana plantation home and features five "shotgun" cottages on 165 acres of ancestral land. Rooms are tastefully decorated and very homelike. The more private cottages have all the conveniences.

9 Rooms • Price range: $95-175
7463 Tunica Trace, St. Francisville, LA 70775
☎ **(225) 635-4232**

St. Francisville
Lake Rosemound Inn Bed & Breakfast

Located on three acres of land overlooking picturesque Lake Rosemound, this former country club is a peaceful country retreat in a superb natural setting. A special treat is their old fashioned self-serve ice cream bar.

4 Rooms • Price range: $75-125
10473 Lindsey Ln, St. Francisville, LA 70775
☎ **(225) 635-3176**

Vacherie
⚛ *Bay Tree Plantation Bed & Breakfast*

Two cottages and a former plantation doctor's office make up this wonderful three-acre property. The circa 1850 French-Creole cottage offers one room and a suite. The Rene House has four rooms with a shared kitchen, parlor and dining room. The Vignes Cottage is fully equipped and self-contained. All accommodations have private baths and lovely antique furnishings, which include some exceptionally beautiful bedsteads.

7 Rooms • Price range: $75-195
3785 Hwy 18 (River Rd), Vacherie, LA 70090
☎ **(225) 265-2109**

White Castle
Nottoway Plantation Restaurant & Inn
This majestic 1859 antebellum mansion is the largest surviving plantation house in the South. It was fired upon during the Civil War but a young captain, who had once been a guest there, offered his protection so that it would not be damaged. The landscaped grounds sit at the edge of sugarcane fields, just over an hour from New Orleans. The Bridal Suite features a private courtyard and a swimming pool.

13 Rooms • Price range: $105-250
30970 Hwy 405, White Castle, LA 70788
☎ **(225) 545-2730**

Notes:

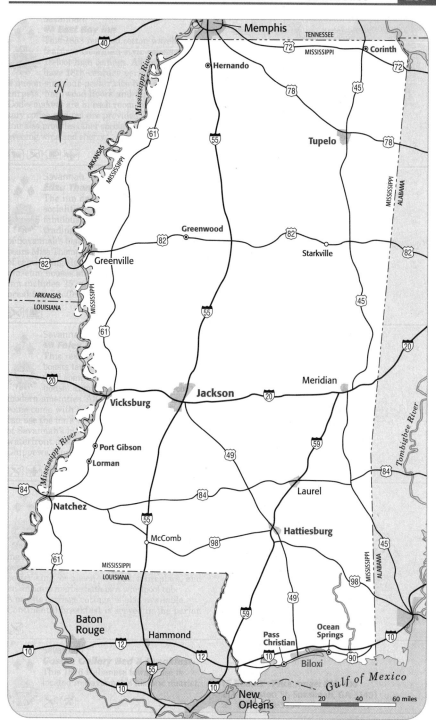

Biloxi
 Father Ryan House Bed & Breakfast Inn

This attractive inn has the unique feature of a palm tree growing through the center of its wide front steps. Built in 1841, the house was once the home of Father Abram Ryan, Poet Laureate of the Confederacy. The house and grounds have been restored, and the rooms—most of which overlook the Gulf—have been furnished with hand-crafted furniture and antiques. A pool is available for guests.

15 Rooms • Price range: $100-175
1196 Beach Blvd, Biloxi, MS 39530
☎ **(228) 435-1189**

Biloxi
Green Oaks Bed & Breakfast

Built in the early 1800s on a Spanish land grant, Green Oaks is the oldest remaining beachfront residence in Biloxi. The two handsome buildings that make up the inn house an impressive collection of period antiques. Each room is elegantly appointed and has a private bath. The inn sits on two acres of landscaped grounds dotted with century-old oaks. A veranda provides a view of the Gulf and the pristine barrier islands.

8 Rooms • Price range: $125-150
580 Beach Blvd, Biloxi, MS 39530
☎ **(228) 436-6257**

Biloxi
Lofty Oaks Inn B & B

Surrounded by six acres of wooded property, this French Country-style farmhouse inn provides a perfect refuge for the weary traveler. Guests will enjoy the pool, the enclosed outdoor hot tub, the deck with a grill, and the breezy front porch complete with a swing. At breakfast guests are treated to a truly delicious meal. The inn is located close to casinos, sandy beaches and an impressive golf course.

4 Rooms • Price range: $99-125
17288 Hwy 67, Biloxi, MS 39532
☎ **(228) 392-6722**

Biloxi
 The Old Santini House B&B

Across the road from the beach, this historic inn has an inviting front porch.

4 Rooms • Price range: $100-175
964 Beach Blvd, Biloxi, MS 39530
☎ **(228) 436-4078**

Corinth
 *The Generals' Quarters Bed and Breakfast Inn*

Originally a church, this structure was built in 1870 and is located in the historic district. The property boasts period antiques and modern conveniences to accommodate any traveler. A second-floor veranda looks down onto the surrounding grounds that feature a pond, azaleas, roses and magnolias. Guests will enjoy the B&B's breakfast made by the resident chef. Nearby activities include boating, fishing, and hiking.

5 Rooms • Price range: $75-120
924 Fillmore St, Corinth, MS 38834
☎ **(662) 286-3325**

Greenwood
Bridgewater Inn

This 1910 Greek-Revival home is located on the Yazoo River in the Mississippi Delta. Each room is attractively appointed and has a private bath. Some boast a view of the river and open onto a columned porch with swings and rocking chairs. Other rooms feature French doors and a claw-foot tub. Nearby are the Florewood Plantation, the Cottonlandia Museum and the downtown Cotton District.

4 Rooms • Price range: $65-90
501 River Rd, Greenwood, MS 38930
☎ **(662) 453-9265**

Hattiesburg
Dunhopen Inn

Built by the grandfather of the present owner, this inn boasts time-honored architecture. The tasteful decor of the home includes Colonial-style furniture which was hand-crafted by the original owner and elegant antiques acquired over the years. Guests can choose to eat in a bistro or in a more upscale restaurant that serves world-class cuisine, both of which are on-site. The surrounding area boasts seven golf courses.

12 Rooms • Price range: $85-175
3875 Veterans Memorial Dr,
Hattiesburg, MS 39401
☎ **(601) 543-0707**

Hernando
Sassafras Inn Bed & Breakfast

Set in a rural area outside of town, this English Tudor-style home is a perfect getaway. Each guestroom is decorated with a different motif and features grand beds, modern amenities and thoughtful details such as terry cloth robes and stereos. On-site is a kidney-shaped indoor pool, waterfalls, a hot tub and tropical gardens. While enjoying rural peace, guests are not far from attractions such as Sun Studios and Graceland.

4 Rooms • Price range: $75-245
785 Hwy 51, Hernando, MS 38632
☎ **(662) 429-5864**

Jackson
⨀ Fairview Inn

This grand three-story Colonial-Revival mansion is one of the few remaining landmark properties in Jackson. Surrounded by flowering magnolia, crepe myrtle trees and formal gardens that include box hedges and statuettes, this 1908 inn exudes an aura of elegance. The house features such details as Venetian marble floors and a crystal chandelier in the foyer, and fine antiques throughout. The eight rooms are divided between the main house and carriage house, where the Hayloft Honeymoon Suite is found. The inn is able to accommodate weddings and large gatherings.

18 Rooms • Price range: $100-290
734 Fairview St, Jackson, MS 39202
☎ **(601) 948-3429**

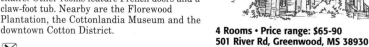

Jackson
Millsaps Buie House

Back in the 1880s, Jackson's social elite built mansions along State Street and gathered in each other's homes for events such as dinner parties, tea dances and croquet. This National Register Victorian mansion was one such place. It survived a disastrous fire before being fully restored in 1987. Rooms on the first and second floors are furnished with fine period antiques and reproductions, while those on the third floor have a more contemporary design. The buffet breakfast has received rave reviews for its first-class cheese grits.

11 Rooms • Price range: $90-175
628 N State St, Jackson, MS 39202
☎ **(601) 352-0221**

Jackson
Old Capitol Inn

Each morning, daily newspapers and coffee await guests just outside their bedroom door. The rooftop gardens feature a private setting for sunning

or relaxing in the hot tub. Bicycles are available for sightseeing or exercise.

24 Rooms • Price range: $85-165
226 N State St, Jackson, MS 39201
☎ **(601) 359-9000**

Lorman
Rosswood Plantation

Once a 1250-acre cotton plantation, Rosswood now grows Christmas trees on its grounds. Built in 1857 in the Greek-Revival style, the inn features 14-foot-high ceilings, columned galleries and a winding stairway. Each room is attractively appointed with fine antiques, a canopy bed, fireplace and a private bath. A heated pool and spa have been added. The inn also invites guests to examine an 1857 diary of plantation life.

4 Rooms • Price range: $115-135
Rt 1, Box 6, Lorman, MS 39096
☎ **(601) 437-4215**

Natchez
Monmouth Plantation

Located on 26 beautifully landscaped acres, Monmouth Plantation offers a look back at the days of the antebellum South. Accommodations are provided in the main house, slave quarters and cabins, the carriage house and plantation suites. All have been carefully restored and rebuilt, and are elegantly outfitted with antique furnishings. Many of the rooms have a fireplace. Monmouth Plantation offers five-course dinners, touted as the "the best in Natchez." This inn offers a romantic setting for weddings, receptions and honeymoons, and has conference space for up to 100 people.

30 Rooms • Price range: $160-270
36 Melrose Ave, Natchez, MS 39120
☎ **(601) 442-5852**

Natchez
🏛 *Cedar Grove Plantation*

Once a prosperous cotton plantation, Cedar Grove is now a country estate tucked away on 150 acres of rolling forest and farmland. This 1830 Greek-Revival house has been fully renovated and features eight fireplaces, a library, a den and a pool. There is also an expansive rear gallery overlooking the rose garden and one of the five stocked ponds on the property. Kennels are provided for guests with dogs.

7 Rooms • Price range: $120-200
617 Kingston Rd, Natchez, MS 39120
☎ **(601) 445-0585**

Natchez
🏛 *Governor Holmes House*

Built in 1794, this two-story brick house is one of the oldest homes in Natchez. It later became the residence of David Holmes, who served as the last governor of the Mississippi Territory and the first governor of the State of Mississippi. Many of the house's original features remain. The inn is decorated with period furnishings and Oriental rugs. A traditional plantation breakfast is served every morning.

4 Rooms • Price: $115
207 S Wall St, Natchez, MS 39120
☎ **(601) 442-2366**

Natchez
🏛 *Linden*

The Linden is a historic Federal antebellum home that has been in the same family for six generations. The front doorway was copied for Tara in "Gone With the Wind." Most of the rooms open onto the galleries and feature one of the finest collections of Federal furniture in the South. In the stately dining room, a magnificent cypress fan hangs over a Hepplewhite banquet table surrounded by Audubon prints.

7 Rooms • Price range: $95-130
1 Linden Pl, Natchez, MS 39120
☎ **(601) 445-5472**

Natchez
Riverside B & B

This restored antebellum home was built circa 1858 and is listed on the National Register of Historic Places. The second story of the home was removed during the Civil War by Union troops so that Confederate forces could not signal from it. The second story was rebuilt in 1903. Since the inn is located high on a bluff, all bedrooms feature a view of the Mississippi River. Guests are treated to full Southern breakfasts.

3 Rooms • Price range: $85 room,
$110-150 suite
211 Clifton Ave, Natchez, MS 39120
☎ **(601) 446-5730**

Natchez
Weymouth Hall

On a high bluff overlooking Mississippi River, this inn offers spectacular views.

3 Rooms • Price range: $95-135
1 Cemetery Rd, Natchez, MS 39120
☎ **(601) 445-2304**

Ocean Springs

♦ **Wilson House Inn Bed & Breakfast**
This log cabin is a great spot for a get-away. Rooms are small but nice.

6 Rooms • Price range: $35-79
6312 Allen Rd, Ocean Springs, MS 39565
☎ (228) 875-6933

Pass Christian

♦ ♦ ⊕ *Inn at the Pass*
Built circa 1870, this home is located in the historic district, and faces the Gulf.

5 Rooms • Price range: $85-125
125 E Scenic Dr, Pass Christian, MS 39571
☎ (228) 452-0333

Port Gibson

♦ ♦ ⊕ *Oak Square Country Inn*
In 1863, as he marched his troops through Port Gibson, General Ulysses S. Grant is reported to have said the town was "too beautiful to burn." Oak Square is a part of this history. A circa 1850 Greek-Revival mansion, the inn has been restored. Rooms are spacious and airy, furnished with 18th- and 19th-century antiques. Grounds feature a courtyard, a fountain and a gazebo. The inn has its own collection of Civil War memorabilia.

12 Rooms • Price range: $110-135
1207 Church St, Port Gibson, MS 39150
☎ (601) 437-4350

Tupelo
♦ *The Mockingbird Inn Bed & Breakfast*
Famous as the birthplace of Elvis Presley, Tupelo is also the home of the Mockingbird Inn. This comfortable B&B is located directly across the street from the school where Elvis attended sixth and seventh grades. Rooms at the inn are decorated thematically, each capturing the character and atmosphere of a different part of the world. Each room has a private bath. Special Romance packages can be requested by guests.

7 Rooms • Price range: $79-99
305 N Gloster, Tupelo, MS 38804
☎ (662) 841-0286

Vicksburg

♦ *Anchuca*
Staying at this 1830 Greek-Revival style home is a true pleasure. The inn is magnificently furnished with heirlooms, and it features such modern luxuries as a grand swimming pool and a whirlpool tub. Guests are treated to a full breakfast and complimentary evening drinks. Guests are welcome to get together and relax in the sitting room, perhaps even to play or listen to the piano. A turn-down service is provided.

5 Rooms • Price range: $85-140
1010 1st East St, Vicksburg, MS 39183
☎ (601) 661-0111

Vicksburg
⚋ *Annabelle*

This historic Victorian Italianate residence was built just five years after the siege of Vicksburg. A stately brick home, Annabelle provides comfortable accommodations. The inn features original artwork and antiques, and offers guests a view of the river. There is also a pleasant courtyard shaded by giant magnolia and crepe myrtle trees, as well as a swimming pool and fountain. Four floating casinos nearby offer van service to pick up guests from the inn.

7 Rooms • Price range: $83-135
501 Speed St, Vicksburg, MS 39180
☎ **(601) 638-2000**

Vicksburg
⚋ *Belle of the Bends*

Perched on a bluff overlooking the Mississippi River sits the Belle of the Bends. This circa 1867 brick home was named after a 1900s steamboat that belonged to the owner's grandfather. The inn is dominated by its wraparound verandas overlooking the river. It is elegantly decorated with period antiques and memorabilia from the steamboats that traveled the Mississippi in the 1880s and early 1900s.

4 Rooms • Price range: $95-150
508 Klein St, Vicksburg, MS 39180
☎ **(601) 634-0737**

Vicksburg
⚋ *Cedar Grove Mansion Inn*

Built circa 1840, this antebellum mansion retains its original Southern charm while providing the best in modern comfort. Guestrooms are located in the main house, the pool house or the carriage house, and some feature fireplaces. Guests will enjoy the pool and the whirlpool tub, the tennis court and the exercise room. Thoughtful services offered by the innkeepers include sherry and chocolate at tea time and before bed.

29 Rooms • Price range: $95-185
2200 Oak St, Vicksburg, MS 39180
☎ **(601) 636-1000**

Vicksburg
The Corners Bed & Breakfast Inn

This two-story Victorian Greek-Revival style mansion stands on a bluff overlooking the Mississippi and Yazoo Rivers. The inn's 15 rooms range in style from Southern elegance to country simplicity. Each room has a fireplace and whirlpool tub, and some have a private porch. Two-bedroom units are also available. Common areas include a front gallery, a glassed-in veranda and a large double parlor filled with antiques and a grand piano.

15 Rooms • Price range: $80-130
601 Klein St, Vicksburg, MS 39180
☎ **(601) 636-7421**

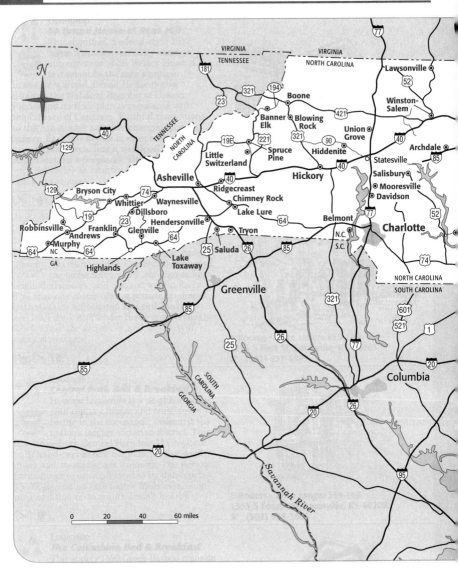

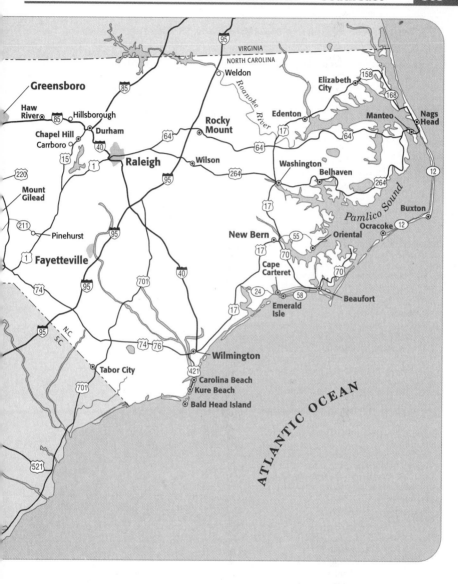

VIRGINIA
NORTH CAROLINA

Greensboro

Haw
River
Hillsborough

Chapel Hill
Carrboro
Durham

Raleigh

Mount
Gilead

Pinehurst

Fayetteville

Weldon

**Rocky
Mount**

Wilson

Edenton

Elizabeth
City

Manteo

Nags
Head

Washington
Belhaven

Roanoke River

Pamlico Sound

Buxton

Ocracoke

New Bern

Oriental

Cape
Carteret

Beaufort

Emerald
Isle

N.C.
S.C.

Tabor City

Wilmington

Carolina Beach
Kure Beach

Bald Head Island

ATLANTIC OCEAN

Andrews

Hawkesdene House Bed & Breakfast Inn and Cottages

The resident llamas at Hawkesdene are just one of the inn's many draws. Situated not far from the Nantahala National Forest, Hawkesdene House offers the comfort and charm of an English country home. A cascading stream runs through the 20 adjoining acres, and several woodland paths weave their way through the surrounding hills. Mornings and evenings, llama treks set out from the inn into the National Forest.

10 Rooms • Price range: $75-175
381 Phillips Creek Rd, Andrews, NC 28901
☎ **(828) 321-6027**

Archdale

The Bouldin House B & B, High Point

The innkeepers at Bouldin House are full of useful information for visitors who have come to shop in nearby High Point. Billing itself as "the home furnishings capital of the world," High Point is the site of America's largest concentration of furniture showrooms. The inn itself offers a splendid gourmet breakfast to start the morning and it is a comfortable place to relax after a full day shopping. All rooms have fireplaces.

4 Rooms • Price range: $95-130
4332 Archdale Rd, Archdale, NC 27263
☎ **(336) 431-4909**

Asheville
Richmond Hill Inn

More than 100 years ago, ambassador and statesman Richmond Pearson built this mountaintop residence overlooking the French Broad River. Saved from demolition some years back, Richmond Hill has been transformed into an elegant inn, consisting of the Mansion, the Croquet Cottages and the Garden Pavilion. The grounds include a parterre garden and plenty of quiet spots to relax. At Gabrielle's, the inn's nationally recognized restaurant, first-class cuisine is served against a background of live piano music.

36 Rooms • Price range: $145-450
87 Richmond Hill Dr, Asheville, NC 28806
☎ **(828) 252-7313**

Asheville
1900 Inn on Montford

This inn was designed in 1900 by Richard Sharp Smith, the supervising architect for Asheville's famed Biltmore House. The inn houses guestrooms furnished with English and American antiques dating from 1730 to 1910. All of the rooms are equipped with private baths and showers, three of which include whirlpool baths. The inn also features a 1,000-square-foot suite with a sitting room and balcony.

4 Rooms • Price range: $120-250
296 Montford Ave, Asheville, NC 28801
☎ **(828) 254-9569**

Asheville
Abbington Green Bed & Breakfast Inn

This 1908 Colonial-Revival house and garden features elegant guestrooms decorated in the English style with canopy beds and antiques. Three of the rooms include working fireplaces, and all are equipped with private baths.

6 Rooms • Price range: $135-225
46 Cumberland Cir, Asheville, NC 28801
☎ **(828) 251-2454**

Asheville
Albemarle Inn

Listed on the National Register of Historic Places, this 1909 Greek-Revival mansion is located in Asheville's upper-crust Grove Park. Guests enter the inn through the parlor with its oak paneling and 11-foot-high ceilings. A massive oak staircase leads upstairs to the richly appointed rooms. Freshly arranged flowers and handmade chocolates are welcome touches. Breakfast is served in the sunporch or by candlelight in the dining room.

11 Rooms • Price range: $130-295
86 Edgemont Rd, Asheville, NC 28801
☎ **(828) 255-0027**

Asheville
⚑ *Applewood Manor Inn*

Giant oak, pine, and maple trees surround this fine old Colonial inn. Rooms are comfortably furnished and most are equipped with a fireplace and a balcony. A full breakfast is served daily, either by the fireside in the formal dining room or on the side porch. Visitors can visit the nearby Smoky Mountain National Park and the Botanical Gardens and go skiing and white-water rafting.

5 Rooms • Price range: $90-120
62 Cumberland Cir, Asheville, NC 28801-1718
☎ **(828) 254-2244**

Asheville
Beaufort House

Previously the home of Charleton Heston, the Beaufort House has guestrooms that tastefully combine antiques with modern amenities. Two of the rooms have entrances off a charming terrace, another from a private deck. A separate carriage house accommodates three more rooms in a more contemporary decor. One of the main attractions here is a magnificent garden, which features more than 8,000 flowering plants.

11 Rooms • Price range: $115-235
61 N Liberty St, Asheville, NC 28801
☎ **(828) 254-8334**

Asheville
⚑ *Black Walnut Bed & Breakfast Inn*

This finely preserved home, with Tudor and Arts and Crafts-style features, was designed by architect Richard Sharp Smith, the supervising architect for the Biltmore Estate. The inn has four guestrooms in the main house and two rooms in a garden cottage. The Dogwood Room is located in the turret, while the Walnut Room and the adjoining Azalea Room can be rented together.

6 Rooms • Price range: $65-225
288 Montford Ave, Asheville, NC 28801
☎ **(828) 254-3878**

Asheville
Cairn Brae Bed and Breakfast

Cairn Brae—Scottish for rocky hillside—perfectly describes the idyllic location of this three-acre mountain retreat. Located above Asheville, the inn combines quiet solitude with spectacular mountain views. The building is a 28-year-old "round house" with four bedrooms, each with large picture windows and a private bath. There is a stone patio outside and the surrounding woodland has walking trails for visitors to explore.

3 Rooms • Price range: $100-140
217 Patton Mountain Rd, Asheville, NC 28804
☎ **(828) 252-9219**

Asheville
⁂ Cedar Crest Victorian Inn

This Queen Anne mansion stands in the hills above Biltmore Village. It is one of the largest and most opulent residences from Asheville's 1890s boom period. Fluted pilasters with Ionic capitals, a majestic stairway, hand-carved woodwork and expansive multilevel verandas are just a few of Cedar Crest's impressive features. Outside the grounds of this inn are graced with dogwoods and English-style gardens.

11 Rooms • Price range: $145-185
674 Biltmore Ave, Asheville, NC 28803
☎ **(828) 252-1389**

Asheville
⁂ The Colby House

Built in 1924, this Dutch Tudor house has been transformed into a charming B&B. The pineapple theme visible throughout symbolizes Southern hospitality. The inn has a parlor with a fireplace, a cozy library, a porch furnished with rocking chairs and well-kept flower gardens—all comfortable places to unwind. Each of the guestrooms features a queen-size bed with a handmade quilt, air-conditioning and a private bath.

5 Rooms • Price range: $125-235
230 Pearson Dr, Asheville, NC 28801
☎ **(828) 253-5644**

Asheville
Flint Street Inns

Known for its cool mountain summers, Asheville is surrounded by a million acres of National Forest. The Flint Street Inns are two adjoining old family homes located in the town's oldest neighborhood. Guestrooms are comfortably furnished with antiques from the 1900s. Nearby places of interest include millionaire George Vanderbilt's Biltmore House and the boyhood home of American writer Thomas Wolfe.

8 Rooms • Price range: $75-110
116 Flint St, Asheville, NC 28801
☎ **(828) 253-6723**

Asheville
⚫ *The Lion and the Rose Bed & Breakfast*

Located in Asheville's Montford Historic District, this residence has been faithfully restored to its original state, one which combines features of Georgian and Queen Anne styles. The interior has high embossed ceilings, golden oak woodwork, Persian rugs and fine antique furnishings. The veranda overlooks parklike grounds bordered by a white picket fence and flower gardens. Breakfast and afternoon tea are served daily.

5 Rooms • Price range: $145-245
276 Montford Ave, Asheville, NC 28801
☎ **(828) 255-7673**

Asheville
⚫ *The Wright Inn & Carriage House*

Set on a tree-lined street amid other stately Victorian homes, the Wright Inn and Carriage House is one of the finest examples of Queen Anne architecture in the area. The inn has elegant public rooms, lovely gardens and a gazebo. Each guestroom has a private bath and two have a fireplace. The Carriage House, with its living room, dining room, fully-equipped kitchen, three bedrooms and two full baths, is just the right size for families or groups.

10 Rooms • Price range: $140-160
235 Pearson Dr, Asheville, NC 28801
☎ **(828) 251-0789**

Bald Head Island
Theodosia's Bed & Breakfast

With its salt marshes, maritime forests and sandy beaches, Bald Head Island is a wonderful place to settle in and relax. The island sits at the mouth of Cape Fear River, just three miles off the coast of North Carolina. Comfortably furnished with bright rooms, the inn offers a myriad of activities, including golf and tennis. Bicycles and golf carts are provided by the inn as cars are not permitted on the island.

13 Rooms • Price range: $160-260
2 Keelson Row, Bald Head Island, NC 28461
☎ **(910) 457-6563**

Banner Elk
Azalea Inn

An impressive collection of birdhouses and an award-winning flower garden are among the first things guests see as they approach this charming establishment. Inside, one can relax in a living room with a fireplace or a sunporch. Guestrooms are comfortable, beds have luxurious down comforters, and all have private baths. Guests awaken in the morning to the aroma of freshly ground coffee and a full buffet breakfast.

8 Rooms • Price range: $109-175
149 Azalea Circle, Banner Elk, NC 28604
☎ **(828) 898-8195**

Banner Elk
Banner Elk Inn Bed & Breakfast

The town is located in the Mount Pisgah National Forest, with hiking, swimming and boating all close by. The B&B itself is situated halfway between the slopes of Sugar Mountain and Beech Mountain. Built in 1912 as a country church, the inn has attractive rooms, which are decorated with an eclectic mix of antique furnishings collected from abroad. The inn has set picnic tables in the gardens. Pets are welcome.

4 Rooms • Price range: $85-130
407 Main St E, Banner Elk, NC 28604
☎ **(828) 898-6223**

Beaufort
Delamar Inn

This restored 1866 home has a charming, well-manicured garden and a patio.

3 Rooms • Price range: $108-118
217 Turner St, Beaufort, NC 28516
☎ **(252) 728-4300**

Beaufort
Pecan Tree Inn

Located just half a block from the waterfront, this Victorian home has been a part of the town since 1866. Its porches, turrets and gingerbread trim evoke the characteristic charm of the Victorian period. Broad-plank pine floors complement the inn's many antiques. Attractive, well-manicured grounds include an English flower-and-herb garden, which is one of the main attractions for sightseers in town.

7 Rooms • Price range: $85-145
116 Queen St, Beaufort, NC 28516
☎ **(252) 728-6733**

Belhaven
River Forest Manor

A classic Victorian mansion. Most of the rooms have a view of the waterway.

6 Rooms • Price range: $65-95
738 E Main St, Belhaven, NC 27810
☎ **(252) 943-2151**

Belmont
Homeleigh Bed & Breakfast

This Renaissance-Revival home was built in 1919 for the A. C. Lineberger family and is listed on the National Register of Historic Places. Guests enter the property by way of 400-year-old wrought-iron gates and pass through three-and-a-half acres of landscaped gardens, which include a brick teahouse. Guestrooms have each been decorated in their own unique style and all are equipped with private baths.

5 Rooms • Price range: $100-125
411 N Main St, Belmont, NC 28012
☎ **(704) 829-6264**

Blowing Rock
Maple Lodge

Located just outside the historic village of Blowing Rock, and near the Blue Ridge Parkway, this charming B&B caters to visitors exploring the region's natural beauty. The inn offers gourmet picnic baskets to accompany day trips spent hiking, while the library is the perfect spot to curl up and relax after a long day's outing. Guestrooms are furnished with antiques and heirlooms and have private baths.

11 Rooms • Price range: $90-170
152 Sunset Dr, Blowing Rock, NC 28605
☎ **(828) 295-3331**

Boone
⚑ *Lovill House Inn*

Situated in the heart of the Appalachian Mountains, the Lovill House Inn is a charmingly rustic 1875 farmhouse nestled in the town named after Daniel Boone. The inn is furnished with a casual elegance, and the 11 wooded acres invite guests to explore. A stream runs along the side of the property, with a waterfall in the woods behind the picturesque barn. There are also large perennial gardens and 30-foot-high hydrangea bushes. The wraparound porch is set up with high-backed rockers for relaxing and taking in the fresh mountain air.

6 Rooms • Price range: $125-195
404 Old Bristol Rd, Boone, NC 28607
☎ **(828) 264-4204**

Bryson City
Hemlock Inn

The Hemlock Inn sits on 45 wooded acres at an elevation of 2,300 feet. Its front porch offers a spectacular view of the surrounding mountains and valleys. Once a mountain farm, the old-fashioned country inn now offers a gateway for those who want to enjoy an outdoor holiday. For walking, hiking, and fishing, the Great Smoky Mountains National Park is just three miles away; for tubing and rafting, Nantahala River is nearby.

26 Rooms • Price range: $140-190
PO Drawer EE, Bryson City, NC 28713
☎ **(828) 488-2885**

Buxton
⚑ *Cape Hatteras Bed & Breakfast*

Visitors to this B&B can enjoy its picnic area, grill and observation deck.

9 Rooms • Price range: $119-149
46223 Old Light House Rd, Buxton, NC 27920
☎ **(252) 995-6004**

Cape Carteret
Harborlight Guest House Bed & Breakfast

The Harborlight Guest House sits on a peninsula overlooking Bogue Sound and the Intracoastal Waterway. The inn property has been expertly landscaped and includes a water garden, palmetto palms and cypress trees. Each guestroom and suite features a private entrance and bath, as well as breathtaking views of the waterway. Boat tours, fishing trips and deep-sea fishing excursions are available nearby.

7 Rooms • Price range: $140-250
332 Live Oak Dr, Cape Carteret, NC 28584
☎ **(252) 393-6868**

Carolina Beach
⊕ *Dolphin Watch Bed & Breakfast*

This ocean-front house built in the 1950s is attractively decorated and includes a beach-front veranda replete with comfy rocking chairs. The guestrooms are pleasantly furnished and each is equipped with a private bath.

6 Rooms • Price range: $115-225
910 Carolina Beach Ave N,
Carolina Beach, NC 28428
☎ **(910) 458-5355**

Chapel Hill
The Inn at Bingham School

This secluded 200-year-old log cabin is listed on the National Register of Historic Places. The spacious guestrooms are individually furnished with period reproductions and antiques; four of them feature gas fireplaces.

5 Rooms • Price range: $65-130
6720 Mebane Oaks Rd, Chapel Hill, NC 27514
☎ **(919) 563-5583**

Charlotte
⊕ *The Inn Uptown*

This gracious century-old home is located in the heart of uptown Charlotte. The inn was constructed by Edgar Andrews as one of the first speculative houses in Charlotte, and today offers guests a haven of charm and hospitality. Each room is appointed with a fireplace, whirlpool tub or private balcony. Corporate guests will appreciate the inn's meeting facilities, telephones with modem capability, as well as a fax and copier.

6 Rooms • Price range: $129-169
129 N Poplar St, Charlotte, NC 28202
☎ **(704) 342-2800**

Charlotte
Morehead Inn

This elegant mansion was built in 1917; its rooms are quiet and attractive.

12 Rooms • Price range: $120-190
1122 E Morehead St, Charlotte, NC 28204
☎ **(704) 376-3357**

Chimney Rock
Esmeralda Inn

The inn is connected to a restaurant, which requires reservations.

14 Rooms • Price range: $99-149
910 Main St, Chimney Rock, NC 28720
☎ **(828) 625-9105**

Davidson
Davidson Village Inn
Located in Davidson's historic district, this inn has a cozy atmosphere. It features a large private library in the common area and handsomely appointed rooms, many of which are furnished with four-poster beds.

18 Rooms • Price range: $100-175
117 Depot St, Davidson, NC 28036
☎ **(704) 892-8044**

Dillsboro
🏩 *Applegate Inn*
This inn has lovely grounds, complete with a fish pond and a scenic stream.

7 Rooms • Price range: $50-100
163 Hemlock St, Dillsboro, NC 28725
☎ **(828) 586-2397**

Durham
Arrowhead Inn Bed and Breakfast
Situated on four acres of trees and gardens, this restored 1775 inn has nine guestrooms located in the Manor House and Carriage House. Each room has a private bath and some are equipped with a two-person whirlpool tub, a wood-burning or gas fireplace, a coffee maker and a refrigerator. Guests may also stay at the Carolina Log Cabin, which includes a sitting room, fireplace, king-size bed and large bath.

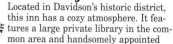

9 Rooms • Price range: $90-250
106 Mason Rd, Durham, NC 27712
☎ **(919) 477-8430**

Edenton
Governor Eden Inn
This refurbished 1920s inn is filled with period furniture.

4 Rooms • Price range: $65-95
304 N Broad St, Edenton, NC 27932
☎ **(252) 482-2072**

Edenton
The Trestle House Inn
Overlooking a pond and lake, the house is located close to scenic walks to nearby sites, including nearby Albemarle Sound. The interior of the house is made of trestle wood. This is a fine choice of lodging for those interested in birding.

5 Rooms • Price range: $60-95
632 Soundside Rd, Edenton, NC 27932
☎ **(252) 482-2282**

Elizabeth City
The Culpepper Inn
This 1936 Colonial-Revival home is set amid magnolias and oak trees on spacious landscaped grounds. Featured here are working fireplaces, two-person baths and a screened porch. The inn also has its own aromatherapy studio.

10 Rooms • Price: $95
609 W Main St, Elizabeth City, NC 27909
☎ **(252) 335-1993**

Emerald Isle
Emerald Isle Inn & Bed & Breakfast
This inn's location near a beach on the lower Outer Banks chain makes it a great place to go for a sun-drenched holiday by the sea. All the suites have full private baths, private entrances and patios with swings.

4 Rooms • Price range: $115-160
502 Ocean Dr, Emerald Isle, NC 28594
☎ **(252) 354-3222**

Franklin
Heritage Inn Bed & Breakfast
This country-style inn, in a wooded
area, has an art gallery on premises.

6 Rooms • Price range: $65-75
43 Heritage Hollow Dr, Franklin, NC 28734
☎ **(828) 524-4150**

Glenville
Innisfree Victorian Inn
Set on top of a mountain, this
Victorian-style inn features a large
wraparound veranda, offering guests
views of Lake Glenville and the long,
undulating form of the Blue Ridge Mountains.
Below lie award-winning gardens in which
guests are welcome to stroll. All guestrooms
are tastefully furnished, most of them have a
private balcony, garden tub and fireplace. The
dining room is octagonally shaped and lit by
an impressive chandelier. Breakfast, which
includes a variety of baked delights, is served
daily and Irish coffee is served every evening
in the parlor.

10 Rooms • Price range: $150-290
108 Innisfree Dr, Glenville, NC 28736
☎ **(828) 743-2946**

Greensboro
Greenwood Bed & Breakfast
Breakfast is a special part of the day at
this B&B. One of the innkeepers is a former New Orleans chef who takes great
pride in serving breakfasts that include
French bread, eggs Benedict or crepes Suzette.
Guestrooms feature king-size, queen-size, or
twin beds, and a private bath. There is also an
upstairs television lounge and an in-ground
pool. Nearby attractions include the Historical
Museum and the Guilford National Battleground.

5 Rooms • Price range: $110-145
205 N Park Dr, Greensboro, NC 27401
☎ **(336) 274-6350**

Haw River
The Victorian Rose
This 1885 Neo-Colonial home features
Italianate trim and antique Victorian
furnishings. The extensive, manicured
grounds are graced with an enchanting

gazebo. Common areas include a spacious
library/game room.

4 Rooms • Price range: $125-125
407 Graham Rd, Haw River, NC 27253
☎ **(336) 578-5112**

Hendersonville
Apple Inn Bed & Breakfast
There's plenty to do during a stay at
the Apple Inn. Guests can play badminton, horseshoes, croquet, billiards,
or simply relax in one of the rocking
chairs or hammocks on the inn's wraparound
porch. Guests are also invited to the Oak Hill
Racquet Club for a complimentary game of
tennis, handball or racquetball, or to use the
club's swimming pool. The inn has five guestrooms, each equipped with a private bath.

5 Rooms • Price range: $75-95
1005 White Pine Dr, Hendersonville, NC 28739
☎ **(828) 693-0107**

Hendersonville
Claddagh Inn

The word "Claddagh" is a Gaelic term meaning love, loyalty and friendship. The innkeepers try to incorporate all these qualities into this 1900s inn. Each of the 16 guestrooms has its own unique style, and all come with a private bath and telephone. Guests are welcome to enjoy the inn's parlor and library. A full home-cooked breakfast is served in the dining room every morning.

16 Rooms • Price range: $99-150
755 N Main St, Hendersonville, NC 28792
☎ **(828) 697-7778**

Hendersonville
The Waverly Inn

Located just 20 miles south of Asheville, this 1898 inn is located near several attractions, including the Carl Sandburg National Historic site, the Folk Art Center and the Brevard Music Center. Fourteen guestrooms and one suite are available, each featuring special items such as a four-poster canopy bed, a claw-foot tub and an old-fashioned pedestal sink. The inn's full breakfast includes homemade jams and stone-ground grits.

14 Rooms • Price range: $100-169
783 N Main, Hendersonville, NC 28792
☎ **(828) 693-9193**

Hendersonville
Echo Mountain Inn

Spectacular mountain views and quiet country charm. Includes motel rooms.

36 Rooms • Price range: $75-175
2849 Laurel Park Hwy,
Hendersonville, NC 28739
☎ **(828) 693-9626**

Hickory
The Hickory Bed & Breakfast

This Georgian-style home is generously decorated with antiques and collectibles from around the world. There are several common areas, including a parlor with a television, a library with a fireplace, and a small office with a phone, fax and PC hook-up. There are four comfortable guestrooms available. In the morning, guests can look forward to coffee, tea, a homemade breakfast and the morning newspaper.

4 Rooms • Price range: $85-125
464 7th St SW, Hickory, NC 28602
☎ **(828) 324-0548**

Hiddenite
Hidden Crystal Inn and Conference Center

This inn is just a short distance from the largest emerald deposit in North America.

13 Rooms • Price range: $85-225
471 Sulphur Springs Rd, Hiddenite, NC 28636
☎ **(828) 632-0063**

Kure Beach

⊕ *Ocean Princess Bed & Breakfast*

Guests at the Ocean Princess are treated to serene surroundings and beautifully landscaped grounds. Among the nearby attractions are bike paths, hiking trails, para-sailing, golf courses, a pool, and, of course, the beach. There are nine rooms, each with its own private bath, color television, microwave, refrigerator and telephone. Some rooms have whirlpool tubs. Breakfast is served daily in the dining room.

12 Rooms • Price range: $119-189
824 Fort Fisher Blvd S, Kure Beach, NC 28449
☎ **(910) 458-6712**

Lake Lure

Gaestehaus Salzburg

Situated on six acres of wooded hillside, this Alpine-style B&B is surrounded by flowering trees and plants with a wealth of bird life. Guests are greeted in the morning with a delicious breakfast, complete with fresh-baked breads. In the evenings, guests can share a glass of wine with their hosts before retiring to one of five spacious, well-appointed bedrooms, complete with private bath.

5 Rooms • Price range: $82-145
1491 Memorial Hwy, Lake Lure, NC 28746
☎ **(828) 625-0093**

Lake Lure

The Lodge On Lake Lure

This picturesque restored lodge is situated on the banks of Lake Lure, at the foot of the Blue Ridge Mountains. Guests can sit outside on the veranda and take in the magnificent view or, in the cooler months, enjoy the cozy fireplace inside. The lodge's lake-front location offers swimming, fishing and boating. Each of the 12 guestrooms features a private bath. The full breakfast, served daily, includes favorite family recipes.

12 Rooms • Price range: $139-165
361 Charlotte Dr, Lake Lure, NC 28746
☎ **(828) 625-2789**

Lake Toxaway

⊕ *The Greystone Inn*

This restored Edwardian mansion provides an unmatched view of Lake Toxaway and the Blue Ridge Mountains. Nineteen rooms are available in the Mansion, each decorated with antiques and period reproductions. There are another 12 rooms in the adjacent Hillmont; every room has a fireplace, wet bar, sitting area and balcony overlooking the lake. The Greystone Inn also includes two Lakeside Suites, complete with king-size bed, a bath with an oversize Jacuzzi and a sitting room. Guests can look forward to mid-afternoon tea and a gourmet dinner.

33 Rooms • Price range: $315-560
Greystone Ln, Lake Toxaway, NC 28747
☎ **(828) 966-4700**

Lawsonville
◆◆ *Southwyck Farm Bed & Breakfast*

This charming B&B off the beaten path offers a touch of New England south of the Mason-Dixon line. Antiques decorate the guestrooms and common areas. The property includes a pond for fishing.

6 Rooms • Price range: $75-125
1070 Southwyck Farm Rd, Lawsonville, NC 27022
☎ **(336) 593-8006**

Little Switzerland
◆◆ *Switzerland Inn*

Located adjacent to the Blue Ridge Parkway, this mountaintop property provides guests with stunning views. Accommodations range from rustic cottages to luxurious one-bedroom condominiums. All feature a private entrance and private bath.

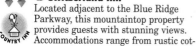

64 Rooms • Price range: $105-180
PO Box 399, Little Switzerland, NC 28749
☎ **(828) 765-2153**

Manteo
◆◆ *The Tranquil House Inn*

This waterfront inn, facing Shalowbag Bay, tries to live up to its name by providing guests with a peaceful break, away from the nearby beaches. Guestrooms offer a wide variety of decor that includes designer wallpaper, Oriental or Berber carpets and dried flower arrangements. Each room is connected to a beautiful, hand-tiled bath. Guests are greeted each morning with a continental breakfast.

25 Rooms • Price range: $149-189
405 Queen Elizabeth St, Manteo, NC 27954
☎ **(252) 473-1404**

Manteo
◆◆ *The White Doe Inn*

This 1910, Queen Anne-style home is one of the most photographed houses in the area. Each of the attractive guestrooms includes a private bath, a ceiling fan, a fireplace and fine linens. Some rooms have a two-person whirlpool tub. Other areas of interest in the inn include the parlor, study, dining room and entry foyer, all illuminated by exquisite chandeliers. A Southern-style breakfast is served daily.

8 Rooms • Price range: $155-250
319 Sir Walter Raleigh St, Manteo, NC 27954
☎ **(252) 473-9851**

Mooresville
◆◆ *Spring Run Bed & Breakfast*

Since 1990, the restful appeal of the Spring Run B&B has drawn visitors to sample its pleasures from countries as far away as India and Brazil. Situated on lovely Lake Norman, this three-story brick home has two guestrooms, each of which features a private bath, a private living room and dining room, and is furnished with a queen-size bed, ceiling fan, air-conditioning and cable television.

2 Rooms • Price range: $135-135
172 Spring Run, Mooresville, NC 28117
☎ **(704) 664-6686**

Mount Gilead
The Pines Plantation Inn

Once the center of a 1,500-acre working plantation, this antique-filled mansion now welcomes a host of international visitors. Built on Lake Tillery, on the edge of Uwharrie National Forest, the Pines Plantation Inn has five guestrooms, each with a private bath, and some with a fireplace. Among the pleasant attractions of this 1878 inn are the 14-foot-high ceilings, an elegant staircase, a sunroom, a parlor and a library.

5 Rooms • Price range: $55-80
1570 Lilly's Bridge Rd, Mount Gilead, NC 27306
☎ **(910) 439-1894**

Murphy
Huntington Hall Bed & Breakfast

Here's an inn tucked away in the foothills of the Great Smoky Mountains. A cozy 1800s home, the inn draws guests who wish to enjoy the local scenery. Each of the individually decorated rooms features tall windows, which offer views of the mountains. Other features include claw-foot baths, a spacious front porch and nightly turndown service. The inn is also renowned for its Murder Mystery weekends.

5 Rooms • Price range: $65-140
272 Valley River Ave, Murphy, NC 28906
☎ **(828) 837-9567**

Nags Head
First Colony Inn

The First Colony Inn is the only historic B&B on the Outer Banks. Built in 1932, it was restored to its original grandeur in the 1980s. A continental breakfast begins the day, served either in your room on a silver tray or in the breakfast room. Guests can spend the rest of the day lounging by the pool, walking along the boardwalk, picnicking at the Cape Hatteras National Seashore or visiting the Pea Island Wildlife Refuge. At the end of the day, visitors retire to their guestrooms, each of which has a tiled bath. Luxury suites include a wet bar or kitchenette.

26 Rooms • Price range: $80-165
6720 S Virginia Dare Tr, Nags Head, NC 27959
☎ **(252) 441-2343**

New Bern
The Aerie Inn

This Victorian-style house, which was built in the 1880s by Samuel Street, is located in the heart of the New Bern's Historic District. It is within a four-block radius of Tryon Palace, the Fireman's Museum, the Civil War Museum, fine restaurants and river-front parks. Each room is furnished with antiques and has a private bath. An English tea is served in the afternoon and fresh-baked foods are available in the evenings.

7 Rooms • Price range: $69-99
509 Pollock St, New Bern, NC 28562
☎ **(252) 636-5553**

New Bern
Harmony House Inn

This 1850 Greek-Revival home was once divided in half and expanded to accommodate a growing family. A new hallway and stairs were built in the Victorian style so that unusually spacious suites could be added. One suite now features a king-size bed and a heart-shaped Jacuzzi for those on a romantic getaway. Harmony House is located in New Bern's Historic District, and is a short walk from Tryon Palace and its formal gardens.

10 Rooms • Price range: $79-109
215 Pollock St, New Bern, NC 28560
☎ **(252) 636-3810**

New Bern
King's Arms Inn

This restored inn is a few miles from Tryon Palace in the Historic District.

7 Rooms • Price range: $70-100
212 Pollock St, New Bern, NC 28560
☎ **(252) 638-4409**

Ocracoke
Berkley Manor Bed and Breakfast

A charming B&B, on three acres of landscaped property at the south end of the island, this B&B is near the Cedar Island Ferry and has great

tower views of Ocracoke Island. Guestrooms are paneled with juniper or aromatic cedar.

12 Rooms • Price range: $135-195
PO Box 220, Ocracoke, NC 27960
☎ **(252) 928-5911**

Oriental
The Cartwright House

Victorian elegance is the hallmark of this three-story inn that manages to maintain a casual, comfortable ambience. Guests enjoy the view of the river while relaxing on the wraparound porch. Public areas and guestrooms are decorated with antiques. All guestrooms have a private bath and one room features a gas fireplace. Those with allergies should know that there is a cat living on the premises.

5 Rooms • Price range: $90-145
301 Freemason St, Oriental, NC 28571
☎ **(252) 249-1337**

Raleigh
The Oakwood Inn Bed & Breakfast

This 1871 Victorian home with an Italian-Revival influence is located in the Historic Oakwood district, an intact 19th-century neighborhood that includes an array of architectural styles, from Greek Revival to "Steamboat" Gothic. Antique furnishings and a gas-log fireplace are featured in each of the rooms. The parlor is a welcoming room with a gracious ambience. Full breakfast and afternoon tea are included.

6 Rooms • Price range: $85-135
411 N Bloodworth St, Raleigh, NC 27604
☎ **(919) 832-9712**

Raleigh
The William Thomas House Bed & Breakfast

This 1881 Victorian home is a historic landmark, which features attractive public areas and large, comfortable rooms. Guests are free to relax on any of the porches, to visit the library with its original Victorian paneling, or to enjoy the 1863 Steinway grand piano in the parlor. The inn's downtown location puts it within easy walking distance of museums, shopping, the Governor's Mansion, the State Capitol, and other historic properties.

4 Rooms • Price range: $115-185
530 N Blount St, Raleigh, NC 27604
☎ **(919) 755-9400**

Ridgecrest
Inn On Mill Creek

Set amid seven scenic acres in the Pisgah National Forest, this B&B is a modern home with an old-fashioned attitude toward hospitality. The building features a two-story great room with a piano corner, a cozy stone hearth and four newly appointed guestrooms or suites, each with its own private bath. Breakfast is served in the dining room or in the solarium by the goldfish pond and waterfall.

4 Rooms • Price range: $100-160
SR 1407 Mill Creek Rd, Ridgecrest, NC 28770
☎ **(828) 668-1115**

Robbinsville
⑩ *Blue Boar Inn*

The recently renovated Blue Boar inn is hidden deep in western North Carolina's Smoky Mountain country, just a short walk from the shores of Lake Santeetlah. It stands on the site of a former hunting lodge. Its upscale accommodations include private porches, sitting areas, king- or queen-size beds, large private baths, air-conditioning and refrigerators. Guests can enjoy a gourmet breakfast served in the dining room.

8 Rooms • Price range: $85-135
200 Santeetlah Rd, Robbinsville, NC 28771
☎ **(828) 479-8126**

Salisbury
Rowan Oak House

Built in 1901, this Queen Anne-style, Victorian home still features the original gas and electric fixtures as well as seven fireplaces, intricate wood carvings, wainscoting and stained-glass windows. It is listed on the National Register of Historic Places. A gourmet breakfast is served on china with crystal and sterling silver. Afterwards guests are encouraged to stroll through the beautifully kept English garden.

4 Rooms • Price range: $100-140
208 S Fulton, Salisbury, NC 28144
☎ **(704) 633-2086**

Saluda
The Oaks Bed & Breakfast

A charming Victorian country home decorated in period-style furnishings.

6 Rooms • Price range: $120-125
339 Greenville St, Saluda, NC 28773
☎ **(828) 749-9613**

Spruce Pine
⚋ *Richmond Inn*

Towering white pines shade this rambling country estate. The eight spacious guestrooms, one of which is a large suite, are each furnished with a private bath, fine antiques and cherished family treasures. The inn also features a stone fireplace in the living room and a wide flagstone terrace and veranda. Nearby Spruce Pine offers fine restaurants, craft studios and an indoor fitness center.

8 Rooms • Price range: $65-110
51 Pine Ave, Spruce Pine, NC 28777
☎ **(828) 765-6993**

Tabor City
Four Rooster Inn

Located on more than an acre of lawns landscaped with camellias and azaleas, this 1949 family home is a real bargain. The rooms are decorated in soft colors and furnished with a variety of antiques. Southern hospitality means that there is afternoon tea, featuring cucumber sandwiches and scones, an evening turndown service and a morning coffee tray brought to your door. Myrtle Beach is just 24 miles away.

4 Rooms • Price range: $55-90
403 Pireway Rd/ Rt 904, Tabor City, NC 28463
☎ **(910) 653-3878**

Tryon
⚋ *Pine Crest Inn*

In the early 1900s, this inn was a favorite retreat for those who could afford to get away from the heat of the low country. Today the building has been restored to its original beauty with richly upholstered furnishings, stone fireplaces and hardwood floors. Visitors can choose to stay in the Main Lodge or in one of the cottages. The inn's restaurant serves full breakfasts and gourmet dinners. Fox hunting and the Block House Steeplechase, still held each spring, are time-honored traditions in Tryon. Other activities include golf, tennis, riding, swimming and hiking in the Foothills Equestrian Nature Center.

35 Rooms • Price range: $160-220
85 Pine Crest Ln, Tryon, NC 28782
☎ **(828) 859-9135**

Union Grove
Madelyn's in the Grove, A Bed & Breakfast

This 1934 cottage and carriage house are located in a secluded rural setting on nine acres of land. All rooms are decorated with family antiques and have a private bath and twin, king- or queen-size beds. The Vance Room has a two-person Jacuzzi, while the Garden Room features a private deck. The area is steeped in musical tradition. Union Grove hosts the Old Time Fiddler's Convention. Enjoy afternoon snacks and evening treats.

5 Rooms • Price range: $75-145
1836 W Memorial Hwy, Union Grove, NC 28689-0249
☎ **(704) 539-4151**

Washington
Pamlico House

Southern hospitality rules in this circa 1900 home with its classic Victorian parlor and family antiques. Guestrooms feature either king-size wicker beds, queen-size four-poster canopied beds, brass twin beds or hand-painted Eastlake beds. Each room is also equipped with a private bath and a sitting area. A historic walking tour of Washington, N.C. begins just outside the front door.

4 Rooms • Price range: $75-95
400 E Main St, Washington, NC 27889
☎ **(252) 946-7184**

Washington
Acadian House Bed & Breakfast

High ceilings and heart-pine floors accent this 1900s home set in an historic district. The proprietors' New Orleans background has prompted Louisiana additions to their breakfasts, such as pain perdu and café au lait.

4 Rooms • Price range: $60-70
129 Van Norden St, Washington, NC 27889
☎ **(252) 975-3967**

Waynesville
Herren House Bed & Breakfast

Before being restored, this charming B&B was operated continuously from 1897 to 1989 as a boarding house. Today, Herron House combines period charm with modern comfort. Gracious Victorian decor and vintage antiques are enhanced by the owners' handmade furniture and paintings. Each room also has its own private bath and sitting area. An aromatic herb garden and wraparound porch add to the inn's attractions.

6 Rooms • Price range: $95-140
94 East St, Waynesville, NC 28786
☎ **(828) 452-7837**

Waynesville
The Yellow House on Plott Creek Road

Situated on a hilltop overlooking the misty Blue Ridge Mountains, this inn is decorated in the colors of the French impressionists. Guests can use the library, several balconies and a veranda. All rooms have a private bath, fireplace and a wet bar or refrigerator. Outside, guests can explore the vast grounds, complete with lily pond and footbridge. Breakfast can be served in your room if desired.

7 Rooms • Price range: $115-145
89 Oakview Dr, Waynesville, NC 28786
☎ **(828) 452-0991**

Whittier
The Chalet Inn

Guests of this B&B can enjoy any number of activities, including white-water rafting, trout fishing, horseback riding, biking and golfing. Located on 22 acres of a forested mountain region, the inn property features hiking trails as well as a waterfall and a pond. Each guestroom provides a private balcony and bath. The Great Room has a fireplace and a library. A candlelight breakfast is served on request on the brook-side patio.

6 Rooms • Price range: $103-127
285 Lone Oak Dr, Whittier, NC 28789
☎ **(828) 586-0251**

Wilmington
◆◆◆◆ Ⓐ *Graystone Inn*

An historic landmark and one of the most elegant structures in Wilmington, this inn has recently undergone extensive renovations. The ground floor features a ballroom, a mahogany-paneled library, a parlor, a music room and a formal dining room. A Renaissance-style oak staircase leads to the large guestrooms upstairs, each of which is decorated with period furnishings. Some rooms also feature working fireplaces and all are equipped with a private bath, fine linens, and robes. This popular setting for weddings also features a honeymoon suite with a walk-in shower and claw-foot tub—both built for two.

7 Rooms • Price range: $159-329
100 S Third St, Wilmington, NC 28401
☎ **(910) 763-2000**

Wilmington
◆◆◆ *The Curran House*

Guests have easy access to a number of attractions when staying at the Curran House. It's only a short walk to downtown, where St. John's Museum, Chandler's Wharf with its shops and the Ice House bar beckon. After a day of exploring, guests return to rooms that feature a private bath and a king- or queen-size bed. Breakfast in the dining room is accompanied by candlelight, crystal and freshly cut flowers.

3 Rooms • Price range: $89-119
312 S 3rd St, Wilmington, NC 28401
☎ **(910) 763-6603**

Wilmington
◆◆◆ Ⓐ *Rosehill Inn Bed & Breakfast*

This 1848 neo-Classic Revival home is located in the Historic District near the Cape Fear River. Guestrooms are spacious and comfortable, and each is individually decorated and named after a special theme such as the Tea Rose with its accents of rose, teal and ivory and the Indochina Room with its Asian appointments. The inn's chef offers breakfast creations including vegetable-garden quiche or macadamia-nut French toast.

6 Rooms • Price range: $149-219
114 S Third St, Wilmington, NC 28401
☎ **(910) 815-0250**

Wilmington
◆◆◆ *The Verandas*

Named for its inviting front and rear verandas, this Victorian Italianate mansion is located in Wilmington's Historic District. Other features include a distinctive cupola providing a panoramic view of the downtown. The well-appointed guest units are tastefully decorated, each in a unique style, and provide luxurious comforts. The inn is near shopping and restaurants and a short drive from Wrightsville Beach.

8 Rooms • Price range: $130-185
202 Nun St, Wilmington, NC 28401-5020
☎ **(910) 251-2212**

Wilmington
The Worth House Bed & Breakfast

This 1893 Queen Anne-style home features a parlor, a library and a formal dining room, each decorated with antiques and period paintings. Some guestrooms have a fireplace and enclosed porch, and all have a sitting area and private bath. A full breakfast is served in the dining room, or on the rear porch overlooking the gardens. Modem connections and fax machines are available to business travelers.

7 Rooms • Price range: $95-150
412 S 3rd St, Wilmington, NC 28401
☎ (910) 762-8562

Wilmington
Taylor House Inn Bed & Breakfast

An inn built in the Neo-Classic Revival style, with high ceilings, a magnificent open staircase and stained-glass windows. Each of the guestrooms has a bed of mahogany, cherry or oak and is equipped with a private bath.

5 Rooms • Price range: $65-135
14 N 7th St, Wilmington, NC 28401
☎ (910) 763-7581

Wilson
Miss Betty's Bed & Breakfast Inn

This gracious Victorian home set in Wilson's historic downtown, captures the elegance of another era. Each of the guestrooms is beautifully appointed and is equipped with a private bath. In addition, four Executive Suites cater to long-term business visitors. Breakfast here is another attraction. Donning her white bonnet, blue dress and white sneakers, Miss Betty prepares and serves such favorites as homemade sausage and grits.

10 Rooms • Price range: $50-80
600 W Nash St, Wilson, NC 27893-3045
☎ (252) 243-4447

Winston-Salem
⑭ Augustus T. Zevely Inn

This brick home, constructed circa 1844, offers comfortable guestrooms.

12 Rooms • Price range: $80-125
803 S Main, Winston-Salem, NC 27101
☎ (336) 748-9299

Winston-Salem
The Henry F. Shaffner B & B Inn

It took two years, from 1905 to 1907, to build this Queen Anne-style house. But the job of restoring the structure took longer. The tiger oak woodwork that decorates the interior was painstakingly refinished, and all guestrooms—including the ornate fireplaces used to heat them—have been restored to their original grandeur. The rooms are all equipped with modern amenities.

9 Rooms • Price range: $99-239
150 S Marshall St, Winston-Salem, NC 27101
☎ (336) 777-0052

Winston-Salem
Lady Anne's Victorian Bed & Breakfast

Guests are invited to a gourmet breakfast on weekends at this Victorian B&B, while a buffet breakfast is served during the week. Built in 1880 in a genteel residential district, the building is decorated with period antiques.

4 Rooms • Price range: $60-85
612 Summit St, Winston-Salem, NC 27101
☎ (336) 724-1074

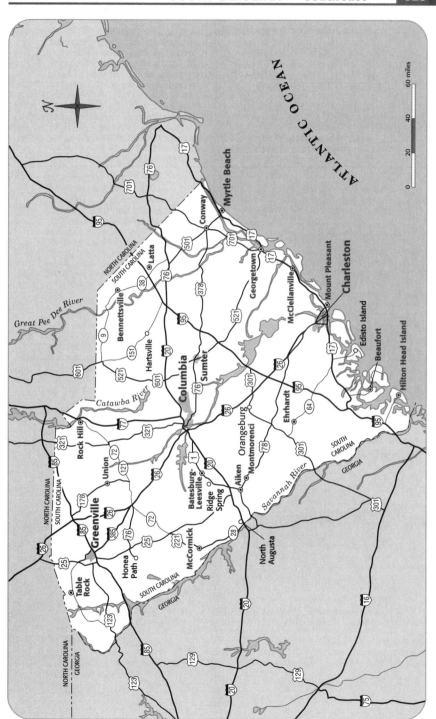

Aiken
Sandhurst Estate Bed & Breakfast Inn

A pillared, white-stuccoed set piece, the Sandhurst Estate is situated in Aiken, a town known as the "Winter Colony" for East Coasters. This 12,000-square-foot home, built in 1883, displays luxuries of a bygone era, including Victorian claw-foot baths in marble bathrooms, oversize glass showers, English antiques and pieces of fine art. Some rooms feature a working fireplace and private veranda. A full gourmet breakfast is served.

10 Rooms • Price range: $90-200
215 Dupree Pl, Aiken, SC 29801
☎ **(803) 642-9259**

Aiken
⚜ *The Willcox Inn*

In the heart of thoroughbred country, this elegant inn has fine dining.

30 Rooms • Price: $100
100 Colleton Ave SW, Aiken, SC 29801
☎ **(803) 649-1377**

Aiken
Town & Country Inn

For guests seeking a warm welcome and a homelike environment, this pleasant inn is the place to be. Spacious bedrooms offer private baths and com-fortable furnishings. Common areas are ideal for socializing or quiet relaxation.

5 Rooms • Price range: $65-95
2340 Sizemore Cir, Aiken, SC 29803
☎ **(803) 642-0270**

Batesburg-Leesville
The Able House Inn

Comfortable rooms and a relaxed atmosphere are what you can expect to find at the Able House. Five distinctively decorated guestrooms offer the luxury of plush towels and linens and extra pillows. Each room has a private bath. There is also a cozy living room with a fireplace and a sunroom with a television. Guests also have access to a refrigerator, a swimming pool and a patio. An enhanced continental breakfast is served.

5 Rooms • Price range: $60-75
244 E Columbia Ave, Batesburg-Leesville,
SC 29070
☎ **(803) 532-2763**

Beaufort
⚜ *Beaufort Inn*

Located in beautiful South Carolina Low Country, the Beaufort Inn is situated only a short distance away from the Intracoastal Waterfront Park. The inn was built in 1897. Today it offers imaginatively appointed guestrooms, each named after a local plantation, the history of which is detailed in the room. Some guestrooms also include special features such as a fireplace, wet bar or Jacuzzi. Every morning a full gourmet breakfast is served in the dining room, where fine cuisine is available nightly. Local attractions include carriage tours, museums, beaches, boating, golf, horseback riding, gift and antique shops, and sidewalk cafes.

12 Rooms • Price range: $125-225
809 Port Republic St, Beaufort, SC 29902
☎ **(843) 521-9000**

Beaufort
The Rhett House Inn

 This 1820 authentic antebellum plantation is located in Beaufort's historic district, and borders the Intracoastal Waterway. The Rhett House Inn's sprawling verandas and white columns foreshadow the elegance inside. The ambience is warm and welcoming; fresh-cut flowers add to the atmosphere. All guestrooms feature cable television, a telephone, CD player and private bathroom. Each room in the newly renovated cottage features a private entrance and porches. A delicious breakfast, including Southern grits, is served daily. A gourmet picnic basket is available on request.

17 Rooms • Price range: $125-350
1009 Craven St, Beaufort, SC 29902
☎ **(843) 524-9030**

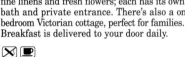

Beaufort
The Craven Street Inn

 It was only in 1997 that this 1870 Victorian house became an inn and it still retains much of the charm of a private residence. Situated on a half-acre of land, it's only one block away from the water. Seven rooms feature original artwork, fine linens and fresh flowers; each has its own bath and private entrance. There's also a one-bedroom Victorian cottage, perfect for families. Breakfast is delivered to your door daily.

8 Rooms • Price range: $139-229
1103 Craven St, Beaufort, SC 29902
☎ **(843) 522-1668**

Beaufort
Cuthbert House Inn

 Listed on the National Register of Historic Places, the Cuthbert House is a short walk from excellent golfing, the beach and an array of fine restaurants. Guestrooms combine the best of the 18th and 19th centuries, with original carved moldings and period furniture, and such modern amenities as cable television, telephone and refrigerator. Each room has a private bath. A gourmet breakfast starts the day off right.

7 Rooms • Price range: $135-225
1203 Bay St, Beaufort, SC 29902-5401
☎ **(843) 521-1315**

Beaufort
Two Suns Inn Bed & Breakfast

 One of Beaufort's grand historic homes, this 1917 inn has six guestrooms, each with a spectacular bay view, a private bath, a phone and central air-conditioning. Common room amenities include a video library and a self-serve refrigerator. Visitors can play croquet or horseshoes on the front lawn, and guest bicycles are available. The breakfast menu changes daily, and an informal "Tea & Toddy Hour" is a high point of the afternoon.

6 Rooms • Price range: $105-160
1705 Bay St, Beaufort, SC 29902
☎ **(843) 522-1122**

Bennettsville
The Breeden Inn, Carriage House & Garden Cottage

This 1886 inn has carried 19th-century beauty into modern times, as seen in its stained, beveled and leaded glass, in the original light fixtures, the unpainted, time-seasoned oak, in the heart-pine wainscoting and in the ornate oak and pine archways. The six guestrooms are decorated with fine bed linens, family heirlooms and interesting artwork. In-room breakfast is available on request.

6 Rooms • Price range: $85-135
404 E Main St, Bennettsville, SC 29512
☎ **(843) 479-3665**

Camden
Lord Camden Inn

A grand 1832 antebellum home conveniently located near many area attractions. Enjoy a game of badminton or horseshoes on the spacious landscaped grounds, or cool off with a dip in the pool. The individually decorated guestrooms are tastefully appointed with antiques and feather beds.

4 Rooms • Price range: $75-110
1502 Broad St, Camden, SC 29020
☎ **(803) 713-9050**

Charleston
⊕ *John Rutledge House Inn*

This inn is one of only two homes still intact that once belonged to signers of the Constitution. Built in 1763, it has been declared a National Historic Landmark and is located in Charleston's Historic District. The restored structure boasts carved Italian marble fireplaces, the original plaster moldings, inlaid floors and intricate iron work. All 19 bedrooms display antiques and historically accurate reproductions, and are located either in the original main house or in one of two carriage houses. Guests can choose between a continental or full breakfast.

19 Rooms • Price range: $195-295
116 Broad St, Charleston, SC 29401
☎ **(843) 723-7999**

Charleston
⊕ *Planters Inn*

An attractive inn in the heart of Historic Charleston, this property represents Southern elegance and hospitality at its best. Guests will marvel at the decor. Rooms feature high ceilings, canopied four-poster beds and museum-quality furnishings. Many have a fireplace, whirlpool bath or piazza overlooking a picturesque garden courtyard. The Courtyard is the perfect place for breakfast, or guests can opt to have their morning meal delivered to their rooms on a silver platter. In the afternoons, guests can have tea, sherry or port in the parlor.

62 Rooms • Price range: $200-300
112 N Market St, Charleston, SC 29401
☎ **(843) 722-2345**

◆ ◆ Charleston
◆ ◆ **⑭ *Vendue Inn***

Authentic antiques and 18th-century furnishings are abundant here at Charleston's Vendue Inn. Each junior and deluxe suite features a gas fireplace, a marble bath, a separate shower and a Jacuzzi tub. Guests staying in a deluxe suite will appreciate the living room and complimentary stocked wet bar. This European-style inn features a Southern breakfast buffet or a continental breakfast delivered right to your room. In the afternoon, complimentary wine and cheese are offered in the Garden Room. Lunch or cocktails are served on the rooftop terrace overlooking the harbor.

45 Rooms • Price range: $145-305
19 Vendue Range, Charleston, SC 29401
☎ **(843) 577-7970**

◆ ◆ Charleston
◆ ◆ **⑭ *Wentworth Mansion***

This 1886 Second Empire mansion is an excellent example of America's Gilded Age. The immense home showcases superb 19th-century craftsmanship in its detailed English tile floors, marvelous woodwork, marble fireplaces and Tiffany stained-glass windows. The grand guestrooms are lavishly decorated with the finest antiques, fireplaces and baths. Enjoy wine tasting and hors d'oeuvres in the parlor or relax with a book in the library. Do not miss the terrific panoramic view from the rooftop cupola deck. At every turn the Wentworth provides uncommon service and satisfaction.

21 Rooms • Price range: $195-425
149 Wentworth St, Charleston, SC 29401
☎ **(843) 853-1886**

◆ Charleston
◆ ◆ ***1837 Bed & Breakfast***

A wealthy cotton planter's home and a brick carriage house are the setting for this 1837 B&B. Located in Charleston village, the inn is close to boat tours, antique shops and restaurants. Guestrooms feature canopied beds and period pieces. The formal parlor has original red cypress wainscoting, cornice molding and wide-plank heart-pine floors. The Southern-style breakfast includes sausage pie, ham frittata and grits casserole.

9 Rooms • Price range: $79-149
126 Wentworth St, Charleston, SC 29401
☎ **(843) 723-7166**

◆ Charleston
◆ ◆ **⑭ *27 State Street Bed & Breakfast***

Built just after 1800 in the city's French Quarter, this is an excellent location from which to explore major points of interest in the area, and to enjoy superior dining and shopping. Carriage-house suites are furnished with antiques and reproductions, and each has a kitchenette and private bath. A private entrance overlooks the courtyard. Special amenities include a morning paper, fresh fruit and flowers.

2 Rooms • Price range: $160-190
27 State St, Charleston, SC 29401
☎ **(843) 722-4243**

Charleston
Ashley Inn Bed & Breakfast

Breakfast is not to be missed at this B&B. The aroma of fresh-brewed coffee sets the pace for such treats as Carolina sausage pie with fluffy sweet potato biscuits, crunchy French toast with orange honey sauce or peaches-and-cream stuffed waffles with praline sauce. After this kind of meal, guests may be tempted to return to their room or suite to rest but should also consider taking a tour through historic Charleston.

8 Rooms • Price range: $80-250
201 Ashley Ave, Charleston, SC 29403
☎ **(843) 723-1848**

Charleston
🆔 Battery Carriage House Inn (1843)

All 11 guestrooms in the Battery Carriage House Inn overlook the mansion's lovely private gardens. Number 20 on the Battery also boasts helpful staff who will be more than happy to serve a continental breakfast in your room or in the garden under the Lady Bankshire rose arbor. After breakfast, guests can take a stroll to the picturesque White Point Gardens and the Battery, facing Charleston Harbor.

11 Rooms • Price range: $209-259
20 South Battery, Charleston, SC 29401
☎ **(843) 727-3100**

Charleston
Belvedere Bed & Breakfast

This Colonial-Revival style B&B is known for its elegant Adamesque woodwork, including rare carved door and window surrounds, eye-catching mantels, chair rails and wainscoting. Guestrooms are equally beautiful, with high ceilings, antique furnishings, personal collections and splendid views of Colonial Lake. A continental breakfast starts a day that could include guided tours, a visit to an art gallery or a picnic at the beach.

3 Rooms • Price range: $160-175
40 Rutledge Ave, Charleston, SC 29401
☎ **(843) 722-0973**

Charleston
Cannonboro Inn Bed & Breakfast

This 1853 historic home offers Southern hospitality in the tradition of Old Charleston. Six guestrooms, featuring four-poster and canopy beds, are available. Guestrooms also have private baths. Cable television, air-conditioning and off-street parking are other special amenities Breakfast includes home-baked cinnamon muffins and is served either on the columned piazza or in the formal dining room.

6 Rooms • Price range: $80-225
184 Ashley Ave, Charleston, SC 29403
☎ **(843) 723-8572**

Charleston
The Elliott House Inn

Built in 1861, this historic inn is furnished with Victorian antiques.

25 Rooms • Price range: $135-160
78 Queen St, Charleston, SC 29401
☎ **(843) 723-1855**

Charleston
⚞ *The Lodge Alley Inn*
Renovated waterfront warehouses taste-
fully decorated with period reproductions.

**95 Rooms • Price range: $165-325
195 E Bay St, Charleston, SC 29401
☎ (843) 722-1611**

Charleston
Maison DuPre
A complex of five historic "Charleston
single houses" and two carriage houses.

**15 Rooms • Price range: $98-215
317 E Bay St, Charleston, SC 29401
☎ (843) 723-8691**

Columbia
Richland Street Bed & Breakfast
Here's an enticing 1992 Victorian-
styled home situated in the heart
of Columbia's Historic Preservation
District. The inn's seven spacious
guestrooms are furnished with king- or
queen-size beds. All rooms have private
baths; two have whirlpool baths. A deluxe
continental breakfast as well as afternoon
refreshments are served daily in the breakfast room or on the front porch. Interesting
museums are within walking distance.
Antique shops, restaurants, city parks and
the Riverbanks Zoological Park are only a
short drive away.

**8 Rooms • Price range: $90-150
1425 Richland St, Columbia, SC 29201
☎ (803) 779-7001**

Columbia
Chestnut Cottage Bed & Breakfast
There is historical significance to
Chestnut Cottage: In 1864 President
Jefferson Davis gave a speech from the
front porch. Since then, this 1850 home
has accommodated all kinds of guests. Five guestrooms, ranging from comfortable to luxurious, are
available. The Carriage House suite features
double French doors, which open to a king-size
bedroom. The B&B has a Civil War library, which
is open to guests. Breakfast is served daily.

**5 Rooms • Price range: $125-200
1718 Hampton St, Columbia, SC 29201
☎ (803) 256-1718**

Conway
⚞ *The Cypress Inn*
Fifteen miles outside of Myrtle
Beach on the water's edge of
Conway's Riverfront area, stands
the Cypress Inn. The inn offers solitude in picturesque surroundings. The
guestrooms each have cable television and
a fireplace; some have a Jacuzzi. A daily
breakfast is served before guests visit local
attractions, such as the endless stretches
of South Carolina beach. Bird-watching
and nature tours are other popular options.
Guests who wish to relax are welcome to
take advantage of the Carolina rockers
on the porch.

**12 Rooms • Price range: $125-175
16 Elm St, Conway, SC 29528
☎ (843) 248-8199**

Ehrhardt
Ehrhardt Hall Bed & Breakfast Inn

This 1903 antebellum mansion has all kinds of comforts to make guests feel pampered, including wide porches with wicker rockers, a formal living and dining room, an indoor pool and a sauna. All six guestrooms are oversize and include ceiling fans, individual armoires, sitting areas, private baths, gas fireplaces and double, queen- or king-size beds. Special business-traveler services are offered. A continental breakfast is served daily.

6 Rooms • Price: $65-85
400 S Broadway St, Ehrhardt, SC 29081
☎ **(803) 267-2020**

Georgetown
1790 House

Located in Historic Georgetown, the 1790 House is noted for its mix of post-Revolutionary War and West Indies styles of architecture. Six guestrooms and one cottage with a whirlpool are available. Common rooms include a drawing room with a fireplace, a gorgeous dining room and a parlor-cum-games room. Guests may use one of the inn's complimentary bikes or visit local attractions such as the Kaminski House Museum.

6 Rooms • Price range: $95-135
630 Highmarket St, Georgetown, SC 29440
☎ **(843) 546-4821**

Georgetown
Alexandra's Inn

Because of this inn's striking resemblance to Tara, the home of Scarlett in "Gone with the Wind," the rooms at the Alexandra's are named after characters in the movie. Scarlett's Room, for instance, features a deep Jacuzzi surrounded by three bay windows and a fireplace. All rooms have private baths and telephones. The pool-side carriage house has two bedrooms and a full kitchen. Full breakfasts can be served in your room.

6 Rooms • Price range: $95-165
620 Prince St, Georgetown, SC 29440
☎ **(843) 527-0233**

Georgetown
Ashfield Manor

Southern hospitality is the name of the game at Ashfield Manor. Each of the four guestrooms has a queen-size bed, cable television and a ceiling fan. Queen Ann-style reproductions are scattered throughout. Guests can enjoy warm evening breezes in the backyard hammock or in a rocking chair on the screened back porch. Nature lovers may catch a glimpse of deer or alligators. Continental breakfast is served.

4 Rooms • Price range: $60-80
3030 S Island Rd, Georgetown, SC 29440
☎ **(843) 546-0464**

Georgetown
DuPre House Bed & Breakfast Inn

Five individually decorated rooms, each with its own charm, await visitors of the 1743 DuPre House. For instance, the Screven Room features a built-in bookcase and a fireplace. The Caine Room has a veranda overlooking the DuPre grounds, and the Arthur Room includes a queen-size bed dressed up in Kingsberry linens. All rooms have private baths. A full breakfast is served daily and a nightly turn-down service is available.

5 Rooms • Price range: $105-125
921 Prince St, Georgetown, SC 29440
☎ **(843) 546-0298**

Georgetown
Live Oak Inn Bed & Breakfast

Lovely original details such as nine fireplaces, hardwood floors and an ornate staircase enhance the natural charm of this 1905 home. Located on a quiet tree-lined residential street within walking distance of Georgetown's historic district, shops and antique stores, the inn's rooms offer the comforts of a home-away-from-home. A screened-in veranda is shaded from the sun by a 500-year-old oak tree

4 Rooms • Price range: $65-115
515 Prince St, Georgetown, SC 29440
☎ **(843) 545-8658**

Georgetown
The Shaw House

A spacious two-story Colonial-style home, the Shaw House has a sweeping view of miles of marshland making this 3,200-square-foot inn a perfect setting for bird-watching. Out front, a striking, wide front porch is enhanced by tall white columns. All three guestrooms are air-conditioned, feature family antiques and have private baths. A full Southern breakfast is served and every guest leaves with a small keepsake.

3 Rooms • Price range: $55-75
613 Cypress St, Georgetown, SC 29440
☎ **(843) 546-9663**

Georgetown
ShipWright's Bed & Breakfast

Rooms have a nautical theme in this home on the Willow Bank Plantation.

2 Rooms • Price range: $60-65
609 Cypress Ct, Georgetown, SC 29440
☎ **(843) 527-4475**

Greenville
Pettigru Place Bed & Breakfast

Home-baked breads are included with breakfast every morning in Pettigru Place. Located in South Carolina upcountry, the B&B stands on a pretty tree-lined street close to downtown Greenville. A 1920s Georgian Federalist-style home, it has five guestrooms, each decorated in a different theme. Rooms may have queen- or king-size beds, a feather mattress, a ceiling fan or cable TV. All rooms have private baths with showers.

5 Rooms • Price range: $99-185
302 Pettigru St, Greenville, SC 29601
☎ **(864) 242-4529**

Hilton Head Island
🕸 *Main Street Inn*

This delightful small hotel is situated on a secluded area of the resort island where wealthy planters once entertained their guests in luxurious mansions surrounded by gardens fragrant with jasmine and gardenia. Fine imported furnishings and handsome artwork decorate all of the rooms, which range from cozy doubles to the lavish king-size courtyard room with a private walled garden. Guests can stroll through the Charlestonian public gardens, plunge into the lap pool or be pampered in the exclusive European spa. Southern food specialties are prepared with care.

33 Rooms • Price range: $185-240
2200 Main St, Hilton Head Island, SC 29925
☎ **(843) 681-3001**

Latta
🕸 *Abingdon Manor*

Halfway between New York and Miami, you'll find this Greek-Revival mansion, tucked away in the village of Latta. This small luxury hotel features comfortable guestrooms featuring antique furnishings, private baths and fireplaces. A gourmet breakfast is served daily, as are early evening refreshments and a complimentary sherry. A hot tub and exercise machines are popular items with visitors, and a guest refrigerator is made available for their use. Nearby activities include golfing, antique shopping and touring heritage sites.

5 Rooms • Price range: $120-160
307 Church St, Latta, SC 29565
☎ **(843) 752-5090**

McClellanville
Laurel Hill Plantation

The original 1850 Laurel Hill Plantation was destroyed by Hurricane Hugo in 1989. This faithful reconstruction carries all the warmth of the original building, with the additional advantage of modern conveniences. Four guestrooms are furnished with antiques and feature a spectacular view of the landscape. All rooms have a private bath. A full country breakfast is served in the dining room.

4 Rooms • Price range: $100-125
8913 N Hwy 17, McClellanville, SC 29458
☎ **(843) 887-3708**

McCormick
Fannie Kate's Country Inn & Restaurant

Rumor has it that this historic 1882 hotel was built over gold mine tunnels. The rooms are decorated with a homespun touch and some of the furnishings belonged to the original proprietors. Ceiling fans on the porch ensure comfortable summer dining.

8 Rooms • Price range: $70-85
127 S Main St, McCormick, SC 29835
☎ **(864) 465-0061**

Montmorenci
Annie's Inn Bed & Breakfast

This Greek-Revival plantation farm-house, surrounded by cotton fields, features charming common rooms, a swimming pool and quaint little cottages for guests who desire more private accommodations. The house narrowly escaped destruction during the Civil War when a cannon ball destroyed the original third floor. The guestrooms are well appointed with antiques, walk-in closets and private baths.

12 Rooms • Price range: $70-100
3083 Charleston Hwy, Montmorenci, SC 29839
☎ **(803) 649-6836**

Mount Pleasant
Guilds Inn

Experience the charm of an historic South Carolina village only five miles from downtown Charleston. The 1888 Guilds Inn is an enchanting Mount Pleasant getaway located near Shem's Creek. A glass-walled foyer with a distinctly Oriental theme welcomes guests upon their arrival. The uncluttered guestrooms are tastefully decorated in soft colors with antique reproduction furniture. A pleasant hometown environment.

6 Rooms • Price range: $110-165
101 Pitt St, Mount Pleasant, SC 29464
☎ **(843) 881-0510**

Mount Pleasant
The Long Point Inn B&B

Log house set among 300-year-old oaks draped in Spanish moss. Cozy rooms.

5 Rooms • Price range: $89-179
1199 Long Point Rd, Mount Pleasant, SC 29464
☎ **(843) 849-1884**

Myrtle Beach
Brustman House

A scant 300 yards from the grounds of the Brustman House, guests come face to face with the Atlantic. Before heading out for a swim, guests start the day with a hearty breakfast, including 10-grain buttermilk pancakes or organically grown eggs seasoned with fresh herbs from the garden. Guestrooms are decorated with Scandinavian modern furniture and all have private bathrooms.

5 Rooms • Price range: $65-120
400 25th Ave S, Myrtle Beach, SC 29577
☎ **(843) 448-7699**

Myrtle Beach
Serendipity, An Inn

A contemporary Spanish Mission-style inn on a quiet residential street in the north end of Myrtle Beach. Many of the spacious guestrooms look out over a large outdoor pool and surrounding patio. An outdoor gas grill and private sitting area are available for guests who wish to barbecue. There's ping-pong and shuffleboard for those who prefer more activity than soaking in the sun and cooling off in the pool.

15 Rooms • Price range: $89-159
407 71st Ave N, Myrtle Beach, SC 29572
☎ **(843) 449-5268**

Rock Hill
The Book & the Spindle

An English-style inn in the heart of the Old South, this place captures the essence of hospitality. The brick Georgian home, which overlooks the Winthrop University campus, is close to a number of cultural events. All suites and rooms have private baths and coffeemakers. Suites have fully stocked kitchen facilities. Charlotte's Douglas International Airport is less than 30 minutes away.

4 Rooms • Price range: $65-85
626 Oakland Ave, Rock Hill, SC 29730
☎ **(803) 328-1913**

Rock Hill
East Main Guest House

Three guestrooms are available in the East Main: the Honeymoon Suite, with a canopy bed, a fireplace and a whirlpool; the East Room, with a queen-size bed and a fireplace; and the Garden Room, with twin beds and a private bath. Built in the early 20th century, the East Main only opened to guests in 1991. Other rooms include a dining room and a parlor-cum-games room. A continental breakfast is served daily.

3 Rooms • Price range: $69-89
600 E Main St, Rock Hill, SC 29730
☎ **(803) 366-1161**

Sumter
The Bed & Breakfast of Sumter

Evidence of the past can been seen throughout this 1896 building. From French doors that open into a Victorian parlor to a European soapstone fireplace with turned columns and a hand-carved mirror, the house's features bring history to life. Rooms are decorated with heirlooms; some have fireplaces, all have private baths. A gourmet breakfast, which may include Belgian waffles with strawberries, is served daily.

4 Rooms • Price range: $70-80
6 Park Ave, Sumter, SC 29150
☎ **(803) 773-2903**

Sumter
Calhoun Street Bed & Breakfast

The intimate, inviting atmosphere of this 1890s family home keeps guests coming back. Four guestrooms are all furnished with family antiques. Guests are welcome to use the various libraries or wander in the rose gardens. A wholesome breakfast, which usually includes homemade breads and muffins, is served daily in the dining room, on the back porch or in-room. Golfing and antique shopping are two of several nearby activities.

4 Rooms • Price range: $65-75
302 W Calhoun St, Sumter, SC 29150
☎ **(803) 775-7035**

Sumter
Magnolia House

This Greek-Revival home is conveniently located in Sumter's Historic District. The inn has many features that guests will appreciate, including five fireplaces, stained-glass windows and inlaid oak floors. Visitors can choose from five guestrooms, each decorated with antiques from a different era. Breakfast is served in the large dining room and afternoon refreshments are available in the formal backyard garden.

4 Rooms • Price range: $85-95
230 Church St, Sumter, SC 29150
☎ **(803) 775-6694**

Table Rock
The Schell Haus, A Resort Bed & Breakfast

Situated in the foothills of the Blue Ridge Mountains, Schell Haus is the perfect rest stop for romance or business. Each of the six guestrooms is tastefully decorated with antiques or antique reproductions. A full breakfast, including local seasonal fruits and berries, is served daily. Afternoon refreshments are available in the parlor, which has a fireplace, a pub table and a grand piano.

6 Rooms • Price range: $85-160
117 Hiawatha Tr, Table Rock, SC 29671
☎ **(864) 878-0078**

Union
The Inn at Merridun

The interior of this antebellum home may be old-fashioned but it displays a contemporary sensibility. The guestrooms are tastefully decorated with period antiques and reproductions. An afternoon tea is available by prior arrangement Thursday to Saturday for an extra charge. Nine acres of quiet woodlands surround the inn.

5 Rooms • Price range: $99-135
100 Merridun Pl, Union, SC 29379
☎ **(864) 427-7052**

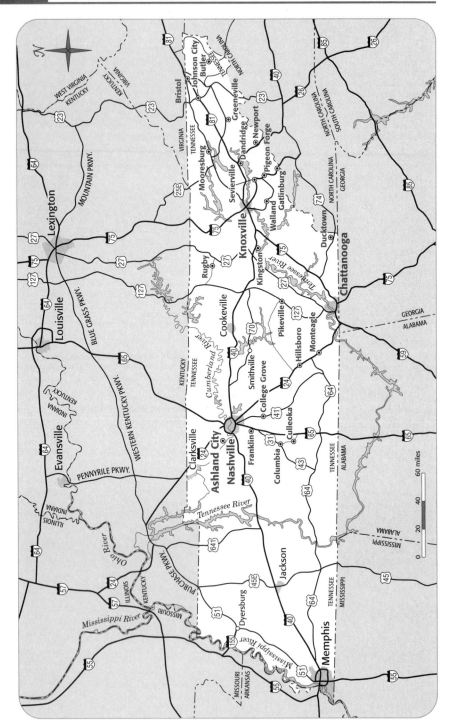

Ashland City
Birdsong Lodge

Originally built as a summer home for the Cheek family of Maxwell House Coffee fame, this circa 1912 log cabin is both luxuriously elegant and rustic. The cross-beamed cedar ceilings and square-cut log walls enhance the warmth of the carefully selected contemporary and antique furnishings in the bedrooms and common rooms. A large screened-in front porch and candlelight dinners complete this picture-perfect setting.

4 Rooms • Price range: $175-295
1306 Hwy 49 E, Ashland City, TN 37015
☎ **(615) 792-1767**

Bristol
New Hope Bed & Breakfast

This large, two-story 1892 house is a good example of Victorian architecture, with its expansive ceilings, transomed doors and hardwood floors. Guestrooms feature private baths and air-conditioning. Bath robes, hair dryers and other amenities are added for good measure. The inn also has a parlor, a game room and a dining room, where breakfast is served daily. Murder-mystery weekends are an extra attraction.

4 Rooms • Price range: $95-155
822 Georgia Ave, Bristol, TN 37620
☎ **(423) 989-3343**

Butler
Iron Mountain Inn

Set high in the Appalachian Mountains where Tennessee, North Carolina and Virginia meet, this two-story log cabin enjoys spectacular views through every season. From the Equestrian Room to the Green Room, the decor of each bedroom reflects the eclectic interests of the innkeeper. Steam showers, Jacuzzis and private balconies are a few of the amenities available. Dinners can be arranged with advance notice.

4 Rooms • Price range: $130-250
138 Moreland Dr, Butler, TN 37640
☎ **(423) 768-2446**

Chattanooga
Adams Hilborne, Mansion, Inn & Restaurant

Winner of Chattanooga's City Beautiful Award, this inn features many luxuries, such as hand-cut, stained and beveled glass, burnished inlaid floors and a grand staircase. Ten guestrooms feature original artworks and exquisite fabrics, along with cable television and Internet access. Guests can dine by candlelight in the Fortwood Ballroom or sip wine by the fireplace under the Rembrandt in the Mayor's Library.

10 Rooms • Price range: $125-290
801 Vine St, Chattanooga, TN 37403
☎ **(423) 265-5000**

Chattanooga
McElhattan's Owl Hill B&B

This attractive B&B is conveniently close to the area's hiking trails.

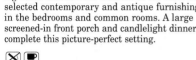

2 Rooms • Price range: $75-125
617 S Scenic Hwy, Chattanooga, TN 37409-1133
☎ **(423) 821-2040**

College Grove
⬥⬥ 🏛 *Peacock Hill Country Inn*

Guests will find themselves in the center of things when they stay in this 150-year-old inn. Popular nearby activities include Shelbyville's Tennessee Walking Horse National Celebration, Franklin's antique shops and several Nashville country-music attractions. Situated on 650 acres of land, the inn is composed of a renovated pre–Civil War farmhouse, a log cabin and a granary, which is now a suite. Guestrooms are done in a variety of decors, including spring garden, Victorian and hearty American denim. A complimentary breakfast is served daily.

10 Rooms • Price range: $125-225
6994 Giles Hill Rd, College Grove, TN 37046
☎ **(615) 368-7727**

Columbia
⬥ *Locust Hill Bed & Breakfast*

Experience down-home hospitality at this 1840 antebellum home and smoke-house. Guests will find this B&B decorated with family antiques, lace curtains, embroidered linens and handmade quilts. All guestrooms feature a private bath. A gourmet breakfast features homemade breads and jam and country ham. Early-morning coffee is served in-room; afternoon tea is served in the parlor.

4 Rooms • Price range: $75-125
1185 Mooresville Pike, Columbia, TN 38401
☎ **(931) 388-8531**

Culleoka
⬥ *Sweetwater Inn*

Located nine miles southeast of Columbia, this inn was built circa 1900.

4 Rooms • Price range: $100-125
2436 Campbell Station Rd, Culleoka, TN 38451
☎ **(931) 987-3077**

Dandridge
⬥ *Mountain Harbor Inn*

Located on the shoreline of Douglas Lake, this inn features spectacular lake and mountain views. Guests can take in the full scope of the surroundings from the inn's front porches. Comfortable guestrooms are furnished with antiques. Situated in the historic town of Dandridge, the inn is ideal for vacationers as well as for weddings or other receptions of up to 200 people.

12 Rooms • Price range: $65-125
1199 Hwy 139, Dandridge, TN 37725
☎ **(865) 397-3345**

Ducktown
⬥⬥ *The Company House Bed & Breakfast*

Lovingly restored, this large 1850s home has quaint rooms.

6 Rooms • Price range: $69-75
125 Main St, Ducktown, TN 37326
☎ **(423) 496-5634**

Ducktown
⬥⬥ *The White House Bed & Breakfast*

Built circa 1900, this home is on the National Register of Historic Places.

3 Rooms • Price range: $64-79
104 Main St, Ducktown, TN 37326
☎ **(423) 496-4166**

Franklin
Country Inn & Suites By Carlson

This inn is part of a worldwide chain of accommodations based on the model of providing comfortable homelike surroundings, friendly personalized service with the addition of hotel-style conveniences. Attractive rooms and common areas are all designed to create the country inn ambience of informal familiarity. Complimentary breakfast, an indoor pool and many other amenities make the Country Inn a good value.

66 Rooms • Price range: $69-89
7120 S Springs Dr, Franklin, TN 37067
☎ **(615) 778-0321**

Franklin
Namaste Acres Country Ranch Inn

Located 25 miles southwest of Nashville, Namaste Acres Barn is in the rural community of Leipers Fork, adjacent to the Natchez Trace Parkway. The guestrooms in this Dutch-Colonial country home have private entrances, private baths, feather-quilted queen-size beds, large seating areas and cozy fireplaces. The inn also has accommodations for horses; the inn can provide horses to ride for guests who arrive without their own.

4 Rooms • Price range: $75-85
5436 Leipers Creek, Franklin, TN 37064
☎ **(615) 791-0333**

Gatlinburg
⚑ Eight Gables Inn

Beautifully decorated guestrooms await visitors to the Eight Gables Inn, all of them with private baths. The home also has a spacious living area and a covered porch, perfect for those balmy summer nights. Located at the foot of the Great Smoky Mountains National Park, the inn is close to golf courses, shopping and nature trails. Nearby activities include white-water rafting, hiking and horseback riding. Downtown Gatlinburg is a two-minute drive away; Knoxville is 30 miles away. The inn is ideal for wedding receptions and company seminars.

12 Rooms • Price range: $129-189
219 N Mountain Tr, Gatlinburg, TN 37738
☎ **(865) 430-3344**

Gatlinburg
Tennessee Ridge Inn
A modern mountaintop stone lodge with walls of glass overlooking the Smoky Mountains and picturesque Gatlinburg. The guestrooms are very spacious and all have that incredible view. A taste of the high life in more ways than one.

7 Rooms • Price range: $75-159
507 Campbell Lead Rd, Gatlinburg, TN 37738
☎ **(865) 436-4068**

Greeneville
Hilltop House B&B
This property boasts beautiful panoramic mountain views.

3 Rooms • Price range: $75-80
6 Sanford Cir, Greeneville, TN 37743
☎ **(423) 639-8202**

Hillsboro
Lord's Landing Bed & Breakfast

From the main house of this B&B, guests have a 360-degree view of their surroundings. Set among wooded hills and rolling fields, the Lord's Landing sits on 50 acres of property. The inn has a landing strip to accommodate private planes. Guests will find six rooms and a two-room suite available. All rooms have large private baths, some have Jacuzzi tubs. Four rooms have a fireplaces. A full breakfast is served daily.

7 Rooms • Price range: $95-150
375 Lord's Landing Ln, Hillsboro, TN 37342
☎ **(931) 467-3830**

Johnson City
The Jam n Jelly Inn Bed & Breakfast

This custom-built log house is close to a number of east Tennessee attractions, including historic Jonesborough. It has six guestrooms with queen-size beds and private baths. Two rooms have telephones. There's a hot tub on the back porch and there are two common areas, one with a large fireplace, the other with a big-screen TV and a large selection of videos. A full breakfast, including homemade jams and jellies, is served daily.

6 Rooms • Price range: $75-85
1310 Indian Ridge Rd, Johnson City, TN 37604
☎ **(423) 929-0039**

Kingston
⟨AAA⟩ Whitestone Country Inn

Those who love nature will be delighted with the Whitestone Country Inn. The 275-acre estate sits on the shores of Watts Bar Lake and is surrounded by a wildlife and waterfowl refuge. Twelve comfortable guestrooms are available at the inn, each with a fireplace, a whirlpool, a TV/VCR and a phone. Guests can also make use of a well-stocked library, a spacious recreation room with exercise equipment, a pool table, a sauna and steam showers. A full country breakfast is served daily. Afterward, guests can take advantage of six miles of walking trails.

18 Rooms • Price range: $125-300
1200 Paint Rock Rd, Kingston, TN 37763
☎ **(865) 376-0113**

Knoxville
⟨AAA⟩ Masters Manor Inn

An excellent example of Victorian vernacular architecture, this 1894 mansion has been in the same family for more than 100 years. Special care was taken during the 1996 renovations to preserve the original woodwork, flooring and fireplaces. The six guestrooms feature private baths, faxes and phone lines. Breakfast is provided every morning and a complimentary dessert is served by candlelight in the dining room each night.

6 Rooms • Price range: $100-200
1909 Cedar Ln, Knoxville, TN 37918
☎ **(865) 219-9888**

Monteagle
Adams Edgeworth Inn

A historic mountain retreat built in
1896, the Adams Edgeworth Inn sits
comfortably in the quaint community
of Chautauqua and is on the National
Register of Historic Places. The comfortable
rooms each have a private bath and some have
a fireplace. Guests are often found relaxing on
one of the inn's many verandas, drinking in the
breathtaking views. Guided nature hikes are
available in the area.

13 Rooms • Price range: $100-395
Monteagle Assembly, Cottage 23,
Monteagle, TN 37356
☎ **(931) 924-4000**

Mooresburg
The Home Place Bed & Breakfast

This home in a woodsy setting has been
in the same family since the 1800s.

4 Rooms • Price range: $45-65
132 Church Ln, Mooresburg, TN 37811
☎ **(423) 921-8424**

Newport
ⓌⒶ Christopher Place, An Intimate Resort

Breathtaking views are the hallmark
of the Christopher Place resort. Set on
200 acres of property in Tennessee's
Smoky Mountains near the national
park, the resort offers a luxurious secluded
retreat. Both one- and two-bedroom suites are
available, some with a whirlpool or a wood-
burning fireplace. Morning coffee is available at
an early hour, and a full breakfast follows at the
convenience of the guests. Poolside picnics and
candlelight dinners are also popular. Guests can
choose to take a dip in the heated pool, play a
game of tennis, or work out in the fitness room,
finishing off in the sauna.

8 Rooms • Price range: $150-350
1500 Pinnacle Way, Newport, TN 37821
☎ **(423) 623-6555**

Pigeon Forge
Hilton's Bluff Bed & Breakfast Inn

This tastefully decorated inn has 10
guestrooms, three of which are honeymoon or special-occasion rooms, each
complete with a heart-shaped whirlpool
tub. There are two executive rooms, with their
own two-person Jacuzzi; and five deluxe rooms
with private baths. Guests have a choice of a
king- or queen-size bed, or a king waterbed. All
rooms open onto a private balcony or a covered
deck. A Southern-style breakfast is served daily.

10 Rooms • Price range: $69-99
2654 Valley Heights Dr, Pigeon Forge, TN 37863
☎ **(865) 428-9765**

Pikeville
Fall Creek Falls Bed & Breakfast

This new country manor home is located on 40 acres of rolling hillside, a mile from Fall Creek Falls State Resort Park. A number of activities are easily accessible, including golfing, hiking, horseback riding, tennis and boating. The highest waterfall east of the Rockies is also nearby. There are eight air-conditioned guestrooms available, each decorated with Victorian and country furnishings. A full breakfast is served daily.

7 Rooms • Price range: $64-130
DeWeese Rd, Pikeville, TN 37367
☎ **(423) 881-5494**

Rugby
Newbury House at Historic Rugby

This restored Victorian boarding house is near a historic village and shops.

6 Rooms • Price range: $60-95
Newbury Rd, Rugby, TN 37733
☎ **(423) 628-2441**

Sevierville
Blue Mountain Mist Country Inn & Cottages

Guests will discover a lily pond and immaculately kept lawns and flower gardens on this family farm, situated on 60 acres in the majestic Smoky Mountains. A huge wraparound porch is the spot from which to take in the magnificent view. Each of the guestrooms is comfortably furnished with such features as vintage wardrobes and heirloom quilts. All have private baths. A Tennessee country breakfast is served daily.

17 Rooms • Price range: $105-149
1811 Pullen Rd, Sevierville, TN 37862
☎ **(865) 428-2335**

Sevierville
Von Bryan Inn

Here's the ultimate mountaintop get-away. Located on the crest of the 2,100-foot Hatcher Mountain overlooking the Wears Valley, this inn offers privacy and comfort. The views from its many porches, decks or balconies are extraordinary. Breakfast is served in the glassed-in breakfast room. Visitors can swim in the pool, soak in the hot tub or work out in the exercise room. After a full day, the large guestrooms beckon.

8 Rooms • Price range: $115-170
2402 Hatcher Mountain Rd,
Sevierville, TN 37862
☎ **(865) 453-9832**

Walland
🏕 *Blackberry Farm*

An ideal spot for either business travelers or vacationers. Situated in the foothills of the Smoky Mountains, this 1,100-acre estate is conveniently located—it's only a half-hour drive from Knoxville airport. Blackberry Farm includes the Chestnut Cottage, which has three meeting rooms that can accommodate up to 80 people. The Cove Cottage, on the other hand, is more suited for pleasure travelers; it has three bedrooms, a full kitchen and a dining room. Guests will find there's much to explore on the grounds, including a boat house, a chapel, a pool and a creek.

44 Rooms • Price range: $395-745
1471 W Millers Cove Rd, Walland, TN 37886
☎ **(865) 984-8166**

Notes:

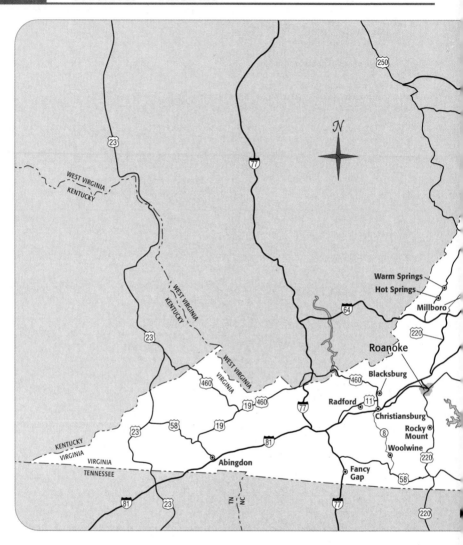

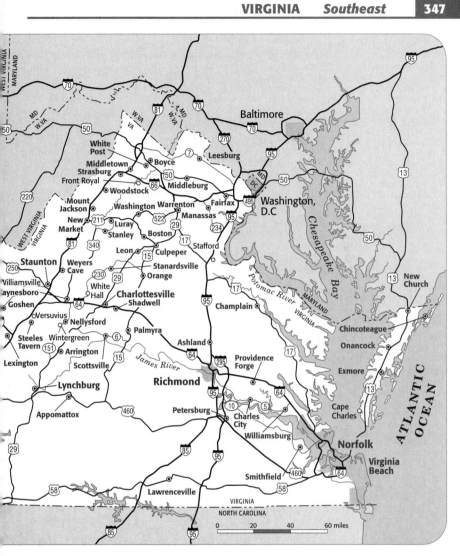

Abingdon
Victoria & Albert Inn
 Located in the historic district of
Abingdon, this 1892 three-story
Victorian home features four inviting
guestrooms. Structural elements such
as high ceilings, bay windows, transom doors
and hardwood floors attest to the inn's Victorian
pedigree. Each room is decorated with period
furniture and is equipped with a working log
fireplace and a large modern bathroom. Guests
are invited to enjoy a daily breakfast that
includes homemade muffins and fresh fruit.
The inn also offers evening refreshments, an
evening turndown service and an extensive
video library.

5 Rooms • Price range: $99-125
224 Oak Hill St, Abingdon, VA 24210
☎ **(540) 676-2797**

Abingdon
Inn on Town Creek
 This brick home features a solarium
and rooms decorated with antiques.

5 Rooms • Price: $125
445 E Valley St, Abingdon, VA 24212
☎ **(540) 628-4560**

Abingdon
Silversmith Inn Bed & Breakfast
Built on the site of a silversmith's shop,
this restored redbrick Italianate house
watches over Abington's Main Street as
it has since 1871. The inn features tree-
shaded porches with rockers and swings and
an outdoor hot tub mounted on a lower deck.
Each room is decorated with period furnishings;
original poplar flooring is accented with floral
rugs. Tea and a full breakfast are served in
the dining room.

5 Rooms • Price range: $100-120
102 E Main St, Abingdon, VA 24210
☎ **(540) 676-3924**

Abingdon
Summerfield Inn Bed & Breakfast
This spacious 1920s-era Colonial-Revival
home combines a private home setting
with the luxurious comfort of a top
hotel. Each of the individually decorated rooms is equipped with a private bath,
five of the rooms have whirlpools. The B&B
also features a large, inviting front porch area,
spacious parlors and a library. Nearby is the
34-mile Virginia Creeper Trail, ideal for hiking, biking and horseback riding.

7 Rooms • Price range: $105-150
101 W Valley St, Abingdon, VA 24210
☎ **(540) 628-5905**

Abingdon
White Birches Inn

This early 20th-century Cape Cod-style home is located in Abingdon's historic district. Although the structure has been completely renovated to incorporate such modern comforts as central air-conditioning, the owners have created an old-fashioned look by furnishing the inn with English and American antiques. The inn also features a wicker-furnished porch with a view of the garden, which has a koi pond and waterfall.

5 Rooms • Price range: $100-130
268 Whites Mill Rd, Abingdon, VA 24210
☎ **(540) 676-2140**

Appomattox
The Babcock House

This early 1900s inn offers five large guestrooms and one suite. All rooms have private baths, ceiling fans and air-conditioning. The amenities of the Bradley Suite include a sitting room, a fireplace and a queen-size sofa bed. A full breakfast is served daily, and lunch or dinner can be arranged by request. There are a number of nearby attractions, including the Lynchburg Fine Arts Center.

5 Rooms • Price range: $95-120
106 Oakleigh Ave, Appomattox, VA 24522
☎ **(804) 352-7532**

Arrington
Harmony Hill Bed & Breakfast

This log home has two guestrooms, each equipped with gas fireplaces.

5 Rooms • Price range: $80-105
929 Wilson Hill Rd, Arrington, VA 22922
☎ **(804) 263-7750**

Ashland
The Henry Clay Inn

This is a faithful replica of the 1906 Georgian-Revival mansion that was destroyed by fire in 1946. Fortunately the inn has managed to capture the former building's period charm. From the pine-floor lobby to the spacious antique-furnished rooms and the upstairs parlor, the inn is true to its past. The guestrooms also feature modern amenities such as private baths and computer modem hookups.

16 Rooms • Price range: $90-165
114 N Railroad Ave, Ashland, VA 23005
☎ **(804) 798-3100**

Blacksburg
Clay Corner Inn Bed & Breakfast

Guests can share full kitchens when staying in this complex of houses.

12 Rooms • Price range: $78-130
401 Clay St SW, Blacksburg, VA 24060
☎ **(540) 953-2604**

Boyce
The River House

This 1780 fieldstone residence is situated on 17 acres of open woodland and river frontage. Tucked away in the foothills between the Blue Ridge Mountains and the Shenandoah Valley, it is truly a secluded get-away. The five air-conditioned guestrooms each feature a private "en-suite" bath and a working fireplace. Guests are welcome to prepare a continental breakfast or snacks in one of two well-stocked kitchenettes.

5 Rooms • Price range: $75-150
3075 John Mosby Hwy, Boyce, VA 22620
☎ **(540) 837-1476**

Champlain
Linden House Bed & Breakfast Plantation

Any one of five porches provide an ideal vantage point to take in the more than 200 acres of landscaped grounds that surround the Linden House. This restored 1750 planter's home is set in rural Essex County, only minutes away from historic Tappahannock. Six guestrooms are available, each with TV, refrigerator, soft fluffy robes and triple sheeting. A full plantation breakfast is served, including homemade biscuits.

7 Rooms • Price range: $95-135
11770 Tidewater Tr, Champlain, VA 22438
☎ **(804) 443-1170**

Charles City
Edgewood Plantation

An exquisite 7,000-square-foot example of Carpenter's Gothic architecture, the Edgewood was once a part of Berkeley Plantation, the ancestral home of President Benjamin Harrison, one of the signers of the Declaration of Independence. Today the inn features rich upholstery, canopy beds, gilded frames and elegant bathrooms. An authentic Victorian Tea Party is available for groups of 10 or more.

7 Rooms • Price range: $138-198
4800 John Tyler Memorial Hwy,
Charles City, VA 23030
☎ **(804) 829-2962**

Charles City
North Bend Plantation Bed & Breakfast

This circa 1819 Greek-Revival style home is set on a 500-acre working plantation. Antiques and heirlooms owned by former occupant General Sheridan decorate the inn, and his china and silverware are still in use in the dining room.

4 Rooms • Price range: $120-135
12200 Weyanoke Rd, Charles City, VA 23030
☎ **(804) 829-5176**

Charlottesville
The Foxfield Inn

Furnishings hand-crafted by the owner decorate the spacious guestrooms of this welcoming inn, which is surrounded by three acres of grounds. All the rooms offer a private bath and three are equipped with Jacuzzis. As well there is a screened teahouse and a heated spa. The inn is situated near the Foxfield steeplechase track and only seven miles from the shops of Charlottesville.

5 Rooms • Price range: $125-160
2280 Garth Rd, Charlottesville, VA 22901
☎ **(804) 923-8892**

Charlottesville
The Inn at Monticello

Located just two miles from Monticello, Thomas Jefferson's beloved home, the Inn at Monticello is steeped in Virginia history. Other nearby attractions include Ash Lawn-Highland, the home of another former president, James Monroe. The five guestrooms feature hardwood floors, Oriental rugs, and a variety of antiques. Each also has a private bath. A lavish gourmet breakfast is served every morning.

5 Rooms • Price range: $120-150
Rt 20 S/1188 Scottsville Rd,
Charlottesville, VA 22902
☎ **(804) 979-3593**

Charlottesville
The Inn at Sugar Hollow Farm

This country B&B retreat is surrounded by 70 acres of majestic mountains, hardwood forests and woodland streams. The inn features a family room with a stone fireplace, a study, and a sunroom. Guestrooms are decorated with hand-sewn quilts, custom-designed window treatments, and cozy comforters. Each room also has a connecting private bath, and two of these feature whirlpool tubs.

5 Rooms • Price range: $95-160
6051 Sugar Hollow Rd, Charlottesville, VA 22905
☎ **(804) 823-7086**

Charlottesville
Silver Thatch Inn

The buildings making up this charming rural inn span over 200 years, the original section being one of the oldest structures in central Virginia. Today guests may choose from seven guestrooms, each decorated in period antiques and named after a Virginia-born president. All are equipped with private baths and many offer fireplaces and canopy beds. The inn also invites guests to a vintage English pub and three-diamond dining.

7 Rooms • Price range: $148-190
3001 Hollymead Dr, Charlottesville,
VA 22911-7422
☎ **(804) 978-4686**

Chincoteague
Cedar Gables Seaside Inn

Here's a seaside inn that is perfect for those who enjoy the water. Guests can fish for crab, relax on the inn's seaside dock or take a walk to Assateague beach. There's also a nearby wildlife refuge, as well as boating, canoeing and sea kayaking. Comfortably furnished guestrooms feature private exterior entrances with direct access to a water-front deck, full-size gas fireplaces, and private baths with Jacuzzi. Guests can also take a dip in the inn's pool or curl up with a book in the secluded shade garden. A gourmet breakfast is served in the dining room or "al fresco" on the screened waterfront porch.

4 Rooms • Price range: $145-180
6095 Hopkins Ln, Chincoteague, VA 23336
☎ **(757) 336-1096**

Chincoteague
The Inn at Poplar Corner

Elegance and country comfort characterize this inn, which has a wraparound porch where afternoon refreshments are served. All of the guestrooms have adjoining private baths, some of which are equipped with oversize whirlpool tubs. Located in the heart of Chincoteague, the inn is within walking distance of shops, and restaurants. Popular activities include biking and beachcombing, and playing tennis and golf.

4 Rooms • Price range: $109-159
4248 Main St, Chincoteague, VA 23336
☎ **(757) 336-6115**

Chincoteague
The Watson House

This restored 1898 Victorian home is within walking distance of several fine shops, restaurants and cafés. Tennis facilities are also nearby as is biking. The inn features a wraparound porch and a dining room. A hearty breakfast is served across the street at The Inn at Poplar Corner. Guestrooms include private baths, some with whirlpools. Cottages are available for families with children under 10 years of age.

6 Rooms • Price range: $79-119
4240 Main St, Chincoteague, VA 23336
☎ **(757) 336-1564**

Christiansburg
The Oaks Victorian Inn

All kinds of amenities are available in this 1893 Queen Anne Victorian inn. Guestrooms have new king- or queen-size orthopedic mattresses, and private bathrooms stocked with plush towels, fluffy terry cloth robes and toiletries. The aroma of freshly ground coffee precedes a generous breakfast, which includes such inn specialties as curried eggs served in white wine sauce with shiitake mushrooms, raisin and Granny Smith apple quiche, shirred eggs in spinach nests or rum-raisin French toast. For the adventurous traveler, the Appalachian Trail is close by.

7 Rooms • Price range: $85-170
311 E Main St, Christiansburg, VA 24073
☎ **(540) 381-1500**

Christiansburg
Evergreen-The Bell-Capozzi House

This family home is set in a lovely Victorian town and features local art.

5 Rooms • Price range: $85-145
201 E Main St, Christiansburg, VA 24073
☎ **(540) 382-7372**

Culpeper
Fountain Hall

Five tastefully decorated guestrooms and one suite await visitors to the circa 1860 Fountain Hall. Each room has a private bath and some have balcony views. The inn boasts an extensive library and a relaxing parlor. Breakfast is served in the morning room. Freshly baked croissants, coffee, tea, country jams and preserves may all be on the menu. After breakfast, guests can take a self-guided tour to historic Culpeper.

6 Rooms • Price range: $85-150
609 S East St, Culpeper, VA 22701
☎ **(540) 825-8200**

Exmore
Gladstone House

Conveniently located between Assateague and Kiptopeke State Park, the Georgian Gladstone House is perfect for guests who like to explore nature. For those whose tastes are a bit more worldly, antique shops, art and sculpture galleries are also close by. Originally home to the town's doctor, the inn has three rooms with private bath, and central air-conditioning. Fresh-squeezed orange juice is just the beginning of a four-course breakfast.

3 Rooms • Price range: $85-95
12108 Lincoln Ave, Exmore, VA 23350-0296
☎ **(757) 442-4614**

Fairfax
The Bailiwick Inn

The first guests to The Bailiwick Inn arrived nearly 200 years ago. Since then, the inn has welcomed many more visitors, all of them treated to 14 lovely guestrooms, furnished with queen-size or twin beds and a fireplace or a Jacuzzi tub. Guests will notice the polished wood balustrade, the fresh-cut flowers in the foyer, the cheery fire in the book-lined parlor, and the silver and crystal in the breakfast room.

14 Rooms • Price range: $215-350
4023 Chain Bridge Rd, Fairfax, VA 22030
☎ **(703) 691-2266**

Fancy Gap
Inn at Orchard Gap & Cottages

Upholding the timeless tradition of a classic Virginia inn, the Orchard Gap offers comfortable accommodation in a quiet mountain setting. Guestrooms have private entrances, individually controlled heat and air-conditioning and private baths. Some rooms have fireplaces. A bountiful breakfast begins a day that may include hiking, golfing or shopping. The inn can help plan special occasions, including birthdays and weddings.

6 Rooms • Price range: $85-150
4549 Lightning Ridge Rd, Fancy Gap, VA 24328
☎ **(540) 398-3206**

Hampton
Victoria House Bed & Breakfast

Built as a private residence in the late 1800s, this Queen Anne-style home has been faithfully restored. The richly decorated guest units offer queen-size beds, antique armoires and baths that mix modern amenities with the charm of antiques. Two handsome parlors invite guests to chat or read by the fire on cool evenings. A full breakfast, served in the formal dining room, includes a hot entrée and homemade breads.

4 Rooms • Price range: $90-135
4501 Victoria Blvd, Hampton, VA 23669-4137
☎ **(757) 722-2658**

Lawrenceville
Brunswick Mineral Springs B&B Circa 1785

Set on a 27-acre estate, this 1700s plantation home has been stylishly restored.

4 Rooms • Price range: $105-125
14910 Western Mill Rd, Lawrenceville, VA 23868
☎ **(804) 848-4010**

Lawrenceville
Three Angels Inn at Sherwood

It began life in 1883 as a hospital—one of the few committed to serving the local black population—and today it is a charming inn. Surrounded by shady oak and cedar trees, the inn serves as an important reminder of Virginian history. The comfortable guestrooms have both a private bath and a fireplace. The inn also features a library, a parlor and a large screened porch.

4 Rooms • Price range: $90-105
236 Pleasant Grove Rd (SR 681) PO Box 883,
Lawrenceville, VA 23868
☎ **(804) 848-0830**

Leesburg
The Norris House Inn

In the historic district, this Federal inn has three rooms with fireplaces.

6 Rooms • Price range: $105-150
108 Loudoun St SW, Leesburg, VA 20175-2909
☎ **(703) 777-1806**

Leon
The Suites at Prince Michel

An inn with lavishly outfitted luxury suites stands in the middle of a tranquil vineyard. Each suite features a spacious living room and a wood-burning fireplace. Plush furnishings in the French tradition, gracious personal service and up-to-the-minute electronics add to the pleasure of any stay. The nearby Prince Michel Wine Museum is a must-see. A special tour of the winery, where visitors are encouraged to partake of the complimentary samples, is only available to guests. The Prince Michel restaurant serves award-winning French cuisine.

4 Rooms • Price range: $350-400
HCR 4 Box 77, Leon, VA 22725
☎ **(540) 547-9720**

Lexington
Historic Country Inns of Lexington

Twenty-three rooms and suites are available in the three town houses that make up the Historic Country Inns of Lexington. All of the rooms are furnished with a variety of antiques and paintings, and some have working fireplaces. Each room is also equipped with a private bath and offers modern amenities. Guests awake to the aroma of fresh muffins and freshly brewed coffee, served in summer on the veranda.

23 Rooms • Price range: $85-135
11 N Main St, Lexington, VA 24450
☎ **(540) 463-2044**

Lexington
Maple Hall Country Inn

A perfect retreat for business meetings. The 1850 Greek-Revival plantation house is located in a scenic setting amid the rolling green hills of the Shenandoah Valley. The 56 acres of spacious grounds include a tennis court and a swimming pool, as well as nature trails that wind past a stocked fishing pond. Rooms are also available in two nearby outbuildings, some of which feature a gas-log fireplace.

21 Rooms • Price range: $85-135
3111 N Lee Hwy, Lexington, VA 24450
☎ **(540) 463-2044**

Lexington
A B&B at Llewellyn Lodge

Located in the historic town of Lexington, this charming brick Colonial-style house exudes a cozy atmosphere in a comfortable family setting. A haven for anglers, the lodge offers guided fly-fishing trips to the area's trout streams.

6 Rooms • Price range: $65-120
603 S Main St, Lexington, VA 24450
☎ **(540) 463-3235**

Luray
The MayneView Bed & Breakfast

A gazebo graces the attractive grounds of this historic 1865 Victorian home, which stands on the top of a hill, offering guests views of the town and the nearby Blue Ridge Mountains. The B&B also features period furniture along with contemporary amenities such as whirlpool baths. Guests have the choice of staying at a separate cottage, also on the site. A full breakfast is served daily.

6 Rooms • Price range: $90-195
439 Mechanic St, Luray, VA 22835
☎ **(540) 743-7921**

Luray
The Woodruff Collection of Inns

This chef-owned Victorian B&B does its best to make guests feel truly pampered. Start the day with morning coffee brought to your room, followed by a gourmet candlelight breakfast in the dining room or breakfast in bed. A delightful afternoon tea features cakes, cookies and pastries. Guestrooms have private baths, Jacuzzis for two and working fireplaces. The Skylight Fireside Jacuzzi Suite is also available.

9 Rooms • Price range: $145-175
138 E. Main St, Luray, VA 22835
☎ **(540) 743-1494**

Lynchburg
B&B at Federal Crest Inn

Magnificent woodwork and classical columns characterize this 1909 Georgian-Revival style mansion. The inn boasts a range of attractions including a grand central staircase and unique mantels. The inn also has a parlor, a library, and a dining room. Each of the four guestrooms has queen-size beds and private bath. A hot breakfast is served daily and bedroom snack basket adds a special touch.

4 Rooms • Price range: $90-115
1101 Federal St, Lynchburg, VA 24504
☎ **(804) 845-6155**

Lynchburg
Lynchburg Mansion Inn Bed & Breakfast

This 1914, 9,000-square-foot Georgian mansion is situated on a half-acre of land in the Garland Hill Historic District. It has a variety of Spanish-style features and is a marvel of architecture: a six-foot iron fence surrounds the inn; 22 immense columns ring the Spanish-tiled veranda; a double door entry opens to a 50-foot Grand Hall with soaring ceilings. Breakfast is served in the formal dining room on fine china.

5 Rooms • Price range: $104-144
405 Madison St, Lynchburg, VA 24504
☎ **(804) 528-5400**

Manassas
Sunrise Hill Farm Bed & Breakfast

This Federal-period B&B is located on the site of two major Civil War battles. Decorated with 18th- and 19th-century European and American antiques, it features Oriental rugs, working fireplaces, and a library. A full gourmet breakfast is served either in the huge country kitchen or on the flagstone terrace. The inn overlooks Bull Creek Run. There's an 18-stall barn with horses, goats and chickens on the grounds.

2 Rooms • Price range: $88-110
5590 Old Farm Ln, Manassas, VA 20109
☎ **(703) 754-8309**

Middleburg
⦿⦿ *Middleburg Country Inn*

This charming B&B was originally an Episcopal rectory built between 1820 and 1850. Located in a well-preserved historic town, the inn has been beautifully restored. Canopy beds and fireplaces can be found in each of the guestrooms, and all are equipped with private baths, some include Jacuzzis. The B&B also has a three-story balcony, ideal for taking in the surrounding views.

8 Rooms • Price range: $125-265
209 E Washington St, Middleburg, VA 20118
☎ **(540) 687-6082**

Middletown
Wayside Inn Since 1797

Operating continually since 1797, this inn gracefully blends its 18th-century ambience with 21st-century comfort. Appointments include canopy beds, English, French and Oriental antiques, brocades and a variety of fancy accoutrements.

22 Rooms • Price range: $99-159
7783 Main St, Middletown, VA 22645
☎ **(540) 869-1797**

Millboro
Fort Lewis Lodge

A mountain farm on a 3,200-acre nature preserve, the Fort Lewis Lodge is a rustic inn with rooms simply furnished with locally made furniture. Visitors can enjoy miles of wooded trails, fishing in clean streams, and jumping into an old-fashioned swimming hole. The beautifully restored 19th-century grist mill offers contemporary American cuisine, including fresh breads and vegetables from the inn's own garden.

13 Rooms • Price range: $85-210
SR 625 (River Rd), Millboro, VA 24460
☎ **(540) 925-2314**

Monterey
Mountain Laurel Inn

Local shops and restaurants are located nearby the Mountain Laurel Inn. The early 1900s home is set in the highlands of the Allegheny Mountains. Each of the guestrooms is uniquely decorated with antiques and period furnishings. Four of the rooms are equipped with private baths. The inn also features the original owner's piano, which stands in the parlor. Breakfast includes a daily special entrée.

4 Rooms • Price range: $75-110
Main St, Monterey, VA 24465
☎ **(540) 468-3401**

Mount Jackson
The Widow Kip's

Two restored cottages are available for families at this 1830s restored Colonial homestead. For singles or couples there are five antique-filled guestrooms boasting original fireplaces. All rooms come with private bath and four-poster, sleigh and hand-carved Victorian beds. The inn is set on seven acres in the Shenandoah Valley, and has a great view of the Massanutten Mountains. Breakfast is served daily.

7 Rooms • Price range: $85-100
355 Orchard Dr, Mount Jackson, VA 22842-9753
☎ **(540) 477-2400**

Nellysford
The Meander Inn at Penny Lane Farm

Five comfortable guestrooms are available in the 85-year-old Victorian farmhouse, each of them has a plush queen-size bed and is equipped with a private bath. A country breakfast is served daily. The inn is situated on 50 acres of horse-grazed pasture and woods in the peaceful surroundings of the Rockfish Valley. There are a number of activities in the vicinity, including horseback riding, hiking and fishing.

5 Rooms • Price range: $105-125
3100 Berry Hill Rd, Nellysford, VA 22958
☎ **(804) 361-1121**

New Church
The Garden & The Sea Inn

Visitors who like nature and the ocean will appreciate the location of this inn. Situated in the quaint Eastern Shore Village of New Church, it is just minutes from the barrier islands of Chincoteague and Assateague, which offer beautiful beaches and an array of wildlife, including the famous wild ponies. Each guestroom at the inn features a queen-size bed and private bath; some have a whirlpool tub.

8 Rooms • Price range: $75-185
4188 Nelson Rd, New Church, VA 23415
☎ **(757) 824-0672**

New Market
Cross Roads Inn

Built in 1925, this lovely white clapboard farmhouse is surrounded by two acres of gardens. The inn's spacious and elegant interior is highlighted by hardwood floors and period furnishings. The guestrooms are decorated with English floral wallpapers and four-poster and canopy beds. Several rooms also feature a Jacuzzi tub and a fireplace. Guests are invited to a complete breakfast served daily in the sunroom.

5 Rooms • Price range: $65-125
9222 John Sevier Rd, New Market, VA 22844
☎ **(540) 740-4157**

Norfolk
Bed & Breakfast at the Page House Inn

In 1990, this 90-year-old Georgian-Revival mansion went through major renovations and then promptly won Norfolk's Design Award for excellence. Located in the heart of the Ghent Historic District, the Page House is within walking distance to an array of attractions, including the Chrysler Art Museum, the Harrison Opera House and the MacArthur Memorial. Each guestroom features a variety of amenities, including a private bath, phone and custom robes. A full European-style breakfast, including fresh-baked cream scones, is served; snacks are available around the clock.

7 Rooms • Price range: $130-155
323 Fairfax Ave, Norfolk, VA 23507
☎ **(757) 625-5033**

Onancock
Spinning Wheel Bed & Breakfast

Bright, sunny antique-filled rooms make up this 1890s Victorian home.

5 Rooms • Price range: $75-95
31 North St, Onancock, VA 23417
☎ **(757) 787-7311**

Orange
Hidden Inn

Situated in the heart of Virginia wine country, this 1890 Victorian farmhouse is surrounded by eight wooded acres of gardens. Guests can tour several wineries in the area. There are 10 guestrooms at this four-building inn, each with a private bath. A full country breakfast is served in the dining room, and picnics are available by reservation. Nearby activities include swimming, golf, tennis, fishing and hiking.

10 Rooms • Price range: $59-169
249 Caroline St, Orange, VA 22960
☎ **(540) 672-3625**

Orange
Mayhurst Inn

A long, winding tree-lined drive is the fitting entry to this magnificent Italianate-Victorian gem. On the National Registry of Historic Places, the 1859 structure features an oval-spiral staircase that climbs up four flights. Restored to combine the best architectural features of the antebellum era with 21st-century comfort, the guestrooms feature such amenities as double whirlpool tubs.

7 Rooms • Price range: $115-200
12460 Mayhurst Ln, Orange, VA 22960
☎ **(540) 672-5597**

Palmyra
Palmer Country Manor

Chickens and cows are just some of the animals living on this working farm on 180 acres of prime land. The 1834 plantation house offers 13 rooms, either in the main house or in one of the private cottages. Each guestroom is air-conditioned, has a king- or queen-size bed, a full bath/shower and a large private deck. The daring visitor can go tubing in the James River or take a hot-air balloon ride over the countryside.

13 Rooms • Price range: $78-185
Rt 2 Box 1390, Palmyra, VA 22963
☎ **(804) 589-1300**

Petersburg
Mayfield Inn

Saved from destruction several times in its 250-year history, the Mayfield stands as a testament to the perseverance of its many owners. As much a museum as it is a B&B, guests will feel like they are stepping back into Colonial Virginia. Pine floors, seven fireplaces and other features are found throughout the house. The award-winning herb garden makes up a delightful corner in the landscaped grounds.

4 Rooms • Price range: $74-110
3348 W Washington St, Petersburg, VA 23804
☎ **(804) 733-0866**

Providence Forge
🕮 *Jasmine Plantation Bed & Breakfast Inn*

Situated in the heart of Virginia's historic plantation country, this restored 18th-century farmhouse boasts guestrooms decorated with American antiques. Upon arrival, guests are served refreshments in the Country Store. A full country breakfast is served every morning, after which guests can explore the inn's 47 acres of pasture and forest. Seasonal horse racing and fishing can be found in the vicinity.

5 Rooms • Price range: $85-140
4500 N Courthouse Rd, Providence Forge, VA 23140
☎ **(804) 966-9836**

Radford
The Alleghany Inn

Built in 1905, this remodeled Queen Anne-style home still contains all of its original oak and Virginia heart-pine woodwork but also features central air-conditioning and a modem line in each of its rooms. Only minutes from a variety of recreational activities such as boating, fishing and hunting, the inn is surrounded by a landscape rich in beauty and history. Breakfast includes country ham cured on the premises and fresh-baked biscuits with homemade jelly.

5 Rooms • Price range: $75-125
1123 Grove Ave, Radford, VA 24141
☎ **(540) 731-4466**

Rocky Mount
The Claiborne House B&B

Charming English gardens surround this Victorian house. A variety of recreational activities are available, including golfing, biking, tennis, or driving part of the 500-mile shoreline of Smith Mountain Lake. Weekly antique auctions are held in Franklin County, which is peppered with antique shops. The B&B's 130-foot wraparound porch features a lending library. Gourmet breakfasts include homegrown fruit in season, and home-baked breads.

5 Rooms • Price range: $85-125
185 Claiborne Ave, Rocky Mount, VA 24151
☎ **(540) 483-4616**

Scottsville
High Meadows Vineyard Inn

This amalgamation of three former homes holds twilight wine tastings featuring Pinot Noir from its own vineyard. Each room has a whirlpool bath, a private porch and a fireplace. Three secluded contemporary carriage houses are also available to stay in. European-style supper baskets containing gourmet meals, candles and poetry are available for weekday guests. Visitors can tour nearby Monticello or hike up Crabtree Falls.

10 Rooms • Price range: $89-265
55 High Meadows Ln, Scottsville, VA 24590
☎ **(804) 286-2218**

Shadwell
🏵 *Clifton, The Country Inn*

A manor house built in 1799 by Thomas Jefferson's son-in-law, Clifton features ample public spaces in which to relax, including a library and living room. There are also recreational facilities such as a swimming pool with a cascading waterfall, a clay tennis court and a lake. Guests are pampered with fine cuisine, beginning with a sumptuous breakfast and concluding with a gourmet dinner precisely orchestrated by the staff.

14 Rooms • Price range: $150-495
1296 Clifton Inn Dr, Shadwell, VA 22911
☎ **(804) 971-1800**

Smithfield
Smithfield Inn

The inn claims that George Washington really did sleep here. Built in 1752, the Smithfield has more than two centuries of innkeeping tradition under its belt, including a time when it served as an inn on the main stage coach route between Norfolk and Richmond. Two dining rooms, each seating 50, are complemented by an Olde English-style tavern and a cozy front sitting room for quiet conversation.

5 Rooms • Price range: $70-125
112 Main St, Smithfield, VA 23430
☎ **(757) 357-1752**

Smithfield
Smithfield Station

If a vacation by the waterfront is on the agenda then this is the place to be. The main inn is perched over a marina and pier that features a lighthouse with two luxurious suites. Second-floor rooms at the main inn have private verandas and street-level accommodations are thematically decorated. The lighthouse suite features a private rooftop observation cupola. The marina has 60 slips and can dock boats up to 70 feet long.

20 Rooms • Price range: $79-225
415 S Church St, Smithfield, VA 23430
☎ **(757) 357-7700**

Smithfield
Isle of Wight Inn

Large Colonial home in an historic river-port town.

12 Rooms • Price range: $45-119
1607 S Church St, Smithfield, VA 23430
☎ **(757) 357-3176**

Stanardsville
Edgewood Farm Bed & Breakfast

Originally built in 1790, the Edgewood B&B is a restored farmhouse located on a secluded 130-acre farm in the foothills of the Blue Mountains. Each of the antique-decorated bedrooms has its own working fireplace. Wildflower and perennial gardens and stream-crossed woods offer scenic paths for a quiet stroll, while for the more active, the Appalachian Trail is nearby. Many historical attractions are less than 30 minutes away.

3 Rooms • Price range: $80-120
1186 Middle River Rd, Stanardsville, VA 22973
☎ **(804) 985-3782**

Stanley
Milton House Bed & Breakfast Inn

It may be hard to believe, but this elegant manor home was ordered out of a 1915 Sears catalogue. The decor features an eclectic collection of antiques and German memorabilia, and each log cabin suite has a fireplace and private hot tub. The cuisine leans toward German (low-fat on request), and guests are invited to indulge in afternoon cakes and cookies. Recreational areas are close at hand, as are historical and tourist sites.

6 Rooms • Price range: $93-160
113 W Main, Stanley, VA 22851
☎ **(540) 778-2495**

Staunton
Ashton Country House

Built circa 1860, this elegant, red-brick country mansion is set on 25 acres of rolling hills in the scenic Blue Ridge Mountains. Charming Country-style antiques and decor grace every room. The spacious bedrooms feature queen-size beds with down comforters or quilts. All have private baths and four have fireplaces. Three porches provide ample opportunity to relax amid the surrounding natural beauty.

6 Rooms • Price range: $70-150
1205 Middlebrook Ave, Staunton, VA 24401
☎ **(540) 885-7819**

Staunton
The Belle Grae Inn and Restaurant

Forming a little neighborhood of 13 Victorian homes, this complex offers a wide variety of rooms and suites, each with features such as fireplaces, verandas, and wet bars. An armoire filled with games, puzzles and cards stands in the bar, and a comfortable parlor and reading room offer places for quiet conversation and relaxation. Both fine and casual dining are offered in the sitting and dining rooms and in the courtyard.

14 Rooms • Price range: $99-209
515 W Frederick St, Staunton, VA 24401-3333
☎ **(540) 886-5151**

Staunton
Frederick House

This group of restored Victorian homes features a collection of rooms, each with its own unique decor and architectural features, including a private entrance, balcony and fireplace. Visitors may enjoy antiquing, visiting historic sites, or taking in the 19th-century charm of nearby Staunton. Enjoy the culinary herb garden and flowering trees of the terrace gardens.

22 Rooms • Price range: $85-150
28 N New St, Staunton, VA 24401
☎ **(540) 885-4220**

Staunton
The Sampson Eagon Inn

Decorated with fine antiques and fabrics, this restored 1840 home is elegant yet comfortable, traditional yet contemporary. Each room features a canopied bed, private modern bath, and television with VCR and complimentary video library. Breakfasts may include such exotic fare as Grand Marnier souffle pancake and Kahlua pecan Belgian waffles, as well as homemade breads and fresh seasonal fruits.

5 Rooms • Price range: $89-98
238 E Beverley St, Staunton, VA 24401
☎ **(540) 886-8200**

Staunton
Thornrose House at Gypsy Hill

This charming and comfortable Georgian home is surrounded by an acre of gardens. A wraparound veranda provides a quiet place to sit and talk, although there are many recreational facilities nearby. A bottomless cookie jar in the parlor sets the tone for the service—friendly and accommodating. The property is conveniently close to local restaurants and wineries, as well as natural and historic points of interest.

5 Rooms • Price range: $60-90
531 Thornrose Ave, Staunton, VA 24401
☎ **(540) 885-7026**

Steeles Tavern
Steeles Tavern Manor Country Inn

This inn is a 1916 manor home on 55 acres of rolling valley farmland complete with a creek, springs and pond. It is decorated with a great attention to detail using antique oak, lace and ruffles. Each guestroom features a gas-log fireplace and double Jacuzzi bath. Fine dining is offered in the romantic evening glow furnished by candlelight and chandeliers in the dining room.

5 Rooms • Price range: $135-185
Box 39, Rt 11, Steeles Tavern, VA 24476
☎ **(540) 377-6444**

Steeles Tavern
Sugar Tree Inn

Tucked away in the Blue Mountains, the Sugar Tree Inn contains fieldstone fireplaces and exposed logs of hand-hewn chestnut, oak and poplar. The rooms are decorated along themes celebrating special historical personages. Each has a working fireplace. Outside the scenery dazzles throughout the year. Menus change to reflect the best of the season's produce and there is always at least one vegetarian entrée featured.

12 Rooms • Price range: $105-160
145 Lodge Trail, Steeles Tavern, VA 24476
☎ **(540) 377-2197**

Strasburg
⊕ Hotel Strasburg

An appealing collection of antiques and art—most for sale—graces this 1895 hotel. From a pier mirror reflecting a statue of Athena to the china and lace that grace the dining room, these pieces contribute to the hotel's Victorian ambience.

29 Rooms • Price range: $79-175
213 Holliday St, Strasburg, VA 22657
☎ **(540) 465-9191**

Virginia Beach
⚜ *Barclay Cottage*

Built as a summer cottage in 1895, and once used as a schoolhouse, Barclay Cottage is located just two blocks away from the beach and fishing pier in the heart of the Virginia Beach tourist area. Although the building has been completely restored and modernized, antiques preserve the inn's historic ambience. The wraparound porches are ideal for relaxing after a day at the beach or after visiting historic sites in the area.

6 Rooms • Price range: $88-118
400 16th St, Virginia Beach, VA 23451
☎ (757) 422-1956

Warm Springs
The Inn at Gristmill Square

A grist mill dating to 1900 lies at the center of the cluster of buildings that make up the inn's charming mountain village setting. The mill now serves as a restaurant featuring continental and traditional American cuisine, while the outbuildings contain individually decorated and named rooms. Amenities include three tennis courts and a sauna. Horseback riding, hunting, fishing and other recreational activities are available nearby.

17 Rooms • Price range: $60-100
Rt 645 Old Mill Rd, Warm Springs, VA 24484
☎ (540) 839-2231

Warrenton
Black Horse Inn

Twenty acres of Virginia countryside and more than 130 years of history surround the Civil War-era mansion that constitutes the Black Horse Inn. Sumptuously decorated guestrooms provide the best of the past and the present. Four-poster and canopy beds, a rock fireplace and a black marble bathroom are a few of the features found in some rooms. Horses are available for experienced riders.

8 Rooms • Price range: $125-295
8393 Meetze Rd, Warrenton, VA 20187
☎ (540) 349-4020

Washington
⚜ *Middleton Inn*

Built in 1850 by Middleton Miller, the manufacturer of the Confederate uniform, this elegant, Federal-style brick manor house sits atop a knoll facing the Blue Ridge Mountains. From the complimentary wine served on the veranda to the gourmet breakfast, Middleton Inn strives to recreate the gentility of an English country home in a Southern setting. Each of the four charming guestrooms in the main house is equipped with a marble bath and working fireplace. Also on site is the two-story guest cottage, which includes a living room with fireplace, a library and a Jacuzzi.

5 Rooms • Price range: $195-525
176 Main St, Washington, VA 22747
☎ (540) 675-2020

Washington
Foster Harris House Bed & Breakfast

In the 1930s this circa 1900 building was a very popular guesthouse. Later, after an extensive restoration, the current owners re-opened its doors to guests in 1984. All of the guestrooms now have private baths, some have wood-burning stoves. The beds are either queen size or double. Each room commands a special view of the Blue Ridge Mountains or of the B&B's gardens. The breakfast menu changes with the season.

5 Rooms • Price range: $95-200
189 Main St. PO Box 333, Washington, VA 22747
☎ **(540) 675-3757**

Washington
⊕ *The Heritage House Bed & Breakfast*

A quaint 1837 manor house that, according to legend, was used as General Jubal Early's headquarters during the Civil War. Guests can read an extensive history of the house in the parlor and there are lovely gardens to enjoy.

5 Rooms • Price range: $105-185
291 Main St, Washington, VA 22747
☎ **(540) 675-3207**

Waynesboro
Belle Hearth B&B

An impressive 1909 two-story, gabled Victorian-style home with a wraparound porch and warm homelike ambience. Named after its seven beautifully made fireplaces this pleasant inn features high ceilings, heart-pine floors, an outdoor pool and gas fireplaces in some of the guestrooms. Victorian furnishings are mixed with objects and artifacts the innkeepers have collected during their extensive travels.

4 Rooms • Price range: $80-85
320 S Wayne Ave, Waynesboro, VA 22980
☎ **(540) 943-1910**

Waynesboro
The Iris Inn

Concealed beneath The Iris Inn's contemporary exterior is an enchanting country lodge. The Great Room features a massive mural and a stone fireplace that stretches up 28 feet to the peak of the ceiling. The building was designed to take advantage of the stunning scenery and many guestrooms have a wall of windows that look out onto the surrounding forest. Parks and historic attractions are all but a short drive away.

9 Rooms • Price range: $85-150
191 Chinquapin Dr, Waynesboro, VA 22980
☎ **(540) 943-1991**

Weyers Cave
The Inn at Keezletown Road

This pleasant Victorian inn is located in an appealing small town setting. It has its own herb and flower gardens that supply both the kitchen with fresh herbs and edible garnishes and the rest of the inn with fresh-cut flowers. Fluffy comforters and Oriental rugs, porch rockers and a hammock provide old-fashioned comfort. A full breakfast, including Southern delicacies and eggs fresh from the inn's own chicken house, is served every morning.

4 Rooms • Price range: $75-115
1224 Keezletown Rd, Weyers Cave, VA 24486
☎ **(540) 234-0644**

White Post
L'Auberge Provençale French Country Inn

The careful decor and design of this 1753 fieldstone manor on 18 acres re-creates the south of France. The cuisine is superb, prepared by a fourth-generation French master-chef using fruits, herbs and vegetables fresh from the Auberge's own orchard and gardens, and complemented by an extensive wine cellar. Area activities include antiquing, horseback riding and, for the more adventurous, hot-air ballooning.

14 Rooms • Price range: $125-295
13630 Lord Fairfax Hwy, White Post, VA 22663
☎ **(540) 837-1375**

Williamsburg
Liberty Rose Bed & Breakfast

This beautifully restored beaded clapboard home stands at the top of a hill just a mile from the Colonial Historic Village. The style is romantic, and the rooms are individually decorated with European antiques, vintage fabrics and designer wallcoverings. Some rooms have a full canopy bed, fireplace and oversize claw-foot tub in a private bath. Guests are invited to play a tune on the grand piano in the parlor, or to simply relax by the fire. A sumptuous breakfast is served on the sunny morning porch or in the courtyards at intimate tables for two.

4 Rooms • Price range: $145-225
1022 Jamestown Rd, Williamsburg, VA 23185
☎ **(757) 253-1260**

Williamsburg
An American Inn

This stately brick Colonial home was built during the reconstruction of Colonial Williamsburg, and evokes an earlier era when hospitality was a matter of pride, and fine living was an art practiced in restful surroundings. Each guestroom features a gracious queen-size bed and private bath and all are uniquely furnished with fine antiques, rich fabrics and Oriental rugs. Breakfast is a lavish presentation of regional Virginia foods.

5 Rooms • Price range: $109-159
600 Richmond Rd, Williamsburg, VA 23185
☎ **(757) 220-8011**

Williamsburg
Applewood Colonial Bed & Breakfast

A Colonial Flemish-bond brick home, built by craftsmen in 1929.

4 Rooms • Price range: $95-175
605 Richmond Rd, Williamsburg, VA 23185
☎ **(757) 229-0205**

Williamsburg
The Cedars Bed & Breakfast

A three-story brick Georgian home, this B&B is a short walk from Colonial Williamsburg and other attractions. Each room is uniquely decorated with antiques and elegant fabrics. Candlelight and fresh flowers accompany full breakfasts, which are served from a hand-hewn hunt board on the tavern porch. To pass the time guests are invited to play cards or chess, or to just sit and relax on the tavern porch.

9 Rooms • Price range: $95-160
616 Jamestown Rd, Williamsburg, VA 23185
☎ **(757) 229-3591**

Williamsburg
⚹ Colonial Capital Bed & Breakfast

Antique furnishings, Oriental rugs, and ceiling fans create a charming Southern-style atmosphere in this Colonial-Revival home. Guests can relax outdoors on the patio, or stay inside to play games or read books by the fireplace in the traditional plantation parlor. Each room features a four-poster canopy bed and a private bath. For breakfast, special blend coffee, Virginia pork and savory souffle or casserole are offered.

5 Rooms • Price range: $110-150
501 Richmond Rd, Williamsburg, VA 23185-3537
☎ **(757) 229-0233**

Williamsburg
Colonial Gardens Bed & Breakfast

Century-old oaks and charming gardens create a magical woodland setting for this Colonial brick house. Rooms are individually decorated with original artwork, antiques and fresh flowers. Outdoor relaxation takes place on a screened sunporch, or on the rockers and swing on the front porch. A full plantation breakfast, including fresh-baked breads, is served in a formal dining room on elegant china.

4 Rooms • Price range: $115-165
1109 Jamestown Rd, Williamsburg, VA 23185
☎ **(757) 220-8087**

Williamsburg
Fox & Grape Bed & Breakfast

Warm hospitality awaits you in this renovated Colonial-style house. The exterior has been embellished with a wraparound porch; inside the rooms are furnished with antiques, cross-stitch samplers and handmade quilts. On display are a couple of the hosts' collections, one of carved roosters and duck decoys, another of Noah's Arks. The Shaker-style furniture was made by the host.

4 Rooms • Price range: $95-110
701 Monumental Ave, Williamsburg, VA 23185
☎ **(757) 229-6914**

Williamsburg
Hite's Bed & Breakfast

This attractive Cape Cod-style house is decorated with antiques and collectibles. Each room has a private bath with a claw-foot tub. Guests can enjoy birds, flowers and a goldfish pond while they swing on the swing in the garden. Guests are also welcome to amuse themselves playing the antique pump organ and Victrola in the parlor. Nearby attractions include Jamestown, Yorktown, Williamsburg and Busch Gardens.

2 Rooms • Price range: $95-110
704 Monumental Ave, Williamsburg, VA 23185
☎ **(757) 229-4814**

Williamsburg
Indian Springs Bed & Breakfast

A 10-minute walk away from Colonial Williamsburg, Indian Springs is located in a quaint neighborhood, surrounded by gardens and greenery. A patio, lined with rockers, provides a fine opportunity for bird-watching or drinking a quiet afternoon tea. Each room features a private bath and a private entrance, which overlooks a wooded ravine. A hearty breakfast is served, and the hosts are happy to suit specific dietary needs.

4 Rooms • Price range: $95-135
330 Indian Springs Rd, Williamsburg, VA 23185
☎ **(757) 220-0726**

Williamsburg
The Inn at 802

The parlor of this brick inn is a nice spot to sit before the fire and the veranda has comfy wicker furniture ideal for lounging in with a book. The inn itself is right across the street from William and Mary College. It has comfortable guestrooms with queen-size beds, down comforters and private baths. A candlelight breakfast is served in the formal dining room on a table set with silver, crystal and fine china.

4 Rooms • Price range: $125-145
802 Jamestown Rd, Williamsburg, VA 23185
☎ **(757) 564-0845**

Williamsburg
Legacy of Williamsburg Bed & Breakfast Inn

Flickering candlelight and 18th-century antiques evoke the elegance and romance of the past, while cleverly concealed conveniences assure the utmost in comfort of the present. Relax with a game of darts or play billiards on an English-style table in the tavern. Breakfast is served by the grand fireplace in the keeping room, where antique cupboards display 18th-century pewter ware.

4 Rooms • Price range: $125-180
930 Jamestown Rd, Williamsburg,
VA 23185-3917
☎ **(757) 220-0524**

Williamsburg
Magnolia Manor B&B

Georgian home with canopy beds, two suites and fresh-baked goodies.

4 Rooms • Price range: $125-185
700 Richmond Rd, Williamsburg, VA 23185
☎ **(757) 220-9600**

Williamsburg
Piney Grove at Southall's Plantation

This 1857 Greek-Revival plantation houses four comfortable guestrooms, each with private bath, coffeemaker and refrigerator. Fresh flowers are a staple and, during the Christmas season, each guestroom is provided with its own decorated real tree. Guests are treated to mint juleps on the porch swing or hot toddies by a roaring fire. A plantation breakfast, including Virginia ham or sausage, is served daily.

4 Rooms • Price range: $135-270
16920 Southall Plantation Ln,
Williamsburg, VA 23187
☎ **(804) 829-2480**

Williamsburg
⚜ *A Primrose Cottage*

Award-winning gardens surround this adorable Cape Cod-style cottage with bright green shutters. Whimsical decorative touches such as antique ice-box bedside tables and prints from Hans Christian Andersen fairy tales are punctuated by light, spring colors and German folk-art accents. Local birds can be observed at the feeders just outside the breakfast room window. The Williamsburg historical district is within walking distance.

4 Rooms • Price range: $95-145
706 Richmond Rd, Williamsburg, VA 23185
☎ **(757) 229-6421**

Williamsburg
⚜ *War Hill Inn Bed & Breakfast*

In 1968, with the assistance of an architect from Colonial Williamsburg, this 18th-century reproduction home was built on 32 acres of land that includes a vineyard, an orchard, gardens and a forest. Pine floors from a school, stairs from a church and beams from a barn were all incorporated into this incredibly authentic inn. Naturally, all of the modern amenities were also skillfully included. Two cottages are also available.

6 Rooms • Price range: $80-150
4560 Long Hill Rd, Williamsburg, VA 23188-1533
☎ **(757) 565-0248**

Williamsburg
⚜ *Williamsburg Sampler Bed & Breakfast Inn*

This plantation-style Colonial boasts a fine collection of antiques, pewter and samplers. The meticulous attention to detail, as seen in the pegged hardwood floors and multi-membered crown moldings throughout, also adds to 18th-century warmth and atmosphere. Fresh coffee and homemade muffins are just the introduction to the "Skip Lunch®" breakfast served on fine china in the Great Room.

4 Rooms • Price range: $110-160
922 Jamestown Rd, Williamsburg, VA 23185
☎ **(757) 253-0398**

Williamsburg
Holland's Lodge

Family-owned since 1929, this stately Colonial lodge offers Southern hospitality.

5 Rooms • Price range: $65-95
601 Richmond Rd, Williamsburg, VA 23185
☎ **(757) 253-6476**

Woodstock
The Inn at Narrow Passage

This inn, whose oldest section dates to 1740, features rooms with handsome furnishings and an understated elegance. Some guestrooms have pine floors and stenciling, and most have a private bath and working fireplace. After a short walk to the river, guests can watch for ducks or go fishing, then return for lemonade on the porch in summer, or hot spiced tea by the fire in winter. Nearby are wineries, battlefields, caverns, and ski facilities.

12 Rooms • Price range: $75-145
30 Chapman Landing Rd, Woodstock, VA 22664
☎ **(540) 459-8000**

Woolwine
The Mountain Rose Inn

Secluded on 100 acres of mountain meadow, this 1901 Victorian was built from wood that was cut and dried on the property. Excellent quality craftsmanship is evident in the inn's Victorian embellishments and tongue-and-groove woodwork. Breakfasts, which include freshly ground coffee, homemade breads with apple butter and Southern orange pancakes, are served by the glow of oil lamps.

5 Rooms • Price range: $89-119
1787 Charity Hwy, Woolwine, VA 24185
☎ **(540) 930-1057**

Notes:

_____
_____
_____
_____
_____
_____
_____
_____
_____
_____
_____
_____
_____
_____
_____
_____
_____
_____
_____
_____
_____

Southwest

Majestic peaks are a spectacular backdrop for Main Street in Telluride, Colorado.

Scenic Byways
of the Southwest

The Southwest is a land of rock. Bryce Canyon, shown here, is only one of several parks in the region that feature fantastic formations.

San Luis to Santa Fe
The mountain scenery and the rich Spanish and Native American history of northern New Mexico have drawn artists and writers to the region for generations. This route takes drivers through the vibrant cultural and artistic centers of Taos and Santa Fe, as well as hamlets with similar adobe architecture, where visitors may hear Spanish spoken at least as often as English.

Poncha Springs to Durango
The Rocky Mountains form the backbone of the state of Colorado and their western slopes offer some of the continent's most varied mountain scenery. This route makes its way through fertile valleys and mountain passes, offering views of forest, granite peaks and red volcanic cliffs. Stop-offs are equally varied, including a recreational area, a historic museum and an archeological site.

Torrey to Panguitch
Part of Utah's "color country," this short stretch of highway winds through some of the most unusual and wondrous scenery in the region. The route passes through a series of parks, each one dramatically different—from Capitol Reef with its the imposing wall to Bryce Canyon and its fanciful multicolored rock hoodoos.

Mt. Carmel Junction to I-15
This drive reveals a harsh and beautiful country of red rock and sparse vegetation. The highlight is the spectacular Zion National Park. St. George and the other communities of the region feature landmarks dating from Mormon pioneer days.

The San Miguel County Courthouse, built in 1885 and still in use today, is a feature attraction in Telluride, Colorado.

Most people associate the Southwest with brilliant summer sun, but the region can be equally beautiful in the winter.

For further information on the sites along each route, see the Scenic Byways Resource Guide on page 775.

Cameron to Grand Canyon Village

There is simply no site on earth like the Grand Canyon. The short drive along the South Rim is unforgettable. Whether one gazes into the canyon from the lookouts or braves a hike down into the base, it is hard to get one's fill.

San Luis to Santa Fe

Near the beginning of the route in Colorado are the Great Sand Dunes and the Cumbres and Toltec Scenic Railroad. Then, heading south into New Mexico, the road passes between the rugged San Juan and Sangre de Cristo ranges. Near Questa, it enters the magnificent valley of the Rio Grande and then winds along to the historic towns of Taos and Sante Fe.

❶ Great Sand Dunes National Monument and National Preserve

Ever-shifting mountains of sand, these dunes hug the foothills of the Sangre de Cristo Range. The highest on the continent, the dunes rise 750 feet above the desert valley below. The sands support well-adapted plants such as bright prairie sunflowers, but most animals skirt the edges of the 39-square-mile territory. Human visitors can choose the nature trails around the perimeter or can venture out onto the dunes themselves, stepping onto sand undisturbed by anything other than the wind. Special summer activities organized by the visitor center include a kite-flying and sand-castle-building event.

❷ Cumbres and Toltec Scenic Railroad

Once part of the Denver to Rio Grande line, this is the longest narrow-gauge rail journey in the country. The line is actually served by two trains, one starting in Antonito, Colorado, and the other in Chama, New Mexico. They meet at the half-way point of Osier and then each returns to its starting point. Driven by coal-burning engines, the Antonito train climbs into the San Juan Mountains, traveling through deep valleys and across heart-stopping trestle bridges. At Osier, travelers can have lunch and turn back or change trains and continue on. Traveling through high mountain meadows, the train crests at the 10,000-foot Cumbres Pass and then drops precipitously into Chama. Travelers return to Antonito immediately by van. The entire trip can be accomplished in reverse, starting in Chama.

❸ Harwood Museum of Art

A hundred years ago, the artists Ernest Blumenschein and Bert Phillips broke their wagon wheel 20 miles north of Taos. After a coin toss, Blumenschein rode into Taos to have the wheel repaired. Later, after Blumenschein rhapsodized about the beauty of Taos, both men moved to the town. Their enthusiasm for the area's clear mountain light and the rich mix of Hispanic, Native, and Anglo heritage soon drew other artists and writers. In the last century, Georgia O'Keeffe and D.H. Lawrence were among the creative people to call Taos home. Founded in 1915, the Taos Society of Artists has made a significant mark on American art and today the town is considered one of the country's premier artists' colonies. Strolling the narrow streets, visitors can admire Spanish-style adobe buildings, visit several historic homes, and poke their heads into artists' galleries and workshops. The Harwood Museum, which displays paintings, prints, drawings and sculpture of the last 150 years, offers a good introduction to the history and significance of New Mexico art.

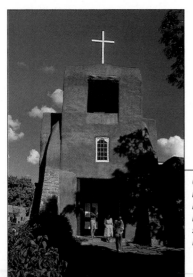

One of the oldest churches in the country, the San Miguel Mission in Santa Fe is typical of the Spanish-style architecture of New Mexico.

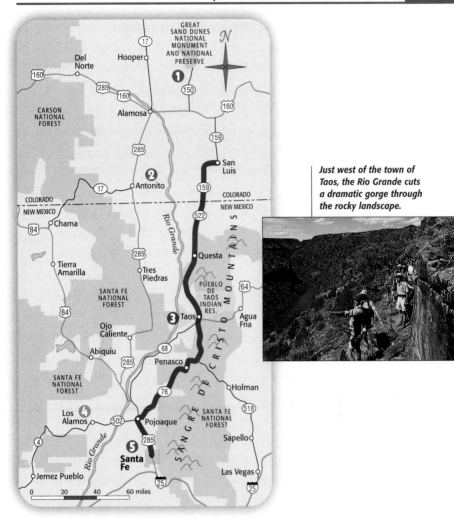

Just west of the town of Taos, the Rio Grande cuts a dramatic gorge through the rocky landscape.

❹ Bradbury Science Museum

Visitors to the museum can learn how scientists at Los Alamos National Laboratory are using the latest technologies to solve issues related to energy, health, the environment and to the end of the Cold War The lab is well known for its historic role in the Manhattan Project, the World War II effort that developed the atomic bomb. More than 40 interactive exhibits and videos showcase the laboratory's historical and current role in national security and some of the technical applications of its science and research.

❺ Santa Fe

First settled by Pueblo peoples in the 11th century, Santa Fe was founded as a Spanish town in 1609. Now the capital of New Mexico, this small city of 56,000 still offers a vibrant cultural mix. Some of the public buildings, such as the Governor's Palace and the Mission of San Miguel of Santa Fe, date from the beginning of the Spanish settlement. The city has a lively cultural life and many museums and galleries. One of the highlights, the Museum of International Folk Art, features artifacts, drama, dance and music from more than 100 countries.

Poncha Springs to Durango

Traveling west on Route 50 from Poncha Springs, drivers quickly rise to the Continental Divide, the backbone of the Rockies. From this high point, the route follows a series of beautiful river valleys and then turns south through the rugged San Juan Mountains. The section south of Ouray passes through old mining towns and climbs the precipitous Red Mountain Pass.

❶ Monarch Aerial Tram

Crossing the Continental Divide at Monarch Pass, cars and bikes can make it only so far. To get right to the top, ride an additional 700 feet on the aerial tram. Only the brave will look down as the gondola rises at a top speed of 400 feet per minute. Located at an elevation of 12,000 feet, the observation tower allows you a breathtaking 360-degree view, one of the best in the Rockies. To the south lie the Sangre de Cristo and San Juan mountains and to the north, the Ruby Mountains and the towering peaks of the Collegiate Range. Telescopes bring the sights right up close.

❷ Pioneer Museum

The small town of Gunnison is a perfect base for fishing and water sports and for exploring the nearby Gunnison National Forest. Worth a visit right in town is the Pioneer Museum, a cluster of restored turn-of-the-20th-century buildings, including a schoolhouse, a post office and a railroad depot. Displays include pioneer farm equipment and household implements, Native American arrowheads and an antique auto collection.

❸ Curecanti National Recreation Area

Damming of the Gunnison River has created three reservoirs that now form the heart of an exceptional recreation area. The three lakes tempt visitors out on the water and anglers favor them for their stock of trout and salmon. The park also boasts hiking and skiing trails and 10 separate campgrounds. The three visitor centers offer guided walks and evening presentations.

❹ Black Canyon of the Gunnison National Park

Carved by the Gunnison River, the walls of Black Canyon drop 2,000 feet. Little light reaches the bottom and heavy shadows are cast on the rock walls, giving the canyon its name. The sparse vegetation includes sagebrush, gambel oak and Douglas fir. Only the very experienced mountaineer should attempt the descent—and even then, only with the permission of the ranger. Visitors can view the canyon from the roads along the north or south rim; the northern access is closed in winter. The visitor center offers information on the canyon's unique geology.

❺ Durango and Silverton Narrow Gauge Railroad

In operation since 1881, this railway once hauled valuable gold and silver ore. It now transports tourists. The train follows the same narrow-gauge track, with rails laid only three feet apart to slip through the narrow mountain passes. The same coal-burning engines pull the train and most of the wood-paneled cars are original as well. The three-hour trip from Durango to Silverton goes from the sagebrush slopes of the San Juans to the conifer forests of the high country. Visitors can return to Durango after a two-hour layover or they can spend the night in the tiny legendary mining town of Silverton. Only part of the route operates in the winter.

Built as a hospital in 1893, this building now houses the Telluride Historical Museum, with collections of photos and artifacts.

Located about three miles east of Telluride, picturesque Bridal Veil Falls urges the Bridal Veil Creek over a 365-foot drop. A mining road leads hikers, mountain bikers and jeeps to the falls.

❻ Mesa Verde National Park

The massive Cliff Palace rises several stories and encompasses about 150 rooms. Made of the same sandstone as the cliffs behind it, it manages to almost disappear. The Palace is one of thousands of ruins in the Mesa Verde archeological preserve, once the home of the ancestral Pueblo people. These people inhabited the region as long ago as A.D. 500. They were farmers, potters and basket weavers and beautiful artifacts have been recovered in the area. The first housing was constructed by digging pits in the ground, which were lined with stone, and later free-standing pueblos were built. About 1200, for reasons not understood, they moved into cliff dwellings built in alcoves in canyon walls. By 1300 the area was a bustling trade center of 5,000 people. And then, within a generation, the people had left. It is generally thought that their descendants are the Pueblo peoples of northern New Mexico and Arizona. Visitors to the mesa can view various sites from paved lookouts. Others can be reached and explored on foot.

Torrey to Panguitch

Heading south from Torrey, Highway 12 offers a view of imposing Boulder Mountain to the west and the ridge of the Capitol Reef to the east. It then passes in quick succession through pine and aspen woods, desert plateaus, and high plains. A series of spectacular state and national parks line the route, each with unique geology. Visitors end their trip in the historic ranching town of Panguitch.

Hikers at the Calf Creek Recreation Area between Escalante and Boulder can follow a trail to this lovely 126-foot waterfall.

guided trail through 20 of them. There is a replica of an Anasazi home showing the way of life of the inhabitants and a museum displaying artifacts found at the site.

❶ Capitol Reef National Park
A 100-mile-long bulge in the earth's crust, the cliffs of the Capitol Reef rise 1,000 feet in a series of multicolored layers. The whole is topped with a layer of white Navajo sandstone. The sandstone forms huge domes resembling the U.S. Capitol building (hence the park's name) and is pitted with eroded water pockets, some as large as swimming pools. The park follows the length of the ridge and presents fascinating geological oddities—there are stone arches, domes and alcoves to explore and canyons that send back a repeating echo. The park can be explored on foot from the visitor center or by car along various scenic drives. Horseback tours are available through local outfitters. Running through the park is the fertile Fremont River valley, first inhabited by Native Americans whose petroglyphs are still visible along the banks of the river. Later, Mormon pioneers settled the valley and the remnants of the village of Fruita can be visited. In season, travelers can pick their own fruit at local orchards.

❷ Anasazi Indian Village
Inhabited by the Anasazi people from about A.D. 1050 to 1200, this site has been partially excavated—87 rooms have been uncovered so far and visitors can follow a self-

❸ Escalante Petrified Forest State Park
Visitors stop at this park primarily to view the colorful petrified forest. The wood of stumps and tree trunks, thought to have been toppled by volcanic flow, has been gradually replaced with minerals, leaving unnatural-looking rings of red, yellow and metallic gray. The park has its own campground and the Wide Hollow Reservoir offers attractive swimming and fishing.

❹ Bryce Canyon National Park
This park has been described as one of the most beautiful in the world. The enormous amphitheater-shaped hollows are studded with multicolored rock formations in vivid yellows and reds. The formations, called "hoodoos," have been sculpted by nature into extraordinary, fanciful shapes—one is even said to resemble Queen Victoria. Because of the instability of the soil, most of the trees are dwarfed and twisted, giving the area the look of a huge bonsai garden. Spring brings a wonderful variety of flowers and the park is also home to more than 170 species of birds. The most spectacular vantage points along the rim can be reached by car. There are also trails zigzagging down into the hollow, but the climb back up can be quite arduous. The park is at its most wondrous at sunrise and sunset and is particularly magical following a light dusting of snow.

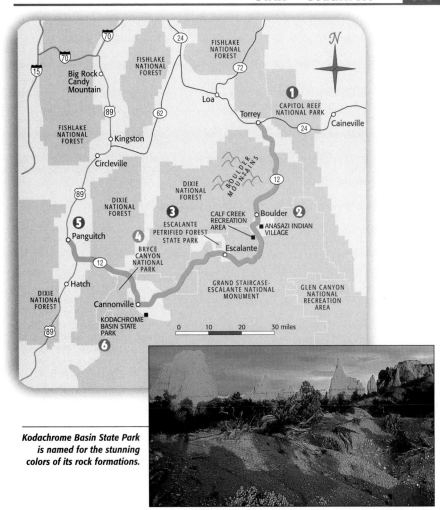

Kodachrome Basin State Park is named for the stunning colors of its rock formations.

❺ Paunsagaunt Western Wildlife Museum

Located in the Old West town of Panguitch, this museum displays more than 400 mounted animals of North America as well as many exotic animals from other parts of the world. The animals are displayed in scenes representing their natural habitat and photography is encouraged. There are also displays of animal skulls and Native American artifacts from several western tribes as well as a large butterfly collection.

❻ Kodachrome Basin State Park

The mood of this park is dramatic and ever-changing—as the light and weather shift, the multicolored rock formations change color from ashen to red, then from red to yellow. Visitors can discover tranquil spots among the formations from which to admire the majestic desert scenery. The park also features massive white spires with such imaginative names as "the Ballerina" and "the Patriarch." These towering spires are thought to be columns of minerals from ancient springs or geysers—as the surrounding soft red sandstone was eroded, the white columns were left standing. Camping facilities are available in the park and the area can be enjoyably explored on horseback.

Mt. Carmel Junction to I-15

Heading west from Mt. Carmel Junction, travelers will quickly spot the looming cliffs of Zion National Park. The route goes through one section of the park and then continues west through a rugged landscape of rock outcroppings and sagebrush. Some of the towns in the area, one of them now a virtual ghost town, offer an intriguing glimpse at Mormon history.

❶ Cedar Breaks National Monument

Looking like it would seat a crowd of millions, Cedar Breaks is an enormous natural amphitheater carved from the edge of a plateau. The slopes drop 2,000 feet below the plateau rim, forming stone spires and arches resembling the buttresses of a Gothic cathedral. Clinging to the slopes are twisted and stunted bristlecone pines, among the oldest trees on the planet. The intense yellows, browns and reds of the rock shift as the light changes and occasional wisps of clouds floating along the slopes add to the eerie effect. There are no roads or trails down to the base, but a road and hiking trails follow the rim and offer fabulous views. The road is closed in the winter and the hiking trails are taken over by adventuresome cross-country skiers and snowshoers.

❷ Coral Pink Sand Dunes State Park

The coral color of these ever-changing sand dunes contrasts with the red of the surrounding cliffs and the intense blue of the sky. The desert landscape has served as a backdrop for several movies. The sands are a playground for motorcyclists and fans of dune buggies and all-terrain vehicles. Others can enjoy the trails along the perimeter of the park.

❸ Zion National Park

West Temple, Court of the Patriarchs, Towers and Temples of the Virgin—the names of the dramatic peaks and stone monoliths of Zion National Park pay tribute to the reverence inspired by the place. A scenic drive, accessed by shuttle bus from April until October, offers visitors stunning views of one of the highlights, Zion Canyon. Walking trails lead to lookouts and special rock formations throughout the park. There is also a region of undisturbed back country to tempt enthusiastic campers. The trees and plants of the park vary according to elevation; the lower slopes sustain a variety of desert plants, while higher up are forests of fir and aspen. More than 270 species of birds have been spotted in the park, which is also home to a variety of animals, including bobcats, elk, black bears and gray fox—although they usually manage to stay out of sight. The park is particularly enchanting right after a rain, when rivulets cascade down the cliff faces. The visitor center has exhibits to help tourists plan their visit. Rangers lead guided walks and a children's program runs in the summer.

❹ Grafton

Founded in 1859 by Mormon families, all that is left of this community near Rockville is a well-preserved and picturesque ghost town. The town has served as a backdrop for several movies, including "Butch Cassidy and the Sundance Kid."

The first Mormon settlers to encounter the fantastic cliffs and canyons of Zion National Park saw them as a place of peaceful refuge.

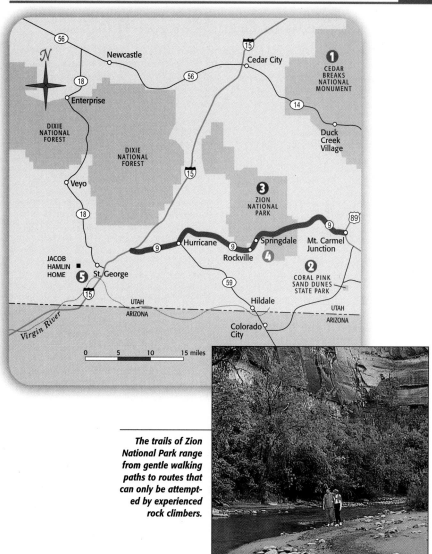

The trails of Zion National Park range from gentle walking paths to routes that can only be attempted by experienced rock climbers.

5 St. George

The original Mormon settlers of this town came to take advantage of its warm climate to grow cotton. St. George soon became known as "Utah's Dixie." Two of the city's landmarks date from the early days of Mormon settlement. The Temple, a pristine white building in a Gothic-Revival style, was built by local men called on by the church to give one day out of 10 to the construction. The Tabernacle, built as a meeting house for 2,000, is a red sandstone building with a slender white steeple. Brigham Young wintered in St. George and visitors can tour his restored 1873 adobe house. In Santa Clara, a suburb of St. George, the 1863 sandstone home of Mormon missionary Jacob Hamlin also offers guided tours. Both homes feature period furnishings and implements. A pioneer museum in St. George displays items dating from the beginning of the settlement.

Cameron to Grand Canyon Village

This drive offers views of the sheer walls of the Little Colorado River Canyon, but this, of course, is just a warm-up for the splendor of the main attraction. Continuing west, drivers will find themselves following the rim of the incomparable Grand Canyon. After trying to absorb the grandeur from the various lookouts, those who decide to spend more time can base themselves in Grand Canyon Village.

❶ Tusayan Museum and Ruin

This site was inhabited by about 30 ancestral Pueblo people near the end of the 12th century. After a few decades they moved elsewhere, leaving behind their 15-room dwelling. Visitors can tour the ruin and a small museum features exhibits on the life of the ancient people as well as that of some of the Native American peoples currently living in the area.

❷ The Grand Canyon

The majestic Grand Canyon is truly one of the greatest masterpieces of nature. Its size is humbling: 277 miles long, a mile deep and 10 miles across. Gazing into the depth of the canyon, one loses all sense of perspective and the powerful Colorado River at the base seems like a tiny stream. The towering walls of the canyon display distinctly colored layers that serve as a record of two billion years of Earth's history. Most visitors view the canyon from its South Rim, where a road leads to a series of breathtaking lookouts—although one section is off-limits in the summer and must be explored by bicycle or shuttle bus. Some of the lookouts can also be reached by a short, easy trail suitable for the whole family. A free shuttle bus system provides access to many spots on the South Rim, and is the only way to get to the Canyon View Information Plaza. The visitor center here has displays to help travelers plan their time at the canyon. Ranger-conducted walks, talks and evening programs are offered at several locations on the South Rim throughout the year. The North Rim, open from mid-May until late fall, is even higher than the South and offers its own dramatic vistas. However, although it is only 10 miles away as the crow flies, it is more than 200 miles by car. Because of the depth of the canyon, hikers who decide to descend to its base will pass through as many ecological zones as on a trip from British Columbia to the Mexican border, with vegetation ranging from pine forest near the top to desert scrub at the bottom. Although there are a number of trails into the canyon, only few are maintained. Even these should only be attempted by the experienced hiker and only with plenty of water. A slightly less arduous way to explore the canyon is by mule—these tours must be booked as much as a year in advance. And for those looking for a combination of comfort and awesome views, a number of companies in the area offer bus, plane and helicopter tours.

❸ Kaibab National Forest

Split into a northern and southern section by the Grand Canyon, this area is a great base from which to visit the canyon, but is also worth a visit in its own right. There are both primitive and developed campsites available. Visitors can enjoy horseback riding, hiking and cross-country skiing and the lakes offer good fishing. Dominated by ponderosa pine trees, the forest is home to large

Formed in the last few million years, the awesome Grand Canyon is one of the great natural wonders. About 277 miles long and 5,700 feet deep, it offers a spectacle of color and depth in the shapes of rock and earth.

Aboard the Grand Canyon Railway, passengers can look forward to a Wild West shoot-out, a museum and 65 miles of canyon scenery.

game such as elk, mule deer and antelope. Turkey and coyote are quite common and mountain lions and black bears can be spotted occasionally. The Kaibab squirrel, a dark gray squirrel with a white tail and tufted ears, is unique to this forest.

❹ Havasu Canyon

A smaller side branch of the Grand Canyon, Havasu Canyon belongs to the Havasupai people. The canyon offers a lush beauty of rich vegetation and turquoise waters. There are no roads to the base, so visitors must descend the steep switchbacks on foot or by mule. At the base of the canyon is the Native American village of Supai, where visitors can stop to eat and rest. There are no cars here and the locals travel by foot or on horseback. The peacefulness is only occasionally marred by the arrival of a helicopter that carries tourists and supplies. Just beyond the village is the campground and the jewels of the canyon—four waterfalls that plummet down the canyon walls. One of them, Havasu Falls, plunges into a beautiful turquoise pool, perfect for bathing.

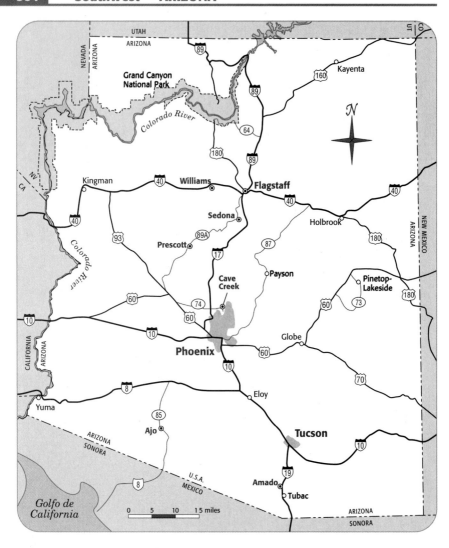

Ajo
The Guest House Inn

The picturesque town of Ajo is the site of this 1925 inn, which was originally built to accommodate local mining officials. The inn has since been completely renovated in the rich traditions of the Sonoran Desert region. All the guestrooms are equipped with private baths and each has been given an individual theme. The inn features desert views from the deck at the rear of the house. A full breakfast is served in the dining room.

4 Rooms • Price range: $69-79
700 Guest House Rd, Ajo, AZ 85321
☎ **(520) 387-6133**

Amado
⑨ *Amado Territory Inn*

This two-story ranch house located in the mountainous Amado territory is a great spot for both a relaxing getaway and some interesting sightseeing. Activities include exploring nearby Tubac with its world-class arts-and-crafts galleries, as well as hiking and horseback riding. All rooms feature patio or deck access and are equipped with private baths. The inn's café offers a variety of Southwestern specialities.

9 Rooms • Price range: $105-135
3001 E Frontage Rd, Amado, AZ 85645
☎ **(520) 398-8684**

Cave Creek
Gotland's Inn Cave Creek

A four-acre retreat terraced into a hillside, this inn offers a choice of four luxury suites. Each enjoys mountain views and is decorated in typical Southwestern fashion. All suites have private access, living areas and kitchenettes. Visitors are welcome to enjoy the whirlpool tubs and working fireplaces. The inn is an ideal stopover en route to the Grand Canyon and is close to the Cave Creek historic center.

4 Rooms • Price range: $140-199
38555 N Schoolhouse Rd, Cave Creek, AZ 85327
☎ **(480) 488-9636**

Flagstaff
⑨ *The Inn at 410 Bed & Breakfast*

Just a short walk from historic downtown Flagstaff, this charming 1907 Craftsman house has been redecorated in true Southwestern style. Each of the nine rooms and suites is comfortably furnished with antiques and has been given its own distinctive character. All rooms have a private bath; some feature a fireplace and a Jacuzzi. The inn's garden has a gazebo. Gourmet breakfasts are served daily in the dining room.

9 Rooms • Price range: $135-190
410 N Leroux St, Flagstaff, AZ 86001
☎ **(520) 774-0088**

Flagstaff

Jeanette's Bed & Breakfast

Standing among the pines at the foot of Mount Elden, this stately Victorian-style home is known for its romantic ambience. Some of the touches that add to the atmosphere include antique-filled rooms, handmade soap, claw-foot tubs, rooms adorned with flowers and a fireplace for the cool Arizona nights. In the afternoon, guests are invited to join the hosts for fresh-squeezed lemonade and homemade cookies.

4 Rooms • Price range: $99-130
3380 E Lockett Rd, Flagstaff, AZ 86004
☎ **(520) 527-1912**

Phoenix
Maricopa Manor Bed & Breakfast Inn

This restored 1928 Spanish Mission-style house is surrounded by fruit trees. The one and two-bedroom suites are beautifully decorated and some feature gas or wood-burning fireplaces. The inn also boasts a library, a pool with fountains and hot tubs.

7 Rooms • Price range: $139-229
15 W Pasadena Ave, Phoenix, AZ 85011
☎ **(602) 274-6302**

Prescott
Dolls & Roses Bed & Breakfast

Located near the Prescott courthouse, this 1883 Victorian has been restored to its original condition. Antiques, paintings and—true to the inn's name—an extensive doll collection add to the atmosphere. Guests are invited to relax on the large veranda and enjoy the rose garden—the other inspiration behind this charming B&B's name. Each guestroom is equipped with a private bath, and a full breakfast is served daily.

4 Rooms • Price range: $89-99
109 N Pleasant St, Prescott, AZ 86301
☎ **(520) 776-9291**

Prescott
Pleasant Street Inn

This 1906 Victorian home presides over downtown Prescott and is within walking distance of the town square. The interior was renovated in 1991. Today visitors are offered a choice of a room or a suite. The downstairs suite features a private deck, while the upstairs one has a working fireplace. All accommodations have a private bath. Guests can have either a full or a continental breakfast.

4 Rooms • Price range: $89-135
142 S Pleasant St, Prescott, AZ 86303
☎ **(520) 445-4774**

Prescott
Lynx Creek Farm Bed & Breakfast

Quiet countryside surrounds this Western-style log cabin and guest house. The attractively decorated guestrooms have a country flair, and two of them have separate parlors and their own full kitchens.

6 Rooms • Price range: $85-180
5555 Onyx Dr, Prescott, AZ 86302
☎ **(520) 778-9573**

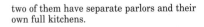

Prescott
♦ ♦ *Prescott Pines Inn Bed & Breakfast*

This 1902 Country-style Victorian inn has rooms in a chalet and cottages. All rooms are equipped with private baths and are decorated with authentic

Victoriana. The three-bedroom two-story chalet includes a deck and a wood-burning stove.

13 Rooms • Price range: $65-115
901 White Spar Rd, Prescott, AZ 86303
☎ **(520) 445-7270**

Sedona
♦ ♦ *Adobe Village & Graham Inn*
♦ ♦

This inn, a "village" of adobe-style casitas, offers a unique vacation setting that combines authentic Southwestern design and decor with exquisite luxury. Each of the 850-square-foot casitas has been given an individual theme and the results are impressive. Each unit's one-of-a-kind furnishings are complemented by a double Jacuzzi tub, a waterfall shower, two fireplaces and a fully furnished kitchenette. The casitas enclose a central courtyard with a delightful pond and waterfall. Guests are invited to a traditional breakfast of Southwestern specials each morning.

10 Rooms • Price range: $159-499
150 Canyon Circle Dr, Sedona, AZ 86351
☎ **(520) 284-1425**

Sedona
♦ ♦ *Apple Orchard Inn*

Set on two wooded acres a half mile from uptown Sedona's art galleries and shops, this inn combines to great effect contemporary luxury and spectacular natural scenery. Each of the seven custom-designed rooms is equipped with a Jacuzzi and a private patio that invites guests out to enjoy the red-rock vistas. The richly furnished Great Room, with its large stone fireplace, is a perfect spot to relax in the evenings. Other amenities include a swimming pool and an eight-person outdoor Jacuzzi with a waterfall. Breakfasts are full gourmet affairs with a changing menu.

7 Rooms • Price range: $140-235
656 Jordan Rd, Sedona, AZ 86336
☎ **(520) 282-5328**

Sedona
♦ ♦ *Canyon Villa Bed & Breakfast Inn*
♦ ♦

This Mediterranean-style property with its stucco walls and red-tiled roof is the perfect complement to the spectacular Sedona rock formations surrounding it. Huge arched windows frame the views and custom-made stained glass adds more bright color. Other features include a library and a tranquil reading garden. Each of the guestrooms has a private balcony or a patio, great for watching the stars or simply relaxing. All rooms are also equipped with a whirlpool tub and four of them have a fireplace. The breakfast, prepared by the hostess, is one of the high points of the day.

11 Rooms • Price range: $150-160
125 Canyon Circle Dr, Sedona, AZ 86351
☎ **(520) 284-1226**

Sedona
⟐ *Casa Sedona*

Located on an acre of quite secluded property, this Southwestern-style building was designed by an architect who was influenced by Frank Lloyd Wright. The inn melds perfectly with the natural surroundings. The gardens include an outdoor hot tub—an ideal spot for stargazing. Each of the 16 guestrooms is individually decorated, and all feature fireplaces and large Jacuzzis. Guests are invited to have a full breakfast and afternoon appetizers, both usually served outdoors. The hosts also offer hiking and driving maps and a day-trip plan for those visiting the Grand Canyon.

16 Rooms • Price range: $135-250
55 Hozoni Dr, Sedona, AZ 86336
☎ **(520) 282-2938**

Sedona
⟐ *The Inn on Oak Creek*

Designed and built as a Sedona art gallery by the owner's family almost 30 years ago, this attractive building has been remodeled and refurnished to accommodate 11 guestrooms. The B&B is situated at the edge of Oak Creek on a private creekside park, and so it offers guests vistas of the waterfront and of the nearby red rocks. Also nearby are some of the Southwest's finest galleries and restaurants. Each guestroom is equipped with a whirlpool bath—most are large enough for two—as well as a working fireplace. A gourmet breakfast, prepared by a professionally trained chef, is served daily.

11 Rooms • Price range: $150-260
556 Hwy 179, Sedona, AZ 86336
☎ **(520) 282-7896**

Sedona
Adobe Hacienda

This unique five-room Spanish-style hacienda overlooks the Sedona Golf Resort and also boasts spectacular red-rock views. Decorated with Native American and Mexican furniture, each of the guestrooms has the ambience of the Southwest. Rooms are equipped with private baths; whirlpool tubs and fireplaces are also available. Every morning, guests are invited to a breakfast of huevos rancheros and jalapeño cornbread.

5 Rooms • Price range: $139-169
10 Rojo Dr, Sedona, AZ 86351
☎ **(520) 284-2020**

Sedona
Alma de Sedona Inn

This inn's hilltop setting is a great place to enjoy the region's views and spectacular nighttime skies. Each guestroom is decorated differently. The inn

also features a parlor, a pool, and a pool-side patio, where breakfast is served.

12 Rooms • Price range: $149-235
50 Hozoni Dr, Sedona, AZ 86336
☎ **(520) 282-2737**

Sedona
Bed & Breakfast at Saddle Rock Ranch

Situated on a three-acre ranch outside
of Sedona, this historic 1926 stone-
and-adobe homestead is a great desert
 hideaway. Each of the carefully decorated rooms has a wood-burning fireplace
and is equipped with a private bath. Courtyard
gardens, indoor lounges, a pool and an outdoor
Jacuzzi tub are popular with the guests.
Breakfast is served poolside or in the stone-
walled breakfast room.

3 Rooms • Price range: $154-179
255 Rock Ridge Dr, Sedona, AZ 86336
☎ **(520) 282-7640**

Sedona
Boots & Saddles Bed & Breakfast

This B&B celebrates the "gentleman
cowboy." Guests at this B&B are
encouraged to enjoy the splendor of the
 surrounding desert in luxurious style.
Picture yourself soaking in an outdoor hot tub
and gazing up at the stars in the night sky.
Private balconies and skylights in the cathedral ceiling offer views of another kind. The
inn also features in-room whirlpool tubs,
working fireplaces and a full breakfast.

4 Rooms • Price range: $120-225
2900 Hopi Dr, Sedona, AZ 86336
☎ **(520) 282-1944**

Sedona
Creekside Inn at Sedona

Located on the banks of Oak Creek,
this inn borders a black hawk nesting
refuge, where other native wildlife
 also abounds. The inn itself features a
decor of Victorian antiques, while guestrooms
are equipped with whirlpool tubs and private
garden patios. Breakfast is prepared by the
inn's highly rated chef. Visitors interested in
shopping will not be disappointed by Sedona's
selection of shops and art galleries.

5 Rooms • Price range: $175-250
99 Coppercliffs Dr, Sedona, AZ 86339
☎ **(520) 282-4992**

Sedona
The Lodge at Sedona

The wooded acres that surround this
secluded lodge lend a natural
beauty to the site. Each of the B&B's
 rooms and suites is equipped with a
private bath—some also have a Jacuzzi and a
working fireplace—and all are beautifully decorated with country-pine antiques in the earthy
tones of the Southwest. Other features include
a parlor, a library and an enclosed breakfast
porch where breakfast is served daily.

14 Rooms • Price range: $129-249
125 Kallof Pl, Sedona, AZ 86336
☎ **(520) 204-1942**

Sedona

⚌ *A Sunset Chateau B&B Inn*

This B&B features some of the most spectacular, unobstructed views of Sedona's world-acclaimed red rock formations. Guests may choose between the suites or the more economical chalets. The suites have Jacuzzi tubs, separate stand-up showers, gas fireplaces, and include a full, gourmet breakfast. The chalets, which feature 600 square feet of living space, are equipped with private baths and full kitchenettes.

22 Rooms • Price range: $85-220
665 Sunset Dr, Sedona, AZ 86336
☎ **(520) 282-2644**

Sedona

⚌ *A Territorial House Old West Bed & Breakfast*

The decor of this traditional Southwestern home matches the natural setting of Sedona. A large, open gathering room features a native-stone fireplace, and the building is surrounded by red-rock formations and cedar trees. Each of the four individually decorated guestrooms is equipped with a private bath. Whirlpools, working fireplaces and private balconies with telescopes for stargazing are also available.

4 Rooms • Price range: $100-185
65 Piki Dr, Sedona, AZ 86336
☎ **(520) 204-2737**

Sedona

"A Touch of Sedona" Bed & Breakfast

A short walk from the historic uptown Sedona district, this charming five-room inn features panoramic red-rock views and awesome nightly sky watching. Each of the rooms is equipped with a private bath and queen- or king-size beds. A hearty breakfast menu is available in the Great Room, where the floor-to-ceiling windows frame a spectacular vista. Close at hand are the Hike West Fork Trail and ancient cliff dwellings.

5 Rooms • Price range: $109-159
595 Jordan Rd, Sedona, AZ 86336
☎ **(520) 282-6462**

Sedona

Wishing Well Bed & Breakfast

Almost hidden off an unmarked juncture on the highway lies this secluded jewel of an inn. The owners of this establishment have made the privacy and comfort of their guests their primary consideration. All five sumptuous guestrooms have been built to take advantage of Sedona's amazing mountain vistas. Special features in each room include Jacuzzi tubs, private decks and fireplaces.

5 Rooms • Price range: $160-195
995 N Hwy 89A, Sedona, AZ 86336
☎ **(520) 282-4914**

Sedona
Cozy Cactus Bed & Breakfast
This B&B offers guestsrooms in a ranch-style home. Several of the guest rooms share a kitchen and a living room with a fireplace. Sliding glass doors lead to patios that run the length of the property and look out onto the National Forest.

5 Rooms • Price range: $110-135
80 Canyon Circle Dr, Sedona, AZ 86351
☎ **(520) 284-0082**

Tucson
Adobe Rose Inn
Located in the historic Sam Hughes section of Tucson, minutes from the University of Arizona, this 1933 adobe structure is an island of calm. All rooms are furnished in Southwestern style; all have private baths.

7 Rooms • Price range: $105-135
940 N Olsen Ave, Tucson, AZ 85719
☎ **(520) 318-4644**

Tucson
Agave Grove Bed & Breakfast Inn
Located on two-and-a-half acres of desert grounds, this "oasis away from home" captures the serenity and magic of the region. The inn is appointed with Southwestern decor, fine antiques and family heirlooms. The guestroom are all comfortably furnished and equipped with their own baths. The inn also features a sunken living room and a large family room highlighted by a massive flagstone fireplace.

4 Rooms • Price range: $95-165
800 W Panorama Rd, Tucson, AZ 85704
☎ **(520) 797-3400**

Tucson
Car-Mar's Southwest Bed & Breakfast
A quiet setting in the Sonora Desert makes this property a special getaway destination. The handmade furniture, done in the traditional Southwestern style of "lodgepole and saguaro rib," provides each guestroom with an authentic touch. Other features are the courtyards and a pool set in attractively landscaped grounds. Nearby sights include the Arizona-Sonora Desert Museum and the San Xavier Mission.

4 Rooms • Price range: $65-125
6766 W Oklahoma St, Tucson, AZ 85746
☎ **(520) 578-1730**

Tucson
Casa Alegre Bed & Breakfast Inn
This inn has attractive 1915 and 1923 Craftsman-style bungalows. Located near the University of Arizona, it is situated in a neighborhood of shops and interesting eateries. The guestrooms are decorated with comfortable furniture; all accommodations have private baths. Other features of the inn include built-in cabinetry with leaded glass, an inglenook rock fireplace and a dining room where breakfast is served daily.

7 Rooms • Price range: $70-125
316 E Speedway Blvd, Tucson, AZ 85705
☎ **(520) 628-1800**

Tucson
Casa Tierra Adobe Bed & Breakfast Inn

This rustic adobe home recalls the haciendas of old Mexico. The structure features more than 50 arches and includes vaulted brick ceilings and an arched interior courtyard enclosing a tranquil fountain. The three rooms and two suites open onto both the desert and the courtyard. All accommodations are equipped with private baths. A full gourmet-vegetarian breakfast is served in the formal dining room.

4 Rooms • Price range: $125-300
11155 W Calle Pima, Tucson, AZ 85743
☎ **(520) 578-3058**

Tucson
Catalina Park Inn

This 1927 Mediterranean-style home is located in Tuscon's historic district, and showcases fine woodwork and architectural detail. The parlor features a working fireplace and wall cabinets displaying the inn's collection of fine china. All six rooms are equipped with private baths and top-of-the-line beds. Some rooms also include a fireplace, a private porch and a separate entrance. A gourmet breakfast is served daily.

6 Rooms • Price range: $114-144
309 E 1st St, Tucson, AZ 85705
☎ **(520) 792-4541**

Tucson
Coyote Crossing Bed & Breakfast

Just 18 miles from downtown Tucson, this B&B offers guests the chance to experience the full beauty of the Sonoran Desert. Each of the four spacious rooms has a private bath and an entrance that leads to the pool and patio areas. Guests are invited to a healthy breakfast of fresh fruit, yogurt and granola; in the cool desert evening, they are encouraged to lounge by the fireside in the large Arizona Room.

4 Rooms • Price range: $95-120
6985 N Camino Verde, Tucson, AZ 85743
☎ **(520) 744-3285**

Tucson
Hacienda Bed & Breakfast

Centrally located, this B&B has a lot to offer. Guests are invited to lounge by the pool, in the private patio, or use the heated spa. The inn also has two Great Rooms, one of which accommodates a baby grand piano, the other a dance floor. The rooms and suites are each equipped with private baths and complimentary bath robes. The suites, located upstairs, include an Arizona Room with views of the Catalina Mountains.

4 Rooms • Price range: $75-125
5704 E Grant Rd, Tucson, AZ 85712
☎ **(520) 290-2224**

Tucson
Jeremiah Inn Bed & Breakfast

This contemporary-style inn is dramatically situated at the foot of the Catalina Mountain Range. Guests are welcome to swim in the pool and take advantage of the outdoor spa; beneath the starry desert nighttime sky such experiences are unforgettable. All six guestrooms are comfortably furnished with queen-size beds and TVs; all have a private bath. Breakfast is served in the dining room or on the patio.

4 Rooms • Price range: $90-120
10921 E Snyder Rd, Tucson, AZ 85749
☎ **(520) 749-3072**

Tucson
The Peppertrees Bed & Breakfast Inn

A touch of England marks this meticulously restored 1905 Tucson house. Located within walking distance of many downtown Tucson attractions, the inn has a patio garden that is a desert Eden. All rooms feature private baths and the guest houses are equipped with kitchens, living and dining areas, and private patios. Guests are invited to a full gourmet breakfast made with recipes from the innkeeper's cookbook.

6 Rooms • Price range: $98-140
724 E University Blvd, Tucson, AZ 85719
☎ **(520) 622-7167**

Tucson
La Posada Del Valle Bed & Breakfast

An authentic adobe-and-stucco structure in the Santa Fe style, this inn was originally designed as a villa by Tucson architect Josias T. Joesler. Furnishings date from the Art Deco era and each of the five guestrooms has been named after a female entertainer of the 1920s or 1930s. The inn also features landscaped gardens and courtyards. A gourmet breakfast is served in the dining room.

5 Rooms • Price range: $115-145
1640 N Campbell Ave, Tucson, AZ 85719
☎ **(520) 795-3840**

Tucson
El Presidio Bed & Breakfast Inn

This 1886 Victorian adobe mansion features suites with private baths and kitchenettes. Lush gardens flourish in the inn's cobblestoned courtyards, which are further enhanced by fountains. A gourmet breakfast is served in the dining room.

4 Rooms • Price range: $85-125
297 N Main Ave, Tucson, AZ 85701
☎ **(520) 623-6151**

Tucson
The Royal Elizabeth Bed & Breakfast Inn

Listed on the National Register of Historic Places, this 1878 mansion combines Victorian style within a typical Southwestern adobe structure. The inn's renovations feature spacious guestrooms, period antiques and decor, fine linens, private baths, and comfortable seating areas. Most guestrooms can be made into adjoining suites and have private entrances.

6 Rooms • Price range: $140-190
204 S Scott Ave, Tucson, AZ 85701
☎ **(520) 670-9022**

Tucson
The SunCatcher

This contemporary home is located just minutes from Saguaro National Park and offers guests a variety of ways to relax after a day of hiking the trails. The inn features a mesquite bar where afternoon wine and cheese is served, a heated pool and an outdoor hot tub. Guestrooms are named after four great hotels, and each offers such attractions as direct access to the pool and wood-burning fireplaces.

4 Rooms • Price range: $125-145
105 N Avenida Javalina, Tucson, AZ 85748
☎ (520) 885-0883

Williams
The Sheridan House Inn

This inn features comfortable rooms and gourmet breakfasts.

7 Rooms • Price range: $100-225
460 E Sheridan Ave, Williams, AZ 86046
☎ (520) 635-9441

Williams
Terry Ranch Bed & Breakfast

Known as the gateway to the Grand Canyon, this log home has Country-Victorian decor. Spacious guestrooms feature sitting areas, antiques, private baths and, in some rooms, working fireplaces. The building also has a wraparound veranda and a gazebo. Guests can wave to the vintage locomotive and passenger cars as the train arrives from the Grand Canyon. A full family-style breakfast is served daily.

4 Rooms • Price range: $110-155
701 Quarterhorse Rd, Williams, AZ 86046
☎ (520) 635-4171

Williams
⬧ Mountain Country Lodge Bed & Breakfast

Built as a mansion in 1909, this B&B boasts uniquely decorated rooms.

8 Rooms • Price range: $70-109
437 W Rt 66, Williams, AZ 86046
☎ (520) 635-4341

Notes:

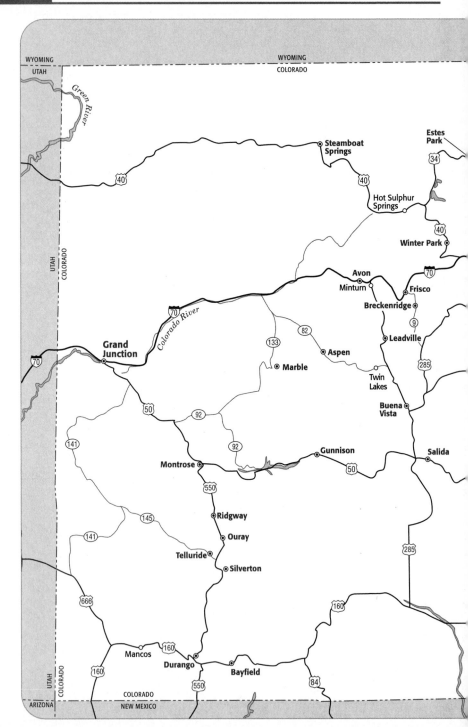

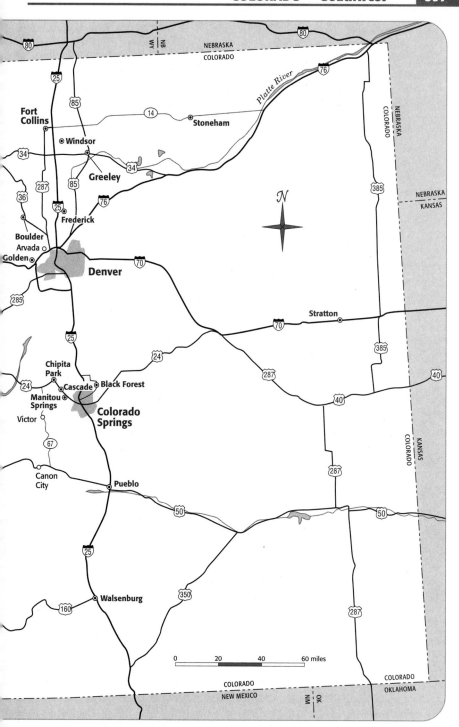

Aspen
Hotel Lenado

Located near a park in the heart of Aspen, this modern inn is a combination of contemporary luxury and rustic ski-lodge charm. A sitting area in the atrium-style lobby features a 28-foot stone fireplace and over-stuffed couches. Guestroom appointments include interior shutters, carved apple-wood beds with down comforters and private decks. After a day on the slopes, the rooftop hot tub or Markham's Bar is the place

19 Rooms • Price range: $275-385
200 S Aspen St, Aspen, CO 81611
☎ **(970) 925-6246**

Avon
West Beaver Creek Lodge
Spacious modern inn with mountain views. Deluxe suite is self-contained.

8 Rooms • Price range: $179-199
220 W Beaver Creek Blvd, Avon, CO 81620-7626
☎ **(970) 949-9073**

Black Forest
Black Forest Bed & Breakfast

This enormous gambrel-roofed log house is set on 20 acres of rolling meadows, golden aspens and Ponderosa pines. The traditional log cabin design and decor has some contemporary touches such as skylights and glass walls with spectacular views. The Haven suite has a 1,600-square-foot atrium, a 44-foot lap pool, an exercise area and a sauna. Breakfast can be served in the privacy of your room or on the terrace.

5 Rooms • Price range: $75-200
11170 Black Forest Rd, Black Forest, CO 80908
☎ **(719) 495-4208**

Boulder
Alps Boulder Canyon Inn
Luxury units, fireplaces, porches and patios mark this 1870 log cabin.

12 Rooms • Price range: $120-225
38619 Boulder Canyon Dr, Boulder, CO 80302
☎ **(303) 444-5445**

Boulder
The Boulder Victoria Historic Inn
Built in the 1870s in an ideal location, this property offers fine hotel amenities.

7 Rooms • Price range: $139-199
1305 Pine St, Boulder, CO 80302
☎ **(303) 938-1300**

Boulder
The Briar Rose Bed & Breakfast

Situated in a residential neighborhood, this brick home was built in the 1890s and became the city's first bed and breakfast. Each of the nine rooms has a distinctive character, complete with period antique furnishings, original art and "Fedderbet" comforters on queen-size beds. The extensive gardens are carefully groomed. A shuttle service is available to transport guests to the Denver airport, one hour away.

10 Rooms • Price range: $119-164
2151 Arapahoe Ave, Boulder, CO 80302
☎ **(303) 442-3007**

Boulder
Earl House Historic Inn
This 1880s Gothic-Revival mansion has
two carriage houses with elegant rooms.

8 Rooms • Price range: $139-199
2429 Broadway, Boulder, CO 80304
☎ **(303) 938-1400**

Boulder
The Inn on Mapleton Hill
An 1899 house, shaded by towering
maple trees, in a quiet residential
neighborhood. One of the second floor
rooms has a private balcony, two rooms
have fireplaces and five have private baths.
One block from the lively Pearl Street mall.

7 Rooms • Price range: $93-139
1001 Spruce St, Boulder, CO 80302
☎ **(303) 449-6528**

Breckenridge
Allaire Timbers Inn
This award-winning contemporary log
B&B is tucked among the trees at the
end of Main Street, in the heart of
Summit County, home to four ski
resorts and four championship golf courses. The
inn's log-and-beam Great Room features a large
stone fireplace, a tiled sunroom and a reading
loft. For a rejuvenating experience, soak in the
spa on the main deck, which offers views of the
town and Ten Mile Range.

10 Rooms • Price range: $155-420
9511 Hwy 9, Breckenridge, CO 80424
☎ **(970) 453-7530**

Breckenridge
Bed and Breakfasts on North Main Street
Originally a prospector's shack before
being reduced to a hangout for ski bums
and hippies, the 1885 Williams House
and adjacent Victorian Willoughby
Cottage were saved and renovated to become the
elegant lodgings they are today. Known as the
honeymoon B&B, the Cottage is a great choice
for a romantic weekend. A Barn Above the
River was added in 1997 to provide five more
suites, all with river and mountain views.

11 Rooms • Price range: $199-375
303 N Main St, Breckenridge, CO 80424
☎ **(970) 453-2975**

Breckenridge
ⒶⒶ The Hunt Placer Inn
Perched on a hill above town, each
room at this inn has a deck or balcony.

8 Rooms • Price range: $170-190
275 Ski Hill Rd, Breckenridge, CO 80424
☎ **(970) 453-7573**

Breckenridge
Evans House Bed & Breakfast
In the heart of the historic district, this
B&B has one room with a mountain view.

6 Rooms • Price range: $100-140
102 S French St, Breckenridge, CO 80424
☎ **(970) 453-5509**

Breckenridge
Ridge Street Inn
An 1890s Victorian home within walking distance to shops and restaurants.

5 Rooms • Price range: $75-175
212 N Ridge St, Breckenridge, CO 80424
☎ **(970) 453-4680**

Buena Vista
The Adobe Inn

The flavor of old Mexico permeates this adobe hacienda located in the Arkansas Valley and surrounded by mountain ranges. There are three unique rooms: the Indian room, with its distinctive corner fireplace and hand-carved headboard; the Mexican room, complete with hand-tooled fixtures; and the Antique room, filled with golden-oak furniture. A Mexican tiled solarium provides a comfortable retreat.

5 Rooms • Price range: $74-95
303 Hwy 24 N, Buena Vista, CO 81211
☎ **(719) 395-6340**

Cascade
🏵 *Black Bear Inn of Pikes Peak*

This inn is the only lodging available along the Pikes Peak Highway. Every room provides views of the mountains; common areas are spacious and pleasantly decorated. An illuminated trail leads to a hot tub in the woods. The inn is set among pine trees on land bordering Pike National Forest, which provides miles of hiking and biking trails. In the winter, visitors can go glacier skiing. Other sightseeing attractions are just minutes away.

12 Rooms • Price range: $70-120
5250 Pikes Peak Hwy, Cascade, CO 80809
☎ **(719) 684-0151**

Cascade
Eastholme in the Rockies B&B

Established in 1885, this former resort hotel is on the National Register of Historic Places. Surrounded by tall pines the authentic Victorian inn is a wonderful mountain hideaway. Former guests include Dwight and Mamie Eisenhower.

8 Rooms • Price range: $75-150
4445 Haggerman Ave, Cascade, CO 80809
☎ **(719) 684-9901**

Cascade
Rocky Mountain Lodge & Cabins

Rustic mountain lodge with a stone fireplace in the common room.

5 Rooms • Price range: $95-115
4680 Haggerman Ave, Cascade, CO 80809
☎ **(719) 684-2521**

Chipita Park
Chipita Lodge B&B

This 1927 log-and-stone lodge, on a knoll at the base of Pike's Peak, has functioned as a general store, post office, community center and land development office. In its current incarnation as a B&B, it has an attractive great room with a stone fireplace and guestrooms decorated with tasteful Native American and Western touches. A hot tub in a gazebo off the deck has an incredible mountain view.

4 Rooms • Price range: $98-125
9090 Chipita Park Rd, Chipita Park, CO 80809
☎ **(719) 684-8454**

Colorado Springs
Old Town GuestHouse

Located in the popular and historic Old Town, this modern brick building provides guests with urban luxury. The rooms are all named after flowers and are individually decorated using such varied themes as Cowboy, Oriental and Moroccan. Many of the private porches and balconies provide views of nearby attractions such as Pikes Peak, the Garden of the Gods and Old Colorado City. For business travelers, guestrooms are equipped with voice and data access; a private conference facility is also available. Guests may chose a full or light breakfast in the dining room or on the patio.

8 Rooms • Price range: $95-175
115 S 26th St, Colorado Springs, CO 80904
☎ **(719) 632-9194**

Colorado Springs
Cheyenne Canon Inn

Guests may choose to stay in a Swiss chalet, an Oriental tea house, a Mexican hacienda or a Colorado lodge at this inn. Once a gambling hall and bordello, the 1921 Mission-style mansion stands in a canyon at the base of the Cheyenne and Almagre Mountains. Each guestroom has a distinctive decor reflecting a different region of the world. The Great Room features seven-foot windows that frame the mountain views.

10 Rooms • Price range: $95-200
2030 W Cheyenne Blvd,
Colorado Springs, CO 80906
☎ **(719) 633-0625**

Colorado Springs
Holden House 1902 Bed & Breakfast Inn

A local family with mining interests in the area built this Colonial-Revival Victorian home and carriage house in 1902. The house sits on a tree-lined street near the historic district of Old Colorado City. The decor is Victorian and each unit has a fireplace, a queen-size bed and an oversize tub for two. Two sittings of the full gourmet breakfast are held in the formal dining room. Beverages and cookies are always on hand.

5 Rooms • Price range: $135-145
1102 W Pikes Peak Ave,
Colorado Springs, CO 80904
☎ **(719) 471-3980**

Denver
Capitol Hill Mansion Bed & Breakfast

Built for the Keating Family this Richardson Romanesque-style mansion was built in 1891 during Denver's so-called Gilded Age. At the top of the stairs in the oak-paneled entry hall is an eight-foot-high stained-glass window. Guestrooms are spacious, their tasteful decor creating a genuine homelike environment. Some guestrooms have balconies or fireplaces; three are two-room suites, several can accommodate four people.

8 Rooms • Price range: $90-175
1207 Pennsylvania, Denver, CO 80203
☎ **(303) 839-5221**

Denver
Castle Marne

This 1889 urban mansion, with its rustic lava-stone exterior and whimsical tower, is considered by many to be the finest work of William Lang, "America's most eclectic architect." It served as a butterfly museum, then a processing center for parolees before being restored to its former opulence. Situated in the heart of the Wyman Historic District, it's just minutes away from fine dining and many of the city's attractions.

9 Rooms • Price range: $80-245
1572 Race St, Denver, CO 80206
☎ **(303) 331-0621**

Denver
⊛ *Holiday Chalet, A Victorian Hotel Bed & Breakfast*

When staying at the Holiday Chalet be sure to ask the innkeepers to tell the fascinating story about their family and this grand, three-story mansion. Many of the beautiful antique furnishings and decorations are family heirlooms that were "excavated" from the basement of the house. All 10 guestrooms include fully equipped kitchens, three have sunrooms and eating areas and two have fireplaces.

10 Rooms • Price range: $99-160
1820 E Colfax Ave, Denver, CO 80218
☎ **(303) 321-9975**

Denver
⊛ *Merritt House Bed & Breakfast Inn*

A handsomely furnished 1889 home with a secluded outdoor patio.

10 Rooms • Price range: $105-175
941 E 17th Ave, Denver, CO 80218
☎ **(303) 861-5230**

Denver
Queen Anne Bed & Breakfast Inn

Facing quiet Benedict Fountain Park in the Clement Historic District stand these side-by-side National Register Victorians, built in 1879 and 1886. A favorite among business travelers because of its downtown location, the inn is a short walk away from the Capitol, the Mint, shops and museums. Rooms are decorated with period furnishings, but guests be warned: There have been reports of restless apparitions.

14 Rooms • Price range: $95-175
2147-51 Tremont Pl, Denver, CO 80205
☎ **(303) 296-6666**

Durango
General Palmer Hotel
Established in 1898, this hotel was named after a Civil War general who left a legacy of railroad lines. Palmer supervised the construction of the Durango to Silverton narrow gauge railway. Now fully restored, the hotel and its adjacent annex are classic Durango landmarks. They feature attractive public rooms adorned with Victorian furniture, and a staff well trained in gracious Southwestern hospitality. Guests are treated to handmade chocolates and in the morning, homemade muffins and croissants. To add a homey touch, there's a teddy bear on each bed.

39 Rooms • Price range: $98-275
567 Main Ave, Durango, CO 81301
☎ **(970) 247-4747**

Durango
Apple Orchard Inn
Located in the beautiful Animas Valley, this farmhouse-style inn stands on more than four acres of landscaped grounds, complete with an orchard and wooden bridges set over gurgling streams. All accommodations are comfortably furnished; three of the six luxurious private cottages have a fireplace. The main house features a parlor with a floor-to-ceiling river-rock fireplace, original artwork and Brazilian cherry-wood floors.

10 Rooms • Price range: $110-195
7758 CR 203, Durango, CO 81301
☎ **(970) 247-0751**

Durango
Leland House Bed & Breakfast Suites
Guests can enjoy the warmth and comfort of a country inn along with the convenience of a downtown hotel at this 1927 restored brick apartment building. Six units are actually three-room suites; all accommodations have kitchen facilities and private baths. The surrounding area is known for first-class skiing. Also nearby is the classic Durango to Silverton narrow gauge steam train, which has been used in many Western films.

10 Rooms • Price range: $139-179
721 E 2nd Ave, Durango, CO 81301
☎ **(970) 385-1920**

Durango
Lightner Creek Inn
This inn, which resembles a French country house, is set in a bucolic valley traversed by a trout stream. The Carriage House offers spacious and private suites. Breakfast is seved in a cheerful sunroom. The gazebo is a highlight of the professionally landscaped flower gardens. The entire property is surrounded by a wildlife refuge, so surprise sightings can occur on even the shortest stroll.

10 Rooms • Price range: $85-175
999 CR 207, Durango, CO 81301
☎ **(970) 259-1226**

Durango
The Rochester Hotel

The Old West theme, inspired by movies filmed in the area, dominates here. This historic downtown 1892 hotel features spacious, tastefully decorated units, all with high ceilings and a full bath. Breakfast is served in the lobby and includes the house specialties—cranberry scones and home-made granola. Skiing at Purgatory or the Nordic Center is close at hand and the Four Corners area provides rafting, fishing and hiking during the summer.

15 Rooms • Price range: $139-189
726 E Second Ave, Durango, CO 81301
☎ **(970) 385-1920**

Estes Park
Mountain Shadows Bed & Breakfast
Modern log cabins with mountain views, gas fireplaces and whirlpools.

8 Rooms • Price range: $189-189
871 Riverside Dr, Estes Park, CO 80517
☎ **(970) 577-0397**

Estes Park
Romantic River Song Inn
The wilderness location and imaginative interior decor endow the rooms at this inn with strong appeal. Guests will marvel at the elk and deer that roam the inn's 27 wooded acres. Inside, each of the cozy guestrooms has unique features: For example, one room has a rooftop shower and another has a whirlpool in a greenhouse with a deck overlooking a pond. A truly romantic getaway in a sensational natural setting.

9 Rooms • Price range: $150-295
1765 Lower Broadview Rd, Estes Park, CO 80517
☎ **(970) 586-4666**

Fort Collins
Edwards House Bed & Breakfast

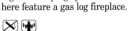

This 1904 neo-Classical home is located in a quiet residential area of the city, within walking distance of Colorado State University and the historic Old Town shopping and restaurant district. Fort Collins has been called the "Choice City" because of its tree-lined streets, temperate climate, and proximity to some of the best hiking, biking, skiing and camping spots in the country. All rooms here feature a gas log fireplace.

8 Rooms • Price range: $89-159
402 W Mountain Ave, Fort Collins, CO 80521
☎ **(970) 493-9191**

Frederick
Hoffman Hideaway Bed & Breakfast
A refurbished 1910 hotel near downtown with a view of the Front Range.

5 Rooms • Price range: $59-109
154 5th St, Frederick, CO 80530
☎ **(303) 833-0444**

Frisco
Creekside Inn

Situated on the bank of Ten Mile Creek, this Rocky Mountain getaway offers well-lit rooms with vaulted ceilings. Each is furnished with antiques and family heirlooms and has a private bath. Guests can choose from nordic trails and five major downhill ski areas just minutes away. A ski storage area is provided. Summer offers opportunities for mountain biking, hiking and golf. Whatever the season, guests revel in the breathtaking views.

7 Rooms • Price range: $170-195
51 W Main St, Frisco, CO 80443
☎ **(970) 668-5607**

Golden
The Alexander Jameson House

Relax in quiet comfort in this home located in the foothills of the Rockies.

4 Rooms • Price range: $80-130
1704 Illinois St, Golden, CO 80401
☎ **(303) 278-0200**

Grand Junction
Los Altos Bed and Breakfast

This hillside retreat has spectacular views of mountains and Grand Mesa.

7 Rooms • Price range: $84-165
375 Hillview Dr, Grand Junction, CO 81503
☎ **(970) 256-0964**

Grand Junction
Mount Garfield Bed & Breakfast

Located in a peach orchard, this B&B features spacious grounds with rose arbors and horse/buffalo corrals. The guestrooms are individually decorated and an upstairs loft provides the best views of Mt. Garfield. A large deck offers a common eating area as well as an outdoor hot tub. Touring the local wineries, a trip to Colorado National Monument or white-water rafting adventures are all popular activities.

4 Rooms • Price range: $72-125
3355 F Rd, Grand Junction, CO 81520
☎ **(970) 434-8120**

Greeley
Sod Buster Inn

This newly built octagonal inn is situated on the site of the original homestead of one of the town's founders. It was built to blend in architecturally with the other houses on the Historic Monroe Corridor. A wraparound veranda accentuates the classic Country-style decor and furnishings. It is located only a few blocks from downtown shopping in one direction and the University of Northern Colorado in the other.

10 Rooms • Price range: $84-124
1221 9th Ave, Greeley, CO 80631
☎ **(970) 392-1221**

Gunnison
Mary Lawrence Inn

In 1885, when the area was still pioneer territory, a local saloon keeper built this Italianate home. Later, when Mary Lawrence settled in Gunnison, where she was a teacher, she operated a boarding house from the building. The rooms offer vivid colors, antiques and interesting collectibles. The inn is well situated as a home base for skiing at Crested Butte or Monarch resorts or fishing in one of three nearby rivers.

7 Rooms • Price range: $85-135
601 N Taylor, Gunnison, CO 81230
☎ **(970) 641-3343**

Leadville
The Ice Palace Inn Bed & Breakfast

Built using materials from the original Ice Palace, this inn has charming decor.

6 Rooms • Price range: $89-159
813 Spruce St, Leadville, CO 80461
☎ **(719) 486-8272**

Manitou Springs
🐾 _Rockledge Country Inn_

The Rockledge is a grand Arts-and-Crafts mansion built in 1912 as a vacation home. Set on three-and-a-half acres at the foot of Pikes Peak, it is considered to be one of Colorado's finest inns. Each of the four very spacious luxury suites has a unique floor plan and its own special amenities. The atrium-style parlor is a favorite with guests and features a two-story stone and copperwork fireplace. Evening cocktails provide another occasion for visitors to mingle and relax. Dinner can be enjoyed at the inn too, upon prior arrangement.

4 Rooms • Price range: $215-295
328 El Paso Blvd, Manitou Springs, CO 80829
☎ **(719) 685-4515**

Manitou Springs
🐾 _Blue Skies Inn_

This quiet refuge has a stream, a gazebo and gardens. The Gothic-Revival buildings feature rooms with tile baths, showers, or Jacuzzis. Breakfast is served in the private courtyard or in the privacy of your room.

10 Rooms • Price range: $125-225
402 Manitou Ave, Manitou Springs, CO 80829
☎ **(719) 685-3899**

Manitou Springs
🐾 _The Cliff House @ Pikes Peak_

In 1873 The Cliff House began welcoming guests to this gold-rush town. Later, the natural mineral springs became the attraction and the inn was converted to a resort hotel. The inn's reputation for elegance, comfort and quality service has attracted such notables as Theodore Roosevelt, J. P. Getty, Thomas Edison, Charles Dickens among others. In-room data ports and free internet access are available.

57 Rooms • Price range: $169-400
306 Canon Ave, Manitou Springs, CO 80829
☎ **(719) 685-3000**

Manitou Springs
🐦 *Red Crags Bed & Breakfast Inn*

This renovated four-story mansion, built in 1880, is prominently situated on a bluff with views of Pikes Peak and the spectacular Garden of the Gods. The two-acre estate has landscaped grounds and herb gardens with a private picnic area. Inside, high ceilings, hardwood floors and attractive antiques predominate. The formal dining room features a rare cherry-wood Eastlake fireplace.

8 Rooms • Price range: $85-185
302 El Paso Blvd, Manitou Springs, CO 80829
☎ **(719) 685-1920**

Manitou Springs
Frontier's Rest Bed and Breakfast Inn

A Victorian-era businessman's home built in 1898. Rooms are small but comfortable; some have a fireplace and all have desks. Conveniently close to a cog railway, mineral springs, hiking trails, shopping and restaurants.

4 Rooms • Price range: $90-195
341 Ruxton Ave, Manitou Springs, CO 80829
☎ **(719) 685-0588**

Marble
Ute Meadows Inn Bed & Breakfast

Located above the Crystal River, this property has spectacular mountain views.

7 Rooms • Price range: $120-150
2880 CR 3, Marble, CO 81623
☎ **(970) 963-7088**

Montrose
Uncompahgre Bed & Breakfast

This B&B is a beautifully renovated 1915 schoolhouse, which is located south of town and has a wonderful view of the San Juan mountain range. It boasts a large common room that was once the school's auditorium.

7 Rooms • Price range: $70-95
21049 Uncompahgre Rd, Montrose, CO 81401
☎ **(970) 240-4000**

Ouray
China Clipper Inn

For sheer pristine beauty it is difficult to match the surrounding area of this modern inn. Located in what has been called the "Switzerland of America," the inn features rooms named for famous clipper ships. Guests can view snow-capped peaks from a hot tub in the garden. In winter rates include half-price lift tickets for skiing at Telluride and half-price tickets for Ouray's Hot Springs.

12 Rooms • Price range: $95-125
525 2nd St, Ouray, CO 81427
☎ **(970) 325-0565**

Ouray
Damn Yankee Country Inn

A great location summer or winter. This contemporary inn has recently undergone extensive remodeling and features a third-floor breakfast room with a fabulous view of the San Juan Mountains. Some of the other embellishments include an enlarged reception room, new carpets and linens. The gazebo hot tub is a soothing way to relax after sightseeing, mountain biking or hiking.

10 Rooms • Price range: $69-195
100 6th Ave, Ouray, CO 81427
☎ **(970) 325-4219**

Pueblo
Abriendo Inn

This 1906 restored inn was voted the best weekend getaway in the local business journal's "Best of Pueblo" contest and is described as an inn that "offers what is quite easily one of the finest bed and breakfast experiences in the state" by local tourist associations. The rooms are richly appointed with antiques and period reproductions, and each has a private bath and in-room phone.

10 Rooms • Price range: $69-125
300 W Abriendo Ave, Pueblo, CO 81004
☎ **(719) 544-2703**

Ridgway
Chipeta Sun Lodge and Spa

This southwestern lodge combines adobe and log-beam construction with passive solar design to produce a bright and airy interior. Unique guestrooms, filled with hand-made rustic furniture, offer stunning views. A rooftop hot tub is hidden away in the inn's tower and guests can enjoy breakfast in the Solarium. As well as serving as a base camp for ski-touring the San Juan Hut System, the inn provides half-price lift tickets.

25 Rooms • Price range: $90-225
320 S Lena, Ridgway, CO 81432-2013
☎ **(970) 626-3737**

Salida
The Tudor Rose Bed & Breakfast

Converted in 1995 from a private estate into a B&B, this modern Tudor-style manor rests on 37 acres of Rocky Mountain countryside. Every guestroom has a terrific view as well as all the modern amenities. A stable, paddock and three pastures are available for guests who wish to bring horses. Outdoor activities include rafting, hiking, llama treks, and all the winter sports.

6 Rooms • Price range: $65-150
6720 CR 104 Rd, Salida, CO 81201
☎ **(719) 539-2002**

Salida
The Thomas House Bed & Breakfast

Originally built as a rooming house in 1888, this inn upholds its long tradition of western hospitality. Guests will discover comfortable rooms, a nice back-yard with a deck, a spa and some very pretty flower gardens.

6 Rooms • Price range: $66-120
307 E First St, Salida, CO 81201
☎ **(719) 539-7104**

Silverton
The Wyman Hotel & Inn

This red-sandstone building, tucked into the peaks of the San Juan Mountains, was originally built in 1902 by Louis Wyman Sr., a trader, trapper and road builder in this isolated mining town. The inn originally housed a ballroom, lodge hall, mining offices, grocery store as well as other amenities. Today, the guestrooms are decorated with period antiques. A full gourmet breakfast and afternoon tea are served daily.

17 Rooms • Price range: $90-183
1371 Greene (Main) St, Silverton, CO 81433
☎ **(970) 387-5372**

Silverton
Silverton's Inn of the Rockies at the Historic Alma House

A charming 1898 home with guestrooms, common areas and one large suite.

9 Rooms • Price range: $68-130
220 E 10th St, Silverton, CO 81433
☎ **(970) 387-5336**

Silverton
Villa Dallavalle B & B

Historic Silverton lives on in this 1901 inn listed on the National Historic Register.

7 Rooms • Price range: $60-100
1257 Blair, Silverton, CO 81433
☎ **(970) 387-5555**

Steamboat Springs
Sky Valley Lodge

Set in the woods, this mountain lodge blends country charm, serenity, and panoramic views. The town is world famous as "Ski-Town USA" and is home to almost 40 winter Olympians. The summer season features the Hot Air Balloon Rodeo. Visitors to the area can explore the millions of acres of National Forest, and partake in some of the world's finest trout fishing. Daily shuttles transport guests to town or the slopes.

24 Rooms • Price range: $105-195
31490 E Hwy 40, Steamboat Springs, CO 80477
☎ **(970) 879-7749**

Steamboat Springs
Steamboat Valley Guest House

Enjoy Swedish pancakes, green chile cheese soufflé or Irish oatmeal when visiting this beautiful Alpine-style log cabin. The cheerful, sunlit guestrooms are very comfortably furnished and the com-

mon room has a fantastic view of the ski jump across the valley.

4 Rooms • Price range: $85-160
1245 Crawford Ave,
Steamboat Springs, CO 80477
☎ **(970) 870-9017**

Stoneham
Elk Echo Ranch Country Bed & Breakfast

This is a family-oriented, 2,000-acre ranch in Pawnee National Grasslands.

4 Rooms • Price range: $89-99
47490 WCR 155, Stoneham, CO 80754
☎ **(970) 735-2426**

Stratton
Claremont Inn

In a quiet location, this property has elegant public areas and luxurious rooms.

7 Rooms • Price range: $99-249
800 Claremont Dr, Stratton, CO 80836
☎ **(719) 348-5125**

Telluride
Bear Creek Bed & Breakfast

The spectacular scenery seen from the rooftop terrace and hot tub as well as the guestroom windows make a visit to The Bear Creek a memorable experience.

Breakfast includes a delicious selection of traditional dishes and homemade treats.

9 Rooms • Price range: $80-230
221 E Colorado Ave, Telluride, CO 81435-2369
☎ **(970) 728-6681**

Telluride
The San Sophia

In the heart of the Telluride National Historic District, this opulent Victorian-style building provides a 1900 country inn atmosphere and is only steps from the gondola. Breathtaking views of St. Sophia Ridge and Ingram Waterfall await guests from the classical turret observatory. Elegant rooms have brass beds with handmade quilts and over-size tubs. The breakfast buffet and complimentary afternoon reception feature gourmet treats.

16 Rooms • Price range: $185-350
330 W Pacific St, Telluride, CO 81435
☎ **(970) 728-3001**

Walsenburg
The Grape Garden Bed & Breakfast

Set in a quiet location, this inn offers some rooms with electric fireplaces.

6 Rooms • Price: $75
24857 US Hwy 160, Walsenburg, CO 81089
☎ **(719) 738-1136**

Windsor
Porter House Bed & Breakfast Inn
In 1898 a local newspaper proclaimed that this Queen Anne home was "the prettiest house in northern Colorado." Today this charming B&B has been lovingly restored and decorated with sophisticated restraint. Three large common rooms are exquisitely furnished in period pieces. Every guestroom is an invitingly cozy retreat. The patio and garden offer a tranquil corner to bird-watch while nibbling on a homemade cookie.

4 Rooms • Price range: $85-145
530 Main St, Windsor, CO 80550
☎ **(970) 686-5793**

Winter Park
The Grand Victorian at Winter Park

Looking like a priceless Victorian doll house, this super luxury-class inn provides stylish decor, turreted sitting rooms and cathedral-like ceilings. Its location on a secluded knoll in an Alpine village, called the "Western Gateway to Rocky Mountain National Park," provides inspiring vistas of the Continental Divide. The après-ski fondues served with complimentary hot toddies are a favorite with the guests.

10 Rooms • Price range: $155-440
78542 Fraser Valley Pkwy,
Winter Park, CO 80482
☎ **(970) 726-5881**

Winter Park
⑩ Gasthaus Eichler Hotel

This is a European chalet-style inn that has all its guestrooms on the second floor. Special amenities include Jacuzzis and free shuttle service to the ski hills. The inn's ski-season meal plan includes break-

fast and dinner at the German restaurant that is located on the main floor.

15 Rooms • Price range: $90-180
(for 2, incl. meals)
78786 US Hwy 40, Winter Park, CO 80482
☎ **(970) 726-5133**

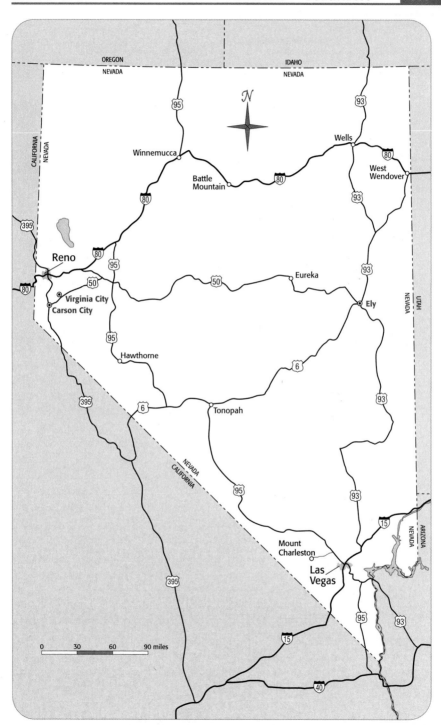

Carson City
Bliss Mansion
This establishment has comfortable rooms with modern amenities.

4 Rooms • Price range: $165-175
710 W Robinson, Carson City, NV 89703
☎ **(775) 887-8988**

Ely
Steptoe Valley Inn
Originally the city's grocery store, this building was completely reconstructed in 1990 as an inn. Each of the guestrooms is named after an Ely city pioneer and features a private bath and a private balcony. Decorative details throughout the inn include wood trim, marble thresholds, tile mosaics and high, embossed ceilings. The grounds boast a gazebo and a rose garden, all under a canopy of lovely spruce and fruit trees.

5 Rooms • Price range: $84-92
220 E 11th St, Ely, NV 89315
☎ **(775) 289-8687**

Virginia City
Gold Hill Hotel
This is Nevada's oldest inn and it exudes an old-fashioned ambience. Guests will enjoy the proximity to downtown Virginia City combined with the atmosphere of yesteryear. Each guestroom features tasteful decor, and several have balconies.

14 Rooms • Price range: $45-200
1540 Main St, Virginia City, NV 89440
☎ **(775) 847-0111**

Notes:

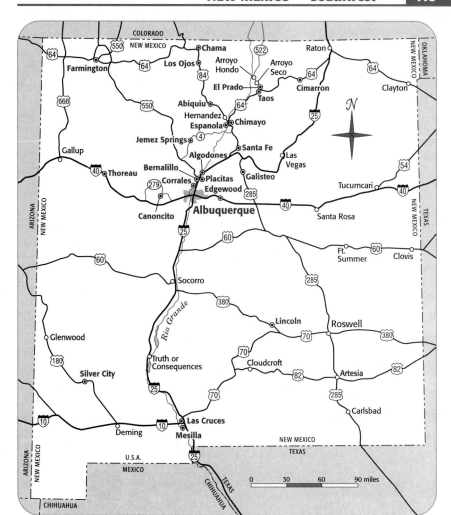

Abiquiu
Casa del Rio

Situated near Georgia O'Keeffe's pink cliffs, this modern residence, built in traditional adobe style, is ideally located for day trips to places such as Rio Grande Gorge, Abiquiu Reservoir and Ghost Ranch Living Museum. Local handmade crafts, rugs, bed coverings and furniture decorate the inn. Guestrooms feature king-size or twin beds and each room has a modern bath finished with handmade Mexican tiles.

3 Rooms • Price range: $100-135
Hwy 84, MM 199.46, Abiquiu, NM 87510
☎ **(505) 753-2035**

Albuquerque
⦾ Bottger-Koch Mansion Bed & Breakfast in Old Town

The character of this inn lies in its details. The elegant Victorian mansion has been around since 1887. Today it is shaded by tall trees. Rooms have grand beds, luxurious linens, dressing robes, private baths and handmade crafts and rugs. Guests are invited to use the sitting room and library, or to take a dip in the whirlpool. English tea is a tradition in which such treats as cucumber sandwiches and sugar cookies are served.

8 Rooms • Price range: $89-179
110 San Felipe NW, Albuquerque, NM 87104
☎ **(505) 243-3639**

Albuquerque
⦾ Brittania & W. E. Mauger Estate Bed & Breakfast

One of New Mexico's grand old homes, this 1897 property has eight rooms, each with a private bath, and some with a television and telephone. Guests can watch the sunset from the 30-foot-long old-fashioned porch, relax in the cozy parlor, or linger over breakfast in the breakfast room. The common rooms are ideal for business meetings. The innkeepers own two well-behaved dogs, Miss Nellie and Mr. Barney.

8 Rooms • Price range: $89-179
701 Roma Ave NW, Albuquerque, NM 87102
☎ **(505) 242-8755**

Albuquerque
⦾ Hacienda Antigua B&B

Massive carved gates lead the way into the 200-year-old Hacienda Antigua. Then visitors are treated to a beautiful flowering courtyard, which leads to the thick, adobe walls of the hacienda. The five guestrooms feature such amenities as traditional bancos (benches), old-fashioned pedestal tubs, kiva fireplaces and brass showers. All rooms include a private bath. A pool is available for guests to use in warmer months.

6 Rooms • Price range: $109-189
6708 Tierra Dr NW, Albuquerque, NM 87107
☎ **(505) 345-5399**

Algodones
Hacienda Vargas Bed and Breakfast Inn

First a stagecoach stop, then a train depot and an Indian trading post, the 18th-century Hacienda Vargas now caters to visitors with eight spacious rooms and suites, each with its own private entrance and bath. A perfect location for guests hosting a private party or wedding, the hacienda boasts a number of nearby activities, including horseback riding and casino gambling. A full breakfast is served.

8 Rooms • Price range: $79-149
1431 SR 313 (El Camino Real),
Algodones, NM 87001
☎ **(505) 867-9115**

Bernalillo
La Hacienda Grande

This adobe great house is said to be the oldest inn in the U S. It has been standing for more than 250 years and exudes a sense of history and tradition. Inside the buckskin colored building are beamed cathedral ceilings and stucco walls. Guests will love the open-air courtyard with its covered portico and the brick-covered dining room where Southwestern treats are served.

6 Rooms • Price range: $99-139
21 Barros Ln, Bernalillo, NM 87004
☎ **(505) 867-1887**

Canoncito
Apachie Canyon Ranch Bed & Breakfast Country Inn

This ranch offers guests the opportunity to observe wild horses, explore nature trails, or go horseback riding. Afterward, the comfortable guestrooms, each complete with a queen-size bed, are the perfect place to relax. There are three dining areas, serving both Southern and Southwestern fare, including inn specialties—green chile omelettes and tutti-frutti breakfast sundaes.

4 Rooms • Price range: $88-265
4 Canyon Dr, Canoncito, NM 87026
☎ **(505) 836-7220**

Chama
⚐ *The Gandy Dancer Bed & Breakfast*

The name Gandy Dancer originates from slang meaning "railroad laborer." This 1913 house was renovated in 1990 and again in 1995 and now boasts seven bedrooms, each with a private bath, and king- or queen-size bed. A hearty breakfast is served in the dining room. Afterward, guests can enjoy the beauty of this part of the southern Rockies, with its lovely lakes and streams and more than 100 species of birds.

7 Rooms • Price range: $75-125
299 Maple Ave, Chama, NM 87520
☎ **(505) 756-2191**

Chama
⚐ *Posada Encanto Bed & Breakfast*

Just one block from the Scenic Railroad, in the Old Town of Chama, sits this charming, rustic inn. A full breakfast is served each morning, preparing guests for a day of trail rides, train trips, fishing, or lake touring.

5 Rooms • Price range: $79-85
277 Maple Ave, Chama, NM 87520
☎ **(505) 756-1048**

Chimayo
Casa Escondida

Situated on six acres of gorgeous land, this inn has an atmosphere of serenity. The adobe home boasts breathtaking views of the area, and the bright colors of the interior decor have been chosen to complement the natural hues of the outdoors.

8 Rooms • Price range: $80-140
64 Rd 0100, Chimayo, NM 87522
☎ **(505) 351-4805**

Cimarron
⚫ Casa del Gavilan

Cimarron, the location of this inn, means "wild" in Spanish. The name reflects the area's majestic natural surroundings, where mountains, valleys and the wide-open sky fill the view. Built in 1905, this hacienda-style ranch house with wonderful vistas has a secluded setting. The inn is a perfect traditional adobe home with 12-foot-high ceilings and 18-inch-thick walls.

5 Rooms • Price range: $75-105
Hwy 21 S, Cimarron, NM 87714
☎ **(505) 376-2246**

Corrales
The Chocolate Turtle Bed & Breakfast

Located in the historic district of Corrales, this newly remodeled Territorial-style home is located on land with an awesome view of nearby mountains. Guestrooms are decorated with Southwestern-style art and furniture, and each features a private bath. Full breakfasts include such items as melons, kiwi, blue corn pancakes, and frittatas. Guests find homemade chocolate goodies in their rooms.

4 Rooms • Price range: $65-135
1098 W Meadowlark Ln, Corrales, NM 87048
☎ **(505) 898-1800**

Corrales
The Sandhill Crane Bed & Breakfast

A winding brick path leads guests through an old turquoise gate up to this adobe hacienda, where the large bedrooms are fitted with feather beds and luxury linens. The inner courtyard is a perfect place to relax. The area is home to a variety of wildlife including hummingbirds and roadrunners. There are many things to do such as horseback riding and bicycling. Massages can be arranged by appointment.

4 Rooms • Price range: $90-160
389 Camino Hermosa, Corrales, NM 87048
☎ **(505) 898-2445**

Corrales
Yours Truly Bed & Breakfast

The emphasis here is on comfort: adobe-padded walls to ensure quiet, private baths, oversize showers, romantic fireplaces and comfy robes. The day begins with morning coffee and homemade fruit bread, which is brought to your door. Afterwards, a full breakfast is served. Nearby activities include river rafting and hot-air balloon rides.

4 Rooms • Price range: $98-135
160 Paseo de Corrales, Corrales, NM 87048
☎ **(505) 898-7027**

Edgewood
Alta Mae's Heritage Inn

Located on famous Route 66, this inn is in a prime position for access to much of the beauty of the American West. The inn boasts views of three mountain ranges and pays tribute to the surrounding nature by styling guestrooms after regional geographical landmarks. Guests enjoy the luxury of down comforters and pillows in their bedrooms, which are decorated with fine art and feature private whirlpools.

5 Rooms • Price range: $95-125
1950 Old Route 66, Edgewood, NM 87015
☎ **(505) 281-5000**

El Prado
Cottonwood Inn Bed & Breakfast

The former residence of flamboyant local artist Wolfgang Pogzeba, the Cottonwood Inn, six miles from Taos Plaza and across from Taos Pueblo, now welcomes visitors. Pogzeba designed the rooms with balconies for views of the impressive Taos Mountain. The two-story inn features original art, set against a backdrop of classic pueblo architecture. Each room has a private bath, kiva fireplace, Jacuzzi and private entrance.

7 Rooms • Price range: $120-230
02 SR 230, El Prado, NM 87529
☎ **(505) 776-5826**

Espanola
Inn at the Delta

A careful attention to detail is what guests will notice at this inn. Hand-carved corbels, portals and handmade Mexican-tile floors predominate. All the artwork in the inn is done by local artists. Guestrooms feature large Jacuzzi tubs, comfortable queen-size beds and Southwestern-style furnishings, all made specifically for the inn by local artisans. A full breakfast is served each morning.

10 Rooms • Price range: $100-150
304 Paseo de Onate, Espanola, NM 87532
☎ **(505) 753-9466**

Farmington
The Casa Blanca Inn

This 1950s Mission-style home sits atop a bluff overlooking Farmington. Guests can participate in a number of nearby activities, including golf and fishing. There are five cozy guestrooms, each with a telephone, TV/VCR and a private tiled bath. The spacious living room, the dining room and the library are all tastefully decorated. Breakfast is served in the formal dining room and features homemade, fresh-baked goods.

6 Rooms • Price range: $68-175
505 E LaPlata St, Farmington, NM 87401
☎ **(505) 327-6503**

Galisteo
The Galisteo Inn

Built by a settler when New Mexico was still a Spanish territory, this property is more than 200 years old. Much of the inn's original character remains: The wide hall with its 12-inch-wide floor planks, plastered white adobe walls and rough-hewn ceiling beams is an prime example. Guestrooms feature Southwestern furnishings and private baths; some have a fireplace. Breakfast may include chile-studded frittatas and quick bread.

12 Rooms • Price range: $80-200
9 La Vega St, Galisteo, NM 87540
☎ **(505) 466-4000**

Jemez Springs
Riverdancer Inn

Set on five secluded acres in a remote mountain area next to an enchanting river, this inn offers guests miles of scenic landscape to explore. Guests may fish, hike, ski, enjoy the hot springs or laze in hammocks. Throughout the inn, floors are radiantly heated Saltillo tiles. Guestrooms, built around a garden plaza with a fountain, feature private baths, phones and TVs. Workshops and body treatments can be arranged.

7 Rooms • Price range: $99-124
16445 Hwy 4, Jemez Springs, NM 87025
☎ **(505) 829-3262**

Las Cruces
Hilltop Hacienda B&B

This two-story arched adobe brick dwelling of Moorish design offers an incredible view of the Mesilla Valley and the Organ and Dona Ana Mountains, as well as Las Cruces. Guests can enjoy iced tea on the wide patios overlooking the 18 acres of property or sit by the fire in the sitting room. Three spacious rooms feature private baths and king- or queen-size beds. Breakfast is served in the dining room or on the patio.

3 Rooms • Price range: $75-85
2600 Westmoreland St, Las Cruces, NM 88012
☎ **(505) 382-3556**

Las Cruces
Lundeen's Inn of the Arts

Old-World charm and western hospitality combine to make this 100-year-old restored Mexican Territorial-style inn special. Two double-story guest houses are joined by a Great Room that has dark wood floors, an 18-foot-high, pressed-tin ceiling, an 1855 German piano and Jacobean-style furniture. Rooms are named after New Mexican or Native American artists. Breakfast and afternoon refreshments are served.

22 Rooms • Price range: $63-77
618 S Alameda Blvd, Las Cruces, NM 88005
☎ **(505) 526-3326**

Las Cruces
T. R. H. Smith Bed & Breakfast

The westward expansion of the railroads in the 1880s put the town of Las Cruces on the map. This particular inn was once the home of the State Bank president who commissioned the building of this Prairie-style house in 1914. The home boasts the original hardwood floors, stained-glass windows and high-beamed ceilings. The garden room is a pleasant place for breakfast, and the Inn's Pool Hall is a great spot in which to relax.

4 Rooms • Price range: $60-132
909 N Alameda Blvd, Las Cruces, NM 88005
☎ **(505) 525-2525**

Lincoln
Casa de Patron Bed & Breakfast Inn

Located 5,700 feet above sea level, this 1860 single-story adobe home is about 30 miles northeast of Ruidos. All seven rooms at the B&B feature private baths and various other amenities, including a fireplace, a private entrance and a Jacuzzi. Both continental and full breakfasts are available. Guests can use the large common room, which has a fireplace and a grand piano. Families with children are welcome in the casitas.

7 Rooms • Price range: $77-117
Hwy 380 E, Lincoln, NM 88338
☎ **(505) 653-4676**

Los Ojos
Casa De Martinez Bed & Breakfast

Located in the historic rural community of Los Brazos, this adobe residence is just minutes away from a number of activities, including fishing, cross-country skiing and sightseeing. The 1859 home has always been owned and operated by the same family. Each of the five antique-filled rooms has a private bath. The casa, open from February to October, is listed on the National Register of Historic Places.

5 Rooms • Price range: $75-125
31 CR 334, Los Ojos, NM 87551
☎ **(505) 588-7858**

Mesilla
Meson de Mesilla

This "pearl of the Rio Grande" boasts views of the majestic Organ Mountains. A peaceful ambience pervades the whole inn, from the lovely guestrooms to the deck and the pool. The European restaurant offers an award-winning wine list.

15 Rooms • Price range: $45-175
1803 Avenida de Mesilla, Mesilla, NM 88046
☎ **(505) 525-9212**

Placitas
Hacienda de Placitas Inn of the Arts

Situated in a small historic village, this is a great jumping-off place for local sightseeing. The inn is comprised of a number of cabins, one of which is a log cabin transported from the wilderness, and all of which are furnished with country decor. There is a pool, a sauna, a fitness room and a hot tub on site. Local activities include hot-air ballooning, hiking and llama trekking.

7 Rooms • Price range: $99-199
491 Hwy 165, Placitas, NM 87043
☎ **(505) 867-0082**

Santa Fe
Adobe Abode

This 1907 residence features a mix of Native American, Hispanic and Anglo influences—which means that no two rooms are exactly alike. Antiques from France and England, a mahogany planter's chair from the Philippines, handmade Aspen pole beds and puppets from Java are some of the furnishings found in guestrooms. Modern amenities are appropriately unobtrusive. A Southwestern-style breakfast is served daily.

6 Rooms • Price range: $125-185
202 Chapelle, Santa Fe, NM 87501
☎ **(505) 983-3133**

Santa Fe
⍨ Alexander's Inn

This 1903 Victorian bungalow is tucked away in Sante Fe's historic residential east side. The inn's attention to detail can be seen in the hand-stenciling that appears throughout the inn. Family antiques, dried flowers, dormer windows, lace curtains and stained-glass windows also add to the decor. Flowers and plants grace every room. Guestrooms feature televisions and telephones. Breakfast includes homemade muffins.

9 Rooms • Price range: $90-175
529 E Palace Ave, Santa Fe, NM 87501
☎ **(505) 986-1431**

Santa Fe
⍨ Casa de la Cuma B&B

Situated on a hill overlooking the Plaza Sante Fe, the Casa de la Cuma is within walking distance of shops, museums and restaurants. In the winter, downhill and cross-country skiing and snowboarding activities are a short drive away. Guestrooms feature air conditioning and televisions. Guests can eat a breakfast in the breakfast room, which has windows framing views of the mountains.

4 Rooms • Price range: $85-145
105 Paseo de la Cuma, Santa Fe, NM 87501
☎ **(505) 983-1717**

Santa Fe
Casapueblo Inn

Just a stroll away from the Plaza, this is a sophisticated, beautiful adobe inn.

32 Rooms • Price range: $179-229
138 Park Ave, Santa Fe, NM 87501
☎ **(505) 988-4455**

Santa Fe
El Farolito Bed & Breakfast Inn

El Farolito offers seven guestrooms situated in four authentic Sante Fe adobe buildings. Each room features a private hand-painted tiled bath, a kiva fireplace, phones and cable TV; some rooms have a refrigerator. All rooms have a private entrance and a patio or a wet bar. Unique items sprinkled throughout reflect Santa Fe's Pueblo, Spanish-Colonial and Anglo cultures. An expanded continental breakfast is served daily.

8 Rooms • Price range: $150-180
514 Galisteo St, Santa Fe, NM 87501
☎ **(505) 988-1631**

Santa Fe
Four Kachinas Inn

Named after the supernatural beings said to reside in the San Francisco peaks, this inn provides guests with very earthly comfort. Guestrooms are decorated with antique Navajo rugs, Hopi Kachina dolls and handmade wooden furniture. Three ground-floor rooms have individual garden patios. All rooms have a private bath and a telephone. Guests can relax in the courtyard. Breakfast is served in the privacy of your room.

5 Rooms • Price range: $140-165
512 Webber St, Santa Fe, NM 87501
☎ **(505) 982-2550**

Santa Fe
Hacienda Nicholas

This traditional adobe home has been decorated with woven textiles in soft tones, rustic Mexican furnishings and tiles, and wrought-iron or carved-wood four-poster beds. The large windows let in the sunlight and the hardwood floors and beamed ceilings make for an elegant interior. Your hosts are more than happy to suggest activities such as visiting nearby Indian pueblos or hiking the trails along the Rio Grande.

7 Rooms • Price range: $110-160
320 E Marcy St, Santa Fe, NM 87501
☎ **(505) 992-0888**

Santa Fe
⑩ El Paradero Bed & Breakfast

Originally a Spanish farmhouse, this 1800s building has 12 guestrooms with such features as fireplaces, porches, skylights and balconies. All rooms are decorated with hand-woven textiles, tiles, folk art and Southwestern furniture. There are two suites in the 1912 double-brick coachman's house. A different gourmet breakfast entrée is served daily. Fresh fruit and orange juice and home-baked breads are always part of the menu.

14 Rooms • Price range: $80-150
220 W Manhattan Ave, Santa Fe, NM 87501
☎ **(505) 988-1177**

Santa Fe
Seret's 1001 Nights

This comfortable inn features absolutely delightful decor. Walls are painted in deep monochromes and the textiles used to decorate the place have bold, vibrant patterns and colors. Wood pieces complement the upholstered furniture, giving the guest units a cozy feel. The units comprise one or two bedrooms, fully-equipped kitchens, private baths and sitting areas. The courtyard is a pleasant place to unwind.

21 Rooms • Price range: $179-249
150 E DeVargas St, Santa Fe, NM 87501
☎ **(505) 992-0957**

Santa Fe

Spencer House Bed & Breakfast Inn

Located on the quiet, semi-residential and historic McKenzie Street corridor, this 1923 Mediterranean-style adobe house is minutes away from Santa Fe's historic plaza. English, Welsh and Colonial-American antiques can be seen throughout the inn. Five guestrooms are offered here, each with a queen-size bed and a private bath; some rooms have a fireplace and cable TV. A gourmet breakfast is served daily.

6 Rooms • Price range: $109-160
222 McKenzie St, Santa Fe, NM 87501
☎ **(505) 988-3024**

Santa Fe
Territorial Inn

This inn blends features of stone and adobe-style architecture. It's an oasis in the heart of historic Sante Fe, boasting a private rose garden, courtyard and lawns shaded by large cottonwoods. Creature comforts are key here where guests enjoy continental plus breakfasts in the morning, and later relax by a roaring fire or soak in the hot tub. The concierge service will assist guests with dinner and theater reservations.

10 Rooms • Price range: $139-219
215 Washington Ave, Santa Fe, NM 87501
☎ **(505) 989-7737**

Santa Fe
The Madeleine
Built in 1886 by a railroad tycoon, this inn has retained many of its original features. Rooms have feather beds and fuzzy robes and most have fireplaces.

The garden boasts a bed of roses and pansies, canopied by aspen and apricot trees.

8 Rooms • Price range: $80-165
106 Faithway, Santa Fe, NM 87501
☎ **(505) 986-1431**

Silver City
The Carter House

This 1906 oak-trimmed home has four private rooms and a larger area for groups. The four guestrooms come with private baths. A more spacious two-room suite is also available. Guests can feel free to relax in one of the inn's sitting rooms or on the large wraparound porch. The inn also has a well-stocked library. Downstairs there is a 22-bed dormitory, complete with a kitchen and a washer/dryer.

5 Rooms • Price range: $62-80
101 N Cooper St, Silver City, NM 88061
☎ **(505) 388-5485**

◆ ◆ Taos
◆ ◆ **⚜ *Casa de Las Chimeneas Bed & Breakfast***
◆ ◆ This inn provides guests with a truly
luxurious, pampered experience. The
 pueblo-style house features beamed-
ceilings, large windows, and fine woodwork. It is decorated with bright colors and
hand-woven textiles. Amenities include a fitness
room, a sauna, an outdoor hot tub and spa, and
massage services. The grounds are in continual
bloom and feature three fountains. The kitchen
herb garden supplies the restaurant with flavors,
which guests enjoy during their complimentary
two-course breakfast and at the evening buffet.
All rooms have private entrances, full baths and
stocked mini-fridges.

8 Rooms • Price range: $150-325
405 Cordoba Rd, Taos, NM 87571
☎ **(505) 758-4777**

◆ Taos
◆ ◆ **Adobe and Stars B&B**
Located just outside Taos and surrounded by the Sangre de Christo Mountains,
 this B&B is the perfect locale for a
 relaxing getaway. The inn, which
opened in 1996, takes full advantage of the
extraordinary view: Big windows, decks and
patios invite star gazing. High beamed ceilings,
kiva fireplaces and outdoor portals are some of
the inn's other attractions. Guestrooms feature a
private bath. A full country breakfast is served.

8 Rooms • Price range: $105-180
584 SR 150, Taos, NM 87571
☎ **(505) 776-2776**

◆ Taos
◆ ◆ **⚜ American Artists Gallery House Bed & Breakfast**
Providing superior hospitality is an art,
an art which has been achieved at
 this B&B. Each morning, guests have
the paper brought to their bedroom
door and then are served a creative and delicious breakfast. Local artwork, be it sculpture,
ceramics, photography or painting, adorns the
gallery and guestroom walls. Possible activities
include world-class skiing, fishing, and white-
water rafting on the Rio Grande.

10 Rooms • Price range: $100-250
132 Frontier Ln, Taos, NM 87571
☎ **(505) 758-4446**

◆ Taos
◆ ◆ **⚜ The Brooks Street Inn**
A casual, yet stylish inn that features
both fine art and recycled paperbacks,
the Brooks puts the emphasis on
relaxation. Six guestrooms are furnished with hand-crafted furniture, photographs
and fresh-cut flowers. The large common room
features a fireplace, artwork and a pair of towering hand-carved African giraffes. Breakfast is a
real treat, with white chocolate apricot scones,
blue corn pancakes and pineapple salsa.

6 Rooms • Price range: $113-150
119 Brooks St, Taos, NM 87571
☎ **(505) 758-1489**

Taos

Casa Encantada

A crooked blue door opens into this B&B's shady courtyard with its hammocks and fountain. Once inside the house, guests discover comfortably furnished guestrooms with amenities. Rooms also have outdoor patios.

9 Rooms • Price range: $95-150
416 Liebert St, Taos, NM 87571
☎ **(505) 758-7477**

Taos

Casa Europa Inn & Gallery

This spacious 17th-century Pueblo-style adobe inn is surrounded with open pastures and majestic mountain views. An enclosed courtyard with a fountain and flower gardens adds to the ambience. Inside, spacious guestrooms feature private baths and a sitting area with a fireplace. Two rooms come with full-size Jacuzzis. Guests can also enjoy the dining room, where a gourmet breakfast is served daily.

7 Rooms • Price range: $95-185
840 Upper Ranchitos Rd, Taos, NM 87571
☎ **(505) 758-9798**

Taos

⑭ Dreamcatcher Bed & Breakfast

The gleaming wood ceilings, stone-tiled floors and brightly colored walls make this inn cheery and bright. The bedrooms feature grand beds and traditional stone fireplaces. Guests can relax on a hammock, curl up by the fire, or take a soak in the hot tub. Delicious refreshments are prepared daily by the innkeepers. This inn is perfectly situated for touring historic Taos and the northern part of New Mexico.

7 Rooms • Price range: $84-119
416 La Lomita Rd, Taos, NM 87571
☎ **(505) 758-0613**

Taos

⑭ Inn on La Loma Plaza

This hacienda is listed on the National Register of Historic Places. An authentic example of Pueblo-Revival architecture, the inn stands on one of the oldest residential plazas in the Southwest. It has a gracious front lawn and lovely gardens. Inside, there is a sunroom with plants and local artwork. Guestrooms feature private baths, telephones and private entrances. Breakfast is a gourmet affair.

7 Rooms • Price range: $115-275
315 Ranchitos Rd, Taos, NM 87571
☎ **(505) 758-1717**

Taos
Orinda Bed & Breakfast

This pueblo-style home is surrounded by pastures, giant elms and cotton-woods. Guestrooms are decorated in Southwestern style and feature Mexican-style viga ceilings and private baths. The living room boasts a fireplace nook, large picture windows and a book, music and video library for guests to enjoy. Breakfasts of fresh-baked breads, fresh fruit and other delights are served under the skylights in the art gallery.

5 Rooms • Price range: $70-240
461 Valverde, Taos, NM 87571
☎ **(505) 758-8581**

Taos
La Posada de Taos

Tucked away on a cul-de-sac in the Taos Historic District, La Posada de Taos offers seclusion and quiet. The 100-year-old adobe house is decorated with 19th-century antiques and hand-woven rugs. Six guestrooms are all located on the ground floor. Five rooms have fireplaces. Breakfast is served every morning. Afterward guests can explore the many nearby galleries, muse-ums, shops and restaurants.

6 Rooms • Price range: $85-155
309 Juanita Ln, Taos, NM 87571
☎ **(505) 758-8164**

Taos
Touchstone Inn & Spa

Surrounded by cottonwood trees, willows, pines, an apple orchard and a wildflower garden, this 1795 adobe hacienda is only a mile from downtown Taos Plaza. On entering their rooms, guests will find an ice bucket, wineglasses and robes. The rooms each have a great view of the mountain or the garden; they also have private patios and entrances. Some rooms have a Jacuzzi or a fireplace. A full break-fast is served daily.

9 Rooms • Price range: $100-350
110 Mabel Dodge Ln, Taos, NM 87571
☎ **(505) 758-0192**

Taos
The Willows Inn Bed & Breakfast

Once the home and studio of a promi-nent local artist, this inn houses cozy rooms with private baths featuring hand-painted tiles. Two of the oldest

willows in North America grow on the property, which also has a lily pond and fountains.

5 Rooms • Price range: $90-160
PO Box 6560 NDCBU, Taos, NM 87571
☎ **(505) 758-2558**

Thoreau
Zuni Mountain Lodge

Guests who love the wilderness need look no further: Here's an inn that is located amid the Zuni mountains over-looking beautiful Bluewater Lake. Local

activities include hiking, sailing and swimming. The inn hosts a gallery of Southwestern artwork.

7 Rooms • Price range: $55-85
40 W Perch Dr, Thoreau, NM 87323
☎ **(505) 862-7769**

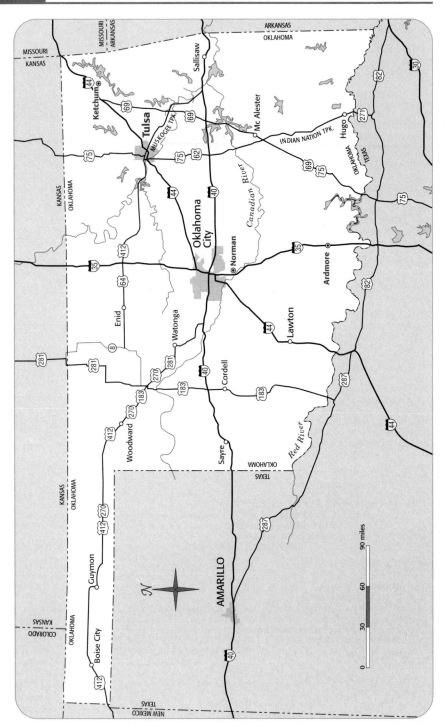

Ardmore
Shiloh Morning Inn

Located on 73 acres of countryside, this inn combines country flair with luxury comfort. Guests can choose from five suites in the main house or two secluded cottages. Each accommodation includes a hot tub or whirlpool for two, a fireplace and a private balcony, patio or deck. The site offers birdwatching and hiking or just watching the sunset over the wide open spaces. A gourmet breakfast is served daily in the dining room.

7 Rooms • Price range: $119-179
RR 1, Box 91E, Ardmore, OK 73401
☎ **(580) 223-9500**

Ketchum
Summerside Inn Bed & Breakfast

This B&B includes the fieldstone Main House as well as a group of peaceful cottages with knotty pine interiors. Cottage guests receive a continental "good morning" basket, while all Main House guests enjoy a full breakfast in the dining room.

7 Rooms • Price range: $85-125
7 Summerside, Ketchum, OK 74349
☎ **(918) 782-3301**

Norman
Montford Inn

The casts of many films, including the cast of "Twister," have stayed here (Helen Hunt's signed photo hangs in the lobby). Situated just 2.5 miles from the University of Oklahoma, this recently built inn exudes old-world character and features antique furnishings and family heirlooms. Each room is equipped with a fireplace and a bathroom, some with a whirlpool tub. Three secluded cottage suites are situated across the street.

16 Rooms • Price range: $75-125
322 W Tonhawa, Norman, OK 73069
☎ **(405) 321-2200**

Tulsa
McBirney Mansion Bed & Breakfast

A baseball star turned banker, James McBirney chose Tulsa to build this beautiful example of an English Tudor-Gothic home. Chosen as a Designer Showcase Home in 1997, the four-level inn features leaded- and stained-glass windows and authentic antique furnishings. Guestrooms are equipped with luxury amenities as well as period decor. Three acres of landscaped grounds surround the inn and overlook the Arkansas River.

8 Rooms • Price range: $119-225
1414 S Galveston, Tulsa, OK 74127
☎ **(918) 585-3234**

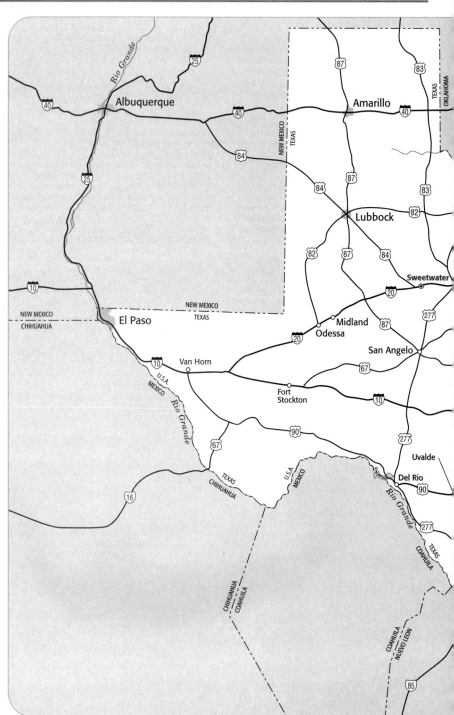

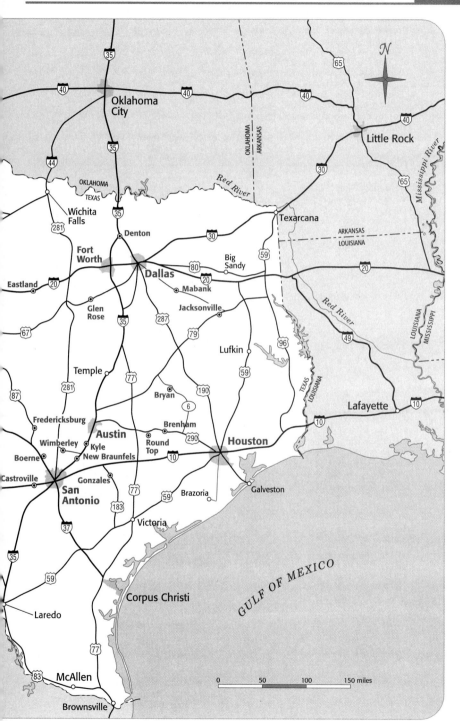

Austin
Austin-Lake Travis Bed & Breakfast

This inn's expansive use of glass and multiple decks capture the incredible vistas of Lake Travis. Each of the four guestroom suites has its own distinctive character, colors and accents. Designed for comfort, the rooms feature half-canopied king-size beds facing the lake and are equipped with private baths. Suites also include a sitting area furnished with an overstuffed love seat, as well as tables and antique chairs.

4 Rooms • Price range: $175-250
4446 Eck Ln, Austin, TX 78734
☎ **(512) 266-9490**

Austin
The Inn at Pearl Street

Surrounded by a shaded 1,600-square-foot deck, this Greek-Revival style estate offers an Old World setting for a comfortable stay. The four guestrooms, which have been professionally decorated by one of Austin's finest interior designers, offer modern comfort in a classic way. Visitors can listen to classical music in the Music Room, which hosts a player grand piano. On weekends, a full breakfast is served in the dining room.

4 Rooms • Price range: $109-200
809 W Martin Luther King Blvd,
Austin, TX 78701
☎ **(512) 477-2233**

Boerne
Boerne Country Inn

This inn features charming rooms and a breakfast menu that changes daily.

14 Rooms • Price range: $60-70
911 S Main, Boerne, TX 78006
☎ **(830) 249-9563**

Brenham
Ant Street Inn

The guestrooms in this 100-year-old building have 12-foot-high ceilings, stained-glass windows, wood floors and private baths. Located in the downtown historical district, the inn boasts museum-quality antiques, including full- and half-tester beds. The Memphis Room includes an original freight elevator as its central element. Owner Pam Traylor has won accolades for her delicious breakfast creations.

13 Rooms • Price range: $95-250
107 W Commerce, Brenham, TX 77833
☎ **(979) 836-7393**

Brenham
Far View Bed & Breakfast

Enjoy Gatsby-era elegance in this 1925 home, which is listed as a Texas Historical Recorded Landmark. The manicured grounds are distinguished by 70-year-old oaks, under which guests may play horseshoes or lounge by the pool. A typical breakfast includes buttermilk oatmeal pancakes topped with home-grown pecans. Blue Bell Creameries and Ellison's Greenhouse are among the nearby attractions.

7 Rooms • Price range: $85-165
1804 S Park St, Brenham, TX 77833
☎ **(979) 836-1672**

Bryan
Reveille Inn

Prior to being turned into a B&B, this 1941 home was a fraternity house at Texas A & M University. Its Southern-Colonial style graces one acre of land shaded by old sentinel oaks. The four large guestrooms each have a private bath and are comfortably decorated. The B&B also features full-kitchen facilities, outside patios and picnic areas. A full gourmet breakfast is served every morning.

4 Rooms • Price range: $120-120
4400 Old College Rd, Bryan, TX 77801
☎ **(979) 846-0858**

Castroville
The Landmark Inn

Originally a stagecoach stop, this 1849 inn is closed Tuesdays and Wednesdays.

8 Rooms • Price range: $45-60
402 Florence St, Castroville, TX 78009
☎ **(830) 931-2133**

Dallas
⚜ *Hotel St. Germain*

This restored 1906 Victorian home is the smallest luxury hotel in Dallas. Each of the seven suites is decorated with early 1900s French antiques and canopied feather beds under 14-foot-high ceilings. Each also has a working fireplace. The inn also hosts a restaurant that has been called the most romantic in the city. Royalty and celebrities check in here regularly. The ivy-covered New Orleans-style courtyard, complete with fountain, is a sight for sore eyes. Here guests enjoy a highly acclaimed seven-course gourmet dinner presented on 75-year-old Limoges china.

7 Rooms • Price range: $300-700
2516 Maple Ave, Dallas, TX 75201
☎ **(214) 871-2516**

Denton
The Redbud Inn

Each of the inn's rooms sports a different theme and color scheme.

5 Rooms • Price range: $65-135
815 N Locust, Denton, TX 76201
☎ **(940) 565-6414**

Eastland
The Eastland

This historic 1918 hotel, features Victorian decor, and high, tin ceilings. Guestrooms have king-size beds, full baths and cable television. An in-room breakfast of coffee, juice, fruit, and home-baked bread and muffins is served daily.

6 Rooms • Price range: $70-90
112 N Lamar St, Eastland, TX 76448
☎ **(254) 629-8397**

Fort Worth
The Texas White House B&B

This Historic Preservation Council award-winning house recreates the elegance of the 1910 original. The guestrooms are all fitted with queen-size beds. A common parlor, a large wrap-around porch, and a gazebo encourage socializing. Centrally located, the house is situated near the Fort Worth Zoo, the Cultural District and the Botanic Gardens. Breakfast is served according to guests' schedules.

3 Rooms • Price range: $105-125
1417 Eighth Ave, Fort Worth, TX 76104
☎ **(817) 923-3597**

Fredericksburg
Creekside Inn

Located just one block from the town's historic Main Street, this inn offers a combination of old and new. The seven large suites overlook Baron's Creek and are furnished with antiques, as well as all the conveniences and luxuries of a modern inn. Facilities include a well-stocked kitchenette and private baths equipped with whirlpool tubs. A full breakfast is served every morning in the dining room.

7 Rooms • Price range: $85-100
304 S Washington, Fredericksburg, TX 78624
☎ **(830) 997-6316**

Fredericksburg
The Magnolia House

This property gets its name from the magnificent magnolia trees that surround the house. Built in 1923 by Edward Stein, a prominent local architect who also designed the county courthouse, the inn is a fine example of the Craftsman style. A Texas Historical Landmark, the inn has had a recent restoration with careful attention to detail. Adjoining the building, a stone patio overlooks a pond and waterfall.

5 Rooms • Price range: $95-115
101 E Hackberry, Fredericksburg, TX 78624
☎ **(830) 997-0306**

Fredericksburg
Das College Haus Bed & Breakfast

This comfortable Victorian residence was built in 1906.

4 Rooms • Price range: $110-125
106 W College St, Fredericksburg, TX 78624
☎ **(830) 997-9047**

Glen Rose
Hummingbird Lodge

A delicious buffet-style breakfast is served daily in this B&B. The lodge is set on approximately 140 acres of countryside. It features hardwood floors,

fireplaces, and a back deck. Guest are invited to visit the property's waterfalls and pond.

6 Rooms • Price range: $89-115
PO Box 128, Glen Rose, TX 76043
☎ **(254) 897-2787**

Gonzales
St. James Inn Bed & Breakfast

Situated in the historic Old Town, this restored south Texas mansion was once the home of the son of David Levi Kokernot, unsung Texas hero and legendary cattleman. Each bedroom has a fireplace and a private bath. The B&B is an hour from both Austin and San Antonio. The town of gonzales is steeped in the history of the Texas Revolution and the Alamo and has many interesting sights.

5 Rooms • Price range: $70-125
723 St James St, Gonzales, TX 78629
☎ **(830) 672-7066**

Houston
Angel Arbor Bed & Breakfast

This 1923 Georgian-style residence is located in the Historic Houston Heights neighborhood. Each spacious room is inspired and named after a different angel. Proprietor Marguerite Swanson hosts well-attended murder-mystery dinner parties. Out back, a resplendent arbor provides shade for those guests who wish to view the garden and pond. A solarium offers the same view.

5 Rooms • Price range: $85-125
848 Heights Blvd, Houston, TX 77007
☎ **(713) 868-4654**

Houston
Hidden Oaks Bed and Breakfast

This plantation-style home was built in 1927 by the great-grandson of Ezekiel Thomas who was a member of one of the first 300 families to receive title to property in Texas. Set on one-and-a-half acres of landscaped grounds, the inn features suites with high ceilings. Guests can also stay in the Carriage House, which has a whirlpool tub. An American- or Mexican-style breakfast is served daily.

4 Rooms • Price range: $95-125
7808 Dixie Dr, Houston, TX 77087-4614
☎ **(713) 640-2457**

Houston
Sara's Bed & Breakfast

This Queen Anne-style inn near the historic Houston Heights district, is furnished with antiques and collectibles. The inn features a spiral staircase, which climbs to a third-level widow's walk for a view of downtown Houston.

13 Rooms • Price: $70-150
941 Heights Blvd, Houston, TX 77008
☎ **(713) 868-1130**

Houston
The Lovett Inn

Some of the rooms in this 1918 Colonial home have a private deck.

8 Rooms • Price range: $75-175
501 Lovett Blvd, Houston, TX 77006
☎ **(713) 522-5224**

Houston
Patrician Bed & Breakfast Inn

This three-story mansion, which was built in 1919, is located in the museum district. Its present owners have restored the building to its former grandeur.

Guests are invited to enjoy breakfast in the large dining room or sunny solarium.

4 Rooms • Price range: $75-145
1200 Southmore Ave, Houston, TX 77004
☎ **(713) 523-1114**

Houston
Robin's Nest Bed & Breakfast Inn
This Victorian-style home was built in 1895.

4 Rooms • Price range: $89-120
4104 Greeley St, Houston, TX 77006
☎ **(713) 528-5821**

Jacksonville
The English Manor
Many original 1932 light fixtures, ceiling fans, and floor coverings still decorate this Tudoresque home. European chandeliers, an Italian vanity, a rosewood secretary and other heritage pieces provide an eclectic elegance to the small hostelry. Rooms have feather beds and large private baths. Full gourmet breakfasts are served. The rolling woodlands of east Texas offer berry picking, golf and bike trails.

4 Rooms • Price range: $75-90
540 El Paso St, Jacksonville, TX 75766
☎ **(903) 586-9821**

Jefferson
Old Mulberry Inn
This large B&B is a newly built home situated in the historic district of Jefferson. All accommodations are furnished with comfortable beds and contemporary amenities. Featured in Southern Living and other periodicals, this attractive inn is an upscale lodging choice for travelers who are seeking a special weekend getaway. Coffee and homemade biscotti are served in the library before breakfast.

5 Rooms • Price range: $99-135
209 Jefferson St, Jefferson, TX 75657
☎ **(903) 665-1945**

Jefferson
The Claiborne House

This restored home of Captain V. H. Claiborne was built in 1872. Furnished with antiques from the period, the original heartwood floors and 13-foot-high ceilings were retained in the restoration. A full, Southern gourmet breakfast is served daily.

6 Rooms • Price range: $115-135
312 S Alley St, Jefferson, TX 75657
☎ **(903) 665-8800**

Kyle
The Inn Above Onion Creek
Located only 25 miles from Austin, this inn provides a tranquil place to stay. Guests enjoy strolling along the banks of Onion Creek and lounging by the outdoor pool. All guest units feature feather mattresses, fluffy duvets, vaulted ceilings and spectacular views of the hill country. Gourmet breakfasts and a light evening meals are served. Nearby Austin and San Marcos offer shops, fine restaurants and entertainment.

9 Rooms • Price range: $140-275
4444 Hwy 150 W, Kyle, TX 78640
☎ **(512) 268-1617**

Mabank
◆ ◆ **The Birdhouse B&B**
This B&B is a contemporary, well-appointed home.

4 Rooms • Price range: $88-88
103 E Kaufman St, Mabank, TX 75147
☎ **(903) 887-1242**

New Braunfels
◆ ◆ ◆ **The Lamb's Rest Inn**
Located on the banks of the Guadalupe River on a secluded acre of trees, gardens and fountains, this charming inn features an expansive deck overlooking the river. The four distinctively decorated rooms each have a sitting area and private bath. Other facilities include a pool and hot tub. A full breakfast is served in the dining room and on the veranda. Activities in the area include shopping, scenic drives, and visiting historical sites.

5 Rooms • Price range: $110-250
1385 Edwards Blvd, New Braunfels, TX 78132
☎ **(830) 609-3932**

Round Top
◆ ◆ ◆ **Heart of My Heart Ranch B&B**
This B&B ranch consists of five buildings for accommodating guests, and a sixth for business meetings. The Main House, is a beautiful Victorian home, nestled among native oaks by the side of a fishing and boating lake. All of the rooms are furnished with antiques, many of which are family heirlooms. A delicious breakfast buffet is served at the Main House in the formal dining room and out on the wraparound porch.

12 Rooms • Price range: $115-225
403 Florida Chapel Rd, Round Top, TX 78954
☎ **(979) 249-3171**

San Antonio
◆ ◆ ◆ ◆ **The Columns on Alamo**
This gracious 1892 Greek-Revival style house and the adjacent 1901 guest house feature elegant rooms furnished with Victorian antiques and period reproductions. All rooms are equipped with a private bath and queen- or king-size bed. Generous gourmet breakfasts are served in the main house. The inn is located in the King William Historic District, a short walk from the Alamo. Also reachable on foot are the River Walk and the convention center. For those who prefer, the downtown trolley stops at the door. Just a short drive away are Sea World and the Spanish Mission Trail.

13 Rooms • Price range: $92-255
1037 S Alamo St, San Antonio, TX 78210
☎ **(210) 271-3245**

San Antonio
Academy House of Monte Vista

This 1897 Victorian home on the Monte Vista hill has both charm and an air of serenity. Each of the B&B's guestrooms is decorated with antique furnishings and has a private bath. Guests are treated to an old-fashioned country breakfast. Afterward, many enjoy strolling through the surrounding Historic District, which offers a profusion of architectural styles—from gingerbread houses to multi-story mansions.

4 Rooms • Price range: $95-175
2317 N Main Ave, San Antonio, TX 78212
☎ **(210) 731-8393**

San Antonio
Adams House Bed & Breakfast

Work by local artists decorates the rooms and hallways of this 1905 Victorian-Italianate house, which features unique wood trim and accents. Built by the owner of a lumber mill, all the wood in the house is made of irreplaceable red pine heartwood. Four verandas offer guests a quiet place to relax. The B&B is located in the King William Historic District, which has many points of cultural interest.

4 Rooms • Price range: $119-179
231 Adams St, San Antonio, TX 78210
☎ **(210) 224-4791**

San Antonio
⚅ Arbor House Inn & Suites

Comprised of four historic houses dating from 1903, recent restorations of this inn garnered the San Antonio Conservation Society's plaque for excellence. The houses are clustered around an interior garden, creating a tranquil oasis in the downtown area. The large and moderately sized suites are each uniquely decorated and feature high ceilings and private baths. Some also have private balconies and kitchen amenities.

18 Rooms • Price range: $125-195
540 S St Mary's St, San Antonio, TX 78205
☎ **(210) 472-2005**

San Antonio
A Beckmann Inn and Carriage House Bed & Breakfast

Named as an exceptional City Historic Landmark, this 1886 inn retains its Victorian charm. White wicker furniture invites guests to relax on the wraparound porch that looks out on a landscaped yard. The front lobby features an intricately designed wood mosaic floor imported from Paris and 14-foot-high ceilings with tall windows. Guestrooms have queen-size beds and are equipped with private baths.

5 Rooms • Price range: $110-150
222 E Guenther St, San Antonio, TX 78204
☎ **(210) 229-1449**

San Antonio
Bonner Garden Bed & Breakfast

Artist Mary Bonner made history in 1910 when she commissioned the construction of this house. Because four of her previous homes had burned down, she hired an architect who was the first in the Southwest to use concrete reinforced with steel. She then added the touches that give this villa its present Italian-Renaissance style. The property also features lovely gardens and a rooftop terrace with a view of the city.

6 Rooms • Price range: $85-135
145 E Agarita Ave, San Antonio, TX 78212
☎ **(210) 733-4222**

San Antonio
Brackenridge House B&B

Located in the King William Historic District, this beautifully restored inn combines a turn-of-the-20th-century ambience with Texan charm. Located only a short walk from the river, the downtown, and the Alamo, the inn is also near the trolley that ferries guests to sightseeing stops farther afield. Guests with pets or children under 12 are invited to stay in the charming self-contained carriage house, which has two bedrooms.

6 Rooms • Price range: $105-200
230 Madison, San Antonio, TX 78204
☎ **(210) 271-3442**

San Antonio
Noble Inns-The Jackson House

The owners of this 1894 home in the King William Historical District are descendants of founding settlers to the area. One ancestor, Samuel Maverick, was prominent in the Texas revolution and his name has entered the English lexicon. The Jackson House boasts a conservatory with a beautiful indoor garden spa. Guests also have the option of staying in the Pancoast Carriage House, with its patio and swimming pool.

6 Rooms • Price range: $110-167
107 Madison St, San Antonio, TX 78204
☎ **(210) 225-4045**

San Antonio
Riverwalk Inn

Located directly on the Riverwalk, this cozy inn with its rustic decor has 150 feet of river frontage. Five 1840 log homes were relocated from Tennessee—log by log—and were used to build two of the main buildings. Each guestroom has been decorated with country antiques suited to the unique flavor of these old cabins. Storytellers and living-history presenters are often invited to entertain guests on weekends.

11 Rooms • Price range: $125-180
329 Old Guilbeau, San Antonio, TX 78204
☎ **(210) 212-8300**

San Antonio
The Royal Swan Bed & Breakfast

This lovely 1892 Victorian house, located in the King William Historic District, boasts large verandas, original fireplaces, stained glass and hand-carved woodwork. Other features include a bridal balcony and an entrance foyer constructed with loblolly pine. Guestrooms amenities include antique furnishings, claw-foot tubs and fine milled soap. Historic restoration of the surrounding neighborhood was initiated in the late 1960s.

5 Rooms • Price range: $110-160
236 Madison St, San Antonio, TX 78204
☎ **(210) 223-3776**

San Antonio
A Victorian Lady Inn

This restored 1898 Victorian mansion is a historical landmark. Each of the guestrooms has been carefully furnished with period antiques and lace curtains, as well as a private bath and air-conditioning. Some also include a fireplace and private veranda. Breakfast is served formally in the dining room or alfresco on the sunporch. A 25-cent trolley ride, available right outside the door, takes guests to local cultural sites.

8 Rooms • Price range: $89-135
421 Howard St, San Antonio, TX 78212
☎ **(210) 224-2524**

San Antonio
A Yellow Rose Bed & Breakfast

Situated in the King William Historic District, this well-restored, late 19th-century house was built in two stages. The Sunday House was built in 1865 and is highlighted by original maple flooring. The Main House was built in 1878 and features a grand staircase, a 25-foot-high ceiling, and original triple-hung, stenciled-glass windows. Some of the large and comfortable guestrooms feature a private porch with rocking chairs.

5 Rooms • Price range: $114-149
229 Madison, San Antonio, TX 78204
☎ **(210) 229-9903**

San Antonio
Christmas House Bed & Breakfast

A Christmas theme is used to decorate the common areas of this B&B.

5 Rooms • Price range: $75-150
2307 McCullough, San Antonio, TX 78212
☎ **(210) 737-2786**

San Antonio
Inn on the River

This carefully restored, early 1900s home overlooks the San Antonio River.

12 Rooms • Price range: $119-139
129 Woodward Pl, San Antonio, TX 78204
☎ **(210) 225-6333**

Sweetwater
Mulberry Mansion

This restored 1913 California Spanish-style home makes the perfect stop for visitors attending the "World's Largest Rattlesnake Roundup," an annual event held in Sweetwater. Named after the largest tree in Nolan County, the mansion was the county's first hospital from 1923 to 1936. The inn features a luxurious living area with an original 1913 mural. Home-cooked meals are served in the formal dining room.

7 Rooms • Price range: $70-195
1400 Sam Houston St, Sweetwater, TX 79556
☎ **(915) 235-3811**

Victoria
Friendly Oaks Bed and Breakfast

A large veranda shaded by huge 100-year-old oaks welcomes guests to this 1915 building. Each of the four guestrooms is individually decorated and is equipped with a private bath. Guests are invited to enjoy a gourmet breakfast featuring the house specialty, Scottish Pancakes. Local attractions include the nearby historic neighborhood with its 200 restored homes, local festivals, nature walks, birding and boating.

4 Rooms • Price range: $55-85
210 E Juan Linn St, Victoria, TX 77901
☎ **(361) 575-0000**

Wimberley
Blair House Inn

This charming B&B is situated on 85 acres of Texas hill country and minutes from historic downtown Wimberley. Each guest unit is uniquely decorated with a variety of themes—from Southwestern decor to Spanish lace-and-roses decor.

8 Rooms • Price range: $145-225
100 Spoke Hill Rd, Wimberley, TX 78676
☎ **(512) 847-1111**

Notes:

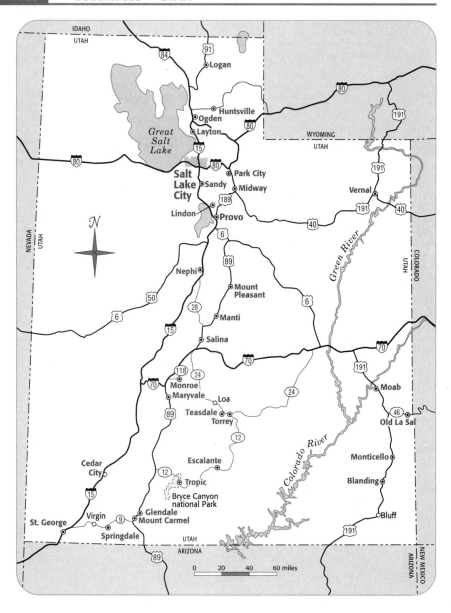

Blanding
Grayson Country Inn

Built in 1908, this structure was once the only hotel in Blanding. Its proximity to famous Cedars State Park makes it a very desirable location. Guests will enjoy country breakfast specialities such as homemade granola and Navajo fry bread.

9 Rooms • Price range: $54-64
118 E 300 South St, Blanding, UT 84511
☎ **(435) 678-2388**

Blanding
Rogers House Bed & Breakfast

Between mountains, valleys and the red rocks of Arches National Park, lies this lovely inn with sophisticated charm. Rooms have queen-size beds and whirlpools.

5 Rooms • Price range: $52-64
412 S Main, Blanding, UT 84511
☎ **(435) 678-3932**

Cedar City
Baker House Bed & Breakfast

Situated high on a hill, this three-story mansion overlooks the Cedar Valley and the mountains beyond. All guestrooms have fireplaces, whirlpool tubs and king-size beds with pillow-top mattresses. After a great sleep, guests will awake to a hearty breakfast of Southwestern delicacies that may include stuffed French toast or breakfast enchiladas. Ski resorts and national parks are nearby.

5 Rooms • Price range: $99-209
1800 Royal Hunte Dr, Cedar City, UT 84720
☎ **(435) 867-5695**

Escalante
Escalante's Grand Staircase Bed & Breakfast-Inn

Decorated in an Old Western style, this new B&B features log furniture and a grand fireplace in the Great Room. Special features include pillow-top mattresses and private baths in the guestrooms, skylights and covered porches, and inside and outside dining. Guests enjoy a gourmet breakfast each morning, and in the evening can dine at restaurants that are just a stroll away. Transportation is provided to/from the airport.

5 Rooms • Price range: $65-105
280 W Main, Escalante, UT 84726
☎ **(435) 826-4890**

Escalante
Rainbow Country Bed & Breakfast Inn

The sundeck at this contemporary B&B is the perfect place to relax and unwind.

4 Rooms • Price range: $50-65
586 E 300 S, Escalante, UT 84726-0333
☎ **(435) 826-4567**

Glendale
Eagles Nest Bed & Breakfast

This contemporary Country-style inn is located in a secluded Utah canyon with outstanding scenery. The innkeepers have collected antiques and artifacts on their travels, and these pieces now adorn the walls. Guests are treated to breakfasts of baked bread and fresh fruit; in the afternoon they are offered wine and cheese. Also offered are massage-by-appointment and turndown service.

4 Rooms • Price range: $79-117
500 W Lydia"s Canyon Rd, Glendale, UT 84729
☎ **(435) 648-2200**

Glendale
Historic Smith Hotel Bed & Breakfast
The new back porch and spa are great for relaxation at this lovely B&B.

7 Rooms • Price range: $44-80
295 N Main St, Glendale, UT 84729
☎ **(435) 648-2156**

Huntsville
Jackson Fork Inn

This unique inn is located in a scenic valley area. Once a modern dairy farm, the structure has been renovated to accommodate guests in the loft area of the barn. Rooms are two-stories, accessible by a spiral staircase, and they have queen-size beds.

8 Rooms • Price range: $60-120
7345 E 900 S, Huntsville, UT 84317
☎ **(801) 745-0051**

Layton
Outwest Bed & Breakfast

Western elegance is key at this atmospheric B&B. Old West decor is featured throughout the inn, and each guestroom has a name, such as "Boots 'n' Spurs" or "Hideout." All rooms feature queen- or king-size beds, fireplaces, and private baths; some feature whirlpools. Guests can enjoy the on-site exercise facilities, sauna and game room, or they can visit nearby attractions such as the golf course or the local aeronautics museum.

9 Rooms • Price range: $65-120
1904 W Gordon Ave, Layton, UT 84041
☎ **(801) 444-0794**

Lindon
Somewhere Inn Time

This newly built inn features whirlpools and fireplaces in each of the guest units.

8 Rooms • Price range: $75-198
175 N State St, Lindon, UT 84042
☎ **(801) 785-9777**

Manti
The Yardley Inn

Elegantly furnished with antiques, this inn also features modern conveniences.

4 Rooms • Price range: $60-65
190 S 200 W, Manti, UT 84642
☎ **(435) 835-1861**

Marysvale
Moore's Old Pine Inn

History enthusiasts will love the inn's proximity to museums and trails of the wild west, and the fact that Butch Cassidy stayed here. It was constructed in 1882 in what was a railroad and gold-mining town and is the oldest hotel in Utah.

9 Rooms • Price range: $50-100
60 S Hwy 89, Marysvale, UT 84750
☎ **(435) 326-4565**

Midway
⚠ Blue Boar Inn & Restaurant

Surrounded by the finest seasonal recreation in Utah, the Huckleberry Inn offers a European sensibility and atmosphere. Each room is a unique blend of European and American decor, furnished with hand-carved European reproduction furniture, and equipped with a gas fireplace and jetted tub or therapeutic/aromatic steam shower. Continental or full-service breakfast is prepared by a chef according to time-honored recipes, and four-course gourmet dinners, to the accompaniment of a pianist, are offered on Fridays and Saturdays.

14 Rooms • Price range: $150-295
1235 Warm Springs Rd, Midway, UT 84049
☎ **(435) 654-1400**

Midway
⚠ Homestead Resort

More than a century ago a farmer unwittingly struck a "hot pot," out of which warm water flowed. Soon visitors from neighboring communities were coming to bathe in the medicinal waters. The enterprising farmer soon developed the spot into the area's first resort. Now individual buildings and quaint cottages are connected by scenic walkways traversing the landscaped grounds. Set in the broad Heber Valley, this resort is surrounded by hills and mountains that offer stunning views. The inn features four restaurants to suit any occasion. Special golf or sleigh-ride packages are available.

151 Rooms • Price range: $129-199
700 N Homestead Dr, Midway, UT 84049
☎ **(435) 654-1102**

Midway
The Kastle Inn Bed & Breakfast

This inn features picturesque views and is near to fishing, hiking and golf.

5 Rooms • Price range: $120-160
1220 Interlaken Ln, Midway, UT 84049
☎ **(435) 657-2755**

Midway
Johnson Mill Bed & Breakfast

This century-old inn is located on 25 acres of unspoiled nature.

6 Rooms • Price range: $115-225
100 Johnson Mill Rd, Midway, UT 84049
☎ **(435) 654-4466**

Moab
Sunflower Hill Bed & Breakfast Inn

This inn is surrounded by more than an acre of woodlands and flower gardens. It is made up of a Cape Cod-style cottage with a wraparound porch, and an adobe farmhouse containing charming guestrooms with private baths—some with a jetted tub—and antique beds. Several rooms have a private balcony or patio. There is also an outdoor grill and an outdoor hot tub for guests to use. Breakfast includes such dishes as yogurt parfaits, western-style eggs with homemade salsa and freshly baked muffins. The inn is located three blocks from the center of town.

11 Rooms • Price range: $105-180
185 N 300 E, Moab, UT 84532
☎ **(435) 259-2974**

Moab
Castle Valley Inn

For world-class skylines and scenic grandeur, look no further. This inn rests on 11 acres of grounds featuring fruit orchards and manicured lawns. The interior of the inn is equally impressive, as each room is decorated with art and artifacts from around the world. The rooms have walls of polished wood and boast textiles in natural earth tones. Natural light from the many windows highlights the interior decor.

8 Rooms • Price range: $105-160
424 Amber Lane, Moab, UT 84532
☎ **(435) 259-6012**

Moab
Dream Keeper Inn

Just a few miles from the Arches and Canyonlands National Parks, the Dream Keeper is tucked away among sheltering trees and flowering gardens. Each room is individually decorated; most have direct access to the pool and garden area. A hearty, healthy breakfast is served in the dining room or on the patio. Secure bike storage and maintenance facilities are available for cyclists wishing to take advantage of the area's vast bike trail system.

6 Rooms • Price range: $80-130
191 S 200 E, Moab, UT 84532
☎ **(435) 259-5998**

Moab
The Mayor's House Bed & Breakfast Inn

Your host at the Mayor's House is indeed the mayor of Moab. Guests are offered relaxation in the heated swimming pool or hot tub, and massage therapy is available by appointment. Many guests sample the cuisine of the local restaurants, others grill their food on the patio. Nearby recreation includes cycling on the Slickrock Bike Trail, white-water rafting on the Colorado River and exploring national parks.

6 Rooms • Price range: $90-200
505 Rose Tree Lane, Moab, UT 84532
☎ **(435) 259-6015**

Moab
Cali Cochitta House of Dreams B&B
Boasting phenomenal views, this inn is near to national parks and forests.

4 Rooms • Price range: $90-130
110 S 200 E, Moab, UT 84532
☎ (435) 259-4961

Moab
The Desert Chalet Bed & Breakfast
This is an authentic log cabin, warmly-decorated, with lovely grounds and views.

5 Rooms • Price range: $65-95
1275 E San Juan Dr, Moab, UT 84532
☎ (435) 259-5793

Moab
Desert Hills Bed & Breakfast
Located in a beautiful setting, this inn offers top-notch views of the surrounding red rocks and mountain peaks. Comfortable rooms have elegant decor, queen-size beds and private baths. There is a whirlpool on-site and a golf course nearby.

5 Rooms • Price range: $35-130
1989 Desert Hills Ln, Moab, UT 84532
☎ (435) 259-3568

Monroe
Petersons Bed & Breakfast
Shaded by a 100-year-old apple tree, Peterson's offers a two-room unit in a private wing with lawn and private entrance. A unique and creative breakfast ensures that no one goes away hungry. Located minutes away from state parks.

2 Rooms • Price range: $60-80
95 N 300 West, Monroe, UT 84754
☎ (435) 527-4830

Mount Carmel
Arrowhead Bed & Breakfast
Situated in a valley, this inn features a pool, a whirlpool and large rooms.

6 Rooms • Price range: $69-125
2155 S State St, Mount Carmel, UT 84755
☎ (435) 648-2569

Mount Pleasant
🅰🅰 *Larsen House Bed & Breakfast*
This attractive inn is becoming famous for its gourmet breakfasts.

6 Rooms • Price range: $55-60
298 S State, Mount Pleasant, UT 84647
☎ (435) 462-9337

Nephi
Whitmore Mansion
Recently renovated to recapture its original Victorian beauty, this 1898 Queen Anne mansion features hand-quarried red sandstone, carved gingerbread designs and turrets with curved glass windows. Rooms, two bridal suites and a family suite are offered. Breakfast is served in the dining room, and evening drinks and snacks are served in the reading parlor and on the veranda. Nearby recreation includes fishing and golf.

9 Rooms • Price range: $60-125
110 S Main St, Nephi, UT 84648
☎ (435) 623-2047

Ogden
The Alaskan Inn

This modern log cabin, secluded among lofty pines and granite-crested mountains, reflects the spirit of its tranquil surroundings. Perched on the bank of the Ogden river, its landscaped environment and tree-shaded patio offer an ideal setting for special occasions of all kinds. Each room is individually decorated in its own Alaskan theme. A full breakfast is served, with pancakes or waffles, delivered directly to your suite any time you like.

23 Rooms • Price range: $115-195
435 Ogden Canyon Rd, Ogden, UT 84401
☎ **(801) 621-8600**

Old La Sal
Mt. Peal Resort/Country Inn
Call for information.

8 Rooms • Price range: $79-150
1415 E Hwy 46, Old La Sal, UT 84530
☎ **(435) 686-2284**

Park City
1904 Imperial Hotel, A Bed & Breakfast Inn

Formerly a boarding house with a colorful history, the 1904 Imperial Hotel offers individually decorated rooms, each with its own unique amenities. Guestrooms include a private bath, and some have a large Roman tub. The parlor, with its Victorian-style furnishings, offers a cozy spot to curl up by the fire. Breakfasts are substantial, with apple granola pancakes, homemade syrups and eggs Julia. An oversized hot tub is available by reservation.

10 Rooms • Price range: $150-245
221 Main St, Park City, UT 84060
☎ **(435) 649-1904**

Park City
Angel House Inn

Painted a beautiful shade of blue, this spacious house is surrounded by flower gardens and manicured lawns. The inn, located in historic Park City, boasts scenic views and provides easy access to hiking and skiing in the surrounding wooded lands and mountains. All guestrooms are designer-appointed and feature grand beds and European and American antiques. Guests are treated to a gourmet breakfast on crystal and china.

9 Rooms • Price range: $169-315
713 Norfolk Ave, Park City, UT 84060
☎ **(435) 647-0338**

Park City
The Goldener Hirsch Inn

This inn stands in prestigious Deer Valley, at the foot of Bald Mountain. Built in the architectural style of a mountain chalet, and decorated with hand-painted and carved furniture from Austria, the inn is cozy and welcoming. Guestrooms are fitted with wood-burning fireplaces, king-size beds and down comforters. The restaurant features gourmet European cuisine in a refined setting. Guests will enjoy the hot tub and sauna.

20 Rooms • Price range: $210-900
7570 Royal St E, Park City, UT 84060
☎ **(435) 649-7770**

Park City
The Old Miners Lodge

Originally built as a miner's boarding house in 1893, the Old Miner's Lodge has suites furnished in period antiques and Country-style pieces, down pillows and comforters. In the evening guests are invited to gather by the fire in the living room for complimentary refreshments. Park City offers exceptional year-round recreation, including golf, tennis, hiking, riding, hot-air ballooning, skiing and snowmobiling.

12 Rooms • Price range: $140-285
615 Woodside Ave, Park City, UT 84060
☎ **(435) 645-8068**

Park City
The Washington School Inn

This inn, a renovated schoolhouse originally built in 1889, offers rooms furnished for comfort with taste. Several of the guestrooms have a fireplace. Outside a sauna and a Jacuzzi, surrounded by locally quarried limestone, help guests relax after a day of skiing or—in the summer—golf, tennis, mountain-biking or fly-fishing. Mornings start with freshly ground coffee and a hearty American breakfast.

15 Rooms • Price range: $135-500
543 Park Ave, Park City, UT 84060
☎ **(435) 649-3800**

Park City
Owl's Roost Country Inn

After a day of skiing, hiking or cycling nearby, guests can relax by the inn's fire.

4 Rooms • Price range: $60-110
2326 Comstock Dr, Park City, UT 84060
☎ **(435) 649-6938**

Providence
Providence Inn Bed & Breakfast

This inn was constructed in 1926 as an extension to the 1869 Old Rock Church. The entire structure is an outstanding piece of architecture and is now listed on the National Register of Historic Places. Each guestroom is individually themed and decorated accordingly. For example, there is the New Orleans room and the Rose Garden room. All rooms are spacious and beautifully decorated, and include private baths with jetted tubs.

15 Rooms • Price range: $65-159 single;
$85-179 double
10 S Main St, Providence, UT 84332
☎ **(505) 758-0613**

Provo
Hines Mansion

Built in 1895, the mansion has been fully restored to offer contemporary comforts in a traditional setting. Each of its nine themed rooms has its own private bath with jetted tub and pillow-top bed to ensure maximum relaxation. Complimentary fresh-baked cookies, fruit and sparkling cider are offered every evening and a gourmet breakfast is served in the morning. The mansion is close to several ski resorts and Brigham Young University.

9 Rooms • Price range: $99-199
383 W 100 S, Provo, UT 84601
☎ **(801) 374-8400**

Salina
The Victorian Inn
This inn features lovely stained-glass
windows and lavish country breakfasts.

4 Rooms • Price range: $60-90
190 W Main St, Salina, UT 84654
☎ **(435) 529-7342**

Salt Lake City
Anniversary Inn at Kahn Mansion
The lavish, themed suites of this 1895
mansion are ideal for romantic getaways.

 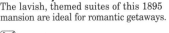

14 Rooms • Price range: $119-369
678 E South Temple, Salt Lake City, UT 84102
☎ **(801) 363-4900**

Salt Lake City
Anniversary Inn at Salt City Jail
Located in a former jail of the Old West,
the Anniversary Inn offers an assortment
of guestrooms uniquely decorated with
unusual themes. Suites include the
Romeo and Juliet , with its sweeping, curved staircase to the second floor, and the South Pacific, with
tiki torches, tropical fish and a volcano hot tub.
Like its sister inn at Kahn Mansion (above), each
room has amenities, such as a fireplace, jetted tub,
waterfall and giant-screen television.

36 Rooms • Price range: $119-369
460 S 10th E, Salt Lake City, UT 84102
☎ **(801) 363-4900**

Salt Lake City
Anton Boxrud Bed & Breakfast
A restored 1901 "mini-mansion," the
Anton Boxrud has many Victorian features such as elaborate pocket doors
and leaded windows of stained and
beveled glass. Guests are invited to relax on the
pillared front porch, or in the hot tub under the
grape arbor. Breakfast begins with an exclusive
blend of freshly ground coffee, continuing on to
such treats as fresh-baked cinnamon buns and
stuffed French toast served on Bavarian china.

7 Rooms • Price range: $70-140
57 S 600 E, Salt Lake City, UT 84102
☎ **(801) 363-8035**

Salt Lake City
Armstrong Mansion Bed & Breakfast
This distinctive century-old Queen
Anne mansion features hand-carved
woodwork, intricate stenciling,
antiques and floral patterns everywhere one turns. Each individually decorated
room has a private bath. Guests may lounge in
the Mayor's Parlor by the fireplace and have
a drink or homemade cookies. Breakfast includes
fresh-baked muffins and a hot entrée such as
quiche in puff pastry.

13 Rooms • Price range: $99-229
667 E 100 S, Salt Lake City, UT 84102
☎ **(801) 531-1333**

Salt Lake City
Haxton Manor Bed & Breakfast
This is a lovely, sunny inn decorated
with antiques, and flowers.

6 Rooms • Price range: $100-170
943 E S Temple, Salt Lake City, UT 84102
☎ **(801) 363-4646**

Salt Lake City
The Inn on Capitol Hill
All rooms in this historic mansion boast
fireplaces, private baths and views.

13 Rooms • Price range: $119-229
225 N State St, Salt Lake City, UT 84103
☎ **(801) 575-1112**

Salt Lake City
The Royal Scotsman at Pinecrest
This beautifully preserved 1915 house
is set under towering pines and in
formal gardens on six acres of land.
It has an eclectic yet refined modern
decor. Each room is individually decorated
on one of a variety of international themes.
Breakfast includes such delectable treats as
banana sour-cream pancakes, and is served
in the dining room overlooking a trout pond
and the gardens.

6 Rooms • Price range: $100-195
6211 Emigration Canyon Rd,
Salt Lake City, UT 84108
☎ **(801) 583-6663**

Salt Lake City
Saltair Bed & Breakfast
Listed on the National Register of
Historic Places, this inn provides memorable accommodation for all its guests.
The bungalow, cottages and many
suites are decorated with 19th-century antiques
and feature grand beds and down comforters.
Guests will enjoy a full breakfast and evening
snacks. The outdoor hot tub and the sundeck
are great for relaxation after a day of skiing at
one of the seven nearby resorts.

7 Rooms • Price range: $55-129
164 S 900 East, Salt Lake City, UT 84102
☎ **(801) 533-8184**

Salt Lake City
Ellerbeck Mansion Inn Bed & Breakfast
This turn-of-the-20th-century mansion is
a perfectly delightful place to stay.

6 Rooms • Price range: $135-175
140 B St, Salt Lake City, UT 84103
☎ **(801) 355-2500**

Salt Lake City
Red Brick Inn
This Victorian-style inn offers comfort-
able rooms with modern amenities.

4 Rooms • Price range: $60-120
1030 E 100S, Salt Lake City, UT 84102
☎ **(801) 322-4917**

Salt Lake City
Wildflowers Bed & Breakfast
This is a charmingly decorated Queen
Ann from the Victorian period.

5 Rooms • Price range: $85-125
936 E 1700 South, Salt Lake City, UT 84105
☎ **(801) 466-0600**

Sandy
Castle Creek Inn
This Scottish castle stands among tall
oak trees. The inn features whirlpools
and fireplaces and each room is tastefully decorated. Guests are treated to a

full breakfast and afternoon tea. The B&B is
located near skiing, hiking, and rock climbing.

10 Rooms • Price range: $99-225
7391 S Creek Rd, Sandy, UT 84093
☎ **(801) 567-9437**

Springdale
Harvest House Bed & Breakfast
This lovely inn boasts several units with
private decks and views of the canyon.

4 Rooms • Price range: $100-150
29 Canyon View Dr, Springdale, UT 84767
☎ **(435) 772-3880**

Springdale
Novel House Inn at Zion
This B&B has a library stocked with
books, games and puzzles. It also has a
covered patio, which offers great views of
the setting sun. Positioned at the base of
the sandstone cliffs of Zion National Park, the
inn is surrounded on three sides by gorgeous
nature and yet is just a stroll to the shops and
restaurants of Springdale. Breakfast and afternoon tea are served in the grand dining room
or on the sunny patio.

10 Rooms • Price range: $80-115
73 Paradise Rd, Springdale, UT 84767-0188
☎ **(435) 772-3650**

Springdale
Zion House Bed & Breakfast
Set amid red-rock mountains, this B&B
has bright rooms with tasteful decor.

4 Rooms • Price range: $75-89
801 Zion Park Blvd, Springdale, UT 84767
☎ **(435) 772-3281**

St. George
Greene Gate Village Historic Bed & Breakfast Inn
This group of nine restored houses dates
back to the 1870s. Many rooms are decorated with antiques, and some offer a
whirlpool tub. Outside, there are some
charming gardens as well as a swimming pool
and a tennis court. Breakfast features homemade
breads, pecan waffles, and whole-wheat pancakes. The Greene Gate is within walking distance of the downtown historic district, and a
short drive from nine golf courses and skiing.

16 Rooms • Price range: $79-139
76 W Tabernacle St, St. George, UT 84770
☎ **(435) 628-6999**

St. George
An Olde Penny Farthing
In a historic district lined with pecan,
mulberry and pomegranate trees,
stands this 1870s mansion. The lava
foundation and thick adobe walls of the
inn keep it cool in the hot Utah sun. Each room
is decorated in deep pastel tones and features
large windows and gleaming hardwood floors.
Breakfast here is a grand occasion in which
guests enjoy such specialities as peach French
toast or cranberry pancakes.

5 Rooms • Price range: $55-125
278 N 100 W, St. George, UT 84770
☎ **(435) 673-7755**

St. George
Seven Wives Inn

Consisting of neighboring pioneer homes built in 1873 and 1883, the Seven Wives Inn offers charmingly decorated rooms, some with balconies, all with a private bath and most with a claw-foot or whirlpool tub. A complimentary breakfast of sausage "en croute," apple pecan pancakes, buttermilk waffles, parfaits and homemade muffins is served in the dining room. Full English high tea is available.

13 Rooms • Price range: $55-125
217 N 100 W, St. George, UT 84770
☎ **(435) 628-3737**

Sterling
Cedar Crest Inn

There's a golf course near this inn, which is located near Palisade Lake.

7 Rooms • Price range: $55-95
819 E Palisade Rd, Sterling, UT 84665
☎ **(435) 835-6352**

Teasdale
Muley Twist Inn B & B

In a grove of pinion pines, surrounded by 30 acres of land, stands this charming contemporary farm house. The wrap-around porch offers views of the Fremont River Valley and the red-rock cliffs of Thousand Lake Mountain. Each guestroom feature a unique decor and is fitted with a grand queen-size bed and a private bath. Breakfast includes specialty omelettes, South Rim eggs, homemade bagels and gourmet coffee.

5 Rooms • Price range: $69-99
125 S 250 W, Teasdale, UT 84773
☎ **(435) 425-3640**

Teasdale
Cockscomb Inn

An old-fashioned farm house, this inn serves full country breakfasts.

4 Rooms • Price range: $55-75
97 S State, Teasdale, UT 84773
☎ **(435) 425-3511**

Torrey
⚇ *Sky Ridge, A Bed & Breakfast Inn*

You won't regret staying here. Situated in the heart of Utah's red-rock canyon country, this Territorial-style inn offers magnificent mountain views in a friendly setting. Antiques, contemporary and folk sculpture, art furniture, and a fireplace hand-decorated with 30 pounds of roofing nails all contribute to the inn's unpretentious Western charm. The guestrooms have many distinctive features, such as cathedral ceilings, private decks or patios and hot tubs. Unique house specialties, including green-chile-cheese frittatas and fresh vegetable or smoked trout omelets make for a hearty and delicious breakfast.

6 Rooms • Price range: $107-132
950 E Hwy 24, Torrey, UT 84775
☎ **(435) 425-3222**

Tropic
Bryce Point Bed & Breakfast
Located in an especially beautiful area, this inn offers a charming country atmosphere. The large second floor sundeck offers sweeping views in all directions. Guestrooms are cozy and provide the perfect location for a relaxing getaway.

6 Rooms • Price range: $70-120
61 N 400 West, Tropic, UT 84776-0096
☎ **(435) 679-8629**

Tropic
Canyon Livery Bed & Breakfast
A haven of comfort overshadowed by the towering monoliths of Bryce Canyon.

5 Rooms • Price: $95
660 W 50 S, Tropic, UT 84776
☎ **(435) 679-8780**

Tropic
Fox's Bryce Trails Bed & Breakfast
This B&B is situated in the heart of southern Utah's scenic park area.

6 Rooms • Price: $70
1001 W Bryce Way, Tropic, UT 84776
☎ **(435) 679-8700**

Tropic
Francisco Farm Bed & Breakfast Inn
This homey log house has comfortable rooms. Breakfast is served.

3 Rooms • Price range: $60-70
51 Francisco Ln, Tropic, UT 84776
☎ **(435) 679-8721**

Vernal
Landmark Inn Bed & Breakfast
Call for information.

10 Rooms • Price: $75
288 E 100 S, Vernal, UT 84078
☎ **(435) 781-1800**

Far West

Day breaks over a vineyard in California's Napa Valley wine region.

Scenic Byways
of the **Far West**

Sunset falls on beautiful Emerald Bay, Lake Tahoe, the site of California's first underwater shipwreck park, the Emerald Bay Historic Barges.

San Luis Obispo to Leggett

With its spectacular coastal scenery, this section of SR 1, known as the Pacific Coast Highway, is a must for any visitor to the Golden State. As well as hundreds of miles of coastal cliffs, tidal pools and marine life, the route offers many cultural stopover sites, ranging from the authentically preserved Spanish missions of Monterey State Historic Park to the stunning opulence of the Hearst Castle.

Lee Vining to Big Oak Flat

Great altitudes and dramatic natural vistas mark this east-west route across Yosemite National Park. Giant sequoias and breathtaking geological formations await the many visitors who file along the mountain passes each summer. Detours off the main route mean following the path less often taken and a chance to experience the varied wonders of this great park and its surrounding region.

Leggett to Nemah

With the great redwood forests on one side and the blue ocean waters and rocky surf on the other, this stretch of the Pacific Coast Highway traces a line of remarkable natural beauty along the California-Oregon coast. Dotting the natural splendor are touches of civilization: charming villages, historic ports and sentinel lighthouses.

Columbia River Highway

The U.S. 30, part of which is a historic highway, runs parallel to I-84 and was built to follow the Columbia River Gorge. Providing visitors with some of the state's most stunning panoramic vistas, the route has numerous lookouts and provides opportunities to visit several of the river's dramatic waterfalls. A detour south takes visitors to Mount Hood, the highest point in the state, and its National Forest.

The Neptune Pool is but one of the attractions at the historic Hearst Castle.

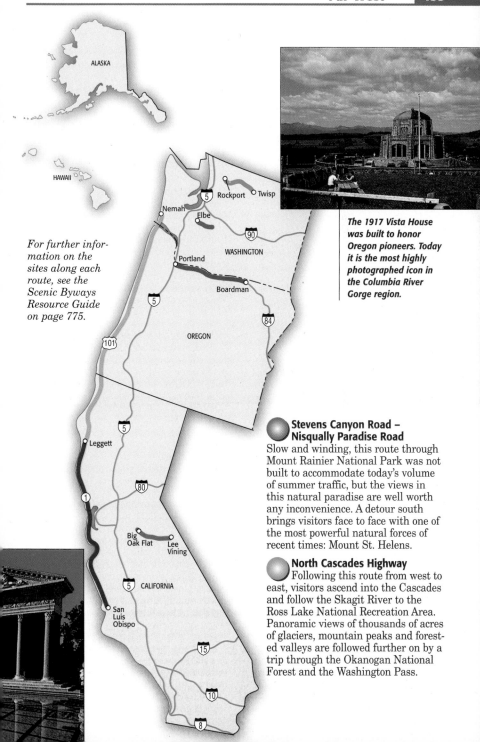

The 1917 Vista House was built to honor Oregon pioneers. Today it is the most highly photographed icon in the Columbia River Gorge region.

For further information on the sites along each route, see the Scenic Byways Resource Guide on page 775.

ALASKA

HAWAII

Rockport · Twisp

Nemah

Elbe

WASHINGTON

Portland

Boardman

OREGON

Leggett

Big
Oak Flat · Lee
Vining

CALIFORNIA

San
Luis
Obispo

Stevens Canyon Road – Nisqually Paradise Road

Slow and winding, this route through Mount Rainier National Park was not built to accommodate today's volume of summer traffic, but the views in this natural paradise are well worth any inconvenience. A detour south brings visitors face to face with one of the most powerful natural forces of recent times: Mount St. Helens.

North Cascades Highway

Following this route from west to east, visitors ascend into the Cascades and follow the Skagit River to the Ross Lake National Recreation Area. Panoramic views of thousands of acres of glaciers, mountain peaks and forested valleys are followed further on by a trip through the Okanogan National Forest and the Washington Pass.

San Luis Obispo to Leggett

Traveling north along the scenic California coastline, many visitors take several days or more to savor this natural wonder. Nearby sites include parkland along the coast and cultural points of interest that are some of the most noteworthy in the country. This route is both a vision of coastal magnificence and a glimpse of California history.

❶ San Luis Obispo de Tolosa

Often called the Prince of Missions, the 1772 San Luis Obispo de Tolosa was the fifth mission constructed by the Spanish in California. In building it, the Franciscans' intention was to convert local Chumash Indians. The mission soon turned into a small industrious colony, attracting the attention and attacks of enemy tribes. This prompted the construction of a new, experimental, fireproof red-tile roof, which soon became the standard for all area missions—and California architecture in general. Much of the structure has been authentically restored and features a museum of Native American and pioneer memorabilia. A visit to the mission should also include a walk through its tranquil gardens.

❷ The Hearst Castle

Grand, palatial, fabulous—finding words to describe the Hearst Castle of San Simeon is as difficult as describing the man behind it. William Randolph Hearst's newspaper empire needed a crown of glory and, with architect Julia Morgan, Hearst spent the latter part of his life—28 years—building it. Dominated by Casa Grande, the cathedral-like structure that houses Hearst's priceless art collection, the estate is a fantastic garden supporting a vast array of exotic flora. Visitors have a choice of four separate walking tours, which include a visit to the enormous guest house, the pools, the gar-

dens and, of course, Casa Grande. An information center at the entrance to the grounds features exhibits highlighting the lives of Hearst and architect Morgan.

❸ Point Lobos State Reserve

Located in proximity to Carmel-by-the-Sea, this spectacular coastal reserve, with its unique geology, covers about 1,200 acres. Known as one of the best cold-water diving sites in the world, some 750 acres are under water. Harbor seals, California sea lions and sea otters live here, and humpback, gray and blue whales can be spotted. Walking along the well-marked trails, visitors may see deer and a variety of bird life.

❹ Monterey State Historic Park

Near the original 1602 landing site of Spanish explorer, Sebastián Vizcaíno, these seven acres preserve the architectural heritage of Old Monterey. Featured are several mid–19th century adobe structures, dating from the time Monterey was the capital of Mexican California. The home of author Robert Louis Stevenson is also part of the site, as is the original Customs House—the oldest standing government building in California. A visitor center offers films about Monterey history.

❺ Big Basin Redwoods State Park

Established in 1902, this 18,000-acre expanse of ancient redwoods near the town of Boulder Creek was California's first state park. Main attractions are the giant redwoods, some of which stand 330 feet tall. The park's visitor center includes a natural history museum and offers naturalist services from June through October. The park has year-round camping.

One of the country's most famous man-made wonders, San Francisco's Golden Gate Bridge is a major attraction.

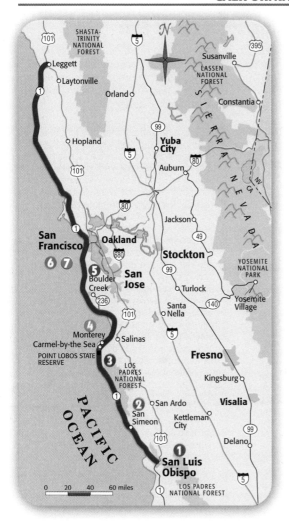

Every turn on SR 1 brings another breathtaking and picture-perfect meeting of land and sea.

⑥ Golden Gate Park

Even with all the other attractions of San Francisco, it's hard to miss Golden Gate Park. This 1,017-acre expanse extends three miles from the bottom of Haight Street to the ocean. Masterful landscaping, a dozen artificial lakes, and a collection of trees and plants from around the world make it a very special urban oasis. Other on-site attractions include an authentic Japanese tea garden, the California Academy of Sciences and the Strybing Botanical Gardens. Visitors can also enjoy tennis courts, an equestrian center and a polo field stadium. Guided tours of various parts of the park are offered from May to October.

⑦ Mission San Francisco de Asis

One of the oldest buildings in San Francisco, this beautiful mission dates back to the dawn of the nation. Its 1776 structure still features rough-hewn redwood roof timbers lashed together with rawhide. On view in the mission's museum are original manuscripts and relics, including original ornate altar decorations imported from Spain and Mexico.

Lee Vining to Big Oak Flat

Heading west along this modernized 1883 mining road, visitors pass by canyons, mountain lakes, fragile subalpine meadows, distant snowy peaks and groves of giant sequoias. Numerous overlooks along the route offer splendid views. Because of the steep grades, this route is not recommended for trailers; heavy snows keep it closed from Lee Vining to Crane Flat during winter.

❶ Mono Basin National Forest Scenic Area

This fascinating area includes the 4,600-acre Mono Lake and the volcanic hills along its borders. This ancient lake, its age estimated at between one and three million years, has a high salt and mineral content. It supports brine shrimp that attract millions of hungry migratory birds. Formations of calcium, tufa, obsidian and pumice have become exposed and rise spirelike from the water. There are many self-guided nature trails and a visitor information center.

❷ Tioga Pass Road

At a dizzying altitude of 9,943 feet, this two-lane paved road provides some of the most dramatic vistas in Yosemite. Entering the park on the east side, it ascends nearly a mile and overlooks a vast canyon. Although portions of the road are more demanding than relaxing, the magnificent scenery is well worth the trip. Due to weather conditions, the road is open only from late May to the first snowfall.

❸ Tuolumne Meadows

Surrounded by lofty peaks, this peaceful domain in the Sierra Nevada is an ideal high-altitude camping spot with access to many fishing and mountain-climbing sites. Prime time in the meadow is early summer, when the wildflowers are at their peak. Nearby points include Waterwheel Falls, Mount Lyell and Tenaya Lake, reached by hiking and horseback tours. A guide service is available and an evening campfire program is conducted throughout the summer.

❹ Yosemite National Park

Despite its fame, many visitors underestimate the size and grandeur of Yosemite. Ancient glaciers carved the area into the colossal landscape of the present, providing sights that leave even the most seasoned traveler breathless. Yosemite Valley comprises only seven of the total 1,169 square miles of parkland. Hundreds of miles of primary roads and trails now make much of this mountain region accessible. The crest of the Sierra Nevada to the east is the origin of the two major rivers running through the park: The Merced River flows through Yosemite Valley and the Tuolumne River carves a magnificent gorge through the northern half of the park. Park services include nature walks conducted by ranger-naturalists, open-air tram tours of the valley, four- to six-day saddle trips and seven-day guided hiking trips. The visitor center in Yosemite Valley offers exhibits and audiovisual programs, while the Wilderness Center provides detailed information about the park's back country.

❺ Mariposa Grove of Big Trees

This stand of giant sequoias is one of the finest in the Sierra Nevada. An easy 36-mile drive south of Yosemite Valley, this section of the park is worth the detour if only to visit Grizzly Giant. This oldest tree

Vernal Fall is one of several spectacular waterfalls in Yosemite National Park. Several local trails provide intimate views of the falls.

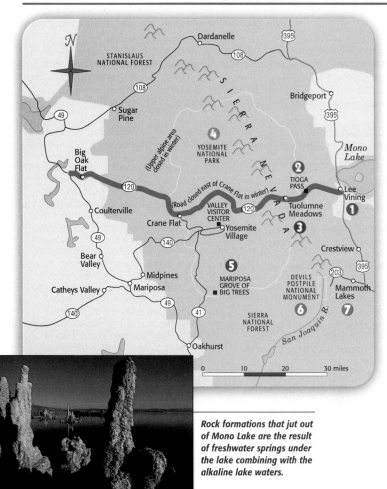

Rock formations that jut out of Mono Lake are the result of freshwater springs under the lake combining with the alkaline lake waters.

in the grove has a base diameter of 30.7 feet and measures 210 feet tall. The grove is also home to one of Yosemite's two "tunnel" trees. The grove museum contains exhibits about these giants and in summer naturalists give public talks daily in the grove. Open-air tram tours are conducted from the grove parking lot for a fee.

❻ Devils Postpile National Monument
Surrounded by Inyo National Forest, this 800-acre site is awesome and inspiring, even by Yosemite's standards. Formed 100,000 years ago and worn smooth by retreating glaciers, these 60-foot-high columns of basaltic rock stand by the San Joaquin River like a wall of enormous

sentinels. Visitors taking the trail leading to the top marvel at the surface, so smoothly eroded that it resembles a tile inlay. Rangers conduct interpretive walks from July to Labor Day.

❼ Mammoth Lakes
Just east of the southern end of Yosemite, this great recreational site is 200,000 acres of trails, lakes and mountains. A year-round resort, the area boasts one of the largest ski areas in the country, with Mammoth Mountain Ski Resort usually staying open until Memorial Day weekend and sometimes even later. The visitors information center organizes guided walks in the summer and ski tours in the winter.

Leggett to Nemah

This route along the coast of northern California and Oregon is both a visit to some of the coast's most stunning vistas and a journey into maritime history. Prospectors, traders and loggers were lured to the region, making settlements in the many natural harbors. Today these settlements have grown into prosperous towns and cities, welcoming visitors and proudly telling their stories.

❶ Avenue of the Giants

The giants are, of course, the magnificent redwoods themselves, which stand high above the surrounding forest, part of the 52,000-acre Humboldt Redwoods State Park. One of more than 100 memorial redwood groves in the region, this 33-mile "Avenue" runs parallel to U.S. 101 and the Eel River. With numerous stops and nature trails, this two-lane road through the forest affords a closer look at some of California's most beautiful trees.

❷ Eureka

When the first prospectors came to Humboldt Bay in 1850 to form the little town of Eureka, they found more trees than gold and the little town turned into a bustling lumber center and port. Today the Old Town district preserves more than 100 Victorian homes and turn-of-the-century warehouses and office buildings. The area boasts a variety of specialty shops, art galleries, restaurants and studios. Also within city limits is Sequoia Park, a 65-acre stand of redwoods, a formal flower garden and a zoo.

❸ Redwood National and State Parks

Forty miles of sweeping Pacific coastline and thousands of acres of forest make Redwood one of the world's most fascinating ecosystems. A World Heritage Site and International Biosphere Preserve, the park protects and explains the natural links between land and sea. The great redwoods are nurtured by the Pacific's summer fogs and a walk through these cathedral-like forests reveals an abundance of blooming flora. Among these redwoods is one of the tallest known living thing on the planet: "Tall Tree" rises 367.8 feet in the air and has a circumference of 44 feet. Beach-combing along the park's shoreline, visitors find rock promontories that afford great spots for whale-watching and viewing numerous sea lion colonies. Within Redwood's boundaries are three state parks and the land that connects them. In addition, a recent acquisition of tens of thousands of acres of clear-cut land will provide for the redwoods of the future.

❹ Oregon Dunes National Recreation Area

Sharing Oregon's coastline of spectacular rock formations is another geological phenomenon: sand dunes. Part of the Siuslaw National Forest, the Oregon Dunes stretch along 40 miles of coast. The dunes average 250 feet in height and extend as far as 2.5 miles inland. An overlook provides access to dune observation platforms. On a river-front boardwalk in Reedsport, the Umpqua Discovery Center lets visitors explore the area's natural and cultural history.

❺ Newport

A resort community for more than 100 years, the turn-of-the-century character of this seaside town has been well preserved in its historic Bay Front district. Other attractions include the Oregon Coast Aquarium, an impressive 39-acre indoor and outdoor facility showcasing coastal

The Oregon Dunes National Recreation Area stretches from Coos Bay to Florence along the coast. The headquarters at Reedsport shows a video on the formation of the dunes.

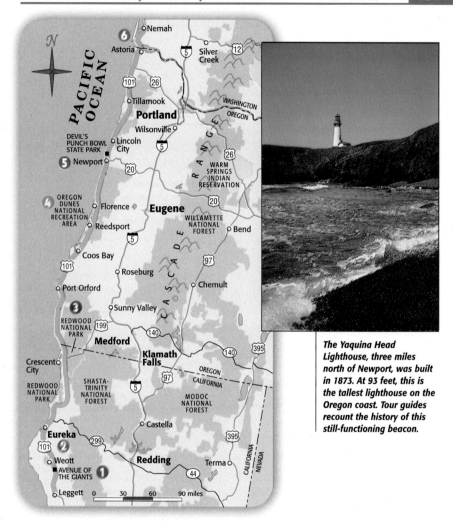

The Yaquina Head Lighthouse, three miles north of Newport, was built in 1873. At 93 feet, this is the tallest lighthouse on the Oregon coast. Tour guides recount the history of this still-functioning beacon.

animals in natural habitats. This state-of-the art facility also boasts one of the largest seabird aviaries in the United States. An eight-mile side trip north of town brings visitors to Devil's Punch Bowl State Park, home of unusual rock formations shaped by wind and waves. Visitors hear the "voice of the sea" as powerful tidal waters surge through the bowl-shaped rock from underneath.

🜲 Astoria

Founded by the Lewis and Clark expedition of 1805, Astoria got its name when it became a fur-trading station under the auspices of John Jacob Astor. This northerly Oregon city has preserved its history in a number of museums and sites. One of the most striking is the Astoria Column. Erected in 1926, the 125-foot column with an observation platform stands on a hill high above the Columbia River. Equally fascinating is the Columbia River Maritime Museum, which has seven galleries focusing on the fur trade, Native Americans and British exploration. Also on view is the keel of a British ship sunk in 1813 and washed ashore in 1973.

Columbia River Highway

Along this road visitors pass majestic rock formations, waterfalls, deep forests and spectacular overlooks. Parts of the route have been designated a National Historic Landmark: Referred to as "a poem in stone," the Historic Columbia River Highway was completed in 1922. Based on a European model, with stone walls and concrete bridges, it brings a touch of the Rhine Valley to this dramatic river gorge.

Wahkeena Falls in the Columbia River Gorge gets its name from the Yakama tribe word meaning "most beautiful." The phrase could easily apply to the entire gorge.

❶ Portland

The "City of Roses," Portland has successfully combined urban growth with a commitment to respect the natural gifts that helped make it prosper. Founded in 1845 on the site of an Indian trading settlement, the city soon grew to straddle the Willamette River. Among the historical institutes tracing the past is the Oregon History Center with its permanent exhibition. The Portland Art Museum, the region's oldest visual arts center, has a large collection of international art treasures and two centers for Northwest and Native American art. But this city's main cultural theme is linked to its official flower and, with the annual summer Rose Festival and numerous permanent rose gardens around the city, Portland is always in bloom.

❷ Columbia River Gorge

This National Scenic Area straddles 80 miles of the Oregon-Washington border and covers 300,000 acres. The region's dramatic terrain ranges from sheer cliffs and mountainous forest to grassy plains. The gorge itself is a geological wonder in which ice age floodwaters have carved out layers of volcanic ash and lava. Rushing through the gorge is the mighty Columbia River in its relentless surge toward the Pacific. The river crashes down cliffs in some spectacu-

lar waterfalls, including Horsetail Falls, named for its unique shape, and Bridal Veil Falls, which has a gorge overlook and walking trails. Added to water and stone are the gorge's distinct ecosystems, ranging from sea-level to sub-alpine vegetation. Crowning the scene are the region's ornithological inhabitants, the peregrine falcon and, the nation's symbol, the bald eagle.

❸ Crown Point State Scenic Area

Situated 733 feet above sea level five miles east of Corbett off I-84, the location of Vista House in this spectacular park is a great place to view the Columbia River Gorge and the surrounding area. Here visitors are offered information about recreation in the Columbia River Gorge and the Mount Hood area, as well as the areas' flora and fauna and geology.

❹ Multnomah Falls

The same ancient river of lava that created the Columbia River Gorge also formed the nearby Multnomah Falls. Measuring 620 awe-inspiring feet, they are Oregon's most famous waterfalls. Upper and lower sections of the falls are linked by a 10-minute walk to Benson Bridge, a magnificent concrete structure built in 1914. Also on site is the Multnomah Falls Lodge with its information center and lookout.

❺ Bonneville Dam

The Adventures of Captain Bonneville by Washington Irving illustrates the explorer's travels and his experiences in the Rocky Mountains region. The impressive dam that

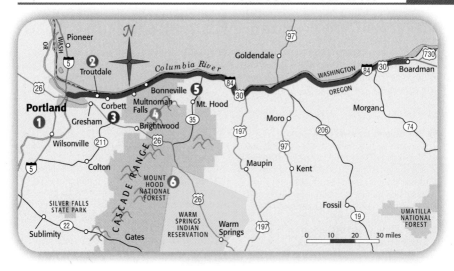

The Hood River Valley is not only one of Oregon's major apple-growing regions, the district is also one of the world's leading producers of winter pears.

carries his name made the Columbia River navigable for other less-adventurous sorts, turning it into a 465-mile waterway. The dam is actually a four section lock and dam system, separated by Bradford, Cascade and Robin islands. This part of the river is also a special place for fish—and anglers. The Bradford Island Visitor Center features a special underwater viewing room from which visitors can see fish swimming up a fish ladder. Adjacent to the dam is the fish hatchery, which has display ponds stocked with sturgeon and trout.

⑤ Mount Hood

Rising 11,239 feet in splendid isolation, Mount Hood presides over the entire region south of the Columbia River and

is the highest point in Oregon. Glaciers extend down the peak to alpine meadows dotted with waterfalls and hot springs. The Mount Hood National Forest surrounds the mountain with a great domain of forested foothills extending to the central Oregon plateau. Running through the forest is the Mount Hood Loop Highway, which follows the SR 35 and the U.S. 26. This route intersects Barlow Pass, which was taken by pioneers traveling the Old Oregon Trail. Another nearby historic spot is the Summit Prairie, a grazing area on the slopes of Mount Hood used by pioneer farmers. The site features the remains of a 19th-century toll house and Summit House, a tourist concession built in the 1880s.

Stevens Canyon Road – Nisqually Paradise Road

Also known as Tahoma, Mount Rainier presides over a land best summed up by the name of one of its lovely meadows: Paradise. But a detour to the domain of Mount Rainier's volatile sister, Mount St. Helens, is a visit to a natural wonder of another kind, the fury of the underworld.

❶ Northwest Trek Wildlife Park

Just north of Elbe, Eatonville is the home of Northwest Trek, a 635-acre wildlife park featuring animals native to the region. Visitors take a guided tram through the park to see moose, caribou, elk, bison and other animals in their natural habitats. A great family spot, the park's facilities include a child's nature discovery center, a theater and a picnic pavilion.

❷ Elbe

Named after the Elbe Valley, this charming town with its historic Little White Lutheran Church adds a touch of rural Germany to the Cascade Mountains. Throughout the summer visitors are attracted to the nearby Mount Rainier Scenic Railroad, a steam-powered scenic excursion train to Mineral Lake, a 14-mile trip through tall timber and over high bridges.

❸ Mount Rainier National Park

With more than 222,000 acres of forest, including 91,000 acres of old-growth trees, this great park is a verdant realm at the feet of its frozen king. Part of the chain of volcanoes running along the Pacific coast known as the Ring of Fire, this dormant volcano could, like Mount St. Helens, erupt one day. With an altitude of 14,411 feet, the mountain supports several different climates. Twenty-five major glaciers cover the upper reaches and the movement of these large bodies has over the years carved out the lakes and valleys on the lower slopes. Abundant rain and snow, particularly on the west side of the mountain, has promoted a rich profusion of moss, wildflowers and trees. Naturalists conduct free guided tours and illustrated talks from late June to Labor Day and the park's numerous visitor centers offer information and exhibits. The 80 miles of roads that snake through the park were engineered many years ago to preserve the natural beauty of the land, but with today's volume of traffic, driving is slow. Only the Nisqually entrance and the Nisqually-Paradise roads are open all year; others close in mid-October or with the first snowfall. For hikers, perhaps the most complete trail in the park is the Wonderland Trail. Three sections, each ranging from 16 to 30 miles, completely encircle the mountain. Some of the interesting sites on the trails are Paradise Meadow, Golden Lake and Box Canyon, one of the most unusual river canyons in America.

❹ Mount St. Helens

After a 123-year-long sleep, Mount St. Helens, one of Washington's snow-capped jewels, awoke with a tremendous jolt one 1980 May morning. More than a thousand feet of the top of the mountain plus much of the bulging north face blew up, releasing smoke and ash 80,000 feet into the air. The pall of ash turned morning into midnight, halting traffic for 100 miles and covering parts of three states with a fine, gray powder. The blast transformed the mountain landscape from lush forested slopes to lava and mud-covered desolation. Since then, biologists, geologists and lay visitors have

Mount Rainier Scenic Railroad's vintage steam train picks up passengers in Elbe for excursions through the stunning landscape.

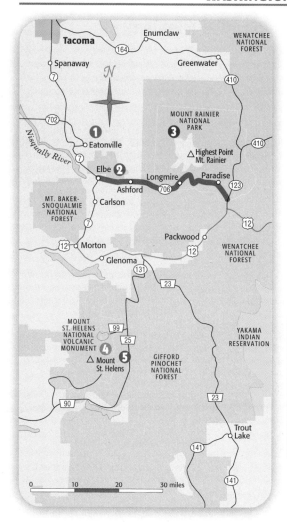

Rising majestically through the mist, 14,411-foot-high Mount Rainier has 25 major glaciers covering its flanks.

had the rare opportunity to study this recovering ecosystem. The landscape is extremely fragile, however, and although the network of hiking trails is growing, park officials have kept many areas restricted. With a permit, it is now possible to climb the southern flank of the mountain, a rigorous 10-hour trek to the summit. For less strenuous sightseeing, a series of forest service roads form a 60-mile link between the principal north and west entranceways. One of the best views from these roads is at the end of Forest Road 99, which passes Meta Lake and comes to

within five miles of the volcano at Windy Ridge. Scenic flights over the park are another option; they leave from many of the area's airports.

⑤ Ape Cave
This 12,810-foot cave tunnel in the Mount St. Helens area is the result of lava flow from an earlier eruption—some 2,000 years ago. The cave got its name in 1946 when it was discovered by the St. Helens Apes, a local boy scout troop. Today visitors equipped with lanterns take guided tours of the cave throughout the summer.

North Cascades Highway

Running east-west through North Cascades National Park, Rockport State Park, Ross Lake National Recreation Area and the Okanogan National Forest, this stretch of SR 20 is a festival of natural wonders. Especially striking is the area between Gorge Lake and Washington Pass, with its panoramic overlooks of glacier fields, mountain peaks and rain forests.

❶ Rockport State Park

Located about 10 miles east of Baker Lake on SR 20, this beautiful stand of old-growth Douglas-fir rain forest is a hiker's dream. Miles of well-marked trails run throughout the park. Other activities include fishing on the Skagit River and camping.

❷ North Cascades National Park Service Complex

A formidable barrier to early explorers, the North Cascades range has been dubbed the "American Alps" and even today represents nature at its most extreme. Names such as Mount Fury, Mount Despair and Forbidden Peak are fitting testimony to this battleground of marauding glaciers. But the 684,245 acres of North Cascades National Park Complex, made up of the park by the same name and the Ross Lake and Lake Chelan Recreational Areas, is not only a collection of jagged peaks. The range gets its name from the many waterfalls cascading from the steep slopes, meltwaters from the many glaciers that still encircle the mountains. The water enriches the verdant floors of the valleys with their forests of Douglas-fir, red cedar and myriad shrubs. At higher elevations, beautiful meadows of wildflowers, heather, moss and phlox can be found, attracting the region's abundant wildlife. Mountain goats, deer, and black bears are common. Very few roads pass through the park besides the North Cascades Highway and part of the unpaved Cascade River Road in the south unit of the park. Many hiking trails wind throughout the back country and they are really the best way to experience the park. Another option, however, is the round-trip ferry on Lake Chelan, the third-deepest lake in the country, which links Chelan with remote Stehekin on the east side of the park.

❸ Ross Lake National Recreation Area

This region lies just west of the Okanogan National Forest and straddles the Skagit River between the north and south units of the North Cascades National Park. It encompasses the lakes formed by the Ross, Diablo and Gorge hydroelectric dams that supply power to Seattle. Today the lakes and the 107,574 acres of glaciers, mountain peaks and forested valleys surrounding them make up this great outdoor recreation spot. A tour of the Diablo Dam includes a walk across the dam, a cruise across Diablo Lake and a ride on an antique incline railway lift. The striking emerald-green color of Diablo and Gorge lakes comes from minerals found in glacial runoff. Both are accessible from SR 20. The more remote Ross Lake, stretching 24 miles northward to the Canadian border, is accessible by car only from the north through Canada, although it can be seen from the overlook on SR 20. In summer a boat taxi to Ross Lake Resort leaves daily from Ross Dam on the Skagit River.

Almost every bend of the road along this stretch of SR 20 brings spectacular vistas of towering forests and awesome peaks.

The Ross Lake Overlook on SR 20 provides a great view of both the shimmering lake and the North Cascades beyond.

④ Okanogan National Forest

This enormous 1,706,000-acre expanse of forest forms a rough triangle bordered by Canada, the Cascade Range, and the Columbia and Okanogan Rivers. SR 20 cuts across the northern section of the forest along the Washington Pass west of Mazama. The Washington Pass Scenic Overlook boasts an elevation of 5,500 feet and spectacular vistas of Liberty Bell Mountain and Early Winter Spires. A short loop trail at the overlook leads to a visitor information center and perhaps the most spectacular picnic area in the country. Another popular walking trail, also off the Cascade Highway, is the Rainy Lake Trail at Rainy Pass. A one-mile paved trail, it is open only from July to September. Other offshoots include a gravel road leading to the highest overlook in the state—7,400 feet—offering a panoramic vista of the North Cascades. Other Okanogan activities include camping, fishing, river rafting and hiking. And in winter, the 300 miles of summer trails are transformed to cross-country ski and snowmobile tracks.

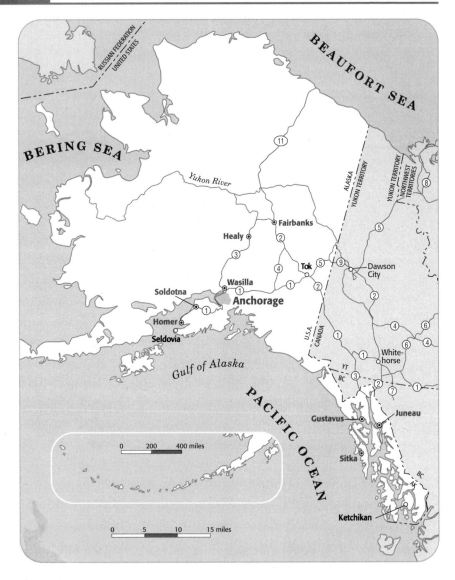

RUSSIAN FEDERATION
UNITED STATES

BEAUFORT SEA

BERING SEA

Yukon River

(11)

ALASKA / YUKON TERRITORY

YUKON TERRITORY / NORTHWEST TERRITORIES

(8)

Fairbanks
Healy ⊙
(2)
(3)
(4) Tok (5) (9)
Wasilla (1) (2) Dawson City
Soldotna (1) Anchorage (1) (2)
Homer ⊙
Seldovia
(5)

U.S.A. / CANADA
(1)
(4) (6)
(6) (4)
White-horse
(1)
YT
BC
(3)
(2) (1)
(7)
Gustavus Juneau

Gulf of Alaska

PACIFIC OCEAN

0   200   400 miles

Sitka ⊙

BC
AK

0   5   10   15 miles

Ketchikan

Anchorage

15 Chandeliers Alaska B&B

An elegant, Georgian-style mansion conveniently located 10 minutes from the airport. All the guestrooms have private baths with heated floors and are nicely appointed in either Victorian, Georgian or Edwardian decor. Summer guests can take advantage of a sunny terrace garden furnished with lounge chairs and tables. For winter guests, ski hills are within easy reach.

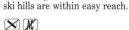

6 Rooms • Price range: $95-125
14020 Sabine St, Anchorage, AK 99516
☎ **(907) 345-3032**

Anchorage
Aurora Winds Resort

Set on two acres of hillside property overlooking Anchorage, this 5,200-square-foot home offers five spacious and tastefully decorated guest accommodations. The enormous McKinley suite features a private sitting area, fireplace, double Jacuzzi and steam shower. Other amenities include an outdoor hot tub, a sauna, an exercise room and a pool table. Breakfast may be taken at the table or in your room.

5 Rooms • Price range: $105-249
7501 Upper O'Malley Rd, Anchorage, AK 99516
☎ **(907) 346-2533**

Anchorage
Lynn's Pine Point Bed & Breakfast

This B&B may be considered small by some standards. However, the comprehensive video library and multiple in-room amenities more than make up for the inn's size. Guests enjoy the complimentary evening beverages, the barbecue, the deck and the whirlpool. Located in a quiet residential area, the inn is not far from tennis courts. The nearby nature and cross-country ski trails are sure to please outdoor enthusiasts.

3 Rooms • Price range: $85-115
3333 Creekside Dr, Anchorage, AK 99504
☎ **(907) 333-2244**

Anchorage
Swan House South B&B

A beautifully landscaped yard with tall trees surrounds this contemporary split-level cedar home. Amenities in the individually appointed guestrooms include cable TV, modem outlets, designer linens, robes and slippers. An eclectic collection of antiques and artifacts from around the world adorn the public rooms. A full gourmet breakfast is served in a lovely dining area

4 Rooms • Price range: $129-249
175 N Augustine Ave., Seldovia, AK 99663
☎ **(907) 234-8888**

Anchorage
Camai Bed & Breakfast

Located on a cul-de-sac in quiet residential area near the University of Alaska Anchorage. Two spacious suites have their own private entrances, sitting areas, kitchenettes and private baths.

3 Rooms • Price range: $65-115
3838 Westminster Way, Anchorage, AK 99508-4834
☎ **(907) 333-2219**

Anchorage
♦♦ *Mahogany Manor*

This 1947 mansion stands on a densely wooded bluff. The redwood interior includes a large common room with two giant fireplaces and a waterfall.

A collection of Alaskan art is displayed throughout.

4 Rooms • Price range: winter $129-299
204 E 15th Ave, Anchorage, AK 99501
☎ **(907) 278-1111**

Fairbanks
♦♦♦ *All Seasons Inn*

On a quiet residential street only a few blocks from downtown Fairbanks, this inn was completely renovated in 1996. The guestrooms, each with a private bath with a tub, were designed specifically with comfort in mind. There are three common areas where guests are welcome to conduct business, socialize or simply relax. Quiche, apple pancakes, egg puffs and fruit-filled crepes are just some of the tempting dishes offered for breakfast.

8 Rooms • Price range: $125-150
763 7th Ave, Fairbanks, AK 99701
☎ **(907) 451-6649**

Fairbanks
♦♦♦ *A Bed & Breakfast Inn on Minnie Street*

In the classic Alaskan tradition of warm and friendly hospitality, the Minnie Street B&B boasts that at the premises "you are a stranger only once."

Centrally located in Fairbanks, the inn offers clean and comfortable rooms

10 Rooms • Price range: $100-195
345 Minnie St, Fairbanks, AK 99701
☎ **(907) 456-1802**

Fairbanks
♦♦♦ *Crestmont Manor Bed & Breakfast*

Near the University of Alaska Fairbanks, this new B&B has a commanding view of the Alaska Mountain Range and Chena River Valley. Antiques, handmade quilts and original art create a pleasant and comfortable environment in the spacious guestrooms. Except for the one economy room, all rooms come with a private bath. Breakfast specialties include orange French toast, quiche and fresh-baked biscuits.

5 Rooms • Price range: $75-120
510 Crestmont Dr, Fairbanks, AK 99708
☎ **(907) 456-3831**

Fairbanks
♦♦♦ *Forget-Me-Not Lodge*

Guests at this B&B have the choice of staying in the main house or one of two renovated historic railway coaches or a caboose. Many of the railway car rooms have been exotically decorated with themes from the 1800s such as Can-Can, Gold Mine and Bordello. The main house features lovely guestrooms and a very spacious living room with a tremendous view of the Tanana Valley and surrounding forest.

10 Rooms • Price range: $75-150
1540 Chena Ridge, Fairbanks, AK 99708
☎ **(907) 474-0949**

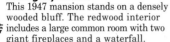

Fairbanks
A Taste of Alaska Lodge
In a secluded location that complements its rustic character, this lodge consists of two fully equipped spacious log cabins. Each cabin was made from massive spruce trees logged from the 220 hillside acres that surround the homestead. Each bedroom, furnished with fine antiques and Alaskan collectibles, faces the majestic Alaska Range for an invigorating panoramic view. Cross-country skiers often spend the evening relaxing in the whirlpool.

10 Rooms • Price range: $150-200
551 Eberhardt Rd, Fairbanks, AK 99712
☎ **(907) 488-7855**

Fairbanks
Fairbanks Downtown Bed & Breakfast
Located in a residential area, close to the downtown, this B&B offers simple, pleasant guest rooms named after people and events important to the history Fairbanks. Rooms have a private entrance and a full kitchen for guests is available.

5 Rooms • Price range: $100-110
1461 Gillam Way, Fairbanks, AK 99701
☎ **(907) 452-7700**

Fairbanks
Midge's Birch Lane Bed & Breakfast
The rooms of this quaint inn have charming Country-style decor.

4 Rooms • Price range: $85-100
4335 Birch Lane, Fairbanks, AK 99708
☎ **(907) 388-8084**

Gustavus
Meadow's Glacier Bay Guest House
Alaska is home to some of the continent's most spectacular scenery and this guest house is situated right in the heart of it all. Visitors enjoy all the modern conveniences of an urban B&B along with the natural splendor of Gustavus. From these comfortable accommodations guests can venture out and discover why Glacier Bay is a UNESCO World Heritage Site.

5 Rooms • Price: $238 for 2 people
12 Meadow Brook Ln, Gustavus, AK 99826
☎ **(907) 697-2348**

Gustavus
Annie Mae Lodge
This inn offers a genuine wilderness experience. The rooms are comfortable.

11 Rooms • Price range: $130-250
#2 Grandpa's Farm Rd, Gustavus, AK 99826
☎ **(907) 697-2346**

Healy

Denali Dome Home Bed & Breakfast

Often referred to as the "Dome House," the rooms in this B&B are actually inside a geodesic dome. There are four floors with living rooms, nine bedrooms, eight bathrooms, a sauna and a fireplace. The comfortable rooms each have satellite TV and a VCR. Ten living-room windows offer views of the Alaskan range and surrounding foothills. Denali National Park is located just 12 miles to the south.

7 Rooms • Price range: $80-110
137 Healy Spur Rd, Healy, AK 99743
☎ **(907) 683-1239**

Healy

Denali Lakeview Inn

Cheerful rooms with decks at this modern inn on tranquil Otto Lake.

8 Rooms • Price range: $110-150
Mile 1.2 Otto Lake Rd, Healy, AK 99743
☎ **(907) 683-4035**

Healy

Touch of Wilderness Bed & Breakfast

Well-appointed guestrooms with contemporary appeal. The dining room has a grand view of the majestic Alaskan range. The spacious common rooms have plenty of room to relax and unwind after a day of outdoor adventures.

9 Rooms • Price range: $95-130
2.9 Stampede Rd, Healy, AK 99743
☎ **(907) 683-2459**

Homer

Victorian Heights Bed & Breakfast

This modern establishment on the shore of Kachemak Bay was built specifically to accommodate visitors. Three of the antique-decorated guestrooms enjoy such amenities as private baths, Jacuzzis and decks. Two rooms share a bath. Every room has a terrific view of the surrounding countryside. The innkeepers are happy to help you plan the day's out-door adventures.

5 Rooms • Price range: $95-125
61495 Race Ct, Homer, AK 99603
☎ **(907) 235-6357**

Juneau

Fireweed House Bed & Breakfast

This property consists of a two-story house and a secluded 1,100-square-foot cedar-beamed guest house. It is situated on four acres of rain forest wetlands on Douglas Island, only six miles from Juneau. A short list of amenities includes Jacuzzis, facilities for children and two friendly Labradors. The Fireweek offers a choice of comfortable rooms and suites to suit a variety of needs.

5 Rooms • Price range: $95-299
8530 N Douglas Hwy, Juneau, AK 99801
☎ **(907) 586-3885**

Juneau
Pearson's Pond Luxury Inn & Garden Spa
This private retreat is surrounded by
rain forest at the edge of the Alaskan
 wilderness next to the Mendenhall
Glacier. The house sits on the bank of
a peaceful pond that was created by the glacier
only 200 years ago. Guests can stroll around
the garden and enjoy the spectacular views
from private hot tubs. The rooms offer a superb
amenity package as well as a private patio in
quiet surroundings.

3 Rooms • Price range: $199-299
4541 Sawa Cir, Juneau, AK 99801-8723
☎ **(907) 789-3772**

Juneau
Alaska Wolf House
The Alaska Wolf House is an impressive cedar-beam structure of some 4,000
square feet. Originally built as a private residence for a prominent local

minister, today, it offers the opportunity to stay
in a rustic yet comfortable setting.

6 Rooms • Price range: $95-165
1900 Wickersham Dr, Juneau, AK 99802
☎ **(907) 586-2422**

Juneau
Blueberry Lodge Bed & Breakfast
The warm, casual tone of Blueberry
Lodge is set by the friendly welcome
you receive when you first arrive.
Expect comfortable rooms and a hearty

breakfast. Specialties of the house include
gingerbread pancakes with lemon curd.

5 Rooms • Price range: $65-95
9436 N Douglas Hwy, Juneau, AK 99801
☎ **(907) 463-5886**

Juneau
The Silverbow Inn Bakery & Restaurant
An on-site bakery and quaint cheerful
rooms make this 1914 inn unique.

6 Rooms • Price range: $122-128
120 2nd St, Juneau, AK 99801
☎ **(907) 586-4146**

Sitka
Alaska Ocean View B&B
The attractive interior design and exterior rock gardens, deck and patio give
this modern house the look and feel of a
country inn in miniature. Located in
the beautiful town of Sitka, once the capital of
Alaska (when it belonged to Russia) this all-
cedar house provides a base for those who wish
to enjoy Alaska's wildlife—including whales and
eagles—and nature trails. The area hosts some
of the best sea-kayaking in the world.

4 Rooms • Price range: $109-179
1101 Edgecumbe Dr, Sitka, AK 99835
☎ **(907) 747-8310**

Sitka
Helga's Bed & Breakfast
Sitting right on the rocky shore of Sitka
Sound, this clean and simple B&B
enjoys a breathtaking view of the surrounding snow-capped mountains.

Every room has a private bath and kitchenette.
A two bedroom suite is also available.

4 Rooms • Price range: $65-88
2827 Halibut Point Rd, Sitka, AK 99835
☎ **(907) 747-5497**

Soldotna
Kenai River Raven Dinner House & Lodge

This spacious contemporary log home sits in a secluded wooded area overlooking the Kenai River. The sunlit guestrooms offer fine linens on comfortable beds and some rooms have Jacuzzis and kitchens. The great room features an impressive riverstone fireplace, Alaskan art and cozy furniture. A sundeck has a walkway down to the river. A hearty breakfast is served every morning before guests head out on their wilderness activities.

8 Rooms • Price range: $80-330
Mile 0.2 Funny River Rd, Soldotna, AK 99669
☎ **(907) 262-5818**

Soldotna
Alaskan Serenity B&B

A log home with a wonderful view of Denise Lake. Guestrooms and two fully equipped cabins are cozy and attractively decorated. One cabin sleeps six while the other accommodates two. Operated by hospitable hosts who like to entertain.

4 Rooms • Price range: $100-135
41598 Aksala Ln, Soldotna, AK 99669
☎ **(907) 262-6648**

Soldotna
Longmere Lake Lodge B&B

This secluded location on the grassy shores of Longmere Lake offers rooms in the main house as well as a separate spacious apartment with a kitchen. Homelike decor. A large seating area, bay windows and a deck afford great views.

6 Rooms • Price range: $110-225
35955 Ryan Ln, Soldotna, AK 99669
☎ **(907) 262-9799**

Soldotna
Salmon Haus Bed & Breakfast

This casual, homey B&B with comfortable accommodations on the Kenai River is a favorite spot for salmon fishing. Friendly innkeepers are members of the local fishing association and will arrange fishing trips and provide equipment.

5 Rooms • Price: $130
44510 Funny River Rd, Soldotna, AK 99669
☎ **(907) 262-2400**

Wasilla
Yukon Don's B&B Inn

Yukon Don has the honor of being voted by locals as both the presider of the best B&B around and the most interesting local personality. At this idyllic country retreat visitors can enjoy the rugged outdoors and yet still have the easy life. All rooms are decorated in Alaskan decor. Each one sleeps four and has at least one queen-size bed. The inn offers splendid views of the Matsu Valley. It is located one hour out of Anchorage.

8 Rooms • Price range: $65-135
2221 Yukon Circle, Wasilla, AK 99654
☎ **(907) 376-7472**

Notes:

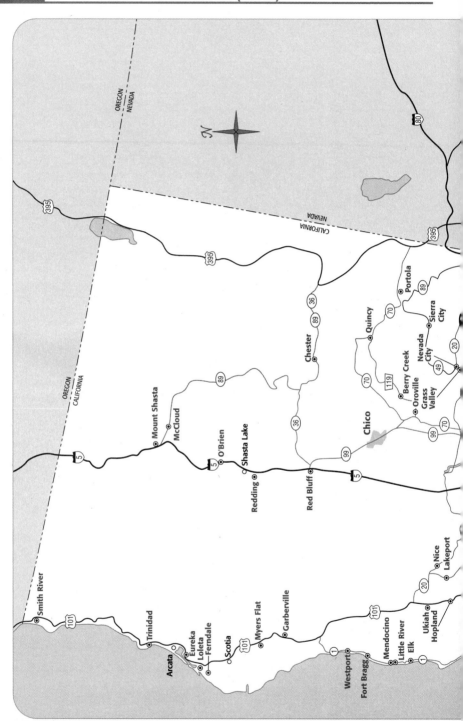

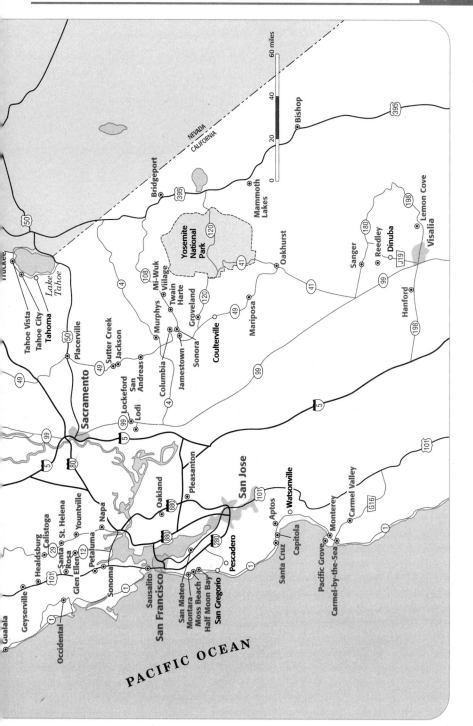

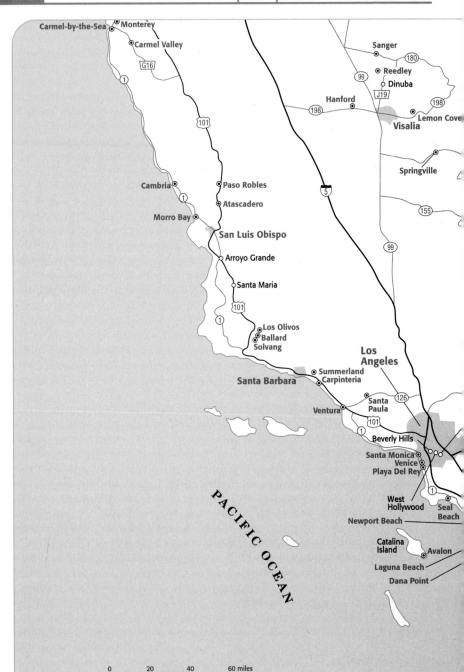

Carmel-by-the-Sea ● Monterey
● Carmel Valley
G16
1
101

Sanger ●
180
● Reedley
99 ○ Dinuba
J19
Hanford ●
198 198
Lemon Cove ●
Visalia

Springville ●

155

Cambria ● ● Paso Robles
1 ● Atascadero
Morro Bay ●
San Luis Obispo
● Arroyo Grande
○ Santa Maria
101
1

5

99

Los Olivos ●
Ballard ●
Solvang

Los Angeles

● Summerland
Carpinteria
Santa Barbara
● Santa Paula
126
Ventura ●
101
1
● Beverly Hills
Santa Monica ●
Venice ●
Playa Del Rey ●

West Hollywood
Seal Beach
Newport Beach
1 ●

Catalina Island ● Avalon
Laguna Beach
Dana Point

PACIFIC OCEAN

0   20   40   60 miles

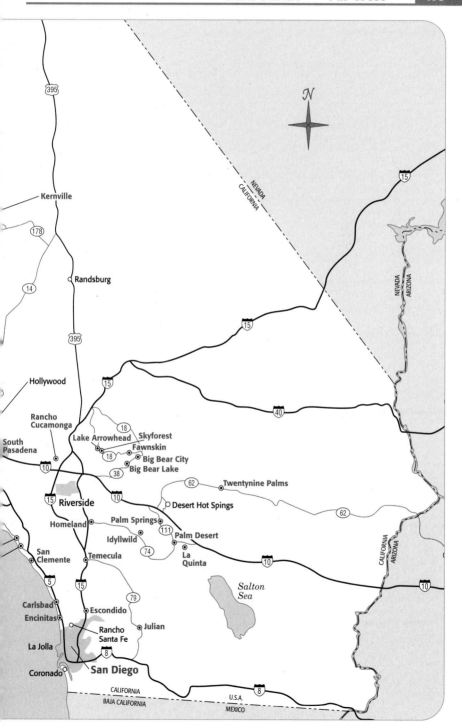

Aptos
Bayview Hotel

This 1878 Italianate Victorian is found where the redwoods meet the sea. The rooms feature antiques, book-lined alcoves and 14-foot ceilings. Guests can stroll through the forest or along the beach or visit the area's award-winning wineries.

11 Rooms • Price range: $140-225
8041 Soquel Dr, Aptos, CA 95003
☎ **(831) 688-8654**

Atascadero
Oak Hill Manor Bed & Breakfast
Nestled among mature oak trees, this English-Tudor manor and carriage house sit atop a hill overlooking the Santa Lucia Mountains. The romantic guest suites are elegantly furnished and decorated in European Country styles. Each suite is also equipped with a working fireplace and private deck or garden patio. Guests are invited to a leisurely breakfast served in the formal dining room. The inn has its own English pub.

8 Rooms • Price range: $145-225
12345 Hampton Court, Atascadero, CA 93422
☎ **(805) 462-9317**

Avalon
The Old Turner Inn
Set in a quiet residential area, this inn has tasteful, elegant decor.

5 Rooms • Price range: $145-200
232 Catalina Ave, Avalon, CA 90704
☎ **(310) 510-2236**

Ballard
The Ballard Inn
The charming Ballard Inn lives up to the colorful history of Santa Ynez Valley. There are several unique common rooms, a dining room with an Italian marble fireplace, the Vintners Room where guests can participate in wine tasting, and the delightful Cafe Chardonnay. Seven guestrooms feature objets d'art, custom-designed quilts and king, queen or twin beds. All rooms have private baths. Breakfast is served every morning in the dining room. Activities include driving through scenic Santa Barbara County, biking through vineyards and exploring nearby mountain trails.

15 Rooms • Price range: $175-265
2436 Baseline Ave, Ballard, CA 93463
☎ **(805) 688-7770**

Berry Creek
Lake Oroville Bed & Breakfast
Set on 40 acres of trees and wildflowers, this enchanting B&B specializes in romantic getaways. There are a variety of attractive features including a sunroom with mountain views, a parlor with a fireplace and an expansive brick patio. All luxury guestrooms are equipped with private baths, five have whirlpool tubs. Not just a meal, breakfast here is an occasion, with guests being offered any number of homemade delights.

6 Rooms • Price range: $75-175
240 Sunday Dr, Berry Creek, CA 95916
☎ **(530) 589-0700**

Big Bear City
Gold Mountain Manor Bed & Breakfast

This 1928 restored mansion is Big Bear's only historic B&B inn. Located on one acre of pine trees and grassy land, it has six guestrooms, each with its own distinct qualities. For instance, the Bouquet Room features brightly colored stencils of jasmine, roses and tulips, while Bessie's Room has antique white wicker furniture. All rooms have private baths. A gourmet country breakfast is served and afternoon hors d'oeuvres are available.

6 Rooms • Price range: $135-200
1117 Anita, Big Bear City, CA 92314
☎ **(909) 585-6997**

Big Bear Lake
ⓐⓐ *Alpenhorn Bed & Breakfast*

Located on nearly two acres of landscaped pine forest in the heart of the City of Big Bear Lake, this B&B offers an atmosphere comparable to some of Europe's finest small inns. Each guestroom is individually decorated and includes a comfortable king or queen bed topped with a hypo-allergenic feather mattress. Each room also features a gas fireplace and private bath with a spa tub for two and separate shower. Other amenities include a full breakfast with a hot entrée, an evening turn-down service and a movie library that includes all the Academy Award Winners for Best Picture from 1939 to 1989!

7 Rooms • Price range: $149-231
601 Knight Ave, Big Bear Lake, CA 92315
☎ **(909) 866-5700**

Big Bear Lake
Apples Bed & Breakfast Inn

Set in the midst of pine trees, guests at this B&B can enjoy the crisp mountain air of Big Bear Lake. Each of the guestrooms is furnished with a king-size bed and private bath, some with Jacuzzi tubs. Also featured is an outdoor hot tub and a specialized court for basketball or volleyball. In addition to breakfast, guests are invited to enjoy sparkling cider and cheese in the afternoon and dessert with coffee or tea in the evening.

12 Rooms • Price range: $130-220
42430 Moonridge Rd, PO Box 7172,
Big Bear Lake, CA 92315-7172
☎ **(909) 866-0903**

Big Bear Lake
Switzerland Haus Bed & Breakfast Inn

Situated at the foot of the most popular ski and mountain-bike resort in Southern California, this B&B is a short distance from powdery slopes and back trails. The Swiss-style inn has five comfortable guestrooms, including a master suite that features a huge stone fireplace, a king-size bed and a private deck. All guestrooms include a private bath and a TV/VCR. A full breakfast is served daily, as are afternoon refreshments.

5 Rooms • Price range: $140-200
41829 Switzerland Dr, Big Bear Lake, CA 92315
☎ **(909) 866-3729**

Big Bear Lake
Truffles Bed & Breakfast

Located in the Moonridge area of Big Bear Lake, this B&B is less than a mile away from a number of attractions, including ski facilities, a nine-hole golf course and lake tours. The inn features traditional furnishings and includes a gathering room with a wood-burning stove and a video library. Guestrooms are decorated in English country-home style. Full breakfasts, afternoon appetizers and evening desserts are served.

5 Rooms • Price range: $138-168
43591 Bow Canyon Rd, Big Bear Lake, CA 92315
☎ **(909) 585-2772**

Big Bear Lake
Eagle's Nest Bed & Breakfast

This charming log cabin B&B is filled with country antiques. Guests may also choose from five cottage units, each equipped with a fireplace, microwave, refrigerator and coffee maker. For these guests, breakfast is available for an extra charge.

10 Rooms • Price range: $85-150
41675 Big Bear Blvd, Big Bear Lake, CA 92315
☎ **(909) 866-6465**

Bishop
Chalfant House Bed & Breakfast

Eight guestrooms are offered at this 1898 restored home. Surrounded by the eastern Sierra Nevada Mountains, the property is close to a theater, a park, gift shops and restaurants. It is also located just a short drive to lakes, streams and museums. Guests are invited to have a cup of hot cider or a frosty orange drink in the parlor before retiring to their rooms, each of which has a private bath and ceiling fan. A full breakfast is served daily.

8 Rooms • Price range: $50-95
213 Academy St, Bishop, CA 93514
☎ **(760) 872-1790**

Bishop
The Matlick House Bed & Breakfast

Built in 1906, this B&B has five charming rooms for guests.

5 Rooms • Price range: $65-85
1313 Rowan Ln, Bishop, CA 93515
☎ **(760) 873-3133**

Bridgeport
⑩ *The Cain House*

This historic Western home has been restored with elegance.

7 Rooms • Price range: $80-135
340 Main St, Bridgeport, CA 93517
☎ **(760) 932-7040**

◆ ◆ Calistoga
◆ ◆ **Foothill House Bed & Breakfast**
This 1892 farmhouse, surrounded by
trees and wildlife offers stunning views
of distant Mt. St. Helena. The spacious
guestrooms have been remodeled for
comfort and are decorated with country antiques.
The color scheme for each room is based on the
colors of the handmade quilts that adorn each
queen-size four-poster bed. Each room is
equipped with a private bath, a wood-burning
fireplace and its own individual entrance.
Breakfast consists of homemade bread and
muffins and is served in the sunroom or on
the terrace. In the afternoon, guests enjoy
wine and cheese, also served in the sunroom.

4 Rooms • Price range: $165-350
3037 Foothill Blvd, Calistoga, CA 94515
☎ **(707) 942-6933**

◆ ◆ Calistoga
◆ ◆ **Christopher's Inn**
This inn combines three Georgian-style
homes and boasts Laura Ashley interiors.

22 Rooms • Price range: $165-395
1010 Foothill Blvd, Calistoga, CA 94515
☎ **(707) 942-5755**

◆ ◆ Cambria
◆ ◆ ⍟ **Blue Whale Inn Bed & Breakfast**
Perched prettily on the green bluffs
of Cambria overlooking the Pacific
Ocean, this B&B mixes a European
Country-style decor with an array of
modern amenities. Cozy mini-suites feature
fireplaces and canopy beds, which are draped
in French and English country fabrics. Each
room also has an armoire, a writing desk,
an oversize dressing room and a tiled bath.
A impressive country breakfast is served in
the dining room. Afternoon tea is served in
the gathering room. There are many nearby local
attractions for guests to explore, including the
legendary Hearst Castle.

6 Rooms • Price range: $210-250
6736 Moonstone Beach Dr, Cambria, CA 93428
☎ **(805) 927-4647**

◆
◆ ◆ Cambria
◆ ⍟ **The J. Patrick House Bed & Breakfast Inn**
The first thing guests will notice on
entering this charming log home is the
smell of homemade goodies such as
cookies, breads and muffins. Not surprisingly, breakfast is a real treat, often including inn specialties such as apple pie bread pudding or blintzes with olallieberry jam. Eight
guestrooms are situated in the main house and
the Carriage House, each one featuring a wood-
burning fireplace and a private bath.

8 Rooms • Price range: $135-200
2990 Burton Dr, Cambria, CA 93428
☎ **(805) 927-3812**

Cambria
Olallieberry Inn

In keeping with their motto, "Where Time Stands Still," the owners of this 1873 restored Greek-Revival house don't even wind their antique clocks. The inn is within walking distance of a number of attractions, including galleries and restaurants. Nine guestrooms are offered, all with private baths. Six rooms have a fireplace. Breakfast may include Alaskan sourdough pancakes or fresh fruit crepes.

9 Rooms • Price range: $100-215
2476 Main St, Cambria, CA 93428
☎ **(805) 927-3222**

Cambria
The Squibb House Bed & Breakfast

This well-preserved 1877 historical house recalls a simpler era. Many furnishings were patterned after original features in the house, which was partially restored in 1993. Guests are invited to relax in the main parlor or stroll through the garden and visit the gazebo. All guestrooms feature private baths and gas fireplaces. A continental breakfast is served. Local attractions include Hearst Castle and whale watching.

5 Rooms • Price range: $95-155
4063 Burton Dr, Cambria, CA 93428
☎ **(805) 927-9600**

Capitola
⑩ Inn at Depot Hill

This turn-of-the-20th century railroad depot has been transformed into a seaside inn with a variety of amenities.
Overlooking Capitola-by-the-Sea, the inn is just a short walk from shops, restaurants and galleries and is also close to Monterey Bay. Each of the guestrooms has been painstakingly redecorated by San Francisco designer Linda A. Floyd. Each features private entrances and gardens, fireplaces, built-in stereo systems, and private white marble baths. The inn also has a formal garden and patio where morning coffee and afternoon tea are served. Guests can also enjoy full, daily breakfast in the elegant dining room.

12 Rooms • Price range: $235-325
250 Monterey Ave,
Capitola-by-the-Sea, CA 95010
☎ **(831) 462-3376**

Carlsbad
Pelican Cove Inn

Only 200 yards from the ocean, this inn is a gateway to uncrowded beaches. Surrounded by gardens of flowers, the inn boasts small romantic rooms, all with individual baths, fireplaces and optional Scandia feather beds. Some rooms have a spa tub. You may eat your breakfast in your room or on the garden patio or sunporch. Beach chairs, towels and picnic baskets are made available to guests on request.

8 Rooms • Price range: $90-180
320 Walnut Ave, Carlsbad, CA 92008
☎ **(760) 434-5995**

Carmel
Sandpiper Inn by the Sea
This 1929 California-style inn is enhanced by award-winning gardens. With no TV or telephone to intrude, guests can hear the crashing of the surf only a half block away. Rooms are decorated with antiques, original paintings and fresh flowers. Some rooms offer fireplaces and ocean views, while all are equipped with private baths. Common areas include a lounge with a stone fireplace where a buffet breakfast is served.

16 Rooms • Price range: $105-285
2408 Bay View Ave, Carmel, CA 93923
☎ **(831) 624-6433**

Carmel
Green Lantern Inn Bed & Breakfast
Here guests get a view of landscaped grounds from their terraced rooms.

18 Rooms • Price range: $129-209
PO Box 1114, Carmel, CA 93921
☎ **(831) 624-4392**

Carmel Valley
⑩ Acacia Lodge-Country Garden Inns
Landscaped grounds, views of mountains and a patio for guests to enjoy.

19 Rooms • Price range: $143-221
20 Via Contenta, Carmel Valley, CA 93924
☎ **(831) 659-2297**

Carmel-by-the-Sea
⑩ Carriage House Inn
Spacious, tastefully custom-decorated rooms await guests at this inn. They feature wood-burning fireplaces, window seats and king-size beds with down comforters. Many rooms have whirlpools and cathedral ceilings. Each morning, guests can expect the morning paper and an expanded continental breakfast, which may include pastries, fruit, granola and juice, delivered to their door. Complimentary hors d'oeuvres and wine and port are served in the library. Carmel is a charming European-style town that boasts more than 150 shops, 90 galleries and 60 restaurants.

13 Rooms • Price range: $279-325
PO Box 1900, Carmel-by-the-Sea, CA 93921
☎ **(831) 625-2585**

Carmel-by-the-Sea
⑩ Briarwood Inn
This inn offers rooms with working fireplaces as well as wet bars.

12 Rooms • Price range: $150-295
PO Box 5245, Carmel-by-the-Sea, CA 93921
☎ **(831) 626-9056**

Carmel-by-the-Sea
Carmel Country Inn
This property is comprised of large suites, which all have wet bars.

12 Rooms • Price range: $115-205
PO Box 3756, Carmel-by-the-Sea, CA 93921
☎ **(831) 625-3263**

Carmel-by-the-Sea
Carmel Garden Court

Oak trees, bougainvillaea and splashing fountains add to the color and sound of this inn's award-winning garden. Guestrooms offer a variety of amenities including fireplaces, sitting areas and private enclosed patios. Each morning, an extended champagne-continental breakfast is served either in-room, in the garden, or in the inn's cozy lobby where guests are invited to enjoy port and sherry in the afternoon.

10 Rooms • Price range: $150-265
PO Box 6226, Carmel-by-the-Sea, CA 93921
☎ (831) 624-6926

Carmel-by-the-Sea
Cobblestone Inn

Beautiful flowering gardens, white sandy beaches and quaint cottages provide the backdrop for this inn. Stone from the Carmel River provides the flooring for the lower level of the inn and also surrounds the fireplaces in the guestrooms. The work of local artists decorates guestrooms, which feature king- or queen-size beds and refrigerators. Breakfast is served on the patio or in the dining room.

24 Rooms • Price range: $115-240
PO Box 3185, Carmel-by-the-Sea, CA 93921
☎ (831) 625-5222

Carmel-by-the-Sea
Crystal Terrace Inn Bed & Breakfast

One of Carmel's landmark inns, this 1927 property has recently been remodeled for further comfort. Modern amenities such as micro-ovens, wet bars and color TVs are featured in some guestrooms. All rooms come with king- or queen-size beds; rooms with king-size beds have a fireplace. A healthy buffet breakfast is served every morning. Afternoon refreshments, including wine, champagne and cheese, are served in the lobby.

17 Rooms • Price range: $95-275
24815 Carpenter St,
Carmel-by-the-Sea, CA 93921
☎ (831) 624-6400

Carmel-by-the-Sea
Sunset House

Located on a quiet residential street a short walk from the beach, this B&B offers guests a first-class seaside getaway. Each guestroom has its own special charm: The South Room has a fireplace and a hand-forged iron California king bed; the North Room has a cozy sitting area and a Hans Christian Anderson king-size bed. All rooms have private baths and refrigerators. An in-room breakfast is served daily.

4 Rooms • Price range: $210-230
PO Box 1925, Carmel-by-the-Sea, CA 93921
☎ (831) 624-4884

Carmel-by-the-Sea
Carmel Wayfarer Inn

This country inn was built in 1929 and is only a short walk to the beach.

17 Rooms • Price range: $125-189
PO Box 1896, Carmel-by-the-Sea, CA 93921
☎ (831) 624-2711

Carpinteria
Prufrock's Garden Inn
This restored 1904 California cottage-style house is only blocks from the beach.

7 Rooms • Price range: $99-259
600 Linden Ave, Carpinteria, CA 93013
☎ **(805) 566-9696**

Chester
⊕ The Bidwell House
This renovated farmhouse sits at the edge of Chester near Lake Almanor.

14 Rooms • Price range: $85-175
1 Main St, Chester, CA 96020
☎ **(530) 258-3338**

Chico
Johnson's Country Inn
Modeled after a Victorian-style farm-house and surrounded by almond tree orchards and flower gardens, this inn is the picture of tranquillity. Each of the four distinctive guestrooms includes a private bath, one has a fireplace and a Jacuzzi. The inn's parlor, with its bay window, looks out over the garden. Coffee is delivered to your door every morning before a gourmet breakfast is served in the dining room.

4 Rooms • Price range: $80-125
3935 Morehead Ave, Chico, CA 95928
☎ **(530) 345-7829**

Chico
Music Express Inn
Bidwell Park, the fourth-largest city park in the country, is just a stroll away from this inn. Other nearby attractions include museum tours and golf. Closer to home, guests can wander in the grounds, play a game of cards or relax in one of the nine well-appointed guestrooms, all of which are equipped with private baths, some with Jacuzzi tubs. A generous breakfast is served daily in the dining room.

9 Rooms • Price range: $60-125
1091 El Monte Ave, Chico, CA 95928
☎ **(530) 345-8376**

Columbia
Columbia City Hotel
This authentically restored hotel of the Gold Rush era was built in 1856.

10 Rooms • Price range: $90-115
Main St, Columbia, CA 95310
☎ **(209) 532-1479**

Columbia
Fallon Hotel
This 1857 Victorian hotel has been restored to its original glory.

14 Rooms • Price range: $60-115
11175 Washington St, Columbia, CA 95310
☎ **(209) 532-1470**

Dana Point
Blue Lantern Inn

The Pacific Ocean gleams through almost every window at this inn. Located on a bluff overlooking the Dana Point Yacht Harbor, the inn has 29 guestrooms, each with a fireplace, a sitting area and an oversize bathroom with a spa tub. Deluxe rooms come with a private deck. In the morning, coffee and the day's newspaper are delivered to your door. You can then choose to sit at a table by a window and enjoy a delicious breakfast featuring fresh fruit, homemade breads and a main course. A fitness center and complimentary bicycles for exploring the coast are available.

29 Rooms • Price range: $150-500
34343 Street of Blue Lantern, Dana Point, CA 92629
☎ **(949) 661-1304**

Elk
Elk Cove Inn

Perched on a bluff overlooking the Mendocino coastline this charming B&B is surrounded by gardens and boasts sweeping ocean views. Originally built in 1883 as a lumber company guest house, it became the first inn of its kind on the northern coast in 1968. In addition to the lovely rooms in the main house there are also oceanfront spa suites. A friendly welcome includes a wine and fruit gift basket presented upon arrival.

15 Rooms • Price range: $148-318
6300 S Hwy 1, Elk, CA 95432
☎ **(707) 877-3321**

Encinitas
Seabreeze Bed & Breakfast Inn

An attractive and modern two-story inn just three blocks away from Moonlight Beach, this establishment is close to a number of other attractions, including the Quail Botanical Gardens and Ecke Poinsettia Ranch. Four guestrooms and one private apartment are available.All have private entrances and baths.

5 Rooms • Price range: $79-160
121 N Vulcan Ave, Encinitas, CA 92024
☎ **(760) 944-0318**

Escondido
Zosa Gardens Bed & Breakfast

This secluded Spanish hacienda on 22 acres of landscaped property stands on a plateau in the mountains of north San Diego. Abundant vegetation grows on the grounds, including guava, citrus and avocado trees. Guests are welcome to take a stroll through the organic gardens or walk to a pond swimming with koi fish. Guestrooms are spacious; a master suite has a fireplace and a private balcony. A breakfast buffet is served.

9 Rooms • Price range: $120-250
9381 W Lilac Rd, Escondido, CA 92026
☎ **(760) 723-9093**

Eureca
Eureka
 ⊕ *Abigail's Elegant Victorian Mansion Bed & Breakfast Inn*

This 1888 award-winning National Historic Landmark features delightful gingerbread exteriors, Victorian interiors and antique furnishings. The restored mansion offers a non-smoking environment in guestrooms. Rooms feature period furnishings, queen-size beds, desks and sitting areas. Some rooms overlook Humboldt Bay and Samoa Peninsula. French gourmet breakfast is served.

4 Rooms • Price range: $79-245
1406 C St, Eureka, CA 95501
☎ **(707) 444-3144**

Eureka
Cornelius Daly Inn, Bed & Breakfast

This 1905 Colonial-Revival home has been restored to its original elegance, while modern amenities have been added. Guestrooms are furnished with fine antiques and feature a range of comforts, including a fireplace and a sitting room. A morning meal is served in the breakfast parlor, on the garden patio or in the dining room. Guests are invited to relax on the wicker rockers, which sit on the porch overlooking the garden.

5 Rooms • Price range: $75-150
1125 H St, Eureka, CA 95501
☎ **(707) 445-3638**

Fawnskin
The Inn at Fawnskin Bed & Breakfast

This two-story log home is surrounded by pine trees at the edge of the lake. It features a knotty-pine interior with country decor. Guestrooms are comfortably furnished. Large stone fireplaces are found in the master suite and common areas.

4 Rooms • Price range: $62-175
880 Canyon Rd, Fawnskin, CA 92333
☎ **(909) 866-3200**

Ferndale
⊕ *Gingerbread Mansion*

This 1899 Victorian mansion is decorated in Queen Anne and Eastlake styles. The work of trompe l'oeil artist Peri Pfenninger is evident throughout the inn and to stunning effect. There are four parlors, each offering a tea service in the afternoon. The elegant dining room boasts a wonderful view of the English garden. There are 11 guestrooms, each with a Victorian bathing area, some with fireplaces, stained-glass windows or claw-foot tubs. An assorted variety of wonderful home-baked goods accompanies afternoon tea and a generous full breakfast is served daily.

11 Rooms • Price range: $120-385
400 Berding St, Ferndale, CA 95536
☎ **(707) 786-4000**

Ferndale
Shaw House Bed & Breakfast Inn

This remarkable 1854 Carpenter Gothic-Revival home is encircled by an acre of the most enchanting gardens. Each room has its own special features, such as bay windows, balconies and vaulted or gabled ceilings.

8 Rooms • Price range: $85-185
703 Main St, Ferndale, CA 95536
☎ **(707) 786-9958**

Ferndale
Victorian Inn

Ferndale is famous for its immaculately preserved Victorian homes and buildings and this 1890 inn, constructed entirely out of redwood, is definitely one of its gems. Every room features period furnishings, architectural details such as bay windows or turret sitting areas, and private baths with claw-foot tubs and pedestal sinks. Curley's restaurant and tavern on the main floor offers fine dining in a casual environment.

12 Rooms • Price range: $85-175
400 Ocean Ave, Ferndale, CA 95536
☎ **(707) 786-4949**

Fort Bragg
⚌ *The Grey Whale Inn*

This 1915 four-story redwood building was originally a hospital. Since 1976 it has been offering guest accommodations. Fourteen spacious guestrooms feature a variety of amenities, including an ocean view, a fireplace, an interior patio, a private deck or a whirlpool tub. Some rooms have wheelchair access; all have private baths. A complimentary buffet breakfast may include homemade coffee bread or casserole.

14 Rooms • Price range: $100-220
615 N Main St, Fort Bragg, CA 95437
☎ **(707) 964-0640**

Fort Bragg
⚌ *The Lodge At Noyo River*

In 1868 Scandinavian shipbuilders were used to construct the original house which was later expanded in the early 1900s. Heartwood fir and redwood were used in the expansion. The lodge has spacious common rooms, private decks and two acres of water-front property overlooking a thriving fishing village harbor. Wander down to the docks and restaurants to watch the fishing boats, sea lions and harbor life.

16 Rooms • Price range: $115-175
500 Casa del Noyo Dr, Fort Bragg, CA 95437
☎ **(707) 964-8045**

Fort Bragg
⚌ *The Weller House Inn*

Listed on the National Register of Historic Places and opened in 1998 by the new owners, this grand 1886 mansion has some very unique features including a 900-square-foot, redwood paneled, ballroom, where breakfast is served and a historic water tower/ observation deck behind the house. Rooms are individually decorated with antiques and homemade quilts. The innkeeper's love for the house is evident everywhere.

8 Rooms • Price range: $95-185
524 Stewart St, Fort Bragg, CA 95437
☎ **(707) 964-4415**

Fort Bragg
Country Inn Bed & Breakfast

This 1890s home has been renovated and decorated in Country-style decor.

8 Rooms • Price range: $89-139
632 N Main St, Fort Bragg, CA 95437
☎ **(707) 964-3737**

Fort Bragg
♦♦ *Old Stewart House Inn*
Call for information.

6 Rooms • Price range: $80-125
511 Stewart St, Fort Bragg, CA 95437
☎ **(707) 961-0775**

Garberville
♦♦
♦♦ *Benbow Inn*
This 1926 English Tudor-style inn has hosted many of the Hollywood elite, including Spencer Tracy and Clark Gable. Listed on the National Register of Historic Places, the inn offers 55 guestrooms, each decorated with antique furniture and fine prints. Terrace bedrooms feature private patios. In their rooms, guests will find a basket of mystery novels and poetry, a decanter of sherry, and coffee and tea. The inn's dining room is open daily for breakfast and dinner. On weekends, musicians help make dining a lively experience.

55 Rooms • Price range: $115-250
445 Lake Benbow Dr, Garberville, CA 95542
☎ **(707) 923-2124**

Geyserville
♦♦ *Hope-Merrill House*
Built in the late 1800s, this Victorian home has four units across the street.

12 Rooms • Price range: $102-215
21253 Geyserville Ave, Geyserville, CA 95441
☎ **(707) 857-3356**

Glen Ellen
♦♦ *Gaige House Inn*
Guests at this exceptional inn may be tempted to take up permanent residence. Set next to a forest stream, in seductively tranquil environs, the inn has been decorated in a discretely luxurious fashion. One suite features a wall of windows and a private deck overlooking the Calabazas Creek. Gourmet breakfasts, a heated pool, complimentary wines—the list of amenities is exhaustive. Heaven in the heart of Wine Country.

15 Rooms • Price range: $150-495
13540 Arnold Dr, Glen Ellen, CA 95442
☎ **(707) 935-0237**

Grass Valley
♦♦ *Elam Biggs Bed & Breakfast*
This Queen Anne Victorian was built in 1892 by Elam Biggs, a successful Grass Valley merchant. Rooms range from cozy to spacious, all with private baths. A large yard is surrounded by tall shade trees and a rose-covered picket fence. Nearby are the Empire Mine and the Malakoff Diggins State Historic Parks, reminders of the early Gold Rush days. The inn is a fine setting for weddings.

4 Rooms • Price range: $80-120
220 Colfax Ave, Grass Valley, CA 95945
☎ **(530) 477-0906**

Grass Valley
Murphy's Inn
Charming 1866 Victorian home with lovely gardens and quaint period decor.

8 Rooms • Price range: $125-175
318 Neal St, Grass Valley, CA 95945
☎ (530) 273-6873

Groveland
Groveland Hotel
This inn consists of a restored 1849 adobe and a 1914 Queen Anne hotel.

17 Rooms • Price range: $135-155
18767 Main St, Groveland, CA 95321
☎ (209) 962-4000

Gualala
North Coast Country Inn
Several rustic redwood cottages perched on a Mendocino coastline hillside make up the North Coast Country Inn. The beautifully landscaped property offers secluded corners: There's a gazebo in the upper garden and a hot tub under the trees. Accommodations include a kitchenette and a fireplace; all are furnished with antiques, and handmade quilts cover the comfortable beds. A peaceful, private hide-away.

6 Rooms • Price range: $175-195
34591 S Hwy 1, Gualala, CA 95445
☎ (707) 884-4537

Half Moon Bay
Mill Rose Inn, Spa & Garden Suites
Surrounded by lush, English-style gardens, this extensively renovated 1902 Victorian cottage offers a retreat for guests looking for peace. The inn is within walking distance of the ocean and the Old Town district of Half Moon Bay. Guestrooms feature European antiques, hand-painted fireplace tiles and sinks, claw-foot tubs and private entrances. An enclosed garden gazebo with a Jacuzzi is located in the inner courtyard and guests may reserve it for private use. Breakfasts are served in the dining room overlooking the rose gardens or they can be served in the privacy of your room.

6 Rooms • Price range: $222-361
615 Mill St, Half Moon Bay, CA 94019
☎ (650) 726-8750

Half Moon Bay
Cypress Inn on Miramar Beach
An in-house masseuse offers soothing massages to guests staying at the Cypress Inn. The inn boasts a colorful collection of native folk art and the guestrooms capture the feel of California beach-side living. All rooms have a view of the sea. There is a myriad of activities in the area, including sailing, whale watching, horseback riding and wine tasting. On weekends, jazz and classical music performances are steps away.

12 Rooms • Price range: $220-358
407 Mirada Rd, Half Moon Bay, CA 94019
☎ (650) 726-6002

Half Moon Bay
Landis Shores

This inn is ideal for business or pleasure. Located only only 30 minutes from San Francisco and Silicon Valley, the inn sits on the rocky shore of Miramar Beach, enjoying an unobstructed ocean view. Pleasantly decorated guestrooms have whirlpool tubs, fireplaces, refrigerators and private decks. Wake up to a gourmet breakfast. Afterward, spend a relaxing morning on the secluded beach, then head off for a late afternoon wine-tasting.

8 Rooms • Price range: $275-345
211 Mirada Rd, Half Moon Bay, CA 94019
☎ **(650) 726-6642**

Half Moon Bay
Old Thyme Inn

A fragrant English herb garden adds a touch of tranquillity to this charming 1899 Queen Anne-style Victorian. Tastefully decorated guestrooms are appointed with hypo-allergenic feather beds and quality linens. Although only some of the rooms have fireplaces and whirlpool tubs, all of them exude the same captivating charm. The inn is just a short walk from the beach and all its attendant pleasures.

7 Rooms • Price range: $130-290
779 Main St, Half Moon Bay, CA 94019
☎ **(650) 726-1616**

Hanford
Irwin Street Inn

Call for information.

30 Rooms • Price range: $69-89
522 N Irwin St, Hanford, CA 93230
☎ **(559) 583-8000**

Healdsburg
⏀ *The Honor Mansion*

This gracious 1883 Italianate-Victorian mansion sits in a quiet residential neighborhood beneath a century-old magnolia tree. The inn is exquisitely decorated with period antiques and hand-painted murals. Guestrooms feature feather beds topped by down comforters. The grounds have been beautifully landscaped: They include gardens, paths, a fountain and koi pond, and a lap pool for those who feel energetic. The separate Squire's Cottage offers accommodations just a stone's throw away on the other side of the pond; it includes a fireplace, a private deck and a well-stocked video library.

9 Rooms • Price range: $180-350
14891 Grove St, Healdsburg, CA 95448
☎ **(707) 433-4277**

Healdsburg

The Grape Leaf Inn
Call for information.

7 Rooms • Price range: $125-250
539 Johnson St, Healdsburg, CA 95448
☎ **(707) 433-8140**

Homeland
Pierson's Country Place
This spacious Mediterranean-style steel-framed home is located just

minutes away from the vineyards of Temecula and the mountains towering above Hemet. Guestrooms are distinctively furnished and three have private balconies that boast magnificent sunset views. Guests are invited to enjoy the inn's outdoor spa and to explore the five-acre property. Complimentary champagne is offered to guests on weekends.

5 Rooms • Price range: $125-125
25185 Pierson Rd, Homeland, CA 92548
☎ **(909) 926-4546**

Hopland
⑭ Thatcher Inn
One of the highlights of this lovely restored 1890s Victorian country inn is the wood-paneled library with its extensive collection of books, cozy seating

and working fireplace. The inn also features a private bar and a landscaped pool patio.

20 Rooms • Price range: $115-175
13401 S Hwy 101, Hopland, CA 95449
☎ **(707) 744-1890**

Idyllwild
Creekstone Inn Bed & Breakfast
This B&B has antiques, fireplaces and whirlpool tubs.

9 Rooms • Price range: $105-155
54950 Pine Crest Ave, Idyllwild, CA 92549
☎ **(909) 659-3342**

Idyllwild
⑭ Strawberry Creek Inn
Located in the San Jacinto Mountains, this large house, with its cedar-shingled exterior, looks completely at home

amid the surrounding pines and oaks. The main building is made up of four adjacent rooms, each with a fireplace and skylight. The inn also has an enchanting cottage with kitchen, fireplace and whirlpool tub—a perfect honeymoon retreat. Full breakfasts are served each morning on the glassed-in porch.

10 Rooms • Price range: $89-115
26370 SR 243, Idyllwild, CA 92549
☎ **(909) 659-3202**

Jackson
Gate House Inn

This Victorian home is set on a hillside surrounded by lovely gardens and a bucolic landscape. Listed on the National Register of Historic Places, the inn features large rooms, high ceilings, private baths and fireplaces. Guests can visit local wineries and sites related to the area's mining history. In the winter, the inn lies above the fog and below the snow. Many national parks and lakes are close by for summer enjoyment.

5 Rooms • Price range: $115-200
1330 Jackson Gate Rd, Jackson, CA 95642
☎ **(209) 223-3500**

Jackson
ⓦ *The Wedgewood Inn*

This quaint Queen Anne-style Victorian replica is furnished in European and American antiques and memorabilia. A Carriage House suite is also available. The grounds are landscaped in English country style. Walking paths lead through a rose arbor to a gazebo. The inn provides a base for exploring Amador County, which has a rich mining history, and the innkeeper is an expert on the subject of gold prospecting.

6 Rooms • Price range: $100-150
11941 Narcissus Rd, Jackson, CA 95642
☎ **(209) 296-4300**

Jamestown
Jamestown Hotel

Dubbed a "Gold Rush treasure since 1858," this B&B has guestrooms named for some of that era's most famous women, such as Lotta Crabtree or Calamity Jane. Each room is individually decorated with old-fashioned furnishings. All of them have private baths—some with antique claw-foot bathtubs, others with whirlpool tubs. Both the Jamestown Hotel Café and the Patio offer first-class California cuisine.

11 Rooms • Price range: $80-135
18153 Main St, Jamestown, CA 95327
☎ **(209) 984-3902**

Jamestown
Palm Hotel Bed & Breakfast

Used for many years as a rooming house for railroad and mining men, this 100-year-old Victorian mansion is located just off historic Main Street. While retaining the grace of its Victorian past, the inn now offers the added comforts of modern amenities. The spacious rooms are light and airy, and are equipped with private baths featuring claw-foot tubs. A homemade breakfast is served at the old marble soda fountain bar.

8 Rooms • Price range: $95-165
10382 Willow St, Jamestown, CA 95327
☎ **(209) 984-3429**

Jamestown
1859 Historic National Hotel, A Country Inn
Call for information.

9 Rooms • Price range: $80-120
18183 Main St, Jamestown, CA 95327
☎ **(209) 984-3446**

Julian
❖❖ ⊕ *Orchard Hill Country Inn*

Native stone from nearby Borrego Springs was used extensively when building this inn. Comprised of a lodge and five California Craftsman-style cottages, the deluxe hostelry has spacious rooms, all of which have been individually decorated using American Country-style decor. Many of them have fireplaces and private verandas. The inn is set in a landscaped four-acre oasis abounding with many varieties of plants; guests are welcome to use the picnic areas.

22 Rooms • Price range: $190-260
2502 Washington St, Julian, CA 92036
☎ **(760) 765-1700**

Julian
❖❖ ⊕ *Butterfield Bed & Breakfast*
Set on a tree-shaded hillside, this charming inn has comfortable rooms.

5 Rooms • Price range: $125-180
2284 Sunset Dr, Julian, CA 92036
☎ **(760) 765-2179**

Julian
❖❖ ⊕ *Homestead Bed & Breakfast*

The historic town of Julian is known for its apples and gold, and is located just one hour from San Diego. The B&B is an attractive mountain home that has been built in a quiet forest spot not far from town. The large gathering room houses a two-story stone fireplace and a game table and provides a 270-degree view of tranquil splendor. All the rooms feature king-size beds, hand-made quilts, Victorian antiques and private baths.

4 Rooms • Price range: $100-150
4924 Hwy 79, Julian, CA 92036
☎ **(760) 765-1536**

Julian
❖❖ ⊕ *The Julian White House Bed & Breakfast Inn*

Although this demure southern Colonial mansion is located in a forested mountain area, it is only five minutes from the center of this historic gold-mining town. The spacious parlor area and guestrooms are individually decorated with antiques and Victorian items, and each room is equipped with a private bath. The inn also features a rose garden with an outdoor spa. A full, candlelight breakfast is served each morning.

5 Rooms • Price range: $130-195
3014 Blue Jay Dr, Julian, CA 92036
☎ **(760) 765-1764**

Julian
❖❖ ⊕ *LeeLin Wikiup Bed & Breakfast*

Some of the guestrooms here have whirlpool tubs and/or fireplaces.

5 Rooms ◦ Price range: $150-175
1645 Whispering Pines Dr, Julian, CA 92036
☎ **(760) 765-1890**

Julian

◆◆ 🏨 *Julian Gold Rush Hotel Bed & Breakfast*
Built in 1897, this historic hotel has
Victorian decor and small rooms.

15 Rooms • Price range: $58-135
2032 Main St, Julian, CA 92036
☎ (760) 765-0201

Kernville
◆ ◆ 🏨 *Kern River Inn Bed & Breakfast*

This inn stands directly across
from Riverside Park and overlooks
wild and scenic Kern River. Some of
the comfortable, individually decorated
units include wood-burning fireplaces and
whirlpool tubs. The inn, which is decorated
with artwork by local artists, features a wide,
furnished veranda. Nearby activities include
white-water rafting, kayaking, fishing, golf,
and gold panning.

6 Rooms • Price range: $89-109
119 Kern River Dr, Kernville, CA 93238
☎ (760) 376-6750

La Quinta
◆◆ *Two Angels Inn*

Reminiscent of an old French
château, this desert resort is surrounded by beautifully landscaped
gardens and trees, framed by the
imposing Santa Rosa Mountains on one side
and tranquil Lake La Quinta on the other.
Each guestroom is individually decorated
with a fireplace and a patio or a balcony
overlooking the lake. Two rooms are situated
in a separate boathouse and feature the
luxury of outdoor hot tubs. Guests can participate
in the area's many activities, including polo,
hiking, casino gambling, golf, tennis and
horse shows.

11 Rooms • Price range: $200-350
78-120 Caleo Bay, La Quinta, CA 92253
☎ (760) 564-7332

Laguna Beach
◆ ◆ *The Carriage House-Bed & Breakfast*

This 1920's designated landmark is
located in a peaceful village setting.
Each of the six individually decorated
suites includes a sitting room and a private bath. The inn also features a secluded brick
courtyard landscaped with a colorful garden and
fountain. Guests are welcomed to the inn with a
carafe of California wine and assorted goodies,
and a full, family-style breakfast is served in the
dining room each morning.

6 Rooms • Price range: $125-165
1322 Catalina St, Laguna Beach, CA 92651
☎ (949) 494-8945

Laguna Beach
◆◆ *Casa Laguna Inn*
The landscaped, terraced grounds of
this inn overlook the ocean.

21 Rooms • Price range: $125-295
2510 S Coast Hwy, Laguna Beach, CA 92651
☎ (949) 494-2996

Lake Arrowhead

Arrowhead Saddleback Inn
This completely restored landmark is surrounded by tall pines and cedars and overlooks Lake Arrowhead. Built in 1917, the inn is a combination of mountain, country and Victorian architecture. There are 34 guestrooms and cottages, each with queen- or king-size beds, stone fireplaces, double whirlpool baths and refrigerators. There is a full-service restaurant and bar, ideal for business meetings or weddings.

34 Rooms • Price range: $99-209
PO Box 1890, Lake Arrowhead, CA 92352
☎ (909) 336-3571

Lake Arrowhead

Bracken Fern Manor
This restored English Tudor-style inn provides a perfect mountain retreat for those who want a secluded holiday. Built in 1929, it offers 10 individually styled guestrooms, each furnished with antiques from around the world. All rooms have private baths. Guests are invited to relax in the backyard hammock under the shade of the dogwoods or sip a glass of wine in front of the fireplace in the parlor.

9 Rooms • Price range: $65-185
815 Arrowhead Villas Rd, Lake Arrowhead, CA 92352
☎ (909) 337-8557

Lake Arrowhead

Chateau du Lac Bed & Breakfast Inn
Perched high on a hill above Lake Arrowhead this appropriately named inn towers over the surrounding landscape. The five enormous guestrooms are very comfortably appointed; three of them feature vaulted beamed ceilings and little extras such as a working fireplace or a private deck. Spectacular views of the lake can be caught at every turn especially from the dining room and the gazebo.

5 Rooms • Price range: $137-248
911 Hospital Rd, Lake Arrowhead, CA 92352
☎ (909) 337-6488

Lakeport

Forbestown Inn
Beautiful little Victorian clapboard farmhouse with a secluded garden pool.

4 Rooms • Price range: $105-115
825 Forbes St, Lakeport, CA 95453
☎ (707) 263-7858

Lemon Cove

Plantation Bed & Breakfast
The Plantation B&B nestles comfortably in the foothills of the Sierra Nevada Mountains in the small citrus community of Lemon Cove. Fruit trees of all kinds grow on the grounds; a Jacuzzi has even been set up in the orange grove. The comfortable guestrooms offer complete privacy and comfort with such extras as sitting areas and terraces. Breakfasts are a feast of fruit fresh from the trees on the property.

8 Rooms • Price range: $69-189
33038 Sierra Hwy 198, Lemon Cove, CA 93244
☎ (559) 597-2555

Lewiston
Old Lewiston Inn
Comfortable rooms and country break-fasts at this inn on Trinity River.

6 Rooms • Price range: $75-95
Deadwood Rd, Lewiston, CA 96052
☎ (530) 778-3385

Little River
Heritage House
This inn is made up of an 1877 farm-house, a historic water tower and numer-ous cottages on 37 acres of landscaped and forested grounds overlooking the

ocean. Many of the spacious suites have fireplaces or wood-burning stoves and awe-inspiring views.

66 Rooms • Price range: $150-375
5200 N Hwy 1, Little River, CA 95456
☎ (707) 937-5885

Lockeford
The Inn at Locke House
Built by Dr. Dean Locke over a period of 27 years for his family and medical practice as they expanded, the 1865 home and water tower are on the National Register of Historic Places. Rustic country decor and modern amenities preserve the past while ensuring comfort. The water tower is an enchanting two-story suite with a private rooftop deck. All rooms offer pleasing views of the lovely gardens and countryside.

5 Rooms • Price range: $115-165
19960 Elliott Rd, Lockeford, CA 95237
☎ (209) 727-5715

Lodi
Wine and Roses Country Inn
Built in 1902, this historic estate is located on five acres of pretty grounds.

10 Rooms • Price range: $94-185
2505 W Turner Rd, Lodi, CA 95242
☎ (209) 334-6988

Loleta
Southport Landing Bed & Breakfast Inn
This 1898 Colonial-Revival house over-looks Humboldt Bay Wildlife Refuge.

5 Rooms • Price range: $95-125
444 Phelan Rd, Loleta, CA 95551
☎ (707) 733-5915

Los Angeles
The Inn at 657
Set in an older neighborhood, this 1848 house has apartments with kitchens.

10 Rooms • Price range: $95-125
657 W 23rd St, Los Angeles, CA 90007
☎ (213) 741-2200

Los Olivos

⊕ *Fess Parker's Wine Country Inn & Spa*

This inn is located in Santa Ynez Valley in the heart of Santa Barbara wine country, surrounded by rolling hills and lush vineyards. There are plenty of entertaining things to do such as horseback riding, bicycling through town or taking a tour of the area's wineries. The inn will prepare gourmet picnic lunches on request. If relaxation is more of a priority, the inn's pool and spa will fit the bill nicely. Guests can also relax in front of the fireplace in the inn's lobby, sit on the veranda or relax in one of the 21 guestrooms, all of which feature wet bars and fireplaces.

21 Rooms • Price range: $180-450
2860 Grand Ave, Los Olivos, CA 93441
☎ **(805) 688-7788**

Mammoth Lakes

⊕ *Cinnamon Bear Inn Bed & Breakfast*

This inn's rooms come in a variety of styles and sizes; some have canopy beds.

22 Rooms • Price range: $79-129
113 Center St, Mammoth Lakes, CA 93546
☎ **(760) 934-2873**

Mammoth Lakes

Snow Goose Inn Bed & Breakfast

Comfortable inn with large gathering room with couches and TV.

19 Rooms • Price range: $78-158
57 Forest Trail, Mammoth Lakes, CA 93546
☎ **(760) 934-2660**

Mariposa

⊕ *Mariposa Hotel-Inn*

Located on the second floor of a classic 1901 Western-style general store in the center of town, this charming inn has very comfortable and nicely appointed guestrooms. All of them have been restored and updated with the addition of private modern baths. The delightful third-floor veranda is a wonderful place to relax over breakfast and watch the hummingbirds. Yosemite National Park is located nearby.

5 Rooms • Price range: $90-125
5029 Hwy 140, Mariposa, CA 95338
☎ **(209) 966-4676**

Mariposa

Little Valley Inn at the Creek

Tucked among the trees beside a meandering stream, the Little Valley Inn offers contemporary rooms with private entrances, a suite with a full kitchen and a private cabin. A tranquil hideaway near Yosemite National Park.

6 Rooms • Price range: $99-125
3483 Brooks Rd, Mariposa, CA 95338
☎ **(209) 742-6204**

McCloud
⚄ *McCloud Hotel Bed & Breakfast*

There are many pleasant places to relax at this 1916 property. The spacious lobby, with its fireplace and patina of aged pine, is an obvious choice. There are also four L-shaped suites, each with a whirlpool tub, a private bath with oversize shower and a sitting area. Another 14 guestrooms have queen, twin or high four-poster beds, a private bath and an antique vanity. A full breakfast is served daily. Afternoon tea is served on Saturday.

17 Rooms • Price range: $98-129
408 Main St, McCloud, CA 96057
☎ **(530) 964-2822**

McCloud
⚄ *McCloud River Inn Bed & Breakfast*

This 1900s Country-Victorian inn is conveniently located for both sporting and recreational activities. The athletic visitor can go hiking, mountain biking, skiing, fishing, boating or golfing—all close by. Sightseers will enjoy nearby art galleries, antique shops, museums and steam-train excursions. The inn provides sack lunches or picnic baskets on request. Guests can start the day with a home-cooked breakfast in the parlor.

5 Rooms • Price range: $85-96
325 Lawndale Ct, McCloud, CA 96057
☎ **(530) 964-2130**

Mendocino
Reed Manor

Guests will appreciate the special touches that make this inn such a standout. For instance, the inn's parlor includes an extensive collection of miniature classic cars, a collection of celebrity dolls and a number of wildlife sculptures. In addition, since the inn is set on a hill and overlooks the historic town of Mendocino, guestrooms that have a deck are provided with a telescope. Rooms also have king- or queen-size beds, fireplaces, large private bathrooms with whirlpools and small refrigerators. A continental breakfast is delivered to the guestrooms.

5 Rooms • Price range: $175-550
PO Box 127, Mendocino, CA 95460
☎ **(707) 937-5446**

Mendocino
Stevenswood Lodge

Nature lovers will appreciate the surroundings of this secluded lodge. Bordered on three sides by the 2,400-acre Van Damme State Park Forest, the inn provides guests with plenty to explore. Visitors can hike through lush Fern Canyon, jog the Pacific Beaches, bike across Mendocino's headlands or canoe Big River. Guestrooms include wood-burning fireplaces, queen-size beds, refrigerators and private baths. Visitors can also take advantage of the private canyon-rim spa pools. Every morning, there is a menu of delicious breakfast treats from which to choose.

10 Rooms • Price range: $125-250
8211 N Hwy 1, Mendocino, CA 95460
☎ **(707) 937-2810**

Mendocino
Agate Cove Inn

Its position on a bluff above the Pacific Ocean provides the Agate Inn's romantic cottages and 1860s farmhouse with unparalleled ocean views. Guestrooms feature king- or queen-size beds, fireplaces and private baths, some have spa tubs, soaking tubs or showers for two. A full country breakfast is served in the farmhouse with its breathtaking ocean view. Amenities include in-room sherry and morning papers.

10 Rooms • Price range: $119-269
11201 N Lansing St, Mendocino, CA 95460
☎ **(707) 937-0551**

Mendocino
Annie's Jughandle Beach Bed & Breakfast Inn

Still in touch with their Southern roots, the innkeepers of this 1880s Victorian farmhouse serve up Cajun cooking with a healthy dollop of Louisiana hospitality. The casually comfortable guestrooms feature queen-size beds and modern baths. Two suites and a loft are also available in the converted barn. The surrounding state reserve and private beach abounds with wildlife and breathtaking scenery.

7 Rooms • Price range: $109-229
Gibney Ln & Hwy 1, Mendocino, CA 95460
☎ **(707) 964-1415**

Mendocino
Glendeven Inn

Here is a tranquil inn composed of an 1867 New England Federal-style farmhouse, a converted barn, a rustic cottage, and a recently built annex. Most of the rooms have fireplaces and some have ocean vistas. Breakfast is served in the sunroom or in the rooms. The owners serve wine and hors d'oeuvres in the farmhouse living room every evening. Glendeven also houses a contemporary gallery, which exhibits the work of local artists.

10 Rooms • Price range: $110-210
8205 N Hwy 1, PO Box 214,
Mendocino, CA 95460
☎ **(707) 937-0083**

Mendocino
⚶ *Hill House Inn*

This charming New England-style inn is located on a bluff overlooking California's spectacular North Coast. It is surrounded by floral gardens, white beaches and abundant wildlife. Whale-watching, deep-sea fishing and canoe trips are easily arranged. Guests can have a meal in the inn's Ocean View Restaurant or relax in Spencer Lounge. Forty-four guestrooms are available, all with polished brass beds and private baths.

44 Rooms • Price range: $165-300
10701 Pallette Dr, Mendocino, CA 95460
☎ **(707) 937-0554**

Mendocino
⚜ *Joshua Grindle Inn*

Situated on two acres of land in historic Mendocino, this 1879 Victorian farmhouse features early American pieces and Shaker furniture. Guestrooms with private baths are found in the main house, the saltbox cottage or the historic water tower. Guests can relax in the parlor and enjoy the cream sherry, tea and fresh-baked sweets served daily. A full breakfast features scones, coffee cake or frittata.

10 Rooms • Price range: $140-235
44800 Little Lake Rd, Mendocino, CA 95460
☎ **(707) 937-4143**

Mendocino
Whitegate Inn

Lush, flower-filled gardens encircle this 1883 doctor's residence. Every room is sumptuously decorated with fine European antiques. All guestrooms feature feather beds, down comforters, fireplaces, private baths and garden or ocean views. Relax on the garden deck or explore the village shops and Mendocino coastline. The friendly staff are happy to help make dinner and activity arrangements.

6 Rooms • Price range: $159-299
499 Howard St, Mendocino, CA 95460
☎ **(707) 937-4892**

Mendocino
⚜ *Dennen's Victorian Farmhouse*

Captivating 1877 farmhouse with Victorian decor in a garden setting.

10 Rooms • Price range: $98-185
7001 N Hwy 1, Mendocino, CA 95460
☎ **(707) 937-0697**

Mendocino
The Headlands Inn

Beautifully remodeled, this 1868 Victorian, with a cottage, has fireplaces.

7 Rooms • Price range: $100-195
Albion & Howard Sts, Mendocino, CA 95460
☎ **(707) 937-4431**

Mendocino
⚜ *The Inn at Schoolhouse Creek*

A historic 1862 farmhouse set on eight landscaped acres that used to be part of a seaside ranch. Some of the accommodations are cottages; all guest quarters offer private baths, TV/VCR's, private entrances and fireplaces as well as an ocean view.

15 Rooms • Price range: $135-250
7051 N Hwy 1, Mendocino, CA 95460
☎ **(707) 937-5525**

Mendocino
John Dougherty House

Gardens highlight the saltbox, cottages and water tower of this 1867 property.

8 Rooms • Price range: $105-225
571 Ukiah St, Mendocino, CA 95460
☎ **(707) 937-5266**

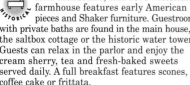

Mendocino
◆◆ *MacCallum House Inn*

A remarkable 1882 family home offering West-coast Victorian elegance at its finest. Every room is richly decorated in period antiques, some of which are original to the house. The popular restaurant and bar serves some the area's best cuisine.

19 Rooms • Price range: $100-190
45020 Albion St, Mendocino, CA 95460
☎ **(707) 937-0289**

Mendocino
◆◆ ⏝ *Rachel's Inn*

This 1860s farmhouse has rooms with fireplaces and balconies; one has a piano.

10 Rooms • Price range: $138-300
8200 N Hwy 1, Mendocino, CA 95460
☎ **(707) 937-0088**

Mendocino Village
◆◆◆ ⏝ *Mendocino Seaside Cottages*

This Victorian-style inn overlooking Headlands State Park boasts beautiful sunset and ocean views. The inn also features sundecks and balconies furnished with grills and lounge chairs. The choice of guestrooms includes a luxurious penthouse suite and suites that include a full kitchen and a working wood stove. A breakfast basket is delivered to each guest's door every morning.

4 Rooms • Price range: $157-300
10940 Lansing St, Mendocino Village, CA 95470
☎ **(707) 485-0239**

Mi-Wuk Village
◆◆ *Country Inn at Sugar Pine*

Call for information.

4 Rooms • Price range: $75-130
19958 Middle Camp, Mi-Wuk Village, CA 95346
☎ **(209) 586-4615**

Montara
◆◆ *Goose & Turrets Bed & Breakfast Inn*

Homey atmosphere in a quiet residential area. Afternoon tea is served.

5 Rooms • Price range: $120-170
835 George St, Montara, CA 94037-0937
☎ **(650) 728-5451**

Monterey
◆◆ ⏝ *Old Monterey Inn*

Once a home and now an inn, this 1929 half-timbered Tudor-style house has 10 guestrooms, each featuring stained-glass windows and skylights, and decorated with period furniture and feather beds tooped with fluffy goose-down comforters. The Garden Cottage has its own private entrance. Inside are linen-and-lace crown canopy beds, tiled fireplaces and white wicker-furnished sitting rooms. Hot beverages and freshly baked cookies are available throughout the day. A hot breakfast can be is served in-room, in the dining room or in the rose garden.

10 Rooms • Price range: $220-390
500 Martin St, Monterey, CA 93940
☎ **(831) 375-8284**

Morro Bay
Marina Street Inn

Guests of this inn have a number of activities to choose from to fill their days. Quiet walks on the beach, sight-seeing, antique shopping and sports such as kayaking or golf are all within reach from the conveniently located inn. The friendly innkeepers strive to create a relaxing and enjoyable environment. From the nicely appointed guestrooms to the spacious, comfortable common areas, the emphasis is on hospitality.

4 Rooms • Price range: $89-170
305 Marina St, Morro Bay, CA 93442
☎ **(805) 772-4016**

Moss Beach
Seal Cove Inn

Set amid wildflowers and bordered by towering cypress trees, Seal Cove Inn is an English-style manor house that looks out to the ocean across acres of country park. The inn is replete with country antiques, reproduction furniture, original water colors and fresh-cut flowers. Guestrooms include features such as wood-burning fireplaces, Jacuzzi tubs, grandfather clocks and French doors opening onto private terraces or balconies. Secluded beaches, tide pools and a tree-lined path along the windswept ocean bluffs contribute to the allure of the Seal Cove Inn.

10 Rooms • Price range: $200-280
221 Cypress Ave, Moss Beach, CA 94038
☎ **(650) 728-4114**

Mount Shasta
Strawberry Valley Inn

Located at the base of majestic Mt. Shasta, Strawberry Valley is a charming 15-room inn built in 1924 by the Italian stonemason Ben Hussing. There are seven suites, each with a separate living area, and some with a fireplace. Breathtaking views of Mt. Shasta are visible from the inn's private garden patio. Nearby, the Upper Sacramento River offers some of the state's best fly-fishing, as well as white-water rafting and kayaking.

15 Rooms • Price range: $58-87
1142 S Mt Shasta Blvd, Mount Shasta, CA 96067
☎ **(530) 926-2052**

Murphys
Dunbar House 1880

Set amid elms and pines in the heart of California's gold country, this 1880 Italianate home offers charming accommodations. Guestrooms feature antiques, down comforters and pillows, a Norwegian gas-burning stove and a refrigerator stocked with a complimentary bottle of local wine. The inn has a large porch for guests to relax on, as well as an attractively landscaped garden. An equestrian taxi service is available.

5 Rooms • Price range: $140-205
271 Jones St, Murphys, CA 95247
☎ **(209) 728-2897**

Myers Flat
✦✦ ⚕ *Myers Inn*

Originally built as a stagecoach stop, this 1867 inn lies in the heart of Redwood country. Avenue of Giants hiking trails are within walking distance. The rooms are furnished with family heirlooms and wicker.

10 Rooms • Price range: $95-195
12913 Avenue of the Giants, Myers Flat, CA 95554
☎ **(707) 943-3259**

Napa
✦✦ ⚕ *The 1801 Inn*

This 1903 Queen Anne Shingle-style house offers an elegant setting.

8 Rooms • Price range: $150-295
1801 First St, Napa, CA 94559
☎ **(707) 224-3739**

Napa
✦✦ ⚕ *Cedar Gables Inn*

The innkeepers here guarantee warm hospitality in luxurious surroundings. Designed by English architect Ernest Coxhead in 1892, the grand country cottage offers deluxe accommodations in a European-style setting. Some of the six guestrooms are furnished with ornate walnut or oak antique beds, most have fireplaces and all have modern baths. Wine and cheese are served every evening in the stately main parlor.

6 Rooms • Price range: $179-299
486 Coombs St, Napa, CA 94559
☎ **(707) 224-7969**

Napa
✦✦ ⚕ *Stahlecker House*

One-and-a-half acres of beautiful flower gardens and manicured lawns surround this sprawling 1940s bungalow. Each of the cozy guestrooms has different features such as spas, fireplaces, window seats or private patios, and all have private baths. A large sundeck is available for guests to enjoy. A delicious breakfast is served every morning by candlelight; other tasty refreshments are always on hand.

4 Rooms • Price range: $1533-298
1042 Easum Dr, Napa, CA 94558
☎ **(707) 257-1588**

Nevada City
✦✦ *Deer Creek Inn*

Deer Creek was famous during Gold Rush days as a "pound-a-day" creek, a term which referred to the amount of gold a miner could expect to pan. The Deer Creek Inn, a three-story Queen Anne Victorian, sits at the edge of this tree-lined creek amid tiered rose gardens. Guestrooms are attractively appointed with period furniture. Some have a private patio or veranda overlooking the grounds and creek.

5 Rooms • Price range: $105-165
116 Nevada St, Nevada City, CA 95959
☎ **(530) 265-0363**

Nevada City
🏵 *Emma Nevada House*

This 1856 Victorian house was the home of the 19th-century opera star Emma Nevada. The inn features a sunroom with floor-to-ceiling antique windows, a living room with a fireplace and a game room with an antique slot machine. The inn also offers wraparound front and back porches. Guestrooms range from grand and high-ceilinged to cozy and intimate. All include a private bath, some have a Jacuzzi or claw-foot tub.

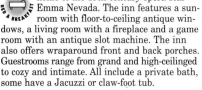

6 Rooms • Price range: $135-195
528 E Broad St, Nevada City, CA 95959
☎ **(530) 265-4415**

Nevada City
🏵 *Grandmere's Inn*

This Colonial-Revival estate was built in 1856 by Aaron A. Sargent, a U.S. senator and prominent publisher. He championed legislation to create the Transcontinental Railroad, and, with his wife Ellen, initiated a bill giving women the right to vote. The elegant house is surrounded by a half-acre of manicured gardens and offers comfortable guest accommodations, including one suite with an enclosed sunporch overlooking the garden.

6 Rooms • Price range: $140-205
449 Broad St, Nevada City, CA 95959
☎ **(530) 265-4660**

Nevada City
Marsh House Bed & Breakfast Inn

Pioneer lumber baron Martin Luther Marsh built this gracious Italianate country villa atop Boulder Hill in 1873. The three-acre estate has been authentically restored, with original period furnishings and personal memorabilia from the Marsh family. Common areas include the Great Room, the wicker-filled glass solarium, the wisteria-covered verandas and the manicured gardens.

6 Rooms • Price range: $150-185
254 Boulder, Nevada City, CA 95959
☎ **(530) 265-5709**

Nevada City
Piety Hill Cottages

These cottages feature American Country-style decor.

9 Rooms • Price range: $80-160
523 Sacramento St, Nevada City, CA 95959
☎ **(530) 265-2245**

Newport Beach
Doryman's Oceanfront Inn

This inn has a rooftop deck. It is conveniently located at the beach.

10 Rooms • Price range: $175-325
2102 W Ocean Front, Newport Beach, CA 92663
☎ **(949) 675-7300**

Newport Beach
Portofino Beach Hotel

This unique hotel overlooks the Pacific Ocean and offers spectacular coastal vistas from Long Beach to San Clemente. The guestrooms, which have a European ambience, combine old-fashioned hospitality with modern amenities.

15 Rooms • Price range: $159-339
2306 W Ocean Front, Newport Beach, CA 92663
☎ **(949) 673-7030**

Nice

Featherbed Railroad Co.
This inn has fabulous views of beautiful Clear Lake. Its guestrooms are located in converted train cabooses. Each of the cars has its own special theme. Amenities include luxurious feather beds and full, hotel-sized baths, most with oversized Jacuzzis. The inn is surrounded by park-like grounds, which include an outdoor swimming pool. Breakfast is served in the adjoining 100-year-old ranch house.

9 Rooms • Price range: $97-146
2870 Lakeshore Blvd, Nice, CA 95464
☎ **(707) 274-4434**

O'Brien

O'Brien Mountain Inn Bed & Breakfast
Guestrooms at this scenic inn have each been given different musical themes. Rooms are equipped with private baths, and guests are invited to a full, healthy breakfast. Local outdoor activities include white-water rafting and hiking.

5 Rooms • Price range: $100-225
18026 O'Brien Inlet Rd, O'Brien, CA 96070-0027
☎ **(530) 238-8026**

Oakhurst

Hounds Tooth Inn
The Hounds Tooth Inn stands amid oaks and towering pines, offering comfortable accommodations with a Victorian flair. Guests can enjoy the views of the surrounding Sierras from the inn's patio while sipping a complimentary glass of wine. Some of the guestrooms have a fireplace and Jacuzzi. Area attractions include Yosemite National Park and Bass Lake. Golf, hiking, fishing and fine dining are just a few of the activities.

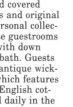

13 Rooms • Price range: $95-185
42071 Hwy 41, Oakhurst, CA 93644
☎ **(559) 642-6600**

Occidental

The Inn at Occidental
This 1860 restored inn has all the special features one would expect from a Victorian property: fir floors, wainscoted hallways and covered porches, to name a few. Antiques and original artwork from the innkeepers' personal collection are on display. The exquisite guestrooms feature luxurious feather beds with down comforters, each with a private bath. Guests can enjoy the veranda, with its antique wicker furniture, or the courtyard, which features a moss mantle fountain and an English cottage garden. Breakfast is served daily in the dining room.

16 Rooms • Price range: $175-270
3657 Church St, Occidental, CA 95465
☎ **(707) 874-1047**

Occidental
The Winding Rose Inn
Comprised of two 1903 homes, this charming inn is decorated with antiques and family heirlooms. Each guestroom is decorated in its own theme, including English, French and Italian motifs. Two of the rooms can be joined to form one suite and share a bath, while the other rooms are each equipped with private baths. The inn also features a private deck and patios. A full breakfast is served in the dining room.

5 Rooms • Price range: $125-175
14985 Coleman Valley Rd, Occidental, CA 95465
☎ **(707) 874-2680**

Oroville
Jean's Riverside Bed & Breakfast
Located on six acres of wooded waterfront on the Feather River, this B&B offers a secluded country atmosphere, yet is near restaurants and shopping.

The inn features a large deck and a parlor with a gold quartz fireplace.

6 Rooms • Price range: $75-145
1142 Middlehoff Ln, Oroville, CA 95965
☎ **(530) 533-1413**

Pacific Grove
🏛 *The Centrella Inn*
This 1890s Victorian has rooms and suites in the main house and five cottages nearby. All accommodations are equipped with private baths. Among the rooms in the house there is one designed specially for romance; it has a view of the garden, a Jacuzzi, a potbelly stove, a wet bar and a canopy bed. The cottages come with fireplaces and wet bars. A buffet breakfast is served each day in the breakfast room; afternoon tea is also served daily.

26 Rooms • Price range: $169-250
612 Central Ave, Pacific Grove, CA 93950
☎ **(831) 372-3372**

Pacific Grove
The Gatehouse Inn
This Italianate Victorian offers stunning views of Monterey Bay.

9 Rooms • Price range: $110-195
225 Central Ave, Pacific Grove, CA 93950
☎ **(831) 649-8436**

Pacific Grove
The Inn at 213 Seventeen Mile Drive
Located in the Monarch butterfly tree zone, this 1920 Craftsman house has been restored to provide guests with comfort and charm. Decorated to reflect the area's character, the inn offers guests a choice between the main house, the rustic cottage units or the redwood chalet. All rooms are equipped with a private bath. The inn also features a wood-paneled dining room, a sitting room and a reading room.

14 Rooms • Price range: $135-240
213 Seventeen Mile Dr, Pacific Grove, CA 93950
☎ **(831) 642-9514**

Pacific Grove
Pacific Grove Inn

 Two properties make up this inn: the 1904 Queen Anne-style Buck Mansion and the 1914 Tuttle House, a charming Victorian cottage. Sixteen rooms and suites are available between the two buildings, each with either a king- or queen-size bed, and a private bath. A homemade breakfast buffet is served. There are several nearby attractions, including Historic Main Street, the Monterey Bay Aquarium and the beach.

16 Rooms • Price range: $140-205
581 Pine Ave, Pacific Grove, CA 93950
☎ **(831) 375-2825**

Pacific Grove
Old St. Angela Inn

 This Shingle-style 1910 home has rooms of distinctive individuality and warmth. Antiques, teddy bears, and other quaint accents make this inn the perfect "home away from home." Guests are invited to sit by the fireplace in the living room where afternoon refreshments (wine, tea, coffee, cookies) are served. The inn also features a garden hot tub. A full buffet breakfast is served in a solarium, which looks out over the garden.

9 Rooms • Price range: $110-195
321 Central Ave, Pacific Grove, CA 93950
☎ **(831) 372-3246**

Palm Desert
Tres Palmas Bed & Breakfast

 Just one block from El Paseo, "the Rodeo Drive of the Desert," with its boutiques, galleries and restaurants, this B&B is also within walking distance of the Palm Desert Town Center, with its movie theaters and indoor skating. After exploring, guests can retire to one of four rooms, each with a private bath, television and queen- or king-size bed. Freshly baked muffins and fresh fruit are part of the daily continental breakfast.

4 Rooms • Price range: $125-195
73-135 Tumbleweed Ln, Palm Desert, CA 92260
☎ **(760) 773-9858**

Palm Springs
The Willows Historic Palm Springs Inn

  This breathtaking 1927 Mediterranean Villa, in historic Palm Springs, has been fully restored. Guests will be impressed by the mahogany beams of the great hall, the frescoed ceiling of the veranda, the mountain waterfall that spills into a pool outside the stone-floored dining room, and the original stone path that climbs through the hillside garden. Guestrooms are equally remarkable, with luxurious private baths, stone fireplaces, private garden patios, and mountain and garden vistas. There is also an outdoor swimming pool. A gourmet breakfast is served.

8 Rooms • Price range: $295-550
412 W Tahquitz Canyon Way,
Palm Springs, CA 92262
☎ **(760) 320-0771**

Palm Springs
Ingleside Inn

Many well-known personalities have made stops at this Palm Springs establishment, including John Travolta, Marlon Brando and Salvador Dali. Situated next to the San Jacinto Mountains, the inn is secluded, yet not far from the finest shopping, dining and nightlife. The inn's guestrooms and villas are complete with terraces, fireplaces and private steam baths. Guests can take a dip in the pool or play a game of croquet.

29 Rooms • Price range: $72-289
200 W Ramon Rd, Palm Springs, CA 92264
☎ **(760) 325-0046**

Palm Springs
⑭ *Villa Royale Inn*

Framed by mountain views, this inn's three acres of landscaped gardens are reminiscent of an estate in Tuscany. Fragrant citrus and lavender grow in the courtyard, which contains two heated pools and a large Jacuzzi. The 31 charming guestrooms are furnished with antiques reflecting a particular region in Europe. Many of the rooms offer special amenities such as fireplaces, kitchens, private patios and spas.

32 Rooms • Price range: $125-300
1620 S Indian Tr, Palm Springs, CA 92264
☎ **(760) 327-2314**

Paso Robles
Arbor Inn Bed & Breakfast

Surrounded by acres of productive vineyards, this Victorian-style inn is decorated in a formal English manner. Upon entering, guests will notice the hardwood floors in the downstairs hall and living room, and the grand staircase leading to second floor guestrooms. Each of the nine rooms features a private balcony, gas fireplace and private bath with separate tub and shower. Breakfast is served every morning in the dining room, and wine and hors d'oeuvres are available in the afternoon. Guest don't have far to go for nearby activities such as kayaking and watching elephant seals.

9 Rooms • Price range: $160-255
2130 Arbor Rd, Paso Robles, CA 93447
☎ **(805) 227-4673**

Petaluma
⑭ *Cavanagh Inn*

A number of attractions are within walking distance of this 1912 inn, including antique stores, a museum, fine dining and walking tours. The decor of the Cavanagh Inn is formal Victorian, with interior walls paneled with rare heart redwood. All seven guestrooms have feather beds. Guests can look forward to an evening turn-down service, which includes warmed electric blankets and tempting evening snacks.

7 Rooms • Price range: $125-150
10 Keller St, Petaluma, CA 94952
☎ **(707) 765-4657**

Placerville

The Chichester-McKee House

This grand 1892 Victorian home was built by a Gold Rush pioneer for his wife. The inn features finely crafted fireplaces, fretwork, stained glass and antiques. There is also a collection of antique dolls. Each guestroom is furnished with Victorian-era beds and matching robes. Rooms are equipped with half baths and share a full bath. Early morning coffee is provided in the solarium before a full breakfast is served in the dining room.

4 Rooms • Price range: $90-125
800 Spring St, Placerville, CA 95667
☎ **(530) 626-1882**

Placerville

Shadowridge Ranch & Lodge

Call for information.

4 Rooms • Price range: $145-175
Fort Jim Rd, Placerville, CA 95667
☎ **(530) 295-1000**

Playa Del Rey

Inn at Playa Del Rey

Located just a few blocks from the beach in the village of Playa del Rey, this inn overlooks the Marina del Rey and the Ballona wetlands, a 350-acre bird sanctuary. Some guestrooms have a clear view of these locales, and those that do also come with a fireplace, deck and Jacuzzi tub. All rooms have private baths. In the morning, guests awaken to the smell of fresh coffee, soon followed by egg soufflés, apple French toast or hot buttered scones.

22 Rooms • Price range: $160-345
435 Culver Blvd, Playa Del Rey, CA 90293
☎ **(310) 574-1920**

Pleasanton

Evergreen Bed & Breakfast

Although this cozy B&B is just minutes away from downtown Pleasanton, it has a secluded ambience. Each of the guestrooms has its own special features. For instance, the Hideaway has a separate private entrance, and features a king-size canopy bed and bath/Jacuzzi, while the Grand View has a fireplace and a private outdoor deck. In the morning, a fresh pot of coffee precedes a hearty full breakfast.

5 Rooms • Price range: $135-250
9104 Longview Dr, Pleasanton, CA 94588
☎ **(925) 426-0901**

Portola

Pullman House

This restored 1910 boardinghouse features a deck overlooking a rail yard.

6 Rooms • Price range: $60-95
256 Commercial St, Portola, CA 96122
☎ **(530) 832-0107**

Quincy
The Featherbed

Built in 1892, this inn reflects the splendor of the Queen Anne era. The inn also features a wide Greco-Roman porch where iced tea is served in the summer. Antiques and fixtures have been hand selected for the guestrooms to complete the inn's evocation of the past. Each rooms has a private bath, some have claw-foot tubs. The inn is famous for its breakfast, which features home-grown blackberry and raspberry smoothies.

7 Rooms • Price range: $85-136
542 Jackson St, Quincy, CA 95971
☎ **(530) 283-0102**

Rancho Cucamonga
Christmas House Bed & Breakfast Inn

This 1904 Queen Anne-style Victorian features stained glass, wood carvings, antiques and gardens.

6 Rooms • Price range: $80-190
9240 Archibald Ave,
Rancho Cucamonga, CA 91730
☎ **(909) 980-6450**

Red Bluff
The Faulkner House

A handsome Queen Anne-style house constructed in 1890.

4 Rooms • Price range: $60-90
1029 Jefferson St, Red Bluff, CA 96080
☎ **(530) 529-0520**

Redding
Tiffany House Bed & Breakfast Inn

This 1930s-era home, built in the Victorian style, is located on a hilltop and offers panoramic views. Guest rooms feature private baths and sitting areas. A gourmet breakfast is served in the dining room or in the gazebo.

4 Rooms • Price range: $85-135
1510 Barbara Rd, Redding, CA 96003
☎ **(530) 244-3225**

Reedley
Reedley Country Inn

These two restored farmhouses are surrounded by orchards and gardens.

5 Rooms • Price range: $85-95
43137 Road 52, Reedley, CA 93654
☎ **(559) 638-2585**

Sacramento
⊕ *Amber House Bed & Breakfast Inn*

Three beautifully restored Craftsman-style mansions make up this charming property. Perfect for everything from intimate gatherings to garden weddings and business meetings, the inn is located in a quiet, historic neighborhood. Early risers usually begin each day with the daily paper and a coffee tray. A generous gourmet breakfast follows, which can be served either in the privacy of the room or in the garden or dining room. Guestrooms feature fireplaces and marbled tiled baths with Jacuzzis. Fresh-baked chocolate chip cookies are served in the evenings.

14 Rooms • Price range: $159-279
1315 22nd St, Sacramento, CA 95816
☎ **(916) 444-8085**

Sacramento

Hartley House Bed & Breakfast
This European-style, old-fashioned hotel is located in historic Boulevard

Park. It features original inlaid hardwood floors, stained woodwork, leaded and stained-glass windows and original brass light fixtures. Period artwork, antique furnishings and collectibles add finishing touches to the parlor, dining room and guestrooms. Breakfasts are served daily and may feature Belgian waffles or blintzes.

5 Rooms • Price range: $124-190
700 22nd St, Sacramento, CA 95816
☎ **(916) 447-7829**

Sacramento
Vizcaya
Located in downtown Sacramento, this stately mansion is minutes away from

the Sacramento Convention Center and the Federal and County Courthouses. The early-20th century property features elegantly furnished guestrooms, all with walnut and mahogany furniture, original art and tiled bathrooms. Some rooms have a Jacuzzi and/or fireplace. A sweeping staircase and impressive entryway lead to the parlor and dining room.

9 Rooms • Price range: $170-350
2019 21st St, Sacramento, CA 95818
☎ **(916) 455-5243**

San Andreas
The Robin's Nest
A Queen Anne-style house, built in 1895, with landscaped gardens.

7 Rooms • Price range: $75-125
247 W St. Charles St, San Andreas, CA 95249
☎ **(209) 754-1076**

San Clemente
⑭ Casa Tropicana Bed & Breakfast Inn
This inn features exquisitely designed rooms, each patterned after a tropical

destination. The Out Of Africa room is decorated in earth colors, and features a four-poster bed with overhung netting, while the bed in the Bali room features bamboo posts and a grass hut overhang. Most rooms have a Jacuzzi and fireplace, and two have a complete kitchenette. Breakfast specialties are served either in-room or on the deck.

9 Rooms • Price range: $120-350
610 Arendia Victoria, San Clemente, CA 92672
☎ **(949) 492-1234**

San Diego
⑭ Heritage Park Bed & Breakfast Inn
A beautifully decorated Queen Anne-style mansion built in 1889.

12 Rooms • Price range: $125-300
2470 Heritage Park Row, San Diego, CA 92110
☎ **(619) 299-6832**

San Francisco
The Archbishop's Mansion

Combining the friendly atmosphere of a country B&B with the elegance of a small European hotel, the inn offers personalized service and exquisitely furnished rooms. Each room has a private bath, some baths have oversized Jacuzzis. Extended continental breakfasts are served in the privacy of the room. The inn, which was built in 1904 for an archbishop, is one of the grandest of San Francisco's Historic Landmark Homes.

15 Rooms • Price range: $195-425
1000 Fulton St, San Francisco, CA 94117
☎ **(415) 563-7872**

San Francisco
Inn 1890

This Victorian inn is centrally located in a historic residential neighborhood, only 10 minutes from downtown San Francisco. Nearby attractions include the Steinhart Aquarium and the Morrison Planetarium. Guestrooms boast 12-foot-high ceilings and expansive bay windows. Some rooms have the original wood fireplace. Bath robes and slippers are provided. A daily continental breakfast features muffins and bagels.

13 Rooms • Price range: $89-129
1890 Page St, San Francisco, CA 94117
☎ **(415) 386-0486**

San Francisco
⑩ Stanyan Park Hotel

This Victorian hotel is a great locale for honeymooners as well as for business clients. Guestrooms feature period decor and full bathrooms. Many rooms have a view of the Golden Gate Park where guests can go bicycling or horseback riding. Some popular nearby attractions include the Japanese Tea Garden and the Natural History Museum. The hotel caters to receptions, meetings and weddings.

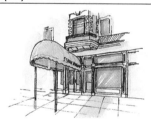

36 Rooms • Price range: $125-180
750 Stanyan St, San Francisco, CA 94117
☎ **(415) 751-1000**

San Jose
The Hensley House Bed & Breakfast

This is the only B&B in downtown San Jose, near the business center of Silicon Valley. The inn combines old-fashioned hospitality with modern convenience, providing great accommodations for weary business travelers. Rooms are decorated with antiques, and feature queen-size beds and private baths, complete with cozy terry cloth robes. Guests can begin each day with a full gourmet breakfast.

9 Rooms • Price range: $200-350
456 N 3rd St, San Jose, CA 95112
☎ **(408) 298-3537**

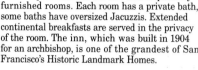

San Luis Obispo
Garden Street Inn Bed & Breakfast

Since its construction almost 150 years ago, this home has seen many incarnations and renovations. The present owners have named all the guestrooms after previous inhabitants, thus keeping alive the house's eventful past. Guests can relax with a book from the well-stocked library and sample local wines and hors d'oeuvres each evening at the Innkeeper's Reception. Breakfast is served daily in the cheerful Morning Room.

13 Rooms • Price range: $110-180
1212 Garden St, San Luis Obispo, CA 93401
☎ **(805) 545-9802**

San Luis Obispo
Heritage Inn Bed & Breakfast
Built more than a century ago, this inn has charming rooms and gardens.

7 Rooms • Price range: $75-85
978 Olive St, San Luis Obispo, CA 93405
☎ **(805) 544-7440**

San Mateo
Coxhead House Bed & Breakfast

This rustic Tudor-Revival home has survived virtually untouched for more than a century. It still features antiques, period furnishings and hand-painted murals in each of the guestrooms, along with amenities such as a queen-size bed and private bath. Visitors will appreciate the inn's special treats, including fresh flowers, cozy robes and hot cocoa. A fresh, hearty breakfast is served in the dining room or in the garden courtyard.

4 Rooms • Price range: $129-250
37 E Santa Inez Ave, San Mateo, CA 94401
☎ **(650) 685-1600**

Sanger
Wonder Valley Ranch Resort
The scenery and recreational facilities at this resort are truly impressive. Guests can enjoy horseback riding, fishing, sailing and any number of other outdoor activities at this ranch by the water. Evenings at the campfire amphitheater are always fun.

50 Rooms • Price range: $86-109
6450 Elwood Rd, Sanger, CA 93657
☎ **(559) 787-2551**

Santa Barbara
⚭ *Bath Street Inn*
Visitors can look forward to home comforts such as big comfortable chairs, a roaring fire and even a resident golden retriever when staying at this 1890 Victorian house. Each guestroom in the three-story main house has a sitting area and a private bath. Rooms in the Summer House have fireplaces; some have a Jacuzzi. The breakfast menu varies; it may include English scones with cheese and egg frittata or peach French toast.

12 Rooms • Price range: $115-230
1720 Bath St, Santa Barbara, CA 93101
☎ **(805) 682-9680**

Santa Barbara

🏵 *The Cheshire Cat*
It is no coincidence that 12 of this inn's 14 rooms are named after characters in "Alice In Wonderland." Antique furnishings were shipped over from England, while the wallpaper and draperies are by a well-known English designer. Each guestroom has a private bath, and some have a Jacuzzi spa-tub, fireplace and private deck. A full breakfast is served on wild strawberry Wedgwood china, either on the flower-filled brick patio or in-room.

21 Rooms • Price range: $140-220
36 W Valerio St, Santa Barbara, CA 93101
☎ **(805) 569-1610**

Santa Barbara

The Parsonage
This 1892 Queen Anne house was originally built for the parson of the Trinity Episcopal Church. Although the house has been restored, it still maintains touches of rare bird's-eye redwood throughout. All guestrooms have a king- or queen-size bed and a private bath. A home-made breakfast is served on the sundeck or in the parlor.

6 Rooms • Price range: $125-350
1600 Olive St, Santa Barbara, CA 93101
☎ **(805) 962-9336**

Santa Barbara

The Secret Garden & Cottages
This quiet retreat consists of brick cottages with private entrances, as well as guestrooms in a main house. Four rooms feature a private redwood patio and outdoor whirlpool. The buildings rest on tree-shaded, beautifully landscaped grounds. Guests can take advantage of the residential location while being only blocks from downtown. Complimentary dessert and hot beverages are served in the evening.

11 Rooms • Price range: $120-160
1908 Bath St, Santa Barbara, CA 93101
☎ **(805) 687-2300**

Santa Barbara

🏵 *Tiffany Country House*
Decorated with antiques and period furnishings, this 1898 Colonial-style home is a wonderful place to relax and enjoy the surroundings. Guests are only a stroll away from the boutiques and restaurants of Santa Barbara. All rooms are fitted with queen-size beds, some have fireplaces and whirlpools. Breakfast at Tiffany's is always a grand affair, served on the veranda overlooking the garden or in the formal dining room.

7 Rooms • Price range: $145-295
1323 De La Vina St, Santa Barbara, CA 93101
☎ **(805) 963-2283**

Santa Barbara
The Upham
This 1871 Victorian hotel is the oldest continuously operating hostelry in Southern California. Guestrooms are in the Main House and the Carriage House; there are also five Garden Cottages. King-size, queen-size or twin beds are available. Each of the delightful garden cottages features a gas fireplace and a porch or secluded patio. The continental breakfast includes freshly baked nut breads and pastries.

50 Rooms • Price range: $155-405
1404 De la Vina St, Santa Barbara, CA 93101
☎ **(805) 962-0058**

Santa Barbara
Blue Dolphin Inn
Just two blocks from the beach, this 1860s house offers comfortable rooms.

9 Rooms • Price range: $125-225
420 Montecito St, Santa Barbara, CA 93101
☎ **(805) 965-2333**

Santa Barbara
The Glenborough Inn
These Victorian-era and California-Craftsman homes are just blocks from downtown and the seashore. Most guestrooms have a private entrance and fireplace, and some have a Jacuzzi. A gourmet breakfast is served in-room.

14 Rooms • Price range: $110-300
1327 Bath St, Santa Barbara, CA 93101
☎ **(805) 966-0589**

Santa Barbara
The Mary May Inn
1886 house with gabled roof and porches. Fireplaces, canopy beds in some rooms.

6 Rooms • Price range: $150-170
111 W Valerio, Santa Barbara, CA 93101
☎ **(805) 569-3398**

Santa Barbara
Old Yacht Club Inn
Classic European furniture and Early American antiques decorate this 1912 California-Craftsman home. Fresh flowers and a decanter of sherry are placed in guestrooms, each of which has a private bath. A gourmet breakfast is served.

12 Rooms • Price range: $110-195
431 Corona Del Mar, Santa Barbara, CA 93103
☎ **(805) 962-1277**

Santa Barbara
Olive House Inn
Located in the beautiful Riviera section of Santa Barbara, this 1904 house is close to both the city and the ocean. Full breakfasts begin with fresh coffee and the daily paper. Guests can request rooms with a private deck, fireplace and/or hot tub.

6 Rooms • Price range: $125-195
1604 Olive St, Santa Barbara, CA 93101
☎ **(805) 962-4902**

Santa Cruz
🏵 *Babbling Brook Bed & Breakfast Inn*

This 1909 B&B is the oldest and largest in the Santa Cruz area. It is situated on an acre of land that has a cascading waterfall, a meandering brook and a romantic garden gazebo. The beach is just a walk away. The guestrooms each have a private bath, fireplace and private deck. Some rooms have a deep-soaking jet bathtub. A delicious breakfast is served daily; wine and cheese, as well as tea and cookies are served in the afternoon.

13 Rooms • Price range: $176-242
1025 Laurel St, Santa Cruz, CA 95060
☎ **(831) 427-2437**

Santa Monica
Channel Road Inn Bed & Breakfast

A rare West Coast example of shingle-clad Colonial-style architecture, this 1910 Colonial-Revival house is one block from the beach in Santa Monica Canyon, and just minutes from Brentwood, Malibu and Beverly Hills. Guestrooms are equipped with private baths, fine linens and thick robes. Guests start the day with the rich aromas of coffee and sweet buttery scones, served in the breakfast room.

14 Rooms • Price range: $165-365
219 W Channel Rd, Santa Monica, CA 90402
☎ **(310) 459-1920**

Santa Paula
The Fern Oaks Inn

Situated on expansive grounds, this two-story Spanish-Revival home reflects the design of a bygone era. Palladian windows line the southern exposure of the solarium. A luxurious silk Oriental rug graces the dining-room floor, and an elegant Chinese rug lies in the living room. All rooms have a separate vanity area and a private bath. Gourmet breakfasts are offered daily. A heated pool is available in summer.

4 Rooms • Price range: $95-130
1025 Ojai Rd, Santa Paula, CA 93060
☎ **(805) 525-7747**

Santa Rosa
The Gables Inn

This inn is a good example of Gothic-Revival architecture from the Victorian era. It boasts graceful 12-foot ceilings, three Italian marble fireplaces, a mahogany spiral staircase and 15 gables crowning the unusual keyhole-shaped windows. Guestrooms are furnished with antiques and the inn's private cottage is furnished with handmade, white pine furniture. Breakfast is served in the formal dining room.

8 Rooms • Price range: $150-250
4257 Petaluma Hill Rd, Santa Rosa, CA 95404
☎ **(707) 585-7777**

Sausalito
Casa Madrona Hotel

From its vantage point on a hillside, this inn has stunning views of the San Francisco Bay. The inn is comprised of spacious cottages and casitas, as well as a gorgeous Victorian mansion that has been accommodating guests for more than 115 years. Guests will enjoy luxuriating in the comfortable rooms. Popular and nearby activities include sailing, hiking, picnicking and sightseeing.

34 Rooms • Price range: $240-750
801 Bridgeway, Sausalito, CA 94965
☎ **(415) 332-0502**

Sausalito
The Gables Inn-Sausalito

Built in 1869, this was Sausalito's first hotel. It has been recently renovated and is now a welcoming modern inn. Rooms boast tasteful decor, queen or king beds, oversize tubs, vaulted ceilings, brick fireplaces and private balconies. Guests will feel pampered by the hospitality, which includes a continental breakfast, afternoon wine and cheese tasting, and concierge services. Many galleries, boutiques and restaurants are nearby.

9 Rooms • Price range: $155-300
62 Princess St, Sausalito, CA 94965
☎ **(415) 289-1100**

Seal Beach
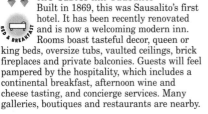The Seal Beach Inn and Gardens

This inn is located in a pleasant waterfront village, only half a block from the beach. It was built in the 1920s and has been extensively restored in recent years. The patio and terraces, which are surrounded by lush, vibrantly colored gardens, are great places to relax and enjoy the sunshine. All guestrooms are furnished with quality antiques and artworks. A full breakfast and evening tea are served daily.

24 Rooms • Price range: $159-399
212 5th St, Seal Beach, CA 90740
☎ **(562) 493-2416**

Sierra City
Holly House

In a historic gold mining town, at the foot of the Sierra Buttes, lies this elegant Italianate mansion. It features high ceilings, classic antiques and airy rooms with either a claw-foot tub or a spa.

6 Rooms • Price range: $85-135
119 Main St, Sierra City, CA 96125
☎ **(530) 862-1123**

Skyforest
Storybook Inn

Rooms at this inn have mountain and valley views. Cozy common area.

7 Rooms • Price range: $89-179
28717 SR 18, Skyforest, CA 92385
☎ **(909) 337-0011**

Smith River
White Rose Mansion Inn

The grounds of this 1869 Victorian mansion feature a creek and a barbecue area.

7 Rooms • Price range: $95-215
149 Fred Haight Dr, Smith River, CA 95567
☎ **(707) 487-9260**

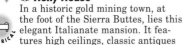
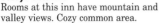
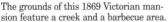

Solvang
Storybook Inn

This newly constructed inn has tastefully decorated rooms, most have a fireplace.

9 Rooms • Price range: $139-205
409 1st St, Solvang, CA 93463
☎ **(805) 688-1703**

Sonoma
MacArthur Place

A grand, 19th-century house, this structure has been renovated into a modern, luxury inn. It lies in the heart of the wine country and the surrounding grounds were originally home to a 300-acre vineyard and working ranch. Guestrooms have king-size beds with custom linens, fireplaces, wet bars and DVD players. Flagstone walkways lead guests through the magnificent gardens, around the fountains and sculpture, to the restaurant.

64 Rooms • Price range: $245-325
29 E MacArthur St, Sonoma, CA 95476
☎ **(707) 938-2929**

Sonoma
Trojan Horse Inn

Guests at this B&B begin the day with a breakfast made from fresh, locally grown ingredients. Complimentary wine and hors d'oeuvres are served in the evenings. The inn itself is located in the heart of California's wine country, just a few blocks from the Historical Sonoma Plaza and City Hall. It is surrounded by an acre of landscaped grounds that include colorful flower gardens. Each guest room has a private bath.

6 Rooms • Price range: $148-185
19455 Sonoma Hwy, Sonoma, CA 95476
☎ **(707) 996-2430**

Sonora
⊛ *Bradford Place Inn and Gardens*

In Old Town Sonora lies this charming inn with a white picket fence and a red shingled roof. As well as guestrooms, the home has several parlors, a veranda and colorful gardens. Guests are treated to their choice of breakfast, from gourmet specialties to the Mother Lode Skillet, which includes scrambled eggs, pan-fried potatoes and ham. For those interested in history, the 1888 courthouse and county offices are just next door.

4 Rooms • Price range: $105-160
56 W Bradford St, Sonora, CA 95370
☎ **(209) 536-6075**

Sonora
Sterling Gardens

This inn is located by the Kincaid Gold Mine, where millions of dollars worth of gold have been recovered since the 1849 Gold Rush. It is an English Country-style home, which features sloping ceilings and oak-paneled walls. Guestrooms are fitted with large beds, private baths and cozy sitting areas. After a scrumptious two-course breakfast, guests can stroll the 10-acre wooded grounds or relax in the hammock.

4 Rooms • Price range: $95-105
18047 Lime Kiln Rd, Sonora, CA 95370
☎ **(209) 533-9300**

South Pasadena
Artist's Inn

Built in 1895 as a farmhouse, this structure has been renovated and redecorated to welcome and pamper guests. Each room is named after an artist and is adorned with art pieces. Guests are invited to enjoy afternoon tea with sweets on the grand porch, and gather around the fireplace in the parlor in the evenings. When the more than 100 roses bloom in the surrounding gardens, the air is heady with perfume.

9 Rooms • Price range: $115-205
1038 Magnolia St, South Pasadena, CA 91030
☎ **(626) 799-5668**

South Pasadena
The Bissell House Bed & Breakfast

Sitting on the corner of Millionaire's Row in the Orange Grove Mansion District, is this gorgeous three-story house. It was built in 1887 and is a recognized Historical Landmark. A collection of antiques decorates the house and the guestrooms feature claw-foot tubs, pedestal sinks and leaded-glass windows. Surrounded by a 40-foot hedge, the landscaped grounds provide privacy and relaxation.

5 Rooms • Price range: $125-175
201 Orange Grove Ave,
South Pasadena, CA 91030
☎ **(626) 441-3535**

Springville
Annie's Bed & Breakfast

Each of the guestrooms at Annie's has a private entrance and bath, and features old-fashioned feather mattresses and homemade quilts. The B&B is situated on five acres of land, surrounded by green pastures and oak-covered hills. Not surprisingly the views of the Sierra Mountains are little short of miraculous. Guests can take in the panorama from one of the decks that overlook the pool and spa, or relax inside by the antique parlor stove.

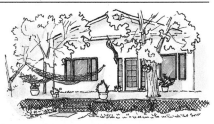

3 Rooms • Price range: $85-95
33024 Globe Dr, Springville, CA 93265
☎ **(559) 539-3827**

St. Helena
Adagio Inn

Call for information.

4 Rooms • Price range: $159-269
1417 Kearney St, St. Helena, CA 94574
☎ **(707) 963-2238**

St. Helena
⚄ *Vineyard Country Inn*

Decorated to complement the natural beauty of the surrounding wine country area, this inn features wood paneling, red-brick, and earth-colored textiles. Suites have large comfortable beds and sitting areas fitted with armchairs, old-fashioned fireplaces and wet bars. Breakfast is served in the bright Morning Room, which boasts floor-to-ceiling windows with views of the pool, the jacuzzi and the inn's own vineyards.

21 Rooms • Price range: $155-230
201 Main St, St. Helena, CA 94574
☎ **(707) 963-1000**

Summerland
⊕ *Inn On Summer Hill*

New England hospitality shakes hands with Southern California beauty at this quaint inn, situated in the foothills of Santa Barbara. Antiques, original artwork and unique furnishings are evident throughout. Guestrooms are fitted with lavish custom fabrics, imported furniture and each one has a private bath with a whirlpool tub. All the rooms offer an ocean view. Days begin with a full breakfast, featuring homemade breads, pastries and seasonal fresh fruit. Refreshments are served in the afternoon, and a mouthwatering dessert ends the day.

16 Rooms • Price range: $229-339
2520 Lillie Ave, Summerland, CA 93067
☎ (805) 969-9998

Sutter Creek
⊕ *The Foxes in Sutter Creek*

An 1857 Gold Rush hotel, this B&B is within walking distance of antique shops, restaurants and art galleries. Also close by are the Amadoe County Museum and the Wheels State Historical Park. Natural attractions include lakes, rivers, reservoirs and El Dorado National Forest, just a few miles away. Each guestroom has a queen-size bed and private bath. Breakfast is served in-room or in the gazebo.

7 Rooms • Price range: $125-195
77 Main St, Sutter Creek, CA 95685
☎ (209) 267-5882

Sutter Creek
⊕ *Grey Gables Bed & Breakfast Inn*

This inn has the look and feel of an English country manor. A red-bricked pathway leads to a terraced garden. Fully carpeted guestrooms are accented with rich wood trim and marble tile and furnished with large armoires. Each room has a tiled bath, and some have a traditional claw-foot tub. A gourmet breakfast, served on fine English bone china, can be served in-room. In the afternoon, tea with cake or scones is available.

8 Rooms • Price range: $133-200
161 Hanford St, Sutter Creek, CA 95685
☎ (209) 267-1039

Sutter Creek
⊕ *Hanford House Bed & Breakfast Inn*

This is a charming inn with red-brick walls and a wraparound porch, brightened with flowers. The innkeepers are friendly and hospitable and will accommodate needs for special occasions. They offer concierge service and there is a massage therapist on call. Plush robes, herbal soaps and delicious tasting truffles welcome guests to their rooms. Breakfast features a variety of delicacies including fresh-fruit smoothies and soufflés.

10 Rooms • Price range: $99-185
61 Hanford St (SR 49), Sutter Creek, CA 95685
☎ (209) 267-0747

Sutter Creek
Sutter Creek Inn

This little inn was the first B&B built west of Mississippi. Rooms are relaxing and many feature wood-burning fireplaces, swinging beds and double bath-tubs. Other attractions include secret gardens, hammocks and private patios.

17 Rooms • Price range: $65-175
75 Main St, Sutter Creek, CA 95685
☎ **(209) 267-5606**

Tahoe City
The Cottage Inn at Lake Tahoe

Museums, shops, restaurants and casinos are all accessible from this conveniently located inn. Built in 1938 in "Old Tahoe" style with knotty pine paneling, all the cottage suites, except the loft suite, are single-level, with a private bath and entrance. Newly remodeled cottage suites are available, with fireplaces and sitting areas; some have kitchenettes. A country breakfast is served in the dining room or on the deck.

15 Rooms • Price range: $150-250
1690 W Lake Blvd, Tahoe City, CA 96145
☎ **(530) 581-4073**

Tahoe Vista
⏍ *The Shore House at Lake Tahoe*

Situated on the North Shore of Lake Tahoe, this secluded getaway is replete with private gardens, a pier and an adjoining sandy beach. Each floor of the inn is surrounded by balconies and decks that offer fabulous views of the lake. Guestrooms are cozy with gas-log fireplaces, private bathrooms and mini-refrigerators. Knotty-pine walls and custom-built log furniture complete the picture.

9 Rooms • Price range: $190-300
7170 North Lake Blvd, Tahoe Vista, CA 96148
☎ **(530) 546-7270**

Temecula
Loma Vista Bed & Breakfast

This Mission-style establishment is conveniently located in the heart of Temecula wine country. Nearby attractions include the Palomar Observatory and the Historical Museum. The guestrooms are all decorated for comfort and each has a private bath. In the evenings, award-winning wine and cheese are served on the patio or in the spa. Full breakfasts are verved daily and feature champagne.

6 Rooms • Price range: $105-165
33350 La Serena Way, Temecula, CA 92591
☎ **(909) 676-7047**

Trinidad
Trinidad Bay Bed & Breakfast

Located in the scenic city of Trinidad, high on a bluff overlooking the California Coast, this inn offers style and comfort. The Cape Cod home features guestrooms with panoramic views of the ocean or of the garden. Breakfast is a grand occasion when guests are treated to specialities such as baked fruit and cinnamon rolls. Whale-watching and visiting the Redwood National Park are just a few of the activities that engage guests.

4 Rooms • Price range: $140-170
560 Edwards St, Trinidad, CA 95570
☎ **(707) 677-0840**

Trinidad
Turtle Rocks Oceanfront Inn

This picturesque inn is located on three acres of ocean-front property, on a bluff 220 feet above the Pacific. It offers views of the surrounding rocks and of the seastacks known as Turtle Rocks. Each guestroom features a private glass-paneled deck, a private bath, a California king-size bed and double-walled construction for privacy. Breakfast includes tasty dishes such as Ukrainian dumplings, quiche or stratta and yeast rolls.

6 Rooms • Price range: $155-210
3392 Patrick's Point Dr, Trinidad, CA 95570
☎ **(707) 677-3707**

Truckee
Richardson House

Surrounded by the Sierra Peaks, this 1880 mansion offers gorgeous views.

8 Rooms • Price range: $100-175
10154 High St, Truckee, CA 96160
☎ **(530) 587-5388**

Twain Harte
⑯ *McCaffrey House B&B Inn*

A white picket fence surrounds this lovely country home, accentuating its picturesque qualities. Oaks, pines and cedar trees shade the house and there is a pretty flower garden. All guestrooms feature impressive black cast-iron stoves, and are brightly decorated with handmade Amish quilts. Most of the rooms have a balcony or a patio so that guests can go outside and enjoy the view of the mountains. An extensive collection of videos and books is available for the use of guests. Data ports have been installed in some of the rooms. After a long day, guests are encouraged to soak in the grand outdoor whirlpool.

7 Rooms • Price range: $125-200
23251 Highway 108, Twain Harte, CA 95383
☎ **(209) 586-0757**

Twentynine Palms
⑯ *Homestead Inn Bed & Breakfast*

A friendly atmosphere pervades this 1928 historic house in a quiet, residential desert area.

7 Rooms • Price range: $75-175
74153 Two Mile Rd, Twentynine Palms,
CA 92277
☎ **(760) 367-0030**

Ukiah
Vichy Hot Springs Resort and Inn
This unique historic resort was originally built in 1854. Guests can soak in the only natural warm, carbonated mineral baths in North America, or

walk on the 700-acre ranch. Massages and facials are also available.

23 Rooms • Price range: $105-245
2605 Vichy Springs Rd, Ukiah, CA 95482
☎ **(707) 462-9515**

Venice
⑯ *The Venice Beach House*

A 1911 California-Craftsman house just a short walk to the beach.

9 Rooms • Price range: $110-250
15 30th Ave, Venice, CA 90291
☎ **(310) 823-1966**

Ventura

Bella Maggiore Inn
This renovated historical landmark, built
in 1926, has an attractive European air.

28 Rooms • Price range: $75-175
67 S California St, Ventura, CA 93001
☎ (805) 652-0277

Ventura
Victorian Rose Bed & Breakfast
A one-of-a-kind establishment, this
extensively restored Victorian-Gothic
Church is more than 110 years old. The
building boasts 26-foot-high beamed
ceilings, stained-glass windows and the original
96-foot-high steeple. Guests can relax in one of
the cozy sitting areas, or examine the inn's collection of eletic antiques. Also on-site are a
double Jacuzzi, a lovely garden and an attractive outdoor veranda.

5 Rooms • Price range: $99-175
896 E Main St, Ventura, CA 93001
☎ (805) 641-1888

Ventura
La Mer European Bed & Breakfast
An 1890 Cape Cod-style Victorian, this
house is a historic landmark overlooking historic San Buenaventura. Each
antique-filled bedroom features a private bath. A Bavarian breakfast is served. The
beach is within walking distance.

5 Rooms • Price range: $90-185
411 Poli St, Ventura, CA 93001
☎ (805) 643-3600

Visalia
Ben Maddox House
Much of the original charm remains
in this 1876 property. The house itself
is constructed of redwood from the
Sequoias, and the parlor, bedrooms and
dining room have 14-foot-high ceilings, dark
pine trim and varnished white oak floors. All of
the rooms feature a sitting area, private bath
and king- or queen-size bed. Guests can also enjoy
a large deck, the spa and the swimming pool.

6 Rooms • Price range: $70-105
601 N Encina St, Visalia, CA 93291
☎ (559) 739-0721

Visalia
The Spalding House Bed & Breakfast Inn
This 1901 Colonial-style house has a
library and parlor with a Steinway.

3 Rooms • Price range: $75-95
631 N Encina St, Visalia, CA 93291
☎ (559) 739-7877

Westport
De Haven Valley Farm
An 1875 farmhouse surrounded by rolling
hills, meadows, streams and woods.

8 Rooms • Price range: $85-140
39247 N Highway One, Westport, CA 95488
☎ (707) 961-1660

Yountville
Maison Fleurie
Three buildings situated on an acre of
landscaped gardens make up this
establishment. Finely crafted furniture,
rich fabrics and a huge stone fireplace
enhance the interior. A pool and spa are available as are full breakfasts and afternoon wine.

13 Rooms • Price range: $115-260
6529 Yount St, Yountville, CA 94599
☎ (707) 944-2056

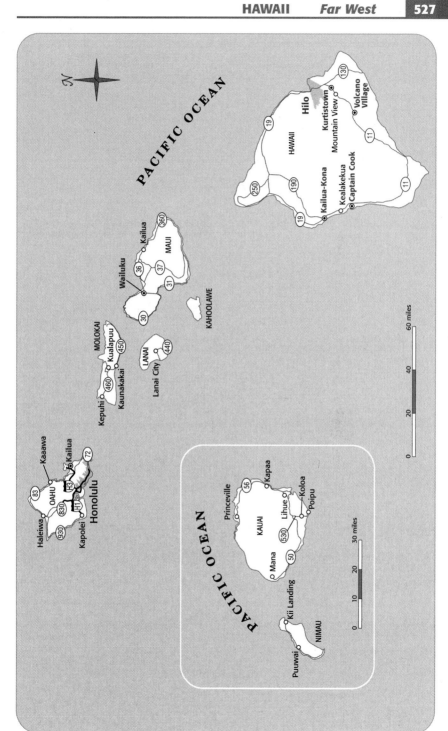

Captain Cook
Areca Palms Estate/Merryman's Bed & Breakfast

Cathedral ceilings and cushioned wicker furniture set the stage in the large living room of Merryman's; guestrooms are spacious and tastefully decorated. Set on a breezy hillside in coffee farm country, and surrounded by expansive lawns and flowering gardens, the B&B has a relaxing country atmosphere. Breakfast includes a daily special and exotic local fruits. Minutes away are shopping, historic attractions and an underwater marine park.

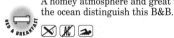

4 Rooms • Price range: $80-125
PO Box 489, Captain Cook, HI 96704
☎ **(808) 323-2276**

Hilo
Hale Kai Bjornen Bed & Breakfast

A homey atmosphere and great views of the ocean distinguish this B&B.

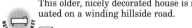

5 Rooms • Price range: $85-110
111 Honolii Pali, Hilo, HI 96720
☎ **(808) 935-6330**

Kailua
Papaya Paradise Bed and Breakfast

A peaceful tropical garden provides a tranquil setting for this inn.

2 Rooms • Price range: $80-100
395 Auwinala Rd, Kailua, HI 96734
☎ **(808) 261-0316**

Kailua-Kona
Hale Maluhia Country Inn B&B

This older, nicely decorated house is situated on a winding hillside road.

6 Rooms • Price range: $85-125
76-770 H Hualalai Rd, Kailua-Kona, HI 96740
☎ **(808) 329-1123**

Kurtistown
Bed & Breakfast Mountain View

Set in a quiet, rural area, this inn has lovely gardens and comfortable rooms.

4 Rooms • Price range: $55-95
PO Box 963, Kurtistown, HI 96760
☎ **(808) 968-6868**

Volcano
Chalet Kilauea-The Inn at Volcano

Six vacation homes decorated in an eclectic blend of Polynesian and contemporary style can be found at this contemporary inn. Guests begin their days with a three-course gourmet breakfast before exploring local sights. Local activities include driving down the crater of an active volcano, walking through a lava tube or a forest of lava trees, and soaking in a naturally heated freshwater tidal pond.

6 Rooms • Price range: $135-395
Wright Rd, Volcano, HI 96785
☎ **(808) 967-7786**

Volcano
Volcano Inn

This inn is located only minutes from Volcanoes National Park and active volcano Kilauea. Guests choose from several fully equipped cedar cottages tucked in among native giant tree ferns. The inn also features an extensive lanai (veranda).

8 Rooms • Price range: $455-145
19-3820 Old Volcano Hwy, Volcano, HI 96785
☎ **(808) 967-7293**

Volcano Village
Kilauea Lodge

Set in wooded Volcano Village, this attractive lodge offers a welcoming atmosphere in the midst of beautiful tropical scenery. The restaurant serves a superb blend of European and local cuisine. Hiking, bird-watching, picnicking and volcano viewing are a stroll away in the spectacular Hawaii Volcanoes National Park. Guests can also explore the black sand beaches and clear lagoons of Hilo's Keaukaha shoreline.

13 Rooms • Price range: $125-165
19-3948 Old Volcano Rd,
Volcano Village, HI 96785
☎ **(808) 967-7366**

Wailuku
The Old Wailuku Inn at Ulupono
Built in 1924 and boasting a rich and colorful history, this restored home is decorated in 1940s "Hawaiiana." Rooms are spacious and cool with floorings made from exotic woods such as eucalyptus and ohia, and furnishings made from bamboo. Each of the rooms is equipped with a private bath and is themed after a verse from a local poet. Decorations match the themes with heirloom Hawaiian quilts and lush plants and flowers.

7 Rooms • Price range: $120-180
2199 Kahookele St, Wailuku, HI 96793
☎ **(808) 244-5897**

Notes:

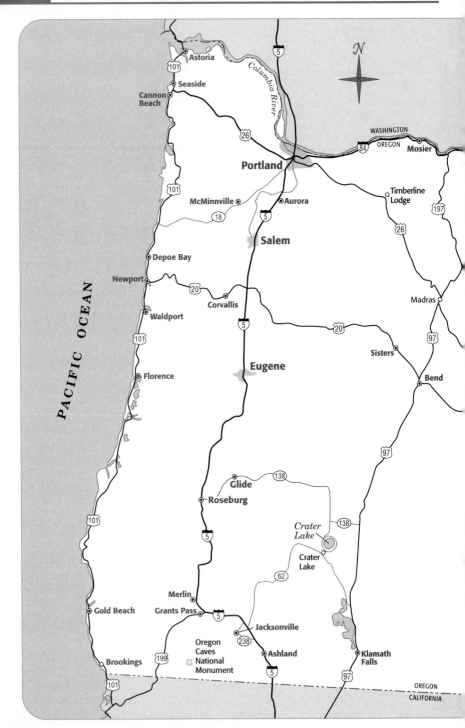

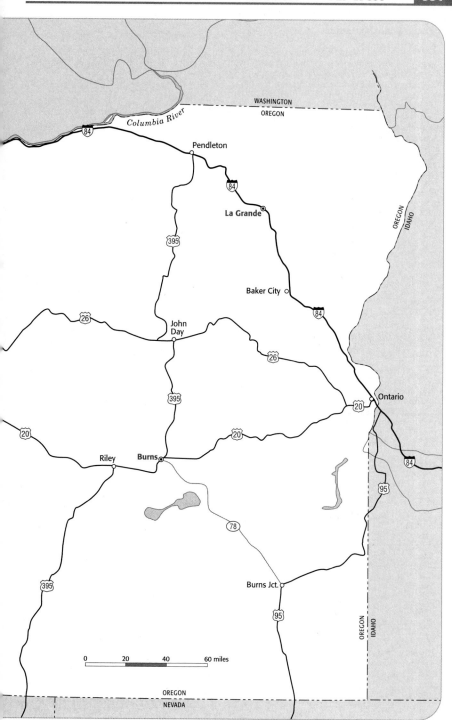

WASHINGTON
OREGON

Columbia River

84

Pendleton

84

La Grande

395

Baker City

84

26

John
Day

26

395

20

Ontario

20

20

Riley

Burns

84

95

78

395

Burns Jct.

95

OREGON
IDAHO

OREGON
IDAHO

0   20   40   60 miles

OREGON
NEVADA

Ashland
Chanticleer Inn

This 1920s Craftsman bungalow is located in a quiet residential neighborhood, a short walk from the Shakespeare Festival and the shops of Ashland's Main Street. Guestrooms are furnished with antiques, firm beds, fluffy comforters, and imported soaps. The spacious living room offers comfy chairs and a warming, open-hearth fireplace. A hearty, healthy, gourmet breakfast is served in the sunny dining room.

6 Rooms • Price range: $145-205
120 Gresham, Ashland, OR 97520
☎ **(541) 482-1919**

Ashland
Country Willows Bed & Breakfast Inn

This restored 1890s farmhouse on five acres of lush farmland is surrounded by the Siskiyou and Cascade Mountains. Guests can take in views of these peaks while relaxing on the willow furniture on two porches, or while rocking on the swing under the inn's namesake willow trees. Homemade breads and muffins are part of a full breakfast served in the sunroom or on the front porch.

9 Rooms • Price range: $95-210
1313 Clay St, Ashland, OR 97520
☎ **(541) 488-1590**

Ashland
🐪 The Iris Inn Bed and Breakfast

This 1905 Victorian home, set in a quiet residential area, is decorated with period flair. Each of the themed guestrooms has its own individual stamp, such as the large windows and magnificent views of the Vista Room and the bright and sunny sitting area of the Blue Room. All rooms, however, are furnished with a private bath and complimentary robes. The inn's elegant breakfast includes such specialties as eggs Benedict and crepes.

5 Rooms • Price range: $75-130
59 Manzanita St, Ashland, OR 97520
☎ **(541) 488-2286**

Ashland
Lithia Springs Inn

Visitors to this Cape Cod-style inn can bath in its natural hot springs.

16 Rooms • Price range: $105-225
2165 W Jackson Rd, Ashland, OR 97520
☎ **(541) 482-7128**

Ashland
Morical House Garden Inn

This restored 1880s Eastlake Victorian farmhouse is surrounded by berries and wildflowers, and stands on two acres of landscaped grounds, which include ponds, a meandering stream and a waterfall. Attractive touches such as leaded- and stained-glass windows, fine woodwork and antiques reveal the inn's 19th-century origins. Visitors can enjoy the sights and sounds of Ashland's festivals, just a short drive away.

8 Rooms • Price range: $95-170
668 N Main St, Ashland, OR 97520
☎ **(541) 482-2254**

Ashland
Mt. Ashland Inn

Located in the country and surrounded by snow-capped mountains, this cozy inn was built from cedar logs cut on the property. Inside, stained glass, hand-carved details, country wallpapers and handmade quilts create a casual elegance. The inn offers guests the use of mountain bikes, skis and sleds in order for them to take advantage of the area's many trails and hills for hiking, biking, and cross-country and downhill skiing.

5 Rooms • Price range: $130-200
550 Mt Ashland Rd, Ashland, OR 97520
☎ **(541) 482-8707**

Ashland
⚭ *Peerless Hotel*

Listed on the National Register of Historic Places, this 1900 brick building is decorated in period style with colorful fabrics and decorative murals and stenciling. The beautifully appointed guestrooms and suites are furnished with an eclectic mix of antique furnishings from New Orleans to Hawaii. The private baths that accompany each room include either a Jacuzzi, a two-person shower or a claw-foot tub.

6 Rooms • Price range: $74-210
243 Fourth St, Ashland, OR 97520
☎ **(541) 488-1082**

Ashland
Romeo Inn

This early 1930s Cape Cod-style inn features traditional decor and a landscaped courtyard with patio, pool and spa. Each of the individually decorated rooms and suites has something unique, such as a marble fireplace or a private patio, and all have king-size beds and private baths. Gourmet breakfasts include melon with blueberry sauce, eggs Florentine, and homemade breads.

6 Rooms • Price range: $130-185
295 Idaho St, Ashland, OR 97520
☎ **(541) 488-0884**

Ashland
⚭ *The Woods House Bed & Breakfast Inn*

Landscaped terraces with herb and rose gardens, majestic trees, and lawns surround this 1908 Craftsman-style inn. Coffee, tea and cookies are always available, as are games, books, magazines and daily newspapers. A three-course breakfast, alternating each day between a sweet and savory main course, is served on fine china in the dining room or in the garden under a spreading walnut tree

6 Rooms • Price range: $105-130
333 N Main, Ashland, OR 97520
☎ **(541) 488-1598**

Ashland
Hersey House

This 1904 Craftsman-style home is located in an attractive residential area that is within walking distance of theaters, shops and restaurants. Each guestroom has its own unique decor, ranging from Victorian to casual contemporary.

5 Rooms • Price range: $125-160
451 N Main St, Ashland, OR 97520
☎ **(541) 482-4563**

Ashland
McCall House Bed & Breakfast

Common areas of this beautifully restored 1883 Italianate manor have bay windows, and are comfortably decorated with period antiques and high back chairs. The B&B itself is located just one block from downtown and the Shakespeare Festival.

9 Rooms • Price range: $145-170
153 Oak St, Ashland, OR 97520
☎ **(541) 482-9296**

Ashland
Oak Hill Bed & Breakfast

This sage-colored 1910 restored farmhouse is located near the city and has a pleasant outdoor deck area. The inn also features a Mediterranean garden, a shady gazebo and a front yard bordered by rhododendrons and two stately oaks.

6 Rooms • Price range: $120-140
2190 Siskiyou Blvd, Ashland, OR 97520
☎ **(541) 482-1554**

Astoria
Clementine's Bed & Breakfast

The rooms in this 1888 Victorian home are furnished with an eclectic array of furnishings, some dating back 100 years. Outside, the inn is surrounded by impressive gardens and across the way stands the Flavel House Museum.

5 Rooms • Price range: $70-135
847 Exchange St, Astoria, OR 97103
☎ **(503) 325-2005**

Bend
Cricketwood Country Bed & Breakfast

Located on 10 acres of quiet countryside, this inn was listed in Time Magazine's "Best Places to Stay." Each guestroom has been given a different garden theme and there is a separate cottage which features cedar-log furniture, knotty-pine walls and a gas fireplace. Breakfast at the inn is an event: Guests get to choose from a very large menu, which includes such delicacies as Moroccan oatmeal and crème brûlée French toast.

4 Rooms • Price range: $85-125
63520 Cricketwood Rd, Bend, OR 97701
☎ **(877) 330-0747**

Brookings
Chetco River Inn

Located only 18 miles inland from the coast, this inn offers 35 acres of birdwatching, fishing, swimming and hiking. Guests are surprised to find the rustic, cedar-log exterior of the inn houses a marble-floored living room full of antiques and fine furniture. Modern amenities at this environmentally sensitive inn are provided by alternative energy sources, including propane gas, and solar power.

6 Rooms • Price range: $125-145
21202 High Prairie Rd, Brookings, OR 97415
☎ **(541) 670-1645**

Brookings
South Coast Inn Bed & Breakfast

This 4,000-square-foot inn offers antique-filled guestrooms, a large dining room and a spacious reading parlor with an original stone fireplace and a vintage grand piano. Located on Oregon's rugged, unspoiled coast, the inn was designed in the Craftsman style and was built in 1917. All rooms are equipped with private baths, and two have a panoramic view of the ocean. The inn also has a separate cottage with a kitchenette.

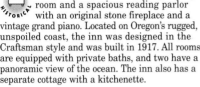

5 Rooms • Price range: $89-109
516 Redwood St, Brookings, OR 97415
☎ (541) 469-5557

Burns
Sage Country Inn B&B
Tastefully appointed guestrooms grace this Georgian-Colonial home.

4 Rooms • Price range: $65-85
351 1/2 W Monroe, Burns, OR 97720
☎ (541) 573-7243

Cannon Beach
⑭ *Stephanie Inn*
This New England-style hotel is located right on the beach, with views of the Pacific Ocean and misty coastal mountains. The inn's four-course gourmet dinners offer innovative Pacific-Northwest cuisine. Unique packages are also available to make special occasions extraordinary: Guests may be greeted with rose petals sprinkled over the bed, or they might discover wine or champagne, chocolates and mementos waiting for them in the room. Suites consist of a sitting room with fireplace and TV/VCR, king-size whirlpool bath beds, a Jacuzzi and a private balcony.

50 Rooms • Price range: $169-449
2740 S Pacific, Cannon Beach, OR 97110
☎ (503) 436-2221

Corvallis
⑭ *Harrison House Bed & Breakfast*
This 1939 Dutch-Colonial house set in a neighborhood of historic homes features Williamsburg-style antiques and an English cottage garden. It was originally owned by a professor at Oregon State University, which is only three blocks away. Individually decorated rooms are large and comfortable. Complimentary afternoon refreshments are offered in the sunroom, and include South Willamette Valley wines and locally made truffles.

4 Rooms • Price range: $90-100
2310 NW Harrison Blvd, Corvallis, OR 97330
☎ (541) 752-6248

Corvallis
A Bed & Breakfast on the Green
Neighboring a private golf course, this inn offers guests a quiet rural setting.

4 Rooms • Price range: $90-100
2515 SW 45th St, Corvallis, OR 97333
☎ (541) 757-7321

Depoe Bay
Gracie's Landing Bed & Breakfast Inn

Built to resemble the New England seaboard inns of the early 1800s, Gracie's Landing offers a relaxing, casual atmosphere with a decidedly nautical ambience. All suites have a deck overlooking Depoe Bay and bridge, and most of them have a fireplace. A full complimentary breakfast is served daily in the dining room. The innkeepers are very accommodating and happy to make special arrangements for their guests.

13 Rooms • Price range: $90-130
235 SE Bay View Ave, Depoe Bay, OR 97341
☎ **(541) 765-2322**

Eugene
⚇ *Campbell House, A City Inn*

A restored 1892 Queen Anne-style home set on an acre of landscaped grounds with gardens and a gazebo, the Campbell House features a variety of guestrooms. Each is thoughtfully decorated and features either a private deck or patio. Other amenities include porcelain tubs and high beds, while some rooms are equipped with fireplaces and Jacuzzis. Located in the historic district of Eugene a few blocks from downtown, guests may attend the local theater or browse the antique shops. Tea and coffee are served in-room, followed by a breakfast of freshly baked scones and mini Belgian waffles.

18 Rooms • Price range: $89-289
252 Pearl St, Eugene, OR 97401
☎ **(541) 343-1119**

Eugene
Excelsior Inn

This 1912 inn offers classic European comfort and style with 14 newly renovated guest suites, each named after a classical composer. Features of the inn include hardwood floors, marble baths, vaulted ceilings, arched windows and cherry wood furniture. All guestrooms are equipped with private baths, two with whirlpool tubs. Guests are invited to eat in the inn's dining room, as well as the more casual breakfast room.

14 Rooms • Price range: $79-150
754 E 13th Ave, Eugene, OR 97401
☎ **(541) 342-6963**

Eugene
The Oval Door Bed & Breakfast

Although recently built, this B&B was designed in the early 20th-century farmhouse style. The inn features a wraparound porch, a spacious living room and a library. Guestrooms are named after Oregon wildflowers and are each equipped with a private bath, two have Jacuzzis. Breakfast here includes a "special of the day" as well as fresh fruit and homemade bread. Nearby are the cafés and restaurants of downtown Eugene.

4 Rooms • Price range: $65-125
988 Lawrence St, Eugene, OR 97401
☎ **(541) 683-3160**

Florence
Edwin K. Bed & Breakfast

This 1914 Craftsman-style home across the street from the Siuslaw River is beautifully accented with landscaped grounds. The six large guestrooms offer a blend of antiques and contemporary comforts, and each is accompanied by a custom-designed private bath. The inn also features a private deck and courtyard, where a waterfall adds to the tranquil mood. Breakfast is served on fine china and crystal in the formal dining room.

7 Rooms • Price range: $85-150
1155 Bay St, Florence, OR 97439
☎ **(541) 997-8360**

Glide
Steelhead Run B&B and Fine Art Gallery

This spacious B&B stands on a bluff overlooking the scenic North Umpqua River. The inn features a variety of themed rooms, a dining room, two decks and an American heritage art gallery. Nearby is Crater Lake National Park.

4 Rooms • Price range: $68-115
23049 N Umpqua (Hwy 138), Glide, OR 97443
☎ **(541) 496-0563**

Gold Beach
Tu Tu' Tun Lodge

Featuring an uncommon blend of sophisticated service and low-key country charm, the Tu Tu' Tun Lodge is located in a secluded, scenic location between the forest and the Rogue River, only seven miles from the Pacific Ocean. A massive stone fireplace is the centerpiece of the contemporary cedar-planked lodge, which also houses an intimate bar, a small library, and a gourmet dining room serving nationally acclaimed cuisine. Each room has a balcony or patio overlooking the river, and several have a fireplace or an outdoor soaking tub. The lodge boasts a heated pool, a four-hole pitch-and-putt course, and a horseshoe course.

20 Rooms • Price range: $135-325
96550 N Bank Rogue, Gold Beach, OR 97444
☎ **(541) 247-6664**

Grants Pass
Flery Manor Bed & Breakfast

This B&B stands on seven acres of mountainside surrounded by a panorama of pine forest. Ponds and a waterfall are located on the grounds and there are hammocks and sitting areas for guests to enjoy. Featured inside are original artwork and family antiques, including canopy beds. A sumptuous breakfast, offering such homemade treats as beignets, frittatas, quiches and kugelis, is served in grand style.

4 Rooms • Price range: $85-100
2000 Jumpoff Joe Creek Rd,
Grants Pass, OR 97526
☎ **(541) 476-3591**

Jacksonville

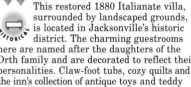 The Historic Orth House Bed & Breakfast, The Teddy Bear Inn

This restored 1880 Italianate villa, surrounded by landscaped grounds, is located in Jacksonville's historic district. The charming guestrooms here are named after the daughters of the Orth family and are decorated to reflect their personalities. Claw-foot tubs, cozy quilts and the inn's collection of antique toys and teddy bears all add to the period decor. The inn also features a wicker-furnished front porch.

4 Rooms • Price range: $95-225
105 W Main St PO Box 1437,
Jacksonville, OR 97530-1437
☎ (541) 899-8665

Jacksonville

Jacksonville Inn

This 1861 inn, located in the first town in America to be named a National Historic Landmark, has a restaurant that offers a five-course table d'hôte, accompanied by a selection of 1,500 wines. Three honeymoon cottages with whirlpool tubs, steam showers and private garden patios are also available. Jacksonville itself has a full slate of festivals and concerts for visitors to enjoy.

11 Rooms • Price range: $125-260
175 E California St, Jacksonville, OR 97530
☎ (541) 899-1900

Jacksonville

TouVelle House Bed & Breakfast

This 1916 Craftsman home is set on two acres of landscaped grounds, just two blocks from the historic downtown. Dark woodwork, antiques, patterned wallpaper and original light fixtures accent the inn's period theme. The guestrooms each include a private bath and an outstanding view. The inn also features a heated pool and an English garden. A three-course gourmet breakfast is served.

6 Rooms • Price range: $135-185
455 N Oregon St, Jacksonville, OR 97530
☎ (541) 899-8938

Klamath Falls

Thompson's Bed & Breakfast

Standing at the foot of a wooded hill, this B&B offers spectacular views of Upper Klamath Lake from the inn's large common room and outdoor deck.

The inn is next door to Moore Park, with its marina and its hiking trail.

4 Rooms • Price range: $75-100
1420 Wild Plum Ct, Klamath Falls, OR 97601
☎ (541) 882-7938

La Grande
Stang Manor Inn

This 1925 Georgian-Colonial home stands in a quiet residential neighborhood. Guestrooms have queen-size beds and private baths. One of the rooms offers a balcony overlooking the rose garden, and the suite features a fireplace in the sitting area. The inn also has a common room, sunroom and dining room, where crystal, fine china and silver set the stage for an elegant breakfast.

4 Rooms • Price range: $78-98
1612 Walnut St, La Grande, OR 97850
☎ **(541) 963-2400**

McMinnville
Steiger Haus Bed & Breakfast Inn

This European-style home is built on terraced landscaping. The five quiet and comfortable guestrooms have private baths and access to the inn's ivy-covered decks. The inn also includes a bright kitchen/dining room and a sunroom/studio.

5 Rooms • Price range: $65-130
360 Wilson St, McMinnville, OR 97128
☎ **(503) 472-0821**

Merlin
⚙ *Pine Meadow Inn Bed & Breakfast*

Set on a wooded knoll with nine acres of meadow and a private forest, the Pine Meadow Inn is styled after a midwestern farmhouse with a wraparound porch. French doors lead to formal English cutting gardens and a koi pond with waterfall in the backyard. Fresh ingredients from the garden are included in the gourmet breakfasts, which feature such hearty fare as Granny Smith pancakes and vegetable frittata.

4 Rooms • Price range: $85-120
1000 Crow Rd, Merlin, OR 97532
☎ **(541) 471-6277**

Mosier
Mosier House Bed & Breakfast

This Victorian-style home is perched on a hill offering picturesque views.

5 Rooms • Price range: $80-125
704 3rd Ave, Mosier, OR 97040
☎ **(541) 478-3640**

Newport
⚙ *Tyee Lodge Oceanfront Bed & Breakfast*

Sitting atop a bluff overlooking Agate beach, the Tyee Lodge is surrounded by a half-acre of park-like gardens. Each guestroom has a magnificent ocean view and is decorated in the Northwestern style with pine furniture, easy chairs and down bedding. A trail leads through a stand of windswept trees to miles of sheltered, sandy beaches, tide pools, and crashing waves. Nearby is Yaquina Head lighthouse.

5 Rooms • Price range: $110-130
4925 NW Woody Way, Newport, OR 97365
☎ **(541) 265-8953**

Portland
The Lion and The Rose Victorian Bed & Breakfast

This 1906 Queen Anne home is listed on the National Register of Historic Places. The house contains ornate decorative plaster work and Oriel windows. Guestrooms are individually decorated and feature private baths—some with claw-foot tubs, others with showers. The inn's comfortable elegance extends out into the grounds, which include fountains, rose gardens and a gazebo. Breakfast is served in the dining room.

7 Rooms • Price range: $95-140
1810 NE 15th, Portland, OR 97212
☎ **(503) 287-9245**

Portland
General Hooker's Bed & Breakfast
This inn's Victorian exterior belies a casual, modern decor.

4 Rooms • Price range: $90-135
125 SW Hooker, Portland, OR 97201
☎ **(503) 222-4435**

Roseburg
House of Hunter Bed & Breakfast
This restored 1900s Italianate home is set in a quiet area bordering downtown.

4 Rooms • Price range: $65-95
813 SE Kane St, Roseburg, OR 97470
☎ **(541) 672-2335**

Salem
A Creekside Inn, the Marquee House
As the name suggests, this B&B features themed guestrooms based on the movies.

5 Rooms • Price range: $60-100
333 Wyatt Ct NE, Salem, OR 97301
☎ **(503) 391-0837**

Seaside
⑩ _Gilbert Inn Bed & Breakfast_

Built in 1892 by a former mayor of Seaside, this Queen Anne B&B retains its Victorian warmth. The home features hand-crafted details such as tongue-and-groove paneling on walls and ceilings. Decorating touches include family heirlooms and period furnishings, such as brass beds and claw-foot tubs. The inn is located only steps away from the beach and Seaside's many shops and restaurants.

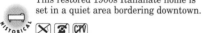 

10 Rooms • Price range: $94-125
341 Beach Dr, Seaside, OR 97138
☎ **(503) 738-9770**

Seaside
⑩ _Sea Side Oceanfront Inn Bed & Breakfast Hotel_
This inn has a fun mix of decorative themes, from rock 'n' roll to seaside.

14 Rooms • Price range: $135-265
581 S Promenade, Seaside, OR 97138
☎ **(503) 738-6403**

Seaside
10th Avenue Inn Bed & Breakfast
Built in 1908, this restored home is bright and modern and close to the beach. The common room that welcomes guests is cheerfully decorated, as are the three guestrooms. The inn also has a completely furnished cottage.

 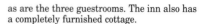

4 Rooms • Price range: $55-129
125 10th Ave, Seaside, OR 97138
☎ **(503) 738-0643**

Seaside
The Guest House Bed & Breakfast

Located across the street from the Necanicum River, this inn offers a blend of contemporary and antique furnishings. Accommodations are decorated in various themes, from the soft tones of the Ladies' Room to the nautical Captain's Room.

4 Rooms • Price range: $70-95
486 Necanicum Dr, Seaside, OR 97138
☎ **(503) 717-0495**

Seaside
Riverside Inn Bed & Breakfast

Close to the beach and downtown, this B&B offers guestrooms of varying size.

11 Rooms • Price range: $60-105
430 S Holladay Dr, Seaside, OR 97138
☎ **(503) 738-8254**

Sisters
Conklin's Guest House

A Craftsman-style home built almost a century ago, Conklin's has been renovated and expanded many times. Landscaped grounds surround a heated swimming pool and ponds are stocked with trout for catch-and-release fishing. Spectacular views of snow-capped mountains rising above a lush valley greet visitors. There are many activities to choose from all year round, including hiking, boating, golf, skiing and snowmobiling.

5 Rooms • Price range: $80-150
69013 Camp Polk Rd, Sisters, OR 97759
☎ **(541) 549-0123**

Waldport
Cliff House

A luxuriously restored historic home, the Cliff House sits on a panoramic bluff with a picturesque ocean view of Alsea Bay and the mountains beyond. The knotty pine paneling and working fireplace create a rustic atmosphere, and the sunsets, viewed from the wraparound deck or one of the private balconies, are breathtaking. On weekends, a gourmet breakfast is served in the dining room with china, crystal, silver and linens.

4 Rooms • Price range: $110-225
1450 Adahi Rd, Waldport, OR 97394
☎ **(541) 563-2506**

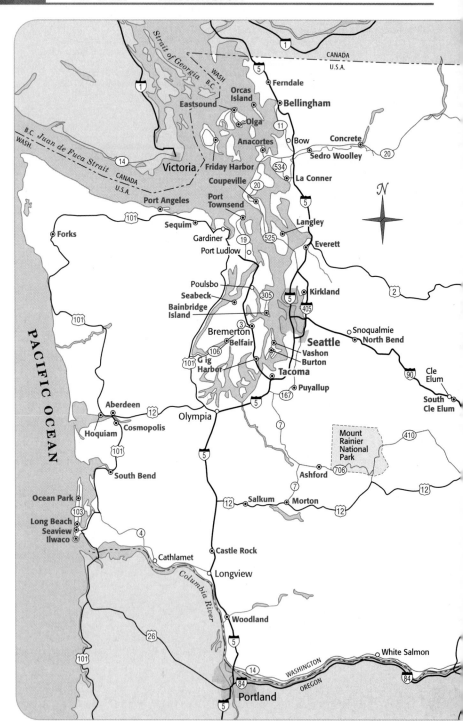

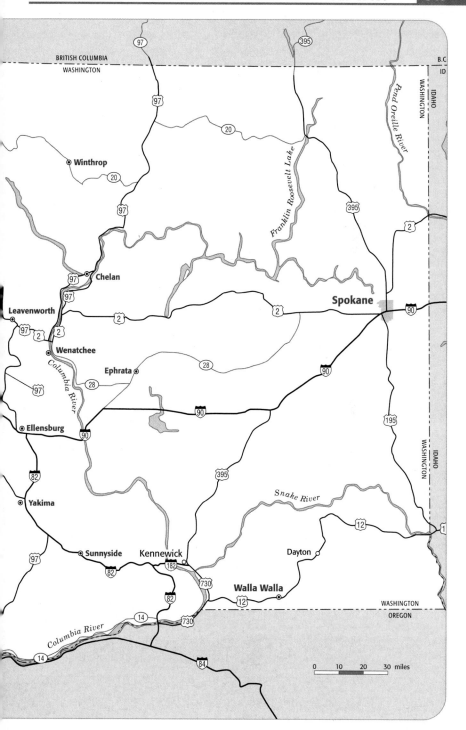

Aberdeen
Aberdeen Mansion Inn Bed & Breakfast

This handsome Victorian mansion was built for lumber baron Edward Hulbert in 1905. Furnished with period pieces and fine antiques, the inn boasts a beautiful entry hall and staircase. All guestrooms have a king-size bed and most have a private bath. The acre of grounds is attractively landscaped and planted with flowering trees and shrubs. Aberdeen is home port for the Lady Washington, which is open for tours by the public.

5 Rooms • Price range: $80-135
807 N M St, Aberdeen, WA 98520
☎ **(360) 533-7079**

Aberdeen
A Harbor View Bed & Breakfast

This Victorian home was originally built in the Colonial-Revival style as a single residence in 1905. Sitting atop a hill overlooking the city and harbor, the inn is a short walk from downtown. The spacious Windsor Room offers a view of downtown Aberdeen and the harbor. Beaches are 20 minutes away and guests are invited to join a Historic Old Homes Walking Tour. Polson Museum and Hoquiam Castle are nearby.

4 Rooms • Price range: $75-130
111 W 11th St, Aberdeen, WA 98520
☎ **(360) 533-7996**

Anacortes
Albatross Bed & Breakfast

Situated on a knoll across from a marina this 1927 Cape Cod offers a splendid view of the waterfront. The quaint guestrooms are comfortably furnished and have private baths. Pleasant innkeepers and a charming ambience complete the picture.

4 Rooms • Price range: $85-95
5708 Kingsway W, Anacortes, WA 98221
☎ **(360) 293-0677**

Anacortes
Channel House

Set in a residential area, this Victorian house is close to Guemos Channel and has a panoramic view of Puget Sound. Adjacent to the main house is a cottage with two guestrooms with fireplaces. Watch the ships sail past from the outdoor hot tub.

6 Rooms • Price range: $85-119
2902 Oakes Ave, Anacortes, WA 98221
☎ **(360) 293-9382**

Ashford
Alexander's Country Inn

Period furnishings set the tone in this nicely renovated historic inn.

14 Rooms • Price range: $110-140
37515 SR 706 E, Ashford, WA 98304
☎ **(360) 569-2300**

Ashford
Mountain Meadows Inn Bed & Breakfast

Set amid cedars on 11 acres of land, Mountain Meadows is just six miles from the entrance to Mt. Rainier National Park. The 1910 home features Native American artifacts and a collection of references on the national parks system.

6 Rooms • Price range: $85-140
28912 SR 706 E, Ashford, WA 98304
☎ **(360) 569-2788**

Bainbridge Island
⬥⬥ *The Buchanan Inn*

Located just 35 minutes by ferry from Seattle, Bainbridge Island offers the peaceful beauty of the Pacific Northwest within easy reach of a major city. This 1912 New England-style barn house sits on one-and-a-half acres of landscaped grounds and gardens. The inn features comfortably appointed rooms, several with an antique-style gas fireplace. A Jacuzzi hot tub is housed in a private rustic cottage for all guests to enjoy.

4 Rooms • Price range: $119-169
8494 NE Odd Fellows Rd,
Bainbridge Island, WA 98110
☎ **(206) 780-9258**

Belfair
Selah Inn

The beautiful Hood Canal is a haven for wildlife and nature enthusiasts alike and the Selah Inn is a wonderful spot to start exploring the area's natural wonders. Start the day with a full breakfast and then head out to the beach to watch the sea lions and otters. After the day's activities, guests retire to a tastefully appointed guestroom or relax in front of the river-stone fireplace in the cozy living room

4 Rooms • Price range: $100-170
130 NE Dulalip Landing, Belfair, WA 98528
☎ **(360) 275-0916**

Bellingham
⬥⬥ *North Garden Inn*

The fancifully ornate exterior of this Queen Anne home overlooking Bellingham Bay is one of the town's finest examples of Victorian domestic architecture. Listed on the National Register of Historic Places, this inn has uniquely decorated guestrooms with views of the harbor or the gardens. The central location makes it easy for guests to explore the nearby historical attractions, restaurants and shops.

8 Rooms • Price range: $60-135
1014 N Garden St, Bellingham, WA 98225
☎ **(360) 671-7828**

Bellingham
Schnauzer Crossing

Situated above Lake Whatcom, midway between Seattle and Vancouver, B.C., Schnauzer Crossing is an attractive, contemporary home that provides gracious accommodations. The Great Room, with its wall of windows, offers a wonderful view of Lake Whatcom. Guestrooms are bright and comfortable, some with a Jacuzzi, a fireplace and a lake view. The inn also features lovely gardens and an outdoor hot tub.

3 Rooms • Price range: $130-215
4421 Lakeway Dr, Bellingham, WA 98226
☎ **(360) 733-0055**

Bremerton
Illahee Manor Bed & Breakfast

The scenic shores of Washington's Kitsap Peninsula provide this grand B&B with a beautiful, tranquil setting. Guests can take refuge in the elegantly appointed guestrooms or enjoy the views from the wraparound porch. Also available is the Honeymoon Cabin, which is ideal for couples seeking a romantic weekend getaway. The Beach House, which sleeps up to 10, is perfect for large families or groups.

7 Rooms • Price range: $125-250
6680 Illahee Rd NE, Bremerton, WA 98311
☎ **(360) 698-7555**

Castle Rock
Blue Heron Inn B&B

Sitting at the edge of Silver Lake on five acres of land, the Blue Heron Inn offers a panoramic view of Mt. St. Helens and its forested valleys. All the guest-rooms have queen-size beds, private balconies and baths. The common areas include a parlor with a fireplace and views of the lake and mountain, a library and a covered veranda. A full country breakfast and dinner are included.

7 Rooms • Price range: $145-165
2846 Spirit Lake Hwy, Castle Rock, WA 98611
☎ **(360) 274-9595**

Chelan
Mary Kay's Whaley Mansion

This 1911 Edwardian-style Victorian home is on a bluff overlooking Lake Chelan. It's close to downtown, the Campbell House, Stehekin Steamer and the lake. The inn specializes in romantic getaways, complete with champagne.

6 Rooms • Price range: $115-135
415 S Third St, Chelan, WA 98816
☎ **(509) 682-5735**

Concrete
Cascade Mountain Inn

Hikers, mountain bikers and bird-watchers are delighted to discover the natural bounty surrounding the Cascade Mountain Inn. Surrounded by five acres of farmland in the foothills of the Cascade Mountains, this modern, gambrel-roofed establishment is near several park trail systems. There is also a 1,500-acre national preserve nearby, which attracts up to 300 bald eagles every spring.

6 Rooms • Price range: $120-140
40418 Pioneer Ln, Concrete, WA 98237
☎ **(360) 826-4333**

Cosmopolis
Cooney Mansion Bed & Breakfast

Built in 1908 for lumber baron Neil Cooney, this attractive mansion features many original American Arts and Crafts-style furnishings. A Jacuzzi, a sauna and an exercise room are available for guests to enjoy, as are the beautiful grounds. The ballroom is ideal for larger functions and formal dinners. The mansion sits next to Mill Creek Park's tennis courts, walking trails and trout-stocked lake and waterfall.

5 Rooms • Price range: $76-185
1705 Fifth St, Cosmopolis, WA 98537
☎ **(360) 533-0602**

Coupeville
◆◆ Anchorage Inn

The elegant Anchorage Inn was built in the style of the Coronado Hotel in San Diego. Guestrooms range from the light and airy Fairhaven, with its bay window and view of Penn Cove and historic Front Street, to the romantic Onward, a turret room with a 13-foot ceiling and views of Main Street and the cove. Elegantly furnished public rooms include a third-floor crow's nest. A sumptuous full breakfast is served daily in the dining room.

7 Rooms • Price range: $75-125
807 N Main St, Coupeville, WA 98239
☎ **(360) 678-5581**

Coupeville
Captain Whidbey Inn

For a refreshing change of pace this is a good place to visit. For almost 100 years this log cabin with its rustic ambience and remarkable seaside setting has been entertaining guests. The current owner, Capt. John Colby Stone, is a certified sailor with many sea adventures in his past. Guests may charter cruises aboard the S.V. Cutty Sark with Stone at the helm.

32 Rooms • Price range: $75-225
2072 W Captain Whidbey Inn Rd,
Coupeville, WA 98239
☎ **(360) 678-4097**

Coupeville
Compass Rose

The Compass Rose is situated on Whidbey Island in Coupeville, the heart of Ebey's Landing National Historical Reserve. The 1890 Queen Anne Victorian has been transformed into an elegant hostelry, replete with antique furnishings, beautiful woodwork and fine objects collected from around the globe by the owners. Tea is served in the afternoon and a generous breakfast is served every morning.

2 Rooms • Price: $85
508 S Main St, Coupeville, WA 98239
☎ **(360) 678-5318**

Coupeville
◆◆ Garden Isle Guest Cottages

Located on beautiful Whidbey Island, the Garden Isle Guest Cottages in historic Coupeville offer a great spot for a romantic honeymoon or anniversary getaway year-round. The comfortably furnished cottages have water and mountain views; in one cottage, there is a gas fireplace. Garden Isle also has a hot tub. Nearby attractions include Whidbey's Greenbank Winery, Meerkerk Rhododendron Gardens and a museum.

2 Rooms • Price range: $75-100
207 NW Coveland St, Coupeville, WA 98239
☎ **(360) 678-5641**

Coupeville
The Inn at Penn Cove

The Inn at Penn Cove consists of two of Coupeville's finest historic homes, the 1887 Kineth House and the 1891 Coupe-Gillespie House. The inn is furnished in Victorian decor and features an antique pump organ, as well as a comfortable sunporch. The Kineth House has an air of quiet luxury, while the Coupe-Gillespie House provides a country atmosphere, with magnificent views of the mountains and the water.

6 Rooms • Price range: $55-125
702 N Main, Coupeville, WA 98239
☎ **(360) 678-8000**

Coupeville
Old Morris Farm Inn
Built around a 1909 farmhouse, this restored home has elegant rooms.

4 Rooms • Price range: $85-125
105 W Morris Rd, Coupeville, WA 98239
☎ **(360) 678-6586**

Coupeville
ⒶⒶ The Victorian Bed & Breakfast

The town of Coupeville, on Whidbey Island, is the second-oldest town in the state and it has more than 100 buildings on the National Historic Register. One of these is the 1889 Italianate home that is the Victorian B&B. The two guestrooms upstairs have queen-size beds and bath. The private guest cottage has a queen-size bed, a trundle, a kitchen and bath. Originally a dentist's office, it was moved here around 1908.

3 Rooms • Price range: $65-100
602 N Main St, Coupeville, WA 98239
☎ **(360) 678-5305**

Eastsound
Otters Pond Bed & Breakfast of Orcas Island

Located on six wooded acres overlooking a protected wetland, the Orcas Island B&B is a bird-watcher's paradise. The modern inn features a deck from which guests can observe swans, blue herons, eagles and many other indigenous birds, while sipping on their morning coffee. Light and airy guestrooms are decorated with comfortable elegance. The secluded haven is close to various island activities and parks.

5 Rooms • Price range: $125-175
100 Tomihi Dr, Eastsound, WA 98245
☎ **(360) 376-8844**

Eastsound
ⒶⒶ Turtleback Farm Inn

This beautifully restored 1890s farmhouse stands on 80 acres of farmland and forest. Located in Crow Valley just six miles from the ferry landing, it commands a spectacular view of lush meadows, duck ponds and lofty Mt. Constitution. The Orchard House is a separate building set in an apple orchard; it offers four bedrooms complete with gas fireplaces and clawfoot tubs.

11 Rooms • Price range: $70-210
1981 Crow Valley Rd, Eastsound, WA 98245
☎ **(360) 376-4914**

Eastsound
Kangaroo House Bed & Breakfast
A 1907 Craftsman-style house with old-fashioned hospitality.

5 Rooms • Price range: $80-140
1459 North Beach Rd, Eastsound, WA 98245
☎ (360) 376-2175

Ellensburg
Murphy's Country Bed & Breakfast
This 1900s bungalow-style frontier home offers fly-fishing on Yakima River.

2 Rooms • Price range: $60-75
2830 Thorp Hwy S, Ellensburg, WA 98926
☎ (509) 925-7986

Ephrata
Ivy Chapel Inn B&B
Located in what was a 1940s Presbyterian church, the recently refurbished Ivy Chapel inn retains much of its original grace and charm. The spacious chapel still boasts its original stained-glass windows and majestic open-beamed cathedral ceiling. There are six different theme rooms, including a Bridal Room, as well as an open-air deck and a hot tub. The inn can accommodate 155 people for weddings or conferences.

6 Rooms • Price range: $75-100
164 D St SW, Ephrata, WA 98823
☎ (509) 754-0629

Everett
Gaylord House
Guestrooms at Gaylord House range from the nautical Commodore's Quarters to the romantic Lady Anne's Chamber. Located on a maple-lined avenue of turn-of-the-century homes, the B&B is a comfortable retreat with a delightful view of Mt. Baker and Mt. Rainier. Gourmet breakfasts are served and excellent dinners are available. A four-course high tea is open to the public by reservation on the first Sunday of each month.

5 Rooms • Price range: $80-175
3301 Grand Ave, Everett, WA 98201
☎ (425) 339-9153

Ferndale
Slater Heritage House
This charming, restored 1904 Victorian home in a rural setting has easy access to the interstate. All the guestrooms are individually decorated in a light and airy style. Charming innkeepers take pride in offering genuine hospitality, quality and service.

4 Rooms • Price range: $65-110
1371 W Axton Rd, Ferndale, WA 98248
☎ (360) 384-4273

Forks
Manitou Lodge
A modern lodge on 10 acres of coastal rain forest with trails leading to popular hiking spots and the coast. The Great Room features a large fieldstone fireplace and some unique furnishings. Enjoy hot beverages with the house's special cookies.

7 Rooms • Price range: $75-125
813 Kilmer Rd, Forks, WA 98331
☎ (360) 374-6295

Forks
Miller Tree Inn Bed & Breakfast

The mountains and the ocean are only a short drive away from this homestead B&B at the edge of town. A comfortable living room has ample reading material on the local tourist spots. The rooms are cozy and have the warm feeling of home.

7 Rooms • Price range: $60-135
654 E Division St, Forks, WA 98331
☎ **(360) 374-6806**

Friday Harbor
Duffy House Bed & Breakfast

English flower gardens, a fruit orchard, terraced rock gardens and a private beach all add to the charm of Duffy House. This 1920s Tudor-style home enjoys a commanding view of Griffin Bay and the snowcapped Olympic Mountains. Eagles' nests can be spotted right out back. Guestrooms are comfortable and all have private baths. Area activities include golfing, sport-fishing, sailing and whale watching.

5 Rooms • Price range: $105-125
4214 Pear Point Rd, Friday Harbor, WA 98250
☎ **(360) 378-5604**

Friday Harbor
⚠ Hillside House Bed & Breakfast

Guests of the Hillside House B&B have to choose between a breathtaking view of Mt. Baker and the Port of Friday Harbor or a room off the incredible two-story garden atrium. All seven comfortable guestrooms have private baths and a variety of amenities. Early risers can take advantage of a light snack to hold them over until the full breakfast is served. The innkeepers' pets include a standard poodle, a parrot and an outdoor cat.

7 Rooms • Price range: $85-250
365 Carter Ave, Friday Harbor, WA 98250
☎ **(360) 378-4730**

Friday Harbor
Trumpeter Inn Bed & Breakfast

Snuggled in a valley on San Juan Island, the Trumpeter Inn offers vistas of meadowlands and the snow-peaked Olympic Mountains. The inn is decorated with sophisticated country character and guest-rooms are tastefully appointed with private baths, down comforters and wonderful views. Many species of wildlife grace the inn's five acres and the inn's hammock and hot tub are fine places to relax. Breakfast features local specialties.

5 Rooms • Price range: $115-150
318 Trumpeter Way, Friday Harbor, WA 98250
☎ **(360) 378-3884**

Friday Harbor
Argyle House Bed & Breakfast

Close to shops, restaurants and the ferry, this 1910 home has old-fashioned charm.

4 Rooms • Price range: $100-145
685 Argyle Ave, Friday Harbor, WA 98250
☎ **(360) 378-4084**

Friday Harbor
Halvorsen House Bed & Breakfast

The property is located in pleasant rural setting just outside of town.

4 Rooms • Price range: $100-175
216 Halvorsen Rd, Friday Harbor, WA 98250
☎ **(360) 378-2707**

Friday Harbor
♦ ♦ **Panacea Bed & Breakfast Inn**
A 1907 traditional Craftsman-style
home with a wraparound porch.

 ⓧ Ⓩ 𝒜

4 Rooms • Price range: $140-180
595 Park St, Friday Harbor, WA 98250
☎ (360) 378-3757

Friday Harbor
♦ ♦ ⦿ **States Inn**
The rooms in this 60-acre horse-board-
ing ranch are all named after different
states. The Arizona has a Spanish influence, while The California is a spacious

room with a spectacular view across the valley
and ponds to nearby hills.

10 Rooms • Price range: $85-140
2687 W Valley Rd, Friday Harbor, WA 98250
☎ (360) 378-6240

ⓧ Ⓩ 𝒜 ⒸⓉⓋ

Friday Harbor
♦ **The Meadows**
Large, comfortable rooms in B&B sur-
rounded by ancient oaks and fields.

ⓧ Ⓩ 𝒜 ⒸⓉⓋ

2 Rooms • Price range: $95-145
1557 Cattle Point Rd, Friday Harbor, WA 98250
☎ (360) 378-4004

Gig Harbor
♦ ♦ **The Rose of Gig Harbor**
Guests can arrive by watercraft at
this pleasant 1917 home in the center
of town; the dock across the street
has moorage. The inn itself has an
unobstructed view of the harbor. Its guestrooms, named after roses and decorated with
floral themes, offer private baths and antique
furniture. Guests can have breakfast in the
dining room or they can have it served in
their rooms.

ⓧ 𝒜 ⒸⓉⓋ

5 Rooms • Price range: $85-150
3202 Harborview Dr, Gig Harbor, WA 98335
☎ (253) 853-7990

Hoquiam
♦ ♦ **Hoquiam's Castle B&B**
Hoquiam's Castle, a 10,000-square-
foot Victorian masterpiece, is both a
state and national heritage property.
Recently restored and converted to a
B&B, this inn is a treasure trove of turn-of-the-
20th-century craftsmanship, luxury and design.
Every room is carefully decorated to evoke the
period. There is possibly no better place than
this marvelous home to get a glimpse of how
late 19th-century captains of industry lived.

ⓧ Ⓩ 𝒜 ⒸⓉⓋ

5 Rooms • Price range: $85-140
515 Chenault Ave, Hoquiam, WA 98550
☎ (360) 533-2005

Hoquiam
♦ ♦ **Lytle House Bed & Breakfast**
High on a hill overlooking Grays Harbor,
lumber baron Joseph Lytle built this
beautiful Queen Anne-style mansion in
1897. The inn's gardens and four parlors
make it a fine place for an intimate wedding,
cocktail party or business meeting. Murder-
mystery dinner parties can also be arranged.
The Lytle House is located next door to Hoquiam's
Castle and is close to Grays Harbor's seaport, a
wildlife refuge and many museums.

ⓧ 𝒜

8 Rooms • Price range: $65-135
509 Chenault Ave, Hoquiam, WA 98550
☎ (360) 533-2320

Ilwaco

🏅 *The Inn at Ilwaco*

Affectionately referred to as "the end of the world" by local residents, Ilwaco is a tranquil little town at the base of the Long Beach Peninsula. Up on a hill overlooking the town and the harbor is The Inn at Ilwaco, a 1928 Presbyterian church converted to a B&B in 1986. Eight pristine rooms and a suite are decorated in a clean, uncluttered fashion. The chapel still has the original pews and is available for conferences and weddings.

9 Rooms • Price range: $79-189
120 Williams Ave, Ilwaco, WA 98624
☎ **(360) 642-8686**

Kirkland

🏅 *Shumway Mansion*

This 1909 award-winning historic mansion sits on almost two-and-a-half acres in a residential neighborhood overlooking Juanita Bay. Lace-covered windows, imported wallpaper and Oriental carpets provide a touch of luxury. The rooms feature antique furnishings from across Europe and North America, carved fireplace surrounds and mantles, and impressive works of art. The sunroom is decorated in white wicker.

8 Rooms • Price range: $95-130
11410 99th Pl NE, Kirkland, WA 98033
☎ **(425) 823-2303**

La Conner

🏅 *The Heron in La Conner*

This friendly Victorian-style inn features cottagelike rooms bedecked with antiques and lace. Phone, TV and bath come with each room. Deluxe king or queen suites are available, all with a spa tub, a fireplace and a deck. Guests can view the surrounding blue hills and glacial peak of Mt. Baker from a spacious backyard hot tub. The town boasts a new museum devoted to art luminaries of the Northwest.

12 Rooms • Price range: $100-160
117 Maple Ave, La Conner, WA 98257
☎ **(360) 466-4626**

Langley

Eagles Nest Inn

This private country retreat offers breathtaking views of Mt. Baker, Camano Island and Saratoga Passage. A registered backyard wildlife sanctuary adjacent to 4,000 acres of public trails, the inn's grounds are home to many birds and woodland creatures. Guests can relax in the outdoor spa or on a private deck. The lobby is a celebration of the island's natural environment, including a floor-to-ceiling mural created by a popular wildlife artist.

4 Rooms • Price range: $95-140
4680 Saratoga Rd, Langley, WA 98260
☎ **(360) 221-5331**

Langley
Saratoga Inn

Whidbey Island and the town of Langley are ideal for visitors who want to take advantage of recreational activities, such as kayaking, biking and hiking or for those who wish to do nothing but relax. At the Saratoga Inn the emphasis seems to be on relaxing but its central location makes it a perfect spot for being active as well. Gracious surroundings, warm hospitality and a beautiful view make the inn an irresistible spot.

15 Rooms • Price range: $110-275
201 Cascade Ave, Langley, WA 98260
☎ **(360) 221-5801**

Langley
Villa Isola B&B Inn

Italian hospitality, Mediterranean ambience and beautiful Northwest scenery come together here. The inn is situated on three-and-a-half pine-filled acres less than two miles from the seaside town of Langley. Guests can take advantage of the professional bocce court in the garden or enjoy the fresh-baked biscotti in the kitchen. Two suites give extra privacy. Mountain bikes are available for touring the island.

6 Rooms • Price range: $75-135
5489 S Coles Rd, Langley, WA 98260
☎ **(360) 221-5052**

Leavenworth
All Seasons River Inn B&B

Nestled among evergreens at the base of the Cascades, this inn provides gorgeous views of the mountains or the Wenatchee River from every room as well as from private decks. For a real treat, guests can watch the river flow by from the spacious Jacuzzi suite. The rooms are furnished with antiques and bear skins or handmade quilts. Seasonal activities—biking, skiing, rafting, golf, fishing—are all near the front door.

6 Rooms • Price range: $105-170
8751 Icicle Rd, Leavenworth, WA 98826
☎ **(509) 548-1425**

Leavenworth
AlpenRose Inn

The AlpenRose inn is managed by the fourth generation of a pioneer family whose artifacts and treasures are on display in the Leisure Room. Located in a Bavarian village, the inn provides the atmosphere of a B&B with the privacy of a small hotel. Some rooms feature balconies and fireplaces; luxury suites include a whirlpool. Depending on the season, guests can enjoy the golf course or the cross-country trails nearby.

15 Rooms • Price range: $80-125
500 Alpine Pl, Leavenworth, WA 98826
☎ **(509) 548-3000**

Leavenworth
Bosch Gärten

Bed, breakfast, hot tub and fabulous views of the Cascade Mountains.

3 Rooms • Price range: $80-115
9846 Dye Rd, Leavenworth, WA 98826
☎ **(509) 548-6900**

Leavenworth
Run of the River

This inn provides log lodgings with panoramic views of the Cascade Mountains and Icicle River. Each room features the hand-hewn craftsmanship of local artisans and is equipped with binoculars to view the area's wealth of birds, including blue herons, eagles and kingfishers. Guests can take a spin on a complimentary mountain bike, enjoy 19 miles of cross-country skiing trails or simply relax on a sunny deck.

6 Rooms • Price range: $205-245
9308 E Leavenworth Rd,
Leavenworth, WA 98826
☎ **(509) 548-7171**

Leavenworth
Haus Rohrbach Pension

A grand Swiss chalet in the Cascade Mountains with nice rooms and a view.

10 Rooms • Price range: $85-110
12882 Ranger Rd, Leavenworth, WA 98826
☎ **(509) 548-7024**

Leavenworth
Pine River Ranch

This ranch provides lodging complete with scenic vistas of the Cascade Mountains and an abundance of recreational activities just minutes away.

Rustic decor including gnarled lodge-pole pine beds are the highlights of each guestroom.

5 Rooms • Price range: $125-175
19668 Hwy 207, Leavenworth, WA 98826
☎ **(509) 763-3959**

Long Beach
ⱿⱿ Scandinavian Gardens Inn Bed & Breakfast

Here's an inn with a touch of Scandinavia, complete with a Finnish cedar sauna and queen-size beds imported from Sweden. Each room is decorated with antiques and is named after a different Scandinavian country. The innkeepers serve breakfast while wearing the region's traditional attire. Of course, they make their own Danish. The inn is conveniently located near the beach.

5 Rooms • Price range: $95-155
1610 California Ave S, Long Beach, WA 98631
☎ **(360) 642-8877**

Morton
St. Helens Manorhouse

Spacious rooms in a 1910 manor house on the edge of a wildlife preserve.

4 Rooms • Price range: $79-89
7476 US Hwy 12, Morton, WA 98356
☎ **(360) 498-5243**

North Bend
ⱿⱿ Roaring River Bed & Breakfast

Surrounded by forest, this rustic inn sits on a bluff above a dramatic bend in the Snoqualmie River. In other words, guests can expect spectacular views, wildlife and nature, nature, nature. The river is full of cutthroat trout, Mt. Si trailhead is nearby, there are four golf courses in the area, and Snoqualmie Falls and Pass are 20 miles away. One room is an old hunting cabin that has been remodeled as a loft and is suitable for four.

4 Rooms • Price range: $95-175
46715 SE 129th St, North Bend, WA 98045
☎ **(425) 888-4834**

Ocean Park
Caswells on the Bay
This contemporary Victorian-style home is on scenic Willapa Bay.

5 Rooms • Price range: $110-160
25204 Sandridge Rd, Ocean Park, WA 98640
☎ (360) 665-6535

Ocean Park
The DoveShire Bed & Breakfast
The extensive and wonderfully kept gardens of this establishment promise hours of pleasurable exploration and relaxation. Fortunately all the guestrooms in the modern bungalow have private entrances to the garden. Rooms have whimsical features. For example, one room has a bedstead with a white picket fence design and several rooms feature hand-painted landscapes on the walls.

4 Rooms • Price range: $100-120
21914 Pacific Way, Ocean Park, WA 98640
☎ (360) 665-3017

Olga
⊛ Buck Bay Farm Bed & Breakfast
The Buck Bay Farm B&B is a quiet traditional farmhouse in a tranquil, natural setting on Orcas Island. The uncomplicated homelike ambience is reflected in the charmingly decorated guestrooms and common rooms. From the fire pit and picnic table in the yard to the friendly hosts and their dog, everything about this B&B speaks of home. Naturally, such accommodations would not be complete without a full home-style breakfast.

5 Rooms • Price range: $95-150
716 Pt Lawrence Rd, Olga, WA 98279
☎ (360) 376-2908

Olga
Spring Bay Inn on Orcas Island
This unique Northwestern home sits between steep ravines, providing great views of Spring Bay. The grounds resemble a private park due to the water frontage and the surrounding 57 acres of fir and madrona forest. More than 250 custom windows bring nature indoors. High ceilings, Rumford fireplaces and walls lined with musical instruments provide a pleasant atmosphere. Daily kayak tours are available.

5 Rooms • Price range: $205-255
464 Spring Bay Trl, Olga, WA 98279
☎ (360) 376-5531

Orcas Island
Windsong Bed & Breakfast
This tranquil location features spacious rooms and down-home comfort.

4 Rooms • Price range: $110-150
213 Deer Harbor Rd, Orcas Island, WA 98280
☎ (360) 376-2500

Port Angeles
BJ's Garden Gate

A Victorian home located in a rural residential area, this inn has views of Juan de Fuca Strait from every room. Fireplaces and large baths are also found in every room. Some rooms feature a private Jacuzzi. Guests can stroll through the garden and watch the ships or even the occasional whale pass by. Farther afield, they can dig for clams, harvest oysters, play golf or visit the rain forest.

5 Rooms • Price range: $130-185
397 Monterra Dr, Port Angeles, WA 98362
☎ **(360) 452-2322**

Port Angeles
Domaine Madeleine

This waterfront inn blends Asian artistry and French pampering with picturesque mountain or water views. The Impressionist Monet Room has a private entrance through a replica of one of the painter's gardens. The Ming Room occupies the top floor and has a private 30-foot balcony. A separate cottage offers romantic seclusion. All rooms feature a fireplace. The multi-course European gourmet breakfasts are legendary.

5 Rooms • Price range: $169-199
146 Wildflower Ln, Port Angeles, WA 98362
☎ **(360) 457-4174**

Port Angeles
The Five SeaSuns B&B

The Five SeaSuns B&B is ideally located near beautiful Olympic Peninsula's parks and natural wonders. The Dutch Colonial property offers European ambience and decor. The cozy guestrooms use the Dutch words for the seasons they are named after. French doors open from the living room onto a beautiful pergola, which overlooks the well-tended gardens.

5 Rooms • Price range: $80-135
1006 S Lincoln St, Port Angeles, WA 98362
☎ **(360) 452-8248**

Port Angeles
Tudor Inn Bed & Breakfast

This English Tudor-style inn was built in 1910 at a time when wood was taken for granted. All the guestrooms feature private baths and views of the Olympic Mountains or the Straits of Juan de Fuca. The inn has many fine European antiques; some are for sale. There is a massage therapist on call, a fortunate occurrence especially for those who spent the day skiing on Hurricane Ridge.

5 Rooms • Price range: $85-135
1108 S Oak St, Port Angeles, WA 98362
☎ **(360) 452-3138**

Port Angeles
Angeles Inn Bed & Breakfast

This contemporary home atop a hill in a quiet residential area has a terrific view of the city and the Strait of Juan de Fuca. The cheerful bedrooms have private baths and the innkeepers are happy to assist with travel and entertainment plans.

4 Rooms • Price range: $65-105
1203 E 7th St, Port Angeles, WA 98362
☎ **(360) 417-0260**

Port Townsend
Ann Starrett Mansion

This classic 1889 "Queen of Queen Annes" features unique architecture, including a solar calendar in the eight-sided dome tower and a freestanding three-tiered spiral staircase, the construction of which has baffled craftsmen for more than a century. Frescoed ceilings, a huge Belgian tapestry, an 1800s "hussy couch," family heirlooms and classic Victorian antiques combine to produce a delightfully eclectic interior decor.

11 Rooms • Price range: $111-245
744 Clay St, Port Townsend, WA 98368
☎ **(360) 385-3205**

Port Townsend
Chanticleer Inn Bed & Breakfast

Located a short ways from the shops, galleries and restaurants of Port Townsend, the Chanticleer is an 1876 Victorian inn offering the classic features of a bygone era in the heart of the town's historic district. In addition to the well-decorated rooms, there is a carriage house that can accommodate up to four for longer stays. It has a fireplace and a fully equipped kitchen. Full gourmet breakfasts feature delicious family favorites.

5 Rooms • Price range: $85-160
1208 Franklin St, Port Townsend, WA 98368
☎ **(360) 385-6239**

Port Townsend
The James House

A grand Victorian mansion built in 1889 and set on a bluff with sweeping views of the waters and mountains of Puget Sound, the James House is a comfortably furnished inn with period antiques. A variety of fine woods were used to build the elegant house and numerous wood-burning fireplaces are found throughout. The inn is a short walk from restaurants, shops, galleries, parks and beaches.

13 Rooms • Price range: $90-225
1238 Washington St, Port Townsend, WA 98368
☎ **(360) 385-1238**

Port Townsend
Old Consulate Inn

The rooms in this Queen Anne mansion are exquisitely decorated with Victorian refinements, fine antiques, family memorabilia, and custom-designed bed linens, comforters, and wall coverings. The building was built in 1889 and served as a German consulate from 1908 to 1911. It has magnificent views of Puget Sound, Mt. Rainier and the Olympic Range.

8 Rooms • Price range: $106-210
313 Walker, Port Townsend, WA 98368
☎ **(360) 385-6753**

Port Townsend
Manresa Castle

This fanciful Rhine-style castle, which commands a view of the area, was built in 1892 and has served as a private mansion, a Jesuit training college and an inn. European antiques and hand-printed wall coverings add to the sense of refinement.

40 Rooms • Price range: $75-95
7th & Sheridan, Port Townsend, WA 98368
☎ **(360) 385-5750**

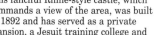

Puyallup
Tayberry Victorian Cottage
The Tayberry Victorian Cottage offers a relaxed and peaceful stay in the country.

4 Rooms • Price range: $45-95
7406 80th St E, Puyallup, WA 98371
☎ **(253) 848-4594**

Salkum
The Shepherd's Inn Bed & Breakfast
A contemporary inn nestled among trees and rolling hills near Mt. St. Helens.

5 Rooms • Price range: $60-85
168 Autumn Heights Dr, Salkum, WA 98582
☎ **(360) 985-2434**

Seabeck
Willcox House

Surrounded by formal gardens, old-growth trees and untouched forest, this secluded 1937 mansion features a copper roof and fish-scale tiled exterior. Inside, oak parquet floors, walnut-paneled walls and a copper-framed marble fireplace continue the Art Deco extravagance. The saltwater lap pool, bar, game room and library offer plenty of opportunities for pleasurable activities. Breakfast fare includes apple pancakes and smoked sausages.

5 Rooms • Price range: $109-199
2390 Tekiu Rd NW, Seabeck, WA 98380
☎ **(360) 830-4492**

Seattle
Capitol Hill Inn
Antiques, brass beds and carved wood moldings in a handsome Victorian.

7 Rooms • Price range: $105-170
1713 Belmont Ave, Seattle, WA 98122
☎ **(206) 323-1955**

Seattle
Gaslight Inn
Comfortable rooms in a B&B made up of two adjacent 1900s homes.

15 Rooms • Price range: $80-180
1727 15th Ave, Seattle, WA 98122
☎ **(206) 325-3654**

Seattle
Hill House Bed & Breakfast
An elegantly restored 1903 Victorian, Hill House is decorated with a graceful mixture of old and new. The inn features choice antiques, beveled windows

and lace curtains, Persian rugs, hardwood floors, and silk-upholstered settees.

7 Rooms • Price range: $75-170
1113 E John St, Seattle, WA 98102
☎ **(206) 720-7161**

Seattle
Inn at Harbor Steps

Just steps away from galleries, antique shops, cafés and the Seattle Art Museum, the Inn at Harbor Steps is located on the lower two floors of a high-rise residential building. Each comfortably furnished, spacious room has a fireplace, a sitting area and beautiful garden views. Amenities include preferred reservations at the Wolfgang Puck Cafe, private parking, and use of the media room and fitness facility.

20 Rooms • Price range: $170-230
1221 First Ave, Seattle, WA 98101
☎ **(206) 748-0973**

Seattle
Mildred's Bed & Breakfast
This double-turreted 1890 Victorian displays traditional B&B hospitality.

4 Rooms • Price range: $120-150
1202 15th Ave E, Seattle, WA 98112
☎ (206) 325-6072

Seaview
The Shelburne Inn

Located between the Columbia River and the Pacific Ocean on the Long Beach Peninsula, the 1896 Shelburne Inn is surrounded by stunning scenery. The peninsula is an unspoiled 28-mile stretch of wild Pacific Coast, with bird sanctuaries, lighthouses and panoramic vistas. The inn is filled with antiques and delightful touches. The inn's Shoalwater Restaurant serves excellent cuisine, while the pub offers lighter fare.

15 Rooms • Price range: $113-159
4415 Pacific Way, Seaview, WA 98644
☎ (360) 642-2442

Sedro-Woolley
South Bay Bed & Breakfast
This inn sits on a hill by Lake Whatcom; rooms have fireplaces and patios.

5 Rooms • Price range: $135-150
4095 South Bay Dr, Sedro-Woolley, WA 98284
☎ (360) 595-2086

Sequim
Blue Whale Inn on the Bay B&B

Situated in the heart of Sequim, this charming inn is minutes away from the John Wayne Marina and beautiful Sequim Bay. Four of the guestroom feature views of the bay, and the living room, with its telescope, is a great place to watch the seals at play. The living room also has a fireplace and the inn's own hot tub is an ideal place to relax after a day of sightseeing. Rooms offer twin, queen- or king-size beds.

5 Rooms • Price range: $75-145
120 Forrest Rd, Sequim, WA 98382
☎ (360) 582-0551

Sequim
Glenna's Guthrie Cottage Bed & Breakfast
This B&B is a restored 1901 farmhouse set in the countryside.

4 Rooms • Price range: $90-125
10083 Old Olympic Hwy, Sequim, WA 98382
☎ (360) 681-4349

Sequim
Greywolf Inn

It is reported that John Wayne was charmed by this village, the harbor of which is named after him. Shaded by towering evergreens, Greywolf Inn stands on five acres of land and is an ideal starting point from which to explore Hurricane Ridge, the Hoh Rain Forest and the Pacific beaches. The inn features a Japanese bathhouse and spa and a nature trail that crosses a stream to a gazebo.

5 Rooms • Price range: $75-135
395 Keeler Rd, Sequim, WA 98382
☎ (360) 683-5889

South Bend
The Russell House
This beautiful Victorian home was built in 1891 and named after its builder John Russell, who constructed it as an anniversary gift for his wife Annie. The house sits atop a hill in the historic section of the city and offers views of Willapa Harbor from every window. The inn's guestrooms are furnished with antiques, the bathrooms feature period fixtures and claw-foot tubs.

4 Rooms • Price range: $75-105
902 E Water St, South Bend, WA 98586
☎ **(360) 875-6487**

South Cle Elum
Iron Horse Inn B&B
Originally built in 1909 as a railroad bunkhouse, the inn is listed on the National Register of Historic Places. Today it features a collection of railroad memorabilia. In addition to the guestrooms, two private caboose suites are available.

11 Rooms • Price range: $50-135
526 Marie Ave, South Cle Elum, WA 98943
☎ **(509) 674-5939**

Spokane
Angelica's Bed & Breakfast
Designed by Spokane architect Kirtland Cutter in 1907, this B&B is housed in an elegant brick mansion that is listed on the National Register of Historic Places. The manor confidently combines fine European sensibility with the humble charm of a country inn. Each of the guestrooms is appointed with antiques and has a queen-size bed. Two rooms have private baths and one, the honeymoon suite, has a fireplace.

4 Rooms • Price range: $95-115
W 1321 Ninth Ave, Spokane, WA 99204
☎ **(509) 624-5598**

Spokane
The Fotheringham House
This late 1800s classic Queen Anne Victorian is tucked away in the historic residential Browne's Addition. The restoration of the home of Spokane's first mayor has produced a beautiful inn that retains many of its original touches. The parlor features a pressed tin ceiling and authentic Victorian furniture, while guestrooms include antique quilts and period furnishings. Porch swings and a Victorian garden add comfort and charm.

4 Rooms • Price range: $95-110
2128 W 2nd Ave, Spokane, WA 99204
☎ **(509) 838-1891**

Spokane
Marianna Stoltz House Bed & Breakfast
This classic American four-square home is situated on a tree-lined street near Gonzaga University and is surrounded by 100-year-old maples. Built in 1908, the inn displays the best craftsmanship of the day and features a wide wraparound veranda, fir woodwork, high ceilings and leaded glass. Old family quilts and lace curtains create a romantic atmosphere in guestrooms.

4 Rooms • Price range: $75-99
427 E Indiana Ave, Spokane, WA 99207
☎ **(509) 483-4316**

Spokane
Waverly Place Bed & Breakfast

A 1902 storybook Victorian home located in the Corbin Park Historical District, the inn offers spacious park-view rooms with queen-size beds and a romantic third-story suite. The Waverly Suite boasts a view of the park from the iron claw-foot soaking tub. Several rooms have a Jacuzzi. Main floor parlors feature built-in window seats and beaded pillars and a veranda overlooks Corbin Park, the rose gardens and a pool.

4 Rooms • Price range: $80-125
709 W Waverly Pl, Spokane, WA 99205
☎ **(509) 328-1856**

Sunnyside
Sunnyside Inn Bed & Breakfast

This inn is conveniently located downtown and is close to 20 area wineries. Made up of two 1919 homes painted pastel blue, the exterior features well-maintained grounds, comfortable lawn furnishings and attractive carriage lamps. The guestrooms are decorated in a warm, country style and are equipped with private baths, most with two-person Jacuzzi tubs. Guests wake to a full, country breakfast served in the dining room.

10 Rooms • Price range: $59-109
804 E Edison, Sunnyside, WA 98944
☎ **(509) 839-5557**

Tacoma
Commencement Bay Bed & Breakfast

On a clear day, the entire Cascade Range from Mt. Rainier to Mt. Baker is visible from the front porch of this hospitable inn. A spectacular view of Commencement Bay is also on tap. Pleasant common areas include an elegant fireside parlor with a grand piano, game and exercise rooms, and a hot-tub deck in the inn's secluded gardens. Guestrooms feature tasteful classic furnishings and private baths.

3 Rooms • Price range: $95-125
3312 N Union Ave, Tacoma, WA 98407
☎ **(253) 752-8175**

Tacoma
The Villa Bed & Breakfast

Rose gardens, fountains and piazzas reminiscent of the Mediterranean surround this handsome 1925 Italian-Renaissance style mansion. Inside, gracefully arched windows, quarter-sawn oak floors and antiques give the inn its beauty. Rooms are spacious and feature four-poster beds, fireplaces and verandas. Common areas include an exercise room, a spa, a parlor and a large veranda with bay and mountain views.

6 Rooms • Price range: $120-120
705 N 5th St, Tacoma, WA 98403
☎ **(253) 572-1157**

Tacoma
Plum Duff House

Call for information.

4 Rooms • Price range: $90-120
619 N "K" St, Tacoma, WA 98403
☎ **(253) 627-6916**

Vashon
Artist's Studio Loft B&B
Surrounded by five acres of gardens, this B&B offers all modern amenities.

4 Rooms • Price range: $95-185
16529 91st Ave SW, Vashon, WA 98070
☎ **(206) 463-2583**

Walla Walla
Green Gables Inn
This Craftsman-style mansion was built on homestead land for Clarinda Green Smith and her husband in 1909. The inn is located in the Whitman College campus area and is within walking distance of historic Main Street. Guestrooms are spacious; some have a wood-burning fireplace, a deck and a Jacuzzi. The Carriage House Cottage has a fully equipped kitchen and is ideal for families. A candlelight breakfast is served daily.

6 Rooms • Price range: $105-135
922 Bonsella, Walla Walla, WA 99362
☎ **(509) 525-5501**

Wenatchee
Warm Springs Inn
A rose-lined lane leads up to this gracious 1917 country estate on the banks of the Wenatchee River. The inn is situated on 10 acres of land and surrounded by majestic trees and gardens. The Great Room boasts a large fireplace and floor-to-ceiling windows that overlook the river. Guests are invited to dine indoors in the dining room or outdoors on the deck. A hot tub is tucked away among the trees.

4 Rooms • Price range: $70-110
1611 Love Ln, Wenatchee, WA 98801
☎ **(509) 662-8365**

Winthrop
The Chewuch Inn & Cabins
The Chewuch is situated in the beautiful Methow Valley on the eastern slopes of the north Cascades Mountains. In spring, the valley opens up to fishing and white-water rafting and more than five million acres of public lands can be explored along hiking trails or on horseback. Winter offers some 110 miles of cross-country ski trails. Deluxe cabins feature full kitchens, and the inn offers billiards and darts in the Game Room.

14 Rooms • Price range: $70-95
223 White Ave, Winthrop, WA 98862
☎ **(509) 996-3107**

Woodland
Grandma's House Bed & Breakfast
This B&B, situated on a family farm, offers a view of pastures and a river.

2 Rooms • Price range: $42-65
4551 Lewis River Rd, Woodland, WA 98674
☎ **(360) 225-7002**

Yakima
Birchfield Manor Country Inn
Antiques, Victorian bric-a-brac and lace give this inn its 19th-century flavor.

11 Rooms • Price range: $90-200
2018 Birchfield Rd, Yakima, WA 98901
☎ **(509) 452-1960**

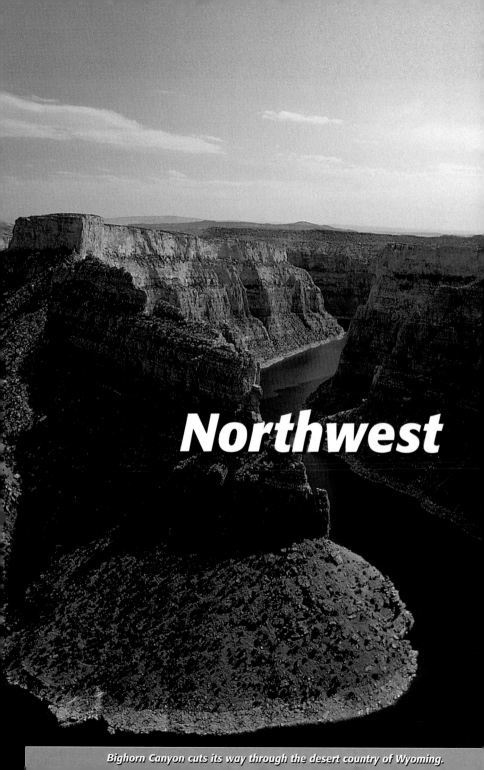

Northwest

Scenic Byways
of the Northwest

In the 1870s thousands of gold hunters and miners boarded trains all across America to seek their fortune prospecting for gold in the Black Hills of South Dakota.

U.S. 93/SR 75

This road follows the Salmon River, also called the "River of No Return" because if you could make it downstream there was no way to make it back. The name only serves to emphasize the nature of this primitive area of Idaho. Following a canyon, travelers are treated to spectacular views. The snow-capped peaks are well known to skiers who flock to Sun Valley every winter.

Going-to-the-Sun Road

Winding through the sometimes treacherous roads of Glacier National Park, this route can't be topped for its awesome scenery. As it climbs over the Continental Divide, various pullouts offer travelers a view of the peaks and canyons. Heading west, the road descends into the McDonald Valley. Here the lush cedar forests more closely resemble the rain forests of the West coast than the Rockies.

U.S. 85

Visitors to The Badlands will soon realize how the area got its name. These eroded hills are fascinating geological wonders that seem desolate and bleak at first. However, there is an abundance of life and history along this route. Buffalo once roamed the neighboring grasslands and many battles were fought here.

U.S. 385

Mount Rushmore brings millions of visitors to South Dakota every year. Although it is an impressive man-made structure, equally impressive are the granite spires of the Black Hills into which it is carved. This route winds through the hills and their abandoned gold mines. The surrounding area is also filled with subterranean caves.

The Wapiti Valley, which offers recreational activities and the possibility of wildlife sightings, links Yellowstone and Cody, home to the Buffalo Bill Historical Center.

The Jewel Cave National Monument was established in 1908 and features beautiful limestone caverns with a series of chambers joined by narrow passages.

St. Mary
West Glacier
MONTANA
Williston
NORTH DAKOTA
Grassy Butte
North Fork
IDAHO
West Yellowstone
Ranchester
Hailey
Pluma
SOUTH DAKOTA
Pringle
WYOMING

For further information on the sites along each route, see the Scenic Byways Resource Guide on page 775.

Yellowstone Park Road

Included in this drive is the majesty of Yellowstone National Park, with its unique blend of thermal activity and vast wilderness. Much of the terrain shows regrowth following the fires of 1988, and wildlife continues to thrive. Motorists should watch out for animals crossing the road and be advised that interior park roads are closed in winter.

U.S. 93/SR 75

● *This route follows the Salmon River, nicknamed the "River of No Return" due to its ferocity, through a primitive landscape of canyons and pristine wilderness. From the steep, winding roads, travelers can enjoy picturesque streams and meadows as well as panoramic views of the snow-topped Sawtooth Mountains. The route also provides access to the popular ski resort of Sun Valley.*

❶ Malad Gorge State Park
The Malad River makes an awe-inspiring 60-foot drop into the Devil's Washbowl, then passes through the Malad Gorge. Here the river takes on a more spectacular appearance due to the spring water that enters at this point. The Malad Gorge State Park encompasses 652 acres around the gorge. Geologists believe that the canyon was created by the retreat of a horseshoe-shaped waterfall. Although the river holds plenty of trout, only foolhardy anglers would attempt to climb down the 250-foot cliffs that form the gorge. There are more accessible locations along the river for dedicated fishermen, such as Niagara Springs. A footbridge suspended above the gorge offers excitement for the adventurous.

❷ Blaine County Historical Museum
More than a century ago the Wood River Valley began to attract attention with the discovery of gold, lead and silver ore. A railroad was built for access to these rich mining towns. They reaped the rewards of their wealth. In 1883 Hailey became the first city in the state to have telephone service and Ketchum pioneered the use of electric lighting. Although the hills of the area are no longer rich in minerals, they are rich in history. The Blaine County Historical Museum in Hailey preserves the local history with pioneer relics, political memorabilia and a replica of a mine shaft.

❸ Sawtooth Fish Hatchery
Stanley is at the north end of the Sawtooth National Recreation Area and is a base camp for hikers and float trips. Redfish Lake takes its name from the spawning sockeye, the vast numbers of which once made the water appear red. However, modern obstructions have now impeded their spawning cycle. The Sawtooth Fish Hatchery rears chinook and sockeye salmon. With the swell of the spring runoff, the young smolts are released from the hatchery on a 900-mile migration to the sea, during which they must safely negotiate eight hydroelectric dams.

❹ Lemhi County Historical Museum
In 1866 five miners discovered gold in this area just west of the Salmon River. The resulting settlement is now a ghost town. The city of Salmon was formed from a more stable tradition of ranching and logging. Famous mountain men, such as Kit Carson and Joe Meek, wandered these hills. Now the city has become a haven for outdoor adventurers and river runners. The Lemhi County Historical Museum preserves the history of gold mining in the area and also offers a display of Native American artifacts and a collection of Oriental art gathered in the 1920s.

❺ Experimental Breeder Reactor
The locals in Idaho Falls simply call it "the site." Created in 1949 as the National Reactor Testing Station, this 890 miles of sagebush and lava contained 52 nuclear reactors. The area was chosen for its isola-

With 750 miles of hiking trails, more than 300 lakes and mountain ranges with peaks exceeding 10,000 feet, the Sawtooth National Recreation Area is an outdoor enthusiast's dream.

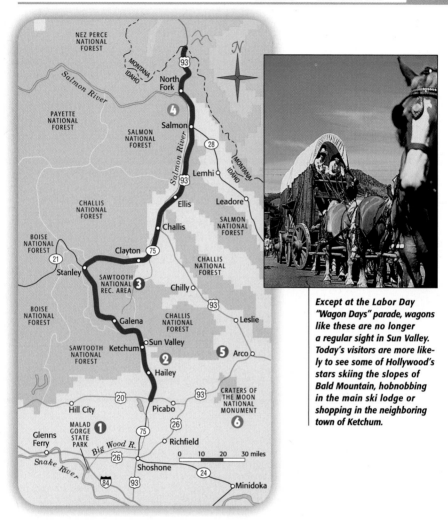

Except at the Labor Day "Wagon Days" parade, wagons like these are no longer a regular sight in Sun Valley. Today's visitors are more likely to see some of Hollywood's stars skiing the slopes of Bald Mountain, hobnobbing in the main ski lodge or shopping in the neighboring town of Ketchum.

tion and uninhabitable terrain. Although seemingly an unlikely place for scientific landmarks, this is where engineers at the Experimental Breeder Reactor No. 1 first produced a usable amount of electricity from nuclear fission in 1951. No longer in use, the site now offers tours of four nuclear reactors, a control room, Geiger counters and other facets of the nuclear age.

⑥ Craters of the Moon National Monument
A seven-mile loop drive provides access to one of the strangest landscapes on the continent. The Craters of the Moon National Monument is comprised of three lava fields, pitted areas of black basalt encompassing 750,000 acres. The name of the monument is very apt: in 1969 NASA astronauts bound for the moon hiked through here in preparation for the Apollo 14 mission. Over the course of eight eruptive periods, 60 lava flows pushed through vents along a series of fissures called the Great Rift. This created an outdoor museum of volcanic activity, rich with cinder cones, lava tubes, spatter cones and tree molds. Visitors can learn more about these beautiful geological attractions at the visitor center. In winter the loop road is groomed for cross-country skiing and snowshoeing.

Going-to-the-Sun Road

This mountain highway winds through Glacier National Park, offering spectacular views. The towering peaks and pristine lakes are a sight everyone should experience. Climbing from the edge of the Great Plains, the road crests over the Continental Divide before dropping into the lush McDonald Valley. As sections of the road are narrow with steep grades, the upper alpine area is closed for the winter.

Contrasting with the spectacular views from the mountain heights are the homey sites of the valley floor, such as this cherry tree in bloom south of Kalispell.

❶ Flathead National Forest

The 2.3 million-acre Flathead National Forest encompasses non-wilderness land and two wildernesses: the Mission Mountains Wilderness, and the Bob Marshall Wilderness Complex, made up of the Scapegoat, the Great Bear and the Bob Marshall. The scenery is a breathtaking mix of snow-crested peaks, glacier-carved valleys and alpine meadows. The forest contains majestic firs and spruce and is crisscrossed by miles of rivers and streams and numerous lakes. Winding through this area is the unbroken facade of jagged peaks that is the Continental Divide, what the Blackfeet call "the backbone of the world." The largest and most geologically interesting area is what the locals call "the Bob." It features the Chinese Wall, a towering 13-mile-long limestone reef riddled with caves. There is no road access in the wilderness areas, which makes for spectacular, but rugged, hiking. The Jewel Basin is a 15,000-acre designated hiking area with 27 alpine lakes. The forest is a refuge for one of the country's largest wildlife populations, including elk, gray wolves, bighorn sheep, bobcats and grizzly bears.

❷ Going-to-the-Sun Road

Quite simply one of the most beautiful drives on the continent, the Going-to-the-Sun-Road climbs over the Continental Divide, passing the lakes, alpine valleys and the stunning glaciers of Glacier National Park. It begins at the east end of the glacier-carved St. Mary Lake. After passing three cascading falls, the route climbs past Jackson Glacier, one of the few active glaciers visible from the road. Logan Pass, at an elevation of 6,646 feet, is the path over the Continental Divide and offers some of the best views from two hiking trails. The pass was formed when two glaciers chewed through a knife-edged ridge called the Garden Wall. The road here descends, following McDonald Creek, into a valley of western red cedars. At Avalanche Creek, crystal-blue waters carve their way through a narrow gorge. Here, a mile-long loop called Trail of the Cedars winds through the rain forest. The western end of the park follows the shoreline of Lake McDonald, with various turnouts offering trails to its beaches. Throughout the journey, wildlife is prevalent.

❸ Museum of the Plains Indians

To the east of Glacier National Park, the mountains level off into vast plains formerly filled with herds of buffalo. These 1.5 million acres are now the grounds of the Blackfeet Indian Reservation. In July this is the site of one of the largest powwows on the continent. Browning is the center of reservation activities and the location of the Museum of the Plains Indians. This living repository is devoted to collecting and exhibiting both contemporary and traditional Native artists. A permanent gallery

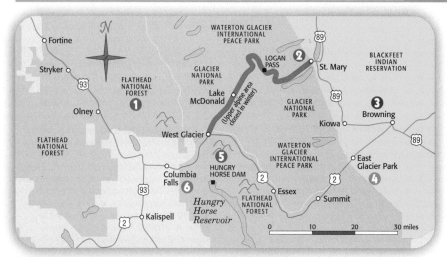

Glacier National Park beckons motorists along Highway 89 west of Browning to stop and smell the flowers.

highlights the artwork of the Blackfeet, Sioux, Arapaho and Indians of the Northern Plains. A multimedia presentation serves to inform viewers of the history of the area as well as inspire new artists.

④ East Glacier Park
Located in the Two Medicine Valley at an elevation of 4,795 feet, East Glacier Park is the recreational center and eastern gateway to Glacier National Park. This small scenic community of 300 still retains its Old West charm. There is a natural mineral lick area that draws mountain goats down to the roadside. Here travelers can take up-close photographs of the wildlife. Marias Pass along Highway 2 offers year-round access to the Glacier National Park.

⑤ Hungry Horse Dam
When it was completed in 1953, the Hungry Horse Dam was the highest concrete dam in the world, reaching an imposing 564 feet. A 30-foot-wide road covers the 2,115-foot-long crest. Several campsites are situated on the Hungry Horse Reservoir, behind the dam. Guided tours of the power-generating area are offered.

⑥ Columbia Falls
Bad Rock Canyon was carved from the union of the north and middle forks of the Flathead River. The town of Columbia Falls, at the canyon's entrance, acts as a gateway to Glacier Park. In summer families can enjoy the Big Sky Waterslide and in winter the Big Mountain Ski Resort.

U.S. 85

Winding through the Great Plains, the scenery on this route is right out of a geological textbook. Much of the trip is through the windswept rock formations of the aptly named Badlands or through the majesty of the prairie. One can imagine the first settlers traveling this route in their wagons, marveling at the landscape while keeping an eye out for angry Sioux warriors.

❶ Fort Union Trading Post

On this site in 1828, Kenneth McKenzie established the Fort Union trading post for his employers, the American Fur Company. It became an important outpost for the thriving fur trade, welcoming the first steamboat on the Missouri River in 1832. A succession of naturalists, scientists and artists visited the post while exploring the Upper Missouri, including John James Audubon. Today the work of these pioneers offers rich historical documentation of the area. In 1837 passengers on a steamboat brought smallpox to the area and the resulting epidemic wiped out thousands of Assiniboine and other Upper Missouri tribes. By the 1850s the Sioux began to displace these tribes, which traded at Fort Union. The trading post was sold to the army in 1867 and soldiers tore it down and used the material to expand nearby Fort Buford. The trading post, established as a National Historic Site in 1966, is now partially reconstructed.

❷ Fort Buford State Historic Site

Fort Buford was built in 1866 at the confluence of the Yellowstone and Missouri rivers as a response to the growing unrest among the Sioux. Now a State Historic Site, this military post once housed six companies of infantry and cavalry who fought the "Indian Wars" until 1895, when the fort was abandoned. This was the infamous location of the final surrender of Chief

Sitting Bull. Even at the formal surrender ceremony, he refused to hand over his arms, passing his rifle to his six-year-old son instead. Sitting Bull and his followers set up their lodges on the south side of the fort, where they stayed for about a week before they were loaded aboard the steamboat *General Sherman*. Some famous Native American leaders were briefly detained at the fort, including Chief Joseph of the Nez Perce and the Sioux warrior, Gall. Also on the site are a stone powder magazine, two officers' residences, a sergeant of the guard office and several historical exhibits.

❸ Theodore Roosevelt National Park

While on a buffalo hunt in 1883, a future president stumbled across an area of rugged terrain known simply as "the Badlands." The buttes, canyons and rock pillars of the region, not to mention the disappearance of the buffalo, sparked his interest in conservation and today this park in the area bears his name. Following the Little Missouri River, the park is divided into three sections: The North Unit is three days by canoe (or 70 miles by car) from the South Unit, which is the largest and is accessible from Medora. Between them, the third unit is the original site of Roosevelt's Elkhorn Ranch. Millions of years of wind, rain and rivers have eroded unique shapes and beautiful patterns out of the rock in the park. The best spots to view the majesty of these rock formations are Painted Canyon Overlook in the south and Oxbow Overlook in the north.

The Fort Union Trading Post offers a well-documented look at the early years of the first fur-trade pioneers in the area.

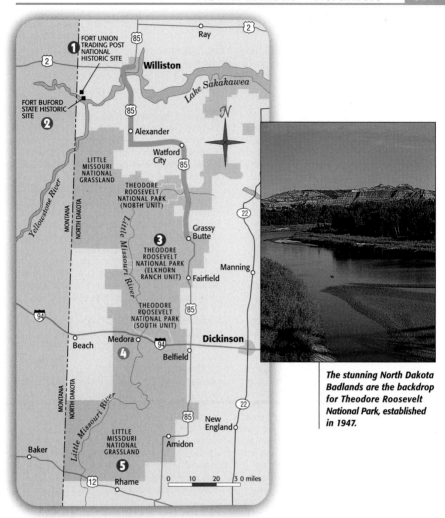

The stunning North Dakota Badlands are the backdrop for Theodore Roosevelt National Park, established in 1947.

❹ de Mores State Historic Site
The town of Medora was founded by a wealthy French nobleman, the Marquis de Mores, in 1883. He had a dream to revolutionize the meat-packing industry. His plan was to slaughter the cattle on the range instead of shipping them East to slaughterhouses. The venture failed, but the town survived. The remains of his operation can be found at the de Mores Historic Site. Here also stands his faithfully restored 26-room chateau with its lavish interior. An interpretive center offers artifacts from his life and times, including a stagecoach and guns.

❺ Little Missouri National Grassland
The Little Missouri National Grassland stretches over a million acres, following the Little Missouri River. At one time crawling with herds of buffalo, the tall grass now moves in wind-blown silence. Offering both prairie and Badlands vistas, visitors to the area today can enjoy hiking, camping, wildlife viewing and fishing. The grasslands are also rich in fossils and archeological sites. At the Burning Coal Vein Area a coal vein 30 feet below the surface has been burning since before the first settlers ever came to these grasslands.

U.S. 385

Winding through the ancient Black Hills, this route offers views of thick pine forests, caves and spectacular rock formations. Buffalo can still be seen roaming the area. Mount Rushmore, a monument to American history, lies near the route. The Native equivalent, the Crazy Horse Memorial, is still being sculpted.

❶ The Homestake Gold Mine

Dominating the hillsides of the town of Lead is the 8,000-foot-deep Homestake Gold Mine, the longest continuously operating gold mine in the world. In 1876 Fred and Moses Manuel staked the claim, but quickly sold out to a big company with access to the large machinery necessary to extract the wealth. Today it produces more than 250,000 ounces of gold annually. Visitors can take a guided tour of surface operations from May through September.

❷ The Black Hills

The Black Hills are the oldest mountains in America. Although Harney Peak is a modest 7,242 feet tall, South Dakotans will remind you that this is the highest point between the Rockies and the Swiss Alps. Named by the Lakota Sioux for the dark, thick swaths of Ponderosa pine that cover them, the hills were sacred to the Native peoples who sought spiritual visions here. One of their prime spots was the conelike geologic rarity known as Bear Butte. The sound of the wind whistling through granite spires, called Needles, often struck fear in the Lakota and can still be heard today. All that changed in the 1870s with the discovery of gold and the coming of settlers. The Centennial and the Mickelson Trails are a good way to see the area up close, on foot, bicycle or horseback. The trails wind through the hills past lakes, streams and abandoned mining encampments.

❸ Mount Rushmore National Memorial

In 1927 the sculptor Gutzon Borglum and his crew of unemployed miners began the 14-year process of drilling, blasting and shaping the granite on the southeast side of Mount Rushmore into 60-foot-high faces of four of America's great leaders: Washington, Jefferson, Lincoln and Theodore Roosevelt. Controversy surrounded the project at first. Some naturalists felt the mountains should not be defaced in the name of personal tributes and some objected to the inclusion of Roosevelt, then dead only eight years. But Roosevelt had owned a ranch nearby and was a friend of the sculptor. The technical challenges were astounding: 450,000 tons of rock were removed before the shapes could emerge. For a better view, travelers can hike from the visitor center and the Viewing Terrace to the sculptor's studio.

❹ Rushmore Borglum Story

Located in Keystone, the Rushmore Borglum Story is a museum dedicated to the 60 years of work by the artist Gutzon Borglum before he embarked on his masterpiece. Although a child of the frontier, he studied in Paris under Auguste Rodin. Visitors can see hundreds of his original sculptures, models he used for Rushmore and a movie about the history of the monument that features dramatic blasting scenes.

❺ Jewel Cave National Monument

Jewel Cave is considered the third-longest cave in the world and it is still being explored. The 125 miles of mapped passages and subterranean chambers feature nailhead calcite crystals lining the walls. Those equipped with a warm sweater and enough nerve to travel underground can witness a maze of unusual boxwork, frostwork and

This charming farm nestles at the foot of the Black Hills.

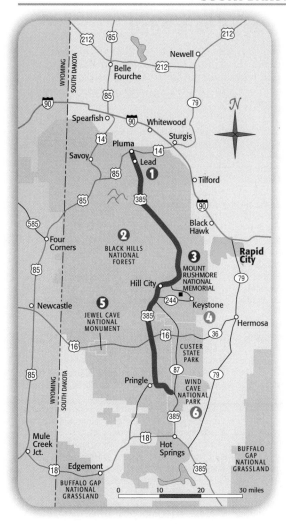

The half-mile-long Presidential Trail provides spectacular views of the famous busts carved into Mount Rushmore.

popcorn formations. Tours requiring various degrees of physical ability are available. Visitors on the Scenic Tour descend in an elevator to a half-mile lighted passageway. The truly adventurous can embark on the Spelunking Tour; this hardy route follows more difficult, unimproved terrain.

❻ Wind Cave National Park

The entrance to the Wind Cave revealed itself in 1881 when Jesse and Tom Bingham heard an unusual whistling sound. It was air escaping from the 96 miles of interconnected underground corridors filled with fragile gypsum beard and helicite balloons. The Wind Cave National Park was established in 1903 in response to the increasing number of curious visitors to the cave, making it the nation's seventh national park. Windy City Lake is 650 feet below the surface and features floating rafts of calcite. Above ground, the park preserves 28,000 acres of prairie grasslands with roaming herds of buffalo and pronghorn antelope.

Yellowstone Park Road

Traveling the North Fork Highway through its gently rolling terrain offers spectacular views and a journey through the history of the Old West. Driving west, the forests become denser and the mountains higher. Geological wonders greet the visitor to Yellowstone National Park, as well as endless vistas of canyons, falls, lakes, and excellent views of wildlife.

❶ Yellowstone National Park

In 1872 reports of the amazing geological wonders and breathtaking wilderness of this area caused Yellowstone to became the world's first national park. Truly a living museum of volcanic activity, the park boasts 500 geysers that erupt in spectacular plumes of steam and hot water. Old Faithful erupts 130 to 140 feet in the air about fifteen times a day. The park is filled with bubbling pools of mud, vents of steam and hot springs. A contrast to this underground cauldron is the peaceful expanse of 2.2 million acres of forests, canyons, lakes and meadows filled with some of the continent's greatest populations of wildlife, such as bison, elk, bear and moose. In summer, unfortunately, the roads can become gridlocked with traffic.

❷ Buffalo Bill Historical Center

Often referred to as the Smithsonian of the West, the Buffalo Bill Historical Center displays memorabilia and historical artifacts of the Old West within its four museums. The main attraction is the museum devoted to the famous hunter, scout and showman. It includes rare motion-picture footage of his Wild West Show, clothing and posters. The impressive Whitney Gallery of Western Art brings together works by the great artists of the West, including Frederic Remington. Also in the center is the Plains Indian Museum, which features a full-scale reproduction of a Lakota camp. The Cody Firearms Museum is a must-see for anyone interested in the history of guns.

❸ Greybull Museum

Local legend claims that a great albino buffalo once roamed the area and this is how the town got its name. Pictographs of the beast are still visible on the river bluffs. The Greybull Museum's diverse collection includes fossils, dinosaur bones, bison heads, century-old clothing and household items such as butter churns and jugs used during Prohibition. Arrowheads and other Native American artifacts such as beadwork and quillwork are also on display.

❹ Medicine Wheel

On a Medicine Mountain ridge in the heart of Bighorn National Forest lies this mysterious archeological site. Measuring 80 feet across, the "wheel" is a circle of stones with 28 spokes radiating from a central hub. Many theories abound as to the origin and purpose of the site. Some believe it was an astronomical observatory used to determine the solstice. Others feel it was a sacred site of worship. Regardless of its original intention, many Native Americans still come here seeking spiritual guidance.

❺ Bradford Brinton Memorial

At the foot of the Bighorn Mountains just south of Sheridan lies this historic ranch and art collection. Established in the early 1890s, the Quarter Circle A Ranch was bought by Bradford Brinton in 1923 for use as his summer home and to raise horses and cattle. It opened to the public in 1961 and today contains works by Frederic Remington, Charles M. Russell, and many

The Brinton Ranch House peeks out from among the trees of its well-kept grounds.

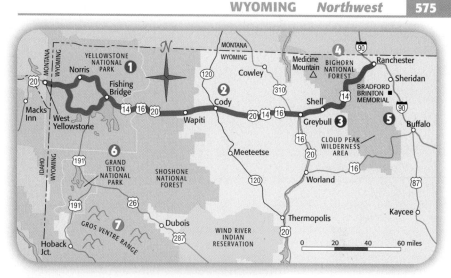

A diverse ecosystem, abundant wildlife and the impressive Teton Range are some of the attractions that draw more than three million visitors to Grand Teton National Park annually.

other of the West's great artists. Also on display are Native American artifacts and other historic memorabilia from the 19th and 20th centuries.

⑥ Grand Teton National Park

The jagged peaks of the youngest mountain range in the Rockies are an alpinist's dream. There are 12 prominent peaks that exceed 12,000 feet, the tallest being the Grand Teton at 13,770 feet. They were formed when the earth's crust split along a normal fault line, one side rising and the other dropping to form Jackson Hole. Glaciers have formed many lakes, which are popular with anglers searching for trout. Huge herds of elk migrate into the area in the summer where they compete with the growing numbers of buffalo. The creation of the park received national attention when local conservationists, concerned about development in Jackson Hole, invited asked J. D. Rockefeller Jr. to buy up the land and donate it to the Park Service.

⑦ Gros Ventre Slide

On June 23, 1925, melting snow and heavy rains caused the entire north end of Sheep Mountain to break off. A section of rock and shale 2,000 feet wide and a mile long slid into the valley below, damming the river and creating Slide Lake. On May 18, 1927, the dam broke, flooding the town of Kelly and killing six people. The entire town was destroyed. Today an interpretive trail winds past the huge gouge and lake remnant.

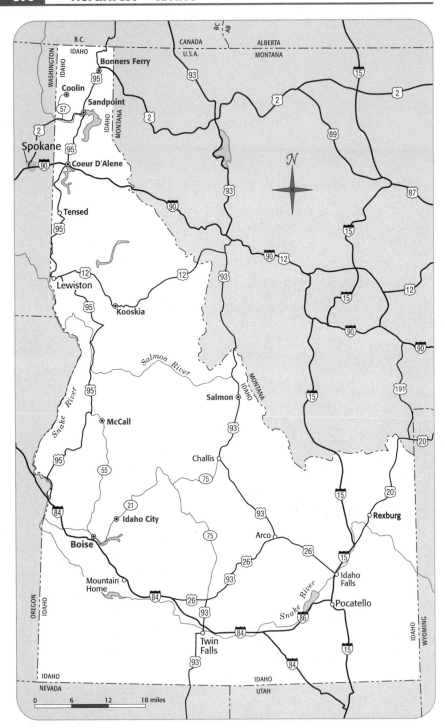

Boise
Idaho Heritage Inn Bed & Breakfast

Listed on the National Register of Historic Places, this 1904 inn was once the home of Idaho governor, Chase Clark. Common rooms feature diamond-paned French doors, oak flooring, and Oriental carpets. Located in the historic Warm Springs District, the inn is within walking distance of downtown, Old Boise and the State University. In the vicinity guests can enjoy skiing, trout fishing or visiting old mining towns.

6 Rooms • Price range: $65-115
109 W Idaho St, Boise, ID 83702
☎ **(208) 342-8066**

Boise
J. J. Shaw House Bed & Breakfast Inn

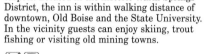

This distinctive 1907 Victorian era Queen Anne is accented throughout with architectural details such as the original leaded-glass windows, exterior and interior columns, decorative moldings and French doors. Many guests like to work the player piano in the sitting room. The inn sits in a quiet residential neighborhood near the city center and Hyde Park. The State University and the Pavilion are a short distance away.

5 Rooms • Price range: $79-109
1411 W Franklin St, Boise, ID 83702
☎ **(208) 344-8899**

Bonners Ferry
Paradise Valley Inn

This lodge-style inn, on 55 acres, offers dramatic views and contemporary decor.

5 Rooms • Price range: $110-175
300 Eagle Way, Bonners Ferry, ID 83805
☎ **(208) 267-4180**

Coeur d'Alene
Coeur d'Alene Bed & Breakfast

Built in 1906, this spacious Colonial house exudes refined comfort. The Art Deco chandelier and carved stairwell of the front hall presage the impressive decor found elsewhere in the inn. Guestrooms are furnished in a modern Scandinavian style; most have private baths. A porch offers sweeping views of the mountains and access to the private gardens, where the luxurious Japanese-style spa and sauna are located.

4 Rooms • Price range: $70-100
906 Foster Ave, Coeur d'Alene, ID 83814
☎ **(208) 667-7527**

Coeur d'Alene
Gregory's McFarland House Bed & Breakfast

Lake Coeur d'Alene has been described by National Geographic as one of the five most beautiful lakes in the world. Explorers of the area can stay at this charming 1905 mansion located in a quiet neighborhood. The dining room displays an antique table that traveled around the Horn from England to San Francisco. A conservatory overlooks a private yard and garden; French doors open onto a deck and a summer house.

5 Rooms • Price range: $115-175
601 Foster Ave, Coeur d'Alene, ID 83814
☎ **(208) 667-1232**

Coeur d'Alene
The Roosevelt, A Bed & Breakfast Inn
Built in 1905 as a schoolhouse, this red-brick structure has spacious rooms, and a Bell Tower suite. One parlor boasts a modern office, the other a Civil War-era chess set. The garden's redwood gazebo houses a spa and sauna, all under a star dome ceiling.

12 Rooms • Price range: $89-249
105 Wallace Ave, Coeur d'Alene, ID 83814
☎ **(208) 765-5200**

Coolin
Old Northern Inn
This inn, which was once a home for railroad workers, has a large deck.

6 Rooms • Price range: $90-140
Sherwood Beach Rd, Coolin, ID 83821
☎ **(208) 443-2426**

Idaho City
A One Step Away B&B Lodging
Was built as a "line shack and barn" for the Idaho Canadian Dredging Company.

4 Rooms • Price range: $45-75
112 Cottonwood St, Idaho City, ID 83631
☎ **(208) 392-4938**

Kooskia
Looking Glass Inn
A quiet retreat on 10 wooded acres with a view of surrounding mountains and river.

7 Rooms • Price range: $55-85
HCR 75, Box 32, US Hwy 12, Kooskia, ID 83539
☎ **(208) 926-0855**

McCall
⚅ Hotel McCall
A 1904 railroad inn by Payette Lake, where guests enjoy hearty breakfasts.

22 Rooms • Price range: $55-210
1101 N 3rd St, McCall, ID 83638
☎ **(208) 634-8105**

McCall
Northwest Passage Bed & Breakfast
Built in 1938 by MGM for Spencer Tracy and film crew of "Northwest Passage."

6 Rooms • Price range: $60-85
201 Rio Vista Blvd, McCall, ID 83638
☎ **(208) 634-5349**

Salmon
Greyhouse Inn Bed & Breakfast
This charming 1894 Victorian gingerbread house, located in a narrow valley of the Salmon River, is set among hay fields and pastures, with views of the mountain ranges. Rafters have dubbed this area the "White-water Capital of the World."

5 Rooms • Price range: $65-90
HC 61, Box 16, Salmon, ID 83467
☎ **(208) 756-3968**

Sandpoint
Coit House Bed & Breakfast
Old-fashioned charm permeates this restored 1907 Victorian manor located in the downtown area of Sandpoint, only minutes to Schweitzer Mountain Resort and a few blocks from the beach. The downstairs master suite boasts a hand-crafted column bed and claw-foot tub. An English garden mural graces the staircase wall. Other rooms are decorated with fine antiques and include pieces such as an ornate brass bed and a sleigh bed.

4 Rooms • Price range: $90-130
502 N Fourth Ave, Sandpoint, ID 83864
☎ **(208) 265-4035**

Sandpoint
Schweitzer Mountain Bed & Breakfast

This chalet retreat is situated on the side of a hill in a beautiful alpine setting in the pristine Selkirks. It has wonderful views, overlooking one of the largest lakes in the West. After a day of skiing guests can enjoy a soak in the hot tub on the covered deck. A special suite contains a loft with a private sitting room and a spacious bathroom. In January, visitors can attend the Winter Carnival; in June they can enjoy Timberfest.

5 Rooms • Price range: $90-175
110 Crystal Ct, Sandpoint, ID 83864
☎ **(208) 265-8080**

Notes:

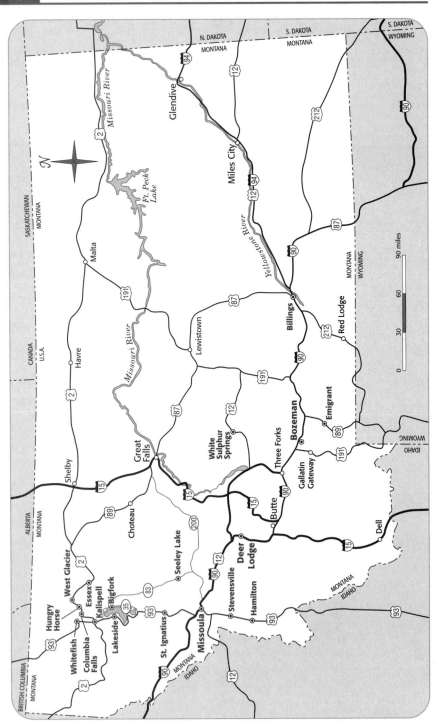

Bigfork
O'Duachain Country Inn

This log lodge is found in a wooded glen between the scenic Mission and Swan mountains. The town of Bigfork has a combination of untamed wilderness and extravagant amenities that has recently made it a favorite destination for the rich and famous. At this inn, guests can enjoy the views from the wraparound deck or the Guest House patio. On the grounds there is a variety of wildlife, including peacocks.

5 Rooms • Price range: $100-120
675 Ferndale Dr, Bigfork, MT 59911
☎ (406) 837-6851

Bigfork
Burggraf's Country Lane Bed N' Breakfast

This B&B is a true log home shaded by evergreen trees on the shores of beautiful Swan Lake. Its eclectic decor is rich in folk art, tribal artwork, and unusual items collected by the innkeeper on her annual trips to third-world countries.

5 Rooms • Price range: $85-95
1 Rainbow Dr on Swan Lake, Bigfork, MT 59911
☎ (406) 837-4608

Billings
The Josephine Bed & Breakfast

This quaint 1915 home offers bright rooms filled with antiques.

5 Rooms • Price range: $78-110
514 N 29th St, Billings, MT 59101
☎ (406) 248-5898

Bozeman
Howlers Inn Bed & Breakfast

On a three-acre wolf sanctuary, this rustic log house boasts mountain views.

8 Rooms • Price range: $85-215
3185 Jackson Creek Rd, Bozeman, MT 59715
☎ (406) 586-0304

Bozeman
Lindley House

Built in 1889 by one of the town's earliest pioneers, this charming Victorian manor house is now listed on the National Register of Historic Places. It is located on a historic tree-lined avenue, close to downtown and the university. The interior features French wall coverings, antique beds, fireplaces, stained-glass windows and an enclosed English garden. Amenities include a hot tub, sauna, and massage. Bicycles are available.

5 Rooms • Price range: $90-350
202 Lindley Pl, Bozeman, MT 59715
☎ (406) 587-8403

Columbia Falls
Bad Rock Country Bed & Breakfast

Scenic mountain views greet guests at this inn, located on 30 rolling acres in its Flathead Valley setting. The main house is filled with Old West antiques. Adjacent to it are two hand-hewn log cabins. Each one contains two rooms with private entrances and log-pole furnishings. Guests often use the inn as a base camp for exploring the magnificent Glacier National Park nearby.

7 Rooms • Price range: $120-179
480 Bad Rock Dr, Columbia Falls, MT 59912
☎ (406) 892-2829

Columbia Falls
Plum Creek House-The Inn on the Flathead River

Set high on a bluff overlooking Flathead River, this inn has panoramic views of the mountains and forests of western Montana. The living areas and guest-rooms have picture windows that frame the scenery and brighten the interior.

5 Rooms • Price range: $105-115
985 Vans Ave, Columbia Falls, MT 59912
☎ **(406) 892-1816**

Deer Lodge
Coleman Fee Mansion Bed & Breakfast
Call for information

5 Rooms • Price range: $65-150
500 Missouri Ave, Deer Lodge, MT 59722
☎ **(406) 846-2922**

Emigrant
Paradise Gateway Bed & Breakfast & Guest Cabins

Minutes away from the north entrance of Yellowstone National Park, this attractive country home is nestled in the Absaroka Mountains with the Yellowstone River running by the back door. Guests can enjoy stunning views from the deck of the main house. A private two-bedroom log cabin with full kitchen is located on 26 acres next to the river and is ideal for fishing the waters for blue-ribbon trout.

6 Rooms • Price range: $85-175
PO Box 84, Emigrant, MT 59027
☎ **(406) 333-4063**

Essex
Izaak Walton Inn

This historic inn was built in 1939 for service crews of the Great Northern Railway. It preserves its railroad heritage while offering country charm in a wooded setting. Located between the Bob Marshall Wilderness and Glacier National Park, it is a nature lover's dream. It is also a treat for fans of the railway—there's a working rail yard 50 feet from the porch. The restored Caboose Cottages can accommodate up to four people.

33 Rooms • Price range: $98-150
290 Izaak Walton Inn Rd, Essex, MT 59916
☎ **(406) 888-5700**

Hamilton
Starfire Farm Lodge

In the heart of the Bitterroot Mountains lies this enchanting Western retreat. Guestrooms are spacious and feature walk-in closets and comfortable sitting areas. Guests are encouraged to fish in the trout-stocked pond and take the time to watch for the white-tailed deer that inhabit the area. Other activities include relaxing in the garden's gazebo, gathering around evening campfires and having picnics.

5 Rooms • Price range: $80-107
387 Fleet St, Hamilton, MT 59840
☎ **(406) 363-6240**

◆◆◆ Helena
Appleton Inn Bed & Breakfast

Built in 1890, this Victorian-style home is complemented by the Appleton Heirloom Furniture Company next door, which custom designs and builds all types of furniture and accent pieces. The house has been restored to its original grandeur and features an arched front porch and architectural details in oak and cherry hardwood. Guests can play the antique rosewood piano, stroll in the gardens, play golf or hike up Mt. Helena.

5 Rooms • Price range: $95-150
1999 Euclid Ave, Helena, MT 59601
☎ **(406) 449-7492**

◆◆◆ Helena
Barrister Bed & Breakfast

This 1874 Victorian mansion has an intimate elegance. Spacious bedrooms have ornate fireplaces, original stained-glass windows, high ceilings and carved staircases. Centrally located downtown, right across from St. Helena Cathedral.

5 Rooms • Price range: $90-105
416 N Ewing, Helena, MT 59601
☎ **(406) 443-7330**

◆◆◆ Helena
The Sanders-Helena's Bed & Breakfast

The state's first senators called this 1875 Queen Anne mansion home. Now restored, the house's walls and floors are embellished with oak, fir and cherry woodwork, incised with stylized leaves and floral patterns. Some of the original furniture is still there, as are collections of ore samples and relics from the Custer battlefield. The surrounding mountainous terrain is perfect for pack-mule trips, rafting, trout fishing, and hiking.

7 Rooms • Price range: $80-110
328 N Ewing St, Helena, MT 59601
☎ **(406) 442-3309**

◆◆ Hungry Horse
Glacier Park Inn B&B

This is a unique octagonal house with two decks that afford expansive views of Glacier National Park and the Flathead River. Rooms have queen-size beds and private baths. A stay of two or more days is recommended to experience the area.

4 Rooms • Price range: $100-120
9128 Hwy 2 E, Hungry Horse, MT 59919
☎ **(406) 387-5099**

◆◆ Kalispell
Creston Country Inn Bed & Breakfast

In a quiet setting amid pastures and fields, lies this charming 1920s farm house. The surrounding area offers many recreational opportunities such as skiing at Big Mountain, hiking at Glacier National Park, or canoeing on Flathead Lake.

4 Rooms • Price range: $74-139
70 Creston Rd, Kalispell, MT 59901
☎ **(406) 755-7517**

Missoula
Goldsmith's Inn

Formerly the residence of the University of Montana's president, this 1911 brick home sits on the banks of the Clark Fork River, so guests can go fishing just outside the front door. The deck offers unparalleled views of the Sapphire and Bitterroot mountains. Each room has a hand-tiled private bathroom, fireplace, reading nook and Victorian bed. The banquet room can handle 60 guests.

7 Rooms • Price range: $89-129
809 E Front St, Missoula, MT 59802
☎ **(406) 728-1585**

Seeley Lake
The Emily A

Named after the innkeeper's grand-mother who ran one of Missoula's first board and rooming houses, this inn stands for the gracious hospitality of the Old West. It is an elegant and spacious log home, which is tucked away in the Rocky Mountains and overlooks a private lake on Clearwater River. Rooms are cozy and comfort-able, featuring such details as feather duvets and fresh flowers.

5 Rooms • Price range: $115-150
SR 83 N, MM20, PO Box 350,
Seeley Lake, MT 59868
☎ **(406) 677-3474**

St. Ignatius
⊕ *Stoneheart Inn*

Here guests are treated to gourmet breakfasts, charming western hospitality, and beautiful mountain scenery. This inn sits at the base of the majestic Mission Mountains and is just a short drive from several national wildlife preserves.

4 Rooms • Price range: $40-65
26 N Main, St. Ignatius, MT 59865
☎ **(406) 745-4999**

Stevensville
Big Creek Pine's Bed & Breakfast

This newly constructed inn provides a relaxing country setting in the heart of Bitterroot Valley. Big Creek runs right through the property. Each of the spacious bedrooms has a private bath and window seat so visitors can sit and enjoy the view. Guests can watch for local wildlife from the porch swing or drink tea by the fire in the Great Room.

4 Rooms • Price range: $70-80
2986 US 93 N, Stevensville, MT 59870
☎ **(406) 642-6475**

West Glacier
A Wild Rose Bed & Breakfast

Located in a lovely mountain meadow setting, just six miles from Glacier National Park, this luxury inn is deco-rated with a Victorian flair. Guests can unwind in a therapeutic spa located in a private outdoor setting. Honeymooners will enjoy one of the Whirlpool Suites, with Victorian oak or cherry furniture, armoire, fireplace and marble-tiled bath with whirlpool tub. Breakfast is served on a 1930s mahogany dining room table.

4 Rooms • Price range: $100-150
10280 US 2 E, West Glacier, MT 59936
☎ **(406) 387-4900**

White Sulphur Springs
Foxwood Inn
Built in 1890, this quaint home offers cozy and comfortable guestrooms.

11 Rooms • Price range: $42-52
52 Miller Rd, White Sulphur Springs, MT 59645
☎ **(406) 547-2224**

Whitefish
Duck Inn Lodge
Situated in a quiet setting on Whitefish River, but only six blocks from downtown, this inn lives up to its name.

Expect duck lamps, duck paintings, duck dinnerware, wooden ducks and even a quacking duck phone. The brass-accented wood interior nicely complements the rough cedar exterior. One room has its own atrium. Some rooms overlook the river and offer guests a glimpse of...ducks!

10 Rooms • Price range: $59-99
1305 Columbia Ave, Whitefish, MT 59937
☎ **(406) 862-3825**

Whitefish
Good Medicine Lodge
Here's a quintessential mountain getaway: a cedar lodge decorated with Western motifs using solid wood furniture and fabrics influenced by Native American textiles. An ideal ski lodge, it features a ski room with boot driers and ski sharpening facilities. Most rooms have a balcony and custom-made lodge-pole beds. The proprietors have received acclaim for their environmentally sensitive business practices.

9 Rooms • Price range: $105-165
537 Wisconsin Ave, Whitefish, MT 59937
☎ **(406) 862-5488**

Whitefish
Hidden Moose Lodge
Each room at this lodge has a private balcony or patio with a flower box.

8 Rooms • Price range: $115-135
1735 E Lakeshore Dr, Whitefish, MT 59937
☎ **(406) 862-6516**

Whitefish
Gasthaus Wendlingen
The beautiful nature surrounding this inn can be viewed from the large front porch, the creek-side patio and the picture windows in all bedrooms. Family recipes are used for the delicious breakfast and afternoon snacks. The steam room is wonderful.

4 Rooms • Price range: $75-125
700 Monegan Rd, Whitefish, MT 59937
☎ **(406) 862-4886**

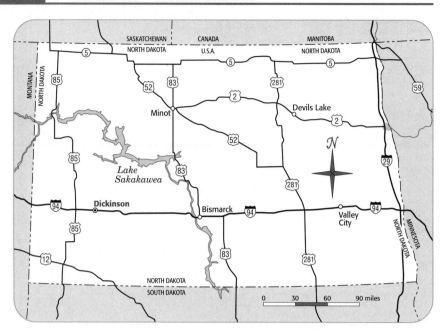

Dickinson
Hartfiel Inn

European flair shines throughout this 1908 home, which boasts original oak fixtures, an elegant dining room with a crystal chandelier, and a handsome living room with a fireplace. Bedrooms are tastefully decorated. Whirlpool on the grounds.

4 Rooms • Price range: $59-89
509 3rd Ave W, Dickinson, ND 58601
☎ **(701) 225-6710**

Notes:

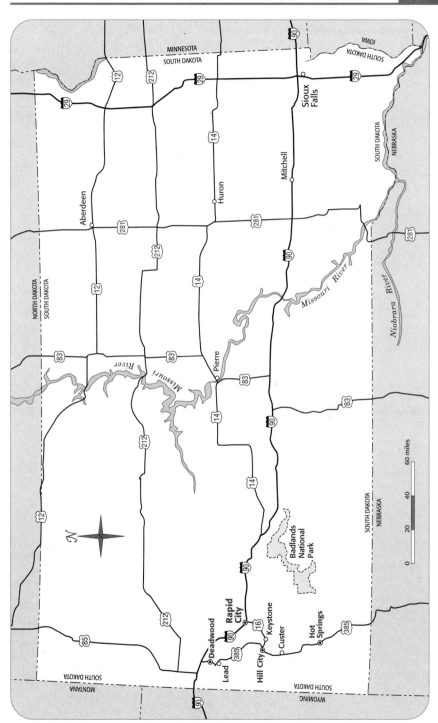

Deadwood
Black Hills Hideaway Bed & Breakfast

Situated on 67 acres of property surrounded by the Black Hills National Forest, this is the ideal getaway for those who want quiet and solitude. Guestrooms are inviting, with private bathrooms and queen-size beds. Most rooms have a deck, a gas fireplace and an indoor two-person whirlpool or outdoor hot tub. A full, hot breakfast is served in the dining room or on the deck. Snacks are served in the afternoon.

8 Rooms • Price range: $99-179
HC 73 Box 1129, Deadwood, SD 57732
☎ **(605) 578-3054**

Hill City
⊛ Country Manor Bed & Breakfast

Surrounded by the Black Hills, this property is located in a sunny valley.

5 Rooms • Price: $95
12670 Robins Roost Rd, Hill City, SD 57745
☎ **(605) 574-2196**

Hot Springs
Villa Theresa Guest House B&B

Built high on a bluff, this 1891 home served as a private club before being converted into a guest house in the 1920s. These days it still maintains an inviting Victorian aura, with crystal and brass chandeliers, Oriental rugs on hardwood floors and 18-foot-high intricately hand-painted ceilings in the octagonal room. Guestrooms are individually decorated, and the Great Room and dining room are furnished with antiques.

7 Rooms • Price range: $70-130
801 Almond St, Hot Springs, SD 57747
☎ **(605) 745-4633**

Rapid City
Abend Haus Cottages & Audrie's Bed & Breakfast

Family-owned and operated, this five-acre estate, surrounded by thousands of acres of National Forest, has suites and cottages furnished with European antiques. A private entrance and bath, patio and hot tub are features of each guestroom. A full Black Hills-style breakfast is served. Nearby activities include biking, fishing and hiking. Bikes and fishing poles are available for guests upon request.

9 Rooms • Price range: $95-175
23029 Thunderhead Falls Rd,
Rapid City, SD 57702
☎ **(605) 342-7788**

Rapid City
Carriage House Bed & Breakfast

Rapid City is centrally located near many of South Dakota's natural and man-made points of interest, such as Wind Cave National Park and Mount Rushmore. However, guests of the Carriage House B&B may decide to forego their sightseeing just to spend as much time as possible in the beautiful house. Every room is decorated to provide the utmost comfort. The hosts also offer a sailing excursion on nearby Lake Pactola.

5 Rooms • Price range: $99-149
721 West Blvd, Rapid City, SD 57701
☎ **(605) 343-6415**

Rapid City
🏨 *Hayloft Bed & Breakfast*

Visitors to this inn located in the beautiful Black Hills can often spot deer, rabbits or wild turkeys in the yard. The day begins with a hearty country breakfast, then guests can take in the view from one of the platform swings or relax in the hot tub on the large deck. Nearby attractions include Mount Rushmore and the Reptile Gardens. Each guestroom has a private entrance and private bath, and some have a marble whirlpool.

8 Rooms • Price range: $105-145
9356 Neck Yoke Rd, Rapid City, SD 57701
☎ **(605) 343-5351**

Notes:

_____
_____
_____
_____
_____
_____
_____
_____
_____
_____
_____
_____
_____
_____
_____
_____
_____
_____
_____
_____
_____
_____
_____
_____
_____
_____
_____
_____

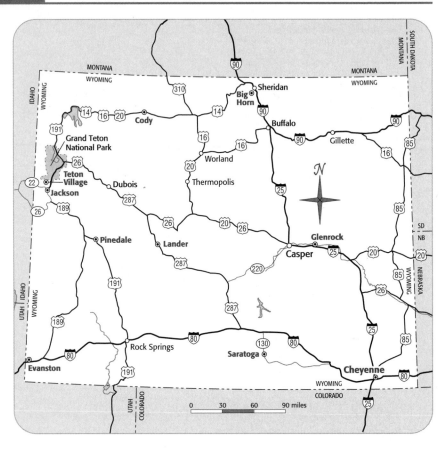

Notes:

Big Horn

Spahn's Big Horn Mountain Bed & Breakfast, L. L. C.

This towering log home, with its cozy cabins, is nestled on the mountainside overlooking the Sheridan Valley. Each guestroom in the main lodge has a private bath and one has a separate entrance. The lodge itself has a three-story living room, an open fireplace, a library, piano and outside deck. The secluded cabins are a five-minute walk from the lodge and feature shower bathrooms. A hearty mountain breakfast is served.

5 Rooms • Price range: $85-140
70 Upper Hideaway Ln, Big Horn, WY 82833
☎ (307) 674-8150

Cheyenne

Nagle Warren Mansion B&B

One of Cheyenne's most elegant residences, this late 19th-century beauty boasts a Victorian Old West decor, with ornate wooden staircases, authentic period wallpaper and 19th-century artwork. Guest accommodations include private baths. There are data ports in each room and the mansion has a fully equipped office. Breakfast is a delight, featuring homemade bread and muffins along with a daily special from the kitchen. Tea and sherry are served every afternoon. Guests who are so inclined can also take advantage of the exercise room and the outdoor hot tub.

12 Rooms • Price: $128
222 E 17th St, Cheyenne, WY 82001
☎ (307) 637-3333

Cheyenne

A Drummond's Ranch Bed & Breakfast

Tucked into the south side of a hill with a wonderful view of the Colorado Rockies, this home sits on 120 acres of land, close to the Medicine Bow National Forest and State Park. Guests will find thick terry-cloth robes, fresh flowers and a treat of fresh fruit or home-baked cake or cookies in their rooms. Breakfasts are custom-tailored and homemade snacks and beverages are always available.

4 Rooms • Price range: $65-160
399 Happy Jack Rd, Cheyenne, WY 82007
☎ (307) 634-6042

Cheyenne

Windy Hills Guest House

Some 7,000 feet atop a rolling vista overlooking Granite Lake sits this guest house. Nature lovers will delight in being surrounded by wildflowers, birds and roaming wildlife. Nearby trails are ideal for hiking and mountain biking, while the lake offers opportunities for fishing, boating and water sports. Visitors can stay in the guest house, suites or three-level log house. Breakfast is served in the great room.

8 Rooms • Price range: $69-175
393 Happy Jack Rd, Cheyenne, WY 82007
☎ (307) 632-6423

Cheyenne
♦♦ *Porch Swing Bed & Breakfast*
Personal attention and European style are features of this 1907 historic home.

3 Rooms • Price range: $50-80
712 E 20th St, Cheyenne, WY 82001
☎ **(307) 778-7182**

Cody
♦♦  *The Lockhart Bed & Breakfast Inn*
This home of author Caroline Lockhart is located just minutes away from the Buffalo Bill Historical Center, Cody Night Rodeo and is 50 miles from Yellowstone National Park. All the country-style rooms are uniquely decorated.

7 Rooms • Price range: $85-95
109 W Yellowstone Ave, Cody, WY 82414
☎ **(307) 587-6074**

Cody
♦♦ *Parson's Pillow Bed & Breakfast*
This 1902 renovated church has small, cozy rooms and is close to downtown.

4 Rooms • Price range: $80-85
1202 14th St, Cody, WY 82414
☎ **(307) 587-2382**

Evanston
♦♦ *Pine Gables B&B Inn*
This 1883 private residence became Evanston's only inn in 1923. An Eastlake Victorian-style mansion, on the Register of Historical Places, this inn is part of the Evanston Historic District walking tour, and is named after the pine trees that are predominant in the area. Rooms have hand-painted murals and marbled walls and are furnished with antiques. French toast and waffles are among the breakfast specials.

5 Rooms • Price range: $100-300
1049 Center St, Evanston, WY 82930
☎ **(307) 789-2069**

Glenrock
♦ *Hotel Higgins*
This 1916 hotel with many original furnishings has a Wild West ambience.

9 Rooms • Price range: $56-80
416 W Birch St, Glenrock, WY 82637
☎ **(307) 436-9212**

Jackson
♦♦ *The Alpine House*
The Alpine House is a Scandinavian-style inn near Jackson Hole Mountain Resort run by two former Olympic athletes. In keeping with the inn's theme, common and private rooms are decorated with clean soft colors, white linens, down comforters and pine furniture. All guestrooms have a fireplace and a private balcony. The spectacular Grand Tetons offer excellent ski slopes and facilities for other winter activities.

21 Rooms • Price range: $95-210
285 N Glenwood, Jackson, WY 83001
☎ **(307) 739-1570**

Jackson
🐪 *Davy Jackson Inn*

Located only three blocks from Historic Jackson Town Square, this country inn features elegant rooms decorated with king-size canopy beds or queen-size beds and modern baths or old fashioned claw-foot tubs. Suites include Jacuzzi steam showers, gas fireplaces and fainting couches. Guests may choose to hike the trails surrounding Jackson Hole or take a ride through Snake River Rapids, then relax in the outdoor hot tub.

12 Rooms • Price range: $199-249
85 Perry Ave, Jackson, WY 83001
☎ **(307) 739-2294**

Jackson
Nowlin Creek Inn

This 6,000-square-foot, family-run inn has maintained its heritage with a blend of antiques, heirlooms, and family photographs, as well as artwork by the innkeepers themselves. The dining room walls have stenciled vines, the living room a flower-and-ivy design, and even the floors are decorated. Eastlake Victorian furniture is featured throughout. Each guestroom has a private bath. Yellowstone National Park is nearby.

6 Rooms • Price range: $160-195
660 E Broadway, Jackson, WY 83001
☎ **(307) 733-0882**

Lander
Blue Spruce Inn

The interior of this 1920 gracious brick home is an outstanding example of the Arts and Crafts style of the early 20th century, with magnificent crown moldings, woodwork and stained-glass windows. The guestrooms are large and comfortable, and each has a private bath. The inn is located in a quiet residential area, and the Pioneer Museum and Sinks Canyon State Park are nearby. A full hot breakfast is served.

4 Rooms • Price range: $70-85
677 S 3rd St, Lander, WY 82520
☎ **(307) 332-8253**

Lander
Piece of Cake Bed & Breakfast

Guests begin the day by taking in the views of the surrounding red and tan sandstone formations and the Wind River Range. A hearty Western breakfast features fresh fruit, home-baked breads and muffins, and healthy granola. Next, guests may want to explore the surrounding mountains and wilderness, sit on one of the private decks or porches, or relax in one of the guestrooms or private cabins.

6 Rooms • Price range: $70-90
2343 Baldwin Creek Rd, Lander, WY 82520
☎ **(307) 332-7608**

Pinedale
Window on the Winds B&B

Located directly on the Continental
Divide Snowmobile Trail, this B&B provides easy access to a number of activities, including stream and lake fishing,
river rafting and hiking. The guestrooms are
decorated in Western and Plains Indian style;
they all have beautiful views and two have a
private bath. All rooms feature lodge-pole pine
queen-size beds with handmade European-
style down duvets. Breakfast is served.

4 Rooms • Price range: $45-95
10151 US 191, Pinedale, WY 82941
☎ **(307) 367-2600**

Pinedale
The Chambers House Bed & Breakfast

This renovated historic log home has
guestrooms that are decorated with
antiques and family heirlooms. Some
have fireplaces. A full breakfast is

served, and picnic lunches, private lunches or
late-night desserts are available upon request.

5 Rooms • Price range: $55-125
111 W Magnolia St, Pinedale, WY 82941
☎ **(307) 367-2168**

Saratoga
Far Out West Bed & Breakfast

This historic home was the winner
of the Saratoga Historical Society
Architectural Award for 1996. Guestrooms are beautifully furnished and are
named after local historical figures. The main
house can accommodate small meetings and has
fax and modem connections. Visitors can relax
in the spa, work out on the exercise equipment
or visit nearby Native American sites and Old
West museums.

6 Rooms • Price range: $85-100
304 N 2nd St, Saratoga, WY 82331
☎ **(307) 326-5869**

Teton Village
Sassy Moose Inn of Jackson Hole

Set in a mountain meadow next to a
golf course, this lovely contemporary log
house enjoys a tremendous view of the
Grand Teton Mountains. Cozy bed-

rooms feature fireplaces or wood-stoves. Ideally
located for summer and winter activities.

5 Rooms • Price range: $169-169
3859 Miles Rd, Teton Village, WY 83014
☎ **(307) 733-1277**

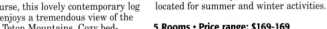

Midwest

Sunrise colors Lake Superior and Palisade Head near Tettegouche State Park, Minnesota.

Scenic Byways
of the Midwest

The Cass Scenic Railroad takes visitors on a trip through West Virginia history.

Elkins to Lewisburg
The unsurpassed natural beauty of West Virginia is no better exemplified than in the area between these two centers. The lush pastureland valleys, broad rolling plateaus and majestic wooded mountains along the western front of the Allegheny Mountains make this a picturesque haven for outdoor recreational enthusiasts and those who just like to stop and smell the flowers.

New Richmond to Friendship
The historic Ohio River marks the southern boundary of Ohio where the state meets Kentucky. The river played an essential role in the exploration and settlement of the area, spawning many towns along its banks. Driving along the river, it is not difficult to imagine a time when riverboats and steamships filled the waterway.

Mackinac Island to Traverse City
Called the "Land of Little Bays" by the locals, the northwest corner of Michigan's Lower Peninsula is a coastal region of scalloped bays, jagged peninsulas and lovely lakeside resort communities. U.S. 31 & SR 119, the main access route to the area, also offers a sizable sampling of Michigan's interior terrain of cherry orchards, vineyards and dense timber.

Great River Road
The "Great River" can only mean the Mississippi and this stretch of SR 35 through Wisconsin puts visitors in touch with the river's northern section and the history traced along its banks. Along the way are charming towns and villages, bucolic dairy farms and even an opportunity to visit the chosen home of America's most famous architect, Frank Lloyd Wright.

The Old Mackinac Point Lighthouse, now a maritime museum, used to keep watch over the Straits of Mackinac and Lake Michigan.

An observation platform beside Blackwater Falls, West Virginia, provides visitors with a superb vantage point.

For further information on the sites along each route, see the Scenic Byways Resource Guide on page 775.

North Shore Drive

Historic and scenic, this route follows the shoreline of the greatest of the Great Lakes, Superior. From the port city of Duluth to the Canadian border, the terrain varies from rolling hills to dramatic lakeside cliffs. Passing by historic water routes and the nearby inland mines of the famed Iron Range, the route tells the story of Minnesota itself.

Elkins to Lewisburg

⬤ *U.S. 219 runs through forested mountains and pasturelands parallel to the western front of the Allegheny Mountains—part of the Appalachian range. This tour is for motorists who have time to spare to take in the picturesque natural beauty of the region. The route traverses the Monongahela National Forest, a 909,000-acre park of many splendid natural wonders.*

❶ Blackwater Falls State Park
One of the most photographed sites in West Virginia is the spectacular falls of the Blackwater River, for which this state park is named. Observation areas along the rim of the falls provide safe vantage points for viewing the river as it plunges down a five-story gorge. For more adventurous visitors, a stairway descends to the foot of the falls. Other recreational activities within the park include paddle-boating, hiking, horseback riding and swimming.

❷ Petersburg
Situated near the gateway to the Seneca Rocks National Recreation Area, Petersburg is a major center for outdoor enthusiasts. Calling itself the "Home of the Golden Trout," Petersburg is also home to the many guides available for hunting, fishing or canoeing trips. A short distance to the west lie the Smoke Hole Caverns. These caverns were used by Native Americans for smoking meat and fish and later by settlers to distill the "devil's brew." A wildlife museum, a log motel and cabins are also on the premises.

❸ Cass Scenic Railroad State Park
In the heart of the Monongahela National forest, the town of Cass remains in many ways relatively unchanged since its inception. The Cass Scenic Railroad, a vintage railway system, continues to run on the same line used to haul lumber from the forest to the town mill. The old logging flat-cars are now refurbished passenger cars where visitors relive the time when the railroad was an essential part of everyday life. The route takes visitors past a re-created 1940s logging camp, allowing an inside view of the living conditions of the loggers. Local museums and shops are filled with relics from the logging trade, including the world's largest band saw.

❹ Droop Mountain Battlefield State Park
On November 6, 1863, one of the largest Civil War battles of West Virginia's history occurred here on a high mountain plateau north of Droop. The fierce battle ended the last serious Confederate resistance in the state. Now a 288-acre park, part of the battlefield is restored and key events during the combat are marked for visitors. A small log-cabin museum contains Civil War artifacts and memorabilia. The park also maintains seven hiking trails that lead to scenic vistas overlooking the panoramic Greenbrier Valley. Picnicking is permitted.

❺ Lost World Caverns
Just north of historic Lewisburg a vast interlocking system of subterranean passageways and caves pierce deep into Earth's mantle, inviting the curious explorer to a fascinating underground world. The cavern, descending nearly 235 feet below the surface, was opened to the public in 1970, when a steep shaft was dug into the main central chamber and a circular stairway was constructed to facilitate visitor access. One of the more impressive natural formations within the cavern is the "Snowy Chandelier." At 30 tons in weight, it is believed to be the largest com-

Historic downtown Lewisburg has retained and revived the architecture of its past.

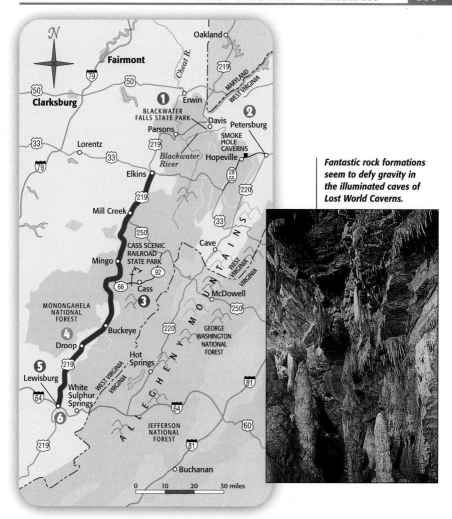

Fantastic rock formations seem to defy gravity in the illuminated caves of Lost World Caverns.

pound stalactite in the nation and one of the world's best displays of pure calcite. Be sure to wear a light jacket or a sweater and comfortable walking shoes.

⑥ White Sulphur Springs/Lewisburg

Mineral springs are believed by many to be a centuries-old cure-all for a multitude of illnesses—a belief that helped to spawn the city of White Sulphur Springs. In 1780, at the springs' source, the city's first inn was built. Over the years this inn evolved into

today's Greenbrier Hotel. During the Cold War, a top-secret government relocation center was built under the hotel to protect Members of Congress in the event of a nuclear attack. Guided tours of the fallout shelter are offered. Nestled amid the natural beauty of the Allegheny Mountains the nearby town of Lewisburg enjoys a rich and colorful history that reaches back some 200 years. The center of town is a 236-acre National Register Historic District with many 18th- and 19th-century buildings.

New Richmond to Friendship

U.S. 52 runs along the soil-rich banks of the majestic Ohio River, a primary tributary of the Mississippi, which defines the southern boundary of the state. There are many historic sites as well as parks and picnic areas along the way. The route tunnels through trees with picture-window openings to the river, then hugs the waterway so closely it feels like you're right on top of it.

❶ Ulysses S. Grant Birthplace

A modest cottage on the banks of the mighty Ohio River marks the birthplace of the 18th president of the United States, Ulysses S. Grant. An outstanding, highly decorated general during the Civil War who is credited as the savior of the Union, Grant would become president in 1869, staying in office until 1877. His birthplace was constructed in 1817 with local white pine and contains one large room (the Grant's original home) and two back rooms, added on later. The cottage is furnished with with antiques and family memorabilia.

❷ Rankin House

During the mid-19th century, the town of Ripley on the Ohio River was a center for steamboat production. It was also—unknown to many of its residents at the time—a safe haven for fugitive slaves seeking freedom in the northern states or Canada. Reverend John Rankin, a local minster, hid many of the slaves in his home, which sits on the aptly named Liberty Hill. It is believed that the reverend would light a lamp hanging in a front window at night to help guide slaves crossing the Ohio River to safety. The novelist Harriet Beecher Stowe visited the reverend and found his story and the harrowing tales of those he helped to be inspirational fodder for her novel, *Uncle Tom's Cabin*. The Rankin

Home is believed to be the one that Eliza, a character in the novel, escapes to after her journey across the frozen Ohio River.

❸ Davis Memorial State Nature Preserve

With more than 500 varieties of plants and trees, this 87-acre preserve is popular with both amateur and professional botanists. One of the rare plants in the preserve is the sullivantia, a rare rock plant that dates back to pre-glacial times and is found here in abundance. Part of the 1,200-mile Buckeye Trail, which encompasses the entire state, passes through the park.

❹ Serpent Mound State Memorial

Lying on a inconspicuous plateau overlooking the Brush Creek Valley, a prehistoric mound of earth resembling the shape of a serpent has for centuries stumped scientists and the public alike. Nearly a quarter of a mile long, about 5 feet high and 20 feet wide at the mouth, it was first outlined with stones and clay and then covered with earth—but no artifacts or other clues have ever been recovered. Nearby conical mounds contain burial artifacts and other archeological remnants of the the ancient Adena people (1000 B.C. to A.D. 700), but it is believed that Serpent Mound was built about 1,000 years ago by the Fort Ancient people to whom the serpent may have had significant religious or mystical symbolism.

An important stop on the Underground Railroad, the Rankin House in Ripley provided refuge for fugitive slaves crossing the mighty Ohio River.

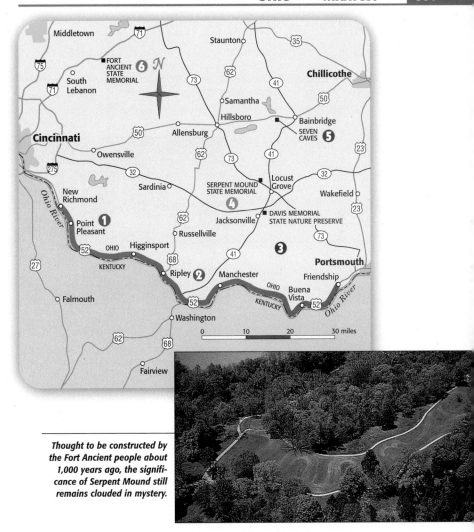

Thought to be constructed by the Fort Ancient people about 1,000 years ago, the significance of Serpent Mound still remains clouded in mystery.

❺ Seven Caves

Not far from Bainbridge, the traditional home of the Shawnee, three well-marked hiking tails lead to the Seven Caves, each with its own uniqueg formations. The caves have paved walkways and handrails and all are easily accessible, although some stair-climbing will be required.

❻ Fort Ancient State Memorial

A National Historic Landmark, Fort Ancient is an important North American archaeological site. Evidence of two different prehistoric indigenous cultures has been found here. Sometime between 100 B.C. and A.D. 500 the Hopewell Indians constructed earthen walls ranging in height from 4 feet to 23 feet that run for 3.5 miles around the 764-acre park. The people also built earthen mounds, several of which seem to have some type of astronomical alignment. About A.D. 900 to 1500, the Fort Ancient people occupied the site, farming the rich floodplains of the Little Miami River. A prehistoric garden replicates crops grown by these two peoples, and a museum provides more information. There are also hiking trails and picnic spots.

Mackinac Island to Traverse City

Highway 31 rambles through a coastal region dotted with dunes and relaxed resort towns filled with many quaint shops and attractions. The numerous roadside fruit stands along the route, selling jams and jellies or cherry pies, provide just a small sample of the special hospitality of the people here.

Colorful catamarans gather along a stretch of beach in Grand Traverse Bay. In Traverse City, these and various other types of watercraft are available for charter.

❶ Mackinac Island

Due to its strategic position in the narrow straits between Lake Huron and Lake Michigan, Mackinac Island has been fought over by many nations wanting to control the continental interior. The original inhabitants were the Ojibwa who came to fish, to plant corn and to bury their dead in its limestone caves. The French first built a fort on the island for missionary purposes. Later the fort was occupied by British forces, who built a new fortress overlooking the harbor. As a result of the War of 1812, it came under American ownership. Many of the historical structures—an officer's quarters, a blockhouse and the fort's original protective stone ramparts—still stand and are open to visitors. The island is accessible only by ferry or aircraft and must be explored on foot, bicycle or horse and carriage—still a popular mode of travel here. Hwy. 185 skirts the perimeter of the island, the only highway in the state that does not allow automobiles.

❷ Colonial Michilimackinac

Located in Mackinaw City, "Gateway to the Straits" and the northernmost city in Michigan's Lower Peninsula, this park is a reconstruction of a French fur-trading village and military outpost that was established in 1715. The visitor center is located in the shadow of the Mackinac Bridge. Called the "Mighty Mac" by local residents, it is one of the world's longest suspension bridges and is considered by many to be a modern engineering marvel.

❸ Divers' Shrine

In many of the coastal villages throughout Michigan, small and sometimes stately monuments stand in remembrance of those who have lost their lives navigating the choppy and unforgiving waters of the Great Lakes. Perhaps the most unique memorial is in Petoskey, a resort community within Little Traverse Bay. Most will never see the peculiarly fitting memorial—however, it still manages to evoke a sense of remembrance in those who just hear of it. The memorial, an 11-foot crucifix, is located 17 feet down at the bottom of the bay. Only accessible to scuba divers, its location in the cold freshwater depths of Lake Michigan is a touching tribute to those lives the Great Lakes have claimed.

❹ Gaylord

Resembling a European hamlet tucked into the hills of Switzerland or Austria, Gaylord is a city full of Alpine-inspired architecture that complements the scenic beauty of the area's shimmering lakes, flowing rivers and expansive wilderness. With more than 20 championship courses, Gaylord is also a golfer's Camelot for aficionados of the sport. The Call of the Wild Museum is well worth visiting. On permanent display are 150 mounted animals, representing a variety of North American species.

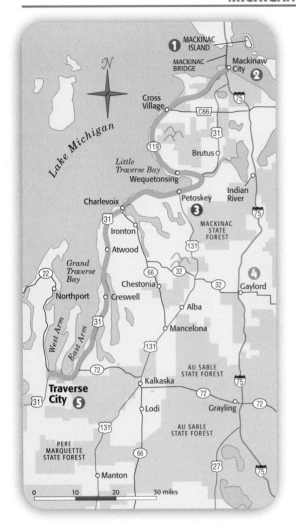

Colonial Michilimackinac State Park (foreground) celebrates Michigan's pioneer past. Ironically, Mackinac Bridge, a poignant symbol of modernity, looms in the background.

❺ Traverse City and State Park

This beautiful resort city and the surrounding region supply about one-third of the world's cherry supplies. What started as a small experiment in the shadow of a failing lumber boom in the late 1800s, cherry farming would go on to become one of the area's largest industries. As one can imagine, the biggest festival of the year here is the National Cherry Festival held in early July. If you're in the vicinity, you'll taste what may be the best cherry pies on the planet. Only two miles to the east of the city's center, Traverse City State Park is a well-maintained 45-acre urban park with a quarter-mile beach on the southern end of the East Arm of Grand Traverse Bay. Inland hiking and biking trails wander through the mature hardwoods and softwoods—the park's interior is completely wooded. For day trips, expect plenty of picnic areas with barbecue grills, as well as a playground for the kids. The park also operates a fully equipped campground.

Great River Road

Rich in history, this picturesque route follows that taken by early fur traders and later by the shipping companies that opened routes between the Mississippi, the St. Croix River and Lake Superior. Many points of interest in the towns and villages along the way make for plenty of opportunities to get acquainted with the past—and present—of America's heartland.

This La Crosse church is one of the charming and poignant memorials to the people who came to settle by the "Great River."

❶ St. Croix Falls

This center for outdoor recreation is located in the scenic St. Croix River Valley. The St. Croix National Scenic Riverway with its 252-mile river reserve offers fishing, canoeing, camping, hiking and cross-country skiing. Also in the area is Interstate State Park, Wisconsin's first state park and one of the nine areas making up the Ice Age National Scientific Reserve. Located along the Dalles, a scenic gorge bordering the east side of the St. Croix River, the site contains fascinating rock formations caused by the swirling current of glacial meltwater.

❷ La Crosse

Named for its location at the juncture of the Mississippi and Black rivers, La Crosse is also a historic meeting and mixing place of the cultures that were attracted here by the two rivers. Originally an Indian trading post, the site's huge stands of pine forests attracted Norwegian and German immigrants. Today the area's rich heritage is celebrated annually with the traditional music festivals, Riverfest and Octoberfest. As for the natural setting, Goose Island County Park makes great use of a wildlife reserve with hiking and cross-country ski trails.

❸ Spring Green

Frank Lloyd Wright chose Spring Green for his home and his architectural school. As a result, this unassuming farming community has collected a great concentration of Wright-influenced structures. Built in 1902 of sandstone and native oak, Wright's home and grounds include living areas, a drafting studio, two galleries containing originally designed furniture and artworks, the school, and a visitor center designed by Wright in 1953. The center conducts guided tours that cover the life and work of Wright. An interesting counterpoint to the Wright complex is Spring Green's other architectural wonder, the House on the Rock. Designed and built by Alex Jordan, Jr.. in the 1940s, this unusual structure sits atop Deer Shelter Rock, a chimneylike formation rising 450 feet above the Wyoming Valley. One of the most striking features of the house is the Infinity Room, a glassed-in 218-foot unsupported extension that gives visitors the impression they are walking on air. Jordan was an avid collector and exhibits ranging from the world's largest theater organs to a re-creation of a 19th-century gas-lit Main Street have turned the site of his home and grounds into a fanciful theme park.

❹ Prairie du Chien

In the mid- to late-1700s the village of Prairie du Chien began to grow around the fur-trading post established after explorers Marquette and Joliette discovered the area in 1673. Control of Prairie du Chien was passed through the years from French to British to American forces. During this time, four different forts were built, the most famous of which is Fort Crawford,

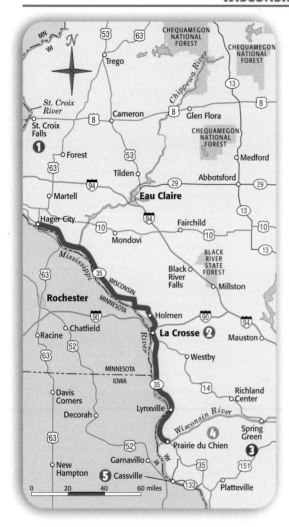

A 19th-century gas-lit Main Street is just one of the attractions at Spring Green's House on the Rock.

where Jefferson Davis and Zachary Taylor were stationed. Today the fort's restored hospital features such displays as an 1850 doctor's office, medical instruments and a history of military medicine. Several miles north, Villa Louis has been authentically renovated and opened as a museum. This 1870 estate was built by the son of fur trader H.L. Dousman. Almost all of the furnishings, art and books on display belonged to the family, and represent one of the finest collections of Victorian decorative arts in the U.S. Also on the site are the Fur Trade Museum and the Old Carriage House.

❺ Cassville

A prosperous Mississippi River community since the early 1800s, Cassville was the home of Wisconsin's first governor, Nelson Dewey. His home is featured at the Stonefield Historic Site. Doors, walls and millwork of the original structure—consumed by fire in 1873—have been incorporated into this authentic reconstruction. Also on the site is a recreated village showing life in small-town Wisconsin around 1900, and the State Agricultural Museum with a reconstructed farmhouse and historical photos, farm machinery and tools.

North Shore Drive

This 150-mile route from Grand Portage to Duluth allows visitors to catch the ever-changing moods and vistas of Lake Superior. An immense forested wilderness cloaking glacier-worn mountains makes a beautiful counterpoint to the vast expanse of water and the mining towns and cities along the way.

❶ Grand Portage National Monument

Grand Portage, just south of the Canadian border on the North Shore, was once the headquarters of the North West Company. Portage is French for "carrying place," which describes the overland route taken by traders at this spot to circumvent the Pigeon River rapids. This national monument offers an authentic re-creation of a 18th-century trading post, with park staffers dressed in period costumes. Several miles south of the monument, Grand Portage State Park features walking trails and a viewing platform with a spectacular vista of Pigeon River. At this point, the river cascades down 120 feet of stone ledges at High Falls, also known as Pigeon Falls, the state's highest waterfalls.

❷ Split Rock Lighthouse

The region's most famous lighthouse is now run by the Minnesota Historic Society, and is in a state park. Rising 54 feet above Lake Superior and overlooking a sheer cliff, the structure was built with materials hauled by ship and hoisted up to its rocky foundations. Today visitors can examine the giant lens, which for many years helped guide ships, and the lighthouse keeper's house, restored to its 1924 appearance.

❸ Gooseberry Falls State Park

This unassuming roadside picnic area has some hidden wonders. Visitors follow trails from the roadside parking to view five beautiful waterfalls, one of which is two-tiered and falls from a height of 60 feet. A visitor center supplies information on the park and other sites along the North Shore.

❹ Two Harbors

This port town's importance—both past and present—is evidenced by the world's largest iron-ore dock, shipping out the produce of Minnesota's Iron Range. And Two Harbors is proud of its past. A visitor center at the north end of town provides walking-tour maps of historic buildings, including the original head offices of the 3M Company, Minnesota Mining and Manufacturing. The town's turn-of-the-century depot and 1892 lighthouse—the first on the North Shore— double as museums. The sepia-toned photos displayed here trace the harbor's history, including some of the tragic shipwrecks that plagued early shipping.

❺ Duluth

The North Shore's traditional gateway, Duluth is a colorful port town that has undergone a decade-long revitalization. Spreading out along 17 miles of shoreline from the mouth of the St. Louis River northward, Duluth with its giant grain-storage facilities is the welcoming place for massive ocean-going freighters. Built on the hills around the lake, the town's streets plunge down the steep escarpment at dizzying angles past the downtown business section and its 1890s jewel, The Depot. This working train station is home to four muse-

Poised dramatically on the cliffs of Lake Superior, the Split Rock Lighthouse is in a state park that also offers trails and campsites.

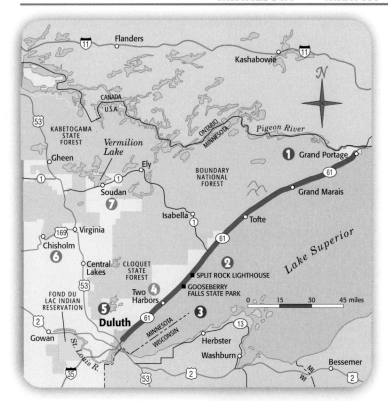

An afternoon's pastime by this inland sea: feeding the gulls in Duluth's Canal Park.

ums and the North Shore Scenic Railroad, which provides excursions to Lester River and Two Harbors, as well as dinner trains. At the bottom of the hill in the lakeside section is the four-mile long Lake Walk. Attractions along this walkway include a working brewery, the Canal Park Marine Museum and the Aerial Lift Bridge, linking the shore and the harbor's Park Point.

❻ Chisholm

Another historic mining center, Chisholm was founded in the 1890s with the discovery of iron ore near the shores of Longyear Lake. The town prospered for many years and today is the site of the Minnesota Museum of Mining and the Iron Ore Miner Memorial. Dedicated in 1987, the memorial features the famous Iron Man statue, the third largest freestanding statue in the U.S.

❼ Soudan Underground Mine State Park

A detour west to the rugged shores of Lake Vermilion brings visitors to this fascinating site. The Soudan Mine was in operation from 1884 to 1962. Today the park's mission is to preserve and display this first iron-ore mine in the state and to interpret the cultural heritage of the people who lived here. Tours include a 2,400-foot journey deep into the heart of the mine via a "cage" and a ride on the mine's railcar.

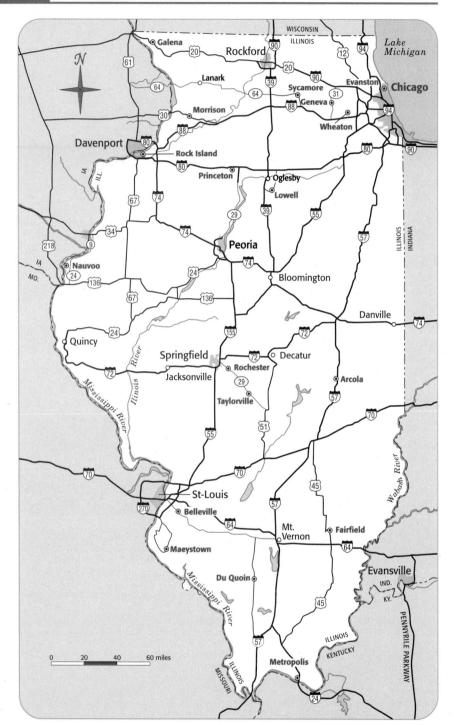

Arcola
The Flower Patch Bed & Breakfast

This Victorian home was built in 1864, expanded in the 1890s and had porches added in early 1900s. Very nicely appointed rooms and elaborate herb and flower gardens create a charming old world ambience. Breakfast consists of seven courses.

5 Rooms • Price range: $60-87
225 E Jefferson, Arcola, IL 61910
☎ **(217) 268-4876**

Belleville
⚇ Swan's Court Bed & Breakfast

This handsome 1883 Victorian home was bought in 1908 by David Baer, who later became known as the "mule king" of the world" because he supplied 10,000 mules a year to the British armed forces during World War I. The inn was restored in 1995 and today houses luxury guestrooms and a delightful screened-in porch. The spacious parlor and dining room make Swan's Court an ideal setting for small receptions or meetings.

4 Rooms • Price range: $45-90
421 Court St, Belleville, IL 62220
☎ **(618) 233-0779**

Belleville
Victory Inn

Situated on a tree-lined street in Belleville, this 1877 home is a beautifully restored Victorian. The decor in the guestrooms ranges from flowery pastels to rich, dark wood and muted colors. Several rooms have a whirlpool tub for two; the Elm Room features a skylight and a large oval picture window. The inn is located within walking distance of downtown Belleville shops, the historic district and the Victorian Home Museum.

4 Rooms • Price range: $60-115
712 S Jackson St, Belleville, IL 62220
☎ **(618) 277-1538**

Chicago
Gold Coast Guest House Bed & Breakfast

In the heart of Chicago's Gold Coast district this renovated 1873 three-story Victorian townhouse offers the best of the new and the charm of the past. Bedrooms feature all the modern amenities in comfortably elegant surroundings. An 18-foot glass wall in the living room looks out onto a verdant private courtyard garden. For a small fee guests may use a nearby fitness club. All of the city's many attractions are close at hand.

4 Rooms • Price range: $129-199
113 W Elm St, Chicago, IL 60610
☎ **(312) 337-0361**

Du Quoin
Francie's Inn On Line

For 39 years, this grand 1908 home was a safe harbor for homeless children. After a major restoration it reopened in 1988 as a B&B. Recently extensive landscaping has turned the three-acre property into a more parklike setting.

5 Rooms • Price range: $60-100
104 S Line St, Du Quoin, IL 62832
☎ **(618) 542-6686**

Fairfield

Glass Door Inn Bed & Breakfast

This is a newly constructed B&B located on two acres of open country-side just a couple of miles outside Fairfield. Guests are free to roam the adjacent 70 acres of open fields and woods. The decor in the guestrooms is contemporary, ranging from the white wicker and tropical colors of the Ocean Room to the soft florals and vaulted ceiling of the Victorian Room.

4 Rooms • Price range: $52-72
RR 3, Box 101, Fairfield, IL 62837
☎ **(618) 847-4512**

Galena
Belle Aire Mansion
This pre-Civil War Federal-style mansion is surrounded by 11 well-groomed acres, which include a barn and a windmill. Guestrooms are warm and inviting, furnished with antiques and reproductions. The Garden Vue Suite features a private veranda, a gas fireplace, a television and VCR, and a whirlpool for two. The inn is located two-and-a-half miles from Main Street, which is lined with historic homes.

5 Rooms • Price range: $90-175
11410 Rt 20 NW, Galena, IL 61036
☎ **(815) 777-0893**

Galena
Park Avenue Guest House
This majestic Queen Anne-style "Painted Lady," which was built in 1893, offers comfortable accommodations. The inn boasts 12-foot-high ceilings, original ornate woodwork and an open staircase. Two formal parlors are open to guests, as is the screened wraparound porch overlooking perennial gardens, ponds and a gazebo. Christmas is a fine time to visit and see the Victorian garlands and the soft glowing lights.

4 Rooms • Price range: $95-135
208 Park Ave, Galena, IL 61036
☎ **(815) 777-1075**

Galena
Queen Anne Guest House
The Queen Anne Guest House was built in 1891 by a self-made Galena merchant named William Ridd. It is located in a quiet residential neighborhood near Grant Park. The home is a fine example of Queen Anne architecture; it has stained- and leaded-glass windows, sliding pocket doors, and oak floors. The Galena area is a haven for artists and photographers. Local activities include riverboat excursions and greyhound races.

4 Rooms • Price range: $85-125
200 Park Ave, Galena, IL 61036
☎ **(815) 777-3849**

Geneva
The Herrington Inn

Tucked away at the edge of the Fox
River in picturesque Geneva sits the
Herrington. This romantic inn blends
the character and intimacy of a French
country inn with the services and amenities
of a grand hotel. Each guestroom is comfortably
appointed, featuring a fireplace, a whirlpool tub
and a river-view terrace. Milk and warm cookies are served in the evening and turn-down
service is available. In the morning guests
awaken to a European continental breakfast.
Atwater's Restaurant offers fine dining with a
casual flair, while the Riverside Spa is a soothing place to start or end each day.

40 Rooms • Price range: $159-450
15 S River Ln, Geneva, IL 60134
☎ **(630) 208-7433**

Lowell
The Brightwood Inn

Newly constructed in 1996 and set on
14 acres of meadow in Matthiessen
State Park, the Brightwood Inn resembles a vintage farmhouse, complete
with veranda and rocking chairs. All guestrooms
have a gas fireplace and private bath, while
some feature an oversize Jacuzzi. Area activities
include hiking the many scenic trails of the
nearby state parks, golfing, rafting, canoeing
and fishing.

8 Rooms • Price range: $75-225
2407 N Illinois Rt 178, Lowell, IL 61348
☎ **(815) 667-4600**

Maeystown
Corner George Inn

The Corner George Inn, built in 1884 as
a hotel and saloon, now occupies a complex of five buildings offering a variety
of guest accommodations as well as a

general store, a ballroom and picturesque lawns
stretching down to a mill stream.

7 Rooms • Price range: $72-169
1101 Main, Maeystown, IL 62256
☎ **(618) 458-6660**

Metropolis
Isle of View Bed & Breakfast

Near a river and a casino boat, this 1885
miller's mansion has a few gas fireplaces.

5 Rooms • Price range: $46-125
205 Metropolis St, Metropolis, IL 62960
☎ **(618) 524-5838**

Morrison
Hillendale Bed & Breakfast

Hillendale is located on the historic
Lincoln Highway—the first paved
transcontinental highway—and was
built in 1891 by E. A. Smith. In 1991
the newly restored building was opened as a
bed and breakfast. Theme rooms range from
Oriental to African. Several rooms feature a
fireplace and a whirlpool spa for two. The inn
also boasts a fitness room, a billiard room, a
Japanese teahouse and a water garden.

10 Rooms • Price range: $63-100
600 W Lincolnway, Morrison, IL 61270
☎ **(815) 772-3454**

Nauvoo

◆ ◆ **⚈ Hotel Nauvoo**

Located in the heart of town is the 1840 two-story Hotel Nauvoo. From the inviting front porch and manicured lawns to the comfortable rooms and modern amenities, this hotel has everything it takes to create a memorable experience.

8 Rooms • Price range: $48-72
1290 Mulholland St, Nauvoo, IL 62354
☎ **(217) 453-2211**

Princeton

◆ ◆ *Yesterday's Memories Bed & Breakfast*

Built in 1852, this Queen Anne house stands at the center of the thriving rural town of Princeton. The inn is surrounded by perennial and vegetable gardens and is furnished with Victorian decor. A private coachhouse suite is attached to the main house. A full breakfast is served each morning, featuring homegrown organic fruit and vegetables. Area attractions include an aquarium, a museum and several sites of historical interest.

3 Rooms • Price range: $60-65
303 E Peru St, Princeton, IL 61356
☎ **(815) 872-7753**

Rochester

◆ ◆ *Country Dreams Bed & Breakfast*

This homey, modern B&B sits on 16 quiet rural acres only 10 minutes from downtown Springfield. Guests are invited to wander through the flower, herb and vegetable gardens, tour the fruit orchard or stroll around the small private lake, where swans, ducks and geese paddle on the water. Guests can also pick and cut their own Christmas trees. One suite features a cozy fireplace and a whirlpool tub.

4 Rooms • Price range: $75-165
3410 Park Ln, Rochester, IL 62563
☎ **(217) 498-9210**

Rock Island

◆ ◆ *Victorian Inn Bed & Breakfast*

This 1876 home was originally built as a wedding gift for the daughter of Rock Island liquor baron Peter Fries. The inn is located on wooded grounds known as the Eaton Gardens, a natural habitat for songbirds in the heart of Old Rock Island's Broadway Historic Area. Rooms are tastefully appointed and the inn still has many Victorian features such as the stained-glass windows in the inn's tower and the beveled plate-glass French doors.

5 Rooms • Price range: $74-149
702 20th St, Rock Island, IL 61201
☎ **(309) 788-7068**

Springfield

◆ ◆ *The Inn at 835*

Hospitable hosts preside over guestrooms in a former luxury apartment building.

9 Rooms • Price range: $89-135
835 S Second St, Springfield, IL 62704
☎ **(217) 523-4466**

Sycamore
Stratford Inn

Guests enjoy the comfortable, homelike ambience of this fine inn, located in the center of a quaint hamlet, close to several fine golf courses and Northern Illinois University campus. A strong sense of the past permeates the inn, from the lobby with its oak wainscoting, fabric wall covering and chandeliers to the antique furnishings and decor elsewhere. The bedrooms are decorated with sophisticated Country-style elegance.

39 Rooms • Price range: $80-139
355 W State St, Sycamore, IL 60178
☎ **(815) 895-6789**

Taylorville
Market Street Inn Bed & Breakfast

A restored 1892 Victorian-era Queen Anne, this home is situated just two blocks from the historic town square. Guestrooms are comfortably furnished with antiques, and several have a whirlpool tub for two. Taylorville is a good spot from which to set out in search of golf; there are numerous courses within a 30-mile radius. Skydiving is also popular. A little further afield are the primary Lincoln sites and a home designed by Frank Lloyd Wright.

8 Rooms • Price range: $85-125
220 E Market St, Taylorville, IL 62568
☎ **(217) 824-7220**

Wheaton
The Wheaton Inn

Some of the large and traditionally styled rooms of this inn have a fireplace.

16 Rooms • Price range: $145-225
301 W Roosevelt Rd, Wheaton, IL 60187
☎ **(630) 690-2600**

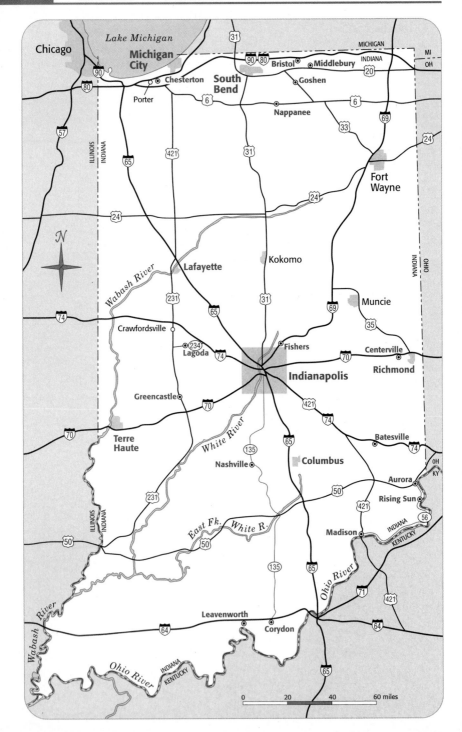

Batesville
🏛 *The Sherman House*

Originally a coaching tavern, the Sherman House first opened its doors to guests in 1852. This unique old inn has a warm, hospitable atmosphere. Guestrooms combine historic charm with modern conveniences; suites and double rooms are available. The pleasant and comfortable Sherman House Restaurant is home to the popular local Raspberry Fest and the Apple Harvest Festival.

23 Rooms • Price range: $50-76
35 S Main St, Batesville, IN 47006
☎ **(812) 934-1000**

Bristol
Rust Hollar Bed & Breakfast

A rustic log house located in a quiet wooded setting in Amish country, just a few miles from Bonneyville Mill Park. Antiques, family heirlooms and Amish decor are featured throughout the nicely appointed guestrooms. The living room has a fireplace.

4 Rooms • Price range: $55-89
55238 CR 31, Bristol, IN 46507-9569
☎ **(219) 825-1111**

Centerville
Historic Lantz House Inn

The 1823 Lantz House is on Indiana's famous Antique Alley, a 30-mile stretch with more than 700 antique dealers. Rooms range from single bedrooms to the Garden Suite with a jacuzzi and cozy private garden. A warm, comfortable getaway.

5 Rooms • Price range: $69-95
214 W Main St, Centerville, IN 47330
☎ **(765) 855-2936**

Chesterton
Gray Goose Inn

Set on 100 wooded acres on the shore of Lake Palomara, the Gray Goose Inn offers urban refinements in a tranquil country setting. The elegantly decorated bedrooms and suites feature private baths and a variety of amenities. An impressive collection of porcelain plates and objects is displayed throughout the inn. Dunes State Park and its system of hiking trails are only three miles away.

8 Rooms • Price range: $80-175
350 Indian Boundary Rd, Chesterton, IN 46304
☎ **(219) 926-5781**

Corydon
🏛 *Kintner House Inn*

This attractively restored inn has many antiques. Guests have kitchen privileges.

15 Rooms • Price range: $49-99
101 S Capitol Ave, Corydon, IN 47112
☎ **(812) 738-2020**

Fishers
Frederick-Talbott Inn

Two wonderfully restored buildings make up the Frederick-Talbot Inn. The 1870 farmhouse and 1906 cottage are decorated with an eclectic mix of local antiques. All the delightful decor and design ideas are a credit to the creative innkeepers. The cottage is the honeymoon suite and provides the privacy newlyweds will appreciate. Just across the street is Conner Prairie, a living history museum.

10 Rooms • Price range: $99-225
13805 Allisonville Rd, Fishers, IN 46038
☎ **(317) 578-3600**

Goshen
Indian Creek Bed & Breakfast

A lovely, new Victorian-style home located in a quiet country setting surrounded by miles of farmland in the heart of Amish country. A full breakfast is served in the dining room overlooking the large deck, which itself is a lovely place to relax and watch for deer. The guestrooms are quaintly decorated with antique furnishings and Country-style decor. Common rooms include a grand living room and a game room.

4 Rooms • Price range: $69-79
20300 CR 18, Goshen, IN 46528
☎ **(219) 875-6606**

Greencastle
Walden Inn

Across from DePauw University in the center of downtown, this charming inn provides a leisurely and quiet getaway. Guests enjoy lounging on the plush

sofas in front of the library's oak-mantled fireplace. The large rooms have an Amish theme.

55 Rooms • Price range: $70-150
2 Seminary Square, Greencastle, IN 46135
☎ **(765) 653-2761**

Indianapolis
The Looking Glass Inn

This lovely, restored 1905 mansion is the sister of the Stone Soup Inn. When guests arrive, they are greeted by their hosts in a large foyer with 10-foot-high ceilings, white crown moldings, chandelier lighting, and glistening hardwood floors. The spacious main parlor has plush white sofas grouped around a fireplace. Each guestroom is appointed with thick down comforters, decorative throw pillows and lovely antique furniture pieces.

6 Rooms • Price range: $105-135
1319 N New Jersey St, Indianapolis, IN 46202
☎ **(317) 639-9550**

Indianapolis
Stone Soup Inn

A spacious B&B, just minutes from downtown, this inn is in the historic Old Northside district. This beautifully restored 1901 home features decoratively painted walls throughout the common areas and guestrooms. A bold use of rich colors and creativity in the guestrooms accent the Mission and Victorian antiques. Three stunning loft-style rooms were influenced by the innkeepers' trip to France.

7 Rooms • Price range: $85-135
1304 North Central Ave, Indianapolis, IN 46202
☎ **(317) 639-9550**

Ladoga
Renaissance Gallery and Towers

A restored 1876 Victorian B&B in the heart of a quaint little town. This inn is the perfect getaway for those who want to take a trip back in time to enjoy

19th-century hospitality. An art gallery on the first floor features the works of local artists.

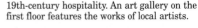

5 Rooms • Price range: $75-250
102 E Main, Ladoga, IN 47954
☎ **(765) 942-2108**

Lafayette
Loeb House Inn

Built in 1882 in the Italianate style, the Loeb House Inn is located in the city just steps away from historic sites and churches, museums, restaurants and a theater. Finely detailed fireplaces, chandeliers, parquet floors and a grand staircase contribute to the overall Victorian charm. Guestrooms have fireplaces, claw-foot tubs, hand-painted tiles and bay windows. Breakfast includes homemade breads and pastries.

5 Rooms • Price range: $89-175
708 Cincinnati St, Lafayette, IN 47901
☎ **(765) 420-7737**

Leavenworth
⚐ *The Leavenworth Inn*

The Leavenworth Inn consists of two restored homes on six acres of land overlooking the Ohio River. Beautiful pine floors, spacious rooms, a tennis court, and walking and bicycle paths are just a few of the amenities guests will enjoy.

10 Rooms • Price range: $69-99
930 SR 62, Leavenworth, IN 47137
☎ **(812) 739-2120**

Leesburg
Prairie House Bed & Breakfast

In a quiet farmland setting surrounded by mature trees and brilliantly colored wild flowers, this charming B&B features warm country decor throughout the common areas and guestrooms. The comfortable reading and music room features a brick fireplace and plenty of books. All of the spacious bedrooms have queen-size beds; two rooms share a bath. Friendly hosts offer a relaxed environment and old-fashioned hospitality.

4 Rooms • Price range: $45-65
495 E 900 N, Leesburg, IN 46538
☎ **(219) 658-9211**

Madison
Carriage House Bed & Breakfast

Beautifully decorated, this converted 1850s carriage house has bi-level rooms.

1 Rooms • Price range: $90-100
308 W 2nd St, Madison, IN 47250
☎ **(812) 265-6892**

Michigan City
Creekwood Inn

Sitting on 30 acres of walnut, oak and pine trees near a fork in Willow Creek, the Creekwood offers a secluded haven for a peaceful getaway. Spacious rooms, some with a fireplace or a private terrace, are comfortably decorated in an eclectic mix of traditional styles. The Ferns restaurant offers gourmet regional American cuisine, making use of fresh local ingredients. A complimentary breakfast includes homemade breads, fresh fruit and coffee.

13 Rooms • Price range: $155-190
Rt 20 - 35 at I-94, Michigan City, IN 46360
☎ **(219) 872-8357**

Middlebury
Varns-Kimes Guest House

A clapboard Victorian built in 1898, the Varns-Kimes House is surrounded by gardens filled with herbs and perennials in bloom all year long. Guests can enjoy the gardens—candlelit at night—from the paths and seating areas, or from the porch. Guestrooms show great attention to detail and creativity. Lavish breakfasts, including home-baked breads, muffins and coffee cakes, are served on antique china in the dining room.

5 Rooms • Price range: $65-95
205 S Main St, Middlebury, IN 46540
☎ **(219) 825-9666**

Middlebury
The Country Victorian Bed & Breakfast

Built more than a century ago, this updated Victorian, located in Amish country, celebrates the style and way of life of a bygone time. Visitors can relax on the front porch and watch the buggies drive by, or curl up in front of the fire with a good book. Each room is distinctively decorated with period furniture and treatments and has a full bath. Some rooms have a whirlpool or a claw-foot tub.

5 Rooms • Price range: $69-129
435 S Main St, Middlebury, IN 46540
☎ **(219) 825-2568**

Middlebury
Essenhaus Country Inn

A lovely Amish-style inn located on a beautifully manicured estate with an animal farm, various country craft shops and a restaurant. Located in the heart of Amish country, rooms are decorated with Amish-made wood furniture and quilts.

40 Rooms • Price range: $60-92
240 US 20, Middlebury, IN 46540
☎ **(219) 825-9447**

Monticello
Sportsman Inn

Phone for information.

20 Rooms • Price range: $55-80
12340 N Upper Lake Shore Dr,
Monticello, IN 47960
☎ **(219) 583-5133**

Nappanee
Homespun Country Inn

Built in 1902, the inn features quarter-sawn oak and stained- and leaded-glass, reminders of time past. Guests can relax on the porch swing, keeping an eye out for a passing horse and buggy. Rooms are named after the original house occupants or their descendants. Breakfast is served in the dining room, a fine beginning to a day of antique shopping and sightseeing in Amish country.

5 Rooms • Price range: $59-79
302 N Main St, Nappanee, IN 46550
☎ **(219) 773-2034**

Nappanee
Olde Buffalo Inn Bed & Breakfast

Built in 1840, this renovated farmhouse is located in a residential locale.

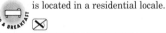

6 Rooms • Price range: $69-169
1061 Parkwood Dr, Nappanee, IN 46550
☎ **(219) 773-2223**

Nappanee
Victorian Guest House

Built in 1887 by a local businessman, this remarkable Victorian home features stained-glass windows, wood paneling, antique tubs and an abundance of exceptional furnishings, many of which are original to the house. Breakfast is served on an 11-foot oak table in the grand dining room. Guests enjoy the quiet residential setting of this grand home. The lovely front porch makes a fine place to sit and unwind at the end of a long day.

6 Rooms • Price range: $69-149
302 E Market St, Nappanee, IN 46550
☎ **(219) 773-4383**

Nashville
⊕ *Artists Colony Inn & Restaurant*

Located in the heart of a historic artisan village, the Artists Colony Inn was built to remember the town's history. Local craftspeople have created furnishings inspired by the past: Windsor chairs, four-poster beds, cherry wood furniture, hand-stitched quilts and hand-loomed rugs. The inn features a full-service dining room with a large stone fireplace and beamed ceilings; paintings by early local artists are on display.

23 Rooms • Price range: $90-220
105 Van Buren St, Nashville, IN 47448
☎ **(812) 988-0600**

Nashville
Cornerstone Inn

The Cornerstone Inn is a newly constructed Victorian-style B&B. Guests are invited to relax in the comfortable rocking chairs on the octagonal second- floor balcony. The bright, cheerful guestrooms are tastefully decorated with fine antiques.

20 Rooms • Price range: $115-135
54 E Franklin St, Nashville, IN 47448
☎ **(812) 988-0300**

Richmond
Philip W. Smith Bed & Breakfast

This stately Queen Anne home, built in 1890, is located in a historic district only a short distance from local attractions. Hand-carved wood and stained-glass windows recall a time when houses were built by craftsmen. Distinctive rooms, each with a private bath, are individually decorated. Homemade refreshments are offered in the evening; in the morning, the aroma of baking bread announces the full breakfast.

4 Rooms • Price range: $75-102
2039 E Main St, Richmond, IN 47374
☎ **(765) 966-8972**

Rising Sun
Mulberry Inn & Gardens Bed & Breakfast

Cozy rooms with antique-style furnishings in an inn surrounded by a lovely garden.

5 Rooms • Price range: $89-125
118 S Mulberry St, Rising Sun, IN 47040
☎ **(812) 438-2206**

South Bend
Book Inn B&B

A quality used bookstore adds to the unique atmosphere of this restored 1872 mansion. Listed as an outstanding example of French Victorian architecture, the B&B has a mansard roof with ornamental arched dormer windows. The entry doors won first place for design at the 1893 Chicago Exposition. Inside 12-foot ceilings, hand-carved butternut woodwork and other remarkable flourishes can be found throughout. Guestroom decor ranges from tender light florals to dramatically rich brocades. The irresistibly comfortable parlor is a favorite spot for guests to relax and socialize with one another.

5 Rooms • Price range: $95-160
508 W Washington St, South Bend, IN 46601
☎ **(219) 288-1990**

South Bend
The English Rose Inn
The English Rose is a charming 1892 rose and plum colored Victorian home set in the quiet historic district of South Bend. Each room is attractively done up with floral patterns and features four-poster beds and fine antique furniture.

6 Rooms • Price range: $75-155
116 S Taylor, South Bend, IN 46601
☎ **(219) 289-2114**

South Bend
The Oliver Inn Bed & Breakfast
This 1880s Queen Anne-style mansion is the largest B&B in town. Shaded by more than 30 tall maples, it sits on a one-acre estate with a carriage house and playhouse from the 1920s. Guests can indulge in a "three-mansions-in-one" trip, which includes dinner at the Studebaker Mansion next door and a tour of Copshaholm House Museum. A computerized piano brings guests out of their rooms to enjoy the entertainment.

9 Rooms • Price range: $115-145
630 W Washington St, South Bend, IN 46601
☎ **(219) 232-4545**

South Bend
Queen Anne Inn
Built in 1893, this Queen Anne-Neoclassic is furnished with antiques.

6 Rooms • Price range: $80-120
420 W Washington St, South Bend, IN 46601
☎ **(219) 234-5959**

Terre Haute
Farrington Bed & Breakfast

The original woodwork throughout this late 19th-century house has been almost completely restored. Located in the Historic District, it offers Victorian charm and elegance. Four of the rooms have uniquely designed fireplaces and full baths, while the fifth has a private covered porch. The large parlor on the first floor was originally used for ballroom dancing. Many of the original chandeliers have survived intact.

5 Rooms • Price: $85
931 S 7th St, Terre Haute, IN 47807
☎ **(812) 238-0524**

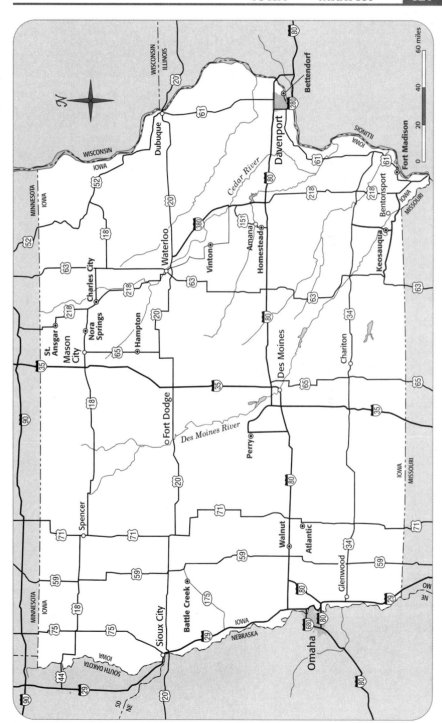

Atlantic

Chestnut Charm Bed & Breakfast

This 1898 Victorian mansion has many attractive features including a parlor with a piano, a sunroom and natural hardwood floors. Outside, a courtyard with a fountain and a gazebo decorate the grounds. Nearby activities include golf, antique shopping and sightseeing, all of which are easily accessible from the inn. There is a choice of guestrooms or well-appointed suites, complete with fireplaces and Jacuzzi tubs.

9 Rooms • Price range: $60-225
1409 Chestnut St, Atlantic, IA 50022
☎ **(712) 243-5652**

Battle Creek

The Inn at Battle Creek

This elegantly restored 1899 Queen-Anne Victorian property is one of the finest in Northwest Iowa and is listed on the National Register of Historic Places. Guestrooms feature period antiques and brass light fixtures and they include private baths with terry cloth robes set out for the use of guests. A private dining room serving gourmet cuisine features an open oak staircase, pristine woodwork and fine antique furnishings.

4 Rooms • Price range: $64-79
201 Maple, Battle Creek, IA 51006
☎ **(712) 365-4949**

Bettendorf

⑩ *The Abbey Hotel*

Situated on a bluff overlooking the Mississippi River, this marvelous Romanesque structure used to be a cloistered Carmelite monastery, and it includes a magnificent Gothic chapel. The Grand Banquet Room and formal dining room are ideal for any type of gathering; together they can accommodate up to 325 people and both have access to the garden courtyard and outdoor pool. Guestrooms feature marble bathrooms and queen- or king-size beds. Most rooms also offer attractive views of the Mississippi River. A complimentary continental breakfast is served each morning.

19 Rooms • Price range: $99-149
1401 Central Ave, Bettendorf, IA 52722
☎ **(319) 355-0291**

Charles City

Sherman House Bed & Breakfast

This fine Victorian home in the city center has been completely restored.

5 Rooms • Price range: $100-150
800 Gilbert St, Charles City, IA 50616
☎ **(515) 228-6831**

Fort Madison
⊕ *Kingsley Inn*

This inn provides the best in modern amenities while maintaining a fine attention to detail. Guests enter the inn under soaring archways above gleaming smoked-glass doors. Next, the exquisite atrium leads the way to guestrooms furnished with restored antiques, comfortable beds with authentic period headboards and private baths—some with whirlpools. The inn is also home to Alphas, a full-service restaurant.

15 Rooms • Price range: $85-105
707 Ave H, Fort Madison, IA 52627
☎ **(319) 372-7074**

Hampton
Country Touch Bed & Breakfast

A B&B offering guestrooms with whirlpools, fireplaces and balconies.

6 Rooms • Price range: $60-120
1034 Hwy 3, Hampton, IA 50441
☎ **(641) 456-4585**

Homestead
Die Heimat Country Inn

Legend has it that this 1858 inn was the original stagecoach stop for the colonies. Today, decor combines period canopy beds with contemporary private baths. The inn also features a large common area and dining room where breakfast is served.

19 Rooms • Price range: $50-80
4430 V St, Homestead, IA 52236
☎ **(319) 622-3937**

Keosauqua
Mason House Inn of Bentonsport

Both Abraham Lincoln and Mark Twain stayed at this 1846 inn.

8 Rooms • Price range: $49-84
Rt 2, Box 237, Keosauqua, IA 52565
☎ **(319) 592-3133**

Nora Springs
Cupola Inn Bed & Breakfast

Set in a charming country area, this B&B uses authentic barn pieces in its decor.

4 Rooms • Price range: $52-84
20664 Claybanks Dr, Nora Springs, IA 50458
☎ **(641) 422-9272**

Perry
Hotel Pattee

This one-of-a-kind historic hotel invites guests to relax in a setting that celebrates the sights and sounds, people and memories of small town life. Each of the hotel's 40 luxurious rooms and suites is decorated to honor individuals and themes important to Perry and the region. The meticulously restored 1913 hotel features Colonial-Revival exterior and Arts and Crafts interior. The inn's facilities include David's Milwaukee Diner, a railroad-themed restaurant presided over by a world-class chef, a cozy library filled with books and movies, a health spa and even a restored, state-of-the-art bowling alley.

40 Rooms • Price range: $105-265
1112 Willis Ave, Perry, IA 50220
☎ **(515) 465-3511**

St. Ansgar
Blue Belle Inn Bed & Breakfast

This 1896 Queen Anne Victorian features fireplaces, tin ceilings with ornate moldings and eight-foot maple pocket doors. Leaded-glass, stained-glass and crystal chandeliers set in bay and curved window pockets further enhance the decor. Guestrooms are influenced both in name and style by some well-known tales, such as that of Robin Hood. Other features include a piano bar and a kitchenette.

5 Rooms • Price range: $65-140
513 W 4th St, St. Ansgar, IA 50472
☎ **(641) 736-2225**

Vinton
The Lion & The Lamb B&B
This 1892 Queen Anne Victorian has been beautifully restored with an exterior painted in a stunning array of colors. Inside features include fireplaces with ornate wood and tiled mantels, 10-foot ceilings and parquet floors.

5 Rooms • Price range: $75-105
913 2nd Ave, Vinton, IA 52349
☎ **(319) 472-5086**

Walnut
Clark's Country Inn Bed & Breakfast
This attractive 1912 home features remodeled guestrooms and baths.

3 Rooms • Price: $58
701 Walnut St, Walnut, IA 51577
☎ **(712) 784-3010**

Walnut
Antique City Inn Bed & Breakfast
Call for information.

6 Rooms • Price range: $50-60
400 Antique City Dr, Walnut, IA 51577
☎ **(712) 784-3722**

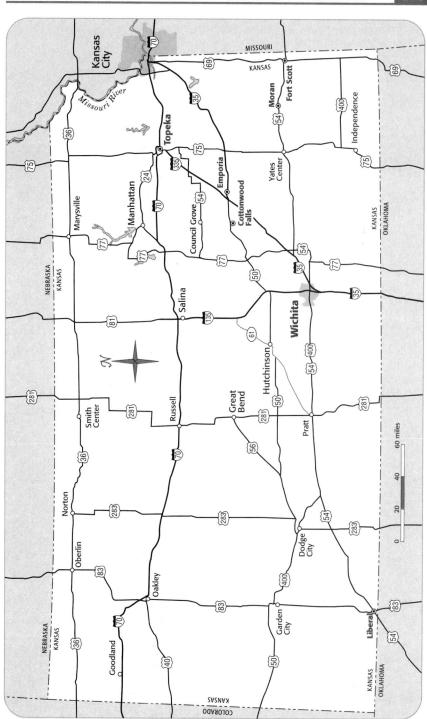

♦♦ Cottonwood Falls
♦♦ **⑳ *The Grand Central Hotel***

Located in the heart of Flint Hills, this hotel is just two miles from the Tallgrass Prairie National Preserve at the Z Bar Ranch. Open since 1884, the hotel features well-appointed and oversize guestrooms with king- or double queen-size beds. The hotel's restaurant offers first-class dining, including fine steaks and entrées. A continental breakfast is served daily. The hotel boasts a number of meeting rooms, ideal for everything from an intimate wedding to a business meeting. Biking, hiking, horseback riding and fishing are all easily arranged from the hotel.

10 Rooms • Price range: $139-169
215 Broadway, Cottonwood Falls, KS 66845
☎ **(316) 273-6763**

♦♦ Emporia
The White Rose Inn

All the rooms at this inn are cozy and individually decorated.

8 Rooms • Price range: $59-129
901 Merchant St, Emporia, KS 66801
☎ **(316) 343-6336**

♦ Fort Scott
♦♦ *Lyons' Victorian Mansion*

Perfect for a leisurely getaway for any occasion, this inn offers great Southern hospitality. Your innkeepers will help you plan such visits as a sweetheart spa retreat, a ladies' spa escape or perhaps a private party. Guestrooms feature king-size beds, dedicated computer lines and complimentary treats. There is a private starlit whirlpool, a gazebo, lovely gardens, a picnic area and a pondside carriage house on the lawn.

4 Rooms • Price range: $89-150
742 S National, Fort Scott, KS 66701
☎ **(316) 223-3644**

♦♦ Independence
♦♦ **⑳ *Glencliff Farm Bed, Breakfast & Spa***

This classy English Tudor estate was named after the glen it overlooks and the stone cliff on which it was built. Guests are treated with first-class hospitality while they stay in this refined and elegant setting. Bedrooms and suites are decorated with Middle Eastern rugs and fine artwork, and boast majestic views of the estate. Special features include a nightly turn-down service, a gift basket, and cozy robes and slippers in all rooms. The business traveler will find all the modern conveniences for work, and the vacationer will no doubt find the heated pool and the oversized Jacuzzi.

4 Rooms • Price range: $79-220
448 Glencliff Rd, Independence, KS 67301-0808
☎ **(316) 331-1277**

Liberal
Bluebird Inn Bed & Breakfast

Surrounded by tall trees and a wrought-iron fence, this inn offers home-style hospitality. Each guestroom is themed after a type of bird and features cozy beds covered by pure cotton linens and handmade quilts. A gourmet breakfast of omelettes, muffins, fruit, fresh coffee and other treats is served each morning in the sunny garden room or in the formal dining room. Guests will enjoy sitting by the fireside in the oak-paneled den.

4 Rooms • Price range: $58-85
221 W 6th St, Liberal, KS 67901
☎ **(316) 624-0720**

Moran
Hedge Apple Acres Bed & Breakfast

This country inn offers a relaxing stay. Guests can try their hand at fishing in the inn's two stocked ponds, or stroll around the surrounding 80 acres, before retiring to their comfortable bedrooms. A full country breakfast is served daily.

4 Rooms • Price range: $54-85
4430 US Hwy 54, Moran, KS 66755
☎ **(316) 237-4646**

Topeka
The Senate Luxury Suites

These completely refurbished suites are decorated with old-fashioned flair, featuring classic tapestries and beautiful furnishings. Different types of rooms are available, including studios and one- and two-bedrooms suites. Guests are free to relax in the hot tub, work out in the exercise room, take in the sights of the Grace Cathedral or the Capitol Dome from one of the balconies, or stroll the landscaped courtyards.

52 Rooms • Price range: $85-155
900 SW Tyler, Topeka, KS 66612
☎ **(785) 233-5050**

Topeka
Heritage House

Formerly the quarters of the Menninger Clinic, this inn has comfortable rooms.

10 Rooms • Price range: $65-140
3535 SW 6th St, Topeka, KS 66606
☎ **(785) 233-3800**

Wichita
⑭ *The Inn at Willowbend*

Golf enthusiasts will appreciate the convenient location of this inn: right next to the Willowbend Golf Club, one of the most noted golf courses in the country. Before setting out for a round, guests can brew a cup of coffee in their room, then enjoy a homemade breakfast either in-room or in the St. Andrew's lounge. All suites feature a king-size bed or two double beds, a fireplace and a whirlpool tub. Some suites also have a small kitchen. Business travelers have access to an IBM-compatible personal computer. A conference room is available for business meetings.

44 Rooms • Price range: $59-185
3939 Comotara, Wichita, KS 67226
☎ **(316) 636-4032**

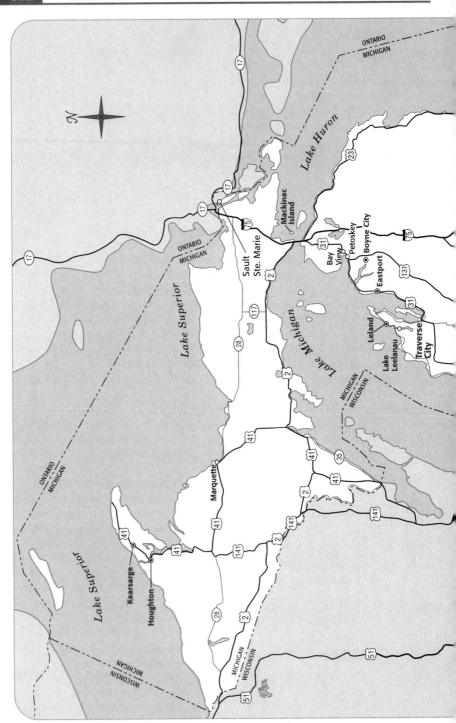

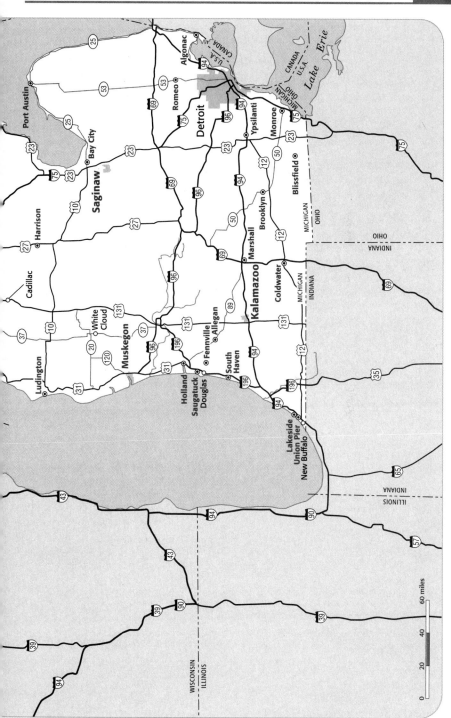

Algonac
◆ ◆ **Linda's Lighthouse Inn**
Built in 1904, this riverside B&B has professionally landscaped grounds with a large outdoor patio deck and hot tub. Cozy guest units offer views of the grounds and the St. Clair River. A gourmet multi-course breakfast is served daily.

4 Rooms • Price range: $85-135
5965 Pte. Tremble Rd (M-29), Algonac, MI 48001
☎ **(810) 794-2992**

Allegan
◆ ◆ **Castle in the Country B&B**
This 1906 Queen Anne-style Victorian is located on five acres of farmland.

5 Rooms • Price range: $75-185
340 M-40 S, Allegan, MI 49010
☎ **(616) 673-8054**

Allegan
◆ ◆ **Winchester Inn**
Built in 1863, this restored home is attractively furnished.

4 Rooms • Price range: $75-105
524 Marshall St, Allegan, MI 49010
☎ **(616) 673-3621**

Bay City
◆ ◆ **Clements Inn**
Originally an industrial baron's mansion, this restored 1886 inn has lovely rooms.

6 Rooms • Price range: $70-175
1712 Center Ave, Bay City, MI 48708
☎ **(517) 894-4600**

Blissfield
◆ ◆ **H. D. Ellis Inn**
A continental-plus breakfast is served daily at this 1883 brick home. The inn features bedrooms and common rooms appointed with fine period furniture. Visitors can ride the nearby historic Adrian and Blissfield Railroad.

4 Rooms • Price range: $80-100
415 W Adrian St, Blissfield, MI 49228
☎ **(517) 486-3155**

Boyne City
◆ ◆ **Deer Lake Bed & Breakfast**
This contemporary waterfront B&B is located on Deer Lake between Boyne Falls and Boyne City. Days begin with fresh coffee or tea, followed by a full breakfast. In the evenings, guests can sit by the fireplace in the parlor or relax with a book before retiring to guestrooms that feature private baths. Two of the rooms have a private balcony overlooking the lake. Nearby activities include golfing, fishing and tennis.

5 Rooms • Price range: $70-105
00631 E Deer Lake Rd, Boyne City, MI 49712
☎ **(231) 582-9039**

Brooklyn
◆ ◆ **Chicago Street Inn**
This Victorian-style inn, which stands in the scenic Irish hills area near downtown, features oak hand-wrought moldings, fretwork, and cherry trim with antique electric chandeliers and European stained glass windows.

6 Rooms • Price range: $65-165
219 Chicago St, Brooklyn, MI 49230
☎ **(517) 592-3888**

Coldwater
Chicago Pike Inn

This 1903 Colonial mansion is an architectural marvel, featuring a sweeping cherry staircase and stained-glass windows. The reception room has a double cherry-mantled fireplace, Staffordshire dogs and a marble-top smoking stand. The library features a Victorian love seat, marble tabletops and a tea table. Guestrooms have private baths, queen-size beds and paddle fans. A full country breakfast is served in the dining room.

8 Rooms • Price range: $100-195
215 E Chicago St (US 12), Coldwater, MI 49036
☎ **(517) 279-8744**

Eastport
Torch Lake Sunrise Bed & Breakfast

Call for information.

3 Rooms • Price range: $100-140
3644 Blasen Shore, Eastport, MI 49627
☎ **(231) 599-2706**

Fennville
The Kingsley House

Located on the west edge of the small town of Fennville, this family-run property is only minutes away from the sandy beaches of Lake Michigan. Hiking and biking trails as well as downhill ski areas are all nearby. Bicycles are provided on request. All rooms come with private baths; some rooms have a whirlpool tub. Antique furnishings are found throughout the inn. A full family-style breakfast is served daily.

8 Rooms • Price range: $90-175
626 W Main (M-89), Fennville, MI 49408
☎ **(616) 561-6425**

Greenville
Gibson House Bed & Breakfast

This Colonial-Revival mansion is a state historic landmark featuring beautiful woodwork, stained glass and Victorian antiques that grace elegant, comfortable rooms. The cherry wood game room includes a billiards table and a movie library.

5 Rooms • Price range: $80-140
311 W Washington St, Greenville, MI 48838
☎ **(616) 754-6691**

Harrison
The Carriage House Inn

The carriage house, which now houses the inn, was originally built by Mennonite carpenters to accommodate a private collection of antiques. Today the inn features 10 guestrooms with private whirlpool baths, and common areas, which include a large room for casual sitting, breakfast, and meetings; a deck; and three acres of landscaped gardens overlooking Budd Lake.

10 Rooms • Price range: $75-175
1515 Grant Ave, Harrison, MI 48625
☎ **(517) 539-1300**

Harrison
Serendipity Bed & Breakfast Inn

This two-story Cape Cod-style home has tastefully decorated guestrooms.

4 Rooms • Price range: $75-150
270 W M 61, Harrison, MI 49625
☎ **(517) 539-6602**

Holland
Dutch Colonial Inn
This B&B was built as a wedding present in 1928 and has since passed through several families before coming into the hands of the present owners, who restored the building to its original state. The perfect choice for special events such as honeymoons and anniversaries, the inn offers executive suites with a king- or queen-size bed, as well as a working fireplace and a private tiled bath with a double whirlpool tub.

4 Rooms • Price range: $70-160
560 Central Ave, Holland, MI 49423
☎ **(616) 396-3664**

Holland
⚠ Bonnie's Parsonage 1908
Built as a parsonage by a Dutch church, this B&B features the original dark oak woodwork, pocket doors and leaded-glass windows. It has two sitting rooms and an outdoor garden patio. Breakfast specialties include baked pancakes.

3 Rooms • Price range: $100-120
6 E 24th St, Holland, MI 49423
☎ **(616) 396-1316**

Houghton
⚠ Charleston House Historic Inn
Located in the historic district and listed on the National Register of Historic Places, this circa 1900 inn blends period elegance with contemporary amenities. Each guestroom has an adjoining private bath and features king canopy beds and in-room coffee and tea. Other facilities include a gathering room tastefully decorated with English antiques, a flower garden walkway with a fountain and a wicker-furnished veranda.

4 Rooms • Price range: $138-238
918 College Ave, Houghton, MI 49931
☎ **(906) 482-7790**

Kalamazoo
⚠ Stuart Avenue Inn Bed & Breakfast
Located in the prestigious Stuart Area Historic District, this inn is actually a collection of Victorian homes and gardens. It includes the Bartlett-Upjohn House, Chappell House, the Carriage House and McDuffee Gardens. Built in the 1880s, they offer fine examples of period decor, including hand-printed art wallpapers and Belgian lace curtains. Guestrooms have private baths, and some are equipped with fireplaces and wet bars.

19 Rooms • Price range: $65-95
229 Stuart Ave, Kalamazoo, MI 49007
☎ **(616) 342-0230**

Kalamazoo
Hall House Bed & Breakfast
Exceptional craftsmanship characterizes this Georgian-Revival house. All guestrooms have private baths. An expanded continental breakfast is served weekdays, with a full breakfast on weekends. Cookies and hot beverages are always available.

6 Rooms • Price range: $79-145
106 Thompson St, Kalamazoo, MI 49006
☎ **(616) 343-2500**

Lakeside
White Rabbit Inn

This B&B's origins as a small hotel are evident in the private, ground-level entrances to each of the guestrooms. With the accent on romance, each of the rooms features a whirlpool bath, a gas fireplace and is charmingly decorated with birch or willow furniture. The inn also offers two pine cabins, each equipped with a kitchen, an outdoor spa and a wood-burning stove. Breakfast is served daily in the large, airy lodge.

8 Rooms • Price range: $95-200
14634 Red Arrow Hwy P.O. Box 725,
Lakeside, MI 49116-0725
☎ **(616) 469-4620**

Leland
⊕ Manitou Manor Bed & Breakfast

This spacious country estate boasts six acres of cherry trees and a landscaped yard. Nearby activities include ferry rides to South Manitou Island, coastal cruises, golfing, biking and hiking. There are also several beaches in the area. The inn features a common room with a fireplace, a glassed-in porch and a deck. All guestrooms have private baths. Coffee is served first thing in the morning, followed by a family-style breakfast.

5 Rooms • Price: $140
147 Manitou Tr W, Leland, MI 49654
☎ **(231) 256-7712**

Ludington
⊕ The Lamplighter Bed & Breakfast

Breakfast here is a three-course gourmet experience served in the inn's elegant dining room. The1896 house has been restored to its former Victorian splendor, preserving important architectural elements while adding modern amenities. Among the features are a golden oak staircase and a Victorian-era fireplace. All guestrooms are equipped with private baths and a mix of period and contemporary furnishings.

5 Rooms • Price range: $110-135
602 E Ludington Ave, Ludington, MI 49431
☎ **(231) 843-9792**

Ludington
⊕ The Inn at Ludington
This circa 1900 home is conveniently located near the ferry dock.

6 Rooms • Price: $100
701 E Ludington Ave, Ludington, MI 49431
☎ **(231) 845-7055**

Mackinac Island
The Inn on Mackinac
Gracious French doors and a beautiful lobby are just some of the features at this completely remodeled 1867 inn. All guestrooms have private baths; some have balconies, skylights or bay windows. A deluxe continental breakfast is served.

44 Rooms • Price range: $125-275
Main St, Mackinac Island, MI 49757
☎ **(906) 847-3360**

Marshall
Rose Hill Inn B&B

This elegant 1860 Italianate mansion is set on 3.5 acres of landscaped grounds that overlook the town of Marshall. Outdoor facilities include a swimming pool and a tennis court. The inn also has a large screened porch and a shaded patio. Inside guestrooms are furnished in period with the modern amenities of private baths and central air-conditioning. Breakfast is served fireside in the dining room under a crystal chandelier.

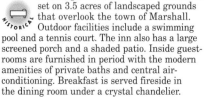

6 Rooms • Price range: $89-140
1110 Verona Rd, Marshall, MI 49068
☎ **(616) 789-1992**

Marshall
The National House Inn

This restored historic inn was built in 1835.

16 Rooms • Price range: $68-145
102 S Parkview, Marshall, MI 49068
☎ **(616) 781-7374**

Monroe
ⓌⒶ Lotus Bed & Breakfast

A beautifully 1870 Italianate mansion with modern amenities.

5 Rooms • Price: $105
324 Washington St, Monroe, MI 48161
☎ **(734) 384-9914**

Muskegon
Port City Victorian Inn

Detailed workmanship distinguishes this 1877 Victorian-era building.

5 Rooms • Price range: $80-150
1259 Lakeshore Dr, Muskegon, MI 49441
☎ **(231) 759-0205**

Port Austin
Lake Street Manor Bed & Breakfast

Situated near Saginaw Bay, this late 1800s Victorian home has nicely landscaped gardens. The guestrooms feature antique furniture and handmade quilts. Breakfast is served in-room, in the dining room or outside in the garden pavilion.

5 Rooms • Price range: $65-75
8569 Lake St (M-53), Port Austin, MI 48467
☎ **(517) 738-7720**

Romeo
Hess Manor Bed & Breakfast

A Greek-Gothic house with small-town charm with comfortable living areas.

5 Rooms • Price range: $79-85
186 S Main, Romeo, MI 48065
☎ **(810) 752-4726**

Saginaw
Montague Inn

This stately Georgian mansion has a reputation as a romantic hideaway. All the guestrooms have working fireplaces. Other features include a library and a dining room, which overlooks the sweeping lawn and Lake Linton. Dining is one of the inn's specialties, with both a gourmet lunch and dinner served daily. Conference facilities are available to facilitate business meetings.

18 Rooms • Price range: $65-160
1581 S Washington Ave, Saginaw, MI 48601
☎ **(517) 752-3939**

Saugatuck
Bayside Inn

Just footsteps from downtown, this waterfront lodging offers easy access to the surrounding antique shops, art galleries, fine dining and live theater. The landmark boathouse has a central living area, complete with a fireplace, and a view of the Kalamazoo River. Guestrooms and suites have private baths and decks. There is also a waterfront spa. A homemade breakfast is served daily.

10 Rooms • Price range: $95-250
618 Water st, Saugatuck, MI 49453
☎ **(616) 857-4321**

Saugatuck
⑩ *Kemah Inn*

Fine antique furnishings, original tile bathrooms and stained-glass windows by artist Carl Hoermann capture the elegance of yesteryear in this impressive circa-1900 mansion. Guests are invited to relax by the fire in the study or take a catnap in the solarium overlooking Lake Kalamazoo. The inn also offers guests the use of the outdoor hot tub.

7 Rooms • Price range: $125-200
633 Allegan St, Saugatuck, MI 49453
☎ **(616) 857-2919**

Saugatuck
⑩ *The Kirby House*

Located a half mile away from Lake Michigan, this 1890 property is a registered state historic site. The house is decorated with a mixture of antique and modern furnishings and has many of its original features, including quarter-sawn oak woodwork and panels, prismed windows, tall ceilings and a six-sided tower. Rooms have private baths. Full breakfasts are by candlelight.

8 Rooms • Price range: $115-155
294 W Center St, Saugatuck, MI 49453
☎ **(616) 857-2904**

Saugatuck
Rosemont Inn Resort

This inn is conveniently located near a number of attractions, including restaurants. Each guestroom is equipped with a private bath, and some feature gas

fireplaces and a lake view. Other facilities include a heated pool and a Victorian gazebo.

14 Rooms • Price range: $155-285
83 Lakeshore Dr, Saugatuck, MI 49453
☎ **(616) 857-2637**

Saugatuck
⑩ *Saugatuck's Victorian Inn*

This inn is an original 1905 Sears Roebuck catalogue house. The craftsmanship involved in restoration is evident in the original oak woodwork and Victorian trim. A variety of spacious guest suites are available—each with a private bath—while the Master Suite includes an oversized Jacuzzi and fireplace. Guests are invited to enjoy the art gallery on the premises. Breakfast is served daily.

7 Rooms • Price range: $110-210
447 Butler St, Saugatuck, MI 49453
☎ **(616) 857-3325**

Saugatuck
Sherwood Forest Bed & Breakfast

Mornings at this Victorian-style home begin with breakfast served in the lace-curtained dining room or on the porch. The morning menu may include blueberry coffee cake, French toast or potato quiche. Guests can take a dip in the large, heated pool or in nearby Lake Michigan. The inn also features leaded-glass windows and an oak-paneled staircase. Guestrooms have queen-size beds and private baths.

5 Rooms • Price range: $105-175
938 Center St, Saugatuck, MI 49453
☎ **(616) 857-1246**

South Haven
⑩ Carriage House at the Harbor

The inn is split into two locations on Lake Michigan, one at the harbor and the other at Stanley Johnson Park (see below). The area is a boater's paradise, with sandy beaches, great fishing and a modern marina. Both Victorian houses are decorated with antiques and Amish furniture. The guestrooms offer scenic views from private decks. Home-baked goodies await guests in the pantry. The richly appointed guestrooms each have a full private bath, a cozy fireplace and a TV with VCR. Some have Jacuzzis. The common rooms include a bright comfortable breakfast room overlooking the harbor and a library.

11 Rooms • Price range: $145-235
118 Woodman St, South Haven, MI 49090
☎ **(616) 639-2161**

South Haven
Inn At The Park

Tucked away in the heart of the Michigan fruit belt, this B&B is a romantic retreat that is in close proximity to fine restaurants, shopping and great golfing. Each guestroom is named after an 18th- or 19th-century horse-drawn carriage and features handsome antiques. Guestrooms have private baths and fireplaces; some are equipped with a deck and a whirlpool. A country breakfast is served daily.

9 Rooms • Price range: $130-195
233 Dyckman Ave, South Haven, MI 49090
☎ **(616) 639-1776**

South Haven
Sand Castle Inn

This centrally located inn has been welcoming people since the 1800s. Visitors can browse through the quaint shops of South Haven, stroll along the Black River walkway or explore nearby Stanley Johnston Park. After an active day, visitors relax on the front porch, complete with a swing and a ceiling fan, before retiring to guestrooms that feature fireplaces, private balconies and private baths. A full breakfast is served.

9 Rooms • Price range: $155-210
203 Dyckman Ave, South Haven, MI 49090
☎ **(616) 639-1110**

South Haven
The Seymour House Bed & Breakfast
Situated on 11 acres of picturesque countryside, this 1862 Italianate-style mansion is a half mile from Lake Michigan. There are well-maintained nature trails and a stocked one-acre pond on the grounds. The inn features a guest living room with a fireplace and a library with books, games and movies. All guestrooms have private baths. A two-bedroom log cabin is available that includes a living room and a kitchen.

7 Rooms • Price range: $135-135
1248 Blue Star Hwy, South Haven, MI 49090
☎ **(616) 227-3918**

Traverse City
Chateau Chantal Bed & Breakfast
This 65-acre estate is located on the Old Mission Peninsula in one of the most scenic areas of the Great Lakes. Casinos, great golf, quiet picnics or wine-tasting tours are some of the activities that guests enjoy while staying at this inn. Nature preserves and a historic lighthouse are nearby attractions. Guest accommodations include private baths, and a full breakfast is served daily.

3 Rooms • Price range: $125-150
15900 Rue de Vin, Traverse City, MI 49686
☎ **(231) 223-4110**

Union Pier
Garden Grove Bed & Breakfast
Days at this B&B begin with a full breakfast that includes fresh-baked muffins and breads, fruits, juices, gourmet coffee and tea. Afterward, the day's activities may include roaming the beach, shopping or biking. Guestrooms are decorated with garden themes and all feature king- or queen-size beds and private baths. Other room amenities include robes and seasonal flowers. Common rooms have fireplaces.

4 Rooms • Price range: $100-160
9549 Union Pier Rd, Union Pier, MI 49129
☎ **(616) 469-6346**

Union Pier
Rivers Edge Bed & Breakfast
This inn is an hour and a quarter from Chicago and it is located near wineries, outlet malls, antique shops, boutiques, great restaurants and beaches. The knotty pine decor includes furniture made by local artists. Guestrooms are equipped with four-poster beds and hickory rockers. Every room also has a fireplace, a TV with VCR and a private bath with a double jacuzzi. Guests can enjoy a full, country breakfast.

8 Rooms • Price range: $99-165
9902 Community Hall Rd, Union Pier, MI 49129
☎ **(616) 469-6860**

Ypsilanti
Parish House Inn
This 1893 Queen Anne parsonage has bright, comfortable guestrooms.

9 Rooms • Price range: $85-135
103 S Huron, Ypsilanti, MI 48197
☎ **(734) 480-4800**

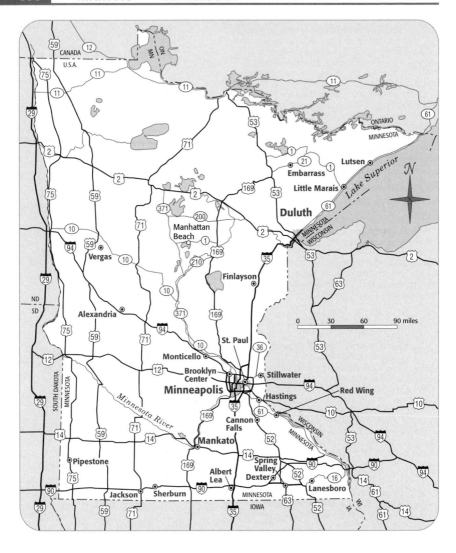

Albert Lea
The Victorian Rose Inn

This delightful 1898 Queen Anne-style home retains much of its early charm, with its grand open staircase, stained-glass windows and beautiful woodwork. Guests are invited to relax in front of the living room fireplace or on the inn's shaded porch. The Kensington Suite features a sitting room, an antique queen-size bed, and a turret surrounded by intricate lace and gingerbread. The Queen Victoria room boasts a marble fireplace.

4 Rooms • Price range: $65-95
609 W Fountain St, Albert Lea, MN 56007
☎ **(507) 373-7602**

Alexandria
Cedar Rose Inn

This romantic inn was built at the turn of the 20th century by one of Alexandria's most successful business-men, Noah P. Ward, in an exclusive area called the "Silk Stocking District." The inn retains all of the original exterior structure, with oversize gables and diamond-paned windows. The interior features antiques, original maplewood floors and stained-glass windows. A wraparound porch and a garden with a gazebo add charm.

4 Rooms • Price range: $75-130
422 Seventh Ave W, Alexandria, MN 56308
☎ **(320) 762-8430**

Brooklyn Center
Inn on The Farm

Housed in a cluster of historic farm buildings, this inn is located on the grounds of a restored Victorian country estate, just minutes from the heart of downtown Minneapolis. The inn is located on the edge of The Green, the estate's landscaped central mall, which features shaded walking paths, extensive lawns, flower beds, and a fountain pool. Rooms all have relaxing whirlpool tubs.

10 Rooms • Price range: $110-150
6150 Summit Dr N, Brooklyn Center, MN 55430
☎ **(763) 569-6330**

Cannon Falls
Quill & Quilt

The combination of traditional elegance and country comfort makes this inn inviting. The spacious home is more than a century old; it has three storys, bay windows and a columned front porch. Guests will enjoy the oak and marble fireplace in winter, the porch swing in summer, and their cozy quilt-covered beds all year round. Wonderful hiking, biking and skiing trails are all nearby.

4 Rooms • Price range: $70-160
615 W Hoffman St, Cannon Falls, MN 55009
☎ **(507) 263-5507**

Dexter
Ice Haus Bed & Breakfast

The rooms at this historic inn are fitted with private bathrooms, modern amenities and family heirlooms. The grounds feature a meadow, a creek and a wildlife sanctuary. Guests will enjoy the B&B's breakfast, afternoon tea and evening snacks.

4 Rooms • Price range: $65-125
65150 220th St, Dexter, MN 55926
☎ **(507) 584-0101**

Duluth
A. Charles Weiss Inn

A. Charles Weiss was the editor and publisher of Duluth's first successful newspaper, the Duluth Herald. He built his stately home in 1895 and today it still retains much of its early Victorian warmth and character. The inn is replete with rich oak, maple and cherry wood, tiled and marble fireplaces, and antique furnishings. Guestrooms are comfortably appointed with private baths, some with whirlpools. A full breakfast is served daily.

5 Rooms • Price range: $95-140
1615 E Superior St, Duluth, MN 55812
☎ **(218) 724-7016**

Duluth
Manor On The Creek Country Inn Bed & Breakfast

Burled African mahogany and tigergrain oak dominate the interior of this handsome Neoclassical Arts and Crafts mansion. On two acres of wooded ravine overlooking Oregon Creek, the Manor has all the charm of an intimate B&B with the added privacy and amenities of a larger, more spacious country inn. A romantic carriage house is available, as are whirlpool suites with fireplaces and treetop porches.

8 Rooms • Price range: $89-279
2215 E Second St, Duluth, MN 55812
☎ **(218) 728-3189**

Duluth
The Olcott House Bed & Breakfast Inn

This brick Georgian-Colonial style home and carriage house were built in 1904 for William J. Olcott, president of Oliver Mining. Soaring pillars, rich mahogany wood and beamed ceilings, as well as hardwood floors, bay windows, and decorative fireplaces, all add to the grandeur of this stately mansion. Several rooms have fireplaces and three-season private porches. Common areas include the music room, library and dining room.

6 Rooms • Price range: $120-175
2316 E 1st St, Duluth, MN 55812
☎ **(218) 728-1339**

Embarrass
Finnish Heritage Homestead

John Kangas began construction on this farm in 1901. His spacious log home served as a "poikatalo," or boarding home, for loggers and railroad workers. Today the inn is a charming blend of Finnish-American architecture and history.

4 Rooms • Price range: $80-90
4776 Waisanen Rd, Embarrass, MN 55732
☎ **(218) 984-3318**

Finlayson
◆◆ *Giese Bed & Breakfast Inn*
Surrounded by woods, this inn is next
to the owner-run antique store.

4 Rooms • Price range: $55-70
13398 130th Ave, Finlayson, MN 55735
☎ **(320) 233-6429**

Hastings
◆ *Rosewood Inn*
◆ ◆
Once a private hospital, this 1880 Queen
Anne-style mansion has been restored
and turned into a romantic retreat. Most
guestrooms have fireplaces and double
whirlpools, while the huge Mississippi Room features skylights, a teakwood double whirlpool, a
copper soaking tub, a European sleigh bed, a
fireplace and a baby grand piano. The inn serves
gourmet dinners and in December offers a traditional English holiday seven-course feast.

8 Rooms • Price range: $127-257
620 Ramsey St, Hastings, MN 55033
☎ **(651) 437-3297**

Hastings
◆ *Thorwood Inn*
◆ ◆
Over 120 years old, this lumber baron's
mansion is a registered Historic Place.

6 Rooms • Price range: $97-257
315 Pine St, Hastings, MN 55033
☎ **(651) 437-3297**

Jackson
◆◆ *The Old Railroad Inn Bed & Breakfast*
Built in 1888, this inn was formerly a
boarding house for railroad workers.

4 Rooms • Price range: $45-75
219 Moore St, Jackson, MN 56143
☎ **(507) 847-5348**

Lanesboro
◆ *Mrs. B's Historic Lanesboro Inn & Restaurant*
◆ ◆
This 1870 limestone structure is on the
Register of Historic Places. It is on the
bank of Root River and is surrounded by
acres of beautiful, unspoiled hardwood
forest. All rooms feature private baths and several have hand-carved Norwegian beds. The parlor
is very inviting with a library of books, games
and a baby grand piano. Country breakfasts are
offered each morning, and fresh, creative lunches
and dinners are available in the restaurant.

10 Rooms • Price range: $65-95
101 Parkway N, Lanesboro, MN 55949
☎ **(507) 467-2154**

Little Marais

Stone Hearth Inn Bed & Breakfast

This spacious and elegant inn sits on the shore of Lake Superior. Guests can enjoy the view while relaxing in the Adirondack furniture on the veranda. Rooms are furnished with full-size antique beds and reading chairs; their private baths boast pedestal sinks and pristine tiles. Bonfires on the shore are hosted by the innkeepers. Breakfast includes regional delicacies. The carriage house and boathouse are perfect for private getaways.

8 Rooms • Price range: $90-150
6598 Lakeside Estates Rd,
Little Marais, MN 55614
☎ **(218) 226-3020**

Lutsen
⑩ Lindgren's Bed & Breakfast on Lake Superior

This rustic 1920s log home on Lake Superior has been extensively remodeled to take full advantage of its spectacular location. The Great Room is flanked by a massive stone fireplace on one side and picture windows overlooking Lake Superior on the other. Guestrooms have wooden interiors with breathtaking views of the lake and the nearby forest. A Finnish sauna is just steps from the main house.

3 Rooms • Price range: $105-150
5552 CR 35, Lutsen, MN 55612-0056
☎ **(218) 663-7450**

Mankato
The Butler House Bed & Breakfast

Once the home of a wealthy confectioner and former mayor of Mankato, this English-style mansion was built in 1905. Special details of the inn include the Steinway grand piano in the main hall, the hand-painted murals in the dining room, and the 15-foot window seat that offers a lovely place to relax. Rooms are fitted with comfortable beds, and feature private baths. Evening refreshment is served on the front porch.

5 Rooms • Price range: $79-129
704 S Broad St, Mankato, MN 56001
☎ **(507) 387-5055**

Minneapolis
Nicollet Island Inn

This building is the last woodworking factory still standing in the area. It was built in 1893 and has since undergone many reincarnations. Built of limestone, in the style of utilitarian architecture, the structure is unique. The dining room was once the loading dock and it has been glassed in so that guests can enjoy a delicious meal while looking out at the Mississippi River flowing by. The bar is more than 150 years old.

24 Rooms • Price range: $135-170
95 Merriam St, Minneapolis, MN 55401
☎ **(612) 331-1800**

Pipestone
Historic Calumet Inn

This historic inn was constructed from hand-chiseled Sioux quartzite block.

40 Rooms • Price range: $60-85
104 W Main St, Pipestone, MN 56164
☎ **(507) 825-5871**

Monticello
The Historic Rand House

During World War II, this 1884 Queen Anne house and its grounds were loaned to the Army Corps for use as officers' quarters for pilots receiving glider training in Monticello. Today the inn's grounds feature an arboretum, a swimming pool and extensive flower gardens. Guestrooms are attractively decorated with period furnishings and private baths. An enormous screened porch overlooks the landscaped lawns and woods.

4 Rooms • Price range: $105-165
1 Old Territorial Rd, Monticello, MN 55362
☎ **(763) 295-6037**

Red Wing
The Candlelight Inn

The superb craftsmanship of this 1877 house is apparent in the cabinetry, the staircase, the parquet floors and the trim. Cherry, butternut, oak and walnut woods add to the beauty of the house as do the original hand-blown glass light fixtures. Guestrooms are appointed with Victorian antiques and private baths, while some include a whirlpool and a fireplace. Nearby are walking, bicycle and ski trails, Treasure Island Casino, and the Mississippi.

5 Rooms • Price range: $99-169
818 W 3rd St, Red Wing, MN 55066
☎ **(651) 388-8034**

Sherburn
Four Columns Inn

Four Columns Inn sits atop a knoll overlooking what was once the Winnebago-Jackson Stage Road. Built in 1884 by George Rhode, the house originally served as an inn for stagecoach travelers. It features a balcony, a deck and a solarium, as well as a 19th-century Victorian gazebo where guests can enjoy their breakfast. Up on the third floor, the Bridal Suite has a pull-down entrance to the roof and the widow's walk.

5 Rooms • Price range: $70-75
668 140th St, Sherburn, MN 56171
☎ **(507) 764-8861**

Spring Valley
Chase's Bed & Breakfast

When William Strong built this house in 1879, it was considered the most handsome private building in the county. The inn was designed in the French Second Empire style, with a shallow mansard roof. Large porches and more than an acre of lawn and gardens surround the house. Large guestrooms have cozy sitting areas and private baths. Area attractions include Forestville State Park.

5 Rooms • Price range: $75-110
508 N Huron Ave, Spring Valley, MN 55975
☎ **(507) 346-2850**

St. Paul
Chatsworth Bed & Breakfast

This spacious 1902 Victorian inn is conveniently located in a quiet family neighborhood just two blocks from the Governor's Mansion on historic Summit Avenue. The inn is in a beautiful wooded setting and surrounded by gardens, with the downtown areas of both St. Paul and Minneapolis minutes away. Distinctive rooms include such features as a private deck, a double whirlpool tub and a Japanese soaking tub.

5 Rooms • Price range: $70-135
984 Ashland Ave, St. Paul, MN 55104
☎ **(651) 227-4288**

St. Paul
The Garden Gate Bed & Breakfast

This inn's guestrooms have been named after different flowers. They are all comfortable and decorated in a modern theme. The shared bathroom features a lovely claw-foot tub. The living room and dining room feature gleaming hardwood floors.

3 Rooms • Price range: $55-65
925 Goodrich Ave, St. Paul, MN 55105
☎ **(651) 227-8430**

Stillwater
William Sauntry Mansion

Built in 1890 by lumber baron William Sauntry, this Queen Anne-Eastlake mansion is nestled in the hills of historic Stillwater. Sauntry's penchant for opulence is visible throughout the mansion: in the parquet floors, the original chandeliers, the painted canvas ceiling, and the cherry and oak woodwork. Guestrooms include whirlpool tubs and fireplaces. Area activities include cruising the St. Croix River and riding the Minnesota Zephyr.

6 Rooms • Price range: $119-199
626 N 4th St, Stillwater, MN 55082
☎ **(651) 430-2653**

Vergas
The Log House & Homestead on Spirit Lake

Set on a sprawling rural property, this historic inn has luxurious guestrooms.

5 Rooms • Price range: $110-195
PO Box 130, Vergas, MN 56587
☎ **(218) 342-2318**

Notes:

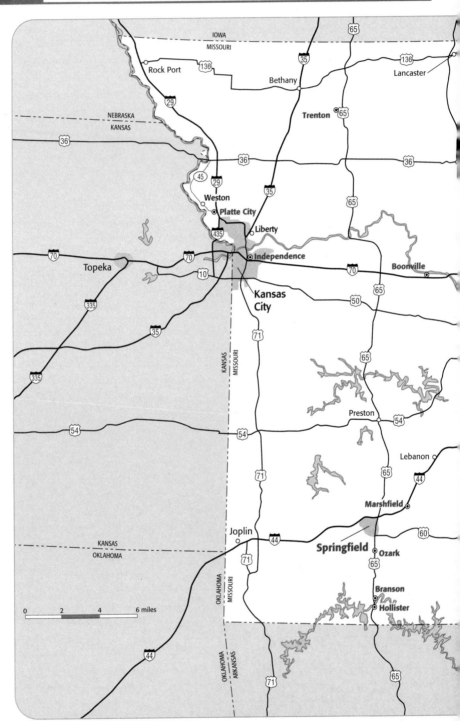

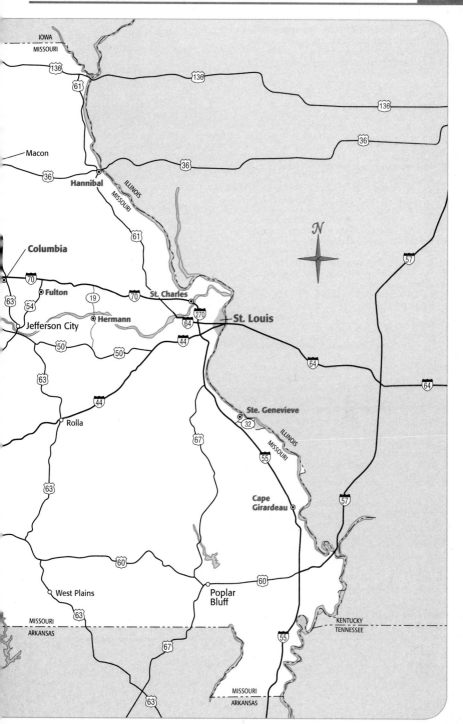

IOWA
MISSOURI

136
61

Macon

36

Hannibal

ILLINOIS

MISSOURI

136

136

36

61

N

57

Columbia

70

Fulton

19

70

St. Charles

270

St. Louis

63

54

Jefferson City

Hermann

64

50

50

44

64

63

44

64

Rolla

Ste. Genevieve

32

ILLINOIS

MISSOURI

67

55

Cape
Girardeau

57

63

60

60

West Plains

Poplar
Bluff

MISSOURI
ARKANSAS

63

67

55

KENTUCKY
TENNESSEE

67

63

MISSOURI
ARKANSAS

Boonville
 Rivercene Bed & Breakfast

This mansion across the Missouri River from Boonville was built in 1864 by an industrious riverboat baron. He imported Italian marble for the nine fireplaces, black walnut for the front doors and hand-carved mahogany for the grand staircase. Now the building has been completely restored and is listed on the National Register of Historic Places. There is a two-room suite and a room with a two-person Jacuzzi.

8 Rooms • Price range: $85-150
127 CR 463, Boonville, MO 65274
☎ **(660) 848-2497**

Branson
Branson Historic Hotel Bed & Breakfast Inn

Built in 1903 with the coming of the railroad, this is the oldest commercial building in town. The author Harold Bell Wright stayed here while writing his novels. The inn also housed the town's first library. Stone columns support the front porch while Adirondack chairs beckon on the verandas. In the morning, guests gather for a full breakfast around the big harvest table in the glass-enclosed breakfast room.

9 Rooms • Price range: $75-105
214 W Main, Branson, MO 65616
☎ **(417) 335-6104**

Branson
The Branson House Bed & Breakfast

The architecture of this 1920s house is unique to the area and the inn itself offers an original English country ambience. The B&B sits on a hillside in downtown Branson overlooking the town and the bluffs of Lake Taneycomo. The former mayor's residence, the B&B is surrounded by rock walls of native fieldstone, old oak trees and flower gardens. Every morning guests are served a gourmet Ozark breakfast.

6 Rooms • Price range: $55-90
120 N 4th St, Branson, MO 65616
☎ **(417) 334-0959**

Branson
The Brass Swan Bed & Breakfast

This contemporary home offers a relaxing environment in a wooded location within view of Lake Taneycomo. Each room has a sitting area and private bath, while some come with a private deck and a spa. The B&B holds an Ozark Mountain Christmas every year. Although the setting is quiet, it takes only minutes to get to the excitement of music, shopping and fine restaurants on the famous 76 Country Boulevard.

4 Rooms • Price range: $70-85
202 River Bend Rd, Branson, MO 65616
☎ **(417) 336-3669**

Branson
Josie's Peaceful Getaway Bed & Breakfast
This romantic getaway features a premier lakefront view of Table Rock Lake from scenic Indian Point. The house itself is decorated with Victorian flair, well-complemented by the cathedral ceilings and a huge stone fireplace. Guests can enjoy a picnic lunch in the gazebo, relax on the large veranda or soak in the lavish spa under the Ozark sky. A delicious candlelight breakfast is served on china and crystal.

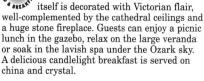

4 Rooms • Price range: $70-125
508 Table Rock Cir, Branson, MO 65616
☎ (417) 338-2978

Cape Girardeau
Bellevue Bed & Breakfast
A 1891 Victorian home with charming rooms and a friendly atmosphere.

4 Rooms • Price range: $70-105
312 Bellevue St, Cape Girardeau, MO 63701
☎ (573) 335-3302

Columbia
The Gathering Place Bed & Breakfast
Built in 1906, this large house was home to numerous fraternities in the 1930s due to its proximity to the University of Missouri. The elegant interior ambience comes from the stained-glass windows, the oak and walnut floors, and the handcrafted wood trim. The rooms are furnished with typical Missouri and American antiques of native walnut. Original and antique works of art hang throughout the house.

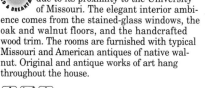

5 Rooms • Price range: $85-145
606 S College, Columbia, MO 65201
☎ (573) 815-0606

Columbia
University Ave Bed & Breakfast
Lovely 1920s brick house on the edge of the University of Missouri campus.

4 Rooms • Price range: $80-90
1315 University Ave, Columbia, MO 65201
☎ (573) 499-1920

Fulton
Loganberry Inn Bed & Breakfast
This inviting 1899 Victorian house once hosted Margaret Thatcher and some members of Scotland Yard. They came for the quiet sanctuary, but they probably would have done well on one of the inn's murder-mystery weekends. Each elegantly appointed guestroom has a private bath and a sitting area. From sipping sodas at the old-fashioned soda fountain to strolling the cobblestone streets, there is lots to do in Fulton.

4 Rooms • Price range: $65-150
310 W 7th St, Fulton, MO 65251
☎ (573) 642-9229

Hannibal
Garth Woodside Mansion

Mark Twain was a childhood friend of the original owner of this 1871 mansion and he stayed here whenever he was in town. Considered one of the top inns in the Midwest, it is set in a quiet area with 39 acres of trees and other flora. The focal point of the lobby is a walnut three-story "flying" staircase. Each room is furnished with Victorian period antiques, many of them heirlooms of the original family.

8 Rooms • Price range: $83-150
11069 New London Gravel Rd,
Hannibal, MO 63401
☎ **(573) 221-2789**

Hannibal
The Rothacker House

This 1847 Greek-Revival house is listed on the National Register of Historic Places and offers views of the Mississippi. Located downtown, it is only a block from city attractions. The third-floor Riverview Suite has a full kitchen, a Jacuzzi in the master bedroom, a second bedroom with a view and a second bathroom with a claw-foot tub. Four other rooms feature either a single or a double Jacuzzi tub.

7 Rooms • Price range: $75-100
423 N 4th St, Hannibal, MO 63401
☎ **(573) 221-6335**

Hannibal
Fifth Street Mansion Bed & Breakfast

Modeled after a 1900s Italian villa, the inn has elaborate Tiffany windows.

7 Rooms • Price range: $78-110
213 S 5th St, Hannibal, MO 63401
☎ **(573) 221-0445**

Hermann
Hermann Hill Vineyard & Inn

This country inn, surrounded by a vineyard, is situated on a bluff overlooking the Missouri River Valley. The rooms are decorated in an Old-World style, featuring high ceilings, arched French doors, solid oak woodwork, stained-glass windows and private balconies with great views. Guests can explore the historic district of town, bike the Katy Trail, walk to the Stone Hill Winery or drive through Missouri wine country.

5 Rooms • Price range: $140-250
711 Wein St, Hermann, MO 65041
☎ **(573) 486-4455**

Hollister
Red Bud Cove B&B Suites

In this country retreat located in a quiet cove on the edge of Table Rock Lake, each suite has a private entrance, a living room, a kitchenette and a private bath; some have a fireplace or a spa. Breakfast is served in the main house dining room overlooking the lake. Guests may rent a fishing or pontoon boat or dock space for their own craft. The area's many attractions are a short drive away along the scenic roads.

8 Rooms • Price range: $82-120
162 Lakewood Dr, Hollister, MO 65672
☎ **(417) 334-7144**

Independence
Woodstock Inn Bed & Breakfast

This updated building was a doll and quilt factory in the early 1900s. Located downtown in the historical district, it is within easy walking distance of Jackson Square, Old Jail Museum, Truman Home, Old Stone Church and many other local attractions. Regardless of the size of room or suite a guest chooses—and there is a variety—the emphasis is on hospitality. Gourmet Belgian waffles are a house specialty.

11 Rooms • Price range: $72-185
1212 W Lexington Ave,
Independence, MO 64050
☎ **(816) 833-2233**

Marshfield
The Dickey House Bed & Breakfast, Ltd.

This Greek-Revival mansion was built in 1913 by a prominent prosecuting attorney. The massive mansion sits in a residential area surrounded by lawns and gardens featuring stately oak trees, a gazebo, a fountain and an outdoor aviary complete with doves and finches. A first glimpse reveals three-foot-diameter columns and intricate woodwork on the beveled windows. The rooms are filled with period antiques and reproductions, some have a Jacuzzi or a private balcony. The area's attractions include wineries, state parks, the Hubble Space Telescope Replica and the Fantastic Caverns.

6 Rooms • Price range: $65-145
331 S Clay St, Marshfield, MO 65706
☎ **(417) 468-3000**

Ozark
Barn Again Bed & Breakfast

The town of Ozark is known as Missouri's antique capital and the antiques in the Barn Again B&B are fine examples of some of the treasures to be found in the area. The two converted barns and Victorian farmhouse are decorated in an eclectic mix of family heirlooms and local pieces. There is a pool, an outdoor basketball court and a path that meanders through the property. Breakfasts are large and satisfying.

4 Rooms • Price range: $69-109
904 W Church St, Ozark, MO 65721
☎ **(417) 581-2276**

Platte City
Basswood Country Inn Resort

The buildings that make up this 73-acre country estate sit in a wooded lakeside setting where the rich and famous once came to relax. Harry Truman and Bing Crosby stayed in the Celebrity Country House suites in the 1940s and 1950s. A cottage built in 1935 has two bedrooms that look out to the lake as well as a private yard and a wood-burning stove. Each of the suites in the main house features a Jacuzzi tub and a private deck.

10 Rooms • Price range: $72-149
15880 Interurban Rd, Platte City,
MO 64079-9185
☎ **(816) 858-5556**

Springfield
Lee-Haydon Bed & Breakfast

In 1930 Mrs. Edna Lee had this impressive Mediterranean-style home built to provide work for unemployed craftsmen. An eclectic assortment of furnishings includes many precious family heirlooms, a large antique doll collection and Civil War memorabilia. All the guest accommodations have queen-size antique beds and private baths. A cottage is also available for those who desire more privacy.

4 Rooms • Price range: $65-125
1036 E Sunshine, Springfield, MO 65807
☎ **(417) 886-1222**

Springfield
Walnut Street Inn
This centrally located historic property has seven guestrooms with fireplaces.

14 Rooms • Price range: $70-159
900 E Walnut, Springfield, MO 65806
☎ **(417) 864-6346**

St. Charles
Boone's Lick Trail Inn Bed & Breakfast

A Federal-style inn built in 1840 on the settler's route, this place was named after the sons of Daniel Boone. Once a home for "flower children" in the 1970s, it is now a key part of the National Register Historic District of town. Guests can enjoy strolling through the district, riding a horse-drawn carriage, hiking or biking the Katy Trail, or visiting museums. Rooms feature private bathrooms, 150-year-old pine floors and river views.

5 Rooms • Price range: $85-175
1000 S Main St, St. Charles, MO 63301
☎ **(636) 947-7000**

St. Louis
Lafayette House Bed & Breakfast
Partially restored, this 1876 home was built by James Eads for his daughter.

6 Rooms • Price range: $70-150
2156 Lafayette Ave, St. Louis, MO 63104
☎ **(314) 772-4429**

Ste. Genevieve
⑳ The Inn St. Gemme Beauvais & Dr. Hertich's House

Built in the 1840s, this three-story brick Colonial mansion is the oldest continuously operating B&B in Missouri. The front veranda is supported by tall pillars. An ornate four-armed brass chandelier is the centerpiece of the front entry and an antique crystal chandelier imported from Florence hangs in the dining room. Antique prints, fresh flowers, old-fashioned wallpaper and curtained windows all contribute to the elegant atmosphere.

14 Rooms • Price range: $75-185
78 N Main St, Ste. Genevieve, MO 63670
☎ **(573) 883-5744**

Trenton
Hyde Mansion Bed & Breakfast Inn
This sprawling two-story gable-roofed
mansion was built by Governor Hyde's
widow in 1949. The six comfortable
rooms have been modified to include
private baths. Guests are invited to take advantage of the common rooms which include a library,
a living room with a grand piano and the new
recreation room with a home entertainment center. In warm weather guests can also enjoy the
patio, which overlooks the pleasant grounds.

6 Rooms • Price range: $60-110
418 E 7th St, Trenton, MO 64683
☎ **(660) 359-5631**

Notes:

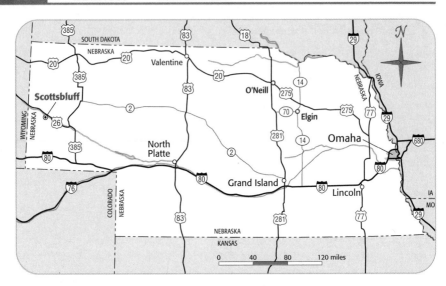

Scottsbluff
Barn Anew Bed & Breakfast

This old barn has been restored and furnished with period antiques. Some of the collectibles in the well-appointed rooms are for sale and the building boasts a tiny museum and antique shop. Refreshments are served in a wicker-furnished sunroom and the leisure room offers games and a selection of books. Breakfast is served in the formal dining room. A golf course and several major attractions are near at hand.

4 Rooms • Price range: $75-90
170549 County Rd L, Scottsbluff, NE 69357
☎ **(308) 632-8647**

Scottsbluff
Fontenelle Inn Bed & Breakfast

Otto John Henke I, West Nebraska's first registered professional architect built this Arts and Crafts-style building in 1917. Listed on the National Register of Historic Places, the inn features first-floor suites with porches and second-floor suites with access to a screened-in veranda. There is also a shaded patio in the flower garden where guests may relax before attending the English high tea in the second-floor tearoom.

7 Rooms • Price range: $55-125
1424 Fourth Ave, Scottsbluff, NE 69361
☎ **(308) 632-6257**

Notes:

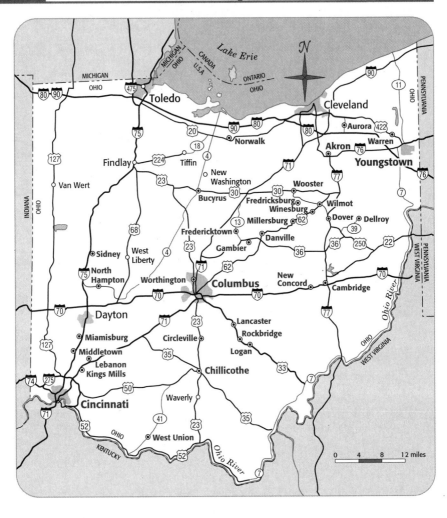

Akron
The O'Neil House Bed & Breakfast

This 19-room Mock Tudor mansion was originally the home of William O'Neil, founder of the General Tire Company. Beautiful woodwork, carved oak panel- ing, oak floors and leaded-glass windows are found throughout the entire house.

4 Rooms • Price range: $70-150
1290 W Exchange, Akron, OH 44313
☎ **(330) 867-2650**

Aurora
The Aurora Inn

The Aurora Inn offers New England-style accommodations right in the heart of Ohio's Western Reserve. The full-service inn offers all the amenities of a large hotel along with the personalized service of a small country inn. Tennis courts, Jacuzzis, two pools and dry-cleaning service are just a few of the extras guests enjoy. Guests may also take advantage of the inn's restaurant and tavern.

69 Rooms • Price range: $175-205
30 Shawnee Tr, Aurora, OH 44202
☎ **(330) 562-6121**

Bucyrus
Hideaway Bed & Breakfast
Call for information.

6 Rooms • Price range: $97-287
1601 SR 4, Bucyrus, OH 44820
☎ **(419) 562-3013**

Burton
⚙ *Red Maple Inn*

Set amid the rolling hills of the fourth-largest Amish community in the world, the Red Maple offers an oasis of uncommon serenity and natural beauty. Guestrooms feature fine Amish crafted furnishings. The library is the perfect place to relax by a fire with a good book or to have a quiet conversation with friends. Enjoy evening hors d'oeuvres and breakfast in the dining room overlooking the valley.

18 Rooms • Price range: $99-200
14707 S Cheshire St, Burton, OH 44021
☎ **(440) 834-8334**

Cambridge
Misty Meadow Farm Bed & Breakfast

The Misty Meadow features rooms overlooking fruit orchards awash with blossoms in the spring and colorful produce in the summer. Miles of scenic country trails weave through the woods nearby, past ravines, streams and wildlife. A pond well stocked with bass offers fishing, swimming and boating. Guests are welcome to enjoy the spa and the sauna. Nightly bonfires are a popular ritual.

4 Rooms • Price: $130
64878 Slaughter Hill Rd, Cambridge, OH 43725
☎ **(740) 439-5135**

Chillicothe

The Greenhouse Bed & Breakfast

This former winter residence of local banker, George Hunter Smith, is a fine example of Queen Anne architecture. Each of the main floor rooms is decorat-ed with cherry wood, leaded glass and frescoes. The guestrooms are elegantly furnished.

4 Rooms • Price range: $70-80
47 E 5th St, Chillicothe, OH 45601
☎ **(740) 775-5313**

Cincinnati
The Parker House

This Queen Anne home dates back to the 1870s. Its 12-foot-high ceilings feature murals framed by ornate wood-work, paneling and wall coverings. Breakfast is served in the music room beneath the portraits of Mozart and Beethoven.

5 Rooms • Price range: $75-110
2323 Ohio Ave, Cincinnati, OH 45219
☎ **(513) 579-8236**

Cincinnati
The Victoria Inn of Hyde Park

A tastefully restored 1909 home is locat-ed in one of Cincinnati's most charming neighborhoods. Each uniquely decorated room features a feather bed and fine antique appointments such as ornately carved furniture, patterned quilts and brass chandeliers. Most have a fireplace, a whirlpool or a claw-foot tub, or a private sleeping porch. Breakfast, includ-ing fresh-baked bread and scones and gourmet coffee, is available in-room or in the dining room.

4 Rooms • Price range: $99-189
3567 Shaw Ave, Cincinnati, OH 45208
☎ **(513) 321-3567**

Circleville
Penguin Crossing Bed & Breakfast

This Federal-style red brick farm-house on 300 acres of farmland dates to the 1820s. Decorated in bold, cheer-ful colors and patterns framed by origi-nal black-walnut woodwork, Penguin Crossing offers comfortable rooms with antiques and down quilts; some have a wood-burning fire-place. A full gourmet breakfast of all-natural foods—recipes with whole grains and honey are a specialty—is served on weekends.

5 Rooms • Price range: $125-225
3291 SR 56 W, Circleville, OH 43113
☎ **(740) 477-6222**

Columbus
50 Lincoln Inn

The unique brick exterior of this circa 1917 house stands out in Columbus's South Shore Gallery district. The works of local and national artists are on display in the inn and each guestroom is named after an artist.

8 Rooms • Price range: $109-139
50 E Lincoln St, Columbus, OH 43215
☎ **(614) 291-5056**

Columbus
Harrison House Bed & Breakfast

A restored 1890s Queen Anne home on nicely landscaped grounds in Columbus' Victorian historic district. The interior features high ceilings, cut glass windows and a mix of contemporary and antique pieces. Each of the beautifully appointed rooms has a private modern bath and queen-size bed. Breakfasts change regularly, depending on the creative whims of the cook. The owners strive to provide all the comforts of home.

4 Rooms • Price: $109
313 W 5th Ave, Columbus, OH 43201
☎ **(614) 421-2202**

Danville
The White Oak Inn

A comfortable farmhouse located on 14 acres of wooded private property, the inn is adjacent to several hundred acres of conservation land, ideal for hiking, fishing, canoeing and other outdoor recreation. The original white oak for the woodwork and red oak for the floors was cut and milled on the property. Heartland cuisine is served using fresh herbs from the garden, specially cut meats, local poultry, home-baked breads and homemade desserts.

10 Rooms • Price range: $90-140
29683 Walhonding Rd (SR 715),
Danville, OH 43014
☎ **(740) 599-6107**

Dellroy
Whispering Pines Bed & Breakfast

Standing on a gentle slope of century-old pines between rolling hills, Whispering Pines commands a magnificent view of Atwood Lake. Six wood-burning fireplaces warm an atmosphere created by collections of art, glasswork and authentic Victorian lighting. Guestrooms feature fine antiques, private baths and beautiful views. Breakfast consists of home-baked treats on a regularly changing menu.

5 Rooms • Price range: $115-175
PO Box 340, State Rte 542, Dellroy, OH 44620
☎ **(330) 735-2824**

Dover
Olde World Bed & Breakfast

Guests here are invited to enjoy the privacy of individually decorated rooms, take in the serene countryside from the veranda or relax in the parlor over games played by a crackling fire. Sample American regional cuisine with the full homemade breakfast, prepared using the best fresh local ingredients. Afternoon tea and dinner are served with advance reservations.

5 Rooms • Price range: $80-110
2982 SR 516 NW, Dover, OH 44622
☎ **(330) 343-1333**

Fredericktown

Heartland Country Resort
This resort is a remodeled 1878 farm-house and three-suite log home on a wooded hillside overlooking a stream. The rooms are cozy; the suites feature a private entrance and porch, a glass-front stove, and a kitchenette. Horseback riding in an indoor or outdoor arena, a swimming pool, a pool table and a ping-pong table are available; nearby is golfing, boating, hiking and skiing. Picnic lunches and candlelight dinners are available.

7 Rooms • Price range: $85-195
2994 Township Rd 190,
Fredericktown, OH 43019
☎ **(419) 768-9300**

Fredricksburg

Gilead's Balm Manor
This sprawling Mock Tudor home is set on the shore of a lake surrounded by towering pines. Six elegantly furnished guestrooms are individually decorated, most with a deck overlooking the lake. A peaceful country hideaway.

6 Rooms • Price range: $100-165
8690 CR 201, Fredricksburg, OH 44627
☎ **(330) 695-3881**

Gambier
The Kenyon Inn
Classic New England-style full service inn on the grounds of Kenyon College.

32 Rooms • Price range: $76-92
100 W Wiggin St, Gambier, OH 43022
☎ **(740) 427-2202**

Kings Mills

Kings Manor Inn Bed & Breakfast
Built by the town's founding family, this three-story frame house is located in a quiet residential neighborhood. Three charming guestrooms and one two-bed-room suite have private baths; some of the baths have whirlpools.

4 Rooms • Price range: $60-90
1826 Church St, Kings Mills, OH 45034
☎ **(513) 459-9959**

Lebanon
ⓦ The Golden Lamb Inn
Opened in 1803, this inn has been continuously operating ever since. Each guestroom is individually decorated with antique furnishings including some magnificent mahogany dressers and bedsteads. There are three historical exhibit rooms.

18 Rooms • Price range: $67-97
27 S Broadway, Lebanon, OH 45036
☎ **(513) 932-5065**

Logan

The Inn At Cedar Falls
Guests seeking a relaxing, peaceful visit should consider staying at this inn, which consists of a collection of reconstructed 19th-century log cabins set on private wooded sites, each with a deck, porch swing and gas log stove. The inn serves fine American cuisine, using organic vegetables and herbs from its own garden. All kinds of outdoor recreational activities, including riding, fishing and nature hikes, are available nearby.

15 Rooms • Price range: $65-102
21190 SR 374, Logan, OH 43138
☎ **(740) 385-7489**

Miamisburg
English Manor Bed & Breakfast

From the B&B's common areas with their jewel tones and polished hardwood floors to the individually decorated guestrooms furnished with period antiques, this English-style manor house exudes an ambience of refined comfort.

4 Rooms • Price range: $75-95
505 E Linden Ave, Miamisburg, OH 45342
☎ **(937) 866-2288**

Millersburg
⊕ *Port Washington Inn*

This large, English Tudor-style home on 45 acres of sprawling hilltop has a breathtaking view of the surrounding forests and meadows. Tastefully decorated with local handmade Amish furniture and floral wall coverings and fabrics, each room has a character of its own. Three large cottages are also available, featuring Jacuzzis, fireplaces and arched cathedral ceilings. All guests have access to an indoor heated swimming pool.

8 Rooms • Price range: $59-189
4667 SR 312, Millersburg, OH 44654
☎ **(330) 674-7704**

Millersburg
Fields of Home Guest House Bed & Breakfast

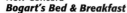

This log cabin guesthouse offers all the comforts of home, set in the bucolic countryside. Enjoy the view of the spring-fed pond, meadows and the sounds of the countryside from rocking chairs on the front porch. Nice Country-style guestrooms.

6 Rooms • Price range: $65-135
7278 CR 201, Millersburg, OH 44654
☎ **(330) 674-7152**

New Concord
Bogart's Bed & Breakfast

Located across the street from Muskingum College, this renovated 1830s Federal home is completely furnished with antiques. There is also a spacious deck and enclosed porch behind the house. Breakfasts are served by candlelight.

4 Rooms • Price range: $75-85
62 W Main St, New Concord, OH 43762
☎ **(740) 826-7397**

North Hampton
Miss Mollie D's Victorian Tea Room/Bed & Breakfast

Built in 1914, this Victorian home is located in a quaint village in rural Ohio. Charmingly modest guestrooms offer cozy furnishings and spacious baths with claw-foot tubs. Lunches and elegant evening meals are served with Victorian style.

4 Rooms • Price: $90
59 E Clark St, North Hampton, OH 45349
☎ **(937) 964-8228**

Norwalk
ⓐ *Georgian Manor Inn*

An elegant Georgian-Revival home built in 1906 and completely renovated, the manor is surrounded by gardens landscaped with a pond, a stream, a waterfall, stoned walks with sitting areas and a large pergola. Suites are decorated in a light Victorian style with fine antiques, reproductions and artwork of English country scenes. Relax in overstuffed love seats or wingback chairs arranged around the living room's fireplace or enjoy a book on the library's leather sofa. A complete breakfast is served on fine china in the mahogany-paneled and -beamed dining room.

4 Rooms • Price range: $95-180
123 W Main St, Norwalk, OH 44857
☎ **(419) 663-8132**

Rockbridge
Glenlaurel, A Scottish Country Inn

A country lodging in a secluded wooded area of Hocking Hills overlooking Camusfearna Gorge, the inn's nicely appointed rooms have a homelike ambience. The cottages offer peace and comfort with with all the modern amenities, such as a private deck with whirlpool. Dine in or dine out on the terraced deck, weather permitting. Afternoon tea is also served. Charming Old World hospitality in the Midwest.

11 Rooms • Price range: $119-289
14940 Mt Olive Rd, Rockbridge, OH 43149
☎ **(740) 385-4070**

Sidney
GreatStone Castle

With a structure of 18-inch-thick Bedford Indian limestone, a wrap-around porch, stone columns, three imposing turrets, stained and leaded glass, and an interior finished in ornately carved, rare imported hardwoods, this aptly named castle has been an Ohio landmark for more than a century. Guests will enjoy the gardens and the front porch swing. Suites feature Victorian furniture.

5 Rooms • Price range: $85-95
429 N Ohio Ave, Sidney, OH 45365
☎ **(937) 498-4728**

Troy
ⓐ *Allen Villa Bed & Breakfast*

When it was built in 1874 this charming 1874 home was described as "the most palatial mansion in town." Little has changed over the years except for the addition of private baths in the guestrooms. A delightful ambience.

5 Rooms • Price range: $65-80
434 S Market St, Troy, OH 45373
☎ **(937) 335-1181**

West Union
The Murphin Ridge Inn
A unique inn with spacious, modern rooms furnished with 18th-century reproductions. The dining room is in an 1810 historic house on the property.

Guests are free to roam the 142 acres of fields and woodlands.

10 Rooms • Price range: $85-115
750 Murphin Ridge Rd, West Union, OH 45693
☎ **(937) 544-2263**

Wilmot
The Inn at Amish Door
Landscaped grounds and nice view of the surrounding Amish countryside.

50 Rooms • Price range: $59-199
1210 Winesburg St, Wilmot, OH 44689
☎ **(330) 359-7996**

Winesburg
The Grapevine House Bed & Breakfast
Call for information.

6 Rooms • Price: $70
2140 Main St, Winesburg, OH 44690
☎ **(330) 359-7922**

Wooster
Historic Overholt House Bed & Breakfast
Call for information.

4 Rooms • Price range: $63-75
1473 Beall Ave, Wooster, OH 44691
☎ **(330) 263-6300**

Worthington
✪ The Worthington Inn
Built in 1831, the Worthington is one of central Ohio's historic landmarks. No two rooms in the inn are alike; all are uniquely decorated with authentic American antiques and 19th-century appointments. The Seven Stars offers an American menu accompanied by an all-American wine list. Located in the center of Olde Worthington, the inn is steps away from tree-lined streets of historic homes, churches and specialty stores.

26 Rooms • Price range: $150-175
649 High St, Worthington, OH 43085
☎ **(614) 885-2600**

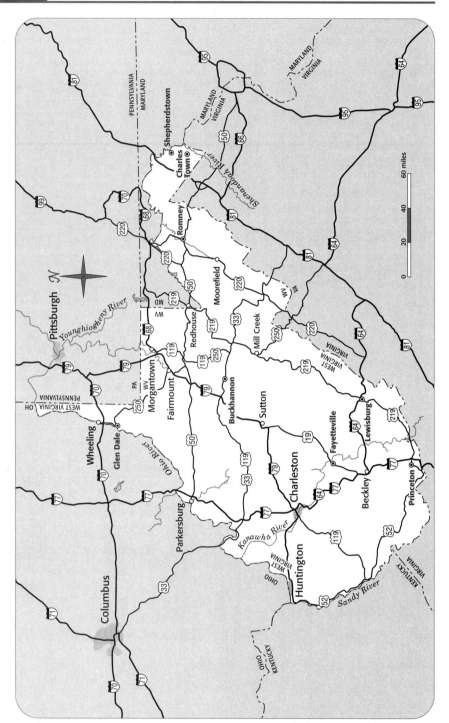

Buckhannon

🏨 *Deer Park Country Inn*

This inn is composed of an 18th-century log cabin, a circa 1900 farmhouse and a new Victorian-style wing. All guestrooms feature private baths, period architectural restoration and such details as ferns, fresh flowers, crisp cotton linens. The surrounding 100 acres of wooded land is great for hiking or just taking a stroll, and guests might see such wildlife as white-tailed deer and Canada geese, which frequent the area.

6 Rooms • Price range: $135-185
Heavener Grove Rd, Buckhannon, WV 26201
☎ **(304) 472-8400**

Charles Town
Cottonwood Inn

A restored 1840s Georgian farmhouse situated on six acres in the Shenandoah Valley, the inn features individually decorated rooms. The property tempts guests out for quiet strolls, while sitting rooms with fireplaces offer the perfect place to curl up with a book chosen from the large library. The inn is an easy drive from a number of historic sites and tours are offered of nearby Civil War battlefields.

7 Rooms • Price range: $65-110
Mill Ln & Kabletown Rd,
Charles Town, WV 25414
☎ **(304) 725-3371**

Charles Town
🏨 *Washington House Inn Bed & Breakfast*

A restored Victorian house built by the grand nephews of George Washington, this inn retains a homey atmosphere with period collectibles and knickknacks. The cozy rooms are decorated with handmade quilts. The owners offer a warm welcome with refreshments in the parlor and abundant breakfasts that include some of their own specialties. The wraparound veranda is a comfortable place to chat or daydream.

6 Rooms • Price range: $99-150
216 S George St, Charles Town, WV 25414
☎ **(304) 725-7923**

Fayetteville
🏨 *Historic Morris Harvey House Bed & Breakfast*

Constructed at the turn of the century by one of Fayette County's most prominent citizens, this house has one of the great wraparound verandas. It also has a unique rain-gathering system and was the first house in the area to boast indoor plumbing. The four guestrooms each feature a private bath and a fireplace. Soft colors and Oriental rugs contribute to the house's elegant decor.

4 Rooms • Price range: $75-95
201 W Maple Ave, Fayetteville, WV 25840
☎ **(304) 574-1902**

Fayetteville
Historic White Horse Bed & Breakfast

Built in 1906 by the county sheriff, this 22-room mansion has been carefully preserved by its owners. Rooms are decorated with comfort in mind and meals are served in the restored dining room, which features a beautiful hand-painted mural.

6 Rooms • Price range: $70-115
120 Fayette Ave, Fayetteville, WV 25840
☎ **(304) 574-1400**

Glen Dale
Bonnie Dwaine Bed & Breakfast

This inn combines Victorian style with modern conveniences. Each professionally decorated room is differently done, but all offer a private bath with a whirlpool tub and a shower, a fireplace, a computer jack and cable TV. Common areas include a library, a living room with an electric grand piano, a patio and a deck. Gourmet candlelight breakfasts are served in the formal dining room and special dietary needs can be accommodated.

5 Rooms • Price range: $70-125
505 Wheeling Ave, Glen Dale, WV 26038
☎ **(304) 845-7250**

Lewisburg
🏛 *General Lewis Inn*

The original wing of this inn dates from 1834, while the larger wing was built in 1928 by the Hock family, who are still the proprietors today. The furnishings are a mix of periods, including Colonial and Civil War-era antiques. A tiny museum displays tools, household implements and musical instruments from pioneer days. In addition to a large breakfast selection, the dining room offers old-fashioned Southern-style dinners.

25 Rooms • Price range: $87-126
301 E Washington St, Lewisburg, WV 24901
☎ **(304) 645-2600**

Romney
Hampshire House 1884

This Victorian home is located in one of the oldest towns in West Virginia. Three of the guestrooms have alcohol-burning fireplaces and antique rifles and pistols are on display. Modern additions include cable television and central air-conditioning. The music room features an 1887 pump organ and a VCR. A full country breakfast is served in the dining room and a health-conscious menu is available. Guests can also enjoy the garden patio.

5 Rooms • Price range: $55-80
165 N Grafton St, Romney, WV 26757
☎ **(304) 822-7171**

Shepherdstown
🏛 *Bavarian Inn*

Overlooking the Potomac River is an establishment right out of the Old World. Built in 1930, this private mansion was purchased in 1962 by Erwin Asam, a native of Bavaria, and his wife Carol. Since then, four Alpine-style chalets and a lodge have been added. The accommodations offer plenty of luxuries—suites feature fireplaces, private balconies and whirlpool baths. Guests make use of the pool, the tennis courts and the exercise room. The dining room serves a range of tempting fare, from wild game to hearty German specialties, and a European-style pub offers a more casual alternative.

72 Rooms • Price range: $115-165
Rt 480 & Shepherd Grade Rd,
Shepherdstown, WV 25443
☎ **(304) 876-2551**

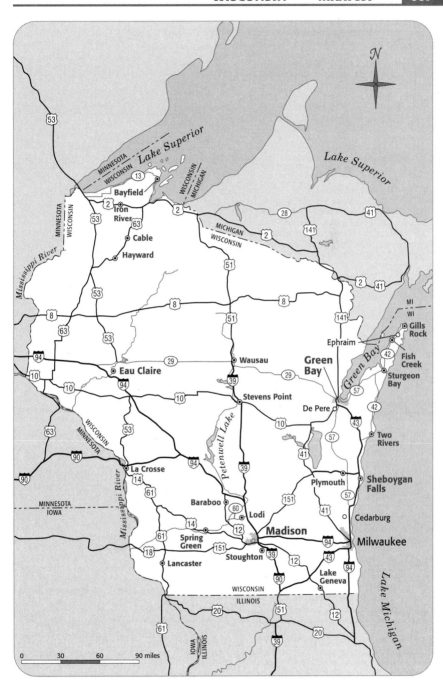

Baraboo

🏵 *Pinehaven Bed & Breakfast*

Tucked into a pine grove, this friendly inn overlooks a spring-fed lake and the Baraboo Bluffs in the distance. Guests can tour the farm and visit with the Belgian draft horses. An upper veranda and a lower deck provide a stunning view of the lake and the bluffs and afford ample opportunity for birding. A paddleboat and a rowboat are available for guests to explore the Baraboo River.

5 Rooms • Price range: $79-95
E13083 Hwy 33, Baraboo, WI 53913
☎ **(608) 356-3489**

Bayfield
Old Rittenhouse Inn

This inn is made up of three late-1800s Victorian mansions, replete with antique furnishings and wraparound verandas. Many elegant features are evident here, such as a beautiful cherry wood staircase and original gas light fixtures. Guestrooms are spacious, with cozy wood-burning fireplaces; some rooms have a whirlpool tub. The inn serves Victorian-style luncheons, dinners and Sunday brunches that are open to the public.

18 Rooms • Price range: $99-249
301 Rittenhouse Ave, Bayfield, WI 54814
☎ **(715) 779-5111**

Bayfield
Cooper Hill House

This quiet, comfortable home offers turn-of-the-20th century charm. The inn boasts spacious grounds for relaxing and birding and is just a short walk from the marina. A two-day stay includes free cross-country or downhill skiing at Mount Ashwabay.

4 Rooms • Price range: $86-99
33 S 6th St, Bayfield, WI 54814
☎ **(715) 779-5060**

Cable
Connors Bed & Breakfast

Located in the heart of Chequamegon National Forest, this estate is just 40 miles south of Lake Superior. There are trails running through the 77-acre property. Guests can view the abundant wildlife or the bright autumn foliage while biking or hiking the back roads. A 110-year-old cabin in an apple orchard next to the house has a kitchenette and fireplace and can accommodate seven people.

4 Rooms • Price range: $85-105
RR 1, Box 255, Cable, WI 54821
☎ **(715) 798-3661**

Eau Claire
Otter Creek Inn

Tucked in among huge trees on a wooded hill, this delightful forest retreat, reminiscent of Snow White's cottage, is approached by a pebblestone walk. The cottagelike English Tudor-style home is almost exclusively a special-event place, so a limousine service is provided. All of the rooms have a private bath with a whirlpool. Breakfast, from a choice of three menus, can be served to guests by the tropical pool or in-room.

6 Rooms • Price range: $55-175
2536 Hillcrest Pkwy, Eau Claire, WI 54720
☎ **(715) 832-2945**

Fish Creek
The White Gull Inn
This country inn built in 1896, has nicely appointed rooms, most with gas fireplaces.

17 Rooms • Price range: $107-265
4225 Main St, Fish Creek, WI 54212
☎ **(920) 868-3517**

Gills Rock
Harbor House Inn
Located in a quaint fishing village, this restored 1904 home offers a view of the harbor and the bluffs from its private porches. Rooms in the main building are decorated in period furnishings and have private baths. Once a carriage house, Troll Cottage has been given a nautical theme, preserving the traditional Scandinavian stove-wood construction of the early settlers. The inn is close to the Washington Island Ferry.

15 Rooms • Price range: $65-175
12666 SR 42, Gills Rock, WI 54210
☎ **(920) 854-5196**

Green Bay
The Astor House
This 1888 home is listed on the National Historic Register and is located downtown in the Astor Historic District. It is only 15 minutes from almost every major attraction in Brown County. Each room is individually decorated and features a fireplace and a whirlpool bath. Themes include the Hong Kong Retreat, a third-floor loft done in an Oriental motif. Another room brings a Monet flower garden to life.

5 Rooms • Price range: $85-152
637 S Monroe Ave, Green Bay, WI 54301
☎ **(920) 432-3585**

Hayward
Lumberman's Mansion Inn
In 1887 the North Wisconsin Lumber Co. built this Queen Anne Victorian showplace for its general manager. The mansion features a restored original

oak staircase, maple floors, white pine pocket doors and a historic carriage stoop.

5 Rooms • Price range: $75-100
15844 E 4th St, Hayward, WI 54843
☎ **(715) 634-3012**

Iron River
Iron River Trout Haus
Located on 40 wooded acres with the Iron River flowing serenely nearby, this renovated 1892 home is built in the lodge-style tradition. Each of the guest-

rooms is decorated with a local theme, featuring wildlife/indigenous artwork and artifacts.

4 Rooms • Price range: $60-75
7420 Drummond St, Iron River, WI 54847
☎ **(715) 372-4219**

La Crosse
⚓ *Chateau La Crosse*
This 1854 stone B&B features ornate wood floors and antique fireplaces.

6 Rooms • Price range: $100-225
410 Cass St, La Crosse, WI 54601
☎ **(608) 796-1090**

Lake Geneva
General Boyd's Bed & Breakfast

This 1867 Colonial-Revival home sits on five acres of landscaped grounds dominated by native white oaks. The inn hosts a large selection of antiques, many of which are original family pieces dating from the 1800s.

4 Rooms • Price range: $95-140
W2915 County Road BB, Lake Geneva, WI 53147
☎ **(262) 248-3543**

Lake Geneva
T. C. Smith Historic Inn Bed & Breakfast

The guestrooms in this inn are decorated with museum-quality antiques and rare paintings, and are furnished in German, French and American styles. The 1845 downtown landmark overlooks the lake and is only steps to the beach. It is an excellent example of a pre-Civil War home, combining Greek-Revival and Italianate styles. Features include intricate woodwork, fine cabinetry and immense pocket doors.

8 Rooms • Price range: $125-375
865 Main St, Lake Geneva, WI 53147
☎ **(262) 248-1097**

Lancaster
Maple Harris Guest House

This 1895 Queen Anne home sits in a residential area. It features the only residential elevator in town as well as detailed oak, maple, and cherry woodwork, double-wide pocket doors, original gas light fixtures, and a three-season porch.

5 Rooms • Price range: $49-69
445 W Maple St, Lancaster, WI 53813
☎ **(608) 723-4717**

Lodi
Victorian Treasure Inn

A national cooking television show featured this inn's memorable breakfast. But the setting of this place is just as memorable as the food. The inn consists of two Queen Anne Victorians: the 1897 Bissell Mansion with its wraparound veranda and formal front parlor; and the 1893 Palmer House, which offers luxurious suites with queen-size beds, gas fireplaces with antique mantles, and private baths with two-person whirlpools.

7 Rooms • Price range: $105-215
115 Prairie St, Lodi, WI 53555
☎ **(608) 592-5199**

Madison
Canterbury Inn

This wonderfully appointed B&B offers upscale guestrooms themed after characters from the Canterbury Tales. The inn is upstairs from a popular bookstore close to the University of Wisconsin and Madison's commercial area.

6 Rooms • Price range: $110-325
315 W Gorham St, Madison, WI 53703
☎ **(608) 258-8899**

Madison

⊕ *Mansion Hill Inn*

A belvedere crowns the gabled roof of this 1858 Romanesque-Revival mansion. Located high on an isthmus between two large lakes, the inn is close to the university campus. The interior features floor-to-ceiling arched windows, ornate cornices, mosaic floors and hand-carved Italian marble fireplaces. An impressive four-story staircase spirals to the rooms above, which boast views of the city, and lakes.

11 Rooms • Price range: $120-340
424 N Pinckney St, Madison, WI 53703
☎ (608) 255-3999

Madison
University Heights Bed & Breakfast

Located close to the university, this four-square has large guestrooms.

4 Rooms • Price range: $80-160
1812 Van Hise Ave, Madison, WI 53705
☎ (608) 233-3340

Madison
The Collins House Bed & Breakfast

This inn is listed on the National Register of Historic Places as a classic example of the Prairie School style of architecture founded by Frank Lloyd

Wright. Perched on the shores of Lake Mendota, it offers spectacular views.

5 Rooms • Price range: $89-180
704 E Gorham St, Madison, WI 53703
☎ (608) 255-4230

Sheboygan Falls
Rochester Inn

Converted from a store built in 1848, the Rochester features a two-level suite tastefully furnished with Queen Anne Victorian furniture. The first floor is a parlor and the second floor is a bedroom and a bath, complete with a double whirlpool. Situated downtown, the inn is close to Kohler, the Kettle Moraine State Forest, upscale shopping and dining. Special touches include breakfast in bed, thick towels and fine linens.

6 Rooms • Price range: $100-160
504 Water St, Sheboygan Falls, WI 53085
☎ (920) 467-3123

Spring Green
Hill Street

This 1904 traditional Queen Anne Victorian is located in a quiet residential neighborhood. The interior is adorned with beautifully carved

antique wood, and the guest units are individually decorated; most include private baths.

7 Rooms • Price range: $70-85
353 W Hill St, Spring Green, WI 53588
☎ (608) 588-7751

Stevens Point
A Victorian Swan on Water
Located near the Wisconsin River and the Green Circle bike trail.

4 Rooms • Price range: $65-135
1716 Water St, Stevens Point, WI 54481
☎ (715) 345-0595

Stoughton
Naeset-Roe Bed & Breakfast

This recently restored 1878 brick Italianate home is situated in the very heart of picturesque Stoughton. Antiques and collectibles make up the decor of the elegant Victorian. The inn features two parlors, a library, a dining room, a patio, gardens, and a spacious front porch. Each of the four individually decorated rooms is equipped with a private bath. The inn also features an on-site gift store.

4 Rooms • Price range: $65-145
126 E Washington St, Stoughton, WI 53589
☎ **(608) 877-4150**

Sturgeon Bay
⍟ Scofield House Bed & Breakfast

The ornamental details of this Queen Anne-style home include beveled-crystal and stained-glass windows, hand-carved window frames, and floors inlaid with patterns made up of five different woods.The house was built in 1902 by the mayor of Sturgeon Bay. The entire third floor has been converted into a luxury suite with three massive gables. The gourmet breakfast has received much praise.

6 Rooms • Price range: $98-202
908 Michigan St, Sturgeon Bay, WI 54235-0761
☎ **(920) 743-7727**

Sturgeon Bay
White Lace Inn

The four historic homes that make up this inn are bordered by a white picket fence and surrounded by gardens. Guests can choose between the Main House, Garden House, Washburn House and Hadley House. All feature rooms furnished with fine antiques, beautiful lace and four-poster or Victorian walnut beds. Other features include private balconies overlooking the gardens and whirlpool tubs.

18 Rooms • Price range: $119-239
16 N 5th Ave, Sturgeon Bay, WI 54235
☎ **(920) 743-1105**

Two Rivers
Red Forest Bed & Breakfast

This 1907 three-story Shingle-style home is highlighted by beautiful beveled- and stained-glass windows. The interior features impressive cross-beam ceilings, a rich wood stairway and an open foyer, complete with a fireplace and window seats. The spacious parlor is ideal for evening gatherings, and the dining room overlooks a garden. Guestrooms feature queen-size beds and ceiling fans. A full breakfast is served.

4 Rooms • Price range: $84-94
1421 25th St, Two Rivers, WI 54241
☎ **(920) 793-1794**

Wausau
Rosenberry Inn

This historic home was built for Judge Marvin Rosenberry in 1908, where he lived until 1916. Today the home features stained-glass windows, wide halls, a carved oak stairway and a sweeping front porch overlooking Franklin Street.

8 Rooms • Price range: $55-160
511 Franklin, Wausau, WI 54403
☎ **(715) 842-5733**

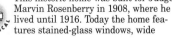

Canada

Lake Moraine makes a perfect picnic stop for hikers in Banff National Park.

Scenic Byways
of Canada

Evangeline, heroine of the Longfellow poem, stands in historic Grand Pré as a perpetual symbol of the Acadian deportation.

The Crowsnest Highway
Running through the southeastern section of British Columbia, this route rolls through breathtaking scenery in the Cascade Mountain Range. Shimmering lakes, mountain ridges, high passes, deep glacier-carved valleys and numerous provincial parks provide photo-stop musts where visitors can capture nature's architectural marvels.

Trans-Canada Highway British Columbia/Alberta
Wildlife and scenery thrill travelers along this strip of the Trans-Canada Highway running along the British Columbia/Alberta border. But spectacular mountain scenery is only part of the charm of this rugged country. There are also fabulous recreational opportunities, such as camping and hiking, and a number of picturesque towns to visit.

The Icefields Parkway
One of the country's most impressive routes, this mid-Albertan byway provides great views of snow-capped mountains, glaciers, emerald-green lakes, powerful rapids and cascading waterfalls. An abundance of wildlife adds to the excitement.

The Gaspé Peninsula
Historical and natural points of interest dot this easternmost region of Quebec. Coastal cliffs reveal the indomitable Atlantic Ocean, which has sculpted coastal cliffs into natural works of art. Historical references go back hundreds of years and retell tales of settlers' first encounters with the Canadian wilderness.

The Port Royal Habitation is an authentic reconstruction of one of North America's first European settlements.

The Icefields Parkway in Jasper National Park has some of the most inspiring roadside vistas in the country.

For further information on the sites along each route, see the Scenic Byways Resource Guide on page 775.

The Evangeline Trail

Sandy beaches, magnificent rocky coastlines and beautiful wooded forests are some of the many attractions along this western Nova Scotia coastline. There are also many man-made sights worth noting, including clapboard homes, pretty farms and impressive lighthouses. Park areas and beautiful lakes are always nearby.

The Crowsnest Highway

From the balmy climate of the Osoyoos region to the thriving fruit region of the Okanagan Valley and the top of Allison's Pass, the Crowsnest Highway offers a range of natural and man-made points of interest. The desert surroundings along the route are diversified by pristine lakes and local flora.

❶ Okanagan Valley
Ever since Thomas Ellis planted the first orchard in 1874, the Okanagan Valley has been known for its thriving fruit industry. Apples, pears, apricots and especially peaches are all produced in the area. In fact, the fruit industry, lumber and tourism are what keep this region thriving. But it's the natural beauty that makes the area so special. Rolling sagebrush hills, lush orchards and radiant lakes delight nature lovers. Those who appreciate beaches and sunny days will find the valley especially appealing since the sun shines more than 2,000 hours per year in this area; that means there's lots of time to enjoy one of 30 easily accessible beaches, water sports or golf—most courses are open from March to October. Visitors may be surprised by the beauty of the region's desert and the huge fabled serpent that supposedly makes its home in one of the lakes.

❷ Osoyoos
This warm, temperate region has a climate very similar to that of Spain and boasts some 12 miles (19 km) of beaches rimming Osoyoos Lake, one of Canada's warmest freshwater bodies. Besides its balmy climate, this small town is home to one of the best museums in the province. Using pictures that detail local history, along with mining and mineral displays and an impressive collection of Native artifacts, the museum gives visitors a taste what B.C. was like in another era. Located in

Community Park, the museum also features a provincial police exhibit and a log building that displays the interior of a late 19th-century pioneer cabin. Also on display are a moonshine still and an extensive butterfly collection.

❸ Manning Provincial Park
This expansive 165,270-acre (66,884-ha) park just north of the U.S. border is bisected by Hwy. 3. From its point of origin in Hope to the summit of Allison Pass within the park, the highway climbs from sea level to 4,400 feet (1,346 m). This picturesque drive is graced in summer with a riot of wildflowers, including blue lupines, yellow arnicas and red Indian paintbrushes. Specific points of interest along the route include remnants of the Dewdney Trail and the Rhododendron Flats—a marked spot off the highway where a footpath wends through vast areas of mauve flowers. Park activities include hiking, camping, mountain biking and horseback riding. A visitor center east of the Lightning Lake campground displays exhibits about the park's natural features.

❹ Boston Bar
Established in the 1860s during the gold rush, Boston Bar got its name from local Natives who called the wave of prospectors Boston men. With the coming of the railway, the town's fortunes turned to logging and trade. One of Boston Bar's feature attractions is the Hell's Gate Airtram, which takes visitors on a 500-foot (153-m) descent into the Fraser River Canyon. The tram then crosses the canyon at its narrowest section, the Hell's Gate Fishways. Two million salmon swim up the fishways in their annual return to the spawning

Cradled in a valley of green and blue, Osoyoos is a great summer recreation spot.

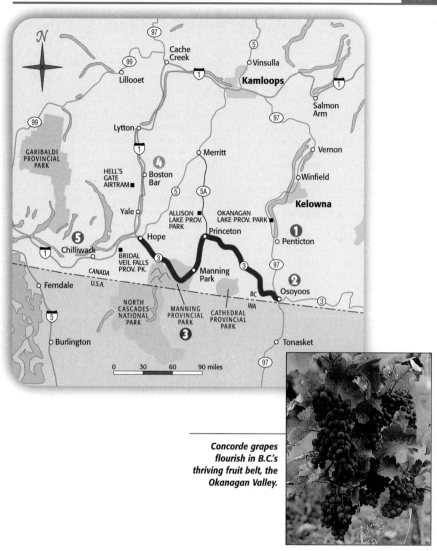

Concorde grapes flourish in B.C.'s thriving fruit belt, the Okanagan Valley.

grounds. A film about this fascinating life cycle is shown at the visitor center. Also found at the site are floral gardens and a suspension foot bridge.

❺ Chilliwack

Nestled in the upper portion of the Fraser Valley, Chilliwack is situated right in the center of a prosperous farming and dairy region. The area is blessed with many lakes, rivers and mountains as well as the Bridal Falls Provincial Park, which fea-

tures a waterfall that drops 400 ft. (122 m) to the valley floor. At the base of the Coastal Mountain Range are the Minter Gardens. Covering nearly 27 acres (11 ha), 11 thematic gardens display seasonal colors, highlighting the distinctive looks of spring, summer and fall. Points of interest in the gardens include a maze, topiary sculptures, a fragrance garden, three aviaries and a Chinese garden. Ideal for families, the gardens also have a children's play area.

Trans-Canada Highway: British Columbia/Alberta

This route has a number of diverse highlights: a world-class golf course, vast national parks, spectacular lakes and mountains, and the takeoff point for a breathtaking helicopter tour over the Rockies. There's history, too. Fossils here date back thousands of years and there is archeological evidence of ancient peoples.

❶ Yoho National Park

Yoho is a Cree exclamation of wonder, a fitting name for this spectacular park, which boasts more than 30 sawtooth peaks that exceed heights of 9,000 feet (2,743 m). Another of the park's wonders is Takakkaw Falls, with its highest drop an incredible 833 feet (254 m), making it one of the highest falls in Canada. Other sights in the park include Lake O'Hara, Natural Bridge, Emerald Lake, Wapta Falls and the Spiral Tunnels of the Canadian Pacific Railway. In 1884 CP laid tracks through Kicking Horse Pass; the Trans-Canada Highway was built in 1959 along this same route. The Burgess Shale Fossil Beds are worth a stop. On display at the park's visitor information center are some 120 species of preserved fossils, including rare soft-bodied creatures dating back 515 million years.

❷ Banff National Park

Banff is Canada's oldest national park, officially established in 1887 after European settlers had arrived. Recent expeditions in the park have revealed a history even older. Evidence suggests that prehistoric habitation dates back some 11,000 years. Remnants of more recent Native settlements, including Blackfoot, Cree and Stoney tribes, have also been found. The glacial-green Bow River flows through the mountain-ringed valley, creating a picturesque backdrop for the town of Banff. The alpine grandeur and mineral hot-spring pools further enhance the area. Banff, which is within the park, is protected by strict controls on development—for instance, residents don't own their land; they lease it from the park. Banff is one of two main centers in this 2,564-square-mile (4,126-sq-km) area of the Canadian Rockies. The other is Lake Louise. At an elevation of just over a mile, this icy blue-green lake gets its color from Victoria Glacier, the meltwaters of which contain silt and rock flour that make the water an opaque turquoise. The tiny village of Lake Louise has a few restaurants and hotels, but the main attraction is the lake itself, which is too cold for swimming but ideal for boating. Visitors can hike to the top of the mountain or take the Banff-Sulphur Mountain Gondola Lift. The open-air observation deck affords spectacular views of Banff and the surrounding mountains.

❸ Canmore

The town of Canmore was the first Canadian Pacific Railroad divisional point west of Calgary and was established as a coal-mining town in 1883. The biathlon and cross-country ski events of the 1988 Winter Olympics were held here and hiking, mountain biking and cross-country skiing are popular activities. During August more than 10,000 people flock to Canmore

Highway 1, the Trans-Canada, links the country from sea to sea and passes through some of the most varied natural regions in the world.

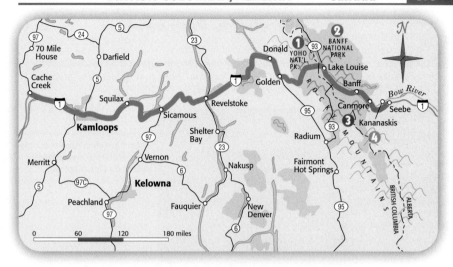

Trail riding is a great way to see some of Banff's lesser traveled spots, such as beautiful Rainbow Lake.

to enjoy the annual Folk Festival. During September, it's time to celebrate the town's Scottish heritage during the Canmore Highland Games, which feature highland dancing, Celtic music and traditional Scottish food. The helicopter sightseeing tours leaving from Canmore are not to be missed. They give a bird's-eye view of alpine valleys, ice fields, the Continental Divide and, of course, the Rockies.

❹ Kananaskis

Kananaskis Country is a four-season recreation area spread over 1,544 square miles (4,000 sq km). The area is situated west of Calgary and encompasses a number of natural points of interest, including Bow Valley, the Elbow-Sheep Wildland, and the Spray Valley and Peter Lougheed provincial parks. Recreational activities include hiking, horseback riding and golfing. The Kananaskis Country golf courses are ranked among the world's best. There are two par-72 championship courses affiliated with the Kananaskis Mountain Lodge, with more than 16 acres (6 ha) of water, 136 bunkers and an elevation of 4,850 feet (1,478 m).

The Icefields Parkway

Nature has been working for centuries to produce the Columbia Icefield. This wonder represents the sheer power and majesty of nature. The route also provides access to the rugged wilds of Jasper National Park and spectacular Maligne Lake—the Maligne Canyon should not be missed.

Columbia Icefield snowcoach tours allow visitors to experience the Athabasca Glacier up close.

❶ Columbia Icefield

One of the many natural beauties inside Banff National Park is the Columbia Icefield. The Icefields Parkway goes right into the area. Completed in 1940, the drive goes through the towns of Lake Louise and Jasper. It follows the headwaters of three major river systems and winds through the impressive mountains of the Eastern Main Ranges. These mountains, which form the Great Divide, are the most rugged of the Canadian Rockies. The route offers spectacular views of snow-topped mountains and several lakes, waterfalls and rivers that drain the Columbia Icefield meltwater into the Atlantic, Pacific and Arctic oceans. There is a wonderful variety of wildlife in this area. Dawn and dusk are the best times to spot the animals, especially the bears and the deer. To get a more intimate view of the terrain, several walking tours are available with one of the area's experienced guides. There are several notable points of interest. The Bow Summit is the highest point on the parkway. Rising 618 feet (2,027 m) above sea level, the summit provides a gorgeous view of blue-green Peyto Lake and, in July and August, an astonishing array of alpine flowers. The Saskatchewan River Crossing is the site of the old horse ford across the North Saskatchewan. A footbridge affords thrilling views into a deep, right-angled canyon where the Sunwapta River turns into the Sunwapta Falls and plunges toward the Athabasca River. And, of course, there is the Columbia Icefield, the largest chain of icefields along the Great Divide. This 126-square-mile (325-sq-km) accumulation of ice feeds eight large glaciers, including the Stufield, the Dome and the Athabasca, all of which can be seen from the parkway.

❷ Maligne Lake

On the way from Lake Louise to Jasper National Park sits lovely Maligne Lake. Separated from the Banff/Jasper Highway by the Maligne range, the Maligne Lake Road travels to the lake just east of Jasper. Along the route to the lake keep a sharp eye out for wildlife. Grizzly bears are common on these isolated hillsides and lake shores, but there have also been sightings of black bears, elk, moose, mules, white-tail deer, big-horn sheep and mountain goats. The Maligne Canyon is one of the region's geological marvels. Some areas of the canyon, carved out by the Maligne River, are only a few feet wide but as much as 160 feet (50 m) deep. On arriving at Maligne Lake, most visitors gasp at the unexpected beauty. The lake is sandwiched between Leah Peak, Samson Peak and Mount Paul on the left and Mount Charlton, Mount Unwin, Mount Mary Vaux and Llysfran

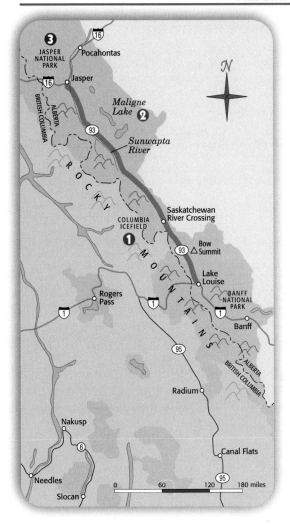

Boat tours on Maligne Lake give visitors a unique view of the surrounding peaks.

Peak to the right. Fish-stocking in the early part of the century has created a fisherman's paradise. Boat tours provide the ultimate lake experience.

❸ Jasper National Park

Banff's northern neighbor is Jasper National Park. Established in 1907, the park was named after Jasper Hawes, the head of the Hudson Bay Company's trading post in the early 1800s. Less developed than Banff, Jasper offers 4,200 square miles (10,878 sq km) of rugged beauty. Majestic mountains, valleys and

lakes are all part of this spectacular Rocky Mountains wilderness. As with other regions along the parkway, wildlife is abundant. Crags and highlands are home to mountain goats and big-horn sheep. Lower slopes and meadows are frequented by deer, elk, moose and bears. Lucky visitors may catch a glimpse of more elusive coyotes, wolves and lynxes. The region's forests of lodgepole pine, spruce, poplar and fir are home to eagles, magpies and jays. The Miette Hot Springs mineral pools are open for bathing from late May to October.

The Gaspé Peninsula

 *This route travels terrain that for the most part has remained largely untouched since the first explorers landed more than 400 years ago. The tip of the peninsula boasts rugged and majestic cliffside sights. Flora and fauna thrive in local national parks. And, of course, there's the unique Percé Rock.*

❶ Percé

This picturesque town is situated on the eastern extremity of the peninsula on the Gulf of St. Lawrence. Percé was a common stop for ships traveling between Québec and France during the 17th century and is still popular today. There are a number of interesting activities such as boat tours, whale watching, art galleries and historic sites. Or, visitors may choose to take an hour-long walk up nearby Mont Ste. Anne. The seven-mile (11-km) drive around the mountain affords spectacular views of nearby villages and offshore islands and passes by some interesting sights, including the Three Sisters Cliffs, the Overlook and the Big Bowl. The region's most photographed sight, however, is Percé Rock. This massive calcerous block, rising abruptly out of the water, measures 1,420 feet (433 m) in length and 288 feet (88 m) in height. It has been pierced by the powerful forces of the sea. The rock changes color depending on the varying light and weather conditions and contains a vast number of fossils. There is a bird sanctuary on Île Bonaventure just offshore and an underwater park for scuba enthusiasts.

❷ Gaspé

On his first voyage to North America in 1534, Jacques Cartier must have been amazed by the spectacular views of the Gaspé Peninsula: sheer cliffs battered by the sea; scores of seabirds; and craggy mountains blanketed by forests. To commemorate the French explorer's arrival, the Jacques Cartier Monument was erected just outside of what is now the town of Gaspé. Six slabs shaped like dolmens recall Cartier's Breton heritage and depict the events of his landing. Next to the monument is the Gaspésie Museum. On display are artifacts, engravings, maps and a range of other items highlighting the region's history. One exhibit, called People of the Sea, focuses on the region's seafaring heritage. Others feature paintings, sculptures, ceramics, photographs and handicrafts. Those interested in learning more about the region and its people can visit the museum's library or archive center, both of which have a large collection of works about the history and people of the Gaspé. Visitors can also see a show in the amphitheater or explore the historic interpretation trail, both of which are on the grounds. Guided tours are available.

❸ Forillon National Park

Located on the northeast tip of the peninsula, this rugged park exhibits jagged seaside cliffs, capes, pebbled beach coves, fir-covered highlands and ocean-terraced lowlands. Throughout the park, geological formations contain rocks from the Ordovician to the Devonian periods. The park is also home to plant groups left over from the ice age. White-tailed deer, moose, black bears, foxes, beavers, minks and coyotes are some

These birds, known as Fou de Bassan, are a common sight on Île Bonaventure in Québec's Gaspé Peninsula region.

At low tide, visitors can approach the Gaspé Peninsula's most famous landmark, Percé Rock.

of the animals that may be seen from the hiking trails. In addition, a number of marine bird species, including double-crested cormorants, black-legged kittiwakes and black guillemots, make their homes in the cliffs and headlands along the coast. The birds share the offshore rocks with gray and harbor seals. From May to October, whales are visible from the clifftops. A program of interpretation activities is offered from late June to mid-October, and includes guided hikes, historical animation, beach walks and slide shows. The interpretation center's four large aquariums represent the underwater habitats found in the park.

❹ Gaspésie Park

Located on the eastern tip of the Gaspé Peninsula near Ste-Anne-des-Monts, this beautiful park covers some 310 square miles (802 sq km) and is known for its abundance of plant and animal life. The region is the only place in Québec where visitors are likely to see moose, wood caribou and Virginia deer all in the same territory. The park includes the Chic-Choc Mountains, with peaks rising to 4,160 feet (1,268 m). Lush flora form a delightfully picturesque backdrop in an area often grazed by caribou in the spring and fall, especially around Mont Albert.

The Evangeline Trail

One of the oldest settlements in Canada, Port Royal, is featured along this route. In fact, history and landscape compete on this scenic drive. From Yarmouth the route passes through old fishing villages, traverses the Annapolis Valley and hugs the shore of the Bay of Fundy, home of the world's highest tides.

❶ Port Royal

This historic village is one of the oldest European settlements in Canada. The modern-day reconstruction of the first Port Royal settlement, known as The Habitation, is set on the north shore of the Annapolis River. The Port Royal colony was founded in 1605 after the landing of French explorer Samuel de Champlain. In 1613 the village was attacked and razed. The Port Royal Habitation was built using Champlain's plan and studies of early 17th-century architecture on what is believed to have been the original site. The reconstruction is protected by a palisade and a canon platform and is centered around a courtyard in the style of a 17th-century French farm. A governor's residence, a priest's house, a chapel, a blacksmith's house and an artisan's workshop are among the buildings in the settlement. They are furnished with early 17th-century reproductions and the staff is outfitted in period dress.

❷ Granville Ferry

The small village of Granville Ferry, which sits on the north side of the Annapolis River, boasts many houses built in the late 1700s. If you look closely, you can see "Holy Lord" door hinges—in the shape of Hs and Ls—brought by New England settlers who thought that the hinges would fend off the powers of witchcraft. One of these residences is the North Hills Museum. Featured here is a fine collection of Georgian hardwood furnishings, as well as porcelain, paintings, ceramics, glass and silver. Guided tours are available.

❸ Annapolis Royal

In the 1630s the French built Fort Port Royal on the south shore of the Annapolis Basin opposite the original Port Royal settlement. When the British took control in 1710, they renamed it Annapolis Royal in honor of Queen Anne. It was the capital of Nova Scotia until Halifax was founded in 1749. At the junction of the Annapolis River and Allen's Creek is the Fort Anne National Historic Site and Museum. The British and the French traded control of this fort during different periods in history. Surviving structures include a powder magazine, a storehouse, ramparts, bastions and ravelins. The old officers' quarters has been restored to house the Fort Anne Museum. Displays showcase the history of the Acadian people as well as of Port Royal and Annapolis Royal. Also on display are maps and Mi'kmaq artifacts. Outdoor monuments honor significant figures, including Pierre Du Gau de Mons, who discovered the basin, and Samuel Vetch, first governor of Acadia. The Annapolis Royal Historic Gardens provide more glimpses into the town's vivid history. The Acadian section of the park showcases the lifestyle of the area's early

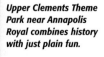

Upper Clements Theme Park near Annapolis Royal combines history with just plain fun.

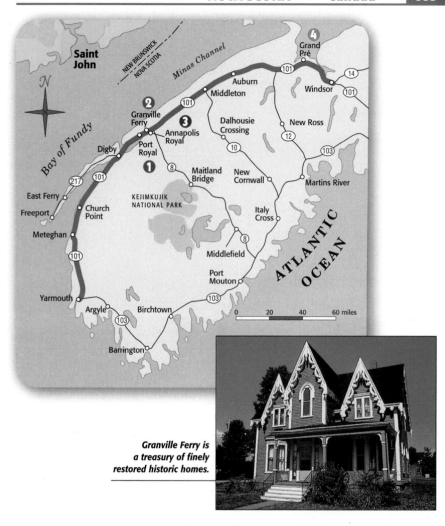

Granville Ferry is a treasury of finely restored historic homes.

settlers. The gardens themselves are divided into themes, including the Governor's Garden, the Rose Garden and the Innovative Garden, where new trends in plant material and garden techniques are demonstrated. Located 10 minutes southwest of Annapolis Royal is Upper Clements Theme Park, the area's newest attraction; its mission is to educate the public about Nova Scotia's legends, history and geography. The park ingeniously applies different types of rides, such as rollercoasters and train rides, as educational tools. Local crafts are also showcased.

❹ Grand Pré National Historic Site of Canada

The Grand Pré National Historic Site, which features a memorial church and museum, pays tribute to the Acadian settlers who made the village one of the most important in the region. In 1755, 40 years after the British took control of the area, the Acadians were deported when England and France declared war; many fled as far south as Louisiana. There is also a bust of Henry Wadsworth Longfellow, who captured the sorrow of the deportation in his poem, *Evangeline*.

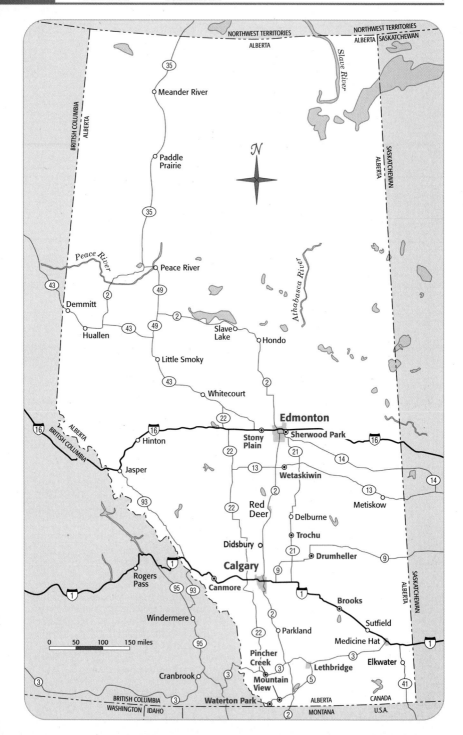

Brooks
Ⓐ *The Douglas Country Inn 2000*

A charming country inn invites guests to relax in casual luxury. Rooms are beautifully appointed; a suite with deck, fireplace and a deep soaker tub is available. Full country breakfasts and sherry nightcaps are complimentary; dinner is served at the licensed restaurant. Dinosaur National Park, one of the world's most prolific fossil grounds, is nearby. Hunters and fishers will like the cleaning facilities, freezer and kennel.

7 Rooms • Price range: $67-99
PO Box 236, Brooks, AB T1R 1B3
☎ **(403) 362-2873**

Calgary
Ⓐ *Calgary Westways Guest House*

The Calgary Westways Guest House is a wonderfully preserved and restored 1912 heritage house in one of the city's oldest districts. Box beam ceilings, leaded-glass windows and hardwood floors grace many of the common rooms and bedrooms. A cozy backyard deck overlooking a park lends a country-like ambience to the urban setting. Interesting shops and restaurants are just a short walk away on 4th Street.

5 Rooms • Price range: $74-124
216 25th Ave SW, Calgary, AB T2S 0L1
☎ **(403) 229-1758**

Calgary
Kensington Riverside Inn

This inn is a welcome addition to downtown Calgary. Situated in the trendy Kensington area, the location offers river and cityscape views from some rooms. Despite the central location there is a sense of being completely removed from the city's bustling core. Though classified as a B&B, the structure and design of the Kensington is more like a boutique hotel, ideal for corporate travelers or tourists.

19 Rooms • Price range: $214-224
1126 Memorial Dr NW, Calgary, AB T2N 3E3
☎ **(403) 228-4442**

Calgary
Ⓐ *Maison Hillcrest House*

On a hill close to trendy 4th Street, this 1914 Craftsman-style home has been immaculately kept. Common rooms feature beamed ceiling, Tiffany-style light fixtures and cabinets with leaded-glass doors. Rooms have private baths, free internet access.

4 Rooms • Price range: $80-120
600 Hillcrest Ave SW, Calgary, AB T2S 0M9
☎ **(403) 228-6164**

Calgary
Ⓐ *Inglewood Bed & Breakfast*

Located in one of Calgary's oldest neighborhoods, this Victorian home has gracious modern rooms, each with a private bath. Only minutes away are the Calgary Zoo, Stampede Park, and the city center, featuring the famous tower.

3 Rooms • Price range: $70-125
1006 8th Ave SE, Calgary, AB T2G 0M4
☎ **(403) 262-6570**

Calgary
⊛ *Paradise Acres Bed & Breakfast*

Spacious, contemporary home located on prairie land just outside the city. Comfortable seating areas and cheerful bedrooms, with ensuite or private bathrooms, feature pleasant homelike decor. A quiet countryside setting convenient to the city

5 Rooms • Price range: $75-85
243105 Paradise Rd, Calgary, AB T2M 4L5
☎ **(403) 248-4748**

Canmore
The Georgetown Inn

This contemporary Tudor-style inn offers the comforts of a B&B with the privacy of an old-fashioned inn. Each of the rooms has a view of the Rocky Mountains. Many of the antiques are from England as are the memorabilia in the pub-style lounge. Banff National Park and Lake Louise are a short drive away. Recreational activities nearby include kayaking, mountain climbing, skating and golf.

24 Rooms • Price range: $119-139
1101 Bow Valley Tr, Canmore, AB T1W 1N4
☎ **(403) 678-3439**

Canmore
⊛ *The Lady Macdonald Country Inn*

Only 15 minutes east of Banff but worlds away from the resort crowds, the Lady MacDonald has country inn charm and hotel-style amenities and services. The tastefully appointed guestrooms range from cozy to spacious, several have breathtaking views of the surrounding mountains. Enjoy rock climbing, skiing, canoeing and biking, then spend the evening relaxing in front of the parlor's fireplace.

11 Rooms • Price range: $145-210
1201 Bow Valley Tr, Canmore, AB T1W 1P5
☎ **(403) 678-3665**

Canmore
⊛ *McNeill Heritage Inn*

Set among the trees on the banks of the Bow River, this 1907 estate has been fully restored. Its many windows provide breathtaking views of the surrounding mountains. The guestrooms feature high ceilings, claw-foot tubs, down duvets and antique pine furniture. Hiking, biking and cross-country skiing are available right outside the door. Fishing, golf, rafting and dog-sledding, as well as historic and scenic sites, aren't far away.

5 Rooms • Price range: $145-155
500 Three Sisters Dr, Canmore, AB T1W 2P3
☎ **(403) 678-4884**

Drumheller
Inn at Heartwood Manor

 Originally built in 1921 as a boarding house, this gambrel-roofed inn has been completely renovated and outfitted with all the modern luxuries. Most of the spacious guestrooms have Jacuzzis and half of them have fireplaces. All rooms are furnished with antiques. The works of Western Canadian artists are on display in the inn. Local attractions include the Royal Tyrrell Museum and the remarkable badlands.

10 Rooms • Price range: $99-249
320 N Railway Ave E, Drumheller, AB T0J 0Y4
☎ **(403) 823-6495**

☒ Ⓓ

Drumheller
Heartwood Haven Country Inn

 This B&B, which is located only a short distance from downtown shops and restaurants, is conveniently close to other area attractions as well. Public spaces and guestrooms are creatively decorated. The spa offers the full range of treatments.

5 Rooms • Price range: $99-225
356 4th St W, Drumheller, AB T0J 0Y3
☎ **(403) 823-4956**

☒ ▣ Ⓩ Ⓓ

Drumheller
Newcastle Country Inn

 The Newcastle Country Inn is situated in a quiet residential area that is close to downtown shopping and restaurants. Guestrooms are pleasantly decorated with an eye to comfort. They all have queen-size beds and private baths.

11 Rooms • Price range: $80-100
1130 Newcastle Tr, Drumheller, AB T0J 0Y2
☎ **(403) 823-8356**

☒ Ⓩ ⒸⓋ Ⓓ

Drumheller
Taste The Past Bed & Breakfast

A large, beautifully restored circa 1910 home originally built by a coal baron. The guestrooms are all on the second floor and each of them has a private bath. The summer gardens are a lovely place to spend some time reading and relaxing.

3 Rooms • Price range: $70-85
281 2nd St W, Drumheller, AB T0J 0Y0
☎ **(403) 823-5889**

☒ Ⓩ Ⓚ ⒸⓋ Ⓓ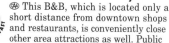

Edmonton
Glenora Bed & Breakfast Inn

Located in an old neighborhood renowned for its art galleries, stylish restaurants and upscale shops, the Glenora was built in 1912, and has been fully restored and decorated with a comfortable urban elegance. Large enough to offer privacy, but small enough to assure a warm and friendly stay, the inn offers individually designed guestrooms that are tastefully furnished with antiques. A full break-fast is served.

21 Rooms • Price range: $70-140
12327 102nd Ave, Edmonton, AB T5N 0L8
☎ **(780) 488-6766**

☒ ▣ Ⓚ Ⓓ

Edmonton
Union Bank Inn

 Luxurious down comforters, fireplaces, individual climate control and dataports in every room make the Union Bank Inn ideal for business or pleasure. The lobby level dining room serves fine cuisine in an incomparable setting. Ideally located.

34 Rooms • Price range: $119-255
10053 Jasper Ave, Edmonton, AB T5J 1S5
☎ **(780) 423-3600**

Ⓨ ☒ ✚ Ⓓ Ⓢ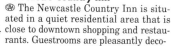

Lethbridge

◆ ◆ ⓐ *Chellsea House Bed & Breakfast*
Comfortable rooms, varying in style
and size, in a contemporary setting.

☒ ☒ 🖋 D

4 Rooms • Price range: $50-100
9 Dalhousie Rd W, Lethbridge, AB T1K 3X2
☎ (403) 381-1325

Mountain View

◆ ◆ ⓐ *Mountain View Inn*
An affiliate of the Rocky Ridge Inn
down the road, this is an ideal location
for family reunions, weddings or simply
a night in a picturesque setting. Guests

eat all meals at the Rocky Ridge and also have
use of their recreational facilities

7 Rooms • Price range: $95-115
PO Box 117, Mountain View, AB T0K 1N0
☎ (403) 653-1599

☒ ☒ 𝒦 🖋 D

Mountain View

◆ ◆ ⓐ *Rocky Ridge Country Resort*
This is an attractively decorated contemporary inn with rustic charm. There
are well-appointed common areas with
wood-burning fireplaces. Guestrooms

vary in size and style, three have private baths.
Extras include a sauna, a hot tub and a pool.

7 Rooms • Price range: $80-95
Box 117, Mountain View, AB T0K 1N0
☎ (403) 653-2350

☒ ☒ 𝒦 🖋 D

Pincher Creek

◆ ◆ ⓐ *Aspen Grove B&B*
The Aspen Grove B&B is a true gem
in set in the foothills of the Rocky
Mountains, convenient to the skiing at
Candle Mountain. The serenity of the

setting and the pastoral views from the rooms at
this inn are well worth the drive.

4 Rooms • Price range: $40-80
PO Box 250, Pincher Creek, AB T0K 1W0
☎ (403) 627-2928

☒ ☒ 𝒦 🖋 D

Sherwood Park

◆ ⓐ *The Berry Inn Bed & Breakfast*
All the facilities in this log house are
set up for guests with reduced mobility.

4 Rooms • Price range: $55-75
5127 Range Rd 203,
Sherwood Park, AB T8G 1E8
☎ (780) 662-3313

🏨 ☒ 🖋 D

Stony Plain

◆ ◆ ⓐ *The Lakehouse Bed & Breakfast*
This modern country home offers warm
hospitality in a peaceful lakefront environment. A canoe and a row-boat are
available for guests who wish to spend

some time on the lake. A private two-bedroom
suite with a kitchen is also available.

3 Rooms • Price range: $50-70
Box 56, Site 8, RR2, Stony Plain, AB T7Z 1X2
☎ (780) 963-9330

☒ ▣ ☒ 𝒦 🖋 D

Trochu

◆ ◆ ⓐ *St. Ann Ranch Bed & Breakfast*
This centennial farmhouse, located on
what was the original town site before
the railway arrived, is operated by
descendants of the original owners.

Charming old-fashioned decor awaits guests at
this adult-oriented property

7 Rooms • Price range: $50-85
St. Ann Ranch; PO Box 670, Trochu, AB T0M 2C0
☎ (403) 442-3924

☒ ▣ ☒ 𝒦 🖋 D

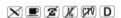

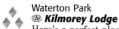

Waterton Park

ⒶＡ *Kilmorey Lodge*

Here's a perfect place to enjoy spectacular scenery and wildlife, and outstanding recreational opportunities. The lodge, which is located on the shore of Waterton Lake and surrounded by towering, snowcapped peaks, was built by the first warden of Waterton Lakes National Park. Each of the charming guestrooms has its own personality. The dining room offers a first-class menu and an extensive list of top-quality Canadian wines.

23 Rooms • Price range: $93-144
117 Evergreen Ave, Waterton Park, AB T0K 2M0
☎ **(403) 859-2334**

Ⓧ Ⓩ Ⓚ Ⓟ Ⓓ

Wetaskiwin
ⒶＡ *The Karriage House Bed & Breakfast 1908*

A wonderfully preserved house with charming Country-style decor and a great assortment of antiques and collectibles. A quaint little cottage in the garden is available for guests who desire a more private environment.

4 Rooms • Price range: $55-85
5215 47th St, Wetaskiwin, AB T9A 1E1
☎ **(780) 352-5996**

Ⓧ Ⓩ Ⓚ Ⓟ Ⓓ

Notes:

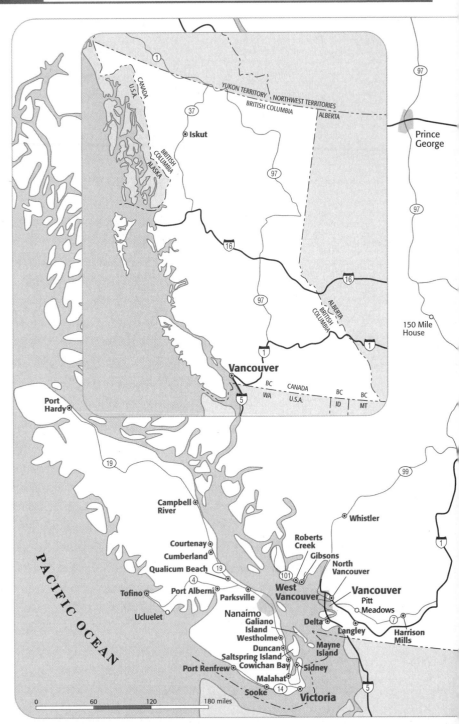

PACIFIC OCEAN

Prince George

150 Mile House

Iskut

Vancouver

Port Hardy

Campbell River

Whistler

Courtenay
Cumberland
Qualicum Beach

Roberts Creek
Gibsons
North Vancouver

Tofino

Port Alberni

Parksville

West Vancouver

Vancouver
Pitt Meadows

Ucluelet

Nanaimo
Galiano Island
Westholme
Duncan
Saltspring Island
Cowichan Bay
Port Renfrew
Malahat
Sooke

Delta

Langley

Harrison Mills

Mayne Island

Sidney

Victoria

YUKON TERRITORY
NORTHWEST TERRITORIES
BRITISH COLUMBIA
ALBERTA

CANADA
U.S.A.

BRITISH COLUMBIA
ALASKA

ALBERTA
BRITISH COLUMBIA

BC CANADA
WA U.S.A.
BC ID
BC MT

0   60   120   180 miles

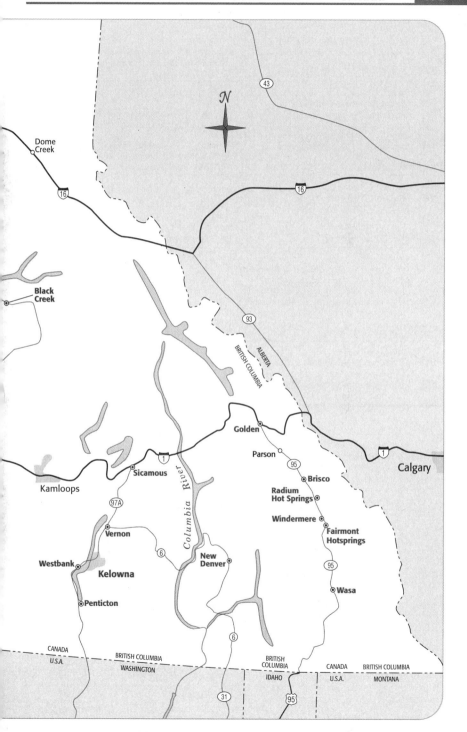

Black Creek

◆ 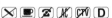 *Tudor Acres Bed & Breakfast*

This Tudor-style home has rooms and one suite with a kitchen and bathroom.

3 Rooms • Price range: $50-80
2065 Endall Rd, Black Creek, BC V9J 1G8
☎ **(250) 337-5764**

Brisco

◆ ◆ *Inn Amongst Friends*

A modern, log-frame, stucco house on a small acreage set back from the highway. Good-size guestrooms have comfortable futon beds, duvets, and a few simple homelike touches. Lovely outdoor decks offer splendid views of Columbia Valley.

4 Rooms • Price range: $55-95
4930 Nelson Rd, Brisco, BC V0A 1B0
☎ **(250) 346-3366**

Campbell River

◆ *Arbour's Guest House*

Call for information.

4 Rooms • Price range: $65-95
375 S Murphy St, Campbell River, BC V9W 1Y8
☎ **(250) 287-9873**

Courtenay

◆ ◆ *Greystone Manor Bed & Breakfast*

The secluded 1918 home is situated on a quiet piece of land overlooking Comox Bay. During the spring and summer the spectacular English gardens are awash with colorful blooms. Pleasant guestrooms and gracious hosts in an idyllic setting.

3 Rooms • Price range: $65-85
4014 Haas Rd, Courtenay, BC V9N 8H9
☎ **(250) 338-1422**

Cowichan Bay

◆ ◆ ⓐ *Dream Weaver Bed & Breakfast*

A towering, contemporary Victorian-style home right in the heart of town, featuring private entrances, gas fireplaces and whirlpool tubs. It is situated very close to some of the town's best shops and restaurants.

4 Rooms • Price range: $55-130
1682 Botwood Ln, Cowichan Bay, BC V0R 1N0
☎ **(250) 748-7688**

Cumberland

◆ ◆ ⓐ *Wellington House Bed & Breakfast*

The expansive backyard garden of this modern home features the remains of an original scale used to weigh coal wagons during the early part of the century. Each of the nicely appointed guest suites includes a private sitting room.

4 Rooms • Price range: $60-85
2593 Derwent Ave, Cumberland, BC V0R 1S0
☎ **(250) 336-8809**

Delta

◆◆ *River Run Cottages*

ⓐ Clustered near a community of houseboats, these individual cottages stand by the delta of the mighty Fraser River. Accommodations include an wonderfully crafted floating cottage or two cottages on the bank with a private boardwalk deck with river views. In the historic fishing village of Ladner, guests can bird-watch, go kayaking or biking, and admire the sunsets beyond the returning fishing boats.

4 Rooms • Price range: $150-210
4551 River Rd W, Delta, BC V4K 1R9
☎ **(604) 946-7778**

Delta
🏵 *Southlands House "By The Sea"*

This expansive country estate overlooks the ocean and the Boundary Bay Regional Park. The area is an internationally significant Pacific flyway, a must-see for birders. Guests can enjoy the spacious landscaped grounds or take a walk to Centennial Beach. The home is located just 30 minutes from Vancouver, 20 from the airport, and 10 from the ferries to Victoria. Each room has a private bath, fireplace, and ocean view.

6 Rooms • Price range: $135-195
1160 Boundary Bay Rd, Delta, BC V4L 2P6
☎ **(604) 943-1846**

Delta
🏵 *Erika's on Twelfth Bed & Breakfast*

Set in a residential setting just a block or so from local shops and restaurants. The homelike setting offers two rooms upstairs and one room downstairs with a patio door that leads out to large deck area. Inquire about trying the on-site beauty salon.

3 Rooms • Price range: $95-120
5447 12th Ave, Delta, BC V4M 2B2
☎ **(604) 943-4378**

Delta
🏵 *Primrose Hill Guest House*

Built in 1913 and moved to its present location in 1985, this Craftsman-style home was converted into a B&B in 1994. Today, this grand old home welcomes guests into its spacious, graceful rooms and coddles them in warm and cozy bedrooms.

6 Rooms • Price range: $75-145
4919 48th Ave, Delta, BC V4K 1V4
☎ **(604) 940-8867**

Duncan
🏵 *Fairburn Farm Country Manor*

Built in 1884, Fairburn Farm was known as a millionaire's country estate. Today the working farm B&B invites guests to help out with the daily chores.

Guestrooms are pleasantly decorated, two have gas fireplaces. A truly unique experience.

6 Rooms • Price range: $95-150
3310 Jackson Rd, Duncan, BC V9L 6N7
☎ **(250) 746-4637**

Fairmont Hot Springs
🏵 *McMillan Chalet B&B*

A warm welcome awaits guests at the McMillan Chalet B&B. The comfortable guestrooms are individually decorated and extremely cozy. The friendly hosts are well known for their wonderful breakfasts.

The nearby hot springs are popular with guest looking to relax.

4 Rooms • Price range: $65-95
5021 Fairmont Close,
Fairmont Hot Springs, BC V0B 1L0
☎ **(250) 345-9553**

Galiano Island
🏵 *Woodstone Country Inn*

This modern country inn is located in a pastoral setting with sweeping views of nearby farmland. Through the surrounding nine acres meander paths around towering cedars and a marsh alive with birds. Fresh fish is served every evening in the award-winning dining room or adjacent lounge and terrace. The Dogwood Boardroom is available for meetings. Guests can spend their days kayaking, fishing for salmon or beachcombing.

12 Rooms • Price range: $105-130
743 Georgeson Bay Rd,
Galiano Island, BC V0N 1P0
☎ **(250) 539-2022**

Galiano Island
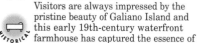
The Bellhouse Inn

Visitors are always impressed by the pristine beauty of Galiano Island and this early 19th-century waterfront farmhouse has captured the essence of this special place. Very cozy, contemporary rooms and stunning scenery.

4 Rooms • Price range: $125-195
29 Farmhouse Rd, Galiano Island, BC V0N 1P0
☎ **(250) 539-5667**

Gibsons

Bonniebrook Lodge Bed & Breakfast

Although Gibsons is probably more famous for The Beachcombers television series than it is for B&Bs, the Bonnybrook Lodge is working hard to change all of that. Recent renovations have only improved on what was already terrific. All of the amenities guests have come to expect from first-class inns have been integrated into this 1920s waterfront home. The main floor houses marvelous Chez Phillipe restaurant.

7 Rooms • Price range: $140-180
1532 Oceanbeach Esplanade, RR5,
Gibsons, BC V0N 1V5
☎ **(604) 886-2887**

Golden

Kapristo Lodge

This secluded family-style European lodge, with its distinctive Canadian flavor, is perched on the side of Kapristo Mountain, offering great views from some of the tastefully decorated rooms. Guests can enjoy the peaks from an open-air terrace, complete with sauna and Jacuzzi. For thrill seekers, an eight-day adventure package is available, including white-water rafting, horseback riding and heli-hiking.

6 Rooms • Price range: $175-240
1297 Campbell Rd, Golden, BC V0A 1H0
☎ **(250) 344-6048**

Golden

Columbia Valley Lodge

This Alpine-style chalet is located in a wetlands area, so it is of great interest to birders. The guestrooms all have a large bathroom. Each second-floor room has a private balcony with panoramic views of the mountain valley.

12 Rooms • Price range: $50-75
2304 Hwy 95 S, Golden, BC V0A 1H0
☎ **(250) 348-2508**

Harrison Mills
Historic Fenn Lodge Bed & Breakfast

Originally built in 1903 as a weekend retreat for friends and family, this lodge retains many of its original guestrooms and furnishings. The surrounding woodlands are a nature lover's delight.

7 Rooms • Price range: $110-160
15500 Morris Valley Rd,
Harrison Mills, BC V0M 1L0
☎ **(604) 796-9798**

Iskut

Red Goat Lodge

The Red Goat Lodge is tucked away in a remote wilderness area just a few steps from Eddontenajon Lake. The property is also the site for a small RV park and a youth hostel. Guestrooms offer simple decor with a nice homelike ambience.

4 Rooms • Price range: $73-95
Box 101, Iskut, BC V0J 1K0
☎ **(250) 234-3261**

Kelowna
⊕ *The Grapevine Bed & Breakfast*

Surrounded by orchards, this exceptional home offers country charm close to the city. Located in the Okanagan Valley, it is close to wineries, golf courses and beaches. From a private patio in the garden guests can admire the great number of birds that frequent the feeder and splash in the waterfall. In the winter the famous powder of Big White and Silver Star Mountains is a treat for skiers.

4 Rooms • Price range: $85-105
2621 Longhill Rd, Kelowna, BC V1V 2G5
☎ **(250) 860-5580**

Kelowna
⊕ *Otella's Guest House*

Situated in a parklike setting with lovely views of the valley and surrounding mountains. Various patios and extensive gardens add to the appeal of the guest house. A trained chef prepares the gourmet breakfasts.

4 Rooms • Price range: $95-125
42 Altura Rd, Kelowna, BC V1V 1B6
☎ **(250) 763-4922**

Langley
⊕ *Eagle's Reach on the Bluff at Fort Langley Bed & Breakfast*

This magnificent home is situated on a bluff with panoramic views of Fraser River and the mountains. It is surrounded by six wooded and landscaped acres, which include a pitch-and-putt practice golf course. Here guests often have impromptu sightings of bald eagles and deer. There are plenty of on-site entertainment facilities. A full Coach House sleeps six. Historic Fort Langley is just minutes away.

4 Rooms • Price range: $80-135
24658 87th Ave, Langley, BC V1M 2R3
☎ **(604) 888-4470**

Malahat
⊕ *The Aerie Resort*

This Mediterranean-style luxury retreat is located in the mountains, providing spectacular views over the ocean. The decor is elegant and rather fanciful, with rococo furnishings and soft pastel colors. In the dining room, guests can enjoy the freshest in Northwest cuisine with a French touch, while also savoring the stunning view. Sometimes visitors join the chef in hunting for mushrooms growing on the surrounding 10 acres. The waters in the area are a playground for seals, orcas and gray whales. The Aerie even has a helicopter pad on-site for high-flying adventurers.

23 Rooms • Price: $285
600 Ebadora Ln, Malahat, BC V0R 2L0
☎ **(250) 743-7115**

Mayne Island
⊕ *Oceanwood Country Inn*

A mock-Tudor home on 10 acres of forested land overlooking Navy Channel.

12 Rooms • Price range: $149-329
630 Dinner Bay Rd, Mayne Island, BC V0N 2J0
☎ **(250) 539-5074**

New Denver
⊛ *Sweet Dreams Guesthouse & Dining*
This inn offers modest and contemporary room decor, wicker furniture and duvets.

⊠ ⊠ ⊠ ⊠ D

5 Rooms • Price range: $45-85
702 Eldorado St, New Denver, BC V0G 1S0
☎ **(250) 358-2415**

North Vancouver
⊛ *A Gazebo in the Garden B&B*
Built in 1910, this home is a fine example of Frank Lloyd Wright's Prairie-style architecture. In the spring and summer the gardens are a sight to

behold and for those who enjoy a bit of solitude there is a charming gazebo.

4 Rooms • Price range: $100-200
310 St James Rd, North Vancouver, BC V7N 1L2
☎ **(604) 983-3331**

⊠ ⊠ ⊠ D

Parksville
⊛ *Marina View B&B*
Overlooking the ocean, this inn offers rooms with a personal touch.

⊠ ⊠ ⊠ ⊠ D

3 Rooms • Price range: $70-95
895 Glenhale Crescent, Parksville, BC V9P 1Z7
☎ **(250) 248-9308**

Penticton
⊛ *Riordan House Bed & Breakfast*
Built in 1921, this classic home is known as "the house that rum built" as the original owner was a well known bootlegger. The current owner of the

B&B has an impressive collection of gesso art from the years 1887 to 1936.

3 Rooms • Price range: $50-85
689 Winnipeg St, Penticton, BC V2A 5N1
☎ **(250) 493-5997**

⊠ ⊠ D

Port Alberni
⊛ *Cedar Wood Lodge*
This thoroughly modern lodge features comfortable guestrooms designed with both the business and vacation traveler in mind. All rooms have queen-size beds

with duvets, air-massage tubs, gas-log fireplaces and many other comforts.

8 Rooms • Price range: $115-125
5895 River Rd, Port Alberni, BC V9Y 6Z5
☎ **(250) 724-6800**

⊠ ⊠ D

Port Hardy
⊛ *Hamilton's Bed & Breakfast*
The owners of this suburban B&B serve continental breakfast.

⊠ ⊠ ⊠ ⊠ D

3 Rooms • Price range: $48-65
9415 Mayor's Way, Port Hardy, BC V0N 2P0
☎ **(250) 949-6638**

Port Renfrew
⊛ *Arbutus Beach Lodge*
Located along the waterfront and beach, this inn offers modest-size rooms.

⊠ ⊠ ⊠ D

5 Rooms • Price range: $55-95
5 Queesto Dr, Port Renfrew, BC V0S 1K0
☎ **(250) 647-5458**

Qualicum Beach
⊛ *Bahari Bed & Breakfast*
A Japanese theme influences the decor of this establishment. The guestrooms are comfortable and three of them have spectacular views overlooking Georgia

Strait. There is also a hot tub secluded up on a hilltop.

4 Rooms • Price range: $105-175
5101 Island Hwy W, Qualicum Beach, BC V9K1Z1
☎ **(250) 752-9278**

⊠ ⊠ ⊠ D

Radium Hot Springs
⊛ *Village Country Inn and Tea Room*
This modern Victorian inn has European hospitality and hand-crafted furniture.

🎐 ∩ ⊠ ◪ D

13 Rooms • Price range: $95-115
7557 Canyon Ave, Radium Hot Springs,
BC V0A 1M0
☎ **(250) 347-9392**

Roberts Creek
⊛ *Welcome Inn Bed & Breakfast*
The comfortable rooms at this inn are in the house or in a garden cottage.

⊠ 🕿 🄺 🄿 D

4 Rooms • Price range: $75-100
1176 Flume Rd, Roberts Creek, BC V0N 2W0
☎ **(604) 740-0318**

Saltspring Island
⊛ *Anne's Oceanfront Hideaway B&B*
All rooms in this newly constructed inn boast an ocean view—many have a private balcony—and feature a unique hydro-massage tub. The wraparound veranda also provides breathtaking views of the water and mountains. Guests have only a short stroll down an ocean path to canoe, swim, suntan or lounge among the arbutus and oak trees. This adult-oriented home is also allergy-aware; the owners can accommodate special diets.

∩ ⊠ 🕿 🄿 D

4 Rooms • Price range: $185-250
168 Simson Rd, Saltspring Island, BC V8K 1E2
☎ **(250) 537-0851**

Saltspring Island
⊛ *The Old Farmhouse Bed & Breakfast*
Rooms have private bath and a balcony or patio. Near a lake, golf and tennis.

⊠ 🕿 🄺 🄿 D

4 Rooms • Price: $170
1077 Northend Rd, Saltspring Island, BC V8K 1L9
☎ **(250) 537-4113**

Sicamous
⊛ *Rainbow Valley Bed & Breakfast*
Accommodations in this modern stucco house are enhanced by a fully equipped guest kitchen and recreation room. For larger groups and families there is a 1,500-square-foot, three-bedroom apartment and a two-bedroom cottage. Breakfast is an all-you-can-eat extravaganza that includes homemade breads and preserves. The beautiful Shuswap and Mara lakes are very popular summer resort areas with Calgarians.

⊠ 🕿 🄺 D

4 Rooms • Price range: $65-105
1409 Rauma Rd, Sicamous, BC V0E 2V0
☎ **(250) 836-3268**

Sidney
⊛ *Shoal Harbour Inn*
This unique heritage log home was built in 1920 for B.C.'s lieutenant-governor. The Country-style luxury suites are well appointed and offer a wealth of historic detail. The halls are finished in great panels of native fir. "Euro-Pacific" cuisine is served on the sundown terrace overlooking the harbor. The inn provides private cruises for up to five guests aboard its yacht and a variety of salmon fishing charters are also available.

⊠ 🄺 D

7 Rooms • Price range: $129-299
2328 Harbour Rd, Sidney, BC V8L 2P8
☎ **(250) 656-6622**

Sooke

 ⌘ *Sooke Harbour House*
This inn, with terraces and a garden of
edible flowers, overlooks ocean and peaks.

28 Rooms • Price range: $297-512
1528 Whiffen Spit Rd, Sooke, BC V0S 1N0
☎ **(250) 642-3421**

Sooke

⌘ *Ocean Wilderness Country Inn*
A secluded, comfortable B&B near the
town of Sooke, the Ocean Wilderness
Country Inn provides access to a natural setting of uncommon beauty. The
surrounding rain forest and views of the Strait
of Juan de Fuca are simply unforgettable.

9 Rooms • Price range: $110-180
109 W Coast Rd, Sooke, BC V0S 1N0
☎ **(250) 646-2116**

Tofino

⌘ *Cable Cove Inn*
Contemporary decor is featured in this
thoroughly modern inn. All of the pleasantly spacious guestrooms have fireplaces and private decks. Some of the
decks feature hot tubs and all of them have a
wonderful view of Clayoquot Sound. Every
morning, juice and a hot beverage are left outside the bedroom doors and breakfast is served
later in the dining room. Guests also have the
use of a kitchen stocked for late-night snacks

6 Rooms • Price range: $160-205
201 Main St, Tofino, BC V0R 2Z0
☎ **(250) 725-4236**

Vancouver

⌘ *Barclay House in the West End*
One of the few remaining houses in
Vancouver's West End district this one
is a true gem. The owners of the recently renovated 1904 Victorian home have
created an antique-decorated B&B that has the
genuine ambience of a family home. Suites have
twin, queen- or king-size beds, their own TV
with VCR, and private baths (some with a claw-
foot tub). Private entrances, wet bars, and gas
fireplaces are also featured in some suites.

5 Suites • Price range: $125-225
1351 Barclay St, Vancouver, BC V6E 1H6
☎ **(604) 605-1351**

Vancouver

Cherub Inn
Built in 1913, this grand and carefully
restored house features an assortment
of stained-glass windows. Its large,
comfortable guestrooms are decorated
in rich wood accents. Located in a quiet neighborhood, it has easy access to the beaches, book-
stores, cafés, Granville Island Market and
downtown. The proprietors can communicate
in six languages. All the beds are queen-size
and have designer linens.

4 Rooms • Price range: $124-175
2546 W 6th Ave, Vancouver, BC V6K 1W5
☎ **(604) 733-3166**

Vancouver
ⓦ *Johnson Heritage House Bed & Breakfast*

If home restoration is a labor of love then it can be said that the innkeepers of this 1920s Craftsman-style house are passionate about their B&B. They also have an extraordinary collection of antiques, which includes carousel animals, gramophones, clocks and coffee grinders as well as furniture and Oriental carpets. The grounds around the B&B have been landscaped. Breakfasts are guaranteed to be healthy and hearty.

4 Rooms • Price range: $105-180
2278 W 34th Ave, Vancouver, BC V6M 1G6
☎ **(604) 266-4175**

Vancouver
ⓦ *"O Canada" House*

The Canadian national anthem was written in this 1897 Queen Anne-style home. The city council gave the owners the right to operate the inn in exchange for maintaining the authenticity of the building. It is located in a quiet neighborhood, only steps away from downtown shops and a few blocks from Stanley Park. Besides rooms, a huge penthouse is available with two queen-size beds. Every morning a gourmet breakfast is served.

5 Rooms • Price range: $158-225
1114 Barclay St, Vancouver, BC V6E 1H1
☎ **(604) 688-0555**

Vancouver
West End Guest House

A renovated pink exterior and intimate guestrooms furnished in Victorian antiques are the hallmarks of this old-fashioned guest house. The parlor, veranda, sundeck and garden offer guests a choice of restful spaces. Located downtown, it is one block from cafés and boutiques, and six blocks from the beaches, trails and renowned aquarium at Stanley Park. Inquire about the resident ghost (if you dare).

8 Rooms • Price range: $105-225
1362 Haro St, Vancouver, BC V6E 1G2
☎ **(604) 681-2889**

Vancouver
Camilla House Bed & Breakfast

This New York-style home is located in the tree-lined Kitsilano area, close to public transit, the University of British Columbia, Nitobe Japanese Gardens and beaches. It features attractively decorated guestrooms with just a touch of the Far East.

5 Rooms • Price range: $65-145
2538 W 13th Ave, Vancouver, BC V6X 2T1
☎ **(604) 737-2687**

Vancouver
ⓦ *Chelsea Cottage B&B*

Located in a lush and well-treed residential neighborhood, within easy walking distance to area restaurants, shopping and transit. Guest rooms are lovingly decorated with many little "extras" to guarantee a pleasant visit.

4 Rooms • Price range: $95-150
2143 W 46th Ave, Vancouver, BC V6M 2L2
☎ **(604) 266-2681**

Vancouver
◆ ◆ **Columbia Cottage**

Lovely gardens surround this charming neighborhood B&B with pleasant guestrooms. Guests who left the car at home will appreciate being only a few minutes from downtown and within walking distance of Granville Island Market.

5 Rooms • Price range: $125-135
205 W 14th Ave, Vancouver, BC V5Y 1X2
☎ (604) 874-5327

Vancouver
◆ ◆ **Windsor Guest House B&B**

This grand old Victorian manor is located in one of Vancouver's oldest neighborhoods. Inside guests will find simple, comfortable rooms and a friendly multi-lingual staff. The central location makes it convenient to all the sights of the city.

10 Rooms • Price range: $65-145
325 W 11th Ave, Vancouver, BC V5Y 1T3
☎ (604) 872-3060

Vernon
◆ ◆ **LakeSide Illahee Inn**

A contemporary resort-like inn, the Illahee is located on beautiful Kalamalka Lake, which offers a sandy beach with excellent swimming and canoeing. Surrounded by 3,300 acres of provincial park, the setting offers nature at its best. Each guestroom has a private bath, private entrance and access to a large semi-private balcony with lake view. The living room features red cedar cathedral ceilings and a picture-window wall.

5 Rooms • Price range: $119-169
15010 Tamarack Dr, Vernon, BC V1B 2E1
☎ (250) 260-7896

Vernon
◆ ◆ **The Tuck Inn Bed & Breakfast**

Some things just keep getting better with age and the The Tuck Inn happens to be one of them. Built around the early 1900s, this pleasant home was expanded in 1969 and underwent extensive renovations in 1992 when it opened as a B&B. Many of the original details of the house have been carefully preserved while additions such as the tea room's circular fireplace have enhanced its historic charm.

5 Rooms • Price range: $50-85
3101 Pleasant Valley Rd, Vernon, BC V1T 4L2
☎ (250) 545-3252

Vernon
◆ ◆ **The Maria Rose Bed & Breakfast**

A private homelike B&B situated between the town of Vernon and Silver Star Mountain Resort. Every guestroom has a private entrance, but due to the hillside setting there are a number of stairs to navigate. Breakfast is served in the main house.

4 Rooms • Price range: $50-80
8083 Aspen Rd, Vernon, BC V1B 3M9
☎ (250) 549-4773

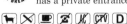

Victoria
 *Abbeymoore Manor Bed & Breakfast*

The Abbeymoore Manor is a fine example of Edwardian residential architecture. Located in the center of the historic Rockland neighborhood of Victoria, this home, which once served as the residence of the provincial lieutenant-governor, has been renovated and is now a popular B&B. Guests who desire more independence and privacy may choose to stay on the self-contained main floor or in the penthouse suites.

7 Rooms • Price range: $99-245
1470 Rockland Ave, Victoria, BC V8S 1W2
☎ **(250) 370-1470**

Victoria
Abigail's Hotel

This distinctive 1930s Tudor-style residence is surrounded by colorful English gardens. Guests can choose from simple corner and country rooms or the more extravagant "celebration" rooms, which feature a king-size bed, a marble-framed double Jacuzzi and a fireplace. Some of the most luxurious rooms are found in the adjacent Coach House. Guests can expect a wonderful breakfast, as the chef used to work in the Empress Hotel.

22 Rooms • Price range: $199-329
906 McClure St, Victoria, BC V8V 3E7
☎ **(250) 388-5363**

Victoria
Andersen House Bed & Breakfast

Formerly the residence of a sea captain, this charming Queen Anne-style home successfully blends rich historic detail with comfortable, contemporary furnishings and original art. Most rooms are quite spacious, each with its own designated balcony, hardwood floors, and private entrance. The surrounding Victorian gardens are well tended and contain century-old fruit trees, sculptures and, of course, flowers.

4 Rooms • Price range: $175-250
301 Kingston St, Victoria, BC V8V 1V5
☎ **(250) 388-4565**

Victoria
The Beaconsfield Inn

This Registered Designated Heritage Building was built in 1905 by a former mayor. The rooms reflect their Edwardian heritage, with leaded-glass windows, Oriental carpets, wainscoting, mahogany wood floors and fine antiques. Some rooms have a fireplace, a Jacuzzi tub and a chandelier. A wicker-furnished conservatory, lush with greenery and a trickling fountain, is a perfect spot for relaxing.

9 Rooms • Price range: $239-325
998 Humboldt St, Victoria, BC V8V 2Z8
☎ **(250) 384-4044**

Victoria
Dreemskerry Heritage Home

Built in 1932 as a wedding gift for the daughter of a lumber baron, the Georgian-Revival mansion has retained much of its original splendor. Very spacious guestrooms and common areas feature elegant window treatments, antique furnishings and Oriental carpets. Some of the guestrooms have private decks overlooking the wonderfully landscaped gardens. A full English breakfast is served in the dining room.

4 Rooms • Price range: $100-145
1509 Rockland Ave, Victoria, BC V8S 1W3
☎ (250) 384-4014

Victoria
A Haterleigh Heritage Inn

From the moment guests step onto the remarkable front porch of this 1901 Victorian masterpiece they will sense that they are about to experience something special. From the stunning porch pillars and stained-glass windows in the parlor to the duvets on the antique beds of the extra spacious guestrooms, The Haterleigh leaves a lasting impression. Personal service, fabulous breakfasts and minutes from the harbor.

6 Rooms • Price range: $217-333
243 Kingston St, Victoria, BC V8V 1V5
☎ (250) 384-9995

Victoria
Holland House Inn

Close to downtown Victoria, this elegant inn has a subtle Mediterranean flavor. Deep jewel tones, floral patterned upholstery and Oriental carpets grace the inn's public and private rooms. The romantic café-style breakfast room opens onto a private little patio with a charming Italian wall fountain. Comfortable guestrooms with luxurious appointments feature sitting areas, fireplaces and balconies or patios.

17 Rooms • Price range: $100-300
595 Michigan St, Victoria, BC V8V 1S7
☎ (250) 384-6644

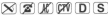

Victoria
⑳ *Markham House Bed & Breakfast*

A Tudor house, sitting on a 10-acre estate with landscaped gardens, tall trees and a picturesque trout pond, this B&B is located in a small coastal community between Victoria and the rugged West Coast beaches. Guests enjoy the internationally famous marine and alpine trails, whale watching, salmon fishing and kayaking. A 50-year-old secluded cottage offers a romantic escape with its deck, whirlpool, and kitchenette.

4 Rooms • Price range: $95-195
1853 Connie Rd, Victoria, BC V9C 4C2
☎ (250) 642-7542

Victoria
Prior House B&B Inn

Formerly the home of one of British Columbia's lieutenant-governors, the Prior House B&B is indubitably one of Victoria's finest lodgings. The regal mansion is surrounded by gardens. Inside it offers the refined ambience of a gilded past with the comforts and conveniences of the present. Guest accommodations are elegantly appointed with quality antiques and fine bedding, each with its own unique features.

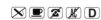

8 Rooms • Price range: $160-285
620 St. Charles St, Victoria, BC V8S 3N7
☎ **(250) 592-8847**

Victoria
Ryan's Bed & Breakfast

This 1892 tastefully restored heritage home reflects the atmosphere of a bygone era. It is situated in the historic James Bay District, within walking distance of the Inner Harbour and downtown. The public areas feature lace curtains, cabinets with fine china and oil paintings in heavy, ornate gilded frames. Guests are treated to a hearty Irish breakfast complete with homemade scones.

6 Rooms • Price range: $135-185
224 Superior St, Victoria, BC V8V 1T3
☎ **(250) 389-0012**

Victoria
Heathergate House Bed & Breakfast

This house features antiques and Mediterranean-style gardens. At the front of the property is a two-bedroom English-style cottage with a private garden patio and full kitchen. Set in the James Bay District just blocks from the Inner Harbor.

5 Rooms • Price range: $120-135
122 Simcoe St, Victoria, BC V8V 1K4
☎ **(250) 383-0068**

Victoria
Humboldt House Bed & Breakfast

Near downtown, this elegant 1895 home was renovated in Victorian style.

 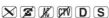

5 Rooms • Price range: $245-315
867 Humboldt St, Victoria, BC V8V 2Z6
☎ **(250) 383-0152**

Victoria
Iris Garden Country Manor Bed & Breakfast

Named for the more than 3,000 irises growing around the B&B. The charming character home has large comfortable guest rooms with down duvets and views of the three wooded acres of countryside. Just minutes from Buchart Gardens.

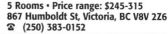

4 Rooms • Price range: $110-160
5360 W Saanich Rd, Victoria, BC V9E 1J8
☎ **(250) 744-2253**

Victoria
King's House Bed & Breakfast

An exceptional B&B in a quiet, residential area, close to the Gorge Vale Golf Course, offering beautifully appointed guestrooms. A full breakfast is served in the dining room overlooking the lush Victorian gardens.

4 Rooms • Price range: $115-155
945 Dellwood Rd, Victoria, BC V9A 6P2
☎ **(250) 382-2460**

Victoria
◆◆ ⑧ *Oak Bay Guest House*

This restored Tudor-style manor features attractive wood paneled walls and open beam ceilings. The cozy guestrooms have been charmingly decorated.

Guests can enjoy the beautifully landscaped yard. It's but a short walk to the ocean.

11 Rooms • Price range: $149-199
1052 Newport Ave, Victoria, BC V8S 5E3
☎ **(250) 598-3812**

Victoria
◆◆ ⑧ *Sunnymeade House Inn*

A comfortable country house in Cordova Bay, a few miles from downtown Victoria. Suites are available with a fireplaces, Jacuzzis, and ocean views. Adventurous

travelers will can take to the hiking trails in Mount Douglas National Park.

6 Rooms • Price range: $79-169
1002 Fenn Ave, Victoria, BC V8Y 1P3
☎ **(250) 658-1414**

Victoria
◆◆ ⑧ *Villa Blanca Bed & Breakfast*

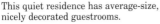

Graciously decorated home with comfortable guestrooms and a lovely yard.

4 Rooms • Price range: $75-150
4918 Cordova Bay Rd, Victoria, BC V8Y 2J5
☎ **(250) 658-4190**

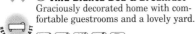

Victoria
◆ ⑧ *An Ocean View Bed & Breakfast*

This quiet residence has average-size, nicely decorated guestrooms.

6 Rooms • Price range: $100-175
715 Suffolk St, Victoria, BC V9A 3J5
☎ **(250) 386-7330**

Wasa
◆◆ ⑧ *Wasa Lakeside B&B Resort*

Casual, fun-loving, young family ambience. This lakeside property with a wonderful panoramic mountain view offers two guestrooms in main house

and two others in a cabin by the lake with private detached bathrooms. Perfect for kids.

4 Rooms • Price range: $90-150
4704 Spruce Rd, Wasa, BC V0B 2K0
☎ **(250) 422-3688**

West Vancouver
◆ ⑧ *Beachside Bed & Breakfast*

Located on a quiet cul-de-sac along a beach, this inn has a variety of rooms.

4 Rooms • Price range: $150-300
4208 Evergreen Ave,
West Vancouver, BC V7V 1H1
☎ **(604) 922-7773**

Westbank
◆◆ ⑧ *Chateau Christian Laurenn Bed & Breakfast*

An unobstructed panoramic view of the city, Okanagan Lake and the mountains can be seen from the B&B's four different dining areas and from the hillside terrace where guests can enjoy a five-course breakfast or afternoon espresso. Rooms are decorated in Battenburg lace and mahogany furniture. Downtown Kelowna is a short drive away.

2 Rooms • Price range: $119-159
3542 Ranch Rd, Westbank, BC V4T 1A1
☎ **(250) 768-9695**

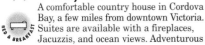

Westbank
⊛ *Wicklow by the Lake B&B*

Gardens extend to a private sandy beach at this home on Okanagan Lake.

 ☒ ☎ Ⓓ

4 Rooms • Price range: $85-95
1454 Green Bay Rd Westbank,
Westbank, BC V4T 2B8
☎ **(250) 768-1330**

Westholme
⊛ *The White House B&B*

This inn has large homey rooms. Breakfast is served in the kitchen.

☒ ☎ 𝒜 ℘ Ⓓ

3 Rooms • Price range: $65-79
7905 Trans-Canada Hwy,
Westholme, BC V0R 3C0
☎ **(250) 748-4480**

Whistler
⊛ *The Durlacher Hof Alpine Inn*

Hand-carved pine furniture and duvets await guests in this Austrian chalet.

ⓕ ☒ ☎ 𝒜 ℘ Ⓓ

8 Rooms • Price range: $225-305
7055 Nesters Rd, Whistler, BC V0N 1B0
☎ **(604) 932-1924**

Whistler
⊛ *Lorimer Ridge Pension*

This mountain lodge has been modeled after the European pensions, while still displaying a touch of the Canadian West Coast. The alpine pension has an outdoor whirlpool on a large deck with stunning views of Fissle, Blackcomb and Rainbow mountains. There are wood-burning fireplaces made with rocks from the river in both the living and billiards rooms. The lodge is only a short walk to the village and the ski hills.

☒ ☎ 𝒜 ℘ Ⓓ

8 Rooms • Price range: $190-255
6231 Piccolo Dr, Whistler, BC V0N1B6
☎ **(604) 938-9722**

Whistler
⊛ *Chalet Luise*

This charming alpine chalet has eight guestrooms, all of which feature pine furniture and down duvets. There's also a comfortable common room

upstairs where guests can sit and relax by the fire.

☒ ☎ 𝒜 ℘ Ⓓ

8 Rooms • Price range: $220-280
7461 Ambassador Crescent, Whistler, BC V0N 1B0
☎ **(604) 932-4187**

Windermere
⊛ *Emerald Grove Estate Bed & Breakfast Inn*

Spacious, elegant rooms and a veranda afford great views of valley and peaks.

ⓕ ☒ Ⓓ

5 Rooms • Price range: $83-124
1265 Sunridge Rd, Windermere, BC V0B 2L0
☎ **(250) 342-4431**

Windermere
⊛ *Windermere Creek Bed & Breakfast Cabins*

Sheltered in a valley on 107 wooded-acres, the Windermere Creek B&B is an ideal mountain hideaway throughout the year. Five secluded log cabins offer a variety of amenities. Four have loft bedrooms, kitchenettes and Jacuzzis. The 1887 log cabin has been renovated to include all the modern comforts. The main house offers a one-bedroom suite with sitting room. Picnic lunches can be arranged for those who wish to go exploring.

☒ ▭ ☎ 𝒜 ℘ Ⓓ

6 Rooms • Price range: $80-105
1658 Windermere Loop Rd,
Windermere, BC V0B 2L0
☎ **(250) 342-0356**

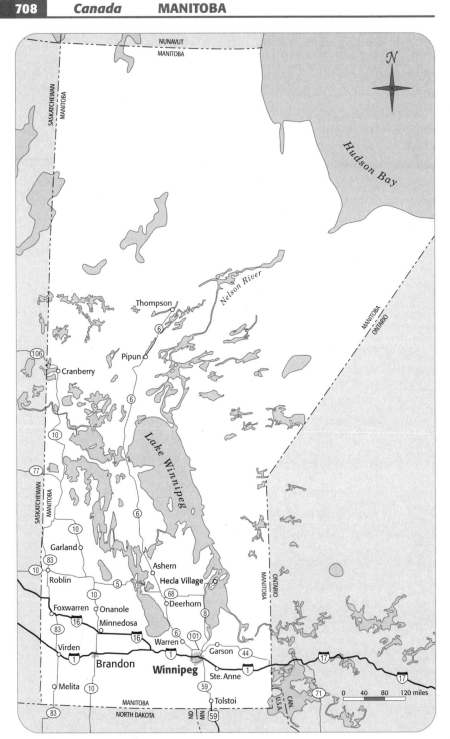

Riverton

◆ ◆ ⒶⒶ *Solmundson Gesta Hus*
Set in an original Icelandic settlement,
this inn offers compact but pleasantly
decorated rooms.

4 Rooms • Price range: $55-75
Box 76, Riverton, MB R0C 2R0
☎ **(204) 279-2088**

🛏 ✕ ☎ 🅚 📺 Ⓓ

Winnipeg
◆ ⒶⒶ *Twin Pillars Bed & Breakfast*
This 1901 brick house, across from a
park, has well-appointed rooms.

4 Rooms • Price range: $40-55
235 Oakwood Ave, Winnipeg, MB R3L 1E5
☎ **(204) 284-7590**

🛏 ✕ Ⓓ

Notes:

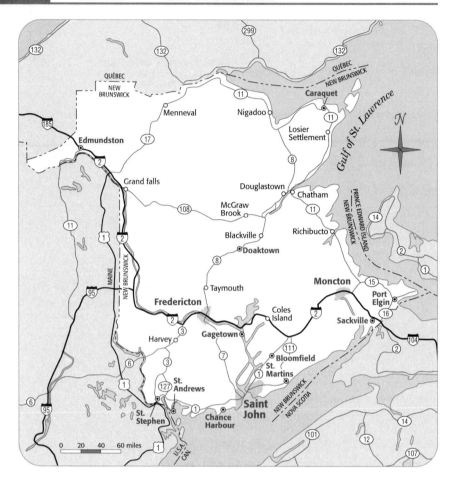

Bloomfield

@ *Evelyn's Bed & Breakfast*
This 400-acre working dairy farm has
rooms furnished in period antiques.

4 Rooms • Price range: $55-75
374 Rt 121, Bloomfield, Kings County, NB E5N 4T4
☎ **(506) 832-4450**

Caraquet
Le Poirier Bed & Breakfast

Built in 1928 by local judge Charles
Poirier using his own plans and
designs, this handsome home has been
restored to its original splendor and is
furnished with antiques. The five guestrooms
offer queen, double or twin beds, and all are
equipped with adjoining private baths. Guests
are invited to a full Acadian breakfast in the
dining room before heading out to enjoy nearby
sights and activities.

5 Rooms • Price range: $78-88
98 St Pierre W, Caraquet, NB E1W 1B6
☎ **(506) 727-4359**

Chance Harbour

@ *The Mariner's Inn*
Set in a secluded spot above the Bay of
Fundy, this inn offers spectacular views
of the world's most dramatic tides.
Some of the rooms have their own patio
or deck, and guests can choose between an
ocean or forest view. The inn is a nature lover's
paradise—hiking, sea kayaking and beachcombing are all nearby. Guests can even select a
package that includes a day excursion with the
inn's resident naturalist.

11 Rooms • Price range: $85-125
32 Mawhinney Cove Rd,
Chance Harbour, NB E5J 2B8
☎ **(506) 659-2619**

Doaktown

@ *The Ledges Inn*
Well-appointed guestrooms in a comfortable log home near the Miramichi.

7 Rooms • Price range: $95-135
30 Ledges Inn Ln, Doaktown,
NB E9C 1A7
☎ **(506) 365-1820**

Edmundston

@ *Auberge Le Fief Inn*
This 1927 two-story brick inn offers a
variety of rooms and a video library.

8 Rooms • Price range: $70-90
87 Church St, Edmundston,
NB E3V 1J6
☎ **(506) 735-0400**

Fredericton

@ *Carriage House Inn*
This attractive 1875 Victorian home
features modest-size rooms.

11 Rooms • Price range: $75-90
230 University Ave, Fredericton,
NB E3B 4H7
☎ **(506) 452-9924**

Gagetown
⑩ *Steamers Stop Inn*

Built in the early 1900s, this inn, looking out over the St. John River and Gagetown Island, has a pleasant and homey feel. Rooms feature rich woodwork and paneling, and most offer a river view. Guests can participate in art workshops offered by the art gallery on the property. For the energetic, kayaks, canoes and mountain bikes are available and box lunches can be ordered. St. John and Fredericton are both nearby.

6 Rooms • Price range: $65-95
74 Front St, Gagetown, NB E5M 1A1
☎ **(506) 488-2903**

Moncton
⑩ *Auberge Wild Rose Inn*

The large, airy rooms here tastefully blend antiques with every modern comfort. Several of the guestrooms feature a Jacuzzi, television and VCR, microwave and mini-fridge, as well as a gas fireplace. The inn's facilities include a game room with pool table, sitting rooms with fireplaces, and a large roofed veranda. Nearby activities include an 18-hole golf course—just a chip shot away!

9 Rooms • Price range: $85-140
17 Baseline Rd, Moncton, NB E1H 1N5
☎ **(506) 383-9751**

Moncton
⑩ *Archibald Bed & Breakfast*

Centrally located in a residential area, this circa 1909 home is spacious and elegantly furnished. The B&B offers guestrooms with both private and shared baths and a pleasant front porch—perfect for summer afternoon and evening lounging.

6 Rooms • Price range: $49-85
194 Archibald St, Moncton, NB E1C 5J9
☎ **(506) 382-0123**

Port Elgin
⑩ *Little Shemogue Country Inn*

Set against a tranquil backdrop, this inn is a restored 1859 home. Guestrooms are available in the original house as well as in a modern wing. Known particularly for its food, the inn offers sumptuous gourmet five-course dinners in its intimate dining room. A private beach is just a short meander away and canoeing, biking, snowshoeing and cross-country ski excursions can be arranged by the inn.

9 Rooms • Price range: $89-155
2361 Route 955, Port Elgin, NB E0A 2K0
☎ **(506) 538-2320**

Sackville
⑩ *Marshlands Inn*

This beautiful 1854 home has hosted visiting celebrities, including the Queen. The interior is furnished with many fine antiques and the upscale dining room is famous for such dishes as fiddleheads and a dessert called Fundy Fog.

17 Rooms • Price range: $79-95
55 Bridge St, Sackville, NB E4L 3N8
☎ **(506) 536-0170**

Saint John
⍟ *Homeport Historic Bed & Breakfast*

Originally constructed for a prominent shipbuilder in 1858, this inn has five individually themed guestrooms, each with a private bath. The Rose Room, the owner's favorite, is decorated in rich hues of red with brass accents. The spring garden colors of the Shore Garden Room give it a light, open feel. The Adriana Room, once the master bedroom, is adorned in mahogany, and the Habour Master suite was named for its view.

10 Rooms • Price range: $85-150
80 Douglas Ave, Saint John, NB E2K 1E4
☎ **(506) 672-7255**

Saint John
⍟ *Inn on the Cove*
Located on the Bay of Fundy, this pleasant inn borders Irving Nature Park.

5 Rooms • Price range: $95-175
1371 Sand Cove Rd, Saint John, NB E2M 4X7
☎ **(506) 672-7799**

Saint John
⍟ *Red Rose Mansion*

The extensive use of oak throughout this lovely 1904 red brick mansion helps to contribute to a romantic Old-World ambience. The inn is located along a tree-lined street in one of the city's most historic neighborhoods and surrounded by picturesque, beautifully maintained grounds. The guestrooms are tastefully decorated, and each is equipped with a private bath. Afternoon tea is available on request.

5 Rooms • Price range: $125-175
112 Mount Pleasant Ave,
Saint John, NB E2K 3V1
☎ **(506) 649-0913**

Saint John
⍟ *Shadow Lawn Inn*

This stately Victorian manor house offers a variety of attractive rooms.

10 Rooms • Price range: $109-185
3180 Rothesay Rd, Saint John, NB E2E 5V7
☎ **(506) 847-7539**

Saint John
⍟ *Five Chimneys Bed & Breakfast*

An 1850s Greek-Revival house with attractive rooms in different sizes.

3 Rooms • Price range: $80-90
238 Charlotte St W, Saint John, NB E2M 1Y3
☎ **(506) 635-1888**

St. Andrews
⍟ *Pansy Patch*

Built in 1912 in the French Normandy tradition, and recently designated as a Canadian Heritage Property, this home is considered to be one of the most photographed in New Brunswick. If the guests are not too busy taking in the architecture, they can stroll on the garden terraces savoring the ocean breeze or browse through works by local artists and artisans displayed in the Gallery Dining Room. All the rooms have a view of the harbor.

9 Rooms • Price range: $165-250
59 Carleton St, St. Andrews, NB E0G 2X0
☎ **(506) 529-3834**

St. Andrews
Tara Manor Inn
Quiet and secluded, this historic estate
offers rooms with a balcony or patio.

28 Rooms • Price range: $89-169
559 Mowat Dr, St. Andrews, NB E0G 2X0
☎ **(506) 529-3304**

St. Andrews
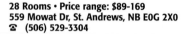 *Treadwell Inn*
This attractive 1820 inn has pleasant
rooms overlooking Passamaquody Bay.

6 Rooms • Price range: $85-185
129 Water St, St. Andrews, NB E0G 2X0
☎ **(506) 529-1011**

St. Andrews
The Windsor House of St. Andrews
North America's largest collection of
Sir Edwin Landseer prints, as well as
exquisite cabinetry and more than 150
other authentic 19th-century works of
art bring this fully restored Loyalist home to life.
Four of the six guestrooms are equipped with
wood-burning fireplaces, adding to the ambience.
The inn offers a full breakfast service, afternoon
tea and four-diamond French cuisine in one of
two dining rooms.

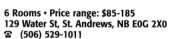

6 Rooms • Price range: $225-300
132 Water St, St. Andrews, NB E5B 1A8
☎ **(506) 529-3330**

St. Martins
Quaco Inn
Attractive guestrooms in both the main
building and new annex of this inn.

12 Rooms • Price range: $95-150
16 Beach St, St. Martins, NB E0G 2Z0
☎ **(506) 833-4772**

St. Martins
St. Martins Country Inn
Located in a historic seaside village
that was once a bustling shipbuilding
port, this dignified Queen Anne manor
sits on a hill overlooking the now quiet
bay. Built in 1857 by St. Martins' leading shipbuilder, who helped launch some of the community's 500 ships, the inn offers a step back in time
without sacrificing any modern amenities. The
two dining rooms feature some of the finest
Maritime cuisine.

16 Rooms • Price range: $95-145
303 Main St, St. Martins, NB E0G 2Z0
☎ **(506) 833-4534**

St. Stephen
Blair House Heritage Inn
Many of the guestrooms at this 1850s
home offer attractive river views.

5 Rooms • Price range: $75-95
38 Prince William St, St. Stephen, NB E3L 1S3
☎ **(506) 466-2233**

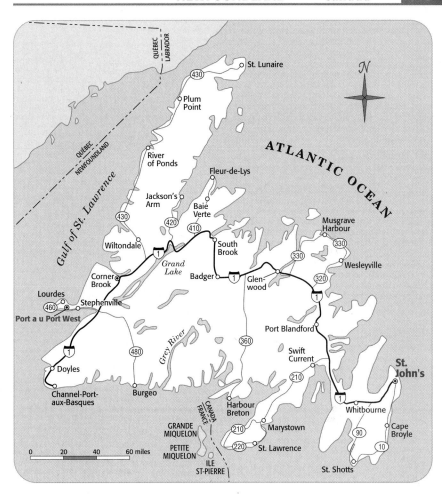

N

Gulf of St. Lawrence

QUEBEC
LABRADOR

QUEBEC
NEWFOUNDLAND

ATLANTIC OCEAN

St. Lunaire

430

Plum
Point

River
of Ponds

Fleur-de-Lys

Jackson's
Arm

Baie
Verte

Musgrave
Harbour

330

Wesleyville

Wiltondale

430

420

410

South
Brook

330

Grand
Lake

Corner
Brook

Badger

Glen-
wood

320

1

Lourdes

Stephenville

Port a u Port West

460

Grey River

Port Blandford

Swift
Current

480

360

210

St. John's

Doyles

210

Harbour
Breton

Whitbourne

Cape
Broyle

Channel-Port-
aux-Basques

Burgeo

GRANDE
MIQUELON

PETITE
MIQUELON

ILE
ST-PIERRE

CANADA
FRANCE

210

220

Marystown

St. Lawrence

90

10

St. Shotts

0   20   40   60 miles

Port Au Port West

Ⓐ *Spruce Pine Acres Country Inn*

Six acres of wooded trails and ocean-front land await visitors to this property. The inn features meeting facilities, a private guest dining room, an extensive multimedia library and a television lounge with a working fireplace. There is also a fitness room, a hot tub and a sauna. Guestrooms are spacious and each one is equipped with a private bath. A two-bedroom deluxe cottage with a fireplace is also available.

6 Rooms • Price range: $84-94
Rt 460, Port Au Port West, NF A0N 1T0
☎ **(709) 648-9600**

St. John's

Ⓐ *Leaside Manor Heritage Inn and Bed & Breakfast*

"The Lea" is a 1921 Tudor-Revival mansion, and is as elegant and as luxurious today as the year it was built. The home features a large reception area with a beamed ceiling and paneled walls, inspired by the hall in the homestead of the Doulton family of Royal Doulton fame. Guestrooms and suites are spacious and furnished with antiques, and all are equipped with private baths.

11 Rooms • Price range: $90-200
39 Old Topsail Rd, St. John's, NF A1E 2A6
☎ **(709) 722-0387**

St. John's

Ⓐ *Banberry House B&B*

This quaint home was built in 1892 and retains its original wood trim, hardwood floors and ornate stained-glass windows. The lovely, well-appointed guestrooms offer modern amenities, and most have a wood-burning fireplace.

4 Rooms • Price range: $89-109
116 Military Rd, St. John's, NF A1C 2C9
☎ **(709) 579-8006**

St. John's

Ⓐ *A Gower Street House*

Set in a quiet residential area, this inn has small cozy rooms.

5 Rooms • Price range: $50-100
180 Gower St, St. John's, NF A1C 1P9
☎ **(709) 754-0047**

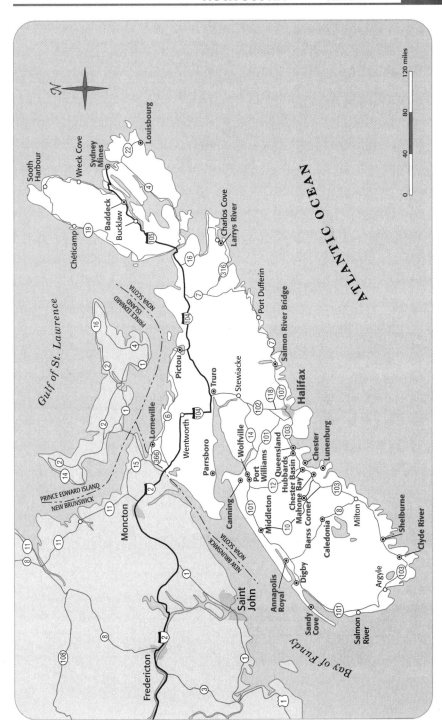

Annapolis Royal
The King George Inn

Once a sea captain's home, this lovely 1868 inn has rooms with private decks.

8 Rooms • Price range: $69-299
548 Upper St George St,
Annapolis Royal, NS B0S 1A0
☎ **(902) 532-5286**

Annapolis Royal
Garrison House Inn

This 1854 inn is in the heart of the downtown area, close to many attractions and just across the street from historic Fort Anne. Bedrooms vary in size and decor and some feature antique furnishings. The atmosphere is casual and homey.

7 Rooms • Price range: $80-119
350 St George St, Annapolis Royal, NS B0S 1A0
☎ **(902) 532-5750**

Baddeck
Castle Moffett

This luxurious property is centrally located near a number of Cape Breton's attractions, including the Cabot Trail, the Bell Museum, Fortress Louisbourg and the Bell Bay Golf Club. It is situated on 185 mountainside acres overlooking Bras d'Or Lakes. The Great Hall has a grand piano and a fireplace. Deluxe suites feature four-poster queen or canopied beds, a whirlpool bath and a fireplace.

4 Rooms • Price range: $250-500
PO Box 678, Baddeck, NS B0E 1B0
☎ **(902) 756-9070**

Barss Corner
100 Acres & An Ox

This beautiful Gothic-Revival home sits on 100 acres of fields, forests, lakes and salmon ponds. Guests can swim, fish, canoe, or just relax in the library or on the decks. All guestrooms have private baths. Guests are treated to a daily five-course breakfast and can even learn some regional recipes at the "Gourmet Ox" cooking classes offered by the Cordon Bleu-trained chef and host.

4 Rooms • Price range: $85-110
4127 Cornwall Rd, Barss Corner, NS B0R 1A0
☎ **(902) 644-3444**

Caledonia
The Whitman Inn

Set in a quiet country area, this property has a variety of rooms and a casual air.

    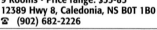

9 Rooms • Price range: $55-85
12389 Hwy 8, Caledonia, NS B0T 1B0
☎ **(902) 682-2226**

Canning
The Farmhouse Inn

Located in the historic village of Canning, this 1850s inn features parlors with stately bay windows and fireplaces. Rooms have private baths. Family and deluxe suites with fireplaces are available. Breakfast is served.

5 Rooms • Price range: $55-139
9757 Main St, Canning, NS B0P 1H0
☎ **(902) 582-7900**

Chester

◆◆ Ⓐ *Mecklenburgh Inn*

This 1890 inn has rooms and a fully equipped suite with a kitchen.

  ⓍⓏⒾⒸⓉⓋ Ⓓ

5 Rooms • Price range: $65-85
78 Queen St, Chester, NS B0J 1J0
☎ **(902) 275-4638**

Chester Basin
◆◆ Ⓐ *The Sword & Anchor Bed & Breakfast*

This 1882 former sea captain's home has a grand view of the bay from the porch.

 ⓍⓏⒾⒸⓉⓋ Ⓓ

8 Rooms • Price range: $80-85
5306 Hwy 3, Chester Basin, NS B0J 1K0
☎ **(902) 275-2478**

Clyde River
◆◆◆ Ⓐ *Clyde River Inn Bed & Breakfast*

This inn is located in a lovely, quiet rural town. The beautifully decorated parlor is full of antiques and period furnishings. There are several places to rest or relax outdoors among the towering trees. Rooms feature Victorian decor and furnishings.

Ⓗ Ⓩ Ⓘ Ⓒ Ⓓ

4 Rooms • Price range: $60-100
10525 Main Hwy, Clyde River, NS B0W 1R0
☎ **(902) 637-3267**

Digby
◆◆ Ⓐ *Harmony Guest House Bed & Breakfast*

This inn is located downtown, just opposite the harbor. It is a century-old lodge, which has a nice, informal atmosphere. All guestrooms are comfortable. Breakfast features ham and eggs, fruit, and freshly baked goods.

  Ⓧ Ⓘ Ⓓ

4 Rooms • Price range: $80-100
111 Montague Row, Digby, NS B0V 1A0
☎ **(902) 245-2817**

Halifax
◆◆ Ⓐ *Halifax's Waverley Inn*

This 1876 three-story Victorian house is close to the business district and the waterfront. Guests can choose a room with a centuries-old Chinese wedding bed or a crocheted lace canopy or opt for a third-floor room with a skylight. All rooms have en suite bathrooms; many have whirlpool tubs. In the morning, guests start the day with a breakfast consisting of flaky croissants, fresh bagels and home-baked muffins.

 Ⓧ Ⓓ

32 Rooms • Price range: $95-155
1266 Barrington St, Halifax, NS B3J 1Y5
☎ **(902) 423-9346**

Hubbards
◆◆◆ Ⓐ *Dauphinée Inn*

On the shore of Hubbards Cove, this establishment offers beautiful views and easy access to the beach. The lovely country home has guestrooms with private baths and also suites with private balconies and double Jacuzzis. The restaurant offers fresh seafood seasoned with organic herbs that come straight from the garden. Guests can hike, cycle or canoe near the Dauphinée.

Ⓨ Ⓧ Ⓩ Ⓘ Ⓒ Ⓓ

6 Rooms • Price range: $89-145
167 Shore Club Rd, Hubbards, NS B0J 1T0
☎ **(902) 857-1790**

Larrys River

⊛ *Seawind Landing Country Inn*
This inn has quaint rooms and it has views of Tor Bay and the sea.

13 Rooms • Price range: $79-129
1 Wharf Rd, Larrys River, NS B0H 1T0
☎ (902) 525-2108

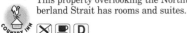

Lorneville

⊛ *Amherst Shore Country Inn*
This property overlooking the Northumberland Strait has rooms and suites.

8 Rooms • Price range: $109-169
RR 2, Lorneville, NS B4H 3X9
☎ (902) 661-4800

Louisbourg

⊛ *Cranberry Cove Inn*
This inn is close to a number of nearby attractions, including Fortress of Louisbourg, which is the largest restored historical site in North America; the S&L Railway Museum; the oldest lighthouse site in Canada; and the Boardwalk. There are also hiking trails and beaches nearby. Guestrooms are decorated in specific themes. Each one has an en suite bath. The inn also features a Jacuzzi and a fireplace.

7 Rooms • Price range: $75-145
12 Wolfe St, Louisbourg, NS B1C 2J2
☎ (902) 733-2171

Louisbourg
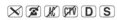
Louisbourg Harbour Inn
A sea captain built this inn on land awarded to his forefather for service in the second siege of Louisbourg of 1758. Sweeping views of the harbor, the ocean and of the historic fortress can be enjoyed from the large second-floor balcony. Guestrooms are beautifully appointed and feature queen beds and private baths. The gorgeous honeymoon suite is fitted with a two-person Jacuzzi and a panoramic picture window.

8 Rooms • Price range: $95-155
9 Lower Warren St, Louisbourg, NS B1C 1G6
☎ (902) 733-3222

Lunenburg

⊛ *Bluenose Lodge*
Dating from the 1860s, this historic mansion has attractive rooms.

9 Rooms • Price range: $95-110
10 Falkland St, Lunenburg, NS B0J 2C0
☎ (902) 634-8851

Lunenburg
Boscawen Inn
An 1888 Victorian mansion built as a dowry gift. The entrance hall features a grand staircase and stained-glass doors that lead the way to three spacious living rooms. An outside deck overlooking Lunenburg's harbor is accessible from each of these living rooms. Guests can choose from different-size guestrooms, some have four-poster or canopy beds, all have private baths. A hearty breakfast is served daily.

19 Rooms • Price range: $60-185
150 Cumberland St, Lunenburg, NS B0J 2C0
☎ (902) 634-3325

Lunenburg
Ⓐ *Kaulbach House Historic Inn*

The award-winning restoration of this home has rendered it beautiful and welcoming. It was built in the 1880s and has been decorated to period with antique furnishings. Not only is this home located in the heart of the National Heritage District, but it is near white sandy beaches and impressive golf courses. The daily three-course gourmet breakfast features such specialties as orange soufflés with strawberry sauce.

7 Rooms • Price range: $88-119
75 Pelham St, Lunenburg, NS B0J 2C0
☎ **(902) 634-8818**

Lunenburg
Ⓐ *The Lunenburg Inn*

Located at the edge of the National Historic District, this 1893 inn is a short distance from the Fisheries Museum of the Atlantic. Sailing, scuba-diving and whale watching are popular nearby activities. All guestrooms have a private bath and two suites have a whirlpool. A common sundeck, covered veranda and sitting room add to the charm. A full breakfast, including casseroles or blueberry pancakes, is served.

7 Rooms • Price range: $90-120
26 Dufferin St, Lunenburg, NS B0J 2C0
☎ **(902) 634-3963**

Mahone Bay
Ⓐ *Bayview Pines Country Inn*

This yellow farmhouse sits on a hill, surrounded by 14 acres of forest and pastures. Guests can sail, kayak, fish, whale watch or just stroll on the beach at this restful getaway. All guestrooms feature private baths and panoramic views of the ocean and of Mahone Bay. Each day begins with a full breakfast of pancakes and maple syrup, blueberry muffins, bacon and eggs and fresh fruit. Guest mooring and kayak storage are offered.

9 Rooms • Price range: $80-100
678 Oakland Rd Indian Point,
Mahone Bay, NS B0J 2E0
☎ **(902) 624-9970**

Mahone Bay
Ⓐ *The Manse at Mahone Bay Country Inn*

Built in the 1870s, this house was the rectory for the United Church for more than a century. Guestrooms have pine floors, en suite baths and twin or queen-size beds. Guests can relax in the Adirondack chairs on the deck or gather by the fireside in the common area. The surrounding area offers restaurants, boutiques, antique shops, and galleries. Mahone Bay is a perfect place for fishing, sailing or kayaking.

4 Rooms • Price range: $95-125
88 Orchard St, Mahone Bay, NS B0J 2E0
☎ **(902) 624-1121**

Middleton

Fairfield Farm Inn

A fully restored 1886 Victorian country inn, this property also includes 110 acres, complete with walking trails and ideal for birding. It is situated close to museums and theaters and is furnished throughout with period antiques. Guestrooms have king- or queen-size beds and en suite private bathrooms. There are also business services, a library and a game room. A wholesome country breakfast starts the day.

6 Rooms • Price range: $65-90
10 Main St, Middleton, NS B0S 1P0
☎ **(902) 825-6989**

Middleton
Falcourt Inn
This recently restored 1920s lodge overlooks the Nictaux River and sits between the North and South Mountains of the Annapolis Valley. It features wainscoting, traditional oak floors, heavy oak-beamed ceilings and a stone fireplace in the dining room. Guestrooms are decorated with Mission-style furniture reproductions and feature private baths and ceiling fans. Nearby attractions include the Annapolis Valley Macdonald Museum.

8 Rooms • Price range: $78-95
8979 Hwy 201, RR 3, Middleton, NS B0S1P0
☎ **(902) 825-3399**

Middleton
Country Charm & Comfort B&B
This 1890 converted farmhouse is located in a peaceful area close to Nictaux Falls. The guestrooms are very clean and well-maintained and vary in size and decor. Several of the guestrooms have en suite baths. Televisions are available to guests.

3 Rooms • Price range: $95-115
2305 Bloomington Rd, Middleton, NS B0S 1P0
☎ **(902) 825-2566**

Parrsboro
The Maple Inn
Built over a century ago, this inn features a variety of tastefully decorated rooms.

9 Rooms • Price range: $55-95
17 Western Ave, Parrsboro, NS B0M 1S0
☎ **(902) 254-3735**

Pictou
Braeside Inn

Located on five acres overlooking historic Pictou Harbour, this inn is within walking distance of town. Built in 1938, it offers guestrooms with private baths. The 150-seat banquet room and 80-seat dining room both overlook the harbor. The inn's conference room is the ideal setting for business meetings and can seat some 60 people. Government-supervised beaches and the Prince Edward Island ferry are minutes away.

18 Rooms • Price range: $70-155
126 Front St, Pictou, NS B0K 1H0
☎ **(902) 485-5046**

Pictou
Consulate Inn & Restaurant
 This 1810 stone Scottish home is a Registered Heritage waterfront property. It has wildflower gardens, a gazebo and stone walls. Rooms are decorated with

period furniture and original quilted hangings; all have private baths. Suites are available.

10 Rooms • Price range: $54-149
157 Water St, Pictou, NS B0K 1H0
☎ **(902) 485-4554**

Pictou
The Customs House Inn
Formerly a customs house, this fine brick and stone inn overlooks the harbor.

8 Rooms • Price range: $119-149
38 Depot St, Pictou, NS B0K 1H0
☎ **(902) 485-4546**

Pictou
Auberge Walker Inn
This 1865 inn features spacious, meticulously renovated guestrooms, each with a private bath. A continental breakfast is served. The inn is just a one-minute walk

from Hector Heritage Quay and a 10-minute drive to the Prince Edward Island ferry terminal.

11 Rooms • Price range: $75-85
34 Coleraine St, Pictou, NS B0K 1H0
☎ **(902) 485-1433**

Pictou
Willow House Inn
A registered historical property built in 1840 by the first mayor of Pictou, this inn is only a short walk from downtown and the waterfront area. Rooms include

private and semi-private baths. A complimentary continental breakfast is served.

8 Rooms • Price range: $59-104
11 Willow St, Pictou, NS B0K 1H0
☎ **(902) 485-5740**

Port Williams
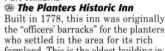 The Planters Historic Inn
Built in 1778, this inn was originally the "officers' barracks" for the planters who settled in the area for its rich farmland. This is the oldest building in the province that has been restored as an inn. The home is a lovely example of early Georgian architecture and boasts manicured grounds. Guests are offered country breakfasts and fresh produce from the garden. A tennis court and mountain bikes are available for guest use.

6 Rooms • Price range: $79-119
1464 Starrs Point Rd, Port Williams, NS B0P 1T0
☎ **(902) 542-7879**

Queensland
Surfside Inn Bed & Breakfast
Overlooking the golden sand and blue water of Queensland Beach, this inn offers refined comfort in a beautiful location. It was built by a sea captain in the late 1800s and has been renovated with all the modern amenities. All guestrooms boast ocean views, grand mahogany beds covered with cozy duvets, and private luxurious whirlpools. Guests are offered a full healthy breakfast each morning. Romance packages are available.

6 Rooms • Price range: $84-169
9609 St Margarets Bay Rd,
Queensland, NS B0J 1T0
☎ **(902) 857-2417**

Salmon River Bridge
◈ *Salmon River House Country Inn*
This on the Salmon River comprises an 1850s house, a cottage and two cabins.

10 Rooms • Price range: $58-84
9931 #7 Hwy, Salmon River Bridge, NS B0J 1P0
☎ (902) 889-3353

Sandy Cove
◈ *The Olde 1890 Village Inn*
This 1890 five-building property is Nova Scotia's longest operating seaside inn. A large wicker-filled sunroom overlooks the tides. Guestrooms have private baths. Breakfast is served daily and candlelight dinners are available on request.

16 Rooms • Price range: $85-120
387 Sandy Cove Rd, Sandy Cove, NS B0V 1E0
☎ (902) 834-2202

Shelburne
◈ *The Cooper's Inn & Restaurant*
This inn is situated on Shelburne's Walking Tour and is across the street from an active cooper's shop. Built in 1784, it is within walking distance of fine beaches, harbor tours, the pristine Roseway River system, a riverside golf course and the Shelburne historical museum complex. Full dining facilities are available in the intimate candlelit dining room. Regional cuisine, fresh local produce and seafood are always on the menu.

7 Rooms • Price range: $85-135
36 Dock St, Shelburne, NS B0T 1W0
☎ (902) 875-4656

Sydney Mines
Gowrie House Country Inn
Casual elegance is key at this lovely 1830s inn. Spectacular gardens surround the original home, the newer annex building and the cottages. Guestrooms are decorated with antiques, have en suite facilities, and most have fireplaces. Breakfast is offered each morning and guests can make reservations for a four-course dinner in the evenings. Specialties include fresh fish and fresh produce from the area.

10 Rooms • Price range: $125-295
139 Shore Rd, Sydney Mines, NS B1V 1A6
☎ (902) 544-1050

Truro
◈ *The John Stanfield Inn*
Comfort and style are hallmarks at this lovely 1902 Queen Anne mansion.

11 Rooms • Price range: $179-229
437 Prince St, Truro, NS B2N 1A6
☎ (902) 895-1651

Wolfville
◈ *Blomidon Inn*
Once a 19th-century sea captain's mansion, this inn features the original hardwood detailing. Rooms and suites offer luxury and comfort. The inn is ideally located for both the history or nature enthusiast. Annapolis Valley boasts the Grand Pré National Historic Site and Longfellow's Evangeline where one can relive the history of the Acadians. The nearby Bay of Fundy features the world's highest and lowest tides.

28 Rooms • Price range: $79-189
127 Main St, Wolfville, NS B0P 1X0
☎ (902) 542-2291

Wolfville

Tattingstone Inn
Built in 1877, this charming inn features many antiques and works of art.

10 Rooms • Price range: $98-175
434 Main St, Wolfville, NS B0P 1X0
☎ **(902) 542-7696**

Wolfville
Victoria's Historic Inn
Comprised of a fine 1893 Victorian home and carriage house, this inn has a refined and intimate atmosphere. All guestrooms are individually decorated and several boast gas stoves, balconies, double Jacuzzis and/or gorgeous sweeping views. The innkeepers are very hospitable and pay great attention to detail. Many guests return year after year to enjoy the peace and relaxation of this luxurious environment.

15 Rooms • Price range: $98-225
416 Main St, Wolfville, NS B0P 1X0
☎ **(902) 542-5744**

Notes:

_____
_____
_____
_____
_____
_____
_____
_____
_____
_____
_____
_____
_____
_____
_____
_____
_____
_____
_____
_____
_____
_____
_____
_____
_____

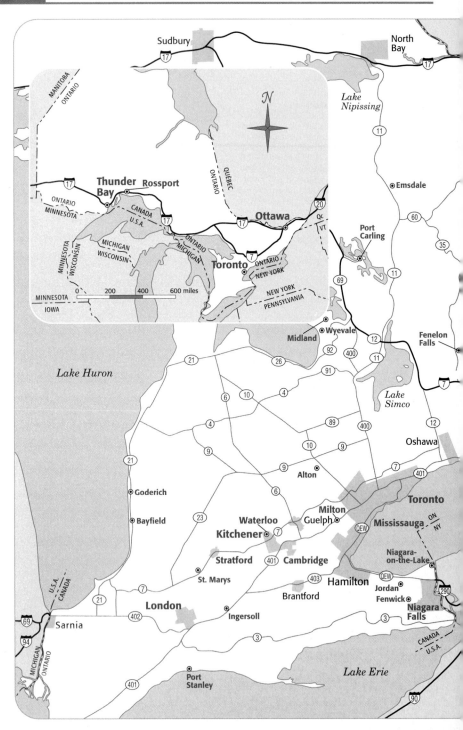

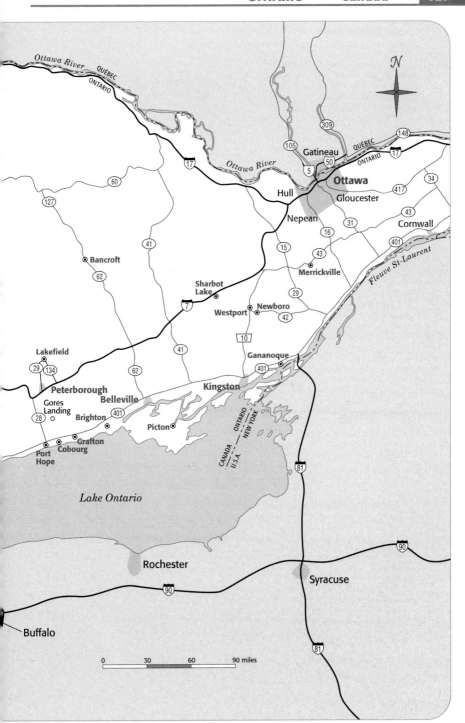

Ottawa River

QUÉBEC
ONTARIO

309

105   Gatineau

QUÉBEC

148

17   Ottawa River   50

ONTARIO   17

5

Hull   **Ottawa**   417   34

Gloucester

60   Nepean   43

127   16   Cornwall

31

41   15   401

Bancroft   43   Fleuve St-Laurent

62   Merrickville

Sharbot
Lake   29

7   Westport   Newboro

42

Lakefield   41   10

29 134   Gananoque

Peterborough   62   401

Gores   **Belleville**   **Kingston**
Landing

28   401   CANADA   ONTARIO

Brighton   USA   NEW YORK

Picton

Grafton
Cobourg
Port
Hope   81

Lake Ontario

90

Rochester   Syracuse

90

90

Buffalo

81

0   30   60   90 miles

Alton

⊕ *The Millcroft Inn*
Only 40 minutes from Toronto, this inn is surrounded by 100 acres of landscaped property in the rolling Caledon Hills. It features guestrooms carefully furnished with European and Canadian antiques. Many rooms offer magnificent views of the waterfalls, the mill pond and the surrounding hills. Each room has a sitting area with comfortable chairs. Guest accommodations are also available at the Manor House adjacent to the main inn and at The Crofts, which embraces 20 self-contained, two-story chalets. Other facilities include an outdoor swimming pool and a gym. The inn also offers four-diamond gourmet dining.

52 Rooms • Price range: $230-295
55 John St, Alton, ON L0N 1A0
☎ **(519) 941-8111**

Bancroft
⊕ *The Brides Gate Inn & Spa*
Charmingly decorated, this inn has well-kept grounds and rooms with lake views.

5 Rooms • Price range: $220-325
2204 Bay Lake Rd, Bancroft, ON K0L 1C0
☎ **(613) 332-0154**

Bayfield
⊕ *The Little Inn of Bayfield*
This 1830s country-style inn is situated on the shores of Lake Huron in the heart of a heritage village. Cycling, golfing, swimming, horseback riding and tennis are some of the things people like to do around here. Visitors may also want to participate in a guided wilderness walk or a fly-fishing expedition. Guestrooms feature up-to-the-minute amenities and most rooms have a double whirlpool, a fireplace and a veranda. The inn's four-diamond restaurant features regional and seasonal dishes prepared with ingredients from local fields, forests, streams and lakes. Children are welcome and so are pets.

29 Rooms • Price range: $85-540
Main St, Bayfield, ON N0M 1G0
☎ **(519) 565-2611**

Brighton
⊕ *Butler Creek Bed & Breakfast*
This Victorian is situated on nine acres near a nature conservation area.

5 Rooms • Price range: $55-75
202 Hwy 30, Brighton, ON K0K 1H0
☎ **(613) 475-1248**

◆◆ Cambridge
◆◆ Ⓐ *Langdon Hall Country House Hotel & Spa*

Recent major renovations at this 1898 converted mansion have added new features such as a three-season arbor over the charming dining terrace. The spa is a multi-level facility with 10 treatment rooms staffed by a team of professionals who offer everything from massage to hydrotherapy. The Cloister Wing has stone floors. The Garden Galleries offer private areas for receptions and meals. The inn also features saunas, steam rooms, whirlpools and a tennis court. The guestrooms have been comfortably furnished and all have a private bath. Most have a fireplace; some have a private terrace.

53 Rooms • Price range: $259-329
RR 33, Cambridge, ON N3H 4R8
☎ (519) 740-2100

◆◆ Cobourg
◆◆ Ⓐ *Woodlawn Terrace Inn*

A restored 1835 home features elegant rooms and a fine dining room.

16 Rooms • Price range: $129-250
420 Division St, Cobourg, ON K9A 3R9
☎ (905) 372-2235

◆◆ Emsdale
◆◆ Ⓐ *Fern Glen Inn*

This century-old farmhouse offers cozy rooms with a tasteful country decor.

5 Rooms • Price range: $65-75
1462 Fern Glen Rd, Emsdale, ON P0A 1J0
☎ (705) 636-1391

◆◆ Fenelon Falls
◆◆ Ⓐ *Eganridge Inn & Country Club*

This restored manor house combines the ambience of the last century with modern luxury. Located on beautifully groomed grounds that feature towering pines and stone fences, the 1837 square-timbered, two-story home, built with hand-hewn logs, is unique in North America. Accommodations are available at the Dunsford House and the five surrounding cottages. The center foyer, the private dining room and the garden room are some of the inn's comfortable common areas. Guestrooms feature four-poster king-size beds and oversize bathrooms with Jacuzzi baths.

11 Rooms • Price range: $190-245
26 Country Club Dr, Fenelon Falls, ON K0M 1N0
☎ (705) 738-5111

◆ Fenwick
◆ Ⓐ *Schaferhof B&B*

Here's a quiet, country retreat just 20 miles from Niagara Falls.

4 Rooms • Price range: $45-85
2746 Moyer St, RR 3, Fenwick, ON L0S 1C0
☎ (905) 562-4929

Gananoque

⊛ *Gray Rock Bed & Breakfast*

The newest and most luxurious B&B in the Thousand Islands region, this inn is located on a two-acre estate of gorgeous rolling lawns. Special features here are the upper deck overlooking the property, an ornately decorated living room and elegant guestrooms with fine bed covers and wood furnishings. Guests are invited to a full breakfast served either in the dining room or, when the weather is warm, outdoors in the courtyard.

4 Rooms • Price range: $89-189
RR 2, Gananoque, ON K7G 2V4
☎ **(613) 382-1255**

Gananoque

⊛ *Trinity House Inn*

This 1859 Victorian red brick inn is located in a historic residential district in the heart of the Thousand Islands region. Features such as open-air verandas and Victorian waterfall gardens give this inn its distinctive ambience. Guestrooms include adjoining bathrooms, and the comfortable suites are equipped with Jacuzzis. Conference facilities are also available. A continental breakfast is served daily.

8 Rooms • Price range: $100-200
90 Stone St S, Gananoque, ON K7G 1Z8
☎ **(613) 382-8383**

Gananoque

⊛ *The Victoria Rose Inn*

A stately 1872 mansion, this home of the first mayor of Gananoque has been beautifully and authentically restored. The inn is characterized by manicured grounds, award-winning gardens and rooms with fine wood furniture and antiques. Each room is also equipped with an en suite bath and air-conditioning. Other features include two dining rooms, a gazebo and a large veranda where afternoon tea is served, weather permitting.

9 Rooms • Price range: $85-190
279 King St W, Gananoque, ON K7G 2G7
☎ **(613) 382-3368**

Gananoque

⊛ *Manse Lane Bed & Breakfast*

This comfortable B&B is centrally located on a residential street within easy walking distance of shopping and local attractions. The inn offers attractive guestrooms and summertime facilities such as an outdoor swimming pool and sundeck.

4 Rooms • Price range: $50-125
465 Stone St S, Gananoque, ON K7G 2A7
☎ **(613) 382-8642**

Goderich
Benmiller Inn

Considered one of Canada's authentic country inns, this 1830s property consists of a series of buildings that form a country village. Guestrooms and conference rooms can be found in each building. The guestrooms feature antique furnishings and historical mill artifacts and have outstanding views of Maitland River or Sharpe's Creek. Deluxe suites have a fireplace and a Jacuzzi. The inn's dining room offers regional dishes and classic country cuisine. Jonathan's Bar serves wine and late evening snacks. A whirlpool and a sauna are available.

47 Rooms • Price range: $125-345
RR 4, Goderich, ON N7A 3Y1
☎ **(519) 524-2191**

Grafton
Ste. Anne's Country Inn & Spa

This inn and spa offers massage, manicure, pedicure, fitness routines and a variety of treatments ranging from aromatherapy to reflexology. Guests who just want to relax will appreciate the guestrooms in the fieldstone main building. The rooms feature working fireplaces and private baths with whirlpool tubs. There is also several guest houses: the Innkeeper's, a renovated Victorian farmhouse; the Farmhouse, the ground floor of an early 1900s brick house; and the Gables, situated on the second floor of the Farmhouse. Meals are included in weekend packages and are tailored to guests' needs.

17 Rooms • Price range: $340-878
RR 1, Massey Rd, Grafton, ON K0K 2G0
☎ **(905) 349-2493**

Ingersoll
Elm Hurst Inn

This country property has pleasant guestrooms and common areas.

49 Rooms • Price range: $126-199
Hwy 401 & Plank Rd, Ingersoll, ON N5C 3K1
☎ **(519) 485-5321**

Jordan
Inn on the Twenty

Located in a village in the Niagara wine region, this inn offers a quiet retreat characterized by an upscale decor and a warm, country ambience. Accommodations include both single-story and two-level suites. All suites have a gas fireplace along with new and antique furnishings. They also feature two double or king-size beds and a bathroom with a Jacuzzi. Suites have modem hook-ups and generous work areas; well-appointed meeting facilities are also available. Guests can tour Niagara's wineries, including the Cave Spring Cellars, a partner with the inn's fine gourmet restaurant.

29 Rooms • Price range: $219-325
3845 Main St, Jordan, ON L0R 1S0
☎ **(905) 562-5336**

Kingston
ⓐ *Hochelaga Inn*
An elegant 1880s Victorian mansion, this inn features an enchanting turret room.

23 Rooms • Price range: $125-155
24 Sydenham St S, Kingston, ON K7L 3G9
☎ **(613) 549-5534**

Kingston
ⓐ *Hotel Belvedere*
This lavishly restored 1880 mansion is considered one of historic Kingston's grandest hostelries. Guestrooms are decorated in classic styles. All rooms have king- or queen-size beds with duvets, pleasant sitting areas and private bathrooms. Conference facilities are available for small groups. The hotel is only minutes away from businesses, restaurants, and downtown shops, galleries and parks.

22 Rooms • Price range: $110-195
141 King St E, Kingston, ON K7L 2Z9
☎ **(613) 548-1565**

Kingston
ⓐ *Painted Lady Inn*
This grand old dame of the Victorian era dates back to about 1870, and it has been beautifully restored to her former elegance. The seven spacious guestrooms are furnished with authentic antiques and they have private baths and central air-conditioning. The inn's luxury rooms include Jacuzzis and working fireplaces. Guests enjoy a full, hot breakfast before heading out to the attractions of the Thousand Islands region.

7 Rooms • Price range: $95-155
181 William St, Kingston, ON K7L 2E1
☎ **(613) 545-0422**

Kingston
ⓐ *The Secret Garden Bed & Breakfast Inn*
This building was built in 1888 by a local fur and leather merchant. The three-story, red-brick structure features antique fireplaces, stained-glass windows and interesting architectural details. The guestrooms have adjoining baths and are appointed with period antiques and king or queen poster beds. A candlelight breakfast is served in the formal dining room.

6 Rooms • Price range: $95-145
73 Sydenham St, Kingston, ON K7L 3H3
☎ **(613) 531-9884**

Kingston
ⓐ *The North Nook Bed & Breakfast*
This circa 1850 limestone building has been fully renovated, yet has retained many original features such as pine flooring, ornate tin ceilings and exposed stone and brick walls. Each guestroom is simply and tastefully decorated.

4 Rooms • Price range: $105-135
83 Earl St, Kingston, ON K7L 2G8
☎ **(613) 547-8061**

Kitchener
ⓐ *Aram's "Roots and Wings"*
This contemporary inn includes a large outdoor swimming pool.

5 Rooms • Price range: $50-100
11 Sunbridge Crescent, Kitchener, ON N2K 1T4
☎ **(519) 743-4557**

Lakefield
◆ ◆ ⓐ *Selwyn Shores Waterfront Bed & Breakfast*
This comfortable home offers pleasant views from several common areas.

5 Rooms • Price range: $70-95
2073 Selwyn Shores Dr, RR 3,
Lakefield, ON K0L 2H0
☎ (705) 652-0277

London
◆
◆ ◆ ⓐ *Idlewyld Inn*
This magnificent 1878 Victorian mansion features ornate wood moldings, intricately carved fireplaces and a massive central staircase. Guestrooms offer a mixture of antique furnishings and modern amenities. Some rooms have leaded-glass windows; some feature framed windows with concealed wooden shutters. Other facilities include in-room fireplaces and whirlpool tubs. A light breakfast is served in the breakfast room.

27 Rooms • Price range: $119-139
36 Grand Ave, London, ON N6C 1K8
☎ (519) 433-2891

Merrickville
◆
◆ ◆ ⓐ *Sam Jakes Inn*
Overlooking the Rideau Canal this heritage limestone jewel is a reflection of more tranquil days. The inn features a garden patio, elegant verandas, a fireside library lounge, a sauna and an exercise room. Guestrooms and suites offer various amenities such as fireplaces, Jacuzzis and sleigh beds. The inn's renowned dining room features fresh local fare accompanied by local micro-brewery beers and Ontario wines.

30 Rooms • Price range: $150-160
118 Main St E, Merrickville, ON K0G 1N0
☎ (613) 269-3711

Midland
◆
◆ ◆ ⓐ *Little Lake Inn Bed & Breakfast*
This 100-year-old home offers guests tranquil views of the lake and park. Features include a large lounge with high-beamed ceilings and a covered veranda—perfect for summer evenings. Each of the comfortable guestrooms is equipped with an ensuite bath, while some offer fireplaces and Jacuzzis. Each morning a full buffet breakfast is served in the parkside dining room. Nearby attractions include the Huron Indian Village.

4 Rooms • Price range: $75-129
669 Yonge St, Midland, ON L4R 2E1
☎ (705) 526-2750

Mississauga
◆
◆ ◆ ⓐ *Glenerin Inn*
This charming 1927 English stone inn is situated in a residential community known as Ivor Woodlands. Decorated in Old World elegance, the inn combines antiques and period reproductions with contemporary luxury. No two guestrooms are decorated alike, and some feature whirlpool tubs and fireplaces. The inn also offers five function rooms, one of which has its own patio. Fine dining is featured at the inn's Thatcher Restaurant.

39 Rooms • Price range: $130-240
1695 The Collegeway, Mississauga, ON L5L 3S7
☎ (905) 828-6103

Newboro

⑭ **Newboro House Bed & Breakfast**
Built in Second Empire style, this
house is located on the main street.

3 Rooms • Price range: $70-75
31 Drummond St, Newboro, ON k0G 1P0
☎ **(613) 272-3181**

Niagara-on-the-Lake

⑭ **The Pillar & Post Inn**
Built in the late 1890s, this inn has
earned the reputation of being one of
the finest in Canada. Guests are invited
to relax in front of a cozy fire in one of
123 inviting guest rooms, experience award-
winning dining in the Cannery and Carriages
dining rooms or indulge in European spa treatment in the world-class Fountain Spa. The inn
also boasts magnificent sky-lit ceilings, exposed
beams and delicate chandeliers. Guestroom
decor features Early-American pine furniture
and handmade quilts. An abundance of fresh
flowers in both the rooms and public areas adds
to the inn's refined ambience.

123 Rooms • Price range: $220-325
48 John St, Niagara-on-the-Lake, ON L0S 1J0
☎ **(905) 468-2123**

Niagara-on-the-Lake
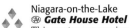
⑭ **Gate House Hotel**
This contemporary inn features a
modern Italian decor.

10 Rooms • Price range: $195-230
142 Queen St, Niagara-on-the-Lake, ON L0S 1J0
☎ **(905) 468-3263**

Niagara-on-the-Lake
⑭ **Moffat Inn**
Tucked away in the Old Town Heritage
District, this 1835 inn offers a range of
uniquely decorated guestrooms. Each
is equipped with queen-size or double
beds and private baths, while some rooms have
a gas fireplace or a patio. The inn also features
a restaurant and pub, which serves meals all
day. Nearby sights include the Niagara River,
Niagara Falls—a 20-minute drive away—Lake
Ontario and the Shaw Theatre Festival.

22 Rooms • Price range: $89-149
60 Picton St, Niagara-on-the-Lake, ON L0S 1J0
☎ **(905) 468-4116**

Niagara-on-the-Lake

⑭ **The Oban Inn**
Here guests will find English-style
gardens and tasteful guestrooms.

25 Rooms • Price range: $220-325
160 Front St, Niagara-on-the-Lake, ON L0S 1J0
☎ **(905) 468-2165**

Niagara-on-the-Lake
⑭ **The River Breeze**
Overlooking the Niagara River, this
elegant home has lovely gardens.

4 Rooms • Price range: $110-140
14767 Niagara Pkwy RR #1,
Niagara-on-the-Lake, ON L0S 1J0
☎ **(905) 262-4046**

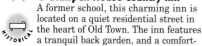

Niagara-on-the-Lake
ⓐ *Blairpen House Country Inn*

A former school, this charming inn is located on a quiet residential street in the heart of Old Town. The inn features a tranquil back garden, and a comfort-able living room. Guestrooms have a cozy decor and ensuite bathrooms.

6 Rooms • Price range: $150-185
287 Davy St, Niagara-on-the-Lake, ON L0S 1J0
☎ **(905) 468-3886**

Niagara-on-the-Lake
ⓐ *Old Bank House*

Located opposite a park and Lake Ontario, this historic home is also close to theater, shops and restaurants. Guestrooms are bright and cozy with charming decor, and the inn offers large, comfortable common areas.

9 Rooms • Price range: $125-199
10 Front St, Niagara-on-the-Lake, ON L0S 1J0
☎ **(905) 468-7136**

North Milton
ⓐ *Country Garden Inn B&B*

This modern, comfortable home in the country offers guests a quiet getaway.

4 Rooms • Price range: $95-150
Winsloe RR 10, North Milton, ON C1E 1Z4
☎ **(902) 566-4344**

Ottawa
ⓐ *Albert House Inn*

This 1875 Second Empire building was both the home and creation of noted Canadian architect Thomas Seaton Scott. In addition to designing his own home, Scott was responsible for many Canadian government buildings, including the West Block of Parliament. Each of the guestrooms is comfort-ably furnished and is accompanied by an ensuite bath. Guests are invited to a sumptuous break-fast served over a three-hour period.

17 Rooms • Price range: $95-140
478 Albert St, Ottawa, ON K1R 5B5
☎ **(613) 236-4479**

Ottawa
ⓐ *Auberge McGee's Inn (Est. 1984)*

This 1886 inn is centrally located the dis-tinguished heritage area of Sandy Hill. A well-preserved Victorian landmark, it is just blocks away from Parliament Hill, the National Arts Centre and Byward Market. Each of the guestrooms has been individually dec-orated and all have adjoining baths. The two themed suites offer double Jacuzzis and fire-places. Breakfast is served in the elegant Art Gallery Dining Room.

14 Rooms • Price range: $88-198
185 Daly Ave, Ottawa, ON K1N 6E8
☎ **(613) 237-6089**

Ottawa
ⓐ *Gasthaus Switzerland Inn*

Built as a private home in 1872, this restored heritage house features guest-rooms with private baths or showers; some have a fireplace. Two specialty suites feature a double Jacuzzi. A complimentary homemade Swiss breakfast is served.

22 Rooms • Price range: $88-208
89 Daly Ave, Ottawa, ON K1N 6E6
☎ **(613) 237-0335**

Peterborough

◆ ◆ ⊛ *King Bethune House*
This spacious, centrally located, Victorian
has a lovely garden.

3 Rooms • Price range: $74-104
270 King St, Peterborough, ON K9J 2S2
☎ (705) 743-4101

Picton
◆ ◆ ⊛ *Merrill Inn*
At this 1870 inn, guests will find
uniquely decorated rooms filled with
period antiques. All have private bathrooms; one room has a Jacuzzi, another
a fireplace. Visitors start the day off with breakfasts that include freshly baked croissants.
Lunches are also available. The inn has a fully
equipped boardroom, ideal for small conferences.
The extensive beaches of Sandbanks Provincial
Park are nearby.

13 Rooms • Price range: $95-175
343 Main St E, Picton, ON K0K 2T0
☎ (613) 476-7451

Picton
◆ ◆ ⊛ *The Waring House Restaurant & Inn*
One of Prince Edward County's best-
known historic buildings, this 1860 inn
is decorated with local memorabilia
and domestic antiques. Each of the
guestrooms is equipped with a private bath,
while other features include air-jet tubs, fireplaces and private patios. Guests can enjoy fine
country cuisine in the Prince Edward Room or
outdoors on the garden-view veranda. The on-
site Barley Room Pub offers live music.

16 Rooms • Price range: $105-155
PO Box 20024, Picton, ON K0K 3V0
☎ (613) 476-7492

Port Carling
◆ ◆ ⊛ *Sherwood Inn*
Set amid mature trees and country surroundings on well-known Lake Joseph,
this inn's location is a long-time favorite
for wealthy cottagers. Guestrooms and
cottages are decorated to reflect the traditional
country character of the region yet they all have
all the modern conveniences. Other features
include whirlpool tubs, private balconies and
stunning views of the lake. The inn is also
famous for its dining room, winner of the coveted
Four Diamond Plate Award. Outdoor activities of
the Muskoka region include boating, swimming
and hiking in summer, and cross-country skiing
and snowmobiling in winter.

49 Rooms • Price range: $139-699
PO Box 400, Port Carling, ON P0B 1J0
☎ (705) 765-3131

Port Hope
⊛ *The Hillcrest*

This mansion is the sole example of Beaux Arts-style architecture in the Port Hope area. One of the area's most impressive homes, it is situated on a ravine lot with terraced gardens and trails. Inn highlights include a living room with a grand piano, a sunroom with a fireplace, a large in-ground heated pool on the south terrace, a social room, a sauna and a private Jacuzzi. Guestrooms are handsomely decorated and they all feature private baths and ample closets. Some rooms have balconies with views of Port Hope and Lake Ontario; others have a working fireplace, a high ceiling and beautiful woodwork.

6 Rooms • Price range: $340-820
175 Dorset St W, Port Hope, ON L1A 1G4
☎ **(905) 885-7367**

Port Hope
⊛ *Butternut Inn Bed & Breakfast*

A towering butternut tree protects this 1847 restored Neoclassic-style home decorated in rich tones. Rooms have queen-size beds and private bats.

Breakfasts include such treats as fruit compote with crème fraîche or poached pears in red wine.

4 Rooms • Price range: $95-125
36 North St, Port Hope, ON L1A 1T8
☎ **(905) 885-4318**

Port Hope
⊛ *The Hill & Dale Manor*

This restored circa 1800 mansion is close to the historic downtown area.

6 Rooms • Price range: $90-150
47 Pine St S, Port Hope, ON L1A 3E6
☎ **(905) 885-8686**

Port Stanley
⊛ *Kettle Creek Inn*

The old-world charm of this 1849 inn is evident throughout: in the parlor, complete with a working fireplace; in the intimate pub; in the foyer, with its bold black and white tiles and antique hutches; and in the three tastefully decorated dining rooms. All rooms feature private baths. Luxury suites also have a whirlpool, a gas fire-place and a private balcony. Conference facilities are ideal for small groups.

15 Rooms • Price range: $100-110
216 Joseph St, Port Stanley, ON N5L 1C4
☎ **(519) 782-3388**

Rossport
⊛ *The Willows Inn Bed & Breakfast*

This contemporary, tastefully decorated B&B overlooks a harbor on Lake Superior. The large, bright guestrooms are indi-vidually decorated and are equipped

with modern bathrooms. Guests are free to enjoy the parlor, library, and sundeck.

4 Rooms • Price range: $60-125
1 Main St, Rossport, ON P0T 2R0
☎ **(807) 824-3389**

Sharbot Lake
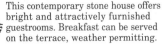
⊛ *Rock Hill Bed & Breakfast*

This contemporary stone house offers bright and attractively furnished guestrooms. Breakfast can be served on the terrace, weather permitting.

The inn's proprietor is fluent in English, Dutch, German and French.

3 Rooms • Price range: $50-90
Hwy 38, Sharbot Lake, ON K0H 2P0
☎ **(613) 279-3006**

St. Marys
⊛ *Westover Inn*

This 1867 limestone Victorian mansion is set amid 19 acres of beautifully landscaped grounds. Guest accommodations are located in the original manor house, the terrace, and the Thames cottage, which features two-bedroom suites with a living room. Guestrooms in the manor house boast original moldings and 11-foot ceilings. The dining room, the lounge, the meeting room and a comfortable common room are also in the manor house.

22 Rooms • Price range: $130-270
300 Thomas St, St. Marys, ON N4X 1B1
☎ **(519) 284-2977**

Stratford
⊛ *Stone Maiden Inn*

Built in 1872 as a private residence, this charming Victorian was converted a few years later to a railway hotel. After many years of service, it was given a complete restoration when its present owners purchased the property in 1982. The furnishings are authentic Victorian, with the accent on comfort. All rooms are decorated in soft colors and options include whirlpools and working fireplaces. Stratford's Shakespeare Festival attracts visitors throughout the summer, but this charming town's other attractions include dozens of antique shops, galleries and fine restaurants.

15 Rooms • Price range: $135-240
123 Church St, Stratford, ON N5A 2R3
☎ **(519) 271-7129**

Stratford
⊛ *Woods Villa*

This 1870 villa is located high on a hill overlooking the river valley and is surrounded by an acre of landscaped grounds. Guestrooms are large; some have fireplaces and all have private baths. French doors on the south side of the ballroom lead to an in-ground swimming pool on the terrace patio. A room-service coffee tray greets guests first thing in the morning, and a full breakfast follows, served in the dining room.

6 Rooms • Price range: $120-215
62 John St N, Stratford, ON N5A 6K7
☎ **(519) 271-4576**

Thunder Bay
ⓦ *The White Fox Inn*

Set on a wooded estate just outside
the city, this elegant mansion overlooks Thunder Bay's most prestigious
golf and country club as well as
the scenic Nor'Wester Mountain Range.
Accommodations are sumptuous and romantic,
with each of the nine guestrooms featuring a
jet tub, fireplace and tasteful decor. Guests
are invited to enjoy a varied breakfast menu,
served daily.

9 Rooms • Price range: $105-279
1345 Mountain Rd, RR 4,
Thunder Bay, ON P7C 4Z2
☎ **(807) 577-3699**

Thunder Bay
ⓦ *Pinebrook Bed & Breakfast*
This inn is in a rural setting on the
eastern outskirts of the city.

4 Rooms • Price range: $70-145
134 Mitchell Rd, Thunder Bay, ON P7B 6B3
☎ **(807) 683-6114**

Toronto
ⓦ *Annex House Bed & Breakfast*
This restored circa 1900 Georgian home
offers a touch of the American South in
the heart of downtown Toronto. Rooms
are furnished with queen or twin beds
and ensuite baths, and guests wake each
morning to a full complimentary breakfast.

4 Rooms • Price range: $75-90
147 Madison Ave, Toronto, ON M5R-2S6
☎ **(416) 920-3922**

Toronto
ⓦ *Beverley Place*
Located in downtown, this property is
composed of two 1887 Victorians.

6 Rooms • Price range: $65-120
235 Beverley St, Toronto, ON M5T 1Z4
☎ **(416) 977-0077**

Toronto
ⓦ *Allenby Guest House*
This restored 1913 B&B is located in a
residential area. Guest units offer modern amenities, including shared kitchen
facilities, and a fully equipped apartment
is also available. Other features include an
attractive sundeck.

7 Rooms • Price range: $55-75
223 Strathmore Blvd, Toronto, ON M4J 1P4
☎ **(416) 461-7095**

Toronto
ⓦ *Jarvis House*
This newly renovated Victorian house
is situated in the heritage district.

11 Rooms • Price range: $89-169
344 Jarvis St, Toronto, ON M4Y 2G6
☎ **(416) 975-3838**

Waterloo

⌂ *Les Diplomates B&B (Executive Guest House)*

Classic elegance in a gracious setting of towering maple trees and manicured lawns. Accommodations have queen-size beds and inviting sitting areas. The soft pastel tones, tasteful lighting, fine linens and down duvets add extra luxury. A five-course gourmet breakfast is served each morning in the dining room, and English-style tea is served to guests each afternoon in the spacious parlor.

4 Rooms • Price range: $69-150
100 Blythwood Rd, Waterloo, ON N2L 4A2
☎ **(519) 725-3184**

Westport

⌂ *Stepping Stone Inn*

Located on 150 acres, this 1840s country inn is near a number of sites, including the Rideau Canal System and the Rideau Trail Hiking System. There is a private swimming pond and a nature trail nearby. The inn features a large country kitchen with an antique cookstove, a solarium and a dining room overlooking the gardens. All rooms have private baths. Luxury suites have a private entrance, a Jacuzzi and a fireplace.

8 Rooms • Price range: $75-175
328 Centerville Rd, Westport, ON K0G 1X0
☎ **(613) 273-3806**

Wyevale

⌂ *A Wymbolwood Beach House B&B*

A contemporary home featuring rooms with private baths and entrances.

4 Rooms • Price range: $65-90
533 Tiny Beaches Rd S, Wyevale, ON L0L 2T0
☎ **(705) 361-3649**

Notes:

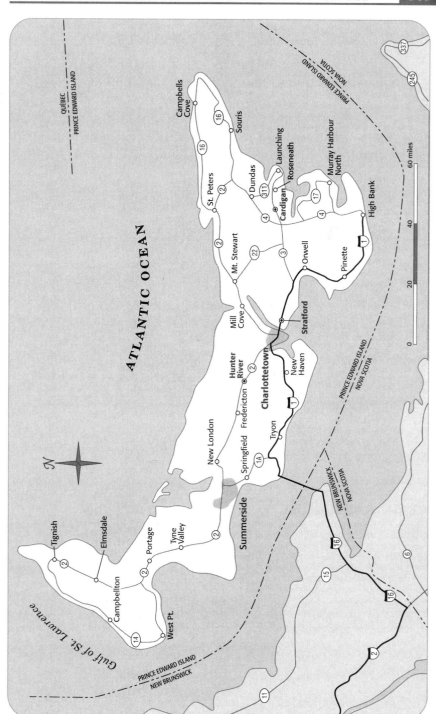

Cardigan

Roseneath Bed & Breakfast

Set in a tranquil riverside location, this 1868 farmhouse inn is decorated with country charm. Featured are antiques, handmade rugs and fascinating artwork collected by the owners on their travels overseas. Other attractions include a working pump organ and a gramophone. The guestrooms are made up with handmade quilts and are equipped with either a private or shared bath. Guests enjoy a home-cooked breakfast daily.

4 Rooms • Price range: $75-90
RR 6, Cardigan, PE C0A 1G0
☎ **(902) 838-4590**

  D

Charlottetown

Anne's Ocean View Haven Bed & Breakfast
This property offers comfortable units and access to a kitchen.

5 Rooms • Price range: $95-165
Kinloch Rd, Charlottetown, PE C1A 7N7
☎ **(902) 569-4644**

 D

Charlottetown

EdenHurst Inn
This 1897 Queen Anne-Revival home with its tower, gables and bay windows, epitomizes the splendor of late Victorian style. The interior of the inn is also impressive, having been restored to its original grandeur. Each of the guestrooms has been given a unique decor, and all are furnished with period antiques. The inn is minutes away from Confederation Square and the heart of the historic downtown.

7 Rooms • Price range: $115-200
12 West St, Charlottetown, PE C1A 3S4
☎ **(902) 368-8323**

Charlottetown

Fitzroy Hall
This well-restored 1872 home has lovely parlors and tasteful guestrooms.

6 Rooms • Price range: $105-225
45 Fitzroy St, Charlottetown, PE C1A 1R4
☎ **(902) 368-2077**

 D

Charlottetown
Hillhurst Inn
The original owner of this 1897 Colonial-Revival home was a shipbuilder, and the common areas display his craftsmanship; quarter-oak paneling, a golden beech finish in the parlor and unique mantelpieces. The guestrooms are furnished with period antiques and a collection of contemporary Island art. From the inn, it is easy to stroll to the harbor front, to hike along the outlying trails or to explore downtown.

9 Rooms • Price range: $99-205
181 Fitzroy St, Charlottetown, PE C1A 1S3
☎ **(902) 894-8004**

D

Charlottetown
The Inns on Great George "The Pavilion"

This block on Great George Street features a unique cluster of heritage buildings that once housed the fathers of Canadian Confederation. The Pavilion Hotel hosted delegates to the 1864 Charlottetown Conference, and The Wellington acted as a gathering place for the legislature. The Pavilion is the largest of this selection of properties and has a variety of elegant rooms, each elegantly appointed with antiques.

27 Rooms • Price range: $155-165
58 Great George St, Charlottetown, PE C1A 4K3
☎ **(902) 892-0606**

Charlottetown
ⓐ *Shipwright Inn*

Built in the 1860s by a shipbuilder, this attractive Victorian home remains true to its heritage by emphasizing a nautical theme. All bedrooms have polished pine floors, some having been converted from ship's planking. Some guestrooms are equipped with a fireplace, a whirlpool and a balcony. Located in the oldest part of one of Canada's oldest cities, a short walk reveals the vintage beauty of historic buildings and the harbor.

8 Rooms • Price range: $135-165
51 Fitzroy St, Charlottetown, PE C1A 1R4
☎ **(902) 368-1905**

Hunter River
ⓐ *Marco Polo Inn*

This pleasant 1925 farmhouse has been completely renovated and is set on part of an attractive campground area. Rooms are comfortable and well-appointed, with bathrooms that offer a choice of shower only or full bath.

6 Rooms • Price range: $65-85
Rt 13, Hunter River, PE C0A 1N0
☎ **(902) 963-2352**

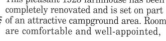

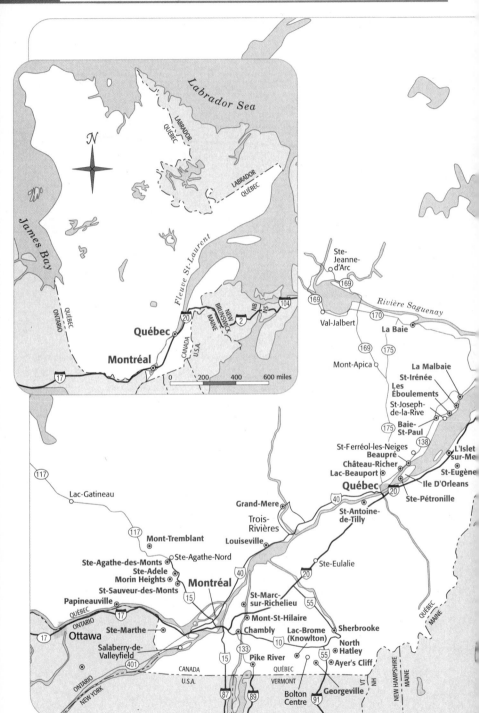

Labrador Sea

LABRADOR
QUÉBEC

LABRADOR
QUÉBEC

James Bay

N

Fleuve St-Laurent

QUÉBEC
ONTARIO

Québec

Montréal

CANADA
U.S.A.

20

MAINE

NEW
BRUNSWICK

NB

NS

2

104

0   200   400   600 miles

17

Ste-
Jeanne-
d'Arc

169

169

Rivière Saguenay

Val-Jalbert

170

La Baie

169   175

Mont-Apica

La Malbaie
St-Irénée
Les
Éboulements
St-Joseph-
de-la-Rive
175   **Baie-**
St-Paul   138

St-Ferréol-les-Neiges
Beaupré
Château-Richer
Lac-Beauport   **L'Islet**
sur-Me
St-Eugène
Ile D'Orleans
Québec   20
Ste-Pétronille

117

Lac-Gatineau

Grand-Mere   40
St-Antoine-
de-Tilly
Trois-
Rivières
117

Mont-Tremblant   **Louiseville**
St-Agathe-Nord   Ste-Eulalie

Ste-Agathe-des-Monts
Ste-Adele   40   20
Morin Heights
St-Sauveur-des-Monts   **Montréal**   **St-Marc-**
sur-Richelieu   55

Papineauville   15
QUÉBEC
ONTARIO
17   **Mont-St-Hilaire**   **Sherbrooke**
Ste-Marthe   **Chambly**   **Lac-Brome**
17   **Ottawa**   **(Knowlton)**   **North**
Hatley
Salaberry-de-
Valleyfield   15   133   **Ayer's Cliff**
401   10   55
Pike River
ONTARIO
NEW YORK   CANADA
U.S.A.   QUÉBEC
VERMONT   **Georgeville**
87   89   **Bolton**
Centre   91   VT   NH
QUÉBEC
MAINE
NEW HAMPSHIRE
MAINE

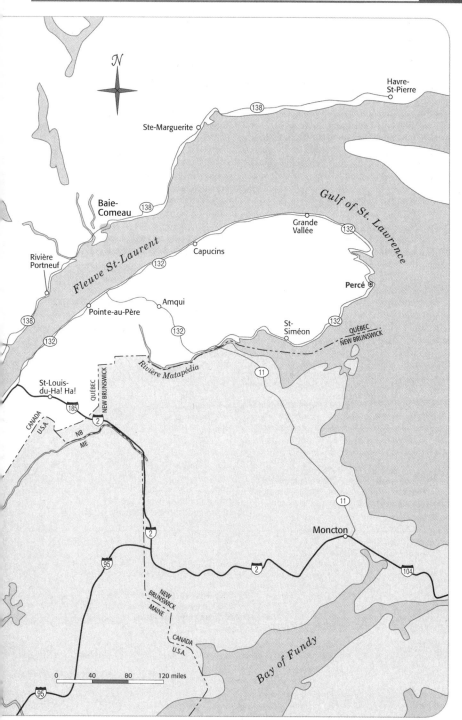

Havre-
St-Pierre

138

Ste-Marguerite

Gulf of St. Lawrence

Baie-
Comeau
138

Grande
Vallée
132

Capucins

Rivière
Portneuf

Fleuve St-Laurent
132

Percé

Amqui

138

Pointe-au-Père

St-
Siméon
132

132

QUÉBEC
NEW BRUNSWICK

Rivière Matapédia

St-Louis-
du-Ha! Ha!

QUÉBEC
NEW BRUNSWICK

11

185

CANADA
U.S.A.

2

NB

ME

11

Moncton

2

95

2

104

NEW
BRUNSWICK
MAINE

CANADA
U.S.A.

Bay of Fundy

0   40   80   120 miles

95

Ayer's Cliff

⊛ *Auberge Ripplecove Inn*

Established in 1945 as a summer resort and fishing lodge, this upscale inn sits on a 12-acre peninsula on Lake Massawippi. Is attractions include two private beaches, a heated pool, and a full range of summer and winter recreation for all ages. Guests can enjoy the lake view from the well-tended gardens or from a private balcony. A formal dinner of French and international cuisine is served in the Victorian dining room. A lakeside terrace and pub provide a more casual atmosphere. An eclectic mix of room styles is available, including lodgings in a century-old log cabin.

26 Rooms • Price range: $140-500
700 Ripplecove Rd, Ayer's Cliff, QC J0B 1C0
☎ **(819) 838-4296**

Baie-St-Paul

⊛ *Auberge Le Cormoran*

Guests have a choice of four different accommodations at this riverfront resort on Baie St. Paul. Children will love the sandy beaches and parents will appreciate the scenery and the tranquillity. Summer or winter, there are plenty of activities.

10 Rooms • Price range: $74-99
196 rue Ste-Anne, Baie-St-Paul, QC G3Z 1P8
☎ **(418) 435-6030**

Beaupré

⊛ *Auberge La Camarine*

Attractive, stylish, comfortable rooms and a lovely garden are all part of this inn.

31 Rooms • Price range: $105-179
10947 boul Ste-Anne, Beaupré, QC G0A 1E0
☎ **(418) 827-5703**

Chambly

La Maison Ducharme

A stately, ivy-covered, historic stone house situated at the foot of Richelieu rapids, this property overlooks Chambly basin. It served as a barracks for nearby Fort Chambly before becoming a hospital, a brewery and then a saddle shop. Now the elegant guestrooms feature lovely antiques, harmonious colors, quality fabrics and magnificent views. Guests can stroll in the garden, swim in the pool or relax on the terrace.

4 Rooms • Price range: $90-125
10 rue de Richelieu, Chambly, QC J3L 2B9
☎ **(450) 447-1220**

Château-Richer

⊛ *Auberge Baker*

This enchanting French Canadian farmhouse built in 1840 offers guestrooms with original pine floors, exposed beams, stone walls, cathedral ceilings and country-style antiques. There is also a charming cottage available in summer.

6 Rooms • Price range: $70-99
8790 ave Royale, Château-Richer, QC G0A 1N0
☎ **(418) 666-5509**

Georgeville
ⓐ *Auberge Georgeville*

Set on a hill overlooking Lake Memphremagog, the 1889 Victorian inn is the oldest continually operated hotel in Quebec. The immaculately preserved historic lodging is well known for its casually elegant decor, delicious regional cuisine and extensive wine cellar. Most rooms have ensuite baths; several have private balconies. Complimentary sherry is served in the sitting room and tea is served on the veranda in summer.

11 Rooms • Price range: $135-250
71 chemin Channel, Georgeville, QC J0B 1T0
☎ **(819) 843-8683**

Grand-Mère
ⓐ *Auberge Santé du Lac des Neiges*

A modern country inn and spa on a peaceful, secluded private lake. Very good-size guestrooms with pleasant decor. Convenient to a public golf course, a ski hill and Mauricie National Park. Motorized boats are not allowed on the lake.

11 Rooms • Price range: $75-105
100 Lac des Neiges, Grand-Mère, QC G9T 5K5
☎ **(819) 533-4518**

Ile d'Orléans
ⓐ *Au Vieux Foyer*

A unique B&B in a rustic early 19th-century Québecois farm home.

4 Rooms • Price range: $55-68
2687 chemin Royal, Ile d'Orléans, QC G0A 4E0
☎ **(418) 828-9171**

L'îslet-sur-Mer
ⓐ *Auberge La Marguerite*

Charming hosts extend a warm welcome to guests visiting their historic 1754 manor in the center of this historic maritime village. Comfortable, guestrooms and inviting common rooms are, like the entire inn, tastefully decorated and impeccably maintained. There are two dining rooms, one for breakfast and the other, which features a stone fireplace, for dinner. The location is ideal for exploring nearby historic attractions.

8 Rooms • Price range: $66-120
88 des Pionniers est,
L'îslet-sur-Mer, QC G0R 2B0
☎ **(418) 247-5454**

La Baie
ⓐ *Auberge des 21*

This contemporary country inn has a variety of nicely appointed rooms.

32 Rooms • Price range: $110-185
621 rue Mars, La Baie, QC G7B 4N1
☎ **(418) 697-2121**

La Malbaie

ⓐ *La Pinsonnière*

La Pinsonnière is perched high above the Saint Lawrence River, surrounded by the breathtaking beauty of Quebec's Charlevoix region, a UNESCO world biosphere reserve. This four-season lodging, originally built as a summer house, has retained much of its warm homelike ambience while offering the luxuries and services of a first-class hotel. Guests will enjoy in-suite Jacuzzis and sweeping views from private terraces. Outdoor activities include whale-watching, golf and tennis, as well as skiing and dog-sledding. Gourmands will appreciate the fine cuisine and one of Canada's largest wine cellars.

25 Rooms • Price range: $145-460
124 rue St-Raphäel, La Malbaie, QC G0T 1B0
☎ **(418) 665-4431**

La Malbaie
ⓐ *La Maison des Berges du Saint-Laurent*

A pleasant waterfront location with nice guestrooms, four with a river view. During the warmer months breakfast is served on the terrace. Within a short driving distance to the Casino de Charlevoix. Hosts speak French, English and Spanish.

9 Rooms • Price range: $50-95
830 rue Richelieu, La Malbaie, QC G0T 1M0
☎ **(418) 665-2742**

Lac-Beauport
ⓐ *Manoir St-Castin*

Since 1938 the Manoir St. Castin has been offering outdoor enthusiasts an exhaustive range of activities. Combining hotel-style services with country inn hospitality, the Manoir provides a number of plans to suit all budgets. Several of the comfortable rooms enjoy balconies with mountain or lake views. Gourmet meals may be enjoyed on the outdoor deck surrounded by spectacular scenery. An active place in all four seasons.

48 Rooms • Price range: $90-160
99 chemin Tour du Lac,
Lac-Beauport, QC G0A 2C0
☎ **(418) 841-4949**

Lac-Brome (Knowlton)
ⓐ *Auberge Lakeview Inn*

Built in 1874, this charming inn is located in the center of Knowlton, an authentic Victorian village. Former Canadian prime ministers have slept in its rooms, now filled with hand-crafted furniture. Studios are available, equipped with a whirlpool bath, a private living room and a balcony. Guests can enjoy the Garden Terrace, the heated pool or an authentic English pub with mahogany woodwork and brass trim.

28 Rooms • Price range: $250-315
50 rue Victoria, Lac-Brome (Knowlton), QC
J0E 1V0
☎ **(450) 243-6183**

Lac-Brome (Knowlton)
ⓐ *Auberge Quilliams Inn*

Located a few miles from the picturesque village of Knowlton, this rustic inn sits between Brome Lake and the Quilliams Wildlife Preserve. Each room has its own private balcony that overlooks one of the beautiful vistas. The area is an all-season playground for outdoor enthusiasts. Guests can windsurf, canoe, golf and hike in the summer; dog-sled, ski, ice-fish and skate in the winter. The restaurant serves refined French cuisine.

38 Rooms • Price range: $129-175
572 chemin Lakeside, Lac-Brome (Knowlton),
QC J0E 1R0
☎ **(450) 243-0404**

Les Éboulements
ⓐ *Auberge Le Surouet*

This contemporary-style inn sits in an enchanting countryside setting next to a delightful artistic village. It offers guestrooms with fireplaces, some with a balcony. There is an art gallery and good-quality gift shop on site. Guests can absorb the view from the large terrace, while indulging in the delights from the Tea Room. On the menu is traditional tarte au sucre, or sugar pie. In the area, guests can ski, dog-sled or go whale watching.

5 Rooms • Price range: $90-135
195 rue Principale,
Les Éboulements, QC G0A 2M0
☎ **(418) 635-1401**

Louiseville
ⓐ *Gite du Carrefour et Maison Historique J. L. L. Hamelin*

Built in 1898 by Docteur Louis-Léandre Hamelin this Queen Anne-style mansion surrounded by lush summer gardens, is an architectural gem. Magnificently preserved and furnished with elegant period antiques, guests enjoy comfortable surroundings in an historic home. The area is the birthplace of some well-known Quebec artists and writers. Local attractions include visiting historical buildings and parks.

5 Rooms • Price range: $50-65
11 ave St-Laurent ouest, Louiseville, QC J5V 1J3
☎ **(819) 228-4932**

Mont-St-Hilaire
Manoir Rouville-Campbell

This impressive Tudor-style home sits on the shores of the Richelieu River amid beautifully tended French and English gardens. It provides a country retreat just 20 minutes from Montreal. The guestrooms offer a choice of quality antique-reproduction furnishings or contemporary-style decor. Guests can take in the majestic natural background of mountain and river from the Manoir's terrace.

25 Rooms • Price range: $149-159
125 chemin des Patriotes sud,
Mont-St-Hilaire, QC J3H 3G5
☎ **(450) 446-6060**

Mont-Tremblant
⑳ *Auberge La Petite Cachée*

This quiet Scandinavian log cabin offers cozy rooms with heated bathroom floors.

10 Rooms • Price range: $95-135
2681 chemin Principale,
Mont-Tremblant, QC J0T 1Z0
☎ **(819) 425-2654**

Mont-Tremblant
⑳ *Auberge Le Lupin Bed & Breakfast*

A family-style B&B within walking distance of Lac Tremblant's private beaches.

9 Rooms • Price range: $99-139
127 rue Pinoteau, Mont-Tremblant, QC J0T 1Z0
☎ **(819) 425-5474**

Montréal
⑳ *Auberge de la Fontaine*

Located in a pleasant residential district, this award-winning inn is near the Latin Quarter, famous for its café terraces and boutiques. It is also across the street from a large park with biking paths. All the spacious rooms have a private bathroom and are sound-proofed. Some have a sitting nook, a work area, or a balcony. Guests can enjoy a view of the park from a summer terrace. A variety of complimentary snacks is available.

21 Rooms • Price range: $145-190
1301 rue Rachel est, Montréal, QC H2J 2K1
☎ **(514) 597-0166**

Morin Heights
⑳ *Auberge Clos Joli*

Family-operated, this renovated farmhouse is located in a quiet rural setting.

9 Rooms • Price range: $105-170
19 chemin du Clos Joli,
Morin Heights, QC J0R 1H0
☎ **(450) 226-5401**

North Hatley
⑳ *Auberge Hatley Inn*

This charming country house sits on a hillside offering magnificent views of Lake Massawippi. Bright, individually decorated rooms with quality furnishings provide plenty of character and charm. Many of the inn's rooms come with a private balcony looking out over the lake and some have a wood-burning fireplace. One of the most celebrated restaurants in Quebec is found within the inn, its salads and herbs coming directly from Auberge Hatley's greenhouse. The wine cellar is exceptional. Recreational activities include kayaking, fishing, cross-country skiing and sleigh rides.

25 Rooms • Price range: $220-525
325 Virgin Rd, North Hatley, QC J0B 2C0
☎ **(819) 842-2451**

North Hatley
⊛ *Hovey Manor*

In a lovely location on a bank overlooking Lake Massawippi, this hostelry lends a welcome touch of Southern flavor to the area by virtue of its antebellum architecture. The rolling farmland, apple orchards and vineyards of this region are only half an hour's drive from Vermont. The original coach house of the manor is now a taproom decorated in antique weaponry. Guests can take advantage of two private beaches or wander the large English garden, enclosed by low stone walls. The manor's distinguished wine cellar and dining room have won many awards.

39 Rooms • Price range: $195-450
575 chemin Hovey, North Hatley, QC J0B 2C0
☎ **(819) 842-2421**

North Hatley
⊛ *Auberge Manoir Le Tricorne*

This charming historic country inn sits on a peaceful hillside surrounded by 90 beautiful acres of fields and woods. The rolling grounds are dotted with ponds and Lake Massawippi can be seen in the distance. The guestrooms are individually decorated and the common areas are well-appointed. Some rooms feature a fireplace, a Jacuzzi and/or a private balcony. Delectable brunches are the host's specialty.

12 Rooms • Price range: $95-185
50 chemin Gosselin, North Hatley, QC J0B 2C0
☎ **(819) 842-4522**

North Hatley
⊛ *Le Coeur d'Or B&B*

Lovely rooms and great breakfasts charm guests visiting this B&B.

8 Rooms • Price range: $75-185
85 School St, North Hatley, QC J0B 2C0
☎ **(819) 842-4363**

Papineauville
⊛ *À L'Orée du Moulin*

This circa 1840 French-Canadian style home has cozy, pleasant guestrooms. Conveniently located to the local attractions such as the Château Montebello and golf course,

Parc Omega nature reserve and the historic Manoir Papineau.

4 Rooms • Price range: $50-65
170 Joseph-Lucien-Malo St, Papineauville, QC J0V 1R0
☎ **(819) 427-8534**

Percé
⊛ *L'Auberge à Percé Lieu Dit au Pirate 1775*

Set on the waterfront, this 18th-century house has small but comfortable rooms.

5 Rooms • Price range: $90-150
169 Rt 132 Centre, Percé, QC G0C 2L0
☎ **(418) 782-5055**

Pike River
⊛ *Auberge-Inn La Suisse*

This country inn features guestrooms with quality duvets and linens.

4 Rooms • Price range: $65-75
119 Rt 133, Pike River, QC J0J 1P0
☎ **(450) 244-5870**

Québec
Ⓐ *Auberge Saint-Antoine*

This restored 18th-century maritime warehouse is located in a neighborhood renowned for its cultural and historical appeal. The inn offers large, bright rooms, all creatively decorated. Some rooms have excellent river views, some have access to a rooftop terrace and some have a private balcony. Its conference facility combines hi-tech and class. Only steps away is Le Petit Champlain, the oldest shopping district in America.

31 Rooms • Price range: $279-399
10 rue Saint-Antoine, Québec, QC G1K 4C9
☎ **(418) 692-2211**

Québec
Ⓐ *Manoir "Mon Calme"*

A lovely Victorian graystone located on Grande-Allée, this manor is within walking distance of fine restaurants, the Plains of Abraham and the attractions of the walled city. It offers tastefully decorated and spacious guestrooms. Guests can soak in the sun and enjoy a generous breakfast on one of two large terraces. The hosts do their utmost to provide all the information necessary for a complete visit to this historic city.

5 Rooms • Price range: $109-149
549 Grande Allée Est, Québec, QC G1R 2J5
☎ **(418) 523-2714**

Québec
Ⓐ *Auberge du Quartier*

Just across the street from the Plains of Abraham and the Quebec Museum, this restored 1852 residence offers elegant public areas and attractive rooms that range from cozy to spacious. Old Quebec and its restaurants and shops are an easy walk away.

15 Rooms • Price range: $75-90
170 Grande Allée ouest, Québec, QC G1R 2G9
☎ **(418) 525-9726**

Québec
Ⓐ *Hotel Manoir d'Auteuil*

In 1931 this 1835 greystone residence was up-dated with Art Deco-style woodwork. Located within the historic walled city makes it accessible to fine restaurants and bistros, and the European ambience that defines this special city.

16 Rooms • Price range: $75-150
49 rue d'Auteuil, Québec, QC G1R 4C2
☎ **(418) 694-1173**

Sherbrooke
Ⓐ *Le Mitchell B&B*

This grand 1939 Tudor-style mansion in Sherbrooke's historic district offers a very comfortable environment and extra spacious rooms. An outdoor pool set in a nicely landscaped yard is quiet, private spot to spend a restful afternoon.

4 Rooms • Price range: $90-135
219 Moore St, Sherbrooke, QC J1H 1C1
☎ **(819) 562-1517**

St-Antoine-de-Tilly

⊕ *Manoir de Tilly*

Established on the shores of the St. Lawrence River in 1702 by some of the country's first pioneers, this town has maintained its old shingled homes and its old-fashioned charm. Built in 1786, the manor, which houses an award-winning dining room, is one of these well preserved homes. The inn itself is a contemporary building. Views of the river and flowering gardens can be had from the tastefully decorated rooms.

30 Rooms • Price range: $120-129
3854 chemin de Tilly,
St-Antoine-de-Tilly, QC G0S 2C0
☎ **(418) 886-2407**

St-Eugéne

⊕ *Auberge des Glacis*

This restored 1840 stone-walled flour mill is set beside a stream on 12 acres of open field and forest between the St. Lawrence River and the Appalachian Mountains. Ten thematically decorated guest-rooms feature local country antiques and modern private baths. A small lake, ideal for swimming becomes a skating rink during the winter. This inn offers the unique ambience of the Quebec countryside in an historic setting.

10 Rooms • Price range: $84-99
46 Route de la Tortue, St-Eugéne, QC G0R 1X0
☎ **(418) 247-7486**

St-Irénée

⊕ *Auberge des Sablons*

This traditional 1902 Charlevoix inn is perched on a hillside overlooking the St. Lawrence River. Decorated with French Country flair, the majority of the rooms have scenic river views. Some rooms have a balcony; others have a fireplace. There are also furnished studio apartments available in a nearby pavilion. The multi-windowed dining room offers continental cuisine with a regional touch.

15 Rooms • Price range: $127-234
290 chemin Les Bains, St-Irénée, QC G0T 1V0
☎ **(418) 452-3594**

St-Marc-sur-Richelieu

⊕ *Auberge Handfield Inn*

Surrounded by farmland, this rustic inn has cottage-style rooms.

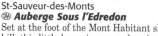

53 Rooms • Price range: $65-240
555 boul Richelieu,
St-Marc-sur-Richelieu, QC J0L 2E0
☎ **(450) 584-2226**

St-Sauveur-des-Monts

⊕ *Auberge Sous l'Edredon*

Set at the foot of the Mont Habitant ski hill, this little home is very welcoming.

7 Rooms • Price range: $64-109
777 rue Principale,
St-Sauveur-des-Monts, QC J0R 1R2
☎ **(450) 227-3131**

Ste-Adèle

ⓐ *L'Eau à la Bouche*

Deep in the heart of one of Quebec's most popular four-season resort regions, L'Eau à la Bouche presents some of the finest cuisine in the country in an environment of casual elegance. The name of the inn means "mouthwatering" and the kitchen of chef Anne Dejardins is renown for its creative use of regional delicacies. This creative flair extends to the bold colors, fine fabrics and unique furnishings in the tasteful, thematically decorated guestrooms. Many rooms feature sitting areas and all look out onto the forest or ski-hills. Special seasonal packages, some that include sleigh rides, are availiable.

25 Rooms • Price range: $170-310
3003 boul Sainte-Adèle, Ste-Adèle, QC J8B 2N6
☎ (450) 229-2991

Ste-Agathe-des-Monts
ⓐ *Auberge du Lac des Sables*
Small but nice rooms near beaches, cycling and cross-country ski trails.

23 Rooms • Price range: $77-126
230 rue St-Venant,
Ste-Agathe-des-Monts, QC J8C 2Z7
☎ (819) 326-3994

Ste-Marthe
ⓐ *Auberge des Gallants*
Lovely gardens surround this very comfortable contemporary country inn.

25 Rooms • Price range: $89-179
1171 chemin St-Henri, Ste-Marthe, QC J0P 1W0
☎ (450) 459-4241

Ste-Petronille
ⓐ *Auberge La Goeliche*
Most rooms in this modern country inn overlook the St. Lawrence River.

16 Rooms • Price range: $125-194
22 chemin du Quai, Ste-Petronille, QC G0A 4C0
☎ (418) 828-2248

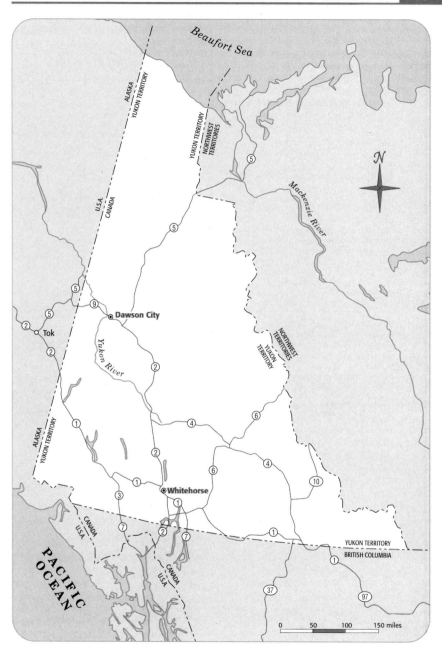

Beaufort Sea

ALASKA
YUKON TERRITORY

YUKON TERRITORY
NORTHWEST TERRITORIES

⑤

Mackenzie River

USA
CANADA

⑤

N

⑤

⑤
⑨
◉ Dawson City

⑤
② ○ Tok
②

Yukon River

②

NORTHWEST TERRITORIES
YUKON TERRITORY

ALASKA
YUKON TERRITORY

① ⑥
② ④
⑥ ④
① ③ ◉ Whitehorse ⑩
①
CANADA
U.S.A.
⑦ ② ⑦ ①
②
CANADA
U.S.A.

YUKON TERRITORY
BRITISH COLUMBIA
①

PACIFIC OCEAN

③⑦ ⑨⑦

0   50   100   150 miles

Dawson City
◆◆ ⓐ *Dawson City Bed & Breakfast*
Located near the museum, this inn has a true homey style and modest rooms.

7 Rooms • Price range: $89-109
451 Craig St, Dawson City, YT Y0B 1G0
☎ **(867) 993-5649**

Dawson City
◆ ⓐ *White Ram Manor Bed & Breakfast*
Overlooking the town, this inn has a well-equipped kitchen for guest use.

10 Rooms • Price range: $50-110
7th Ave & Harper St, Dawson City, YT Y0B 1G0
☎ **(867) 993-5772**

Whitehorse
◆◆◆ ⓐ *Hawkins House Bed & Breakfast*
Located in downtown Whitehorse, this inn features high ceilings, hardwood floors and stained-glass windows that evoke a turn-of-the-20th-century atmosphere. Rooms have modern amenities such as room temperature controls and Jacuzzis. They also have queen-size beds, private bathrooms and balconies and feature art and literature that reflect Yukon culture. Theme breakfasts are served in the Victorian dining room.

4 Rooms • Price range: $136-163
303 Hawkins St, Whitehorse, YT Y1A 1X5
☎ **(867) 668-7638**

Whitehorse
◆◆ ⓐ *Midnight Sun Bed & Breakfast*
This is a bright and modern home only one block from great hiking trails. The owners are very hospitable and their rooms comfortable—and imaginatively decorated. Each guestroom features a different theme, such as Egyptian, Persian or Victorian, and all are fitted with private baths and queen beds. A deluxe breakfast is served each morning in the sunny Deluxe Lounge or Northern Room. Visitors are welcome to use the barbecue.

4 Rooms • Price range: $79-120
6188 5th Ave, Whitehorse, YT Y1A 1N8
☎ **(867) 667-2255**

J K

W X Y Z

The following pages contain helpful information on the sites listed in the Scenic Byways.

NORTHEAST

Rockland to Bucksport:

Farnsworth Art Museum and Wyeth Center.
356 Main St, Rockland, ME. Open daily 9-5, Memorial Day to Columbus Day; Tues-Sat 10-5, Sun 1-5, rest of year. Closed Jan 1, Thanksgiving and Dec 25.
☎ (207) 596-6457

Rockport Marine Park.
André St.
Open daily dawn to dusk.
☎ (207) 236-4404

The Center for Maine Contemporary Art.
162 Russell Ave, Rockport, ME 04856. Open year-round; call for hours.
☎ (207) 236-2875

Camden/Rockport/Lincolnville Chamber of Commerce.
Commercial St, Public Landing, Camden. PO Box 919, Camden, ME 04843.
☎ (207) 236-4404 or (800) 223-5459

Penobscot Marine Museum.
5 Church St, Searsport, ME. Mon-Sat 10-5, Sun 12-5, Memorial Day to Oct 15.
☎ (207) 548-2529

Castine: Bucksport Bay Area Chamber of Commerce.
263 Main St, Bucksport, ME. PO Box 1880, Bucksport, ME 04416
☎ (207) 469-6818

Acadia National Park. PO Box 177, Bar Harbor, ME 04609. Accessible all year.
☎ (207) 288-3338

Kancamagus Highway:

Lost River Gorge. Rte 112 Kinsman Notch, North Woodstock, NH 03262. Open daily 9-6, July to Aug; 9-5 May to June, Sept to Oct.
☎ (603) 745-8031

Kancamagus Pass: The Whale's Tale Water Park. Daily 9-6, July-Aug, 9-5 May-June, Sept-Oct.
☎ (603) 745-8810

North Conway: Mt. Washington Valley Chamber of Commerce. Main St, PO Box 2300, North Conway, NH 03860.
☎ (603) 356-3171 or (800) 367-3364

Crawford Notch State Park. PO Box 1856, Concord, NH 03302.
☎ (603) 374-2272 or (603) 271-3556 off season

Franconia Notch State Park. Rte 3, Franconia, NH 03580.
☎ (603) 823-8800

Cannon Mountain Aerial Tramway. Daily 9-5, July 1 to Labor Day; 9-4:30, mid-May to June 30, Sept to late Oct.
☎ (603) 823-8800

Wilmington to Troy:

Bennington Area Chamber of Commerce. 100 Veterans Memorial Drive, Bennington, VT 05201.
☎ (802) 447-3311 or (800) 229-0252

Stratton Mountain Resort. RR1 Box 145, Stratton Mountain, VT 05155-9406.
☎ (802) 297-4000 or (800) STRATTON

Manchester and the Mountains Chamber of Commerce. 5046 Main St, Suite 1, Manchester Center, VT 05255. Visitors center: Adams Park, Route 7A N.
☎ (802) 362-2100

Hildene House. PO Box 377 Manchester, VT 05254. Tours daily, 9:30-4, mid-May to Oct 31; call for times. Candlelight tours 5-8:30, Dec 27-29.
☎ (802) 362-1788

Plymouth: President Calvin Coolidge State Historic Site. PO Box 247, Plymouth Notch, VT 05056. Daily 9:30-5, late May to mid-Oct.
☎ (802) 672-3773

Shelburne Museum. Rte. 7, VT. Daily 10-5, late May to mid-Oct; 1-4 end of March to late May and mid-Oct to early Dec. Closed major holidays.
☎ (802) 985-3346

Stowe Area Association.
51 Main St, PO Box 1320, Stowe, VT 05672.
☎ (802) 253-7321 or 800-24-STOWE

Sagamore to Orleans:

Heritage Plantation.
67 Grove St, Sandwich, MA. Daily 10-5, mid-May to mid-Oct.
☎ (508) 888-3300

Sandwich Glass Museum.
129 Main St. Daily 9:30-5, Apr-Dec; Wed-Sun 9:30-4:30, Feb-Mar. Closed Thanksgiving and Dec 25.
☎ (508) 888-0251

Trayser Museum. Rte. 6A (Cobb's Hill), Barnstable, MA. Tues-Sun 1:30-4:30, mid-June to mid-Oct.
☎ (508) 362-2092

The Dennis Chamber of Commerce. 242 Swan River Rd, West Dennis, MA. PO Box 275, South Dennis, MA 02660.
☎ (508) 398-3568 or (800) 243-9920

Brewster: Cape Cod Museum of Natural History.
869 Rte 6A, MA. Mon-Sat 9:30-4:30, Sun 11-4:30. Closed major holidays.
☎ (508) 896-3867

Nickerson State Park.
3488 Main St, Rte 6A Brewster, MA 02631. Open year-round.
☎ (508) 896-3491; Camping reservations: (877) 422-6762

Massachusetts Border to I-395:

Quinebaug Valley Fish Hatchery. 141 Trout Hatchery, Central Village. PO Box 441, Central Village, CT 06332. Daily 9:30-3:30. Public fishing pond open Mar 1 to Memorial Day; reservations required.
☎ (860) 564-7542

Roseland Cottage (Henry C Bowen House). Wed-Sun 11-5, June 1 to Oct 15. Tours on the hour; last tour at 4pm.
☎ (860) 928-4074

The Prudence Crandall Museum. Jct Rtes 14 and 169. PO Box 58, Canterbury, CT 06331. Wed-Sun 10-4:30, Feb 1 to mid-Dec; closed Thanksgiving.
☎ (860) 546-9916

Mystic/Groton: Connecticut's Mystic & More! 470 Bank St, PO Box 89, New London, CT 06320.
☎ (860) 444-2206 or (800) 863-6569

Denison Homestead. 120 Pequotsepos Rd, Mystic, CT. Thurs-Mon 11-4, mid-May to mid-Oct.
☎ (860) 536-9248

Fort Griswold State Park. 57 Fort St, Groton, CT 06340. Park open daily 8-sunset. Museum & Monument open daily 10-5, Memorial Day to Labor Day; Sat-Sun 10-5, Labor Day to Columbus Day.
☎ (860) 445-1729

Thomas Lee House Museum. Rte 156, PO Box 112, East Lyme, CT 06333. Open Tues-Sun 1-4, late June to Labor Day.
☎ (860) 739-6070 or (860) 739-5079

Route 30:
Lake Placid: Essex County Visitors Bureau. Olympic Center, 216 Main St, Lake Placid, NY 12946.
☎ (518) 523-2445 or (800) 447-5224

U.S. Olympic Training Center. 421 Old Military Rd, Lake Placid. Daily 8-8, guided tour at 3 Mon-Fri. Closed Dec 25.
☎ (518) 523-2600

Olympic Center. 218 Main St off SR 86. Daily 9-5. Call for hours of tours.
☎ (518) 523-1655 or (800) 462-6236

Whiteface Mountain. Rte 86, Wilmington, NY 12997.
☎ (518) 946-2223 or (800) 462-6236

Blue Mountain Lake Association. Blue Mountain Lake, NY 12812.
☎ (518) 352-7659

Adirondack Museum. Route 30, Blue Mountain Lake, NY 12812. Daily 9:30-5:30, Memorial Day to mid-Oct.
☎ (518) 352-7311

Howe Caverns. Discovery Drive, PO Box 107, Howes Caves, NY 12092. Daily 9-6, Sept to June; 8-8 July to Aug. Closed Jan 1, Thanksgiving and Dec 25.
☎ (518) 296-8900

Iroquois Indian Museum. Caverns Rd, PO Box 7, Caverns Rd, Howes Cave, NY 12092. Tues-Sat 10-5, Sun 12-5, Apr-Dec. Closed Easter Sunday, Thanksgiving and Dec 24-25.
☎ (518) 296-8949

National Baseball Hall of Fame and Museum. 25 Main St, Cooperstown, NY. Daily 9-9, May to Sept 30; 9-5 rest of year. Closed Jan 1, Thanksgiving and Dec 25.
☎ (607) 547-7200 or (888) 425-5633

Springfield Center: Glimmerglass Opera. PO Box 191, Cooperstown, NY 13326.
☎ (607) 547-5704

The Farmer's Museum. Rte 80, Cooperstown, NY. Daily 10-5, June to Sept; Tues-Sun 10-4, Apr to May and Oct to Nov. Closed Thanksgiving.
☎ (607) 547-1450 or (888) 547-1450

SOUTHEAST
Skyline Drive/Blue Ridge Parkway:
The Warren Rifles Confederate Museum. 95 Chester St, Front Royal, VA 22630. Mon-Sat 9-4, Sun 12-4, Apr 15 to Oct 31.
☎ (540) 636-6982 or (540) 635-2219

Luray Caverns. 970 US Hwy 211 W. Daily 9-7, June to Labor Day; reduced hours rest of year. Call for tour times.
☎ (540) 743-6551

Shenandoah National Park. 3655 US Hwy 211 E, Luray, VA 22835. Developed campgrounds open Mar to Dec.
☎ (540) 999-3500

Blue Ridge Parkway. Headquarters: 199 Hemphill Knob Rd, Asheville, NC 28803.
☎ (828) 298-0398

Humpback Rocks Visitor Center. Blueridge Pkwy. Call for hours.
☎ (540) 943-4716

Parkway Craft Center. 667 Service Rd, Blueridge Pkwy, Blowing Rock, NC 28605. Daily 9-5, Mar 15 to Nov 30.
☎ (828) 295-7938

Biltmore Estate. Rte 25, Hendersonville Rd, Asheville, NC. Daily 8:30-5, Apr to Dec; 9-5, Jan to Mar. Closed Thanksgiving and Dec 25.
☎ (828) 255-1700 or (800) 543-2961

Oconaluftee Indian Village. US Hwy 441 N. Daily 9-5:30, May 15 to Oct. 25.
☎ (828) 497-2315

The Buccaneer Trail:
Cummer Museum Of Art & Gardens. 829 Riverside Ave, Jacksonville, FL. Tues-Sat 10-5; Sun 12-5. Closed major holidays.
☎ (904) 356-6857

Kingsley Plantation. 11676 Palmetto Ave, Jacksonville, FL 32226. Daily 9-5; closed Dec 25.
☎ (904) 251-3537

Castillo de San Marcos. 1 Castillo Drive, St Augustine, FL 32084. Daily 8:45-4:45. Closed Dec 25.
☎ (904) 829-6506

Washington Oaks Garden State Park. 6400 N Oceanshore Blvd, Palm Coast, FL 32173. Open daily 8-sunset.
☎ (904) 446-6780

The Kennedy Space Center Visitor Complex. On SR 405. Daily 9-dusk; closed Dec 25 and during certain periods on launch days.
☎ (321) 452-2121

Baton Rouge to Gibson:
Baton Rouge Convention and Visitors Bureau. PO Box 4149, Baton Rouge, LA 70821.
☎ (800) LA-ROUGE

Old State Capital. 100 North Blvd, Baton Rouge, LA 70801. Tues-Sat 10-4; Sun 12-4. Closed holidays.
☎ (225) 342-0500

LSU Rural Life Museum. PO Box 80498, Baton Rouge, LA 70898. Open year-round 8:30-5; closed winter holidays.
☎ (225) 765-2437

The Plaquemine Lock Museum. 57730 Main St, Plaquemine, LA 70764. Daily 9-5; closed major holidays.
☎ (225) 687-7158 or (877) 987-7158

Nottoway Plantation. Off Hwy 1, White Castle, LA. Tours daily 9-5; closed Dec 25.
☎ (225) 545-2730

Tezcuco Plantation. 3138 Hwy 44, Darrow, LA 70725. Daily 9-5, March to Nov; 10-4, Dec to Feb. Closed Jan 1, Thanksgiving and Dec 25.
☎ (225) 562-3929

Oak Alley Plantation. 3645 Hwy 18, Vacherie, LA 70090. Daily 9-5:30, Mar to Oct; 9-5 rest of year. Closed Jan 1, Thanksgiving and Dec 25.
☎ (225) 265-2151 or (800) 44-ALLEY

Wildlife Gardens. 5306 North Bayou Black Drive, Gibson, LA 70356. Daily 8-5; closed holidays.
☎ (504) 575-3676

The Trace:
Adsmore Living History Museum. 304 N Jefferson St, Princeton, KY. Tues-Sat 11-4, Sun 1:30-4; closed holidays.
☎ (270) 365-3114

The Trace: Land Between the Lakes National Recreation Area/Golden Pond Visitor Center. 100 Van Morgan Dr, Golden Pond, KY 42211. Open daily 9-5 year-round.
☎ (270) 924-2016 or (800) 525-7077

The Homeplace in Tennessee. 12 miles S of Golden Pond Visitor Center, 100 Van Morgan Dr, Golden Pond, KY 42211. Open Mon-Sat 9-5, Sun 10-5, Apr to Oct; Wed-Sat 9-5, Sun 10-5, Mar and Nov.
☎ (270) 924-2020 or (800) 525-7077

Fort Donelson. 120 Fort Donelson Park Road, Dover, TN 37058. Visitor center open daily 8-4:30; closed Dec 25. Grounds close at dark.
☎ (931) 232-5706

Tennessee National Wildlife Refuge. PO Box 849, Paris, TN 38242. Daily dawn to dusk.
☎ (901) 642-2091

U.S. 68:
Kentucky Horse Park. 4089 Iron Works Pkwy, Lexington, KY 40511. Daily 9-5, Mar to Oct; Wed-Sun 9-5, rest of year. Closed major holidays.
☎ (859) 233-4303 or (800) 678-8813

Mary Todd Lincoln House. 578 West Main Street, Lexington, KY 40588 Mon-Sat 10-4, Mar 15 to Nov 15; closed holidays.
☎ (859) 233-9999

Shaker Village of Pleasant Hill. 3501 Lexington Rd, Harrodsburg, KY 40330. Open daily 9:30-5:30, Apr to Oct; 10-4:30 rest of year. Closed Dec 24-25.
☎ (859) 734-5411 or (800) 734-5611

Old Fort Harrod State Park. PO Box 156, Harrodsburg, KY 40330. Open daily 8:30-5, Mar 16 to Oct 31; 8-4:30, Nov 1 to March 15.
☎ (859) 734-3314

Maker's Mark Distillery. Loretto, KY. Tours daily year-round; call for times. Closed major holidays.
☎ (270) 865-2099

My Old Kentucky Home State Park. PO Box 323, Bardstown, KY 40004. Daily 8:30-6:30, June 1 to Labor Day; 9-5, rest of year. Closed major holidays.
☎ (502) 348-3502 or (800) 323-7803

Perryville Battlefield State Historic Site. 1825 Battlefield Rd, Perryville, KY 40468. Open daily dawn to dusk, Apr to Oct. Off-season by appointment.
☎ (859) 332-8631

SOUTHWEST
San Luis to Santa Fe:
Great Sand Dunes National Monument & National Preserve. Visitor Center: 11999 Hwy 150, Mosca, CO 81146. Open daily 9-6, Memorial Day to Labor Day; 8:30-4:30 rest of year. Closed Jan 1 and Dec 25.
☎ (719) 378-2312

Cumbres and Toltec Scenic Railroad. Trains depart daily at 10 from Antonito, CO (Hwy 17 & 285) and Chama, NM (500 Terrace Ave), Memorial Day to mid-Oct. Reservations are suggested.
☎ (719) 376-5483 or (888) CUMBRES

Harwood Museum of Art. 238 Ledoux St, Taos, NM. Open Tues-Sat 10-5, Sun 12-5, Apr to Dec; 12-5 Tues-Sun rest of year; closed major holidays.
☎ (505) 758-9826

Bradbury Science Museum. 15th & Central, Los Alamos, NM. Tues-Fri 9-5, Sat-Mon 1-5. Closed Jan 1, Thanksgiving and Dec 25.
☎ (505) 667-4444

Santa Fe Convention and Visitors Bureau. PO Box 909, Santa Fe, NM 87505.
☎ (505) 955-6200 or (800) 777-2489

Museum of International Folk Art. Camino Lejo off Old Santa Fe Trail. Tues-Sun 10-5; closed major holidays.
☎ (505) 476-1200

Poncha Springs to Durango:
Monarch Aerial Tram. Open daily 8-6, Memorial Day to Labor Day (weather permitting).
☎ (719) 539-4091

Pioneer Museum. 803 E Tomichi (US 50), Gunnison, CO. Open Mon-Sat 9-5, Sun 12-4, Memorial Day to Sept 15.
☎ (970) 641-4530

Gunnison Chamber of Commerce. PO Box 36, Gunnison, CO 81230.
☎ (970) 641-1501 or (800) 274-7580

Curecanti National Recreation Area. 102 Elk Creek, Gunnison, CO 81230. Visitor center has limited hours in winter.
☎ (970) 641-2337

Black Canyon of the Gunnison National Park. 102 Elk Creek, Gunnison, CO 81230. Visitor center open daily 8-6 in summer; 8-4:30 in winter.
☎ (970) 641-2337

Durango and Silverton Narrow Gauge Railway. 479 Main, Durango, CO 81301. Excursions year-round; call for times. Reservations recommended.
☎ (970) 247-2733 or (888) TRAIN-07

Mesa Verde National Park and Cliff Palace. PO Box 8, Mesa Verde, CO 81330. Park open year-round; ruins open on limited basis in winter. Call for tour hours. Far View Visitor Center open daily 8-5, May to Sept.
☎ (970) 529-4465 or (970) 529-4461

Torrey to Panguitch:
Capitol Reef National Park. HC 70, Box 15, Torrey, UT 84775. Visitor center open year round, with reduced hours in winter. Closed Dec 25 and some federal holidays.
☎ (435) 425-3791

Anasazi Indian Village. 460 N Hwy 12, Boulder, UT 84716. Daily 8-6, mid-May to mid-Sept; 9-5 rest of year. Closed Jan 1, Thanksgiving and Dec 25.
☎ (435) 335-7308

Escalante Petrified Forest State Park. PO Box 350, Escalante, UT 84726. Visitor center open daily year-round; limited hours in winter.
☎ (435) 826-4466

Bryce Canyon National Park. PO Box 170001, Bryce Canyon, UT 84717. Visitor center open daily 8-4:30 (extended hours during peak season). Closed Jan 1, Thanksgiving and Dec 25.
☎ (435) 834-5322

Paunsaugaunt Western Wildlife Museum. 250 E Center St, Panguitch, UT. Open daily 9-9, May 1 to Oct 1.
☎ (435) 676-2500

Kodachrome Basin State Park. PO Box 238, Cannonville, UT 84718-0238. Trailhead station open Apr to Oct.
☎ (435) 679-8562

Mt. Carmel Junction to I-15:
Cedar Breaks National Monument. Headquarters: 2390 W Hwy 56, Suite 11, Cedar City, UT 84720.
☎ (435) 586-9451

Coral Pink Sand Dunes State Park. PO Box 95, Kanab, UT 84741. Open daylight hours year-round.
☎ (435) 648-2800

Zion National Park. Springdale, UT 84767-1099. Visitor centers open daily 8-7, Memorial Day to Labor Day; reduced hours rest of year.
☎ (435) 772-3256

Grafton: Hurricane Valley Chamber of Commerce. PO Box 101, Hurricane, UT 84737.
☎ (435) 635-3402

St George Area Chamber of Commerce, 96 E St George Blvd, St George, UT 84770.
☎ (435) 628-1658

Jacob Hamlin Home. Santa Clara Drive, St George, UT. Open daily 9-7 in summer; 9-5 in winter.
☎ (435) 673-2161

Cameron to Grand Canyon Village:
Tusayan Museum and Ruin. On Desert View drive in Grand Canyon Park. Open daily 9-5; seasonal closures in winter.
☎ (520) 638-2305

The Grand Canyon National Park. PO Box 129, Grand Canyon, AZ 86023. Visitor center open daily 8-5; hours vary seasonally.
☎ (520) 638-7888

Kaibab National Forest. North Section visitor center: US 89 and SR 67. Open daily May to Oct.
☎ (520) 643-7298 or (520) 643-7395

Kaibab National Forest. South Section visitor center: 200 W Railroad Ave, Williams, AZ 86046. Open daily year-round. Closed major holidays.
☎ (520) 635-4061 or (800) 863-0546

Havasu Canyon. For information: Havasupai Camping Reservations, PO Box 160, Supai, AZ 86435.
☎ (520) 448-2121

FAR WEST
San Luis Obispo to Leggett:
San Luis Obispo de Tolosa. 751 Palm St, San Luis Obispo, CA. Daily 9-5, mid April to end of Oct; 9-4 rest of year. Closed winter holidays.
☎ (805) 543-6850.

The Hearst Castle. 750 Hearst Castle Rd, San Simeon, CA. Hours of tours depend on season. Call for times and to make reservations. Closed Jan 1, Thanksgiving and Dec 25.
☎ (805) 927-2020 or (800) 444-4445

Point Lobos State Reserve.
3 miles S of Carmel on Hwy 1.
Open daily 9-7 Apr to end of
Oct; 9-5 rest of year.
☎ (831) 624-4909
Dive info: (831) 624-8413

Monterey State Historic Park.
20 Custom House Plaza,
Monterey, CA.
Call for hours of tours. Visitor
center open daily 10-5, closed
major holidays.
☎ (831) 649-7118

Big Basin Redwoods State Park.
21600 Big Basin Way, Boulder
Creek, CA 95006.
Visitor center open daily
8 to dusk.
☎ (831) 338-8860

Golden Gate Park, San
Francisco.
Tours May to Oct; call for times.
☎ (415) 263-0991 or
(415) 831-2700

Mission San Francisco de Asis.
3321 16th St at Delores St, San
Francisco.
Open daily 9-4:30, May to Oct;
9-4 rest of year. Closed
Thanksgiving and Dec 25.
☎ (415) 621-8203

Lee Vining to Big Oak Flat:
Mono Basin National Forest
Scenic Area.
PO Box 429, Lee Vining,
CA 93541.
Visitor center open daily 9-5:30
May to Oct; reduced hours and
days rest of year. Closed winter
holidays.
☎ (760) 647-3044

Tioga Pass Road and
Tuolumne Meadows.
In Yosemite National Park.
Open late May to end of Oct,
depending on weather.
☎ (209) 372-0200

Yosemite National Park/
Mariposa Grove of Big Trees.
PO Box 577, Yosemite,
CA 95389.
Open daily all year.
The Mariposa Grove Museum
open daily 9-4:30 late May-
early Oct.
☎ (209) 372-0200

Devils Postpile National
Monument. PO Box 501,
Mammoth Lake, CA 93546.
Interpretive walks early June to
Labor Day; monument open
mid-June to Oct. Ranger station
open daily 8-5, July 1-Labor Day.
☎ (760) 934-2289 or
(760) 872-4881

Mammoth Lakes. Ranger
station: 2500 Main St, Hwy
203; open daily 8-5. Closed Jan
1, Thanksgiving and Dec 25.
☎ (760) 924-5500 or
(888) 466-2666

Leggett to Nemah:
Humboldt Redwoods State
Park/Avenue of the Giants.
PO Box 276, Weott, CA 95571.
Visitor center open daily 9-5
Apr to June and Sept; 9-8 July
to Aug; 10-4 Oct to Mar.
☎ (707) 946-2409 or
(707) 946-2263

Eureka Chamber of Commerce.
2112 Broadway, Eureka,
CA 95501.
☎ (707) 442-3738 or
(800) 356-6381

Sequoia Park, 3550 W St,
Eureka, CA. Open dawn-dusk.
☎ (707) 441-4191

Redwood National and State
Parks. 1111 2nd St, Crescent
City, CA 95531.
☎ (707) 464-6101

Oregon Dunes National
Recreation Center. 855 Hwy
101, Reedsport, OR 97467.
☎ (541) 271-3611

Siuslaw National Forest. PO Box
1148, Corvallis, OR 97339.
☎ (541) 750-7000

Umpqua Discovery Center.
409 Riverfront Way, Reedsport,
OR 97467. Open daily 9-5, June
1 to Sept 30; 10-4, Oct 1 to
May 31. Closed major holidays.
☎ (541) 271-4816

Greater Newport Chamber of
Commerce, 555 SW Coast Hwy,
Newport, OR 97365.
☎ (541) 265-8801 or
(800) 262-7844

Oregon Coast Aquarium.
2820 SE Ferry Slip Rd, Newport,
OR. Daily 9-6, Memorial Day to
Labor Day; 9-8 July to Aug; 10-
5 rest of year. Closed Dec 25.
☎ (541) 867-3474

Devil's Punch Bowl State Park.
c/o Beverly Beach State Park,
198 NE 123rd St, Newport, OR
97365. Open daily dawn-dusk.
☎ (541) 265-4560 or
(541) 265-9278

Astoria-Warrenton Area
Chamber of Commerce.
PO Box 176, Astoria, OR 97103.
☎ (503) 325-6311 or
(800) 875-6807

Astoria Column.
On top of Coxcomb Hill,
Astoria, OR. Daily 8 to dusk.
(503) 325-6311

Columbia River Maritime
Museum. 1792 Marine Dr,
Astoria, OR. Open daily 9:30-5;
closed Thanksgiving, Dec 25.
☎ (503) 325-2323

Columbia River Highway:
Portland Oregon Visitors
Association. Pioneer
Courthouse Sq, 701 SW 6th
Ave, Portland, OR 97204.
☎ (503) 275-8355 or
(877) 678-5263

The Oregon History Center.
1200 SW Park Ave, Portland.
Museum open Tues-Sat 10-5
(Thurs until 8), Sun 12-5.
☎ (503) 222-1741

The Portland Art Museum.
1219 SW Park, Portland.
Open Tues-Sat 10-5
(Wed until 8); Sun 12-5.
☎ (503) 226-2811

Columbia River Gorge.
USDA Forest Service, 902
Wasco Ave, Suite 200, Hood
River, OR 97031.
☎ (541) 386-2333

Crown Pointe State Scenic Area.
PO Box 204, Corbett, OR
97019. Info center open daily
8:30-6, mid-Apr to mid-Oct.
☎ (503) 695-2230

Multnomah Falls.
Lodge open daily 9-8, Memorial Day to Labor Day; 9-5 rest of year. Closed winter holidays.
☎ (503) 695-2372

Bonneville Dam. US Army Corps of Engineers, Bonneville Lock and Dam, Cascade Locks, OR 97014. Daily 9-5; closed Jan 1, Thanksgiving and Dec 25.
☎ (541) 374-8820

Mount Hood Information Center, 65000 E Hwy 26, Welches, OR 97067.
☎ (503) 622-4822 or (888) 622-4822

Stevens Canyon Road - Nisqually Paradise Road:
Northwest Trek Wildlife Park. 11610 Trek Drive E, Eatonville, WA 98328.
Open daily Mar to Oct; Fri-Sun rest of year. Call for hours.
☎ (360) 832-6117

Mount Rainier Scenic Railroad. Excursions Memorial Day to Sept 30 and Dec. Call for times.
☎ (360) 569-2588 or (888) 773-4637

Mount Rainier National Park. Tahoma Woods, Star Route, Ashford, WA 98304.
☎ (360) 569-2211

Mount St. Helens National Volcanic Monument. Headquarters: 42218 NE Yale Bridge Rd, Amboy, WA 98601. Ape Cave open daily in summer. Call for hours of tours.
☎ (360) 247-3900

North Cascades Highway:
Rockport State Park. 51905 SR 20, Rockport, WA 98283. Open daily 6:30 to dusk, Apr to Oct.
☎ (360) 853-8461

North Cascades National Park Service Complex/Ross Lake Recreation Area. 810 SR 20, Sedro-Woolley, WA 98284.
☎ (360) 856-5700

Okanogan National Forest: Okanogan Valley Office, 1240 S 2nd Ave, Okanogan, WA 98840.
☎ (509) 826-3275

U.S. 93 to SR 75:
Malad Gorge State Park. 1074 E 2350 S, Hagerman, ID 83332.
☎ (208) 837-4505

Blaine County Historical Museum. Open Mon and Wed-Sat 11-5; Sun 1-5, Memorial Day to mid-Oct.
☎ (208) 788-1801 or (208) 726-8405

Sawtooth Fish Hatchery. Visitor center open daily 8-5. Guided tours Memorial Day to Labor Day; rest of year by appointment.
☎ (208) 774-3684

Lemhi County Historical Museum. 210 Main St, Salmon, ID. Open May to Oct; call for hours.
☎ (208) 756-3342

Experimental Breeder Reactor. Daily 9-5, Memorial Day to Labor Day; call for rest of year.
☎ (208) 526-0050

Craters of the Moon National Monument. Visitor Center open daily 8-6, Memorial Day to Labor Day; 8-4:30 rest of year, except holidays.
☎ (208) 527-3257

Going-to-the-Sun Road:
Flathead National Forest. 1935 3rd Ave E, Kalispell, MT 59901.
☎ (406) 758-5204

Museum of the Plains Indians. Daily 9-4:45, June-Sept; Mon-Fri 10-4:30, rest of year. Closed Jan 1, Thanksgiving and Dec 25.
☎ (406) 338-2230

Going-to-the-Sun Road/Glacier National Park. PO Box 128, West Glacier, MT 59936. Visitor centers open daily May to late Oct; Apgar Visitor Center open Sat and Sun, Nov to Apr.
☎ (406) 888-7800

Hungry Horse Dam. Visitor center open daily, Memorial Day to Labor Day; call for tour times.
☎ (406) 387-5241

Columbia Falls Area Chamber of Commerce. PO Box 312, Columbia Falls, MT 59912.
☎ (406) 892-2072

Big Sky Waterslide. 7211 Hwy 2 E, Columbia Falls, MT. Open daily 10-8, Memorial Day to Labor Day.
☎ (406) 892-2139

U.S. 85:
Fort Union Trading Post. 15550 Hwy 1804, Williston, ND 58801.
Open daily 8-8, Memorial Day to Labor Day; 9-5:30 rest of year. Closed Jan 1, Thanksgiving and Dec 25.
☎ (701) 572-9083

Fort Buford State Historic Site. RR3 Box 67, Williston, ND 58801. Daily 10-6, May 15-Sept; by appointment rest of year.
☎ (701) 572-9034

Theodore Roosevelt National Park.
PO Box 7, Medora, ND 58645.
☎ (701) 623-4466

de Mores Historic Site. PO Box 106, Medora, ND 58645. Open daily 10-6:30, May 16-Sept 15.
☎ (701) 623-4355

Little Missouri National Grassland. 161 21st St W, Dickinson, ND 58601.
☎ (701) 225-5151

U.S. 385:
The Homestake Gold Mine. Visitor Center: 160 W Main St, Lead, SD 57754. Open year-round; call for hours.
☎ (605) 584-3110

Black Hills, Badlands & Lakes Association.
1851 Discovery Circle, Rapid City, SD 57701.
☎ (605) 355-3600

Mount Rushmore National Memorial.
PO Box 268, Keystone, SD 57751. Open daily 8-10, mid-May to Sept; 8-5 rest of year.
☎ (605) 574-2523 or (605) 574-3165

Rushmore Borglum Story.
Box 650, Keystone, SD 57751.
Open daily mid-May to Sept;
call for hours.
☎ (605) 666-4448

Jewel Cave National
Monument. Visitor center and
museum open daily. Guided
tours daily; call for times.
☎ (605) 673-2288

Wind Cave National Park.
RR 1, Box 190-WCNP, Hot
Springs, SD 57747-9439.
Ranger-guided tours offered
year-round; call for times. Cave
closed Thanksgiving and Dec 25.
☎ (605) 745-4600

Yellowstone Park Road:
Yellowstone National Park.
PO Box 168, Yellowstone
National Park, WY 82190.
☎ (307) 344-7381

Buffalo Bill Historical Center.
720 Sheridan, Cody, WY 82414.
Open year-round; call for hours.
☎ (307) 587-4771

Greybull Museum.
325 Greybull Ave, Greybull, WY.
Open year-round; call for hours.
☎ (307) 765-2444

Medicine Wheel District Office.
PO Box 367, Lovell, WY 82431.
☎ (307) 674-2600 or
(307) 548-6541

Bradford Brinton Memorial.
239 Brinton Rd, Big Horn, WY.
Daily 9:30-5, mid-May to Labor
Day; 10-4 Fri-Sun in Sept.
☎ (307) 672-3173

Grand Teton National Park.
PO Box 170, Moose, WY 83012.
☎ (307) 739-3600

Gros Ventre Slide: Jackson Hole
Chamber of Commerce, PO Box
550, Jackson, WY 83001.
☎ (307) 733-3316

MIDWEST
Elkins to Lewisburg:
Blackwater Falls State Park.
PO Drawer 490, Davis,
WV 26260.
☎ (304)259-5216 or
(800) CALL-WVA

Petersburg: Smoke Hole
Caverns. Rte 55 W. Tours daily
9-5, every half hour.
☎ (304) 257-4442 or
(800) 828-8478

Cass Scenic Railroad State Park.
Daily Memorial Day to Labor
Day; weekends only rest of
Sept and Oct. Call for schedule.
☎ (304) 456-4300 or
(800) CALL-WVA

Droop Mountain Battlefield State
Park. HC 64, PO Box 189,
Hillsboro, WV 24946. Open
daily 6-10 year-round, weather
permitting.
☎ (304) 653-4254

Lost World Caverns.
Fairview Rd, Lewisburg, WV.
Daily 9-7, May 15 to Labor Day;
reduced hours rest of year.
Closed major holidays.
☎ (304) 645-6677 or
(866) 228-3778

Greenbrier County Convention
and Visitors Bureau.
111 N Jefferson St, Lewisburg,
WV 24901. Open 9-5, Mon-Fri,
year-round.
☎ (304) 645-1000 or
(800) 833-2068

Greenbrier Hotel Bunker. 300 W
Main Street, White Sulphur
Springs, WV 24986. Tours Sun
and Wed; call for times.
☎ (304) 536-3595

Monongahela National Forest.
Cranberry Mountain Nature
Center: PO Box HC80, Box 117,
Richwood, WV 26261. Open
daily 9-5, Apr to Nov.
☎ (304) 653-4826

New Richmond to Friendship:
Ulysses S. Grant Birthplace.
1551 SR 232, Point Pleasant,
OH 45153.
Open Wed-Sat 9:30-5 and Sun
12-5, Apr to Oct.
☎ (513) 553-4911 or
(800) 283-8932

Rankin House. 6152 Rankin Rd,
Ripley, OH. Open Wed-Sun 10-5
and Sun 12-5, Memorial Day to
Labor Day.
☎ (937) 392-1627

Davis Memorial State Nature
Preserve. c/o Ohio Division of
Natural Areas & Preserves,
1889 Fountain Sq, Bldg F1,
Columbus, OH 43224.
Open daylight hours year-round.
☎ (614) 265-6453

Serpent Mound. 3850 SR 73,
Peebles, OH 45660. Park open
daily 9:30-8, Memorial Day to
Labor Day (museum 9:30-5);
park also open 10-5 Apr to
Memorial Day and Sept to Oct.
☎ (937) 587-2796 or
(800) 752-2757

Seven Caves. 7660 Cave Rd,
Bainbridge, OH 45612.
Open daily 9 to dusk.
☎ (937) 365-1283

Fort Ancient State Memorial.
6123 SR 350, Oregonia, OH
45054. Open Mar to Nov; call
for hours or to arrange guided
group tours Dec to Feb. Closed
Thanksgiving, Dec 25.
☎ (513) 932-4421or
(800) 283-8904

*Mackinac Island to Traverse
City:*
Mackinac Island Chamber of
Commerce. PO Box 451,
Mackinac Island, MI 49757.
☎ (906) 847-3783 or
(800) 454-5227

Colonial Michilimackinac.
207 W Sinclair, Mackinaw City,
MI. Open daily May to mid-Oct;
call for hours.
☎ (231) 436-4100

Divers' Shrine. Area info:
Petoskey/Harbor Springs/Boyne
Country Visitors Bureau. 401 E
Mitchell St, Petoskey, MI 49770.
☎ (231) 348-2755 or
(800) 845-2828

Gaylord Area. PO Box 3069,
Gaylord, MI 49734.
☎ (989) 732-4000 or
(800) 345-8621

Call of the Wild Museum.
850 S Wisconsin Ave, Gaylord,
OH 49735. Open year-round;
call for hours.
☎ (989) 732-4336 or
(800) 835-4347

Traverse City Convention and Visitors Bureau.
101 W Grandview Pkwy, Traverse City, MI 49684-2252.
☎ (231) 947-3134 or (800) 872-8377

Traverse City State Park.
1132 US 31 N, Traverse City, MI 49686. Open year round.
☎ (231) 922-5270

Great River Road:
St Croix Falls: Polk County Information Center, 710 Hwy 35 S, St Croix Falls, WI 54024.
☎ (715) 483-1410 or (800) 222-7655

St Croix National Scenic Riverway. PO Box 708, St Croix Falls, WI 54024. Visitor center open daily 8:30-5 mid-Apr to mid-Oct; Mon-Fri 8:30-4:30 rest of year.
☎ (715) 483-3284

Ice Age National Scientific Reserve. PO Box 703, St Croix Falls, WI 54024. Interpretive center open daily 8:30-4:30 May to Sept; reduced hours rest of year.
☎ (715) 483-3747

La Crosse Area Convention & Visitors Bureau.
Riverside Park, 410 Veterans Memorial Dr, La Crosse, WI 54601.
☎ (608) 782-2366 or (800) 658-9424

Frank Lloyd Wright's Estate.
5607 County Hwy C, Spring Green, WI 53588. Open daily May to Oct. Call for tour times.
☎ (608) 588-7900

House on the Rock.
5754 Hwy 23, Spring Green, WI 53588. Daily 9-7, mid-March to Oct; Sat-Sun 9-6, Jan to mid-March.
☎ (608) 935-3639 or (800) 947-2799

Prairie du Chien Tourism Council.
PO Box 326, Prairie du Chien, WI 53821.
☎ (608) 326-8555 or (800) 732-1673

Fort Crawford Museum. 717 S Beaumont Rd, PO Box 298, Prairie du Chien, WI 53821.
☎ (608) 326-6960

Villa Louis.
900 W Bolvin St, Prairie du Chien, WI 53821. Tours May to Oct; call for times.
☎ (608) 326-2721

Cassville Stonefield Historic Site. PO Box 125, Cassville, WI 53806. Daily 10-5, July to Aug; 10-4 end of May to June, Sept and Sat and Sun in Oct.
☎ (608) 725-5210

North Shore Drive:
Grand Portage National Monument. PO Box 668, Grand Marais, MN 55604.
Monument grounds, trails and the Grand Portage open year-round. Reconstructed buildings open 9-5, mid-May to mid-Oct.
☎ (218) 387-2788 or (218) 475-2202

Split Rock Lighthouse.
3713 Split Rock Lighthouse Rd, Two Harbors, MN 55616.
Lighthouse open 9-6, May 15 to Oct 15. Visitor center hours vary by season.
☎ (218) 226-6372

Gooseberry Falls State Park.
3206 Hwy 61 E, Two Harbors, MN 55616.
Visitor center open daily 9-4.
☎ (218) 834-3855

Two Harbors Chamber of Commerce.
603 7th Ave, Two Harbors, MN 55616. Open Mon-Fri 8-5.
☎ (218) 834-2600 or (800) 777-7384

Duluth Convention & Visitors Bureau. 100 Lake Place Drive, Duluth, MN 55802-2326.
☎ (218) 722-4011 or 800-4-DULUTH

North Shore Scenic Railroad. 506 W Michigan St, Duluth, MN 55802. Daily Memorial Day to mid-Oct. Call for departure times.
☎ (218) 722-1273 or (800) 423-1273

Chisholm Chamber of Commerce. 10 NW Second Ave, Chisholm, MN 55719.
☎ (218) 254-7930 or (800) 422-0806

Minnesota Museum of Mining.
At west end of Lake St, Chisholm, MN. Open daily 9-5, Memorial Day to Labor Day.
☎ (218) 254-5543

Soudan Underground Mine State Park.
PO Box 335, Soudan, MN 55782. Tours daily, Memorial Day to Sept.
☎ (218) 753-2245

CANADA
The Crowsnest Highway:
Okanagan Valley: Tourism Penticton, 888 Westminster Ave W, Penticton, BC, V2A 8R2.
☎ (250) 493-4055 or (800) 663-5052

Osoyoos and District Chamber of Commerce.
Jct Hwys 3 and 97, PO Box 227, Osoyoos, BC, V0H 1V0.
Open daily 8-8, July to August; 9-5 rest of year.
☎ (250) 495-7142

Osoyoos Museum. Main St, Osoyoos, BC, V0H 1V0.
Open daily 10-3:30, June-Sept.
☎ (250) 495-2582

Manning Provincial Park.
Hwy 3, BC.
Visitor center open daily 8:30-4:30, mid-June to mid-Sept; Mon-Fri 8:30-4, rest of year. Campgrounds open mid-May to Sept.
☎ (250) 840-8836

Boston Bar/Hell's Gate Airtram.
43111 Trans-Canada Hwy, Boston Bar, BC, C0K 1C0.
Open May to Oct; call for hours.
☎ (604) 867-9277

Chilliwack Visitor Information Centre. 44150 Luckakuck Way, Chilliwack, BC, V2R 4A7.
Open daily 9-5, May to June; 9-7, July to Aug; 9-5, Mon-Fri, Sept and April.
☎ (604) 858-8121or (800) 567-9535

Bridal Falls Provincial Park:
BC Lower Mainland Information
Centre. 1610 Mt Seymour Rd,
North Vancouver, BC, V7G 2R6.
☎ (604) 924-2200

Minter Gardens.
52892 Bunker Rd, Rosedale, BC,
V0X 1X0. Open daily 9-5, Apr and
Oct; 9-5:30, May and Sept; 9-6,
June; 9-7, July to Aug.
☎ (604) 794-7191 or
(888) MINTERS

Trans-Canada Highway:
Kananaskis Country General
Inquiries.
800 Railway Ave, Suite 201,
Canmore, AB, T1W 1P1.
☎ (403) 678-5508

Kananaskis Mountain Lodge.
PO Box 10, Kananaskis Village,
AB, T0L 2H0. Open 24 hours.
☎ (403) 591-7500 or
(888) 591-7501

Tourism Canmore.
2801 Bow Valley Trail, Canmore,
AB, T1W 3A2. Open daily 9-6,
Oct to April; 8-8, May to Sept.
☎ (403) 678-5277 or
(800) 661-8888

Banff National Park.
PO Box 900, Banff, AB,
T0L 0C0. Open daily 8-8, July
to August; 9-5, rest of year.
☎ (403) 762-1550

Banff Sulphur Mountain
Gondola.
PO Box 1258, Banff,
AB, T0L 0C0. Open daily 8:30-6,
Apr-Sept; 10-5, rest of year.
☎ (403) 762-2523

Lake Louise Sightseeing Lift and
Gondola.
1 Whitehorn Rd, Lake Louise,
AB, T0L 1E0.
Lift and gondola operate daily
8:30-6, June and Sept; 8-6, July
and August. Lodge open all
year 7:30-6.
☎ (403) 522-3555

Yoho National Park.
PO Box 99, Field, BC, V0A 1G0.
Park open year-round, but most
facilities operate June to Sept.
☎ (250) 343-6783

Burgess Shale Fossil Beds.
201 Kicking Horse Ave, Box
148, Field, BC, C0A 1G0.
Open daily 8:30-4:30.
☎ (250) 343-6006 or
(800) 343-3006

Icefields Parkway:
Columbia Icefield Center.
PO Box 1140, Banff, AB,
T0L 0C0. Open daily 9-5,
April 10 to Oct 20.
☎ (877) 423-7433

Maligne Lake Boat Tours.
Jasper Marketplace, 627 Patricia
St, Jasper, AB, T0E 1E0.
Trips depart daily on the hour
10-5, late June to early Sept;
10-3, mid-May to late June and
mid-Sept to mid-Oct.
☎ (780) 852-3370

Jasper National Park.
PO Box 10, Jasper, AB,
T0E 1E0. Park open year-round,
but many businesses open only
during summer months.
☎ (780) 852-6176

Gaspé Peninsula:
Gaspésie Park. 900 Route du
Parc, Ste-Anne-des-Monts, Gaspé,
QC, G0E 2G0.
Open daily dawn-dusk (weather
permitting).
☎ (418) 763-3181 or
(866) PARCGAS.

Forillon National Park.
122 boul de Gaspé, Gaspé,
QC, G4X 1A9.
Park open year-round.
Reception center open daily
9-6, June 16 to Aug 26;
10-5, June 2 to 15 and Aug 27
to Oct 15.
☎ (418) 368-5505 or
(888) 773-8888

Gaspé Tourist Information
Bureau. 39 York est, Gaspé,
QC, G0C 1R0.
☎ (418) 368-6335

Gaspésie Museum/Jacques
Cartier Monument.
80 boul Gaspé, Gaspé, QC,
G4X 1A9.
Open daily 9-7, June 24 to Sept;
9-5 rest of year. Closed Dec.
☎ (418) 368-1534

Percé Tourism Bureau.
142 Hwy 132 Ouest, Percé,
QC, G0C 2L0.
Open daily 7-11, May 15 to Oct
15; 9-5, Oct 16 to May 14.
☎ (418) 782-5448

Ile Bonaventure and Percé
Rock Park.
162 Hwy 132, Percé, QC,
G0C 2L0. Open daily 8-5,
June 1 to Oct 15. Cruises every
45 minutes daily from 8-5,
May 15 to Oct 15.
☎ (418) 782-2974

The Evangeline Trail:
Port Royal National Historic
Site–The Habitation.
21 Historic Lane, Port Royal,
NS, B0S 1A0. Open daily 9-6,
May 15 to Oct 15.
☎ (902) 532-2898 or
(902) 532-2321

North Hills Museum.
5065 Granville Rd, Granville
Ferry, NS, B0S 1K0.
Open Mon-Sat 9:30-5:30, Sun
1-5:30, June 1 to mid-Oct.
☎ (902) 532-2168

Annapolis District Board of
Trade.
236 Prince Albert Rd,
Annapolis Royal, NS, B0S 1A0.
☎ (902) 532-5769 or
(902) 532-5454

Fort Anne National Historic Site
and Museum.
PO Box 9, Annapolis Royal,
NS, B0S 1A0.
Open 9-6 daily, May 15 to Oct
15; call for off-season hours.
☎ (902) 532-2397 or
(902) 532-2321

Upper Clements Park.
2931 Upper Clements Park Rd,
Annapolis Royal, NS, B0S 1A0.
Open daily 11-7, June 16 to
Sept 3.
☎ (902) 532-7557 or
(888) 248-4567

Grand Pré National Historic Site
of Canada.
2242 Grand Pré Rd, Grand Pré,
NS, B0P 1M0.
Open daily 9-6, May to Oct.
☎ (902) 542-3631

NORTHEAST

21 Courtesy of New Jersey Commerce and Economic Growth Commission

22 *(upper)* Courtesy of Vermont Department of Tourism and Marketing

22 *(lower)* Maxime Thibault

23 Courtesy of Massachusetts Office of Travel and Tourism

24, 25 Courtesy of Maine Office of Tourism

26 William Roy/State of New Hampshire Office of Travel and Tourism Development

27 Dick Hamilton/State of New Hampshire Office of Travel and Tourism Development

28 Jim Mcelholm/Vermont Department of Travel and Tourism, Montpelier, VT

29 Courtesy of Vermont Department of Tourism and Marketing

30, 31 Kindra Clineff/Courtesy of Massachusetts Office of Travel and Tourism

32, 33 John Muldoon/ Connecticut Office of Tourism

34, 35 Courtesy of New York State Economic Development

SOUTHEAST

227, 228 Courtesy of Virginia Tourism Corporation

229, 231 William Russ/ Courtesy of the North Carolina Division of Tourism, Film & Sports Development

230 Tim Thompson/Courtesy of Virginia Tourism Corporation

232 Holland/Florida Department of Commerce, Division of Tourism

233 VISIT FLORIDA

234, 235 Courtesy of the Baton Rouge Area Convention & Visitor's Bureau

236, 237, 238, 239 Courtesy of the Kentucky Department of Travel

SOUTHWEST

371, 372 *(lower)*, 376, 377 Page Teahan/Courtesy of Telluride Visitor Service

372 *(upper)*, 381 John Telford/ Photo Courtesy of the Utah Travel Council

373 Rankin Harvey

374 Michael E. Pitel

375 Jill Caven

378, 379, 380 Frank Jensen/ Photo Courtesy of the Utah Travel Council

382 Courtesy of Flagstaff Convention and Visitor's Bureau

383 Al Richmond/Courtesy of Flagstaff Convention and Visitor's Bureau

FAR WEST

453, 454, 458, 459 Robert Holmes/Courtesy of California Division of Tourism

455, 460, 461 Courtesy of Oregon Tourism Commission

456, 457 Solange Laberge

462 Bob Pool/Oregon Tourism Commission

463 Larry Geddis/Oregon Tourism Commission

464 Courtesy of Tacoma-Pierce County Visitor and Convention Bureau

465 National Park Service

466, 467 Courtesy of Cascade Loop Association

NORTHWEST

563, 564 *(lower)* Courtesy of Wyoming Travel Commission

564 *(upper)* Kristi Hansen/ South Dakota Tourism

565, 572 Photo by South Dakota Tourism

566 Steve Welsh/Idaho Department of Commerce

567 Idaho Department of Commerce

568 Lori Pettenger/Travel Montana Department of Commerce

569 Donnie Sexton/Travel Montana Department of Commerce

570 Clayton Wolt/North Dakota Tourism

571 Dawn Charging/North Dakota Tourism

573 Chad Coppess/South Dakota Tourism

574, 575 Wyoming Travel Commission

MIDWEST

595 MN Office of Tourism

596 *(upper)*, 597 Steve Shaluta, Jr./West Virginia Division of Tourism

596 *(lower)* Courtesy of Travel Michigan

598, 599 David Fattaleh/West Virginia Division of Tourism

600, 601 Ohio Historical Society

602 Terry W. Phipps/Michigan Travel Bureau

603 Vito Palmisano/Michigan Travel Bureau

604 Courtesy of Wisconsin Department of Tourism

605 The House on the Rock/Wisconsin Tourism Development

606, 607 Courtesy of Minnesota Office of Tourism

CANADA

673, 675, 678, 679, 680, 681 Courtesy of Travel Alberta

674, 684, 685 Courtesy of Tourism Nova Scotia

676, 677 Frank Watanabe

682 Pierre Léveillé

683 Rebecca Smollett